COLLECTING MODERN

DESIGN AT THE PHILADELPHIA MUSEUM OF ART SINCE 1876

COLLECTING MOD

DESIGN AT THE PHILADELPHIA

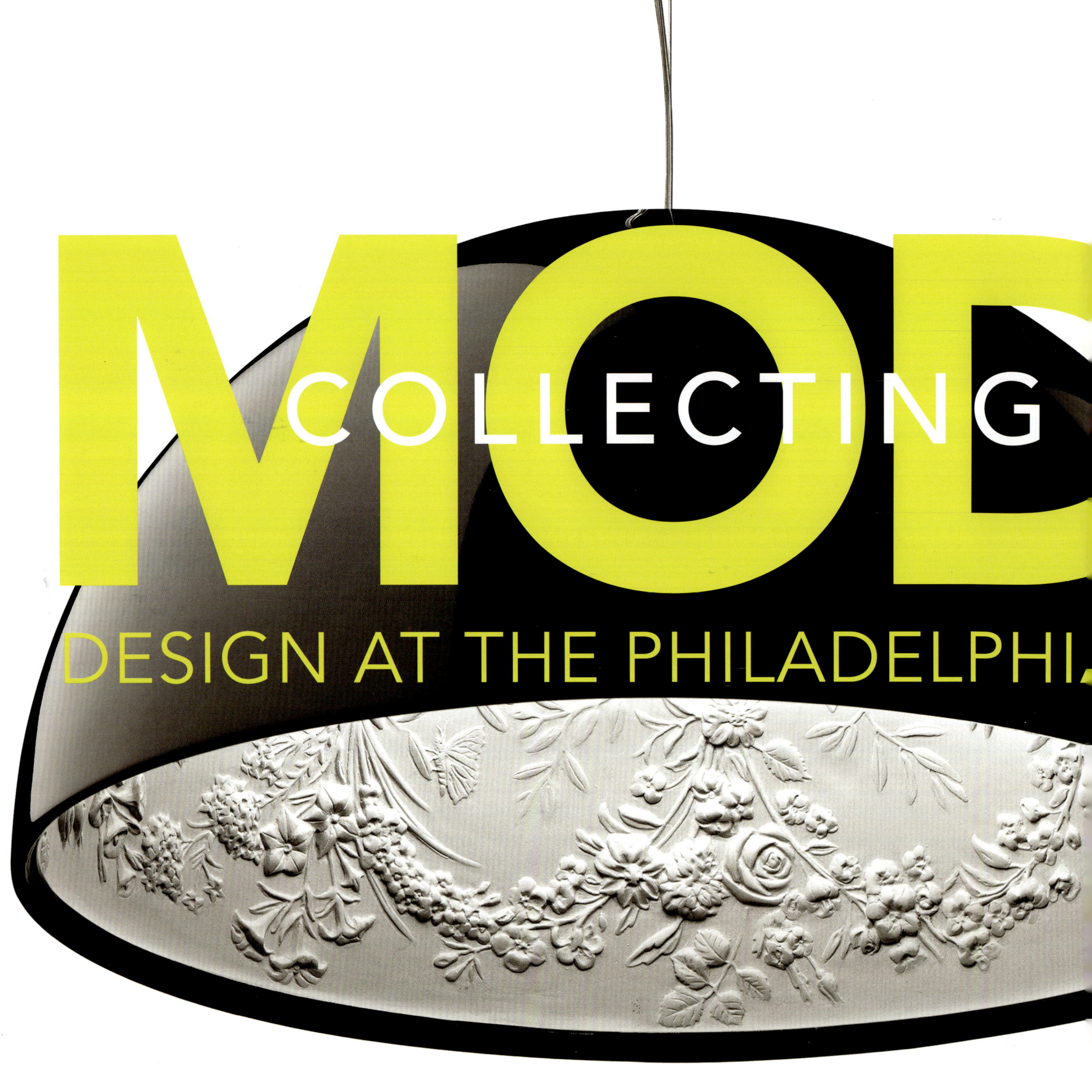

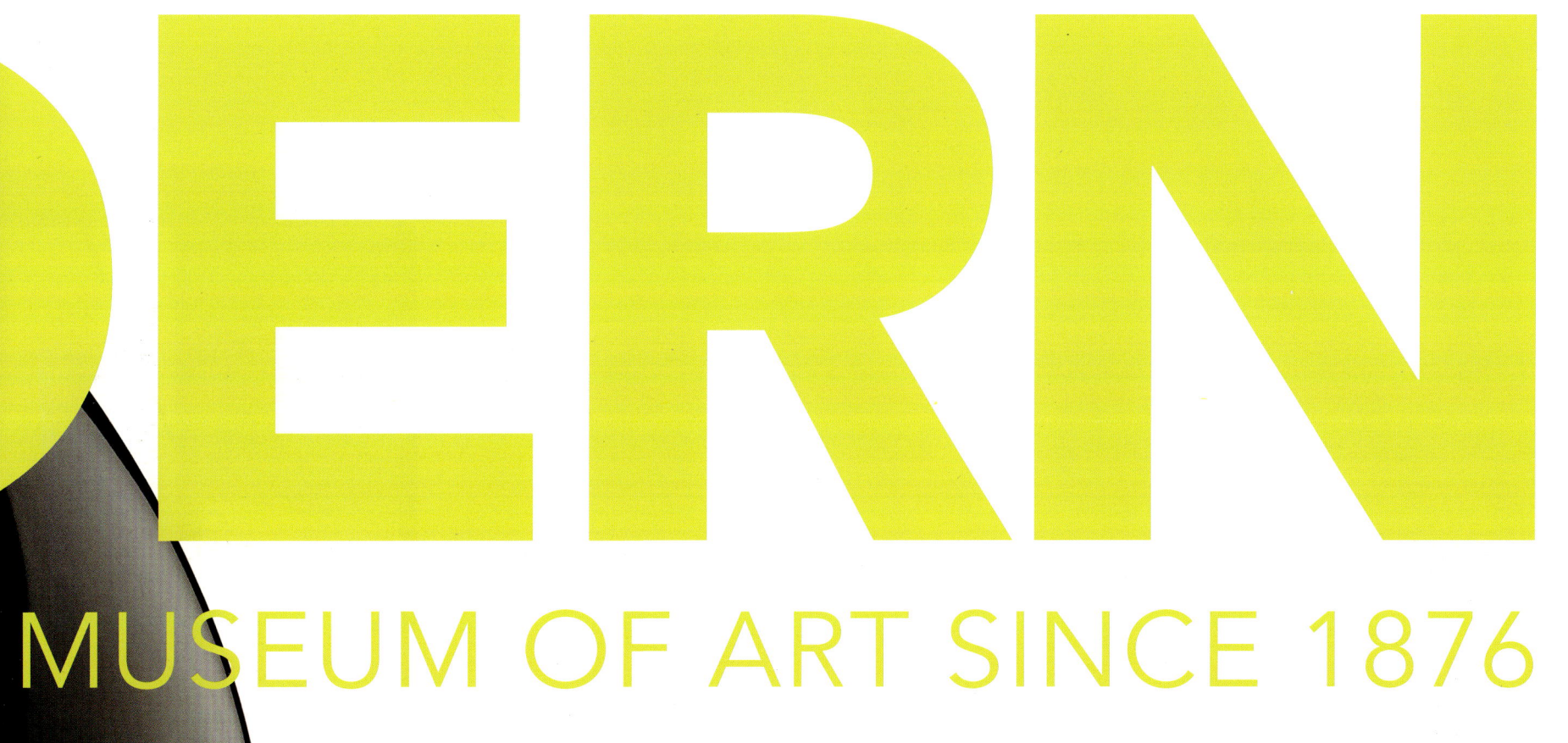

...DERN

...MUSEUM OF ART SINCE 1876

KATHRYN BLOOM HIESINGER

PHILADELPHIA MUSEUM OF ART
published in association with
YALE UNIVERSITY PRESS
New Haven and London

COLLECTING MODERN
Design at the Philadelphia Museum of Art Since 1876

This publication was made possible by Lisa S. Roberts.

Produced by the Publishing Department
Philadelphia Museum of Art
Sherry Babbitt
The William T. Ranney Director of Publishing
2525 Pennsylvania Avenue
Philadelphia, PA 19130
www.philamuseum.org

Edited by Mary Cason
Design and production by Lisa Benn Costigan
Typography composed in Avenir + Bodoni Antiqua
Printed and bound in Italy by Conti Tipocolor S.p.A.

Published in association with
Yale University Press
302 Temple Street
PO Box 209040
New Haven, CT 06520-9040
www.yalebooks.com/art

All rights reserved. No part of this publication may be reproduced or transmitted in any form or by any means, electronic or mechanical, including photocopying, recording, or any other information storage or retrieval system, without permission in writing from the publisher. Every attempt has been made to locate the copyright holders of the works reproduced herein. Any omission is unintentional.

Text and compilation © 2011 Philadelphia Museum of Art

Unless otherwise specified, Museum records and manuscript collections are in the holdings of the Philadelphia Museum of Art, Archives.

Library of Congress Cataloging-in-Publication Data
Philadelphia Museum of Art.
Collecting modern : design at the Philadelphia Museum of Art since 1876 / Kathryn Bloom Hiesinger.
     p. cm.
Includes index.
ISBN 978-0-87633-221-4 (PMA)—
ISBN 978-0-300-12219-0 (Yale)
1. Decorative arts—History—19th century. 2. Decorative arts—History—20th century. 3. Modernism (Aesthetics) 4. Decorative arts—Collectors and collecting—Pennsylvania—Philadelphia.
5. Philadelphia Museum of Art—History. I. Hiesinger, Kathryn B., 1943- II. Title.
NK1382.M63P48 2011
745.09'0407474811—dc22
                    2010039890

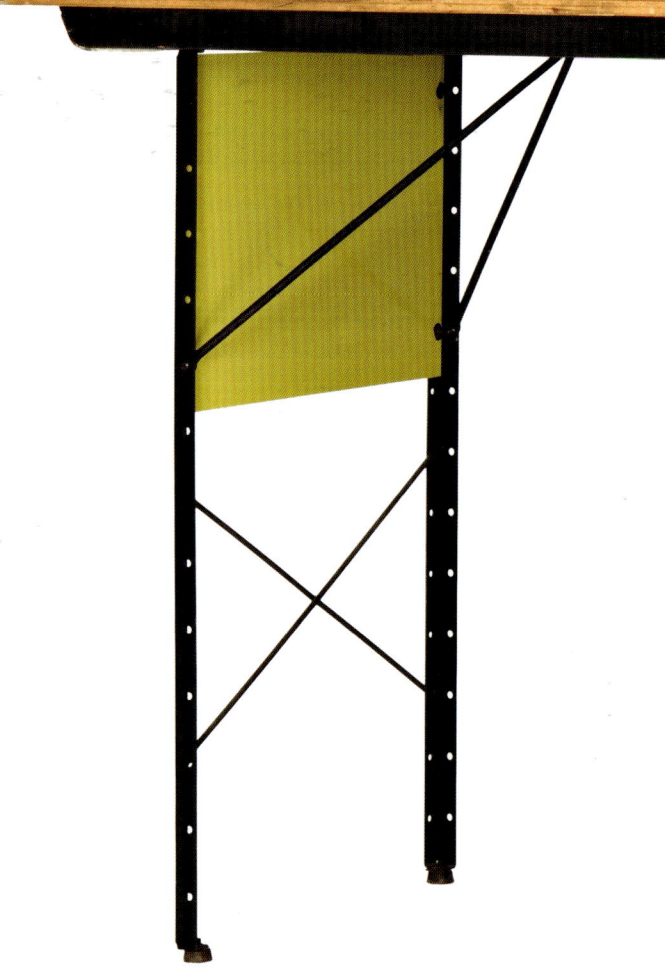

Cover : **Gaetano Pesce** : for B & B Italia : *Up 5* Chair and *Up 6* Ottoman (detail) : 1969 : polyurethane foam, stretch jersey : H (chair) 40 1/2" : D (ottoman) 22 1/2" : 2000-151-1,2 (cat. 145)   Front endpapers : **Jack Lenor Larsen** : woven by Richard Bolan : *Rémoulade* Fabric (detail) : 1956 : linen, jute, cotton, rayon, wool, silk, metallic yarns, other fibers : W 68" : 1984-26-1 (cat. 106)   Title page : **Marcel Wanders** : for Flos : *Skygarden* Lamp : 2007 : aluminum, polycarbonate : D 35 7/16" : 2010-156-2 (cat. 204)   Opposite : **Charles Eames and Ray Eames** : for Herman Miller : *ESU D-10-C* Desk : 1950 : Masonite, birch plywood, steel : H 29 1/2" : 2009-107-1 (cat. 53)   Back endpapers : **Hella Jongerius** : for Maharam : *Repeat Dot Unique* Fabric (detail) : 2002 : cotton, polyester, rayon : W 55" : 2009-93-1 (cat. 95)

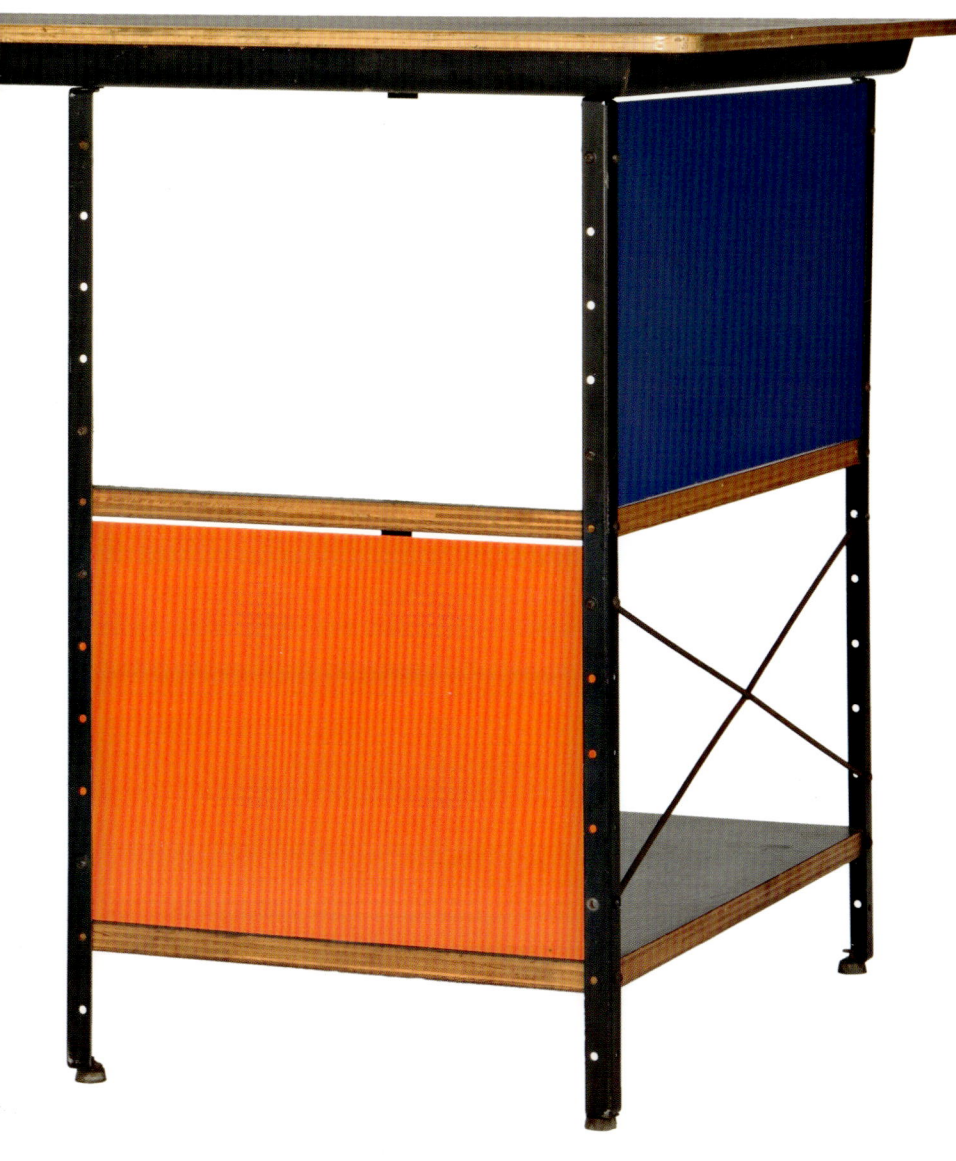

CONTENTS

Foreword : Timothy Rub	7
Acknowledgments	11
1876–1915	13
1916–1964	73
1965–2010	141
Works Illustrated	288
Index	298
Photography Credits	303

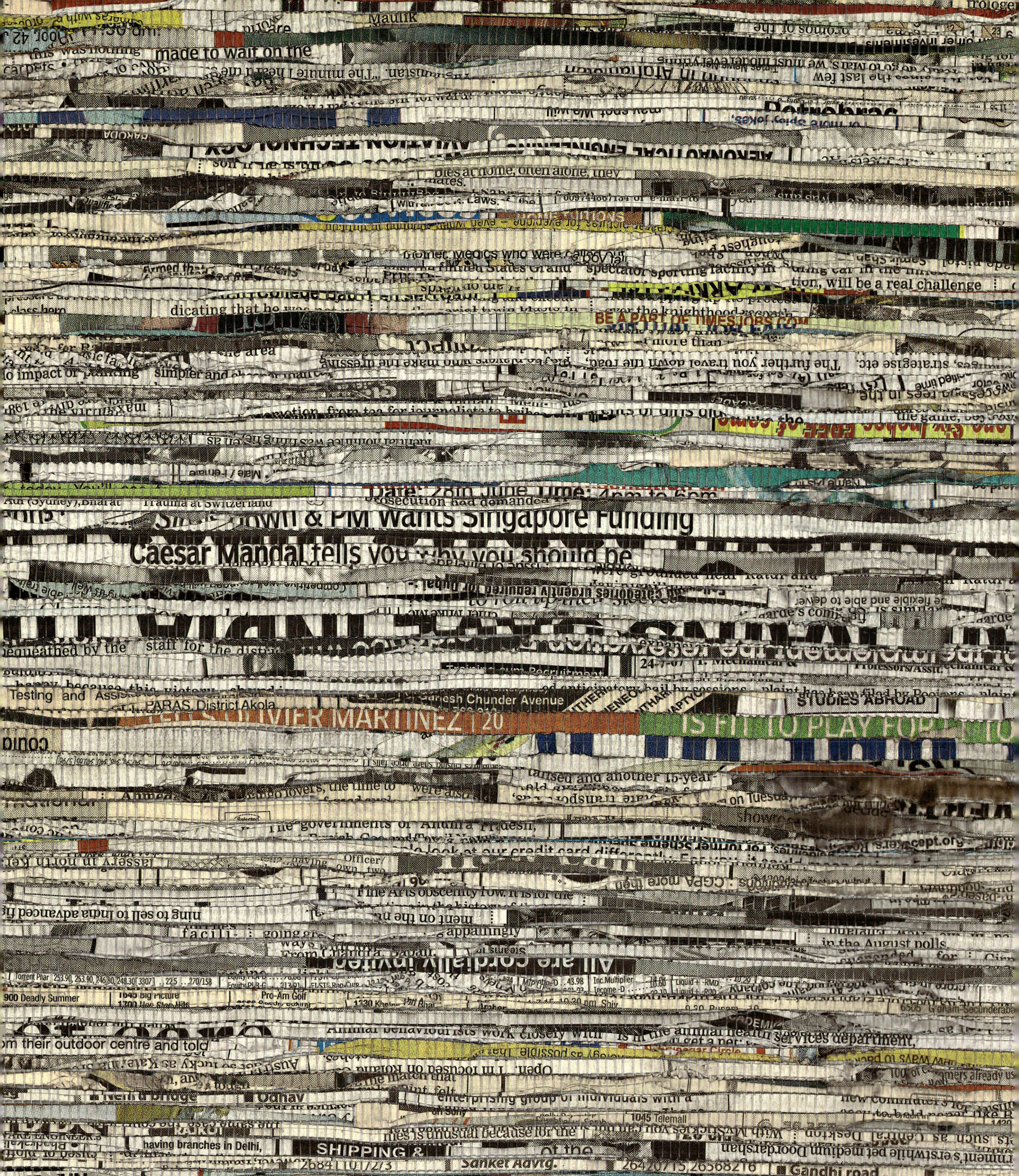

FOREWORD

One of the keys to understanding the development of the collection of the Philadelphia Museum of Art—or, indeed, the history of this institution, especially during the late nineteenth and early twentieth centuries—is the term "industrial art." No longer generally in use, it was once part of the Museum's original title, the Pennsylvania Museum and School of Industrial Art, and clearly expressed the educational goals of its founders and, more specifically, their interest in having the collection serve the useful function of improving the quality of goods designed and manufactured in Philadelphia.

Accordingly, the efforts of the staff of the Museum in the first several decades after its founding in 1876 were directed toward this purpose. In this regard, it is important to note that this endeavor, then as now, encompassed the acquisition not only of significant examples of furniture, ceramics, metalwork, and glass from different historical periods, but also the work of leading designers and manufacturers of the day. This pattern of collecting was purposeful, for it represented the belief that a broad knowledge of the past, of intellectual and artistic traditions, is an essential ingredient of innovation and creativity.

If the author of this study, Kathryn Bloom Hiesinger, the Museum's Curator of European Decorative Arts after 1700, speaks—quite rightly—about the "uneven history" of our collection of decorative arts and design, this should be understood largely as the product, first, of a shift in the educational mission of the Museum, which gradually moved in a direction that no longer directly supported instruction in the disciplines taught at the School of Industrial Art (which eventually separated from the Museum and has since evolved into what is now the University of the Arts) and, second, of the extraordinary changes that occurred in the decorative, or applied, arts during the past century.

If, in retrospect, it is evident that we seemed to have been indifferent to some of those changes or, by contrast, enthusiastic about others, this is not simply a function of the varied judgments of curators and directors that make the shape of any collection like ours distinctive and, at times, even idiosyncratic, but also because of the differing values assigned over time to the acquisition of contemporary work and its relevance to the educational function of this institution. In coming to any judgments about the scope and

Lori Weitzner : for Weitzner Ltd : *Newsworthy* Wallpaper : 2009 : newspaper, nylon : W 47" : 2010-170-1 (cat. 210)

nature of the Museum's collecting efforts in this field throughout its long and distinguished history, the reader should also be mindful of the fact, as Dr. Hiesinger's thoughtful account makes clear, that few fields have changed as dramatically—stylistically, functionally, and technically—as the decorative arts and design have during the period covered by this study.

The publication of Collecting Modern would not have been possible without the encouragement and generous financial support of Lisa S. Roberts, who has served on our board of trustees and as a member of Collab, a collaboration of design professionals who support the modern and contemporary design collections at the Philadelphia Museum of Art. The realization of this work, which provides valuable new perspectives on a central and hitherto underappreciated part of our collection, would not have been possible without her assistance, for which we are deeply grateful.

Many members of our staff made essential contributions to the production of this book. Special thanks are due to Graydon Wood and his colleagues in our Photography Department; Sherry Babbitt, The William T. Ranney Director of Publishing; C. Danial Elliott, Arcadia Director of the Library and Archives; and Susan K. Anderson, The Martha Hamilton Morris Archivist, for their support of Dr. Hiesinger throughout the project. Mary Cason skillfully edited the book, which owes its dynamic design to Lisa Benn.

Finally, and most notably, I would like to express our deepest gratitude to Dr. Hiesinger herself, who devoted several years of study to this topic and, it should not go unremarked, has played a prominent role in the development of the Museum's holdings of the decorative arts and design. No one was better qualified to write Collecting Modern or could have written a more comprehensive or more sympathetic account of this important chapter in our institutional history.

Timothy Rub
The George D. Widener Director and Chief Executive Officer

Fernando Campana and Humberto Campana : for Alessi : Peneira Baskets (3) : 2010 : stainless-steel mesh, natural fiber : D (largest) 15 3/4" : 2010-204-1a–c (cat. 26)

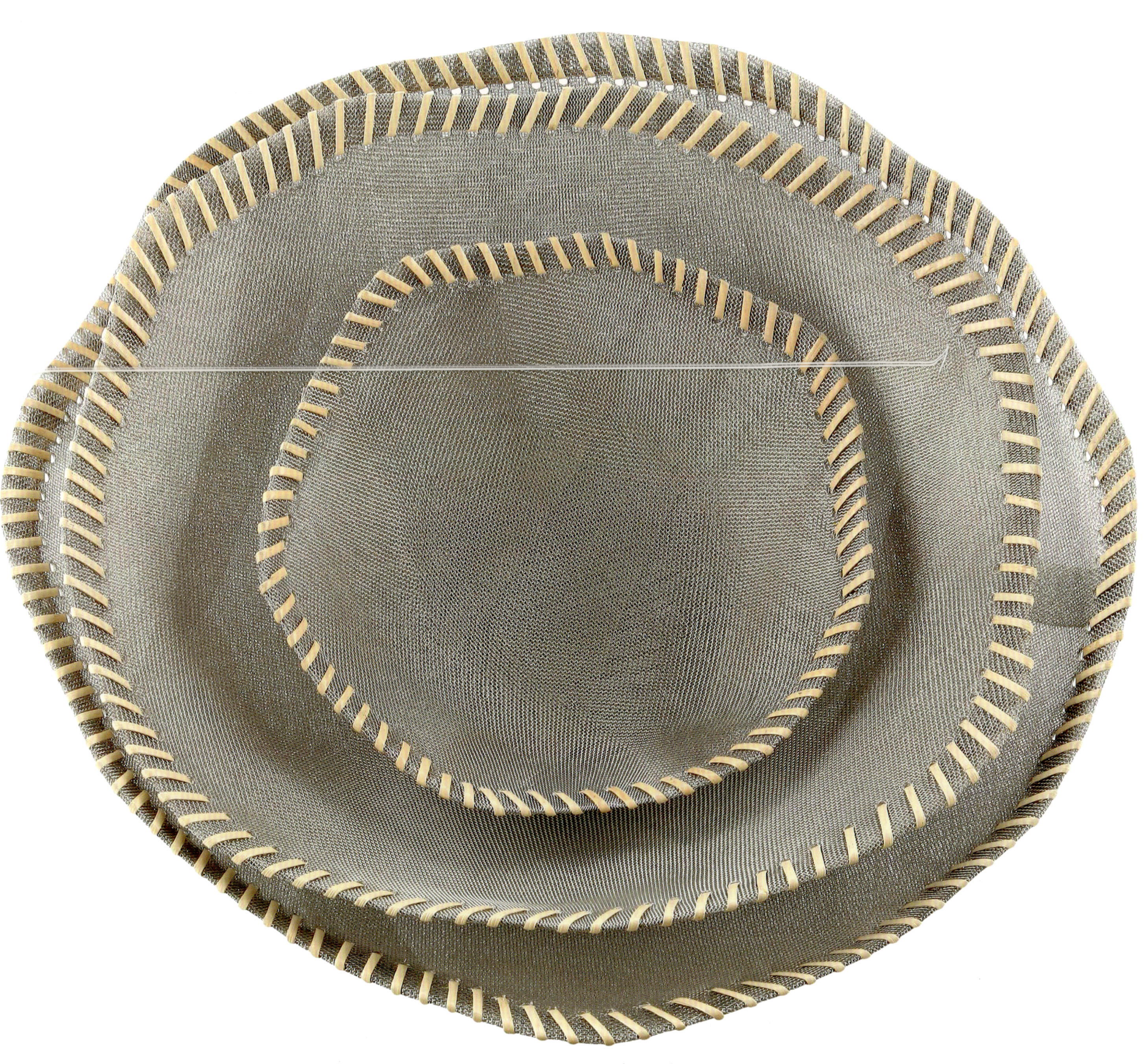

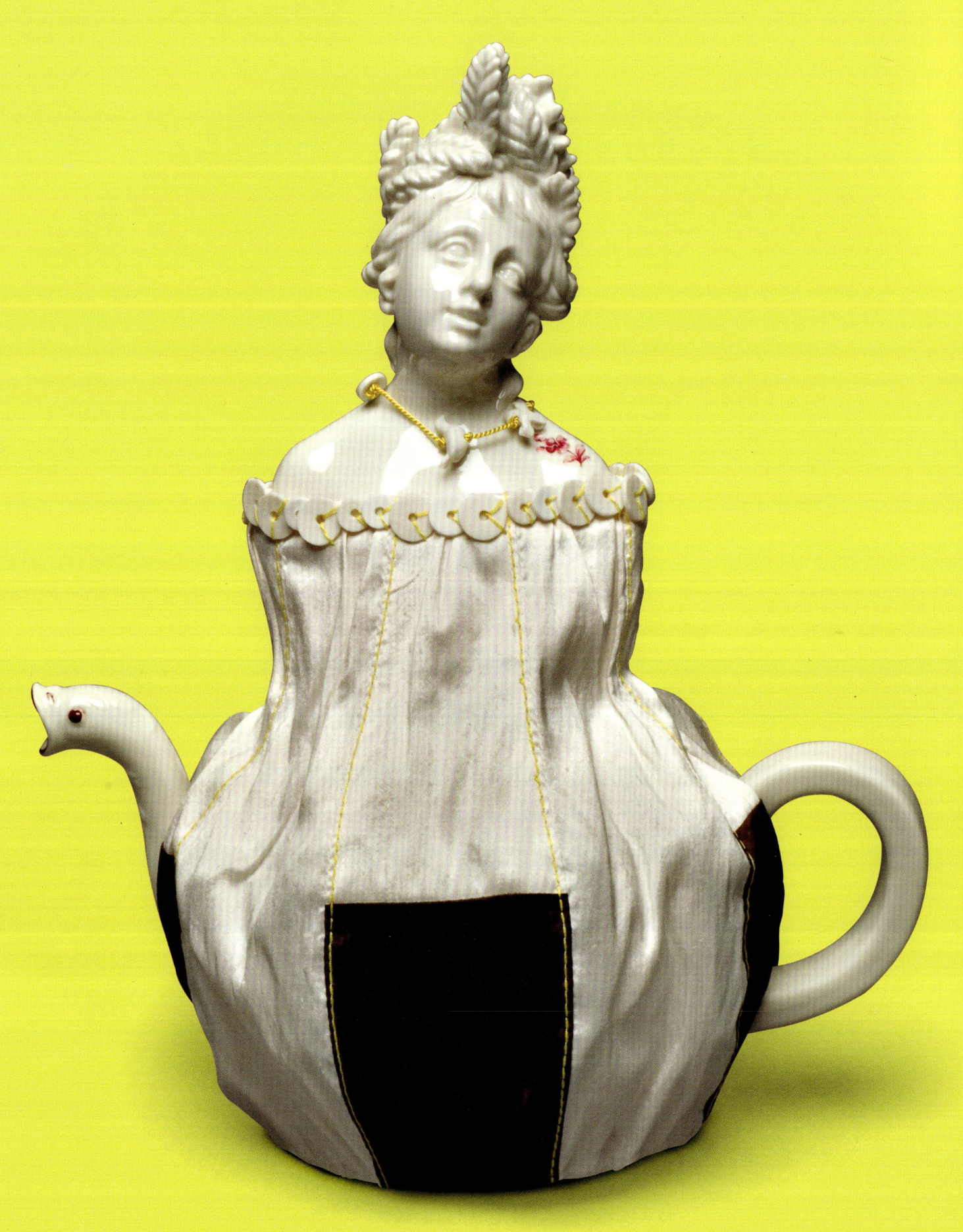

ACKNOWLEDGMENTS

Having enjoyed the singular experience of developing a modern and contemporary design collection for the Philadelphia Museum of Art over my forty-year curatorial career, I am doubly grateful to Lisa S. Roberts for commissioning this book—which has allowed me the pleasure of recording the achievements of my predecessors and reliving my own. For support in building the collections and programs around them, I am more indebted to members of Collab past and present than I can say. The fact that ninety-five percent of the Museum's design collections have been acquired since the founding of Collab in 1970 bears eloquent witness to the perseverance and generosity of this group of architects, designers, and enthusiasts. No book with a concentrated focus on the history of this Museum—seen through the lens of its contemporary decorative arts collections—could be written without access to the Museum's Archives. I owe a great debt to Susan Anderson, Martha Hamilton Morris Archivist, who shared my joy when I made discoveries and provided information and assistance when I needed help, as well as to her most able colleague, Bertha Adams, project archivist. I would like to extend my enduring gratitude to the Museum's library staff who supplied me with countless books and journal articles to advance and illustrate this study: C. Danial Elliott, Arcadia Director of the Library and Archives; Linda Martin-Schaff, library cataloguer; Ryan McNally, library and visual resources assistant; Rick Sieber, assistant reader services librarian; Evan Towle, librarian for reader services; and Mary Wassermann, librarian for collection development. The Museum's photography department made a special campaign to illustrate this book. For his fine work I am especially grateful to Graydon Wood, senior photographer, as well as to photographers Lynn Rosenthal and James Jason Wierzbicki and to Conna Clark, director of rights and reproductions. My curatorial colleagues answered many questions, particularly among them Dilys Blum, The Jack M. and Annette Y. Friedland Senior Curator of Costume and Textiles. Evan H. Turner and James N. Kise kindly read the text and offered valuable suggestions. For his assistance and patience in preparing the manuscript and assembling the illustrations, I would like to express my heartfelt thanks to Joseph McDermott as well as to Rebecca Chewning, who succeeded him. Finally, it is a pleasure to record my gratitude to Sherry Babbitt, the Museum's William T. Ranney Director of Publishing, for her unfailing interest in and enthusiasm for this project; to Mary Cason, associate editor, who perceptively and vigilantly wrestled the text, notes, and illustrations into intelligible proportions; and to Lisa Benn, whose skills as a designer this book so handsomely demonstrates.

Hella Jongerius : for Porzellan Manufaktur Nymphenburg : *Summer* Teapot from *Four Seasons* : 2007 : glazed hard-paste porcelain, silk : H 10 1/2" : 2010-60-1a–d (cat. 96)

1876-1915

THE MUSEUM'S ORIGINS IN A NUCLEUS OF WORKS

The uneven history of the Philadelphia Museum of Art's collections of modern and contemporary decorative arts—known from the later twentieth century as "design"—is the subject of this book. The account rises and falls with the vision and economic fortunes of the institution, its staff, private individuals, and the taste generally for modernism in Philadelphia, which was described by *Good Furniture Magazine* in 1923 as "a big, conservative . . . community that reacts more slowly to innovations than any other city in the country."[1] Over two decades later, in 1944, the Museum's director, Fiske Kimball, reviewed the institution's history of collecting as well as its policies for acquisitions: "It is only fair to say today that prior to 1915, and even down to 1925, the collections of the Museum and of the City, housed at Memorial Hall . . . were—judged by present standards—most inadequate. They comprised . . . the very extensive systematic collections of industrial art assembled by the Museum since 1876 on the model of those at the Victoria and Albert Museum. Valuable for the illustration of types and techniques, they were, with honorable exceptions, lacking in works of high quality." While Kimball noted that the present twentieth-century collections were "very strong," he made an exception for the decorative arts, which were "almost totally lacking."[2] Today, however, the Museum's distinguished collections of modern and contemporary design are among the largest and most important of any comprehensive museum. This is a history with a happy outcome in the present.

The Philadelphia Museum of Art had its origins in the Pennsylvania Museum and School of Industrial Art, which was founded in 1875 on the eve of the Philadelphia International (Centennial) Exhibition of 1876, and given its first home in Memorial Hall (fig. 2), the fine arts exhibition building (the name of the institution would only formally change in 1938; see page 106). In order to form "a nucleus of works of industrial art . . . which, in time, could not fail to have a most beneficial influence upon the industries of our State and City,"[3] a selection committee was appointed by the Museum's newly elected board of trustees to spend $25,000 at the exhibition on the institution's first acquisitions. The committee was headed by William Platt Pepper, vice president of the corporation and managing director of the Museum. Along with Pepper the selection committee consisted of trustees in their capacity as members of four standing committees—on the mechanic arts, materials used in the art industries, the art library, and ornamental art. The latter committee was given overall responsibility for collections, having "entire charge of the purchase and arrangement of works of art as applied to Industry that may be acquired by the corporation."[4] Representing ornamental art on the selection committee were its chair, William Platt Pepper, and Henry C. Gibson; the committee on the art library was represented by its chair, Samuel Wagner, Jr., and Fairman Rogers; and the committees on the mechanic arts and materials used in the art industries, by Thomas Dolan.

The tastemakers on the Museum's board included Philadelphia's educated professional elite as well as self-made men, among them lawyers, physicians, bankers, university professors, civil servants, manufacturers, and art teachers. Some had inherited wealth and social status, others had made their own professional marks and fortunes. William Platt Pepper was a lawyer from a prominent, wealthy Philadelphia family that also included selection committee member Dr. William Pepper, chair and professor of clinical medicine at the University of Pennsylvania (he also served as medical director of the

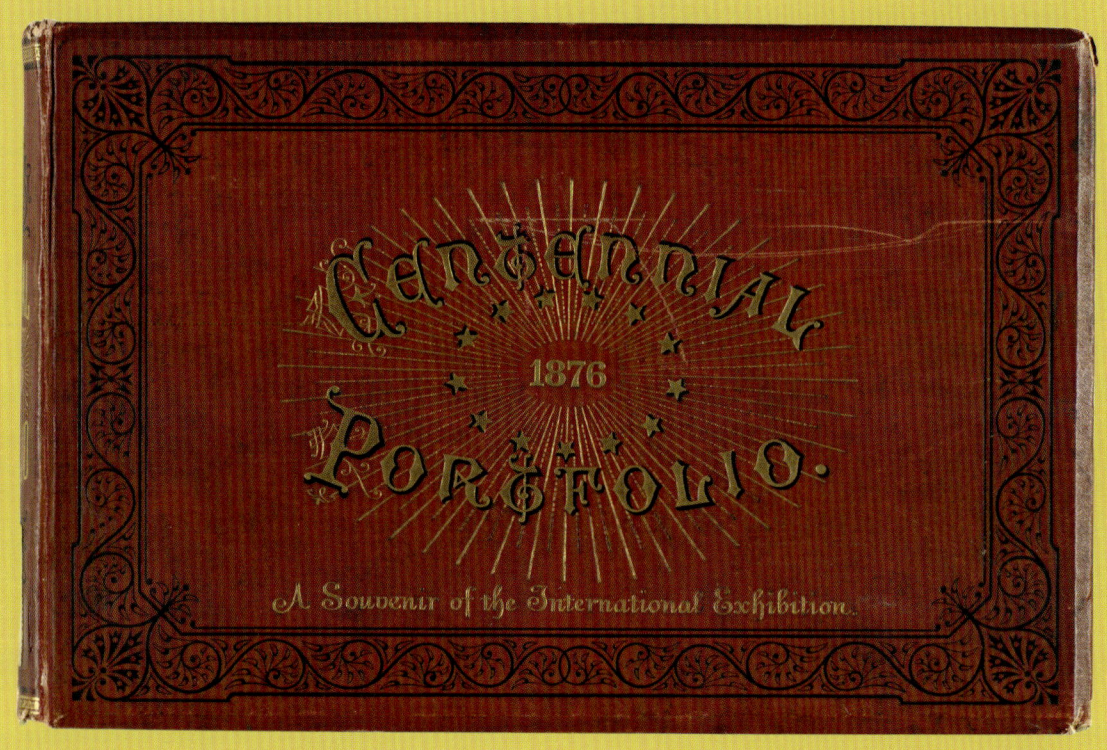

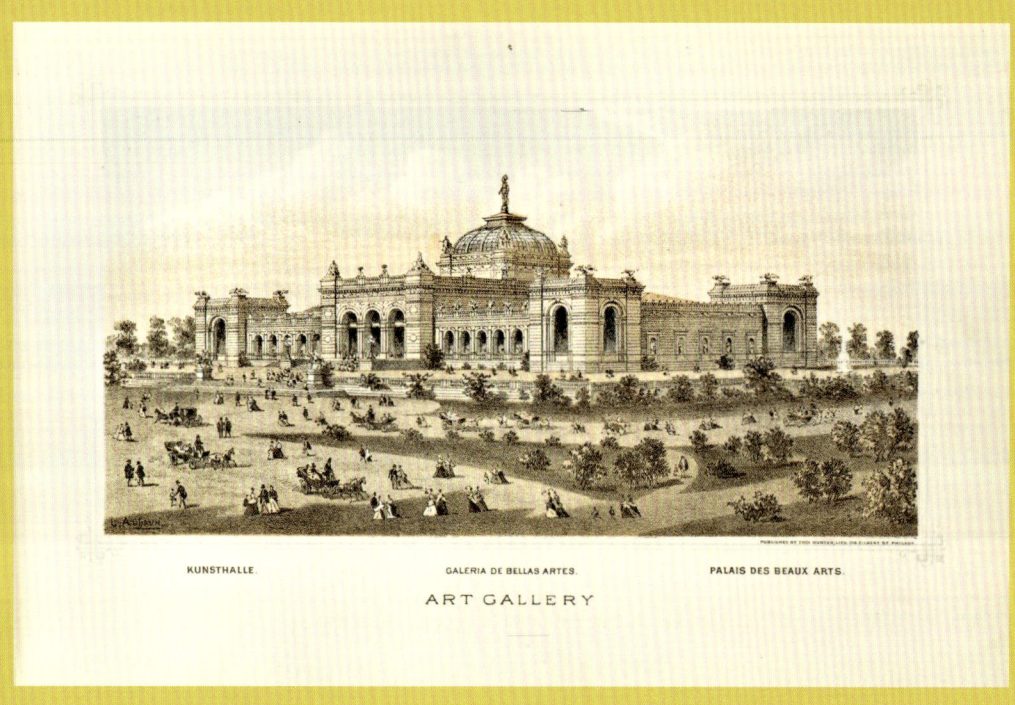

Above, top to bottom : **1. Thompson Westcott** : *Centennial Portfolio: A Souvenir of the International Exhibition at Philadelphia* (Philadelphia: T. Hunter, 1876) (cat. 212)   **2.** Art Gallery, Memorial Hall (later Pennsylvania Museum and School of Industrial Art) : 1876 : from *Centennial Portfolio*
Opposite : **3. Artist/maker unknown** (United States) : *Centennial* Handkerchief : 1876 : printed cotton : W 24¼" : 1913-223 (cat. 14)

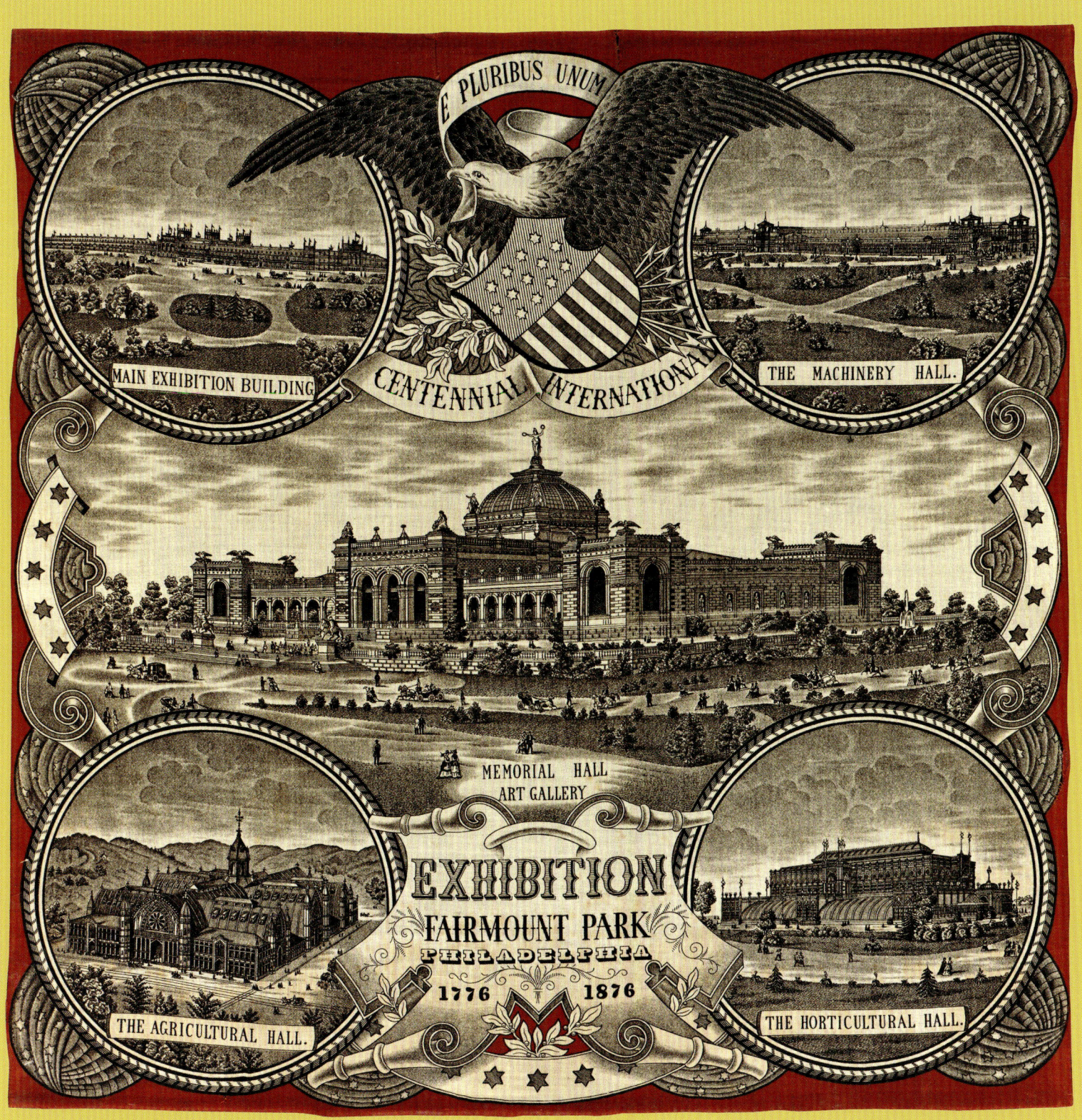

Centennial Exhibition). Unlike the Peppers, Dolan was born "of obscure ancestry"[5] but made his fortune manufacturing textiles and clothing during the Civil War. Gibson was a prosperous real estate developer who inherited money from his father's whiskey-distilling company. Wagner was a lawyer and bibliophile, and Rogers was a civil engineer and professor of civil engineering at the University of Pennsylvania (which he represented on the Museum's board). Rounding out the selection committee were Coleman Sellers and John Baird. Sellers, president of the board of trustees, was a well-known engineer and inventor who also had served from 1870 to 1875 as president of Philadelphia's Franklin Institute, founded for the promotion of the mechanic arts in 1824. His maternal grandfather was the American painter Charles Willson Peale (1741–1827), a pedigree that gave him considerable clout among the art-minded in Philadelphia. Baird was a marble supplier (for the extension of the Capitol in Washington, D.C., among other projects) and chaired the Museum's building committee.

Connected by wealth and civic interest, the selection committee combined members who were considered to have good aesthetic judgment—notably Gibson, Sellers, and William Platt Pepper—with those appointed for their ability to apply an interest in science and technology to art, thereby fusing industry and artistic concerns. As the Museum's didactic mission was intended to demonstrate the inseparability of art and science, the initial program for collecting was not confined to works of art, but also extended to patented inventions as well as plant and animal materials. Among the aesthetes, judged by their later gifts to the Museum, William Platt Pepper seemed personally interested in archaeological and non-Western objects, ranging from Pre-Columbian pottery (given in 1883) to Persian ceramics (1891) to Chinese bamboo screens (1894). Gibson, partnering with fellow trustees Francis W. Lewis and Clarence H. Clark, gave the Museum an eighteenth-century Chinese wall hanging in 1885 and a handsome group of transfer-printed English earthenware in 1889. When Pepper resigned as the Museum's managing director in 1879, the board urged him to continue as vice president (he did), so that the Museum "could continue to enjoy the benefit of his cultivated taste and excellent judgement in those departments of industry and art in which this Institution is particularly interested."[6]

The *Philadelphia Times* reported in the fall of 1876 the selection committee's purchases of both historic and contemporary objects.[7] The latter embraced the fashionable historicizing styles exemplified by Thomas John Bott, Jr.'s porcelain ewer (fig. 4) and stand designed for the Worcester Royal Porcelain Company in imitation of sixteenth-century Limoges copper-ground enamels—an impressive technical feat noted by contemporaries. Bott's ewer and stand were one of thirteen pieces of porcelain

4. **Thomas John Bott, Jr.**: for Worcester Royal Porcelain : Ewer : 1875 : enameled and gilt porcelain : H 11¼" : 1876-1623 (cat. 23)

and earthenware purchased at the Centennial Exhibition for $1,600 from the stand of the London china merchant A. B. Daniell and Son (fig. 6), which represented two firms, Minton and Worcester. The Minton display included parian porcelains with *pâte-sur-pâte* and gilt decoration in the "Greek" style by Marc-Louis-Emmanuel Solon; from this display the Museum purchased two vases, *L'Échange* and *La Grace* (fig. 5)—the first of several pieces by Solon that the Museum would acquire. The selection committee described these works as "remarkable for their excellence of workmanship and artistic design."[8] The committee also bought thirty-three examples of pottery and tiles from the British firm of Doulton & Company for a total of $550,[9] including an oval platter painted by Mary Butterton with a Persian-style design of scattered foliage (fig. 11). The platter perhaps appears more modern to us today than do other pieces from the exhibition because of the decoration's loose arrangement on a plain ground and reliance on a non-Western source. Gifts from manufacturers added to the Museum's initial collection, including a cut-glass wine set made by the Dorflinger Glass Company of White Mills, Pennsylvania, the decanter bearing among other decorations the seal of the city of Philadelphia and the name of its mayor in 1876 (fig. 7). Japanese potter Riokei Nakashima gave the Museum a pair of porcelain jars from his manufactory at Satsuma "in grateful memory [of] the Eminent services rendered to my country by your great Naval Commander Commodore Perry, and the kindness which the Japanese have at all times received from your citizens."[10] The selection committee added an earthenware tray also made (and decorated) by Nakashima, and purchased directly from him (fig. 57).

In retrospect, the committee seems to have overlooked several displays that we would consider important today, among them, that of Vienna's pioneering bentwood furniture firm of Gebrüder Thonet. However, nearly a century later the Museum was able to purchase a collection of twelve bentwood chairs made after the designs of Michael Thonet and his successors (figs. 9, 10). Although wallpapers made by Morris and Company were given to the Museum in 1876 by an anonymous donor, many decades would pass before other examples of British Arts and Crafts would enter the collections, including a marquetry cabinet designed by George Washington Jack for Morris and Company (fig. 12) and a high-back chair designed by Charles Rennie Mackintosh about 1897 for the Argyle Street Tea Rooms in Glasgow (fig. 56). Souvenirs of the exhibition were also acquired in later years, such as Thompson Westcott's handsomely illustrated *Centennial Portfolio* (fig. 1) and a cotton handkerchief printed with views of the Centennial buildings (fig. 3), the latter given by Mrs. William D. Frishmuth, a noted collector of musical instruments and early American decorative arts.[11]

5. **Marc-Louis-Emmanuel Solon** : for Minton : *La Grace* Vase : 1875 : glazed and gilt Parian porcelain : H 15 3/16" : 1876-1620,a (cat. 178)

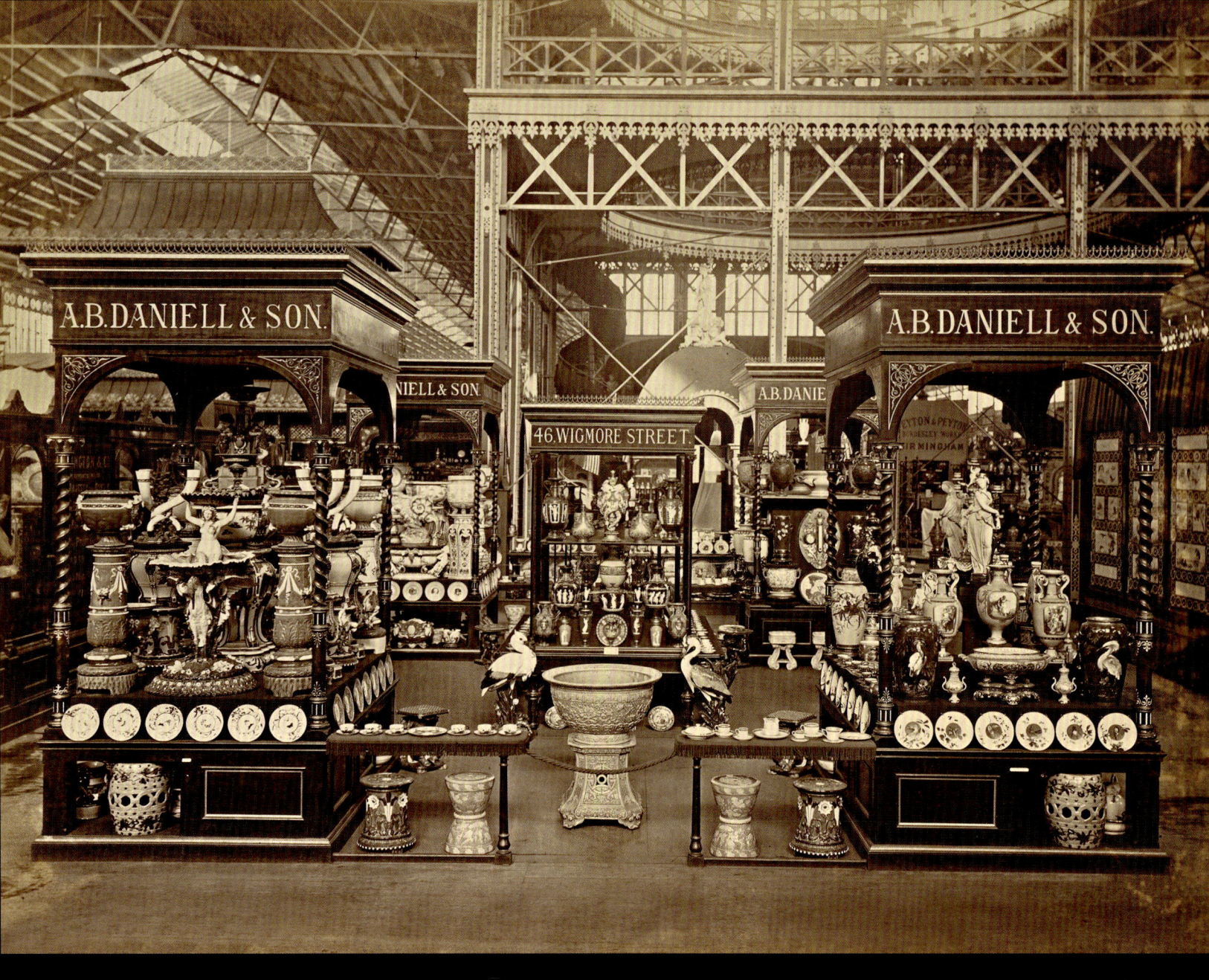
6. A. B. Daniell and Son at the Centennial Exhibition : 1876

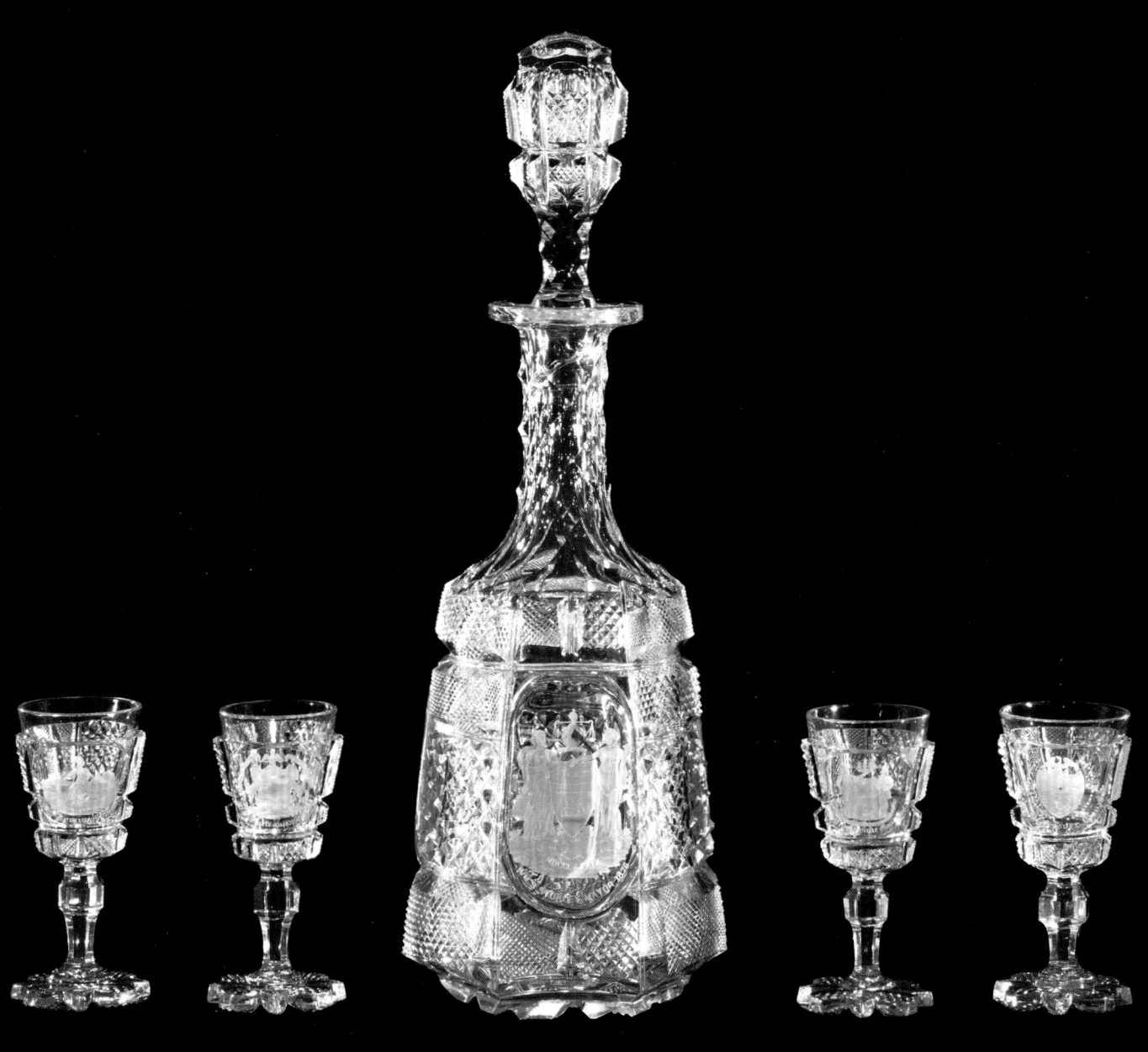

7. Dorflinger Glass Company · Decanter and Wineglasses · 1876 · glass · H (decanter) 16¼" · H (glass) 5" · 1876.1693–1693ll (cat. 46)

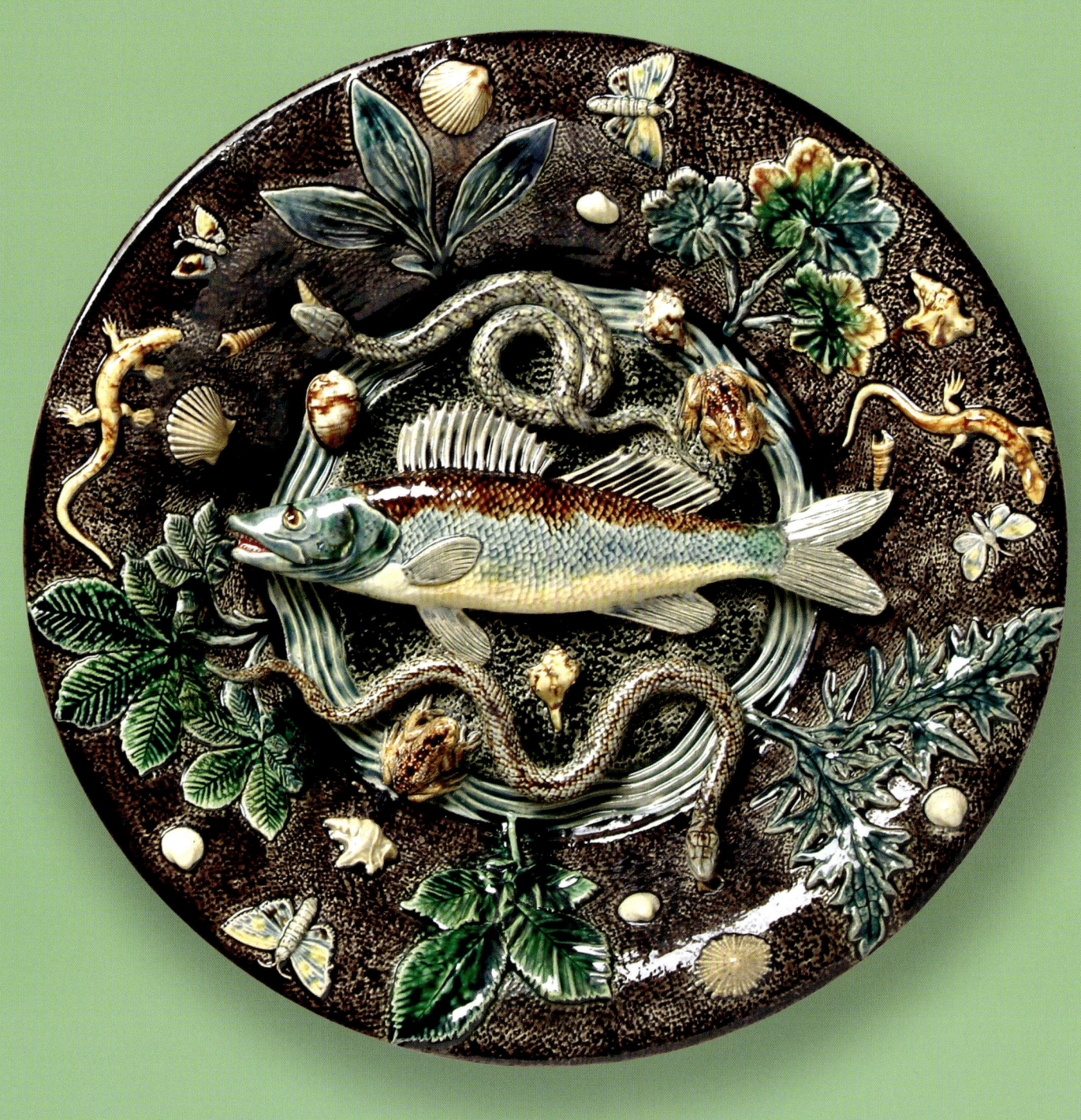

Above : **8. Rörstrand** : Plate : 1876 : glazed earthenware : D 20" : 1897-617 (cat. 162)   Opposite, left to right : **9. Gebrüder Thonet** : Desk Chair, *Model No. 9* : c. 1870 : beechwood, caning : H 29 3/8" : 1969-136-9 (cat. 186)   **10. Gebrüder Thonet** : Chair, *Model No. 51* : c. 1890–1900 : beechwood, caning : H 36 5/8" : 1969-136-8 (cat. 187)

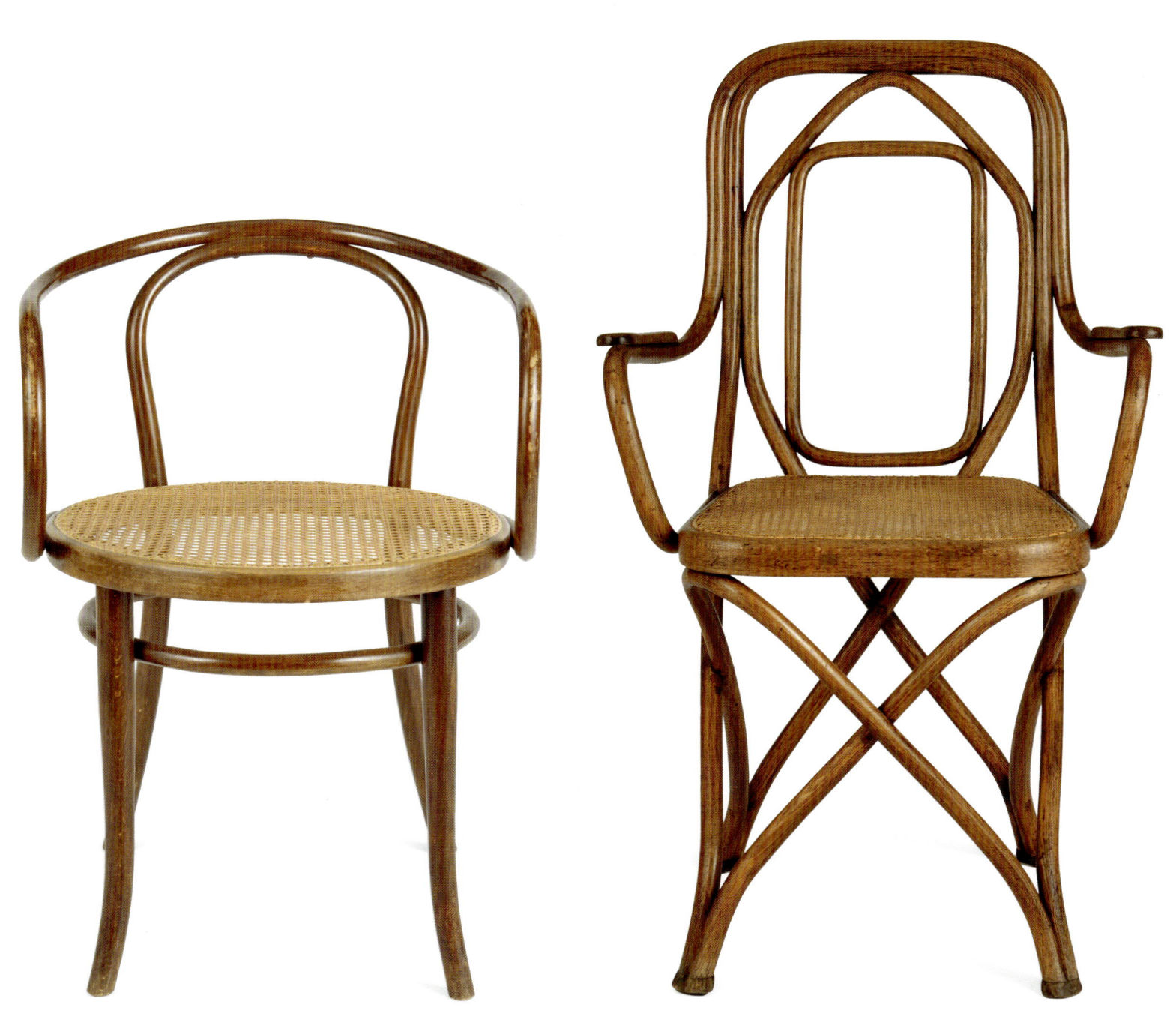

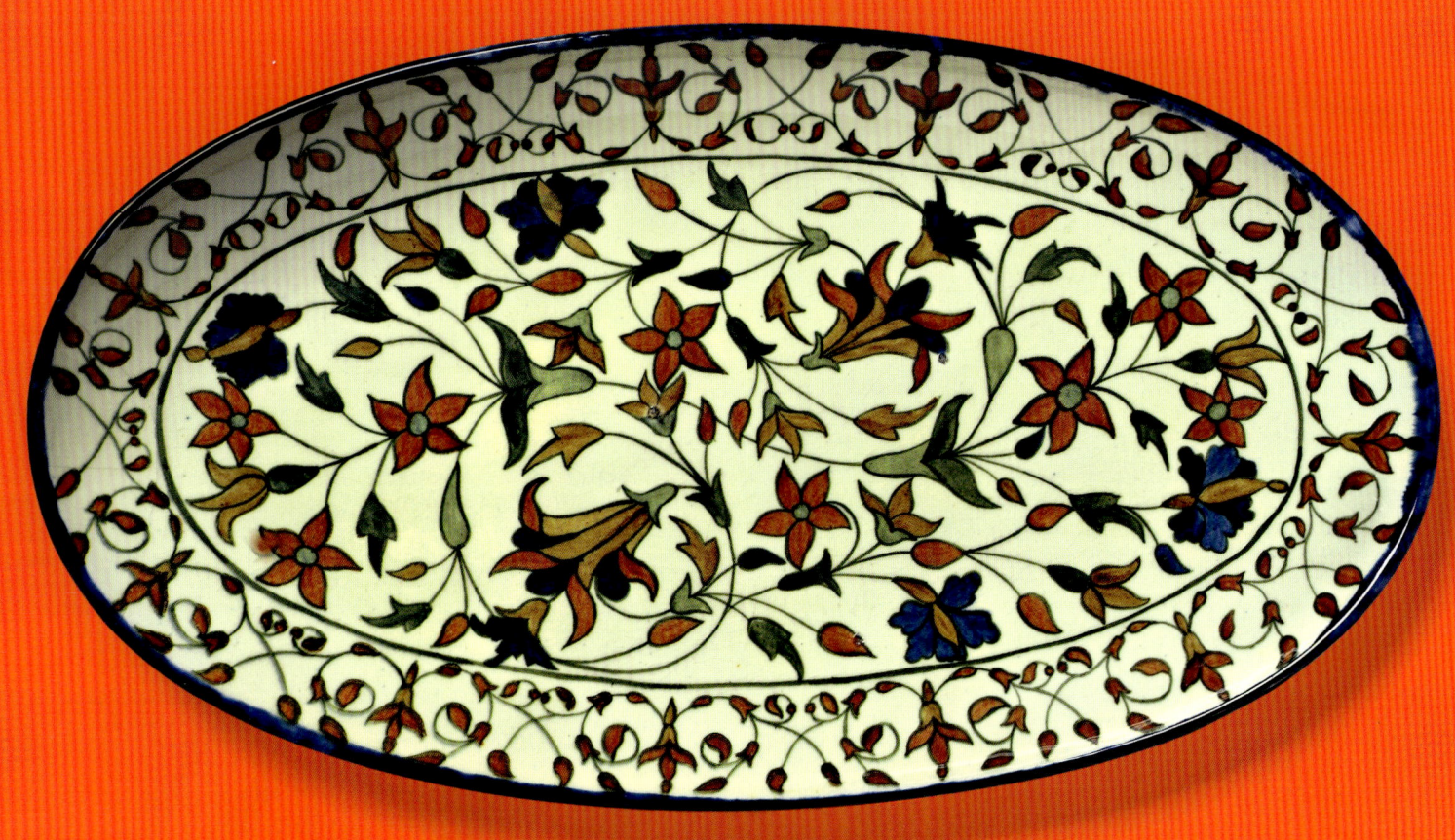

11. Mary Butterton : for Doulton : Dish : c. 1876 : glazed earthenware : W 7⁷/₁₆" : 1876-64 (cat. 25)

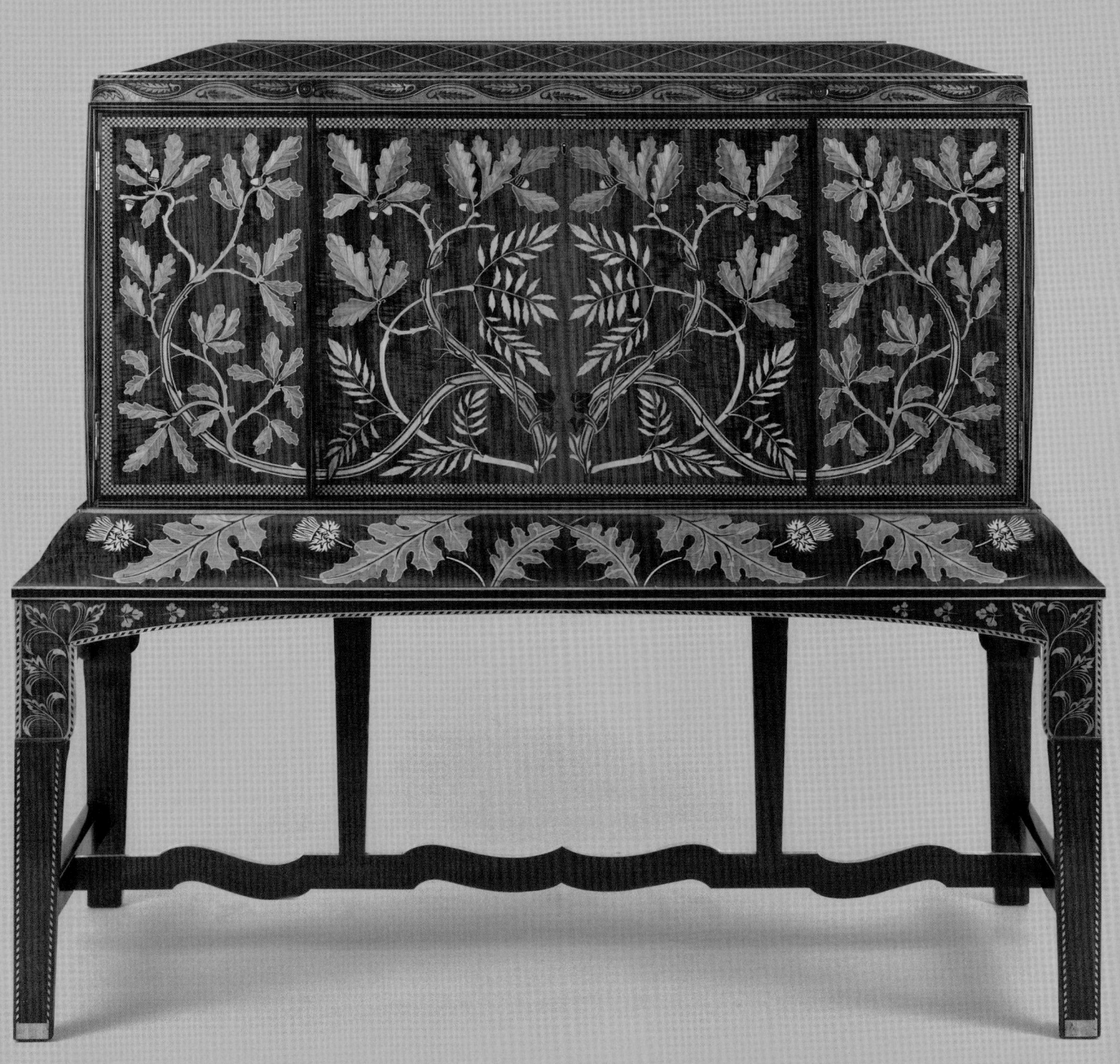

12. George Washington Jack : for Morris and Company : Secretaire Cabinet : c. 1889 : mahogany, hardwoods : H 51½" : 1986-128-1a,b (cat. 87)

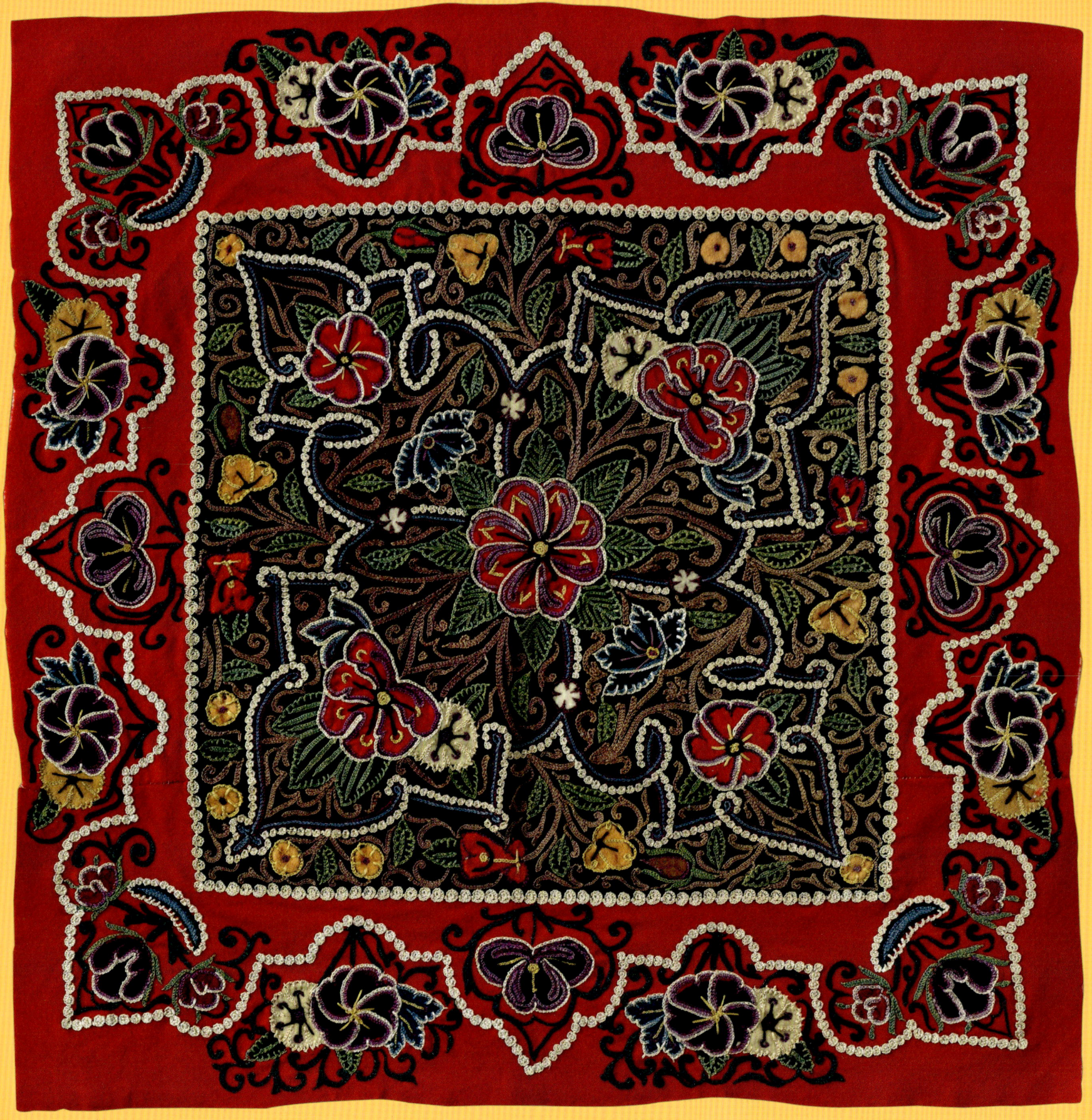

SETTING AN EXAMPLE FOR INDUSTRY AND THE PUBLIC

The character of the institution that the selection committee hoped to form had been defined earlier as "a Museum of Art,"[12] and once, in passing, as a "Museum of Industrial, Decorative and Antiquarian Art."[13] Following a report "on Museums of Art in Europe and in this country" made by the provisional committee that drafted the Museum's charter in 1875, the fledgling institution was created as the Pennsylvania Museum and School of Industrial Art, with a mission "to be in all respects similar to that of the South Kensington Museum of London,"[14] which was also associated with an art school known originally as the School of Design. The Pennsylvania Museum would remain linked to its school until 1964, when the latter achieved independent status as the Philadelphia College of Art (later the University of the Arts).[15] Like the collections of the South Kensington (later the Victoria and Albert) Museum, those of the Pennsylvania Museum were intended to instruct and improve by example the taste of industry and its students as well as that of the general public. Such optimistic faith in the natural abilities of all individuals to learn and judge critically shaped committee members' attitudes toward the Museum's uneducated audience, and toward themselves as connoisseurs and arbiters of taste. Pressure to emphasize the institution's pedagogical purpose through its collections came from the state of Pennsyslvania. In his 1876 annual address Governor John F. Hartranft, who served (ex-officio) on the Museum's board, pointed out that Pennsylvania lacked "industrial education" to train "intelligent farmers, manufacturers, miners, and mechanics," and that the Centennial Exhibition (fig. 14) had brought the opportunity to establish a museum and school in Memorial Hall wherein "to form an art library; special collections, illustrative of industrial processes[;] and a thorough system of instruction in the arts of design as applied to manufactures, accompanied by general and technical lectures." The institution would contain, according to Hartranft, "the nucleus of a collection . . . intended to promote the improvement of American industrial art."[16] Accordingly, along with the fine contemporary English ceramics described above, the selection committee purchased and acquired by gift a wide range of objects and materials in the fields of art, science, and natural history, including historic and contemporary textiles (figs. 13, 20) and fifty-six specimens of Belgian flax meant to enlighten Philadelphia's economically important textile industry. Whether or not related to collecting textiles, in 1879 the Entomological Section of the Academy of Natural Sciences presented the Museum with a collection of insects.[17]

The committee's first acquisition, described by the *Philadelphia Times* as "the most interesting purchase yet," was from Elkington and Company of London: "their complete collection of electrotype reproductions of the original artistic works in gold, silver, bronze, iron and other metals," which had been collected by and then exhibited at the South Kensington Museum. As the newspaper noted, "Those originals represent the artistic work in metal of all ages and all climes, and all that the student can learn from them he can learn from the reproductions" (figs. 17, 19).[18] In addition, the selection committee also reported to the board that it had purchased for $1,500 from the Centennial's Egyptian exhibit "the collections of casts in plaster and zinc of Arabic ornament taken directly from the mosques and tombs for the first time by order of the Khedive."[19] While today we would argue that the value to the student lies more in the experience of an original, unique work of art than in a reproduction of it, the collecting of reproductions and casts for teaching purposes by museums, schools, and universities had a long history in the nineteenth century. Plaster casts of antiquities in particular were assiduously collected to provide access to great works of art at little cost. Art students in Europe and the United States—

13. **Artist/maker unknown** (Caucasus) : Pieced Cover : c. 1876 : wool, silk : H 19¾" : 1876-507 (cat. 8)

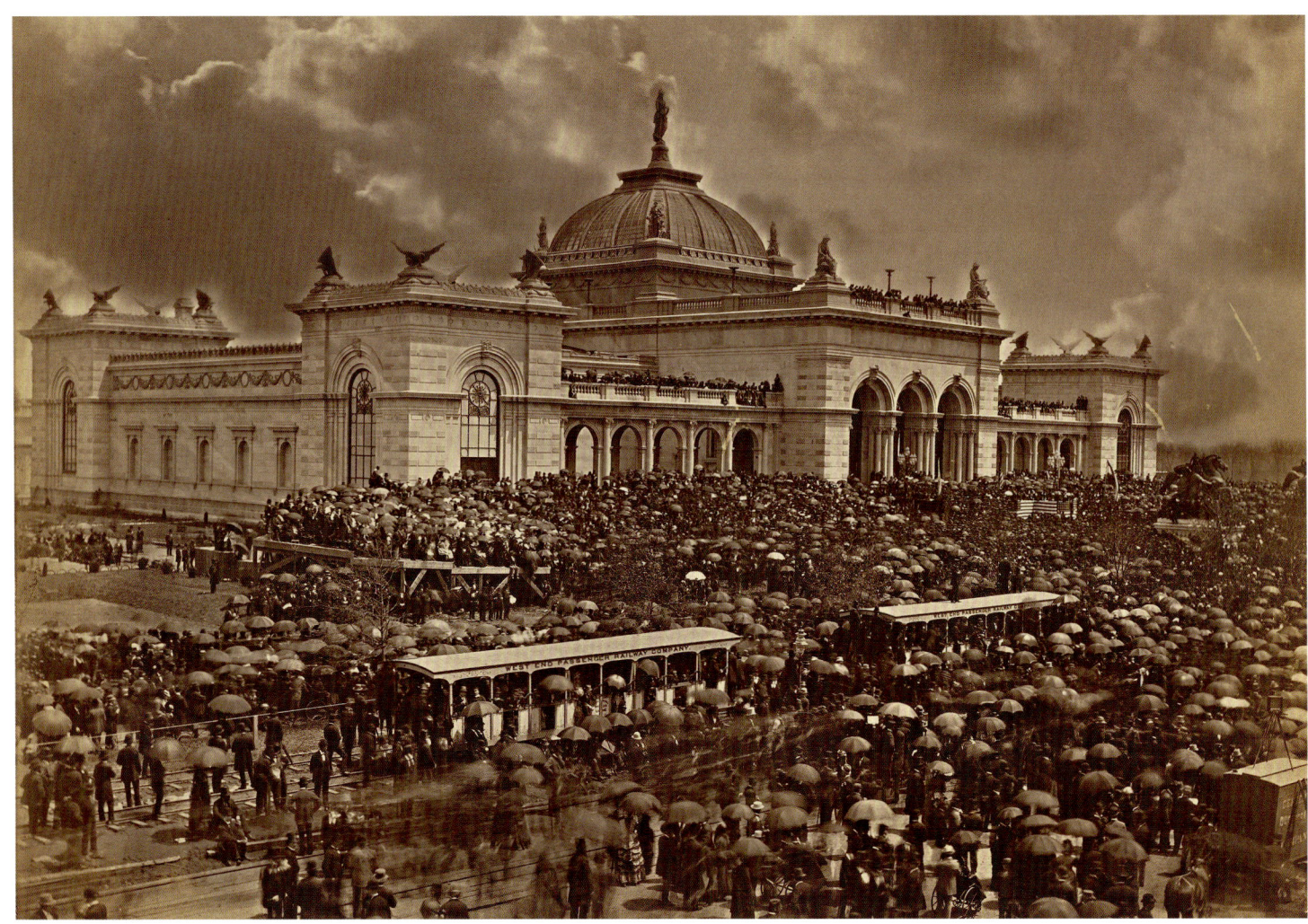

including the Philadelphia painter Thomas Eakins, who studied at the Pennsylvania Academy of the Fine Arts—routinely drew from casts until they were deemed proficient enough to work from live models. By the end of the century, however, the Pennsylvania Museum, along with other American museums, began to shift away from collecting casts to acquiring original works as the latter became available from private European collections and archaeological digs. Still, as late as 1935 the Museum's board of trustees authorized the school principal to purchase three casts from the "Florentine Art Shop" for $35.00.[20]

Already in the fall of 1876, while waiting for Memorial Hall to be refurbished as a museum, the board of trustees asked the committee on ornamental art to inquire into the possibility of exhibiting the Museum's first acquisitions at the Pennsylvania Academy of the Fine Arts.[21] The exhibition was also to include loans, some borrowed from private collections.[22] Smoothing the way for the request to use the academy's space was John Sartain, a well-respected artist and printmaker, member of the Museum's committee on instruction, and long-serving and influential board member of the academy. Sartain had also headed the fine arts section at the Centennial Exhibition in Memorial Hall. Thus from January to March 1877 the Museum's *Art Applied to Industries* exhibition was shown at the academy, tickets required. The exhibition was not financially successful, although the deficit was said to have been "more than repaid by subscriptions from those whose

14. Opening Day Ceremony at the 1876 Centennial Exhibition : Art Gallery at Memorial Hall

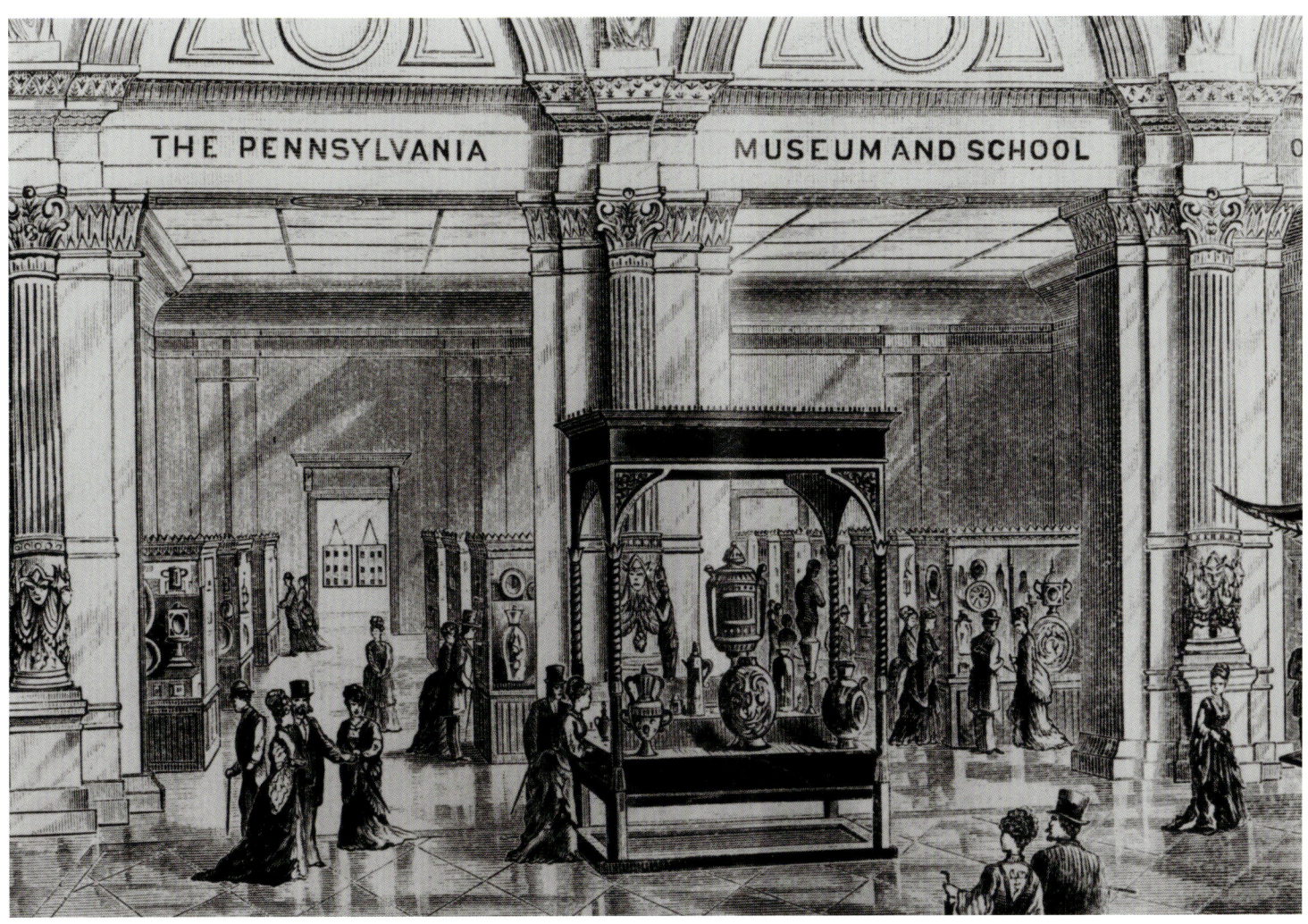

15. Early rendering of the Pennsylvania Museum and School of Industrial Art : c. 1877

interest was aroused."[23] At the close of the exhibition, the objects were moved to Memorial Hall by direction of the committee on ornamental art, and then displayed to the public on May 10, 1877, at the opening of the Pennsylvania Museum and School of Industrial Art (fig. 15).[24]

Following the example of the South Kensington Museum, the Pennsylvania Museum organized and displayed its collections by medium and technique of manufacture, "grouping together, so far as practicable, objects of similar character, and perfecting the plan of labelling, in order that the visitors might be informed of the exact character of each object, and be enabled to study them more intelligently."[25] Contemporary English and French ceramics and glass were lent to the Museum by A. B. Daniell and Son as well as Londros & Co., also of London, along with Spanish glass and pottery recommended by the scholar Juan Riaño, who had catalogued the Spanish objects at South Kensington.[26] These loans were all negotiated and arranged, with an option to purchase, by the director of the South Kensington Museum, Philip Cunliffe-Owen, who had himself purchased a group of Persian objects for the Pennsylvania Museum. Faith in Owen, who had advised the Museum since its inception, was both boundless and well founded. Around this time the Museum corporation also allowed the American Institute of Mining Engineers to display its Centennial exhibition of mining and metallurgy in Memorial Hall, arguing that "this material is of the greatest interest and value as bearing upon one of the most important industries of the State, and although not

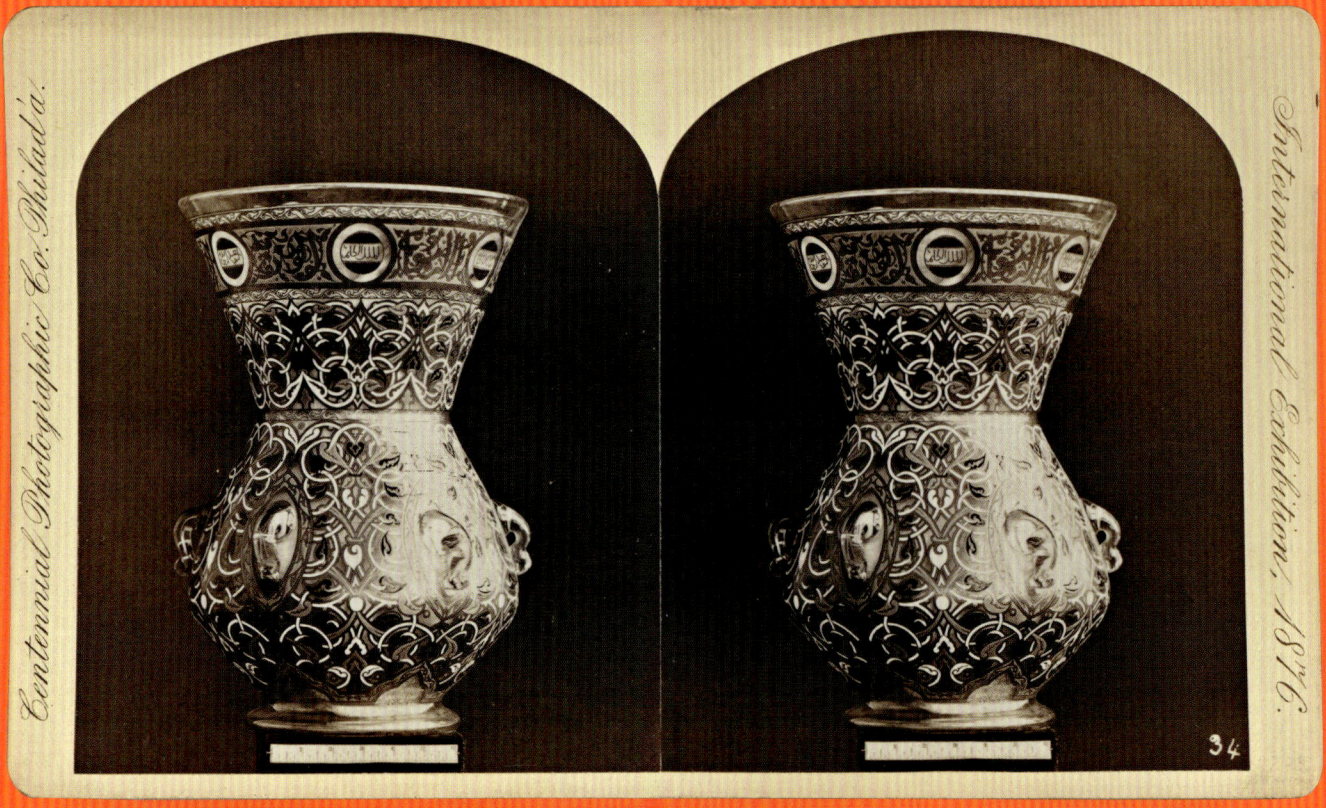
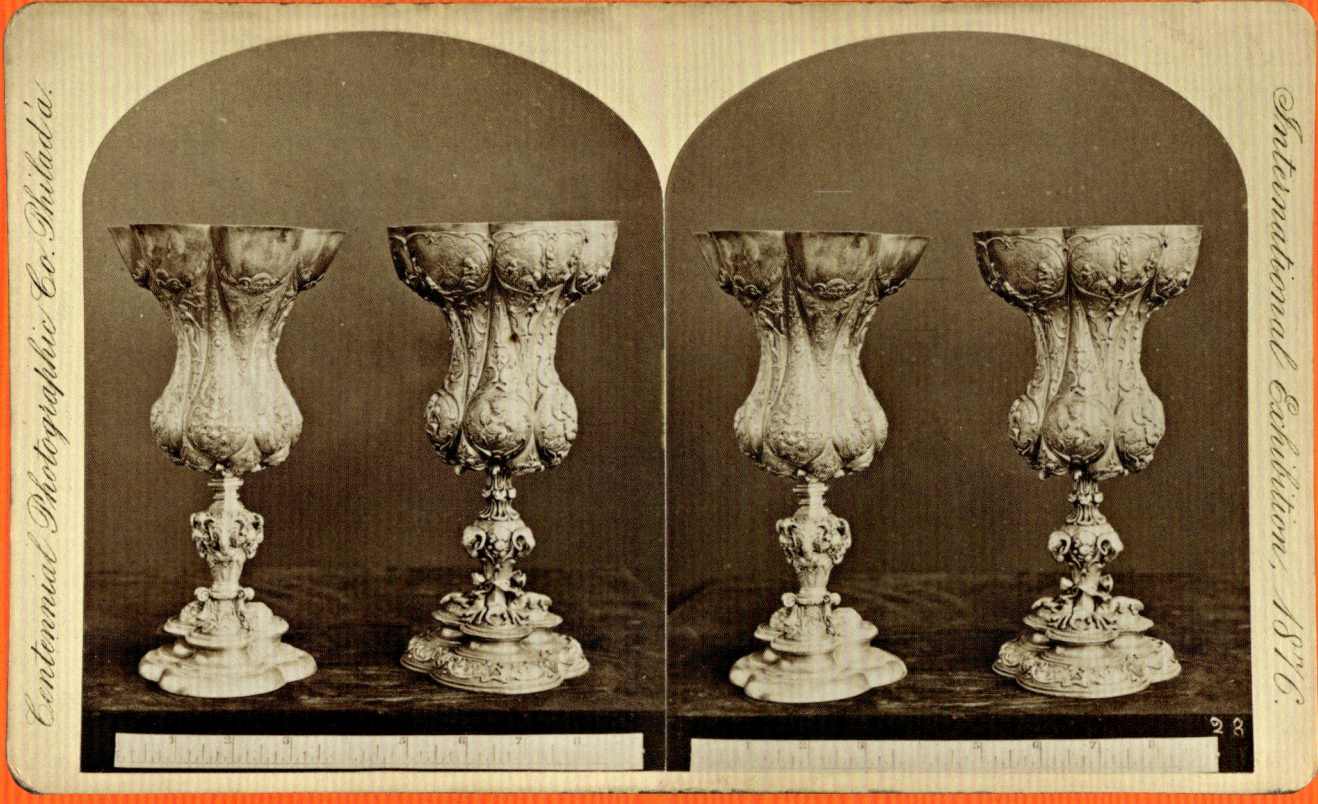

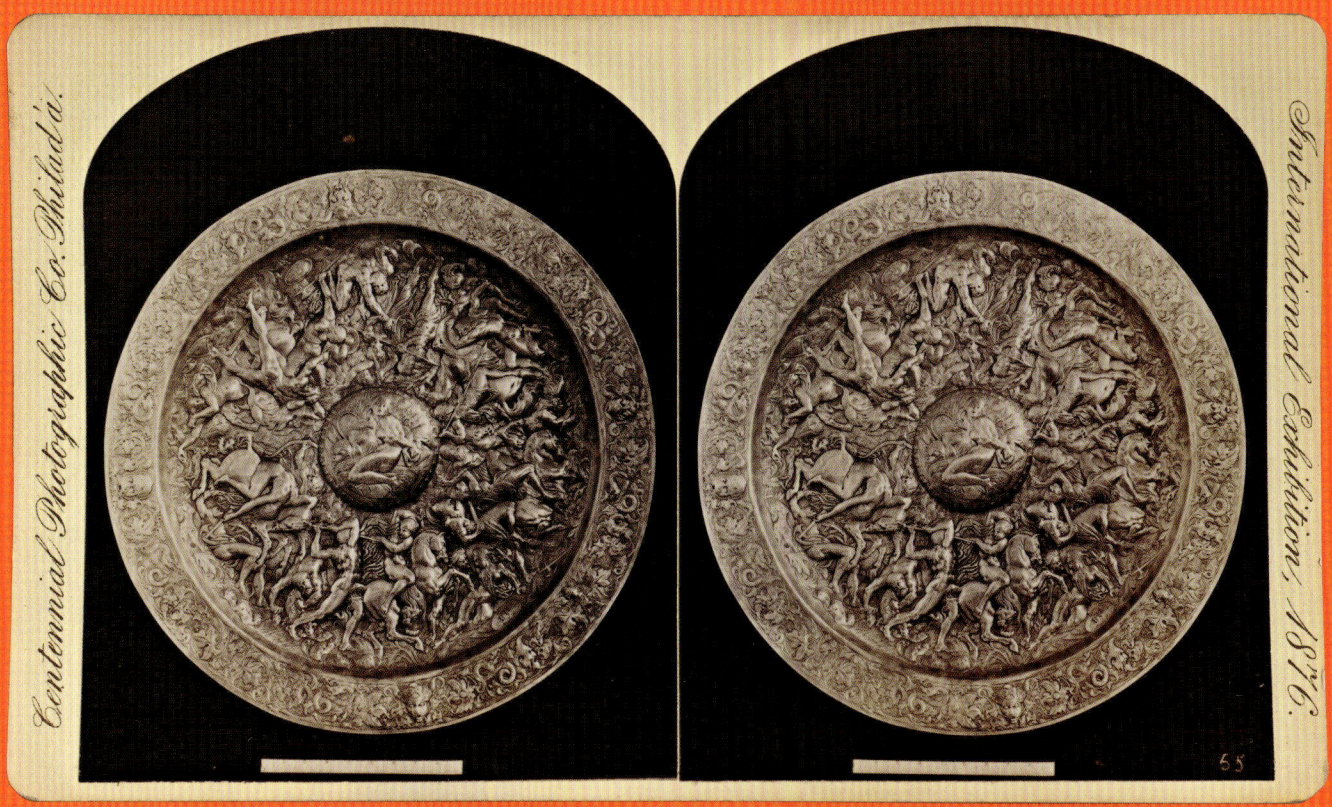

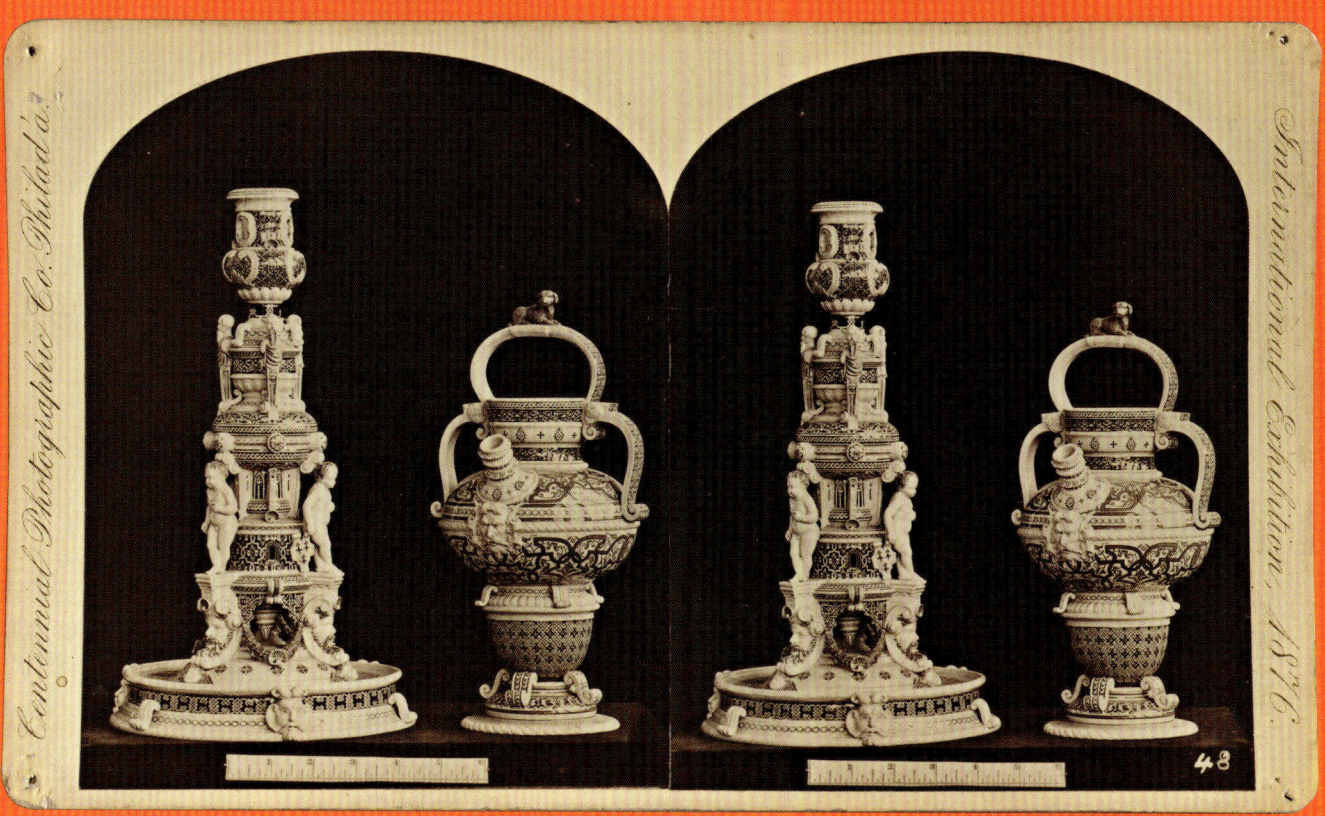

16–19. Stereographs by Edward L. Wilson from *The Collection of the Pennsylvania Museum and School of Industrial Art* (Philadelphia: Centennial Photographic Company, c. 1877) : gelatin silver prints   Clockwise from top left : **16. Philippe-Joseph Brocard** : Lamp : glass   **17. Antoine Vechte** : Salver : silvered electrotype reproduction   **18. Charles Toft** : for Minton : Candlestick and Biberon : glazed earthenware   **19. Artist/maker unknown** : *Jamnitzer* Cup : silvered electrotype reproduction

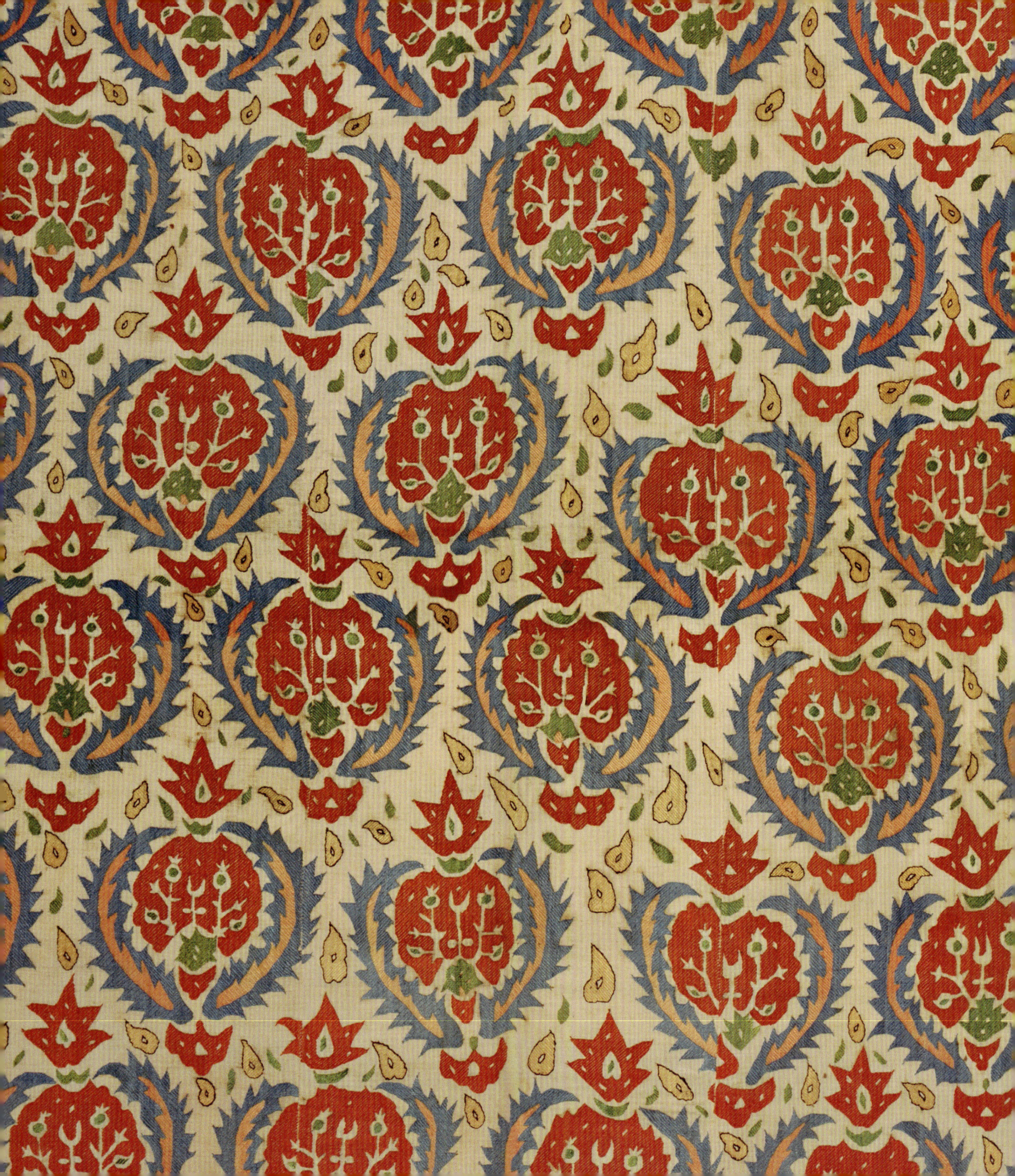

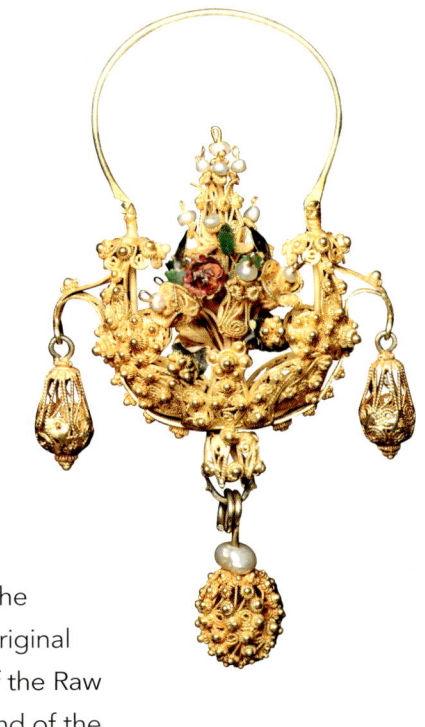
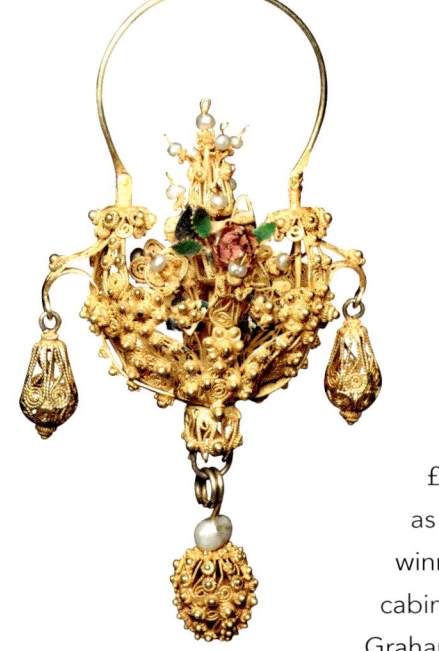

possessing any art character, is quite in keeping with two of the departments of the original Museum plan, that of the Raw Material collection, and of the collection illustrative of the Mechanic Arts."[27] Although supported strongly by the governor and certain trustees, this was a decision the Museum corporation was soon and long to regret: the material occupied much valuable exhibition space, and the parameters of the Museum's collections would change within a decade.

In early 1878 the trustees decided to send the corporation's secretary, H. Dumont Wagner, to the international exhibition being held in Paris from May to October of that year.[28] He was given $1,500 to spend on "works of art applied to Industry as may in his judgment be suitable."[29] Wagner also served as special commissioner for Pennsylvania to inquire into the systems of industrial art education then current in Europe.[30] However, he could find little at the exhibition to buy for the Museum, judging that "the objects exhibited, the value of which was within the means of the Museum, differed little from those of the same class purchased at the Centennial Exhibition." He consequently "bought but few specimens, considering it best to purchase books on industrial art"[31] for the library, to which was added eventually Jules Goury and Owen Jones's important two-volume publication on the Alhambra (fig. 25), which demonstrated to its readers the potential of non-European—particularly Islamic—decoration. At £2,000, objects such as Bruce Talbert's prize-winning Anglo-Japanese cabinet for Jackson and Graham might have been beyond the Museum's budget (it was sold to the khedive of Egypt), or considered too close to the Japanese lacquered cabinet purchased at the Centennial from the Imperial Japanese Commission (fig. 24), but countless other, smaller objects could have been purchased, notably ceramics by Émile Gallé, to further develop the handsome, affordable collection in that medium begun in 1876.

It may have been regret for an opportunity lost that spurred the trustees to purchase the following year examples of enameled glass by Philippe-Joseph Brocard, France's first modern artist-glassmaker, as well as glazed earthenware by Joseph-Théodore Deck, the most influential and technically progressive ceramist in France. These adventurous purchases, described as "interesting specimens of Industrial Art,"[32] were acquired from among the loans made by the firm of Londros to the Museum's inaugural exhibition at Memorial Hall. Sadly, none of these works, like the vast number of acquisitions made by the selection committee in 1876, have survived in the Museum's collections—all sold, unlocated, damaged and destroyed, or transferred to other institutions (figs. 16–19). However, since 1969 a number of works by Deck in the exotic non-Western styles he championed have finally reentered the collections (fig. 22).

Opposite : **20. Artist/maker unknown** (Turkey) : Quilt Facing *(Yorgan Yüzü)* (detail): c. 1300–1919 : linen, silk : W 50" : 1877-18 (cat. 13)
Above : **21. Giacinto Melillo** : Pair of Earrings : c. 1870 : gold, enamel, pearl : L 4 3/8" : 1925-27-337a,b (cat. 127)

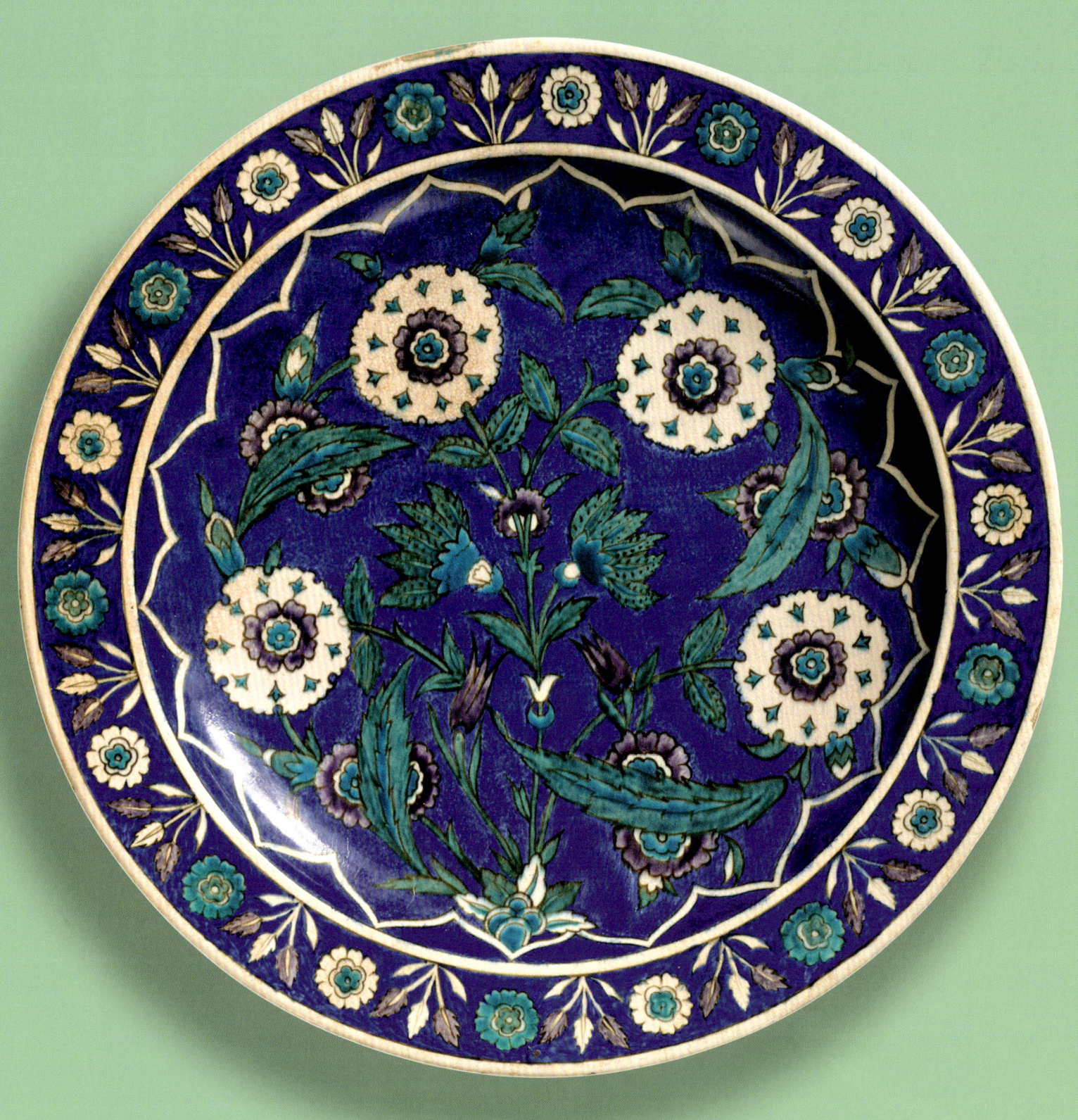

22. Joseph-Théodore Deck : Dish : 1863 : glazed and enameled earthenware : D 18 13/16" : 1978-117-1 (cat. 44)

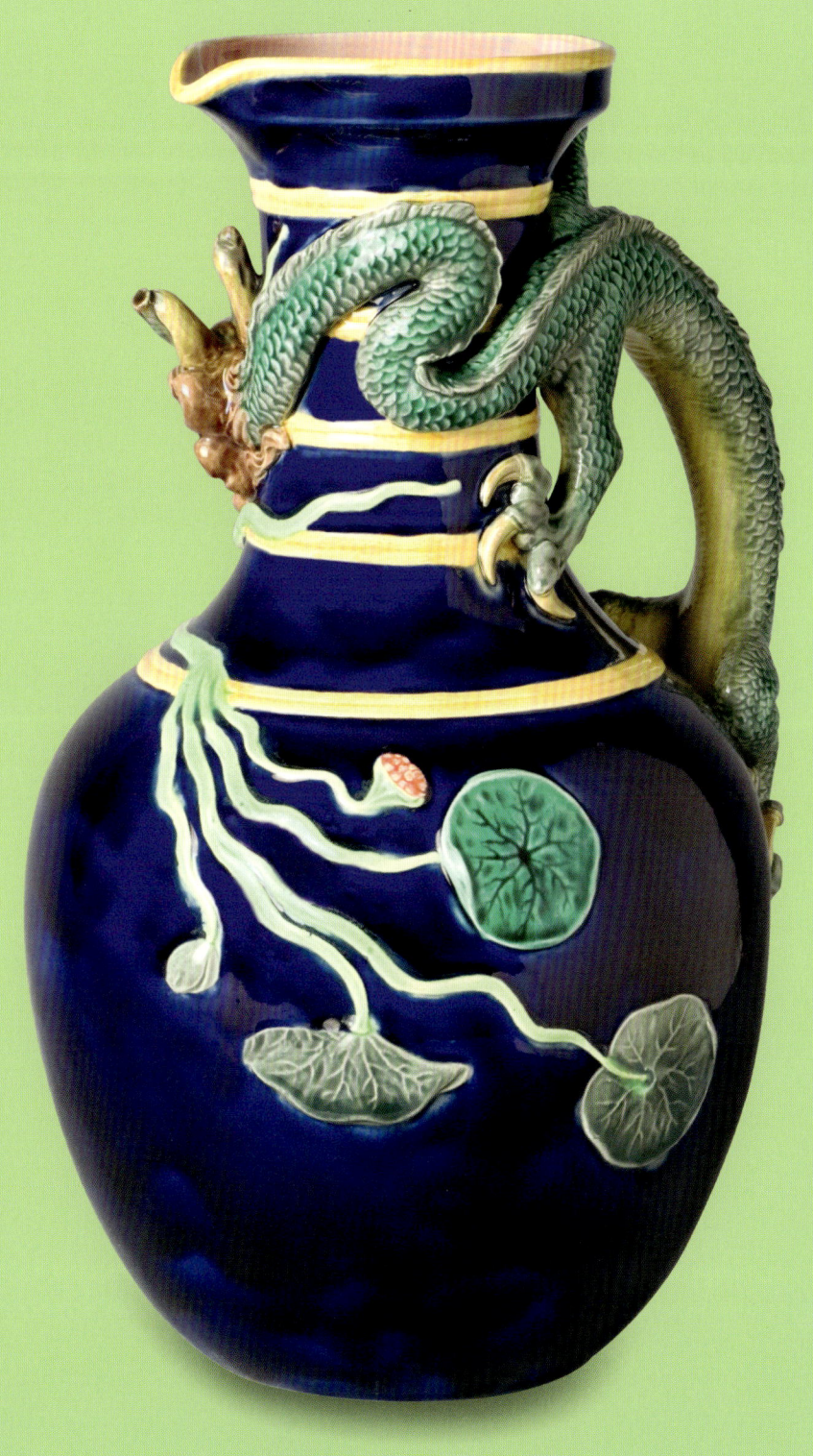

23. W. T. Copeland & Sons : Pitcher : c. 1876 : glazed earthenware : H 10½" : 1897-522 (cat. 37)

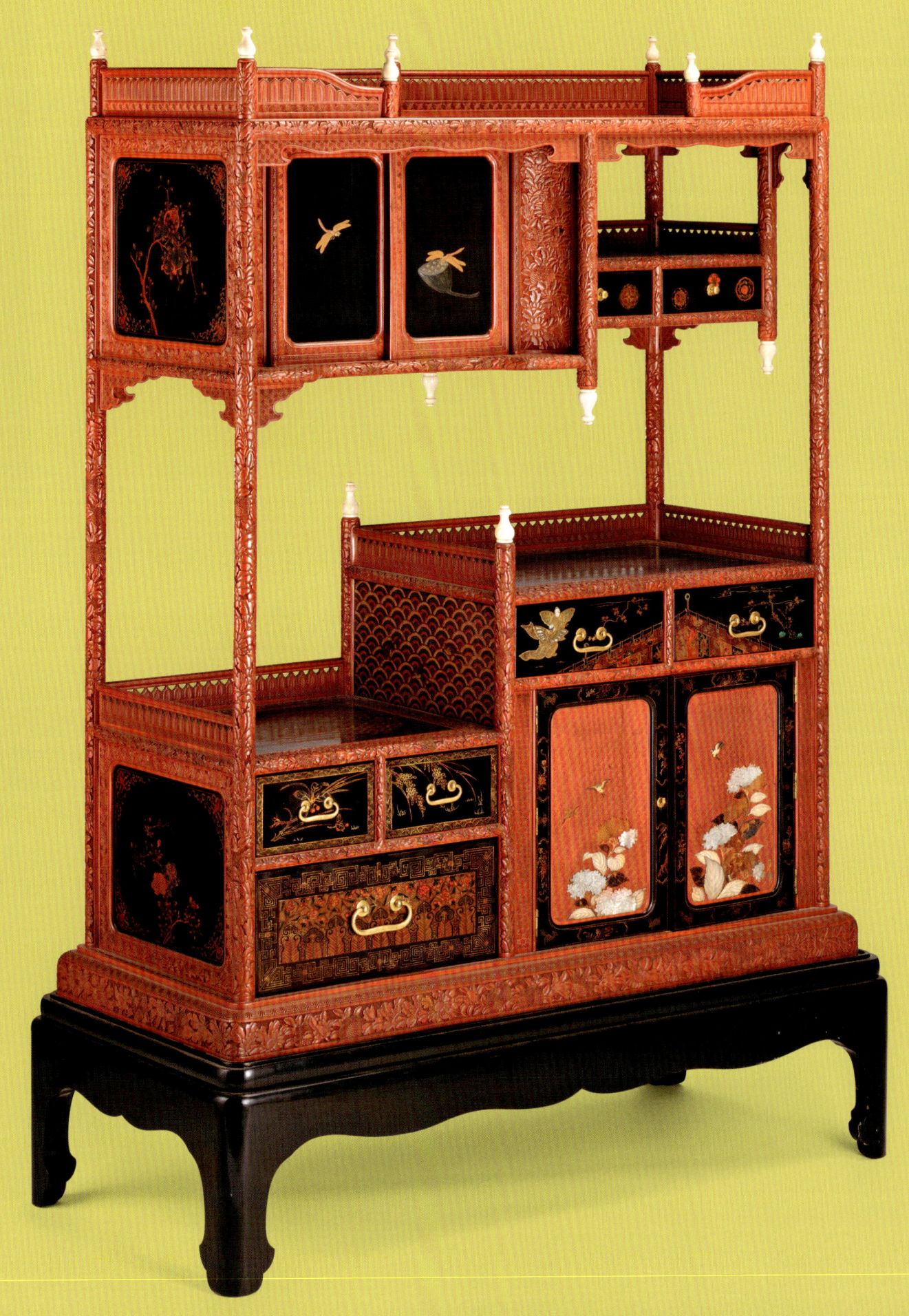

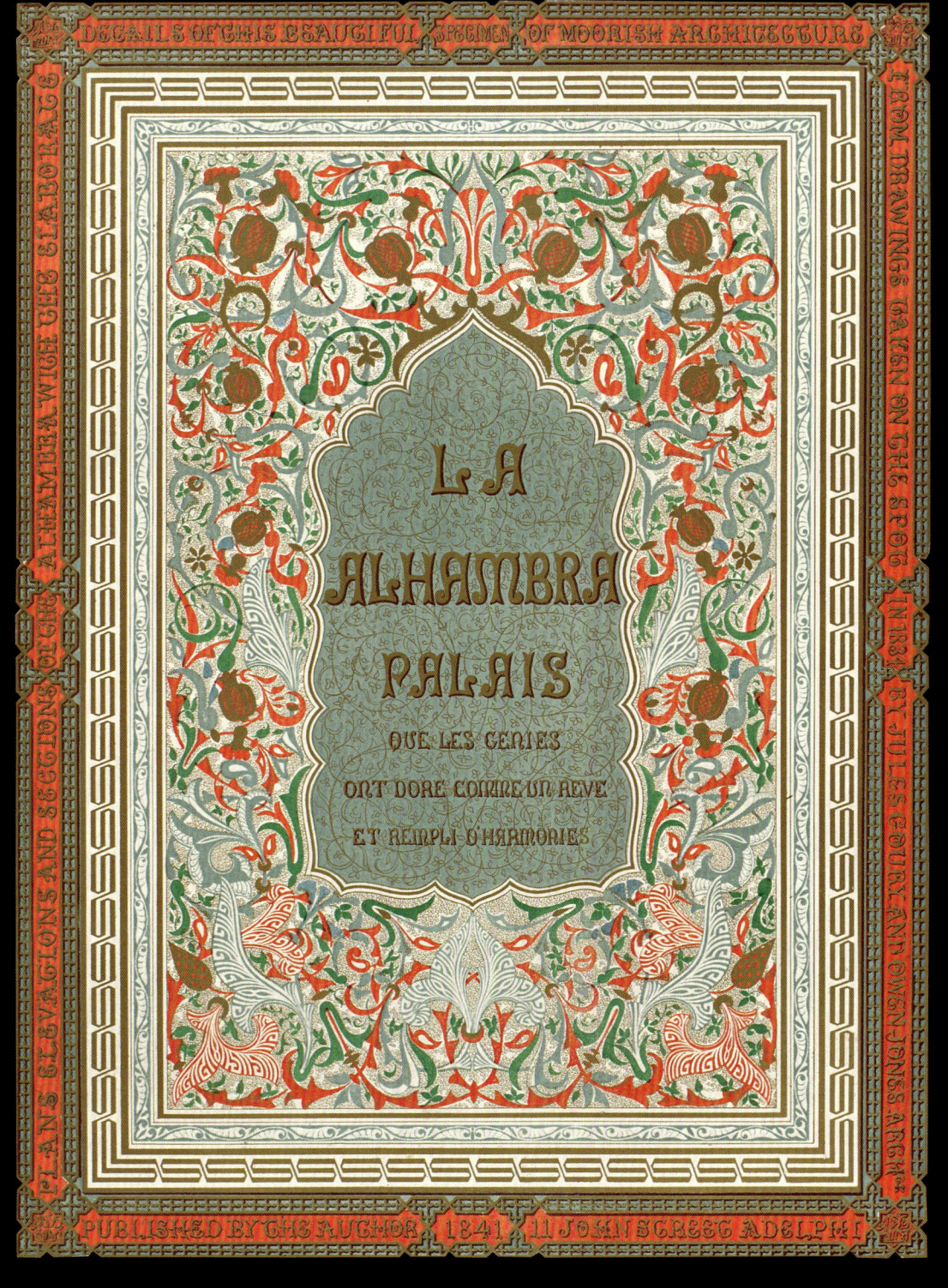

Opposite : **24. Artist/maker unknown** (Japan) : Cabinet : c. 1876 : lacquered wood, horn, mother-of-pearl, jade, bronze, malachite : H 5' 4 1/2" : 1876-1681 (cat. 12)   Above : **25. Jules Goury and Owen Jones** : *Plans, Elevations, Sections, and Details of the Alhambra* (London: Owen Jones, 1842–45) : title page of vol. 1 (cat. 74)

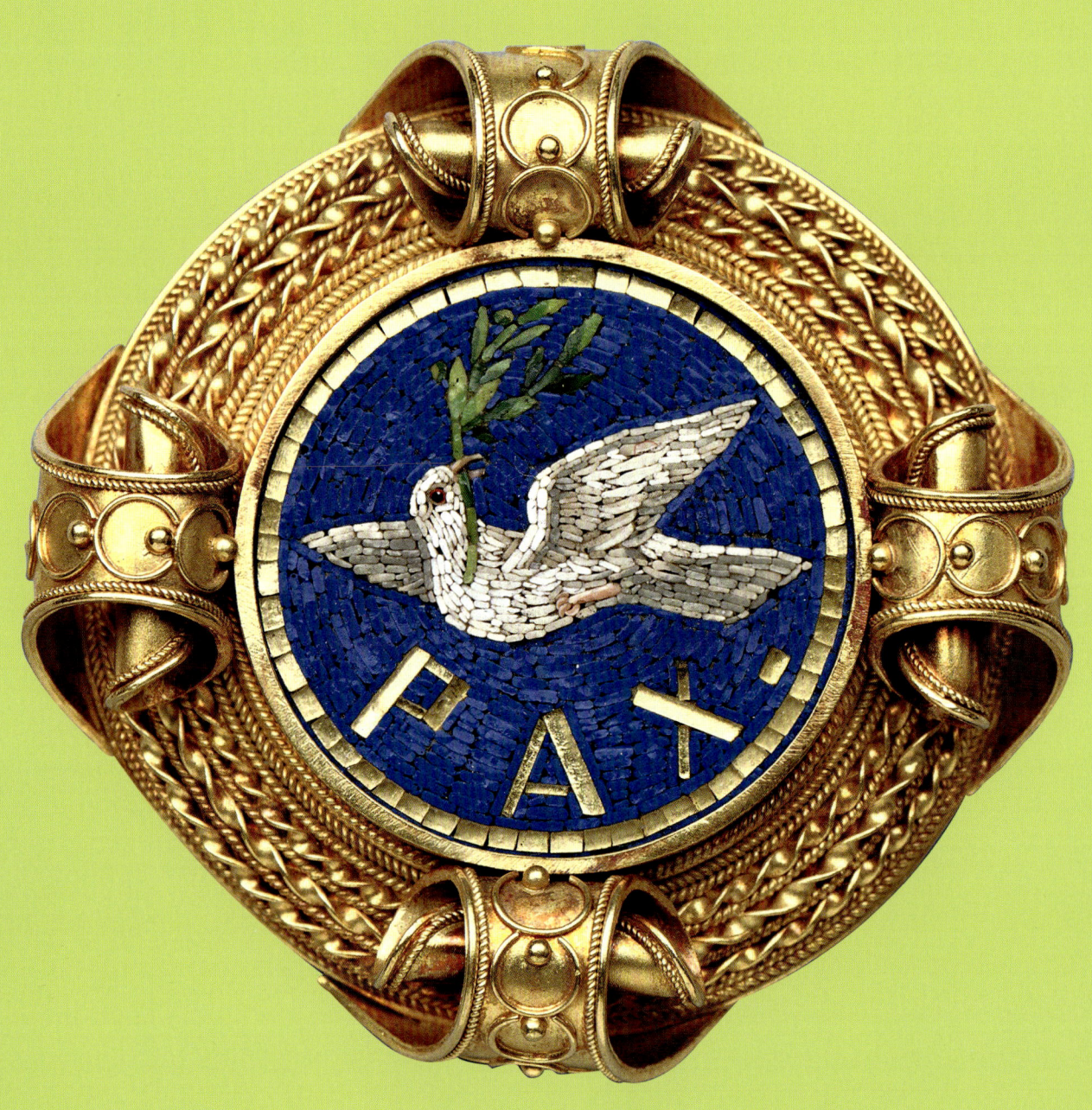

BEYOND NATURAL GOOD TASTE AND COMMON SENSE

Still, Wagner returned from Europe with the very sound opinion that, like the "person(s) of intelligence and knowledge in charge" of the art museums he had visited there, it was important to have "such a person at Memorial Hall," and he urged the appointment of a "Curator."[33] This is the first suggestion that the care and responsibility of the Museum's collections required expertise beyond the natural good taste and common sense of the board. Wagner's advice was duly followed. The office of curator was created in February 1879 (at an annual salary of $1,000),[34] although it was only in 1883 that Wagner's successor, Dalton Dorr, was publicly given the title (together with that of secretary). After Wagner resigned in April 1879, Dorr took over his duties. Son of the clergyman Benjamin Dorr, who had been rector of Christ Church in Philadelphia as well as trustee of the University of Pennsylvania, Dalton Dorr was to serve the Museum until his death in 1901, not only as secretary and curator but also as director from 1893 to 1899 (fig. 27). In its memorial tribute, the board described him as "intelligent and conscientious, systematic and faithful in the discharge of all his duties. . . . With a liberal education and cultivated tastes, he had by constant study acquired much of the special knowledge indispensable to the office of Curator."[35] Dorr collaborated closely with trustee and ornamental art committee chair William Platt Pepper, a strong and dynamic leader (as noted above, he had headed the Centennial selection committee) who himself served the Museum alternately as president and director over a period of almost thirty-five years. A gentleman–museum professional, Pepper was remembered by the board after his death as having voluntarily withdrawn from presidential activities to become "head of the work of the Museum," and for "his ceaseless, untiring endeavor to advance the interests of an Institution for whose success he felt, in so large a measure, a personal responsibility."[36]

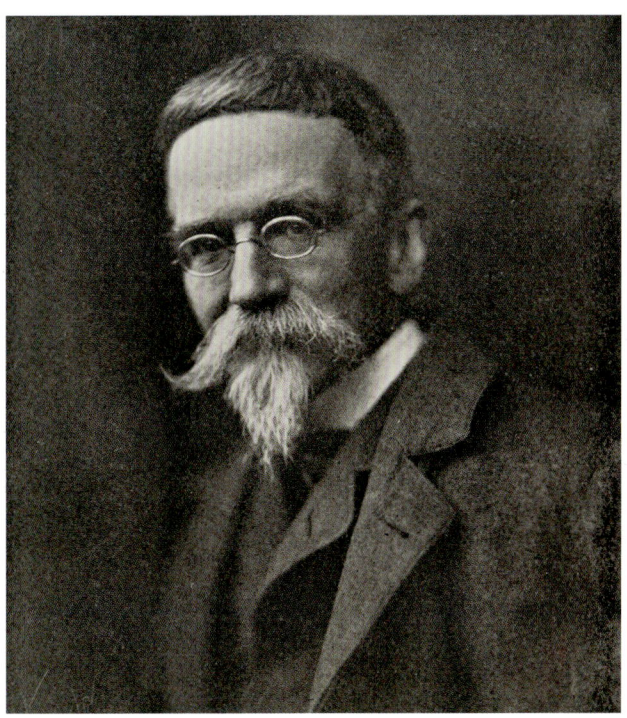

In December 1879 Pepper announced to the board that Mrs. Bloomfield H. Moore intended to donate to the Museum "a collection of industrial art objects . . . as a memorial to her late husband," Bloomfield Haines Moore, head of the prosperous Jessup and Moore paper company of Wilmington, Delaware, who had died the previous year.[37] The Museum's first important gift comprised over two thousand objects that were acquired in two large lots in 1882 and 1899. Mrs. Moore's heterogeneous collection included European and Asian ceramics, enamels, furniture, woodwork, costumes, textiles, fans, glass, metalwork, ivories, painted and wax miniatures, and paintings. The collection was almost entirely historic, and largely eighteenth century, but did include some modern jewelry, such as a handsome gold and mosaic brooch decorated with early Christian symbols in the Italian archaeological style popularized by the firm of Castellani in Rome (fig. 26). Mrs. Moore also gave the Museum modern

Opposite : **26. Artist/maker unknown** (Italy) : Brooch : c. 1850 : gold, mosaic : D 1 1/2" : 1899-923 (cat. 11)   Above : **27.** Dalton Dorr : Museum director, 1893–99

Italian glass in antique styles made by Salviati in Venice, but asked to have these objects returned to her in 1890 (they were). Pepper and the board extended to Mrs. Moore special courtesies in the installation of her collection, for which she paid all expenses, from exhibition cases to the salaries of the attendants who guarded them. She also supervised the initial display, which opened to the public on May 12, 1882, and made additions, as well as subtractions, over the summer and in the years that followed.[38]

The paintings given by Mrs. Moore represented the introduction of fine art to the Museum's collections, a development that was subsequently reflected in the reorganization and redefinition of the board's standing committees. The board voted in January 1882 to merge its art-related committees (ornamental art, mechanic arts, and materials used in the art industries) into a single committee on museum collections that would "have charge of all objects in the Museum and of their arrangement and exhibition."[39] The name of this new committee on museum collections (also known simply as the "Museum Committee") was deliberately generalized to embrace works in all mediums, including paintings. The first chair was trustee Charles E. Dana, a painter who taught in the Museum school and in 1900 would cofound the Philadelphia Water Color Club. A decade later, in 1892, anticipating the arrival of the collection of some 150 paintings formed by William P. Wilstach, the board created a new standing committee on art, "whose chairman must be a Trustee, and, whenever possible, a professional Painter, Sculptor, Architect or recognized Art Expert. . . . To this Committee shall be referred, for their opinion and advice, all proposed purchases for the Museum Collections. The Committee on Art shall have charge of all pictures and statuary, and shall with the Chairman of the Museum Committee and the Curator, arrange for their proper care and display."[40] Thus were the fine arts for a time implicitly separated from the decorative arts (which were the responsibility of the museum committee), reflecting the board's appreciation that the acquisition of works of art in all mediums required a degree of professionalism among both practitioners and experts.

However, between 1880 and 1887 the Museum was able to purchase few works of art, decorative or otherwise. Although the Philadelphia economy was generally prosperous—the city led the nation in the production of textiles, bricks and tiles, pharmaceutical drugs, and chemicals—extended national economic depressions in 1873–79 and 1882–86 made fund-raising difficult for the board. In 1879 Dr. William Pepper urged the creation of an endowment fund, arguing that the "continual begging of small amounts costs the Museum loss of prestige"; two years later the board found it necessary to borrow money "to pay the running expenses of the institution to the end of the fiscal year"; and in 1884 Dr. Isaac Norris urged that an effort be made "to establish a purchasing fund for the Museum."[41] Although no funds were made available for purchases, John T. Morris, member of a large and respected colonial Philadelphia Quaker family, began a long series of distinguished gifts of modern decorative arts to the Museum in 1881. His first donation was recorded as "engraved glass; 2 pieces, modern Austrian";[42] the following year brought "a beautiful white bronze bell, made by the celebrated Italian bell founders, the Poli brothers."[43] Morris had purchased this bell at the Milan Exhibition of 1881, and suggested that all those interested in the Museum who planned to go abroad be made aware "that if each traveler would bring home an object for the Museum, it would help on the good work."[44] Elected to the Museum's board in 1892, shortly after his retirement from business, Morris continued to follow his own philanthropic example of acquiring works of art for the Museum until his death in 1915. As president of the ironworks I. P. Morris and Company, he had built machinery, pumping engines, and pipe fittings (shown at the Centennial Exhibition), but seemed to make effortlessly the transition from modern industry to modern industrial art.

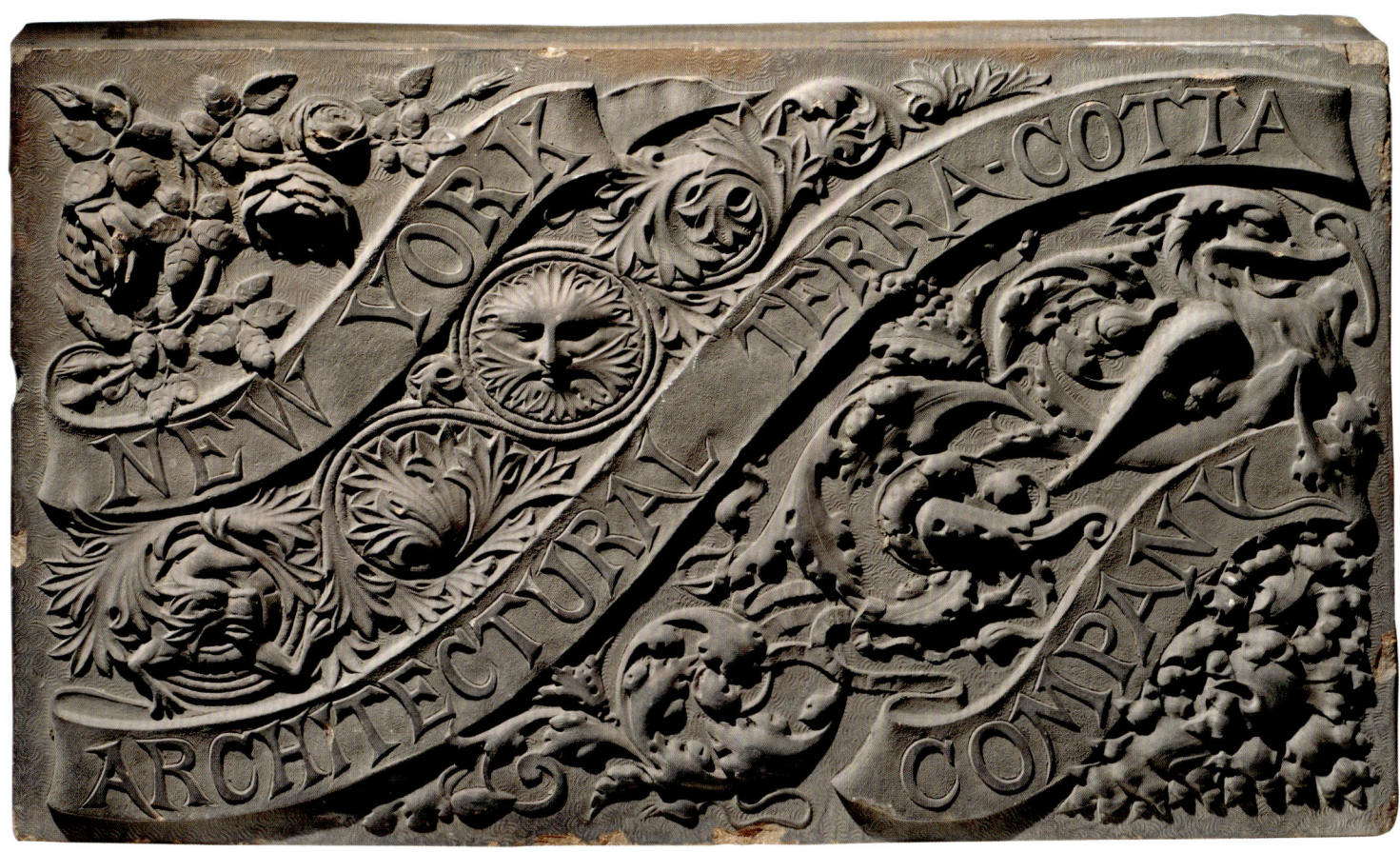

In 1883 the Associate Committee of Women[45] was established by Elizabeth Duane Gillespie, a great-granddaughter of Benjamin Franklin, to assist the board in fund-raising. According to the Museum's annual report, three of their number who were particularly interested in the school were appointed "as a committee auxiliary to the Committee on Instruction."[46] From its earliest years the Associate Committee of Women advanced the interests of the school, reducing its debt with the proceeds of their "entertainments" and creating an annual prize for its best students. In 1899 Mrs. Gillespie boldly organized (and funded through the generosity of Mrs. William L. Elkins) an exhibition of advanced professional work, persuading the Rookwood Pottery Company to send to the school for exhibition some objects that had been prepared for the Paris Universal Exposition of 1900.[47]

Another good example for the struggling institution was set in 1884 by Joseph E. Temple, a businessman in the wholesale dry-goods trade, who gave the Museum an endowment of $50,000 in stocks and bonds: three-fifths of its income was to be used for the purchase of works of art for the Museum (the fund still exists) and two-fifths for scholarships and prizes at the school.[48] Although Temple had made a similarly generous gift to the Pennsylvania Academy of the Fine Arts in 1880 for the purchase of art and awards to students, in 1884 he had apparently "wished to make his gift entirely to the Museum but had been persuaded to give a portion to the School"[49]— the first of many instances wherein the interests of the Museum and the school were divided. The initial purchase made with Temple Fund income in 1887 was a colored photographic reproduction of the Bayeux Tapestry,[50] a

28. **New York Architectural Terra-Cotta Company** : Panel : 1886–89 : terracotta : W 23 1/16" : 1889-169 (cat. 136)

medieval embroidered cloth that depicts the Norman conquest of England. As the income grew, more and larger acquisitions were made. In 1888, for example, a special exhibition of American pottery and porcelain was held at Memorial Hall, from which "five vases and one plaque" were purchased for the Museum with Temple Fund monies.[51] The exhibition was intended to showcase contemporary American ceramics, and "although organized too late for the full co-operation of manufacturers, it was still in a good degree successful in promoting an intelligent interest in furtherance of genuinely artistic work."[52] The exhibition was repeated the following year, resulting in, among other things, a gift to the Museum of a panel made by the New York Architectural Terra-Cotta Company of Long Island City (fig. 28). Circulars had been sent out inviting artists, manufacturers, and workers to participate in the exhibitions, with cash prizes offered ("to American Workmen"), the winning objects to become the property of the Museum.[53]

Complicating the issue of buying or accepting works of art for the Museum was the school's assembly of its own collection. Leslie Miller, principal of the school, went on a buying trip to Europe in 1888 and returned with English furniture, "French and Flemish metal work, original and electro-reproduction, a miniature suit of plate-armor, and an illustrative example of embossed leather work."[54] Donors, too, gave objects separately to the Museum and the school, among them John T. Morris, who in 1895 presented the Museum with contemporary glass made by the firms of J. & L. Lobmeyer in Vienna and Compagnia di Venezia e Murano in Venice, while giving the school Lobmeyer glass and a "collection of embossed and painted leather made by Mora Brothers."[55] In 1894 the Museum's Associate Committee of Women donated to the school contemporary Bavarian pewter that had been purchased the year before at the World's Columbian Exposition in Chicago. In fact, the school became a principal driving force within the institution for collecting and exhibiting contemporary decorative arts (including work by its own distinguished faculty), particularly after it moved in 1893 to a large building at Broad and Pine streets formerly belonging to the Institute for the Deaf and Dumb. The expansion of the school was necessary to accommodate its growing School of Textiles. Trustee William Weightman gave $100,000 toward the purchase of the property, a sum matched heroically but with difficulty by the trustees and the Associate Committee of Women. The purchase of the new building took place just at the beginning of another economic depression in Philadelphia and the nation, lasting from 1893 to 1897.

William Platt Pepper announced to the board in 1898 that "in view of the vast importance of the Textile School in the work of the Institution . . . someone should be at the head, possessing the technical knowledge necessary to develop it." He therefore wished to relinquish the Museum presidency, which he had held for fifteen years, but would continue to serve on the board of trustees.[56] Privately, Pepper wrote Dorr: "I shall continue to do all I can for the Museum, which has been somewhat overshadowed by the success of the School."[57] To meet the need for an individual with the requisite "technical knowledge," Theodore C. Search, a successful businessman who had assumed financial responsibility for organizing and equipping the Textile School when it was first established, was elected president of the corporation. He also served variously as treasurer of Philadelphia's John B. Stetson Company (the world's largest hat manufacturer), president of the Philadelphia Textile Manufacturers Association, and president of the National Association of Manufacturers. Pepper, however, quickly reinvented himself, first becoming chair of the committee on museum collections in 1898 and then director of the Museum in 1899, with Dalton Dorr assuming his former title of curator.[58]

DEVELOPMENT OF THE HISTORICAL AND CONTEMPORARY COLLECTIONS

With the election of John T. Morris (fig. 29) to the board in 1892 and the arrival that year of Edwin Atlee Barber (fig. 30)[59] as honorary curator of the new department of American pottery and porcelain, the Museum began to reposition itself as an institution in which collecting art took precedence over collecting examples of technology and natural science, although the process of redeploying superfluous or redundant collections would only develop in years to come.[60] With Barber's appointment Dorr began to think about the internal organization of the collections, and their further division by object type into departments that would be supervised by specialists in the field. In 1892 Pepper noted that perhaps the Museum's "most important work of the year" had been the establishment of the department of American pottery and porcelain, adding that Barber's "valuable historical collection . . . was purchased and presented to the Museum by Mr. John T. Morris as a nucleus for other collections."[61] In a "preliminary catalogue" of the collection published the following year, Barber described his efforts to gather examples of domestic work from the earliest times to the present as an inducement to contemporary manufacturers to add examples of their best work to the Museum's collections.[62] Also in 1893 Dorr invited Mrs. John Harrison to become honorary curator of the department of textiles, lace, and embroidery, and F. D. Langenheim, honorary curator of the department of numismatics. In 1894 Dorr added a department of goldsmith work, jewelry, and plate with Charles D. Clark as honorary curator. Pepper soon informed Dorr that Clarence Bloomfield Moore, following in his mother's philanthropic footsteps, was giving his own coin collection to the Museum, since the institution now had a department of numismatics and an appointed curator.[63]

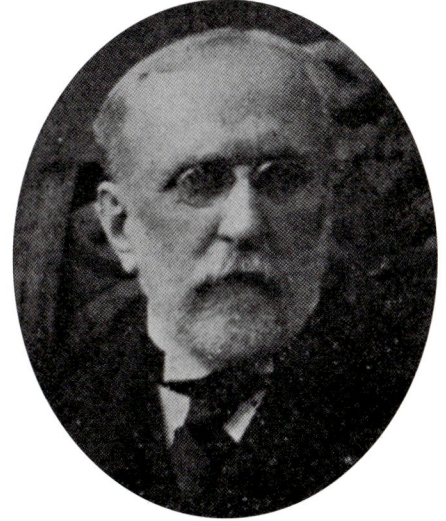

Edwin Atlee Barber had taken his first job as a naturalist, with the Hayden United States Geological and Geographical Survey of 1874–75, traveling in Arizona, New Mexico, Colorado, and Utah; while with the survey he developed a life-long interest in Native American pottery and ceramics in general, becoming a leading authority in the field. Following studies in archaeology, ethnology, and philosophy, Barber received his doctoral degree from Lafayette College in Easton, Pennsylvania, in 1893. The Museum's first trained professional specialist, Barber succeeded Dalton Dorr as curator, secretary of the corporation, and eventually, in 1907, following the death of William Platt Pepper, director. Dorr, Morris, and Barber began to build the collections of contemporary decorative arts, particularly ceramics and glass, following Morris's keen aesthetic instincts as a collector, honed at many international exhibitions and corresponding to Barber's specialized academic interests.

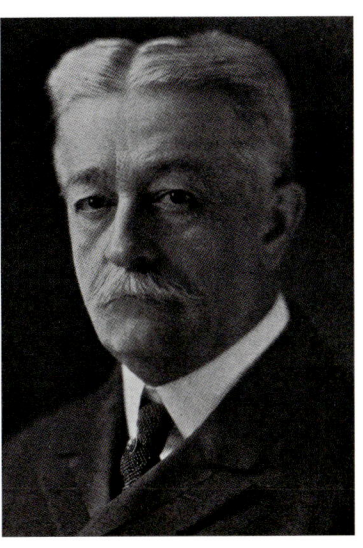

Top to bottom : **29.** John T. Morris : Museum board member, 1892–1915   **30.** Edwin Atlee Barber : named honorary curator in 1892 : Museum director, 1907–16

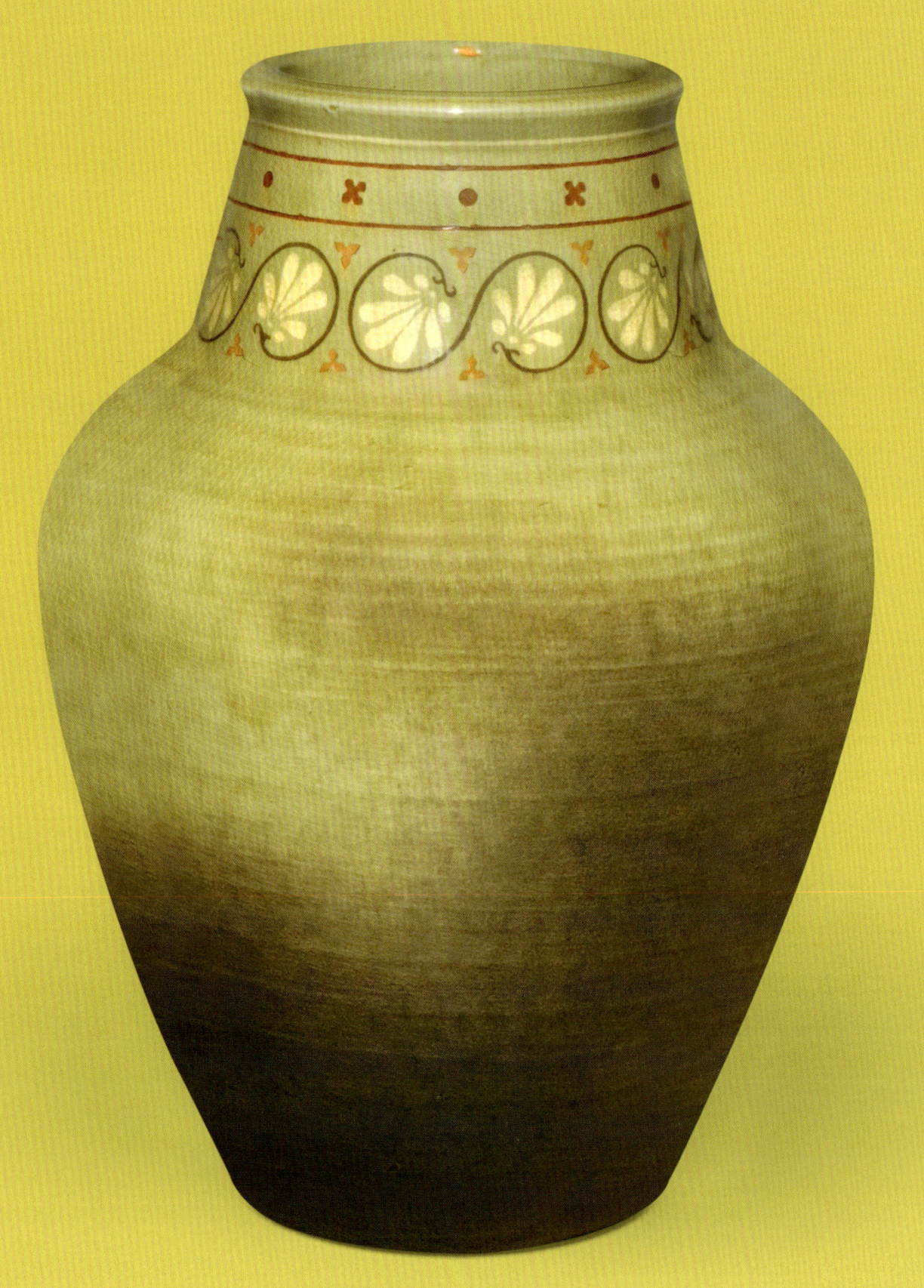

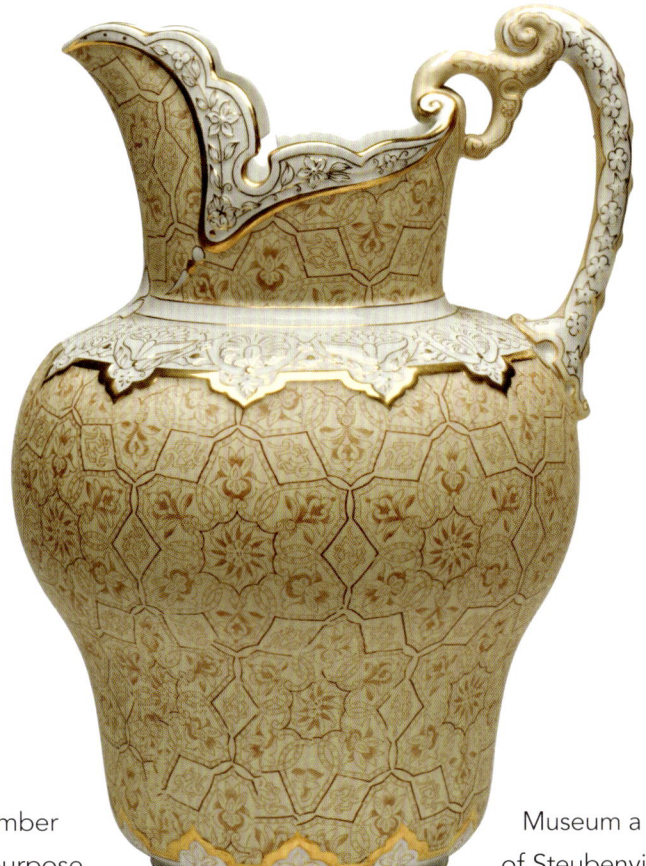

The board recommended in November 1892 that funds be raised for the purpose of purchasing objects the following year at the World's Columbian Exposition in Chicago.[64] Mrs. William Weightman and John T. Morris both advanced the Museum funds to send Dorr and school principal Leslie Miller to Chicago.[65] Dorr, Morris, and Barber went separately to the exposition on behalf of the Museum, and each purchased contemporary ceramics—particularly American art pottery—for the collection. In October 1893 Morris wrote Dorr from Chicago: "How much, *how much* could be done here with $5,000. Think over the propriety of making an appeal in the papers making clear to the people the advantages which can be derived from a little ready cash."[66] Pepper urged Dorr to visit the exposition: "Your trip to Chicago would be of advantage to the Museum and as you have had letters from Exhibitors offering gifts—you would be able to tell whether the proposed gifts are worth accepting for we don't want a lot of trash shunted off on us."[67] When Dorr arrived in Chicago, Barber advised him of his own negotiations with various exhibitors: "I sent you yesterday through the Museum a letter from the Lonhuda pottery of Steubenville, Ohio, in which they offered us some good specimens of their ware. I hope you will see that it is secured before you leave Chicago and packed for shipment."[68] Other manufacturers were equally generous, among them the Ohio Valley China Company of Wheeling, West Virginia, which gave the Museum a spectacular neo-rococo porcelain centerpiece (fig. 35), and the Edwin Bennett Pottery Company of Baltimore, which donated "Numerous Specimens of their Manufacture,"[69] including a Persian-style pitcher with painted and gilt arabesque decoration (fig. 32). Founded only several years earlier, in 1880, by Maria Longworth of Cincinnati, the innovative Rookwood Pottery was a great favorite of Dorr, Morris, and Barber. The collection of "historic" American pottery and porcelain assembled by Barber and sold to the Museum on his appointment as curator included early Rookwood, as well as examples of other American art pottery. In addition, William Watts Taylor, president of Rookwood, presented the Museum with fifteen pieces, of which only one survives today in the Museum's collections (fig. 31).[70]

Opposite : **31. Albert Robert Valentien** : for Rookwood : Vase : 1886 : glazed stoneware : H 11 1/2" : 1976-45-1 (cat. 197)   Above : **32. Edwin Bennett Pottery Company** : Pitcher : 1893 : glazed and gilt earthenware : H 12 1/2" : 1893-368 (cat. 18)

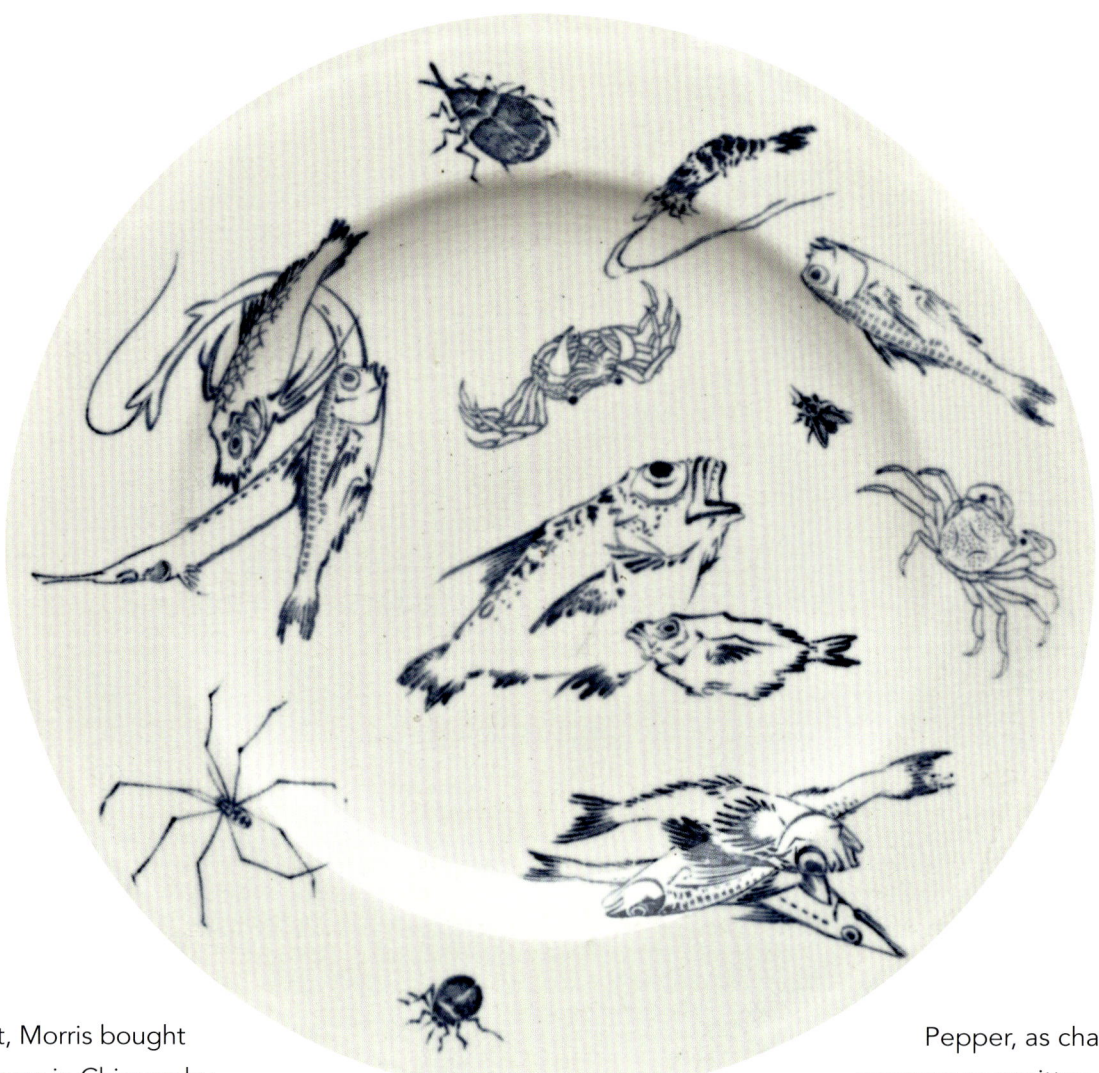

As was his wont, Morris bought a number of pieces in Chicago by different artists and manufacturers, which he or his sister Lydia T. Morris gave either immediately or eventually to the Museum. Among the best and most impressive were a large salt-glazed stoneware jar, lid, and stand with modeled and applied decoration by Susan Frackelton of Milwaukee, Wisconsin (fig. 34), and an important "Greek" vase by Marc-Louis-Emmanuel Solon for Minton. The vase had been made in 1887 and already shown with its pair at the Paris Universal Exposition of 1889. Thoroughgoing, Morris wrote directly to the artist to inquire about its subject. Solon replied: "This time the subject is very simple, and chosen chiefly as an occasion of showing female figures in varied attitudes. It is not to be forgotten that this vase is only one of a pair. On the two vases were contrasted: 'Grace and Strength.'"71 In 1898 Pepper, as chair of the museum committee, proposed to the board the purchase of another masterwork by Solon, the *Jester* vase, from Bailey, Banks and Biddle of Philadelphia.72 The purchase price of $1,500 was drawn from the Temple Fund, and again the artist provided a description of his subject: "In the guise of a Court Jester, the frolicsome Nymph confides to her puppet the secret of the many tricks she has just played. From the branches of a tree hang the masks of various expressions she has worn. . . . On the reverse of the vase a puppet-show is seen, in which little wooden actors are giving a performance of 'Minerva, Goddess of Wisdom, Overpowered and Vanquished by Love'" (fig. 58).73 Pepper, now the Museum's director, wrote Morris about installing the vase and suggested that it deserved "a case of its own—for it is a *most important piece* & worthy of

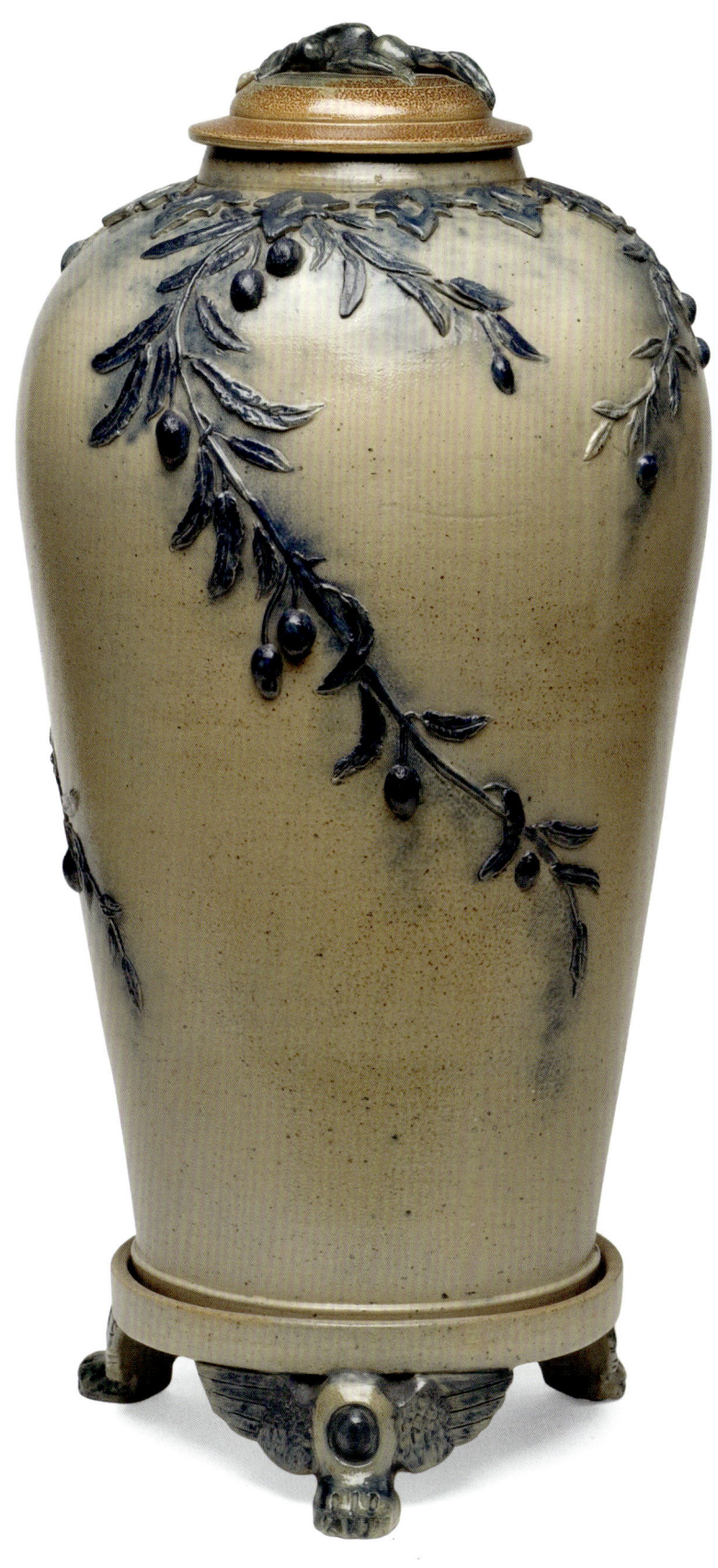

Opposite : **33. Rookwood Pottery** : Plate : 1880 : glazed stoneware : D 8¾" : 1976-104-1 (cat. 161)   Above : **34. Susan Frackelton** : Jar on Stand : 1893 : glazed stoneware : H 25" : 1893-309,a,b (cat. 59)

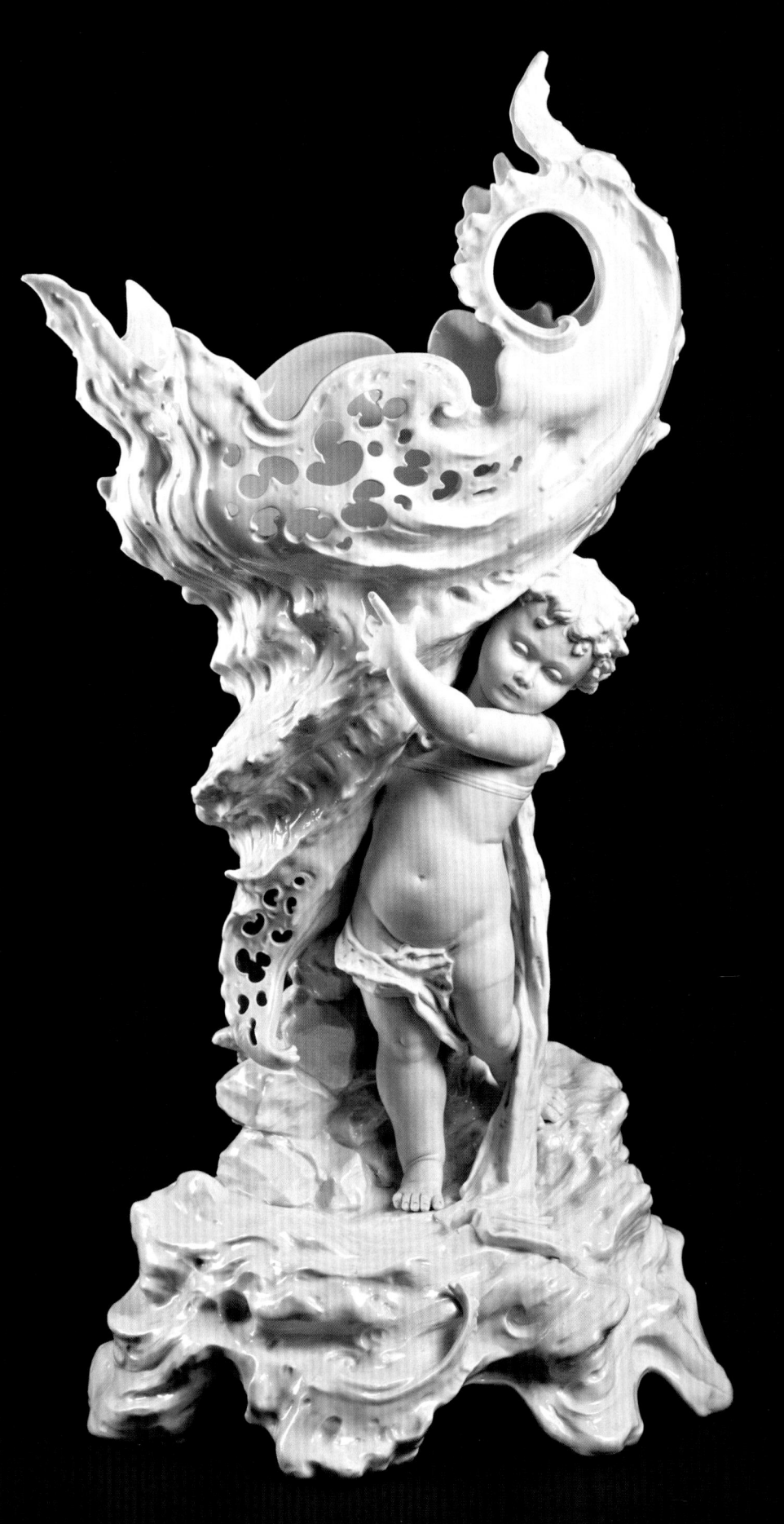

being alone and being made much of. I suppose there is no better specimen in America than that—certainly not in any Museum and it cost a lot of money."[74]

Barber was a serious scholar of ceramics history and technology, writing books, catalogues, and articles that not only did credit to his reputation and that of the Museum, but also made the institution's growing collections—then largely acquired by Barber himself—widely known for the first time in the United States and abroad. In the January 1892 issue of *Popular Science Monthly*, Barber published "Recent Advances in the Pottery Industry," which described the rise of American art potteries in Bennington, Vermont; Phoenixville, Pennsylvania; East Liverpool, Ohio; and Cincinnati, home of Rookwood Pottery, "the first in this country to demonstrate the fact that a purely American art-production, in which original and conscientious work is made paramount to commercial considerations, can be appreciated by the American public."[75] Noting that the Japanese ceramics display at the Philadelphia Centennial Exhibition had perhaps more than anything else inspired the establishment of Rookwood,[76] Barber illustrated the point by means of a dish decorated with fish after Japanese prints (fig. 33). This Rookwood piece came to the Museum with the purchase of Barber's collection in 1892 by John T. Morris, who presented another Rookwood Japanese-style piece the following year; it had been purchased either at the Chicago exposition or, as Barber reported to Dorr, at auction in Philadelphia.[77]

Together Morris and Barber developed the Museum's modern as well as historic ceramic collections, the board member often funding the curator's purchases. The correspondence between the two men about works of art, often on a daily basis and lasting until Morris's death in 1915, records the opinions of two passionate collectors as they acquired objects for themselves and the Museum. Barber's authority in the field of American ceramics was definitively established with the publication in 1893 of his magisterial volume *The Pottery and Porcelain of the United States: An Historical Review of American Ceramic Art from the Earliest Times to the Present Day*, a book that, as he stated in the preface, was the result of "thorough personal investigations . . . study of the products of the potteries in the United States, and . . . consultation with intelligent potters in the leading establishments of the land."[78] As usual, Barber illustrated works from his own collection that had been acquired by the Museum, and in subsequent editions of the book added other Museum pieces.

For the next twenty years Morris and Barber shopped and bought incessantly, visiting potteries, dealers, auction houses, and exhibitions separately and together, submitting their finds to each other for review, agreeing and disagreeing—sometimes strongly but always with great respect. In March 1896 Barber wrote Dorr of his trip to Trenton with Morris: "I brought home a few little pieces as gifts from potters, which I would like to send out to the Museum. . . . Since returning I have written to a couple of the Potteries that we visited, asking for some other small pieces which I happened to see when we were there."[79] Three months later Barber wrote again: "After working for more than a year, I have finally secured some additional examples of recent types of pottery made at the Rookwood Pottery";[80] he later reminded Dorr, "I suppose you have sent an acknowledgment to Mr. W. W. Taylor of Cincinnati, for his recent gift of Rookwood pieces. I had the pleasure of seeing these when I was last out."[81] Taylor's gift included a handsome vase in the *Iris* glaze line, decorated by Constance Amelia Baker in 1896. It was probably during Barber's 1896 trip to Cincinnati that he designed his own tankard for Rookwood, duly stamped with his name and dated 1896. He tended to be an encyclopedic, academic collector, attempting to document each new form or decoration, however slight the variation, as he chronicled the history of American pottery. This was an attitude to which Morris took constant exception, as Barber reported to Dorr with regard to some early nineteenth-century pieces: "I had a talk with Mr. Morris some weeks ago in

35. Carl Goetz : for Ohio Valley China : Centerpiece : 1892 : glazed and unglazed porcelain : H 25 1/2" : 1893-376a (cat. 73)

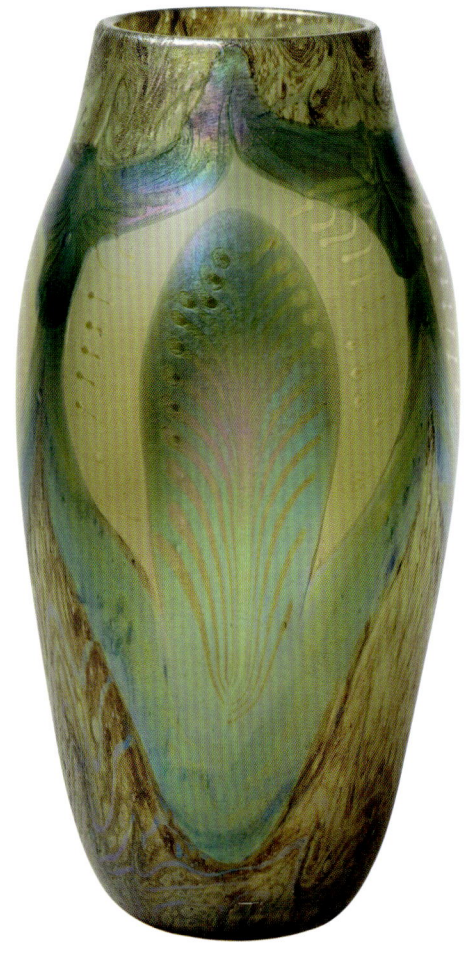
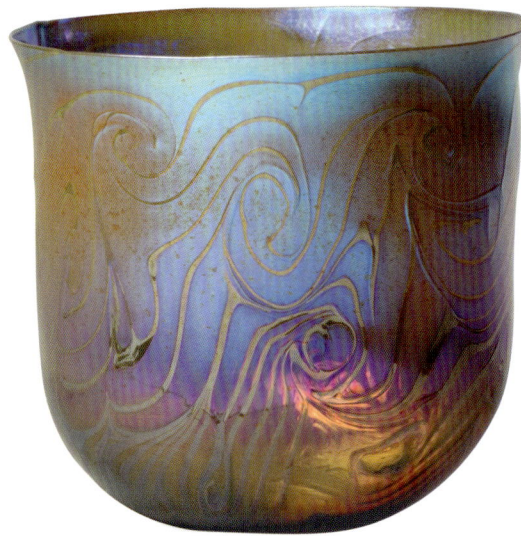

regard to a similar series, though not so complete as this, but did not press the matter as I saw that he felt that the pieces had no artistic value. This is very true, as some of them are extremely crude, but so far as I am concerned personally, I am far more interested in seeing our collection of historic objects complete than in procuring at the present time modern pieces of artistic ware. I desire to see the collection illustrating the progress and development of the art in this country, as complete and unbroken as possible, and for this reason I trust the Museum can afford to raise the small amount necessary to secure this lot."[82]

The 1890s brought to the Museum two important ceramic collections, primarily historic, although each collection included some modern pieces: that of the Reverend Alfred Duane Pell of New York, beginning in 1894 with a gift of English and European porcelain and continuing until Pell's death in 1924 (Pell was named the Museum's honorary curator of European porcelain in 1904[83]); and that of General Hector Tyndale of Philadelphia, bequeathed to the Museum in 1897 by his widow, Julia N. Tyndale. Coproprietor of a fine-ceramics firm, Tyndale had chaired the jury for pottery at the Centennial Exhibition; his bequest included works by contemporary Japanese potters and a pitcher by W. T. Copeland and Sons in the Japanese style (fig. 23). Despite Barber's success in acquiring objects for the collection, he was unhappy about the appearance of the ceramic gallery at Memorial Hall, complaining to Dorr in 1896: "When I was last out I was very much impressed with the unfavorable conditions

Above, left to right : **36. Louis Comfort Tiffany** : for Tiffany : Vase : 1899 : Favrile glass : H 10 3/4" : 1901-59 (cat. 189) **37. Louis Comfort Tiffany** : for Tiffany : Vase : c. 1900 : Favrile glass : H 5 13/16" : 1901-58 (cat. 190) Opposite : **38. Louis Comfort Tiffany** : for Tiffany : Vase : c. 1900 : Cypriote glass : H 9 3/8" : 1901-63 (cat. 191)

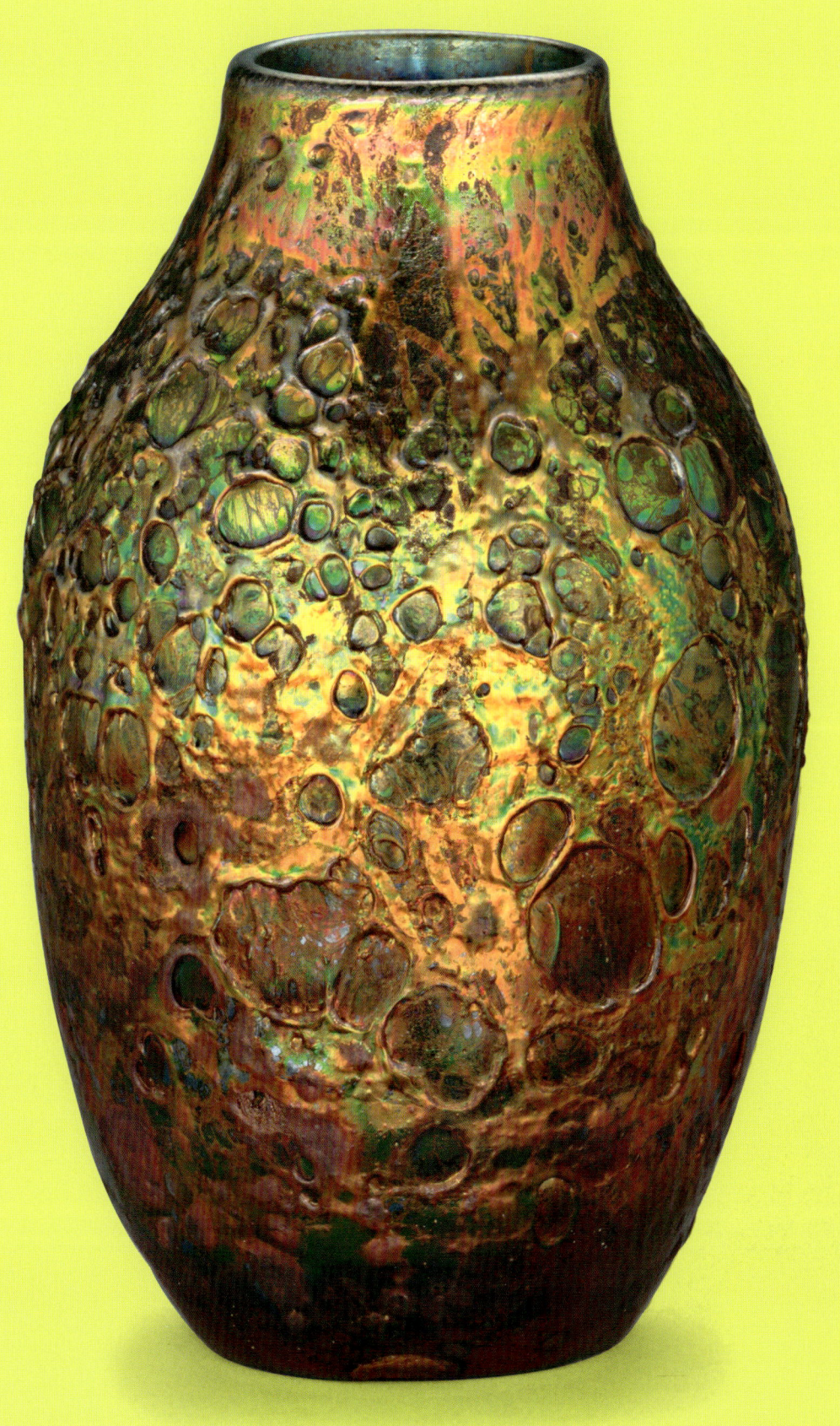

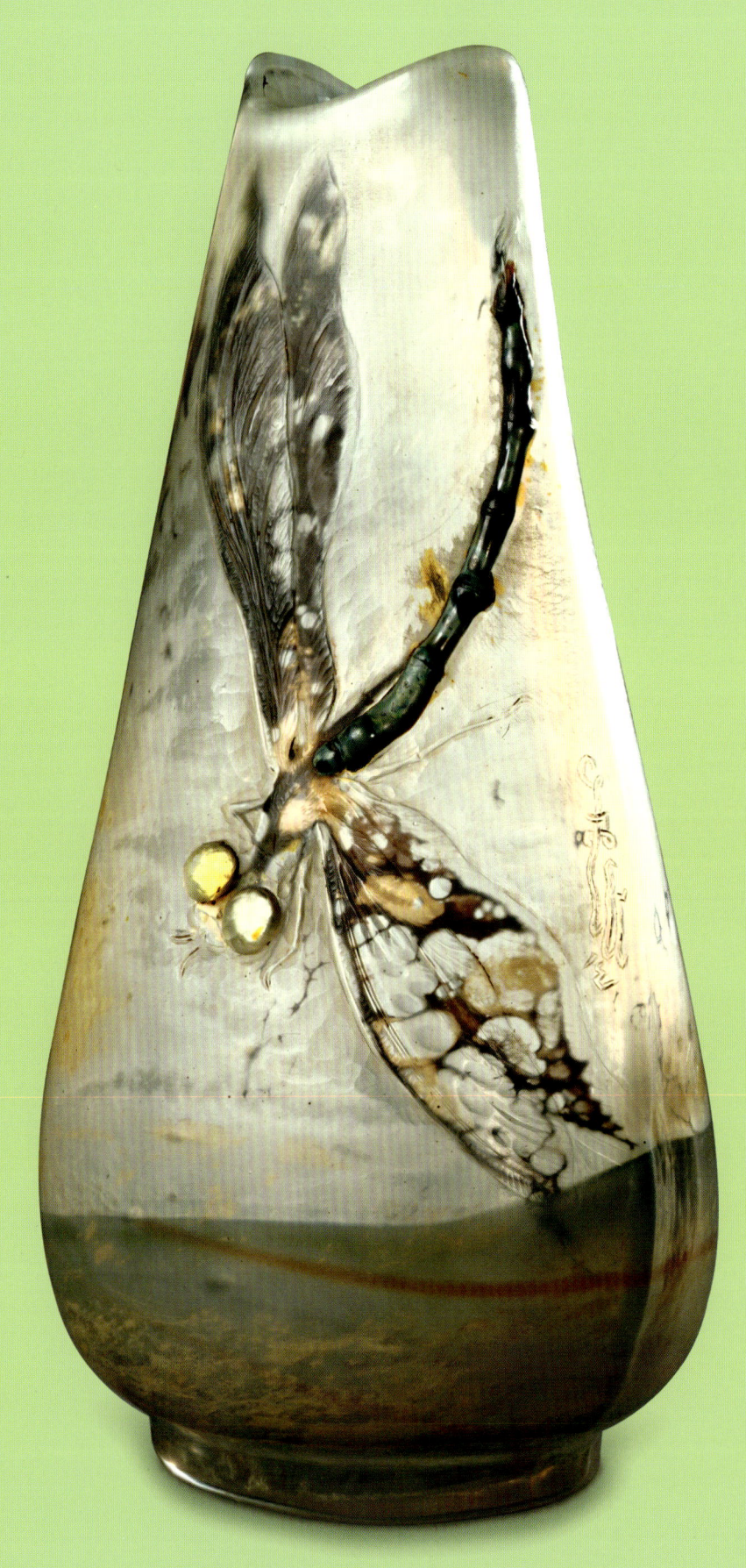

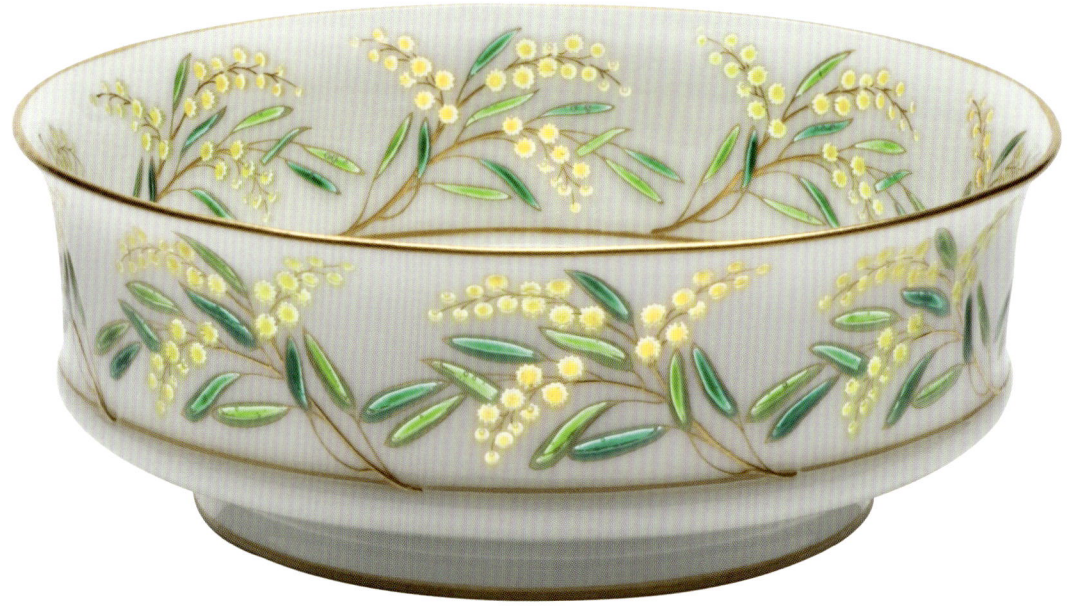

for exhibiting the American collection. The cases are entirely too crowded and the best objects do not show to advantage. The collection also needs rearrangement and I shall be ready at almost any time to arrange it properly when suitable case room has been provided."[84] Nevertheless, in December 1899 he could write to Morris: "On every side I hear nothing but praise for our *American* collection. It is attracting a great deal of interest and several of the papers have called attention to it."[85] This view was seconded by Pepper, who praised the collection as "unequalled by any other Museum."[86]

In 1900, while Barber was working on a revision of his publication *Anglo-American Pottery: Old English China with American Views*,[87] and acquiring the collections to illustrate it, Morris went to Paris to purchase ceramics and glass at the Universal Exposition, returning with Hungarian art pottery from the Zsolnay factory and porcelains from the Parisian firm of Camille Naudot (fig. 40), the Royal Copenhagen Porcelain Manufactory, the Royal Porcelain Manufactory in Berlin, and the Gustavsberg and Rörstrand factories in Sweden, along with ten boxes of Tiffany glass (figs. 36–38), and French glass by Cristallerie de Pantin and Émile Gallé (figs. 41, 42). Morris must have been particularly fond of the pieces by Naudot, as he asked Barber whether he was going to illustrate any of the new objects from Paris in the Museum's next annual report, pointing particularly to "the little cup with inlaid enamel . . . the newest thing in the porcelain line."[88] Barber was not entirely familiar with some of the European pieces Morris had bought, writing: "In making the labels for the Paris pieces, I find that you purchased one of the pieces (cameo

Opposite : **39. Émile Gallé** : Vase : c. 1903–4 : patinated glass with applied decoration, metal foil : H 11 1/2" : 1905-46 (cat. 63)
Above : **40. Camille Naudot, Fils et Cie.** : Bowl : c. 1900 : enameled soft-paste porcelain : D 4 15/16" : 1901-45 (cat. 134)

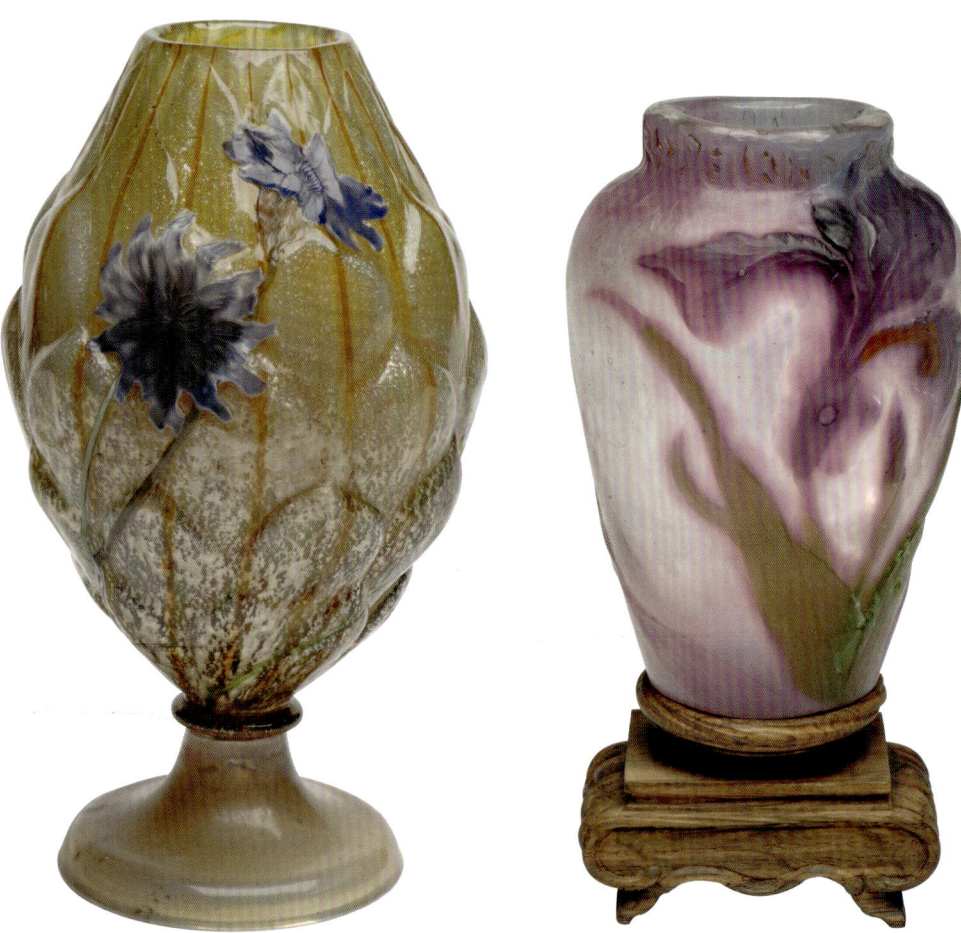

glass) from Stumpf, Violett & Cie., 84 Rue de Paris at Pantain [*sic*]. I am not clear as to whether this firm made the glass or simply sold it to you? Kindly give me the name of the maker, if other than the above" (they were the same; fig. 43).[89] Many decades later the Museum was able to add to the collections two additional groups of European porcelain that had also been shown in Paris: a tea set designed by J. Jurriaan Kok and painted by W. P. Hartgring for the Rozenburg factory in The Hague (fig. 45), and two figures from the *Jeu de l'Echarpe* series designed by Agathon Léonard for Sèvres.

With regard to the ten boxes from Tiffany, Pepper had written to Morris, possibly on Barber's recommendation, requesting that he spend $1,000 of the Temple Fund on a selection of Tiffany Favrile glass at the Paris Exposition.[90] It is likely that Pepper had already seen the glass, as he wrote Dorr: "The Tiffany Favrile Glass people have sent me a notice that the articles they are to send to the Paris Exhibition are now on view at their place in New York. I want to try to get in to see them, if possible toward the close of this week or the middle of next week."[91] Like the works of Solon and the Rookwood Pottery, Tiffany glass was and continued to be a favorite of Morris, Barber, and the board as a whole. Buying in quantity, the Museum became the largest institutional collector of Tiffany glass of the period. While in Paris, Morris also purchased American art pottery, including three Rookwood vases,

Above, left to right : **41. Émile Gallé** : Vase : c. 1900 : glass with marquetry decoration : H 8 1/8" : 1900-219 (cat. 61)   **42. Émile Gallé** : Vase : 1900 : glass with marquetry decoration : H 6 3/16" : 1921-46-71 (cat. 62)   Opposite : **43. Stumpf, Touvier, Viollet & Cie.** : Vase : c. 1900 : glass with wheel-cut decoration : H 8" : 1900-145 (cat. 185)

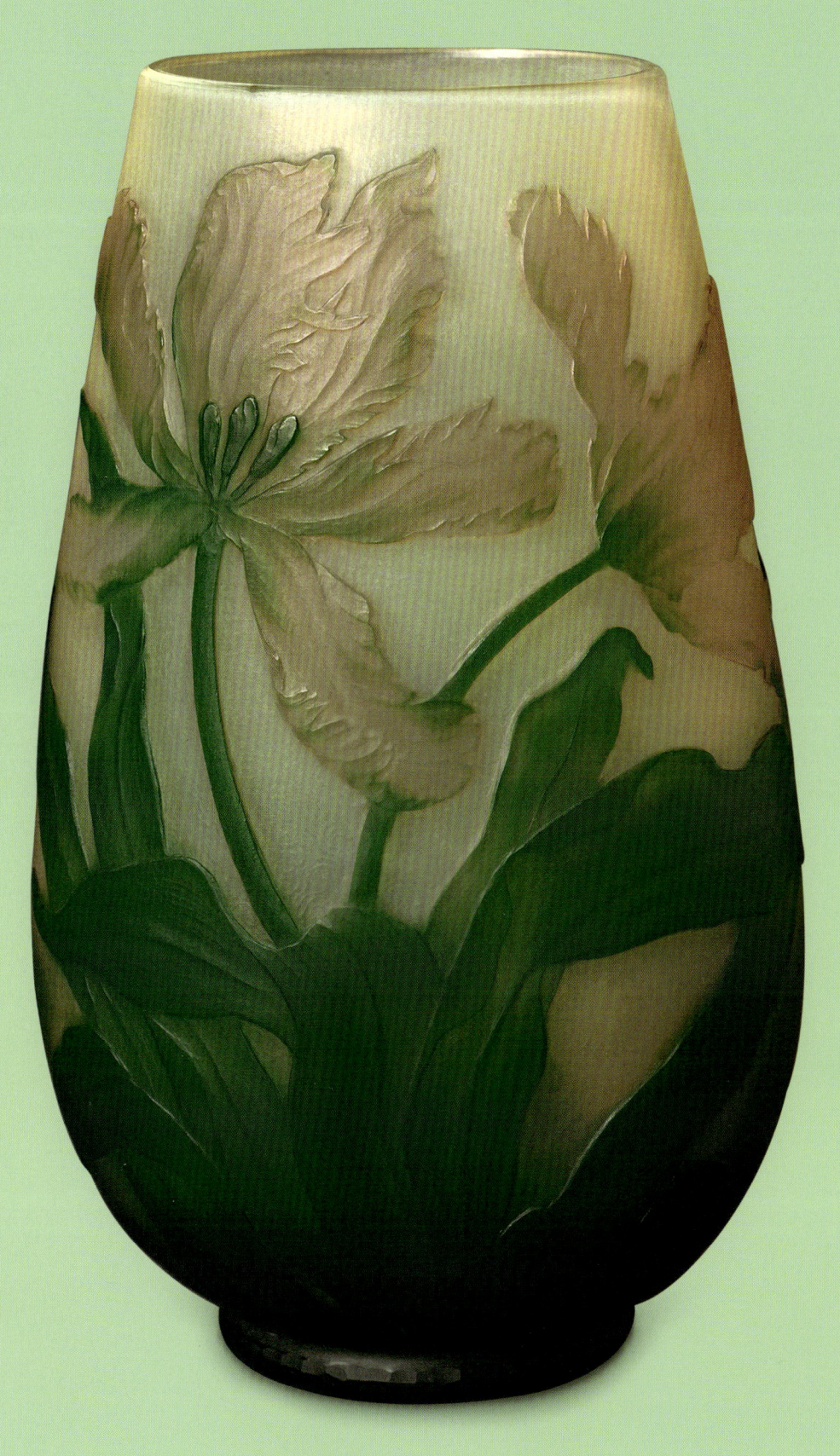

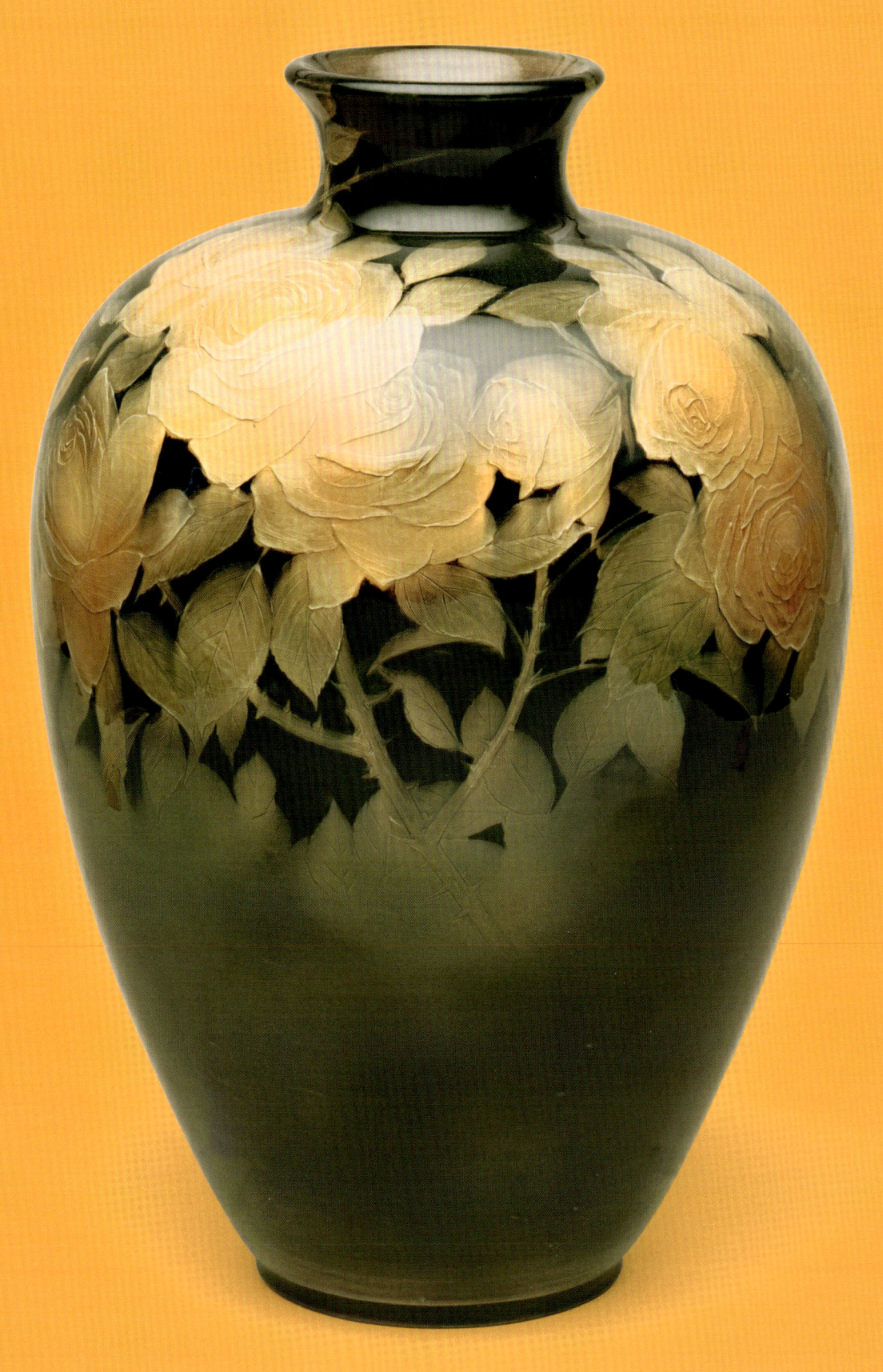

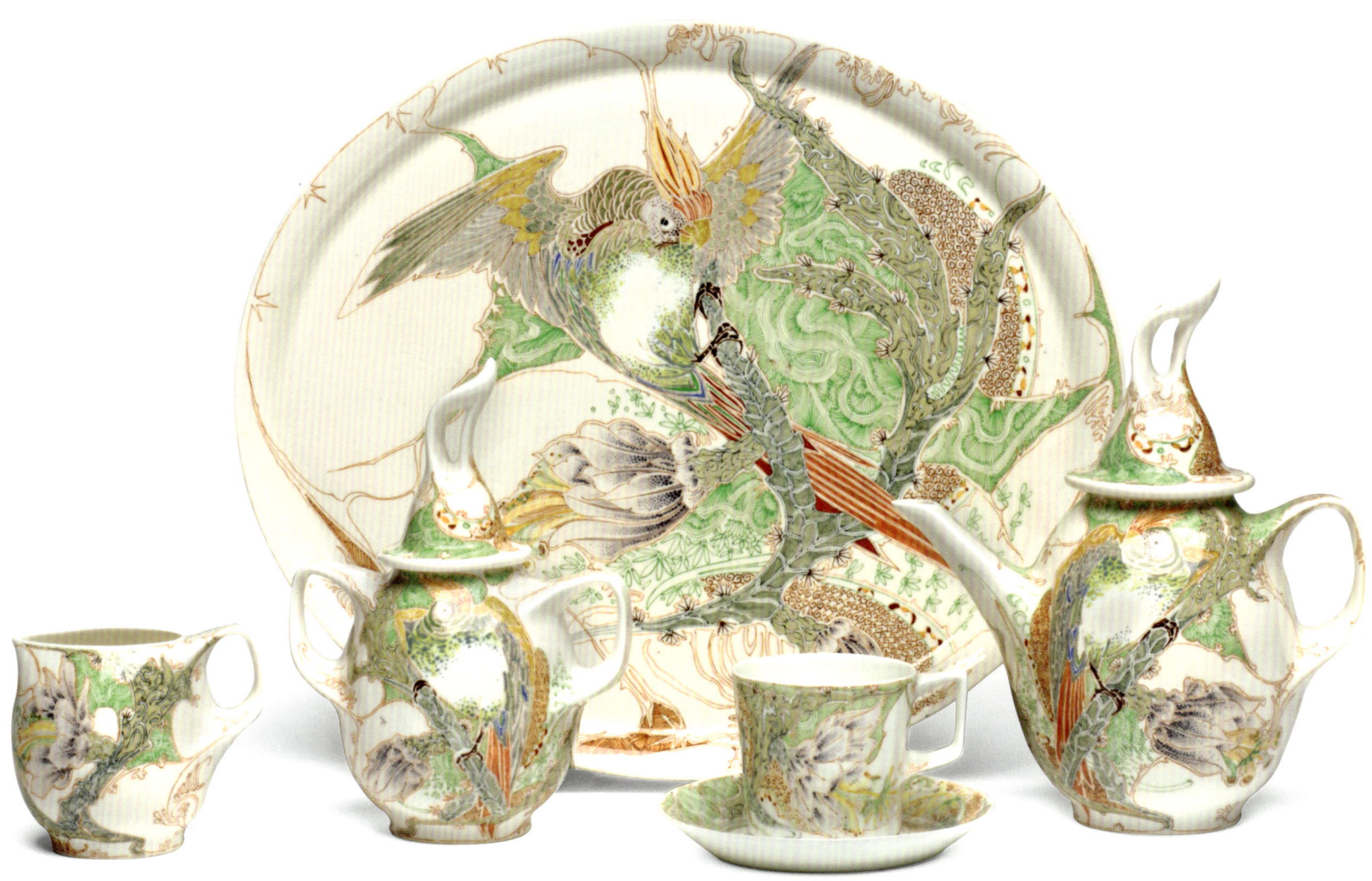

one of them a masterwork, a large vase decorated with delicately translucent roses on a glossy black ground by the Japanese artist Kataro Shirayamadani (fig. 44); Morris also bought six examples of faience from the Boston firm of Grueby.

Barber, meanwhile, had been occupied with his historic collections of American pottery, proposing numerous acquisitions after Morris's return from Paris. Morris, for once, had tired of Barber's constant solicitations: "I have examined the plates sent me and I am sorry to differ with you regarding the desirability of purchasing. I have spent so much money on the Museum this year, and as it seems impossible to secure the 'last plate' I have decided to let someone else have all but #6 for which I send [a] check."[92] Barber was apparently undaunted, as Morris again wrote him, with exasperation, in late 1901: "I agree with you it would be desirable for us to have the small plate but do you not think you are pushing me a little hard?"[93] Once more, three months later, Morris wrote, "The Museum is constantly on my thoughts but really Mr. Barber, sometimes accumulations occur when I must give some attention to my own business."[94]

Opposite : **44. Kitaro Shirayamadani** : for Rookwood : Vase : 1899 : glazed stoneware : H 17 3/8" : 1901-15 (cat. 176)   Above : **45. J. Juriaan Kok and Wilhelmus Petrus Hartgring** : for Haagsche Plateelbakkerij Rozenburg : Tea Service : 1900 : enameled soft-paste porcelain : H (teapot) 7 1/2" : 1975-18-1–6 (cat. 101)

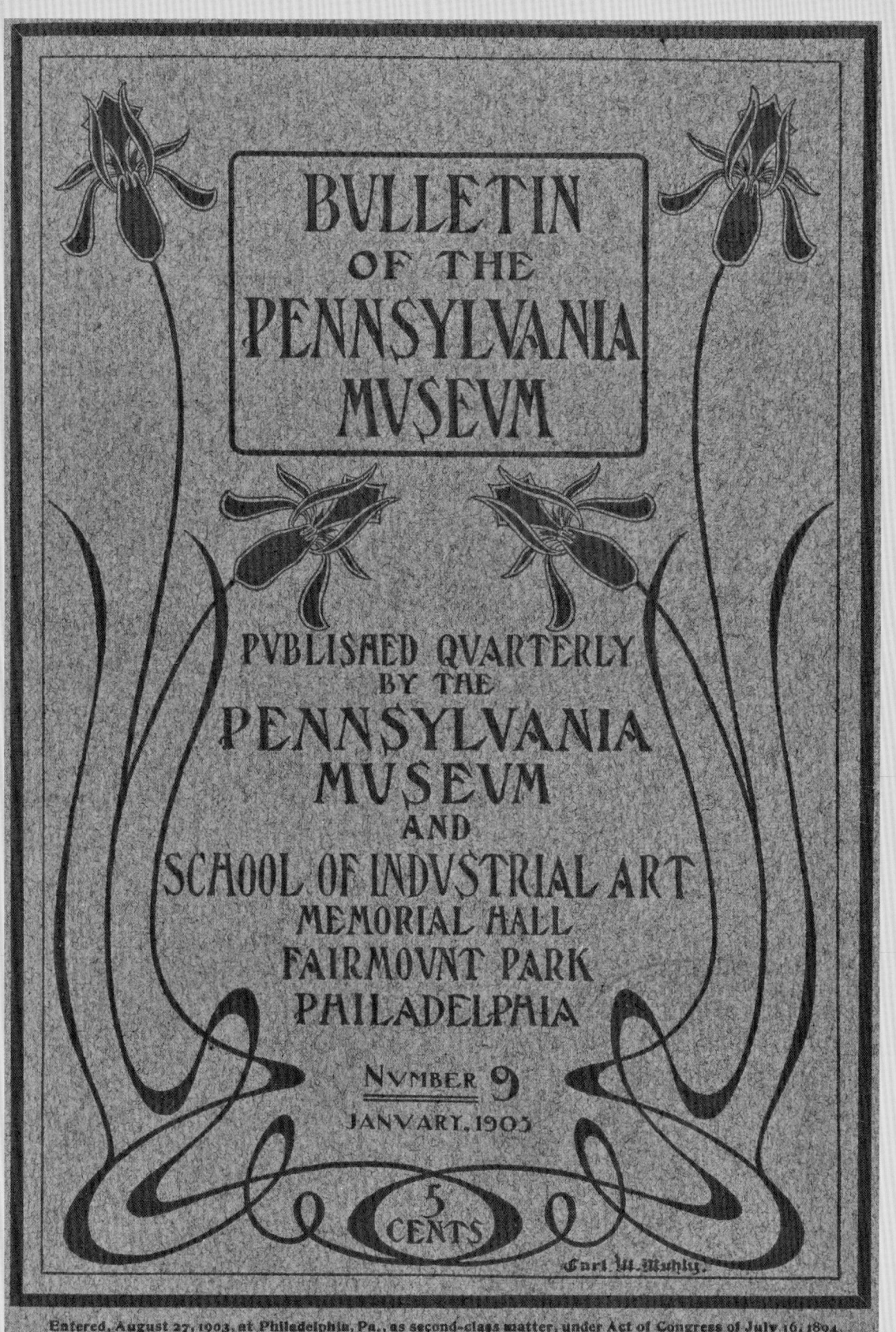

FOLLOWING THE PRINCIPLES OF QUALITY AND INNOVATION

When Dalton Dorr died suddenly in February 1901, Barber was elected to succeed him as the Museum's curator. He continued to consult with Morris regarding most Museum matters, including the new Museum publication that Barber had proposed just weeks before Dorr's death: "I have made arrangements for devoting more time to collecting work and literary work, and it seems to me that there is need of a Museum publication, say a monthly paper, to be devoted to all subjects in which the Museum is interested. Such a publication ought to pay for itself, with possibly a little financial help at the outset, and would attract much attention to the Museum and give it standing among the great Museums of this country."[95] Accordingly, in January 1903 the Museum published its first number of the *Bulletin of the Pennsylvania Museum*, "for the purpose of bringing members of the corporation into closer touch with the work which is being done at the Museum,"[96] as well as to report on the institution's new acquisitions, installations, illustrated art handbooks in preparation, and Temple Fund purchases. The publication also included a plea for establishing similar purchase funds for "modern art glasswares" and other collections.[97] The *Bulletin* was published quarterly until 1919, then irregularly, sometimes more and sometimes less often, frequently serving as a collection handbook or an exhibition catalogue and typically as a vehicle for documenting new acquisitions (fig. 46). Philadelphia's was the first museum publication of its kind in the United States (followed shortly thereafter by the Museum of Fine Arts, Boston *Bulletin*), a fact of which Barber felt justly proud, reporting in 1911, "Other museums followed the example of the Pennsylvania Museum and at present there is scarcely an important public art museum in the United States which does not print its official organ."[98]

As curator, and later director, Barber was eager to professionalize the Museum, endeavoring to broaden its influence and build its collections. He first tackled housekeeping issues, from cleaning Memorial Hall to reclassifying, relabeling, and reinstalling the collections,[99] but he also set about building the size and importance of the Museum's collections by adding more specialized departments staffed with honorary curators. At Dorr's death in 1901 the Museum comprised five departments. Within a year Barber had added six more, including arms and armor; musical instruments; sculpture, marbles, and casts; furniture and woodwork; prints, manuscripts, book plates, and historic seals; and philately—with the hope that they would "prove an important feature in the educational work of the Museum."[100] Barber continued to take personal responsibility for the pottery and porcelain department, which he admittedly favored, years later explaining: "At the beginning of the present administration the Curator endeavored to find at least one department of art in which the Museum might hope to compete with or excel other Museums. The most promising field appeared to be ceramics and around the nucleus of the collection then in possession of the Museum, by filling in gap after gap, the present collection has been assembled, which is admitted to be, if not the largest, the most comprehensive and representative one in this country. . . . The collections include many wares which are not to be found in any other American or foreign museum."[101] The Museum's first "Art Handbook," written by Barber on *Tulip Ware of the Pennsylvania-German Potters*, was published in 1903 along with the first issue of the *Bulletin*.[102] Barber was also responsible for the establishment of a pottery department at the Museum school, writing Morris in late 1902: "I have been talking to Mr. Miller lately in regard to the advisability of establishing a Pottery School and I find that he is quite enthusiastic on the subject" (the department was established the following year).[103]

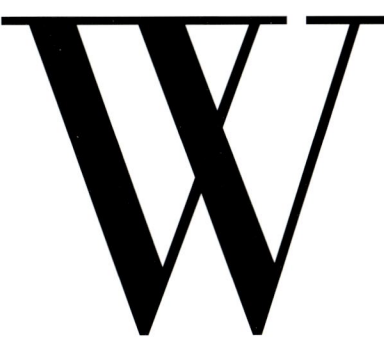

46. *Bulletin of the Pennsylvania Museum*, vol. 3, no. 9 (January 1, 1905)

Abetted and sometimes guided by Morris, Barber continued to acquire contemporary ceramics, telling Morris in 1902: "As I write, the Teco vase from Chicago has arrived and is the best piece of this ware which I have seen" (fig. 49).[104] Morris also continued to buy, offering many of his purchases to Barber for the Museum. "I had a wagon sent to your house," Barber wrote. "I am very much pleased with the contents. . . . There were in the boxes four pieces of Gustafsberg [sic] porcelain [fig. 48], two Rörstrand vases, and a Parian Group."[105] The Louisiana Purchase Exposition of 1904, better known as the Saint Louis World's Fair, provided Morris with ample opportunity for acquisition. Barber apparently was unable to attend and declined an invitation to accept an appointment as juror.[106] The museum committee, which had been chaired since 1897 by trustee John Story Jenks, voted Morris the use of the Temple and Museum Offertory funds for the purchase of art objects at the fair, with the hope, as Barber wrote, that he would "secure some fine things for us."[107] Morris outdid himself in Saint Louis, buying the latest and most advanced ceramics and glass from both the English and French exhibitions—works of James Powell and Sons and the Ruskin Pottery, and by the French artists Eugène Carrière, Auguste Delaherche, Taxile Doat, Émile Gallé, and André Fernand Thesmar. Sadly, only the masterwork by Gallé, a cased glass vase, cut, engraved, and decorated with an applied dragonfly (fig. 39), remains today in the Museum's collections, while a handsome example of Powell glass was added decades later. When the Gallé vase arrived in Philadelphia, Barber wrote Morris that he was "very much pleased with it. It is the best thing that has come from St. Louis, so far."[108]

Morris found an amiable and intelligent colleague in Jenks, who visited the Saint Louis fair and continued negotiations on behalf of the Museum after Morris had returned to Philadelphia. Descended from a colonial Quaker family and coproprietor of Randolph and Jenks, a leading cotton house in Philadelphia, Jenks was particularly interested in numismatics as well as Asian works of art. The previous year, he and Morris had presented the Museum with "a series of antique wood carvings from dismantled palaces of Japan."[109] At the Saint Louis fair Jenks and Morris purchased seven examples, no longer in the Museum's collections, of contemporary Japanese metal. Jenks's letters to Morris from Saint Louis reveal a keen aesthetic sensibility. He describes a Japanese ivory figure of a woman sweeping and an "exquisite" lacquer panel with waves of platinum; the Gallé vase with a dragonfly, "a splendid specimen"; and "superb" enamel cups by Thesmar—"the red one is the finest," he noted. "I think that we had better secure it for the Museum."[110] Typical of Morris's appreciation for high-quality, innovative contemporary decorative arts was his interest in the simple, functional furniture designed for the Vereinigte Werkstätten für Kunst im Handwerk (United Workshops for Art in Craft), established in 1897 in Munich. "The German furniture exhibit is very beautiful," wrote Jenks to Morris from the fair, "Much obliged for calling my attention to it."[111] Although the Museum did not purchase any of the examples,[112] many years later it did acquire an important piece of furniture designed for the Vereinigte Werkstätten by Richard Riemerschmid (fig. 50) along with his stoneware jug and a colored woodcut by Peter Behrens (fig. 51).

During the first decade of the twentieth century, the "modern art glasswares" for which Barber sought special funding in the Museum's *Bulletin* were most consistently made by Tiffany. In the spring of 1905 the board approved the purchase of six pieces of Tiffany glass out of the Temple Fund (fig. 47); in 1908 a Tiffany cameo vase; and in 1912 eight pieces of Tiffany glass (fig. 55).[113] The negotiations over these and other purchases caused Morris and Barber to debate the Museum's collecting policies. In June 1904 W. H. Thomas, secretary and treasurer of Tiffany Furnaces, proposed sending Barber "fifty or sixty" pieces for review: "We regret that our exhibit was not in place at the time Mr. Morris was in Saint Louis, but the exhibit there is quite a small one and we doubt if it will answer the purpose of completing your collection, as well as one specially

47. **Louis Comfort Tiffany** : for Tiffany : Vase : c. 1905 : Favrile glass : H 13 1/8" : 1905-167 (cat. 192)

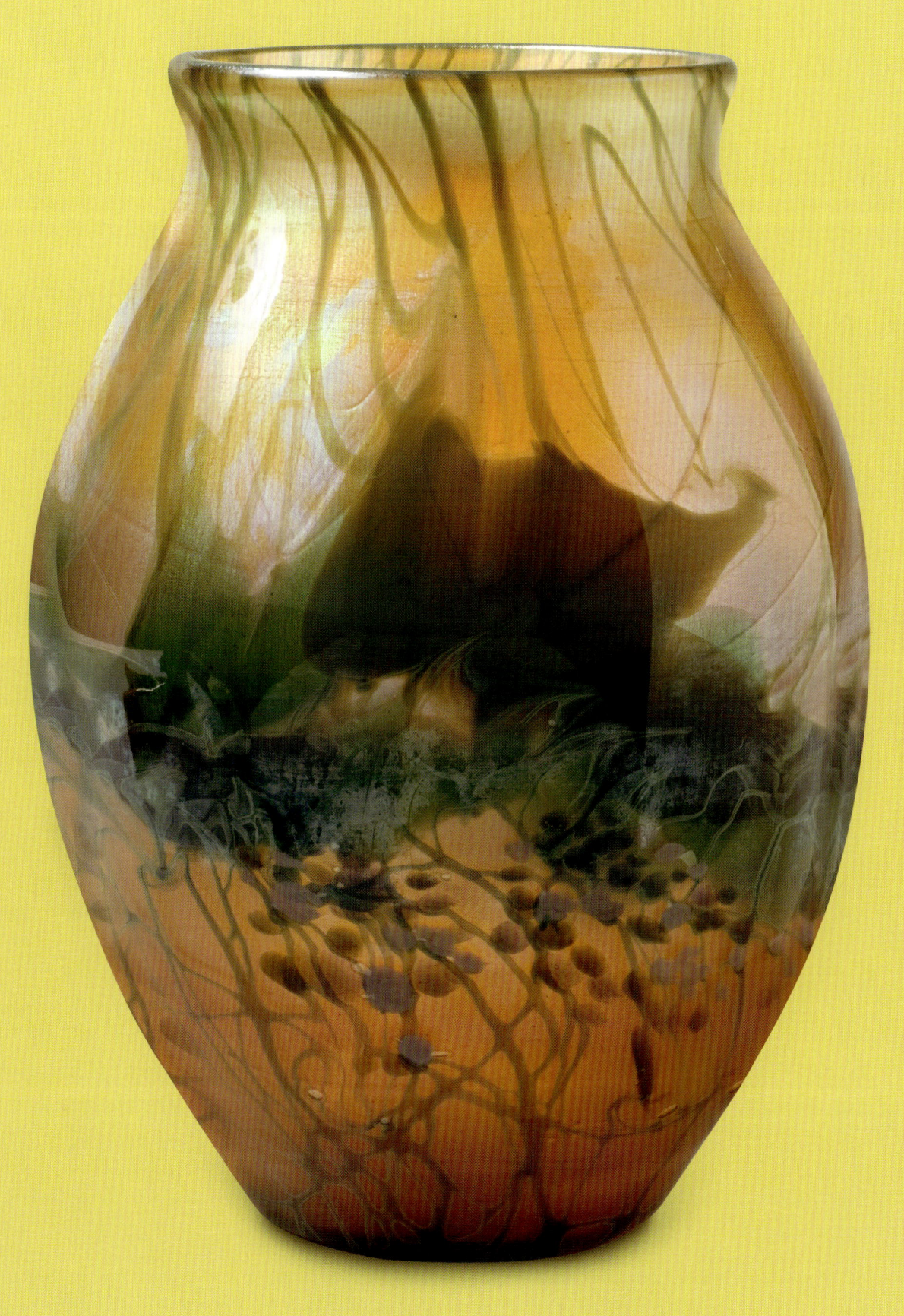

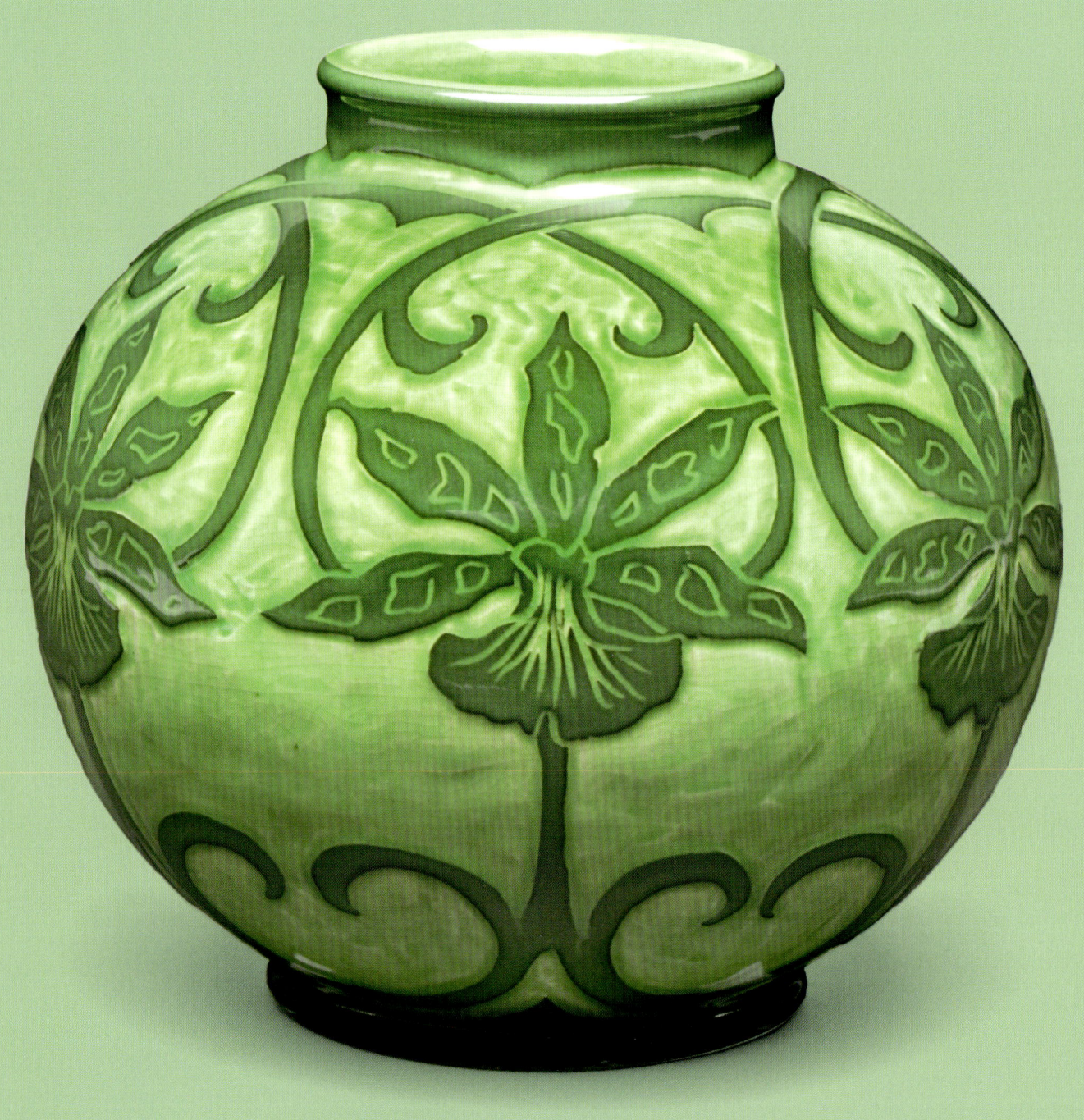

48. **Gunnar Gunnarson Wennerburg** : for Gustavsberg Porslinsfabrik : Vase : 1903 : enameled earthenware : H 5 1/2" : 1903-1693 (cat. 211)

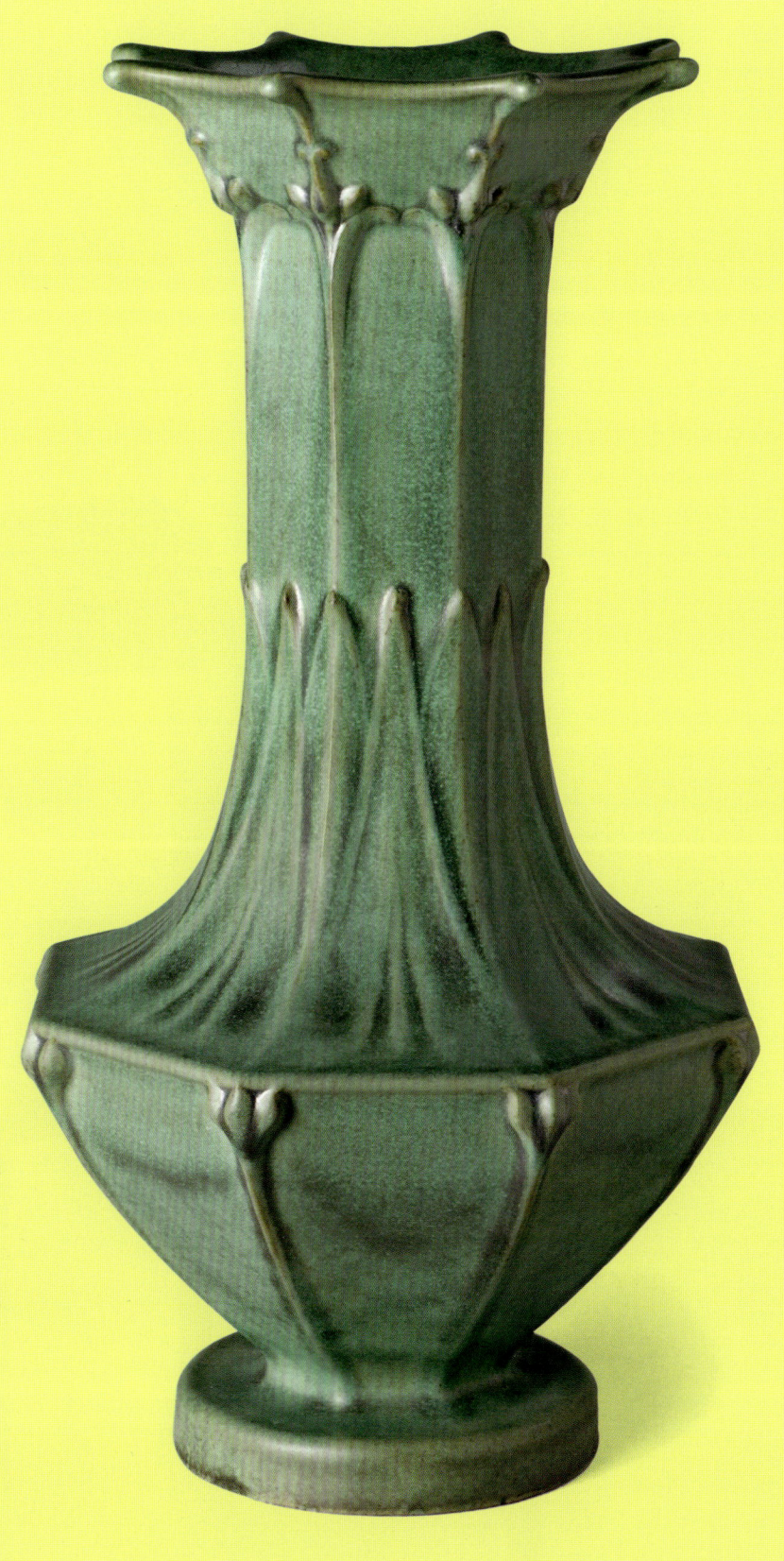

49. **William J. Dodd** : for Teco : Vase : c. 1902 : glazed earthenware : H 13 3/8" : 1902-922 (cat. 45)

selected."¹¹⁴ On reading Thomas's letter, Morris wrote Barber that he liked the idea of buying "in wholesale quantities," although he thought it "pretty risky to have so many specimens sent over. They are delicate and liable to break." He suggested instead that Tiffany send "from time to time on approval specimens of their work as they make new attempts."¹¹⁵ Barber then succinctly wrote Thomas that the Museum "would rather have *one* of your best productions than a *dozen* pieces of lesser merit."¹¹⁶

The principles of quality and innovation, both technical and aesthetic, were articulated by Morris in a letter to Barber the following year: "I think it would be the greatest mistake for us to decide without first visiting the [Tiffany] showroom or factory. . . . Do not let money enter into the question; what we want is the *very best first*; and then the *most distinctive*. Kindly, remember they are not going out of business and for that reason it will be better to buy from time to time their new productions rather than fill up our case at one time. I am so anxious to have a policy of making chronological collections. No one is doing it and some day I think our endeavor would be appreciated."¹¹⁷ He subsequently emphasized, "I am . . . of the opinion that we should not purchase any article upon the sole opinion of the manufacturer."¹¹⁸

Barber did visit the Tiffany showroom in May 1905 and reported to Morris: "I went to New York last week to make the selection of Tiffany glass and was fortunate enough to meet Mr. Tiffany himself. I have selected some very beautiful and novel things. . . . Mr. Tiffany had a case of art pottery which he has been producing in a limited way, none of which has been put on the market and he did not wish to dispose of any of it. I induced him, however, to include two of the best pieces and if we want them, he will let us have them as a great favor."¹¹⁹

Meanwhile, Morris continued to buy Tiffany works both for himself and the Museum, including a piece of the new pottery of which Mr. Tiffany was so possessive. Morris sometimes reversed his opinion about a particular piece, as when he wrote Barber in 1908: "I have been thinking over the small Tiffany vase. Before it is too late to come to a decision regarding it, place it alongside the other specimens and I am inclined to think you will agree with me that it is not interesting enough for us and will rather detract from the collection."¹²⁰

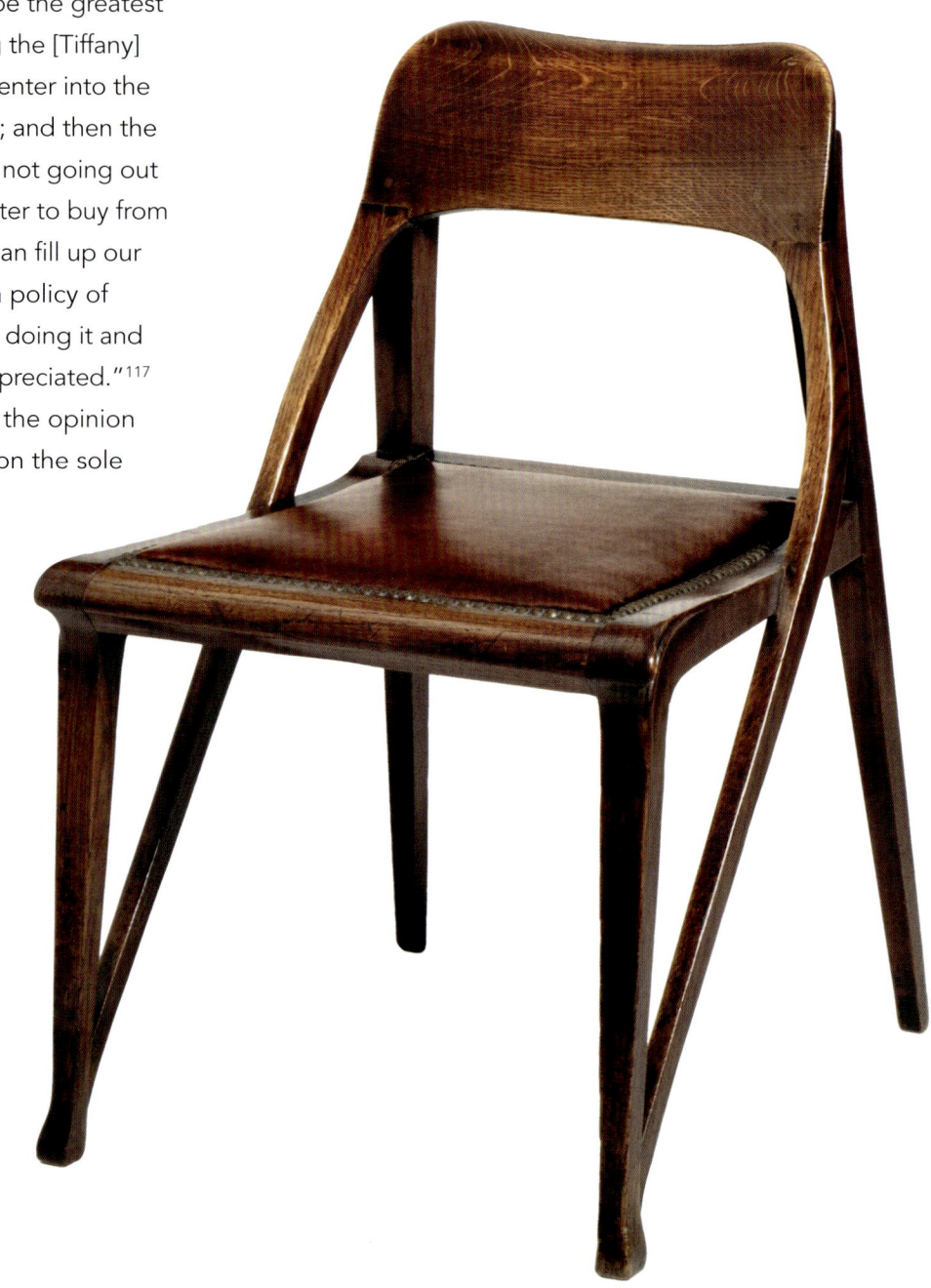

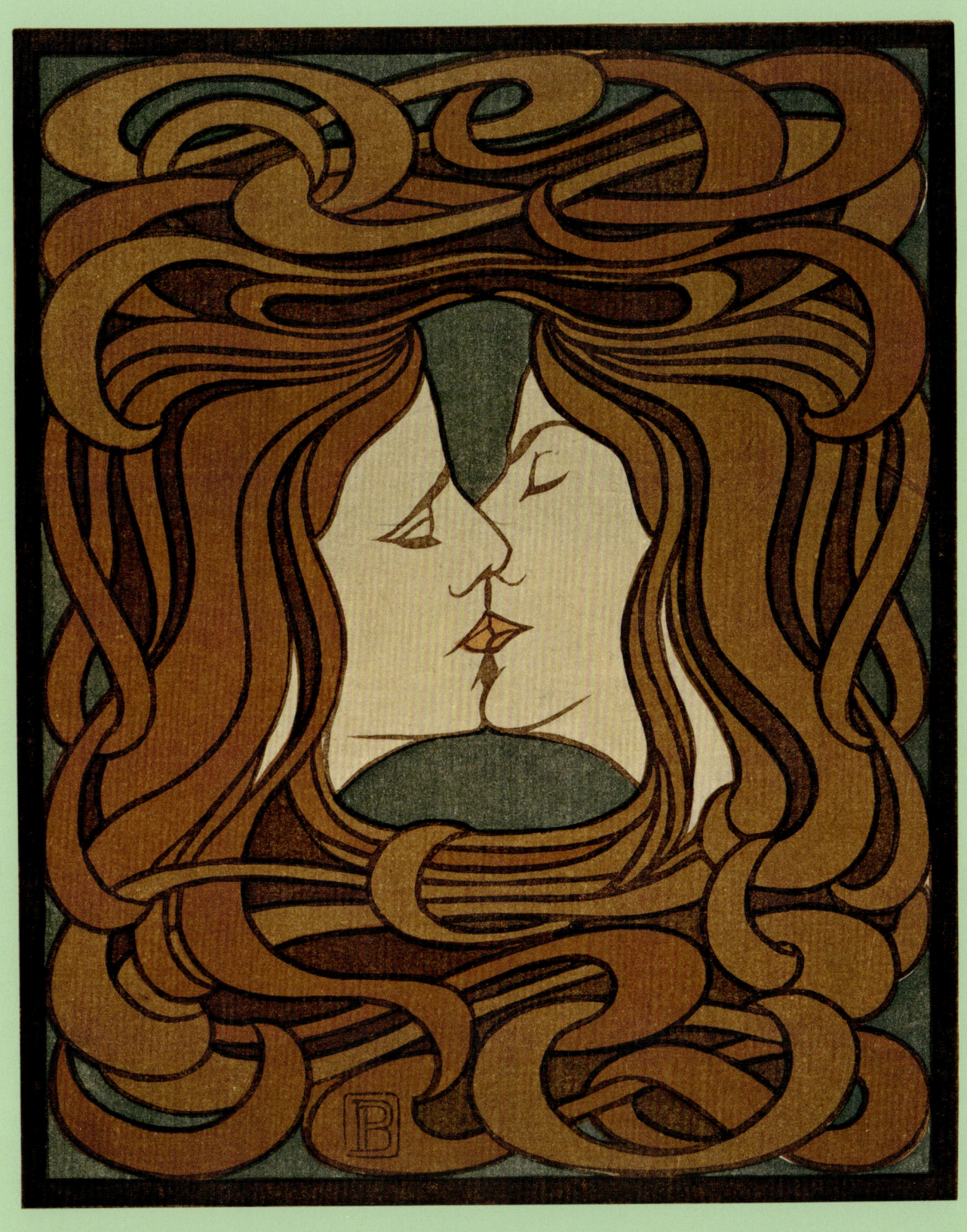

Opposite : **50. Richard Riemerschmid** : for Vereinigte Werkstätten für Kunst im Handwerk : Chair : 1907 : oak, leather : H 30⅝" : 1991-17-1 (cat. 159)   Above : **51. Peter Behrens** : *The Kiss* : 1899 : color woodcut : H (image) 10¾" : 1976–78–1 (cat. 16)

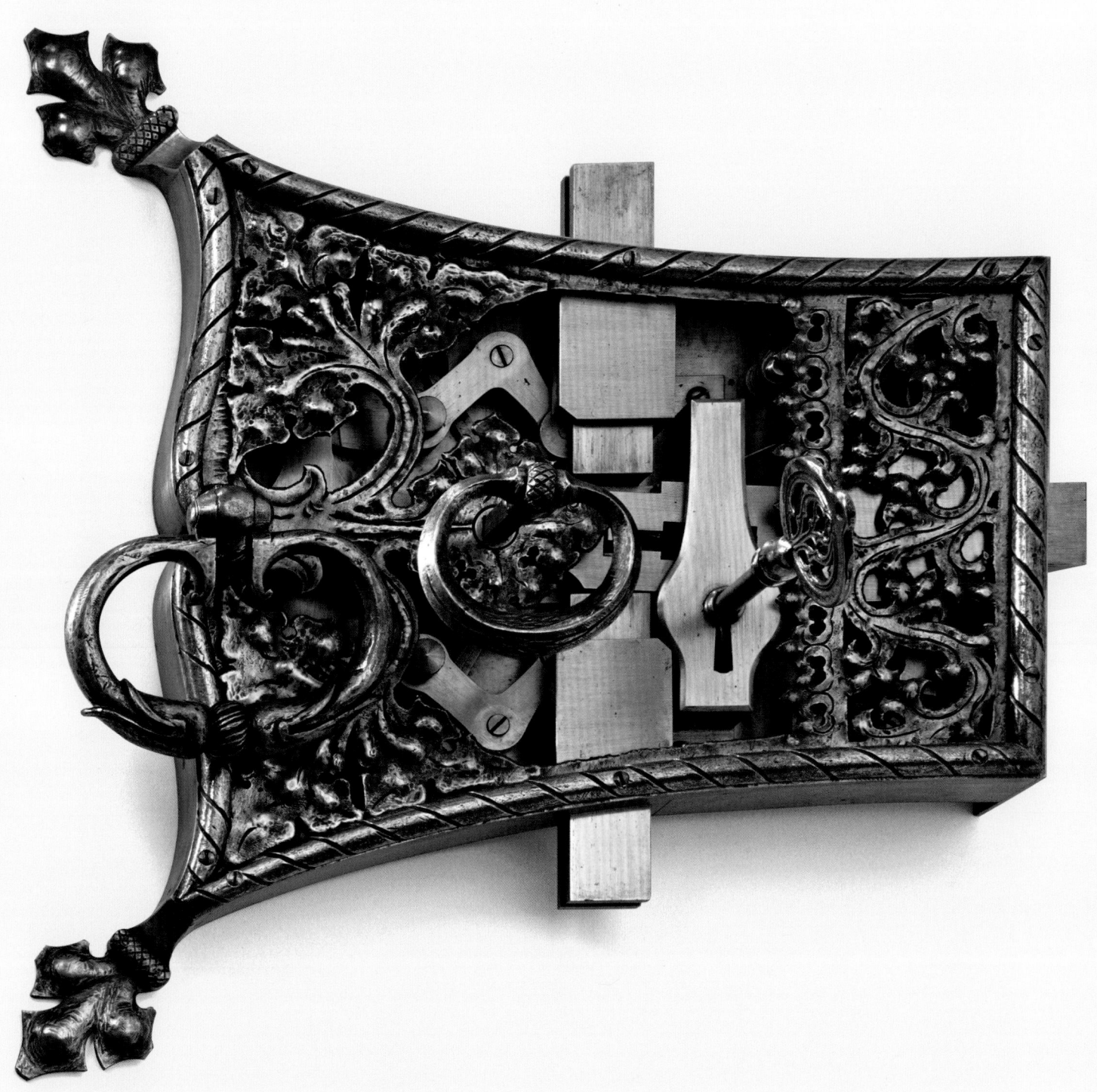

ACQUIRING THE MODERN

Among the most interesting letters between Morris and Barber are those that discuss the importance of acquiring modern and contemporary decorative arts for the Museum. "I am entirely opposed to follow other museums," wrote Morris in 1910, because "they change as their Director's views change. . . . If you care for my interest, the committee will have to take an interest in modern things. Modern things in less than 100 years will be old. Let us get them now and not have our successors wish we had foresight."[121] Barber replied, "I agree with you entirely that we should not neglect modern works of art, and do not think you can accuse me of ever opposing the purchase of such works when they show originality and artistic merit."[122] Accordingly, several months later Barber wrote Morris: "I am sending you a catalogue of a sale of pottery and glass to take place in New York on Tuesday and Wednesday next. This collection is particularly rich in rare modern wares."[123]

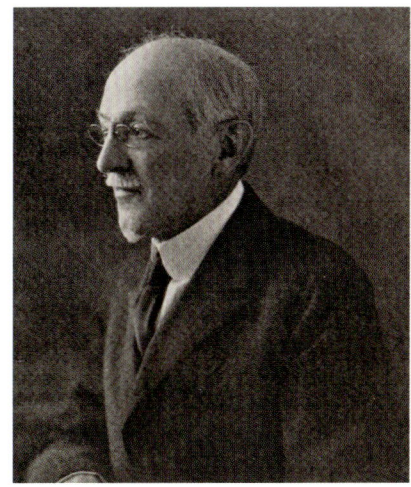

The two men were also aware of local contemporary work, notably that of Samuel Yellin, former student (in 1906), then instructor in metalwork (1907–19) at the Museum school. They acquired for the Museum the first pieces by this craftsman to enter a public collection. "I called at the School, Broad and Pine streets, on Saturday afternoon, to examine the pieces of iron work exhibited by Mr. Yellin," Barber wrote Morris in February 1911. "I was much pleased with a large lock in the collection, and think you would be much pleased with this example of Mr. Yellin's work. . . . While it is not a large work, it is very attractive and the mechanism is of an exceedingly high order. The price which Mr. Yellin asks for the lock is $200."[124] The handsomely embossed and incised "Gothic" lock was purchased that year with the Temple Fund and illustrated in the *Bulletin* in 1913 (fig. 52).[125]

When Barber was named director of the Museum following the death of William Platt Pepper in 1907, he became more directly responsible to a board of trustees with varying art historical interests and whose membership had altered since he had joined the staff in 1892. Among the new trustees were John H. McFadden, a cotton merchant in Philadelphia, New York, and Liverpool, and a serious collector of English paintings;[126] and later Edward T. Stotesbury (representing the commissioners of Philadelphia's Fairmount Park), financier and senior partner of the investment banking firms Drexel, J. P. Morgan, and Morgan Marjes, and a collector of French eighteenth-century decorative arts and sculpture and English portraits. John D. McIlhenny (fig. 53), a principal in his father's gas meter–manufacturing firm,[127] Helme and McIlhenny, as well as a collector of carpets and European furniture, also joined the board. Leading up to and through his appointment as director, Barber had become more ambitious than ever to promote the national and international reputation of the Museum. He continued his campaign of publications, producing a series of "art primers" that began in 1906; a 113-page illustrated *General Guide to the Collections of the Pennsylvania Museum* in 1907; and *The Majolica of Mexico*, a handbook, in 1908. Keenly aware of the need for a national organization of museums,[128] Barber was "in hearty sympathy" with the establishment of the American Association of Museums in 1906.[129] With his expenses supported in part by Morris, in June 1910 Barber made his first trip to Europe, where he visited twenty-two museums.[130] In advance Morris wrote Barber from Vienna: "I am very glad indeed to learn of your

Opposite : **52. Samuel Yellin** : Lock, Key, and Handle : 1911 : iron, mica (now missing) : W 19 3/4" : 1911-237a–e (cat. 221)   Above : **53.** John D. McIlhenny : elected to the Museum's board in 1914 : Museum president, 1920–26

proposed visit to this side of the Atlantic for all you will see will be a revelation and a delight. You are indeed to be envied the pleasure of a first visit; anyone can make a 2d, a 3d & so on, but the pleasure of the first comes but once."[131] Before leaving, Barber had related to Morris what he hoped to accomplish in Europe: "I am anxious to see the Bavarian National Museum in Munich, which Miss Sophy T. Steel said was the best arranged museum of its kind in Europe, particularly in its exhibition of historical interiors."[132] In a report addressed to the trustees on his return from Europe, the director observed:

> One of the most valuable features of many of the European museums is the arrangement of their collections of furniture according to historic periods and with correct historical surroundings. In almost every museum visited, rooms or apartments have been fitted up for the proper display of the furniture of different periods and countries, or as illustrating the habits and customs of the peasantry of different sections. . . .
>
> It is also of great importance that we should gather together a representative collection of American furniture, for the reason that the best Colonial furniture was produced in Philadelphia, and the formation of such an exhibit should be a source of local pride. The installation of a series of apartments illustrating the arts and customs of the early English settlers, the Pennsylvania Dutch, and the refinements of life in our larger cities during the Revolutionary period, would go far toward making this the most representative of American museums.[133]

Among the museum directors whom Barber met in Europe was Justus Brinckmann of Hamburg's Museum für Kunst und Gewerbe (Museum of Art and Design), whose theories of museum planning had led to the creation of composite and period rooms not only in Hamburg, but also in Berlin, Dresden, and Nuremberg. By showing objects in close association, Brinckmann believed, the whole stylistic character of a period or geographic area could be deduced. As he had written in 1894, in his own museum's handbook: "One has to be clear that any product of technical art, worthy of admiration for all times, can only be properly understood in connection with its cultural heritage. . . . The new arrangement, for example, will show us the faiences of the Persians united with their glass, metalwork, and rugs, and thus teach us in a far more incisive way than has been possible in the previous dispersion of material, the nature of their common growth from the soil of a definite culture and inherited taste."[134] Already predisposed, Barber was convinced by what he heard and saw in Europe and began immediately to rethink the presentation of the Museum's collections, writing Morris in August 1910: "As you are doubtless aware, we are now preparing small apartments to answer as historically correct backgrounds for our furniture collections, and I have been wondering where we could procure some suitable paneling for our eighteenth-century French room."[135] Less than a week later he reported: "We are ready to fit up a Spanish room for our Spanish furniture" (fig. 54).[136] When the period "alcoves" opened in October, Barber wrote Morris again: "The reception yesterday was quite successful, as everyone seemed to be very much pleased with the furniture exhibit, so far as it goes."[137] Barber's were among the first period interiors in an American museum. Just the year before, when the Museum of Fine Arts, Boston opened its new building on Huntington Avenue, it had included a Japanese temple room and an interior Japanese garden. In March 1910 the Metropolitan's first curator of decorative arts, W. R. Valentiner, who had been trained at the Kaiser Friedrich Museum in Berlin, installed J. P. Morgan's gift of Georges Hoentschel's collection of medieval and Renaissance objects in composite arrangements with period paneling, just as Barber did a few months later in Philadelphia.

Although Morris was interested in historic objects and had long supported the Museum's collection of eighteenth- and nineteenth-century Pennsylvania German pottery, Barber's plunge into historic interiors and the acquisitions

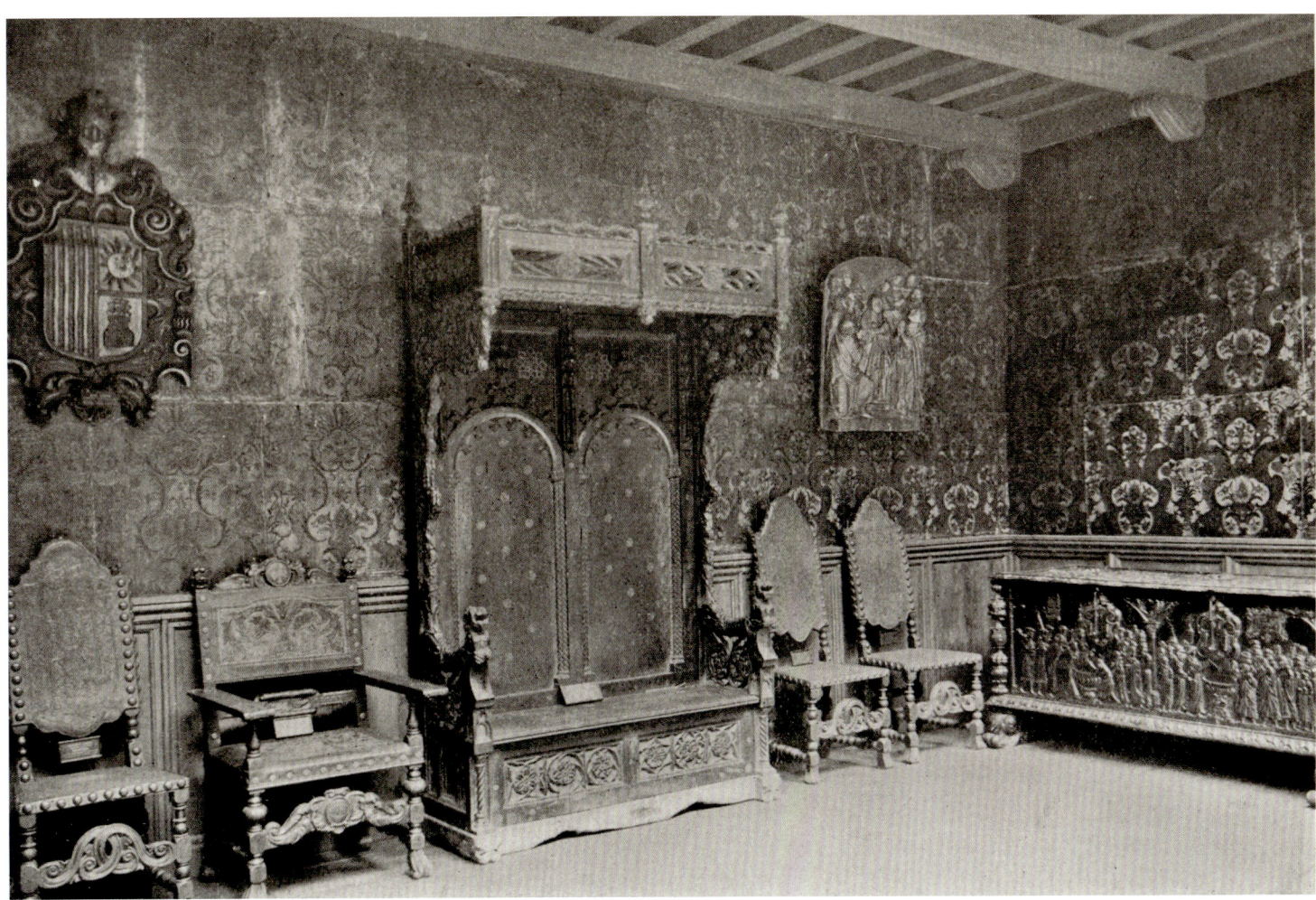

they entailed seemed to dismay him; he privately complained that the Museum in general and Barber in particular were deserting the modernist cause. "I wish I could persuade you to throw away the antique, genuine or fraud, and buy modern work if *very* good," Morris wrote in the summer of 1911. "Bear in mind many of the most valuable collections *today* were nothing more than specimens of contemporary art of the time. Let us do something and not be as far as the end of a dog's tail but behind its brains in following N.Y., Boston & Chicago."[138] Barber replied the following day: "I would be very glad indeed to buy modern work, provided it is as good or better than the ancient. To buy it simply because it is modern, however, and is not as good workmanship as the old, does not appeal to me. I agree with you that the best and rarest pieces, whether old or new, should be procured for the Museum at any price, and in accordance with that view I am exceedingly anxious to secure some of the best modern bronze work, such as I often see exhibited in Tiffany's and other places."[139] Later in the fall Morris again appealed to Barber: "Your question gives me once more the opportunity to beg of you to give up collecting the old (unless *very* good) and to turn your sole attention to the *very* good modern *if* it can be found. Some day it will be old and will be sought after with the same avidity as we hunt the old today. And do you not think it would be pleasant to be remembered for the wisdom in collecting contemporary manufacture."[140] Morris's successful purchase of recent Tiffany glass brought reconciliation in 1912, when he wrote Barber: "It was a pleasure that you approved my selections. I had begun to feel we were growing further and further apart in our views about the Museum."[141]

54. Room in the style of seventeenth-century Spain : Pennsylvania Museum and School of Industrial Art : 1910

THE END OF AN ERA

Morris was increasingly unwell and of necessity began to distance himself from the Museum. Barber, too, was aging. "We shall look forward to a rapid improvement in your health," wrote Morris to Barber in 1914. "Do not get sick, please don't."[142] Their last letters show Morris tart and principled to the end, writing in July 1915: "I think it is well you do not consider yours an *Art* Museum, if you think the specimens sent me to see are examples of *Art*."[143] Barber, ever the academic, replied: "I agree with you that they do not represent a very high degree of art. . . . The collection of American pottery and porcelain . . . is primarily of interest as illustrating the progress and extent of the potter's art in the United States, and the three pieces I sent you for examination would fill in the gaps in the series."[144] Morris died a month later and Barber the following year, marking the end of an era at the Museum and the loss of two of its greatest advocates for collecting modern and contemporary decorative arts. Over half a century would pass before the institution would again find leaders of similar vision and passion.

Morris was remembered by the board as "a generous patron and an intelligent friend . . . ever ready with valuable advice. . . . He had strong views and well defined opinions and these all bore upon his earnest desire to bring to the public, and especially to students . . . the inspiration that the best work of any period never fails to create."[145] In a personal memorial tribute to Morris, published in the Museum's *Bulletin*, Barber noted: "He was always a liberal patron of the Museum and the School and his gifts exceed in importance and value those of any other individual. Possessing rare judgment and gifted with unerring taste, he was largely instrumental in shaping the policy of the Museum, while his advice and approval were always sought by his associates on the museum committee in the selection and purchase of objects of art."[146] The Museum's tribute to Barber was impressive as well, the trustees recording his death a "grievous loss" and describing their academically oriented director as "scrupulously accurate in his work" and an individual "who gave his entire time and such acquirements as he possessed to the discharge of his duties . . . methodical in his habits and sincerely devoted to his trust, with no desire other than a single-minded pursuit of his chosen work as collector and curator."[147]

Adding a long biography and a list of Barber's professional associations, the *Bulletin* noted that "the institution of which he was the head proceeded safely and quietly, under his guidance. . . . We, his colleagues who have been associated with him for many years, deeply deplore his removal from our midst, feeling that his place cannot readily be filled."[148]

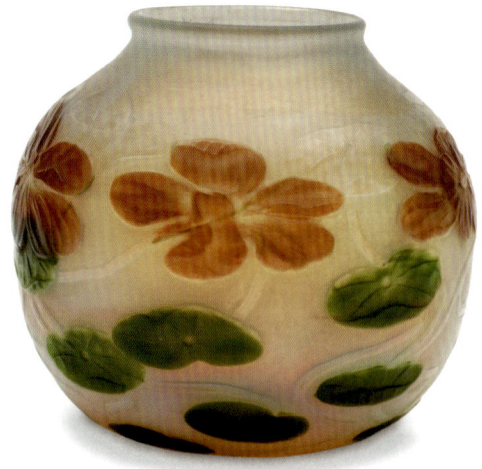

Above : **55. Louis Comfort Tiffany** : for Tiffany : Vase : 1911 : Favrile glass : H 5 1/2" : 1912-1 (cat. 193)   Opposite : **56. Charles Rennie Mackintosh** : probably for Herbert Smith and Son : High-Back Side Chair : c. 1897 : stained oak, rush, horsehair : H 53 7/8" : 1987-71-1 (cat. 109)

1. *Good Furniture Magazine of Furnishing and Decoration*, February 1923, p. 91.

2. "Report of the Director of the Museum," *Annual Report, Philadelphia Museum of Art* [year ending May 31, 1944] (Philadelphia, 1944), pp. 14, 17.

3. *First and Second Reports of the Board of Trustees of the Pennsylvania Museum and School of Industrial Art, 1876–77* (Philadelphia, 1878), p. 7.

4. Board of Trustees Records, Minutes, April 14, 1876.

5. "Dolan, Thomas," *Dictionary of American Biography* (New York: Charles Scribner's Sons, 1946), vol. 5, p. 355.

6. Board of Trustees Records, Minutes, January 13, 1879. Pepper again served as director of the Museum from 1901 until his death in 1907.

7. *Philadelphia Times*, October 12, 1876.

8. Board of Trustees Records, Minutes, June 9, 1876.

9. Ibid.

10. Riokei Nakashima to William Platt Pepper, June 23, 1876, Accession Files, Registrar, Philadelphia Museum of Art.

11. In 1902 Mrs. Frishmuth accepted the Museum's invitation to become honorary curator of the department of musical instruments; Edwin Atlee Barber to John T. Morris, January 13, 1902, Edwin Atlee Barber Records, Correspondence with Morris, Jenks, Miller, and Allan.

12. Board of Trustees Records, Minutes, July 20, 1875.

13. Board of Trustees Records, Minutes, October 12, 1875.

14. Board of Trustees Records, Minutes, October 7, 1875.

15. The school's textile department also became a separate entity, known successively as the Philadelphia Textile Institute, the Philadelphia College of Textiles and Science, and presently as Philadelphia University.

16. John F. Hartranft quoted in *First and Second Reports*, p. 15.

17. Board of Trustees Records, Minutes, June 13, 1879.

18. *Philadelphia Times*, October 12, 1876.

19. Board of Trustees Records, Minutes, June 9, 1876.

20. Board of Trustees Records, Minutes, February 6, 1935.

21. The exhibition was described as comprising "works of art belonging to the Museum together with such articles as may be obtained on loan"; Board of Trustees Records, Minutes, October 13, 1876.

22. The loans included objects belonging to future trustee Dr. Francis W. Lewis; Board of Trustees Records, Minutes, December 15, 1876.

23. *First and Second Reports*, p. 10.

24. Ibid., p. 11.

25. Ibid., p. 12.

26. Juan Riaño catalogued the Spanish objects in the South Kensington Museum in 1872 and subsequently published *The Industrial Arts in Spain* (London: Chapman and Hall, 1879), an art handbook of the South Kensington Museum.

27. *Annual Report, Pennsylvania Museum and School of Industrial Art* [year ending November 30, 1878] (Philadelphia, 1879), p. 13.

28. Board of Trustees Records, Minutes, January 14, 1878.

29. Board of Trustees Records, Minutes, June 23, 1878.

30. Board of Trustees Records, Minutes, July 8, 1878.

31. *Annual Report* [1878], p. 13.

32. Ibid., p. 11.

33. Board of Trustees Records, Minutes, October 14, 1878.

34. H. Dumont Wagner to the Executive Committee, Board of Trustees Records, Minutes, February 14, 1879, and February 1, 1879, as reported therein.

35. Board of Trustees Records, Minutes, March 2, 1901.

36. Board of Trustees Records, Minutes, May 9, 1907.

37. Board of Trustees Records, Minutes, December 8, 1879.

38. Board of Trustees Records, Minutes, December 12, 1884, and June 22, 1894.

39. Board of Trustees Records, Minutes, January 24, 1882.

40. Board of Trustees Records, Minutes, May 5, 1892.

41. Board of Trustees Records, Minutes, October 24, 1879; September 9, 1881; and October 10, 1884.

42. *Annual Report, Pennsylvania Museum and School of Industrial Art* [year ending November 30, 1881] (Philadelphia, 1882), p. 11.

43. *Annual Report, Pennsylvania Museum and School of Industrial Art* [year ending December 30, 1882] (Philadelphia, 1883), p. 8.

44. Ibid.

45. The committee was originally founded as the Women's Centennial Executive Committee "to interest the women of the whole world in the International Exhibition of 1876"; Women's Committee of the Philadelphia Museum of Art Records, Women's Centennial Association Constitution, Centennial Executive Committee scrapbook. Since 1961 the committee has been known as the Women's Committee of the Philadelphia Museum of Art.

46. *Annual Report* [1883], p. 5.

47. Women's Committee of the Philadelphia Museum of Art Records, Minutes, December 8, 1899; see also May 31, 1900.

48. *Annual Report, Pennsylvania Museum and School of Industrial Art* [year ending December 31, 1884] (Philadelphia, 1885), p. 7.

49. Board of Trustees Records, Minutes, October 20, 1885.

50. Board of Trustees Records, Minutes, March 11, 1887.

51. Annual Report, *Pennsylvania Museum and School of Industrial Art* [year ending December 31, 1888] (Philadelphia, 1889), p. 8. See also *Awards and Reports of the Judges* (Philadelphia, 1888); *Catalogue of the Exhibition of American Pottery and Porcelain, Including a Competition of American Workmen* (Philadelphia, 1888); and *Pottery and Porcelain Exhibition, Including a Competition for American Workmen* (Philadelphia, 1888).

52. *Annual Report* [1888], p. 6.

53. *Exhibition of American Art Industry of 1889, Including a Competition for American Workmen* (Philadelphia, 1889).

54. *Annual Report* [1888], p. 8.

55. *Annual Report, Pennsylvania Museum and School of Industrial Art* [year ending May 31,1895] (Philadelphia, 1896), pp. 15, 28.

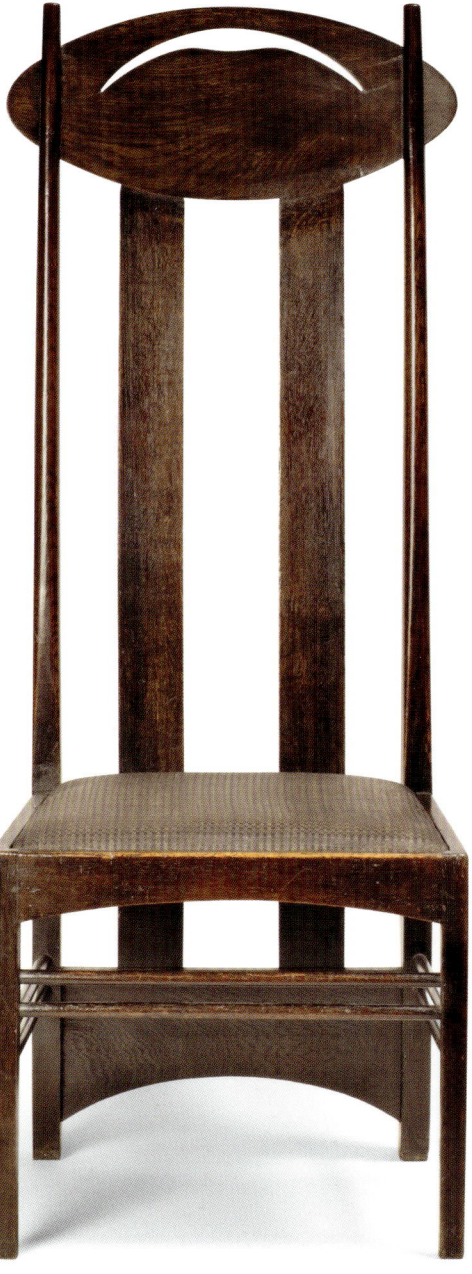

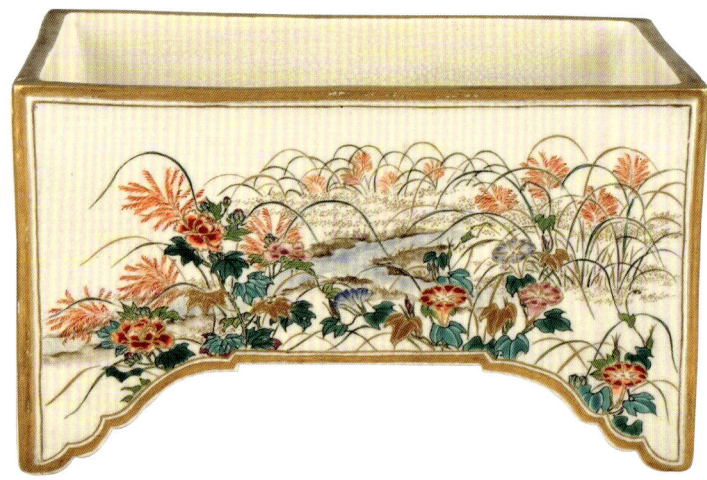

56. Board of Trustees Records, Minutes, January 13, 1898.

57. William Platt Pepper to Dalton Dorr, January 11, 1898, Dalton Dorr Records, William Platt Pepper Correspondence, Pepper Letter Book.

58. Assuming the director's office was not Pepper's idea, as he told Dorr: "I was very much surprised and *not pleased*, the other day when Mr. Search proposed me for the Director of the Museum & I was elected. I should have preferred that position to have still been *your's* [*sic*] for you are on the spot & do it so well. However, you can still be my assistant and in fact the Acting Director & we can work & have always done so, so well for years together." Pepper to Dorr, February 3, 1899, Dalton Dorr Records, Pepper Correspondence, Pepper Letter Book; emphases in the original.

59. Barber spelled his middle name with a capital *L*, as Edwin AtLee Barber, whenever the choice was left up to him; but others usually spelled it with a small *l*, including the Library of Congress.

60. In 1902 "seven boxes of minerals, seeds, and other natural products" were to be offered by the Museum to the Academy of Natural Sciences and elsewhere; Board of Trustees Records, Museum Committee, Minutes, November 3, 1902. In 1913 Barber wrote Morris: "I had a very pleasant conversation with Mr. John H. McFadden at his house, in regard to the Shackleton South Pole collection of geological and natural science specimens and he did not seem at all offended that I suggested that the collection was hardly suitable for an art museum to place on permanent exhibition"; Barber to Morris, January 17, 1913, Barber Records, Correspondence with Morris et al.

61. Barber sold his collection to the Museum for $500, "a sum somewhat less than it had cost him to collect it"; *Annual Report, Pennsylvania Museum and School of Industrial Art* [year ending December 31, 1892] (Philadelphia, 1893), p. 9; and Board of Trustees Records, Minutes, June 10, 1892.

62. Edwin Atlee Barber, *Pennsylvania Museum and School of Industrial Art: Pottery; Catalogue of American Potteries and Porcelains* (Philadelphia, 1893), pp. 3–4.

63. Pepper to Dorr, April 24, 1894, Dorr Records, Pepper Correspondence, Pepper Letter Book: "Hurrah," said Pepper, "so much for having an Honorary Curator appointed!! And this is part of *your* good work and *your* idea, too, I believe"; emphases in the original.

64. Board of Trustees Records, Minutes, November 11, 1892.

65. Pepper to Dorr, October 19, 1893, Dorr Records, Pepper Correspondence, Pepper Letter Book.

66. John T. Morris to Dorr, October 14, 1893, Dorr Records, Museum Letter Book 10; emphasis in the original.

67. Pepper to Dorr, October 19, 1893, Dorr Records, Pepper Correspondence, Pepper Letter Book.

68. Barber to Dorr, November 2, 1893, Dorr Records, Edwin Atlee Barber Correspondence.

69. *Annual Report* [1893], p. 16.

70. Later deaccessioned, this and other early pieces of Rookwood were reacquired by gift and purchase in 1976.

71. Marc-Louis-Emmanuel Solon to Morris, May 2, 1894, Accession Files, Registrar.

72. Board of Trustees Records, Minutes, March 10, 1898.

73. *Annual Report, Pennsylvania Museum and School of Industrial Art* [eighteen months ending May 31, 1899] (Philadelphia, 1899), p. 22.

74. Pepper to Morris, June 24, 1898, Dorr Records, Pepper Correspondence, Pepper Letter Book; emphasis in the original.

75. Edwin Atlee Barber, "Recent Advances in the Pottery Industry," *Popular Science Monthly*, January 1892, p. 303.

76. Ibid., p. 301.

77. Barber to Dorr, October 27, 1893, Dorr Records, Barber Correspondence, Pepper Letter Book: "Mr. Morris has given me a commission to buy for the Museum some Tucker china and Rookwood pieces which are to be sold at Birch's on Monday and Tuesday."

78. Edwin Atlee Barber, *The Pottery and Porcelain of the United States: An Historical Review of American Ceramic Art from the Earliest Times to the Present Day*, 3rd ed., rev. and enl. (New York: G. P. Putnam's Sons, 1893), pp. iii–iv.

79. Barber to Dorr, March 26, 1896, Dorr Records, Barber Correspondence.

80. Barber to Dorr, June 15, 1896, Dorr Records, Barber Correspondence.

81. Barber to Dorr, June 30, 1896, Dorr Records, Barber Correspondence.

82. Barber to Dorr, December 10, 1896, Dorr Records, Barber Correspondence.

83. Referring to Pell's appointment as honorary curator, Barber wrote to Morris: "I think it would help us if we could get his name into this year's report. . . . Such things please him very much and help to interest him in our Museum. . . . He is an expert in [European porcelain] in which I am a little weak." Barber to Morris, July 1, 1904, Barber Records, Correspondence with Morris et al.

84. Barber to Dorr, July 9, 1896, Dorr Records, Barber Correspondence.

85. Barber to Morris, December 4, 1899, Barber Records, Correspondence with Morris et al.; emphasis in the original.

86. *Annual Report* [1899], p. 15.

87. Edwin Atlee Barber, *Anglo-American Pottery: Old English China with American Views; A Manual for Collectors* (1899; Philadelphia: Patterson and White, 1901).

88. Morris to Barber, July 23, 1901, Barber Records, Correspondence with Morris et al.

89. Barber to Morris, July 24, 1901, Barber Records, Correspondence with Morris et al.

90. Board of Trustees Records, Minutes, April 13, 1900.

91. Pepper to Dorr, March 21, 1900, Dorr Records, Pepper Correspondence, Pepper Letter Book.

92. Morris to Barber, May 17, 1901, Barber Records, Correspondence with Morris et al.

93. Morris to Barber, December 20, 1901, Barber Records, Correspondence with Morris et al.

94. Morris to Barber, March 28, 1902, Barber Records, Correspondence with Morris et al.

95. Barber to Dorr, January 9, 1901, Dorr Records, Barber Correspondence.

96. *Bulletin of the Pennsylvania Museum*, vol. 1, no. 1 (January 1903): p. 1.

97. Ibid, p. 5.

98. Edwin Atlee Barber, "Decennial Report," *Bulletin of the Pennsylvania Museum*, vol. 9, no. 34 (April 1911): p. 4.

99. Barber's efforts greatly delighted Pepper, who wrote him in September 1901: "I cannot tell you how much pleased I was with the clean & greatly improved appearance of the walls of the Memorial Hall, and as to the improved light in Vestibule & Rotunda. It amazed me & will be a great boon to the visitors to the Museum & everything will be so much better seen. . . . Let me say again how entirely I approve of what you have done, *so quickly* (it seems to me) under great difficulties & *short handed at that*. I see clearly, with your intelligent assistance, that much good work can be done by us at the Museum, as our views are so much in accord." Pepper to Barber, September 25, 1901, Barber Records; emphases in the original.

Above : **57. Riokei Nakashima** : Tray : c. 1876 : enameled and gilt earthenware : W 7 5/16" : 1876-1665 (cat. 132)   Opposite : **58. Marc-Louis-Emmanuel Solon and Alboine Birks** : for Minton : *Folie* or *Jester* Vase : 1894 : glazed and gilt Parian porcelain : H 23 7/8" : 1898-95 (cat. 179)

100. *Annual Report, Pennsylvania Museum and School of Industrial Art* [year ending December 31, 1902] (Philadelphia, 1902), p. 19.

101. Barber, "Decennial Report," p. 2.

102. Barber made a special plea for a publication fund in that year's annual report: "Of even greater importance than the acquisition of new material, after a museum has grown to the proportions of this, is the publication of original works which shall be accepted as authoritative contributions to the literature of art. A moderate fund would enable the Curator to carry on this important work without embarrassment." *Annual Report, Pennsylvania Museum and School of Industrial Art* [year ending December 31, 1903] (Philadelphia, 1903), p. 19.

103. Barber to Morris, December 29, 1902, Barber Records, Correspondence with Morris et al.

104. Barber to Morris, November 25, 1902, Barber Records, Correspondence with Morris et al.

105. Barber to Morris, December 1, 1903, Barber Records, Correspondence with Morris et al.

106. Barber to Morris, September 19, 1904, Barber Records, Correspondence with Morris et al.

107. Barber to Morris, June 7, 1904, Barber Records, Correspondence with Morris et al.

108. Barber to Morris, January 28, 1905, Barber Records, Correspondence with Morris et al.

109. *Annual Report*, [1903], p. 13.

110. John Story Jenks to Morris, September 15, 1904, Accession Files, Registrar.

111. Ibid.

112. John Wanamaker, however, acquired twenty-one German interiors for display in his Philadelphia store.

113. Board of Trustees Records, Minutes, May 11, 1905; June 8, 1905; January 9, 1908; January, 11, 1912; and October 10, 1912.

114. W. H. Thomas to Barber, June 27, 1904, Barber Records, Correspondence.

115. Morris to Barber, July 1, 1904, Barber Records, Correspondence with Morris et al.

116. Barber to Thomas, July 1, 1904, Barber Records, Correspondence; emphases in the original.

117. Morris to Barber, April 1, 1905, Barber Records, Correspondence with Morris et al; emphases in the original.

118. Morris to Barber, April 20, 1905, Barber Records, Correspondence with Morris et al.

119. Barber to Morris, May 4, 1905, Barber Records, Correspondence with Morris et al.

120. Morris to Barber, January 7, 1908, Barber Records, Correspondence with Morris et al.

121. Morris to Barber, December 2, 1910, Barber Records, Correspondence with Morris et al.

122. Barber to Morris, December 3, 1910, Barber Records, Correspondence with Morris et al.

123. Barber to Morris, May 4, 1911, Barber Records, Correspondence with Morris et al. Morris responded: "I particularly liked *one* piece of new Japan which could be worth having in a *new* collection. I should love to have it in my private little collection but I propose to resist temptation." Morris to Barber, May 5, 1911, Barber Records, Correspondence with Morris et al.; emphases in the original.

124. Barber to Morris, February 27, 1911, Barber Records, Correspondence with Morris et al.

125. Board of Trustees Records, Museum Committee, Minutes, March 8, 1911; and *Bulletin of the Pennsylvania Museum*, vol. 11, no. 42 (April 1913): p. 35.

126. The *Christian Science Monitor* described the collection as "one of the finest of its kind in America"; "Philadelphia Art," *Christian Science Monitor*, May 5, 1916, p. 8.

127. Contrary to published accounts, John McIlhenny, father of John D. McIlhenny, did not invent the gas meter but rather patented in 1895 a gas valve that helped make his company successful, providing the basis upon which the family's fortune was built.

128. [Edwin Atlee Barber], "On the Cooperation of Public Museums," *Bulletin of the Pennsylvania Museum*, vol. 3, no. 10 (April 1905): p. 38.

129. Edwin Atlee Barber to Herman C. Bumpus, May 14, 1906, Barber Records, Correspondence.

130. "If any arrangement is made to send Dr. Barber to Europe this summer, I will be glad to subscribe $100 toward the expenses"; Morris to Jenks, January 4, 1910, Barber Records, Correspondence. The board authorized Barber's trip at its meeting on May 12, 1910, along with the use of "the available fund of the Temple Trust . . . for the purchase of objects for the Museum, should desirable examples be found"; Board of Trustees Records, Minutes, May 12, 1910.

131. Morris to Barber, May 18, 1910, Barber Records, Correspondence with Morris et al.

132. Barber to Morris, April 27, 1910, Barber Records, Correspondence with Morris et al.

133. Edwin Atlee Barber, "Report of the Director of the Museum to the Board of Trustees of the Pennsylvania Museum and School of Industrial Art on the Museums Visited by Him during His Recent European Trip," November 1, 1910, annotated typescript, Edwin Atlee Barber Papers.

134. Justus Brinckmann, *Führer durch das Hamburgische Museum für Kunst und Gewerbe.Zugleich ein Handbuch der Geschichte des Kunstgewerbes* (Hamburg: Verlag des Museums für Kunst und Gewerbe, 1894), pp. v, vii; my translation.

135. Barber to Morris, August 11, 1910, Barber Records, Correspondence with Morris et al.

136. Barber to Morris, August 16, 1910, Barber Records, Correspondence with Morris et al.

137. Barber to Morris, October 26, 1910, Barber Records, Correspondence with Morris et al.

138. Barber to Morris, July 28, 1911, Barber Records, Correspondence with Morris et al.; emphases in the original.

139. Barber to Morris, July 29, 1911, Barber Records, Correspondence with Morris et al.

140. Morris to Barber, October 13, 1911; emphases in the original.

141. Morris to Barber, July 24, 1912, Barber Records, Correspondence with Morris et al.

142. Morris to Barber, March 18, 1914, Barber Records, Correspondence with Morris et al.

143. Morris to Barber, July 16, 1915, Barber Records, Correspondence with Morris et al.; emphases in the original.

144. Barber to Morris, July 17, 1915, Barber Records, Correspondence with Morris et al.

145. Board of Trustees Records, Museum Committee, Minutes, November 1, 1915.

146. *Bulletin of the Pennsylvania Museum*, vol. 13, no. 52 (October 1915): p. 62.

147. Board of Trustees Records, Museum Committee, Minutes, January 2, 1917.

148. "In Memoriam," *Bulletin of the Pennsylvania Museum*, vol. 15, no. 57 (January 1917): p. 1.

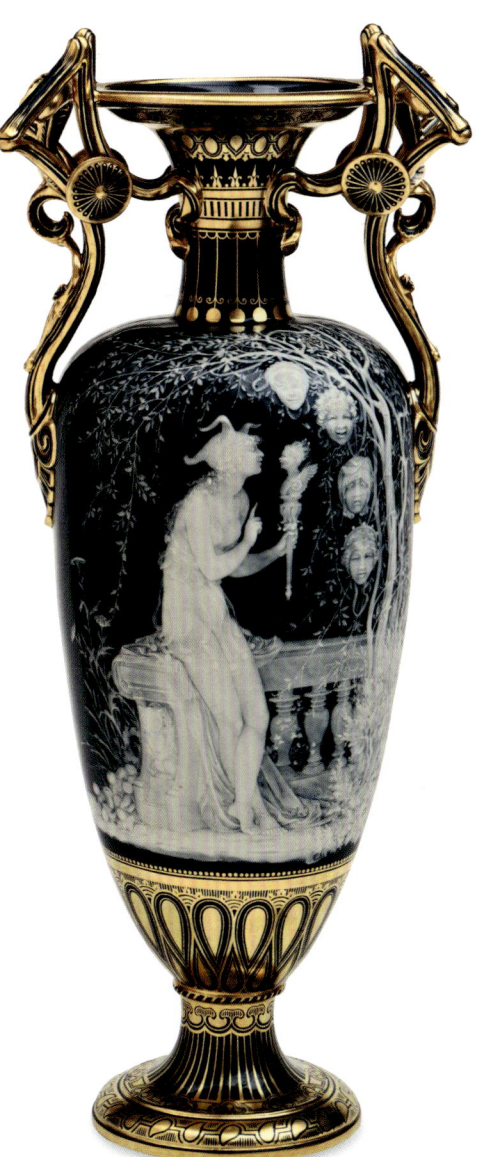

1916-1964

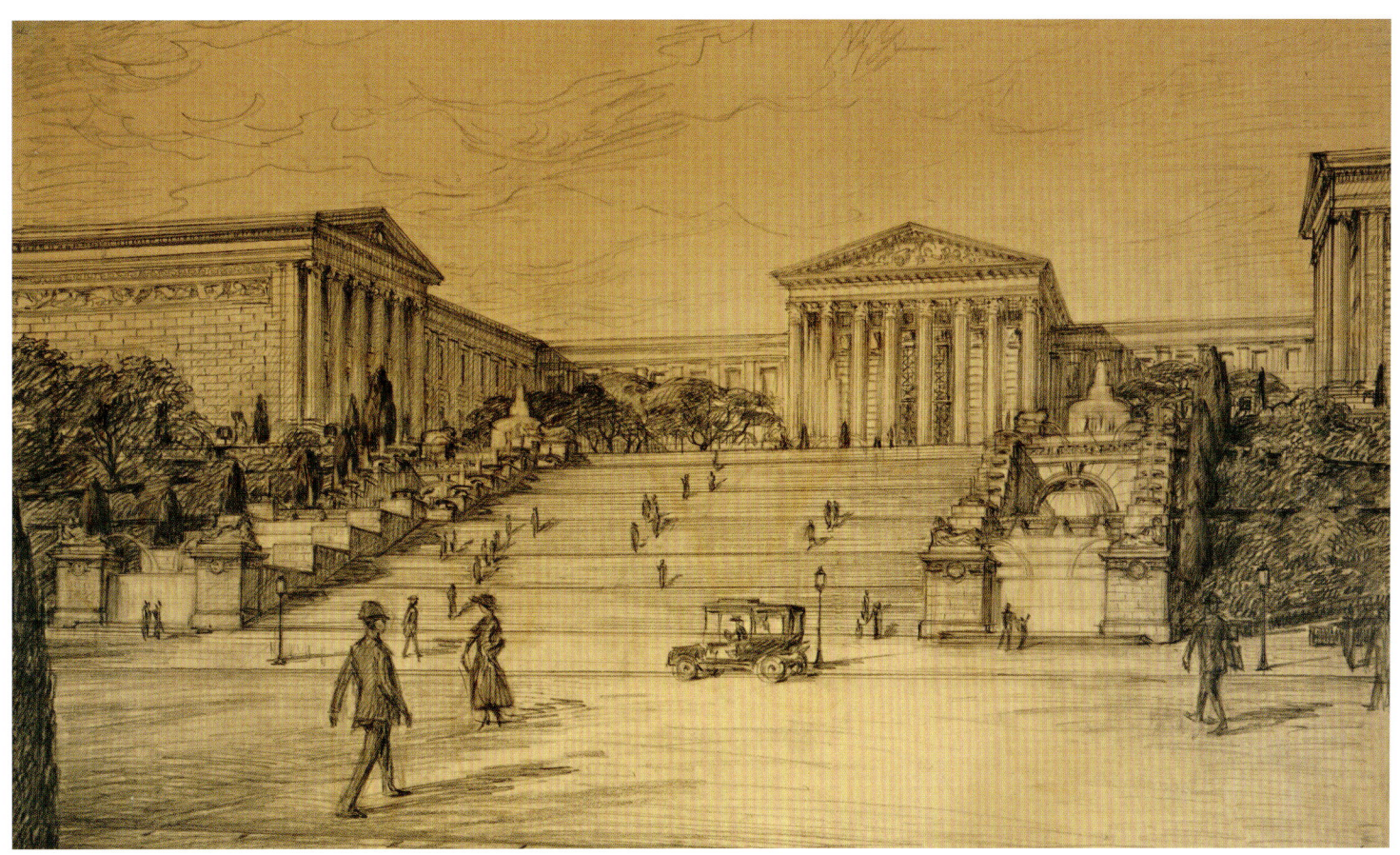

THE MUSEUM PLANS FOR EXPANSION

In the same number of the *Bulletin of the Pennsylvania Museum* that announced the death of Edwin Atlee Barber, the Museum gave notice of its future "removal to the Parkway."[1] Leslie W. Miller, Museum school principal, reported that the project had finally been made possible on December 13, 1916, by the action of the Fairmount Park commissioners, who granted the Museum land to construct a new building on the hill of Fairmount, at the head of the Benjamin Franklin Parkway (fig. 59).[2] From within the Museum it was lawyer Eli Kirk Price, aided by Edward T. Stotesbury, both members of the board of trustees and commissioners of Fairmount Park, who carried the fight for the new Museum building to its successful conclusion, and construction began on Fairmount in 1919. As early as the mid-1890s, the Museum's board had faced issues of overcrowding in Memorial Hall.[3] The planning, construction, and acquisition of objects for the new, much larger building were to occupy the Museum's board, staff, and supporters for the next half-century.

59. **Jacques Gréber** : Rendering of the proposed Museum building on Fairmount : 1917–18 : crayon on tracing paper : W 34" : PDP-1086 (cat. 77)

MODERNISM IN PHILADELPHIA

With a few notable exceptions, the field of modern and contemporary decorative arts little concerned the Museum during this period, lacking champions on the board or among the staff. Still, modernism in general made headway in Philadelphia from the 1920s forward, thanks to such artists, architects, designers, and collectors as Dr. Albert C. Barnes, Alexey Brodovitch, Earl Horter, George Howe, Anna Warren Ingersoll, and R. Sturgis Ingersoll, whose work and purchases of modern painting and sculpture influenced and eventually enriched the Museum's collections. Unfortunately, few of the Philadelphia collectors of modern American and European painting and sculpture collected modern furniture and decorative arts, arguably assigning a lower position to objects of utility in their hierarchy of the arts. Sturgis Ingersoll later recalled that before he and his wife, Marion, began collecting art, the walls of their house "remained bare" according to the modernist "doctrine of bare walls being the appropriate 'décor'";[4] but he and his sister Anna both lived with furniture they had inherited—a handsomely eclectic mix of traditional seventeenth-, eighteenth-, and nineteenth-century styles ranging from Jacobean through Georgian to Renaissance Revival.[5] As in previous years, the faculty and program of exhibitions at the Museum school continued to promote contemporary design, although the work it fostered until about 1930 tended to be historicizing, like that of Samuel Yellin (fig. 52), and directed to the conservative Philadelphia market.

In October 1917 the Museum announced the appointment of Langdon Warner as director. Warner "specialized in Oriental Art" but was also "a man of broad artistic sympathies,"[6] and like members of the Museum board he found "Memorial Hall entirely unsuitable for the exhibition and storage of objects of art."[7] He had come to Philadelphia by way of Harvard College and Harvard University, where he was educated and where he lectured, and the Cleveland Museum of Art, for which he had led an expedition to China. However, within two months of his arrival at the Museum, Warner was sent to East Asia, ostensibly by the Smithsonian Institution—as John D. McIlhenny reported to the museum committee, "in the interests of work previously done"[8]—but in reality, as Warner revealed on his return fourteen months later, "on government service of confidential nature."[9] In Warner's absence his colleague, British-born architect and designer E. Hamilton Bell—concurrently curator of the collection of paintings that John G. Johnson left to the city of Philadelphia in 1917—served as acting director, "deriving many valuable suggestions" from the "mass of notes" left by Warner "for the rearrangement of the collections."[10] Like Warner, Bell was a specialist in Asian art and quick to relocate "the best of the Oriental pottery and porcelain" to a more favorable location in Memorial Hall.[11]

Bell also launched a deaccessioning campaign, arguing: "Among the collections in storage are many things which can never be shown under any circumstances. Can we dispose of these by sale, and how? I understand this has been done in the past. If once we begin doing this I feel sure that a careful combing over of the collections would reveal many an object the money value of which greatly exceeds its artistic. For instance, the two monstrous Berlin porcelain vases which have been retired from the Rotunda. There are also objects on exhibition which are unsuitable and trespass on our valuable space."[12] The two "monstrous" vases made by the Royal Porcelain Manufactory in Berlin had been shown at the World's Coumbian Exposition of 1893 in Chicago and acquired from the Field Museum in Chicago in 1914, when John T. Morris wrote Edwin Atlee Barber:

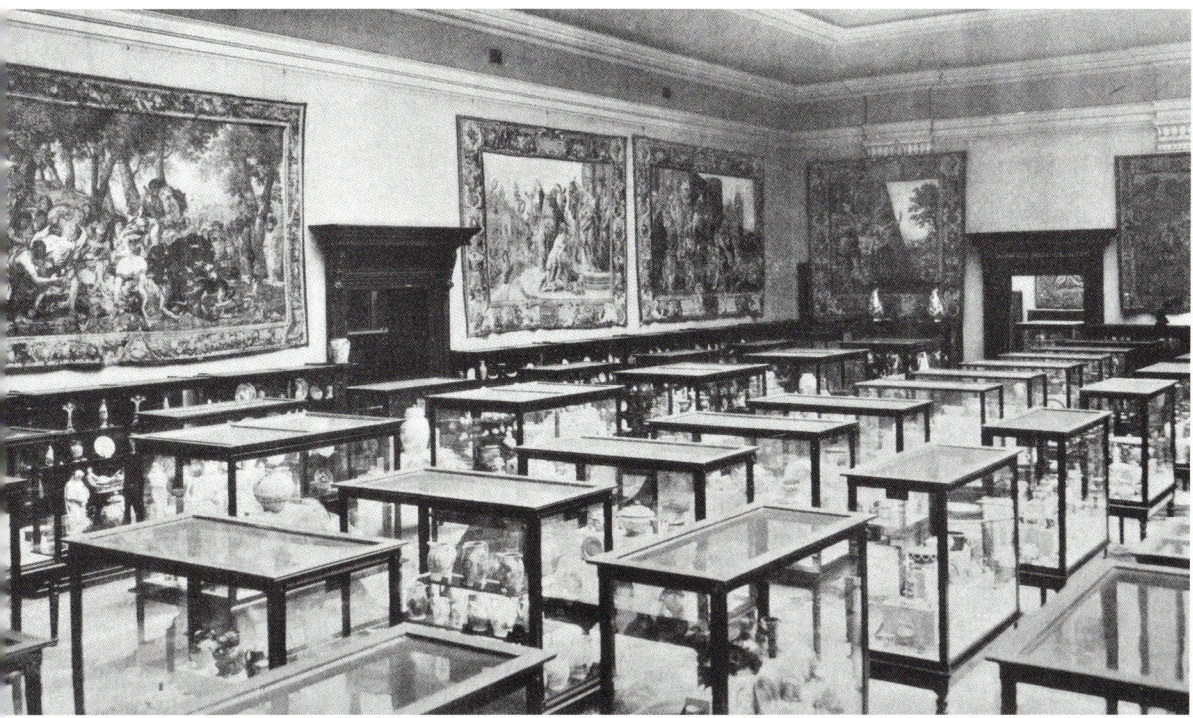

Hamilton Bell had deliberately reduced the Victorian clutter of eighty-eight cases in Barber's East (Ceramic) Gallery (fig. 60) to fifty-two, thus providing "freedom of movement . . . among the potteries and porcelains".[15]

Following Barber, who had initiated a program of special exhibitions in 1915 to increase Museum attendance, Warner's first special exhibition—suggested by John D. McIlhenny, a major lender to the show—took place in 1919 and displayed rugs and other textiles from Asia Minor.[16] Warner insisted that the exhibition be accompanied by a scientific catalogue. After the publication was completed by Bell, Warner announced that he was "particularly pleased to report . . . that it preserves the high standard of scholarship set by Dr. Barber."[17] Again prodded by McIlhenny, Warner promoted acquisitions and exhibitions of early Philadelphia furniture, silver, glass, and architectural elements, a program that continued in force when Theodore Search died in 1920 and McIlhenny became president of the Museum (he continued to serve as chair of the museum committee, a position he had held since 1917).

"Anything of *German Culture* is at a discount today, but I am strongly of the opinion that is no reason why we should not have a representation of the Art of Germany of today. I was very glad to hear you and the Committee are interested in Contemporary Art."[13] Whether for reasons of taste, style, or politics, as World War I continued to drag on, what was appreciated by the Museum as contemporary decorative art in 1914 was disparaged in 1918.

When Warner returned from his leave of absence in February 1919, he immediately announced his acquisition policy for the institution: "I wish to consider the purchase of good examples in the following directions which I consider to be of immediate and constant necessity both to the School, with which we are associated, and the general public to whom we are responsible: Textiles, Furniture, Carved Woodwork, Wrought Iron, Decorative Glass, Near Eastern Pottery, Oriental Pottery and Porcelain, Jewelry. If I were furnished with a small sum to buy, for instance, small examples of Coptic, Peruvian and European textiles I might during the year be able to strengthen our collection materially."[14] Although Warner's taste in objects was largely historic and Asian, his inclination in Museum installation was distinctly modern, as evidenced by the way in which

Much to Warner's delight, in the fall of 1919 the Museum was given an Indian temple that was considered by the director to be the institution's single most important gift, laying the foundation for a department of Indian art.[18] Warner also began to focus on expanding the Museum's collections in anticipation of increased space in the new building in 1921, hiring as "keeper of the collections" Dr. Samuel W. Woodhouse, Jr., a physician and scholar whom he described as having "an unusual capacity for attracting loans and gifts."[19] Warner also supported McIlhenny's mandate from the board that year "to purchase, while in Europe, objects" in an amount "not to exceed $10,000."[20]

60. East Gallery : Pennsylvania Museum and School of Industrial Art, Memorial Hall : 1916

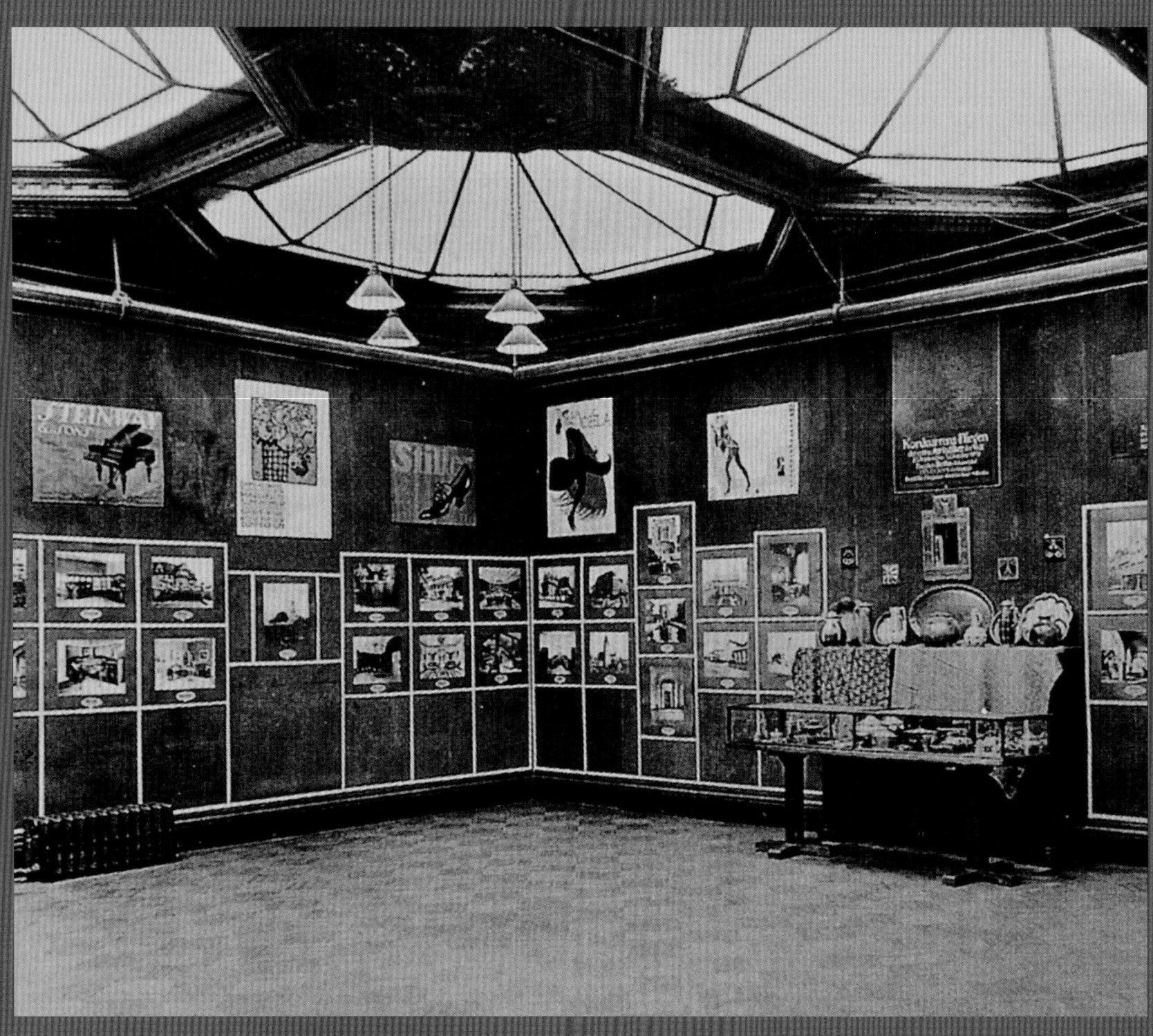

61. *German Applied Arts* exhibition : National Arts Club : New York : 1913

MODERNISM ELSEWHERE

What McIlhenny returned with, most notably, was an eighteenth-century English period room from Tower Hill in London, which was installed and opened to the public in Memorial Hall the following year (fig. 62). Warner and his staff viewed the acquisition of the paneled Georgian room as the first in a series of interiors that, "when complete, will be the ideal way to exhibit the paintings and furniture, the rugs and textiles, and the silver, china and glass of each period. . . . The appeal of the objects themselves is increased, as a closely related historical group their educational value is many times multiplied, and they are given greater esthetic significance. It is hoped that by the time the Museum is prepared to move to its new building, more interiors, illustrating other types of European decoration, will have been added to the collections."[21]

There must have been comments about the Museum's lack of modern direction, because Warner had felt obliged to defend his collecting policy in a *Bulletin* article of 1920:

Museum curators are accused of ignoring the products of modern artists and it is believed that they are entirely hypnotized by mere antiquity. . . . Above all, we are striving to raise the standard of the arts in America. It is believed that this object can best be obtained by the collection and display of objects of the highest standard. . . . Nothing is said about antiquity, nationality, intrinsic value or rarity. It is, of course, true that we are prepared to make greater sacrifices (other things being equal) to obtain objects of great rarity and antiquity for the simple reason that they must be secured when occasion offers and the chance may never come again. . . . But . . . unless [the curator] is pledged to the archeological point of view or to the preservation of antiquities, he must be alert and sensitive to the most modern art.[22]

The Museum corporation voted in 1921 to join the American Federation of Arts (AFA),[23] which had been founded by an act of Congress in 1909 to organize and tour exhibitions of original works "to the hinterlands of the United States,"[24] thereby enriching the public's experience and understanding of art. While certainly not the hinterlands, Philadelphia benefited greatly from a series of AFA exhibitions held at the Museum over the next decades, in particular those that brought modern and contemporary art and design to the city, largely for the first time. The initial exhibition sent to Philadelphia by the AFA in 1921 was a small show of modern prints, followed in December 1922 by an exhibition of American "handicrafts." The Museum's *Bulletin* considered the handicrafts exhibition "a distinct success" and a "step forward, a broadening of the Museum's sphere of activity which in no other way could have been so surely made . . . to give the modern craftsman a source of inspiration . . . to encourage the worker of today by exhibiting and criticizing the results of his efforts."[25] The Pennsylvania Museum school was deeply embedded in the AFA exhibition: Samuel Yellin, former instructor in metalwork, served on the steering committee, and Huger Elliott, Museum school principal since 1920 (Leslie Miller had retired after forty years of service), was a member of the jury of selection.[26] Objects shown in the exhibition were available to the public for purchase, something that Warner was willing to allow, as he said, "because few things are more important than the encouragement of the craftsmen of America through the sale of their best things."[27] The Museum, however, acquired no works from the exhibition.

The field of modern and contemporary decorative arts, slow to advance at the Museum after 1910, found fertile soil for growth in other American institutions, first and notably in Newark, New Jersey. In 1909 John Cotton Dana established the Newark Museum Association at the city's Free Public Library (where he had served as library director since 1901), and until his death in 1929 it was the most progressive design museum in the country. The *New York Times* obituary for Dana celebrated him as a man of original ideas and accomplishments, who brought contemporary mass-produced, machine-made objects into museums, finding art—as well as democratization—in "machine art, collective art, art which is the result not merely of one person's self-expression, but the creative expression of a great, conscious group."[28] In 1912 Dana's groundbreaking exhibition, *German Applied Arts*, which opened in Newark and toured the United States through the following year, featured some three hundred objects from the Deutsches Museum in Hagen (fig. 61).[29] He brought another large exhibition of German manufactures to Newark in 1922, which Warner refused, arguing that the "show will be of small benefit to the cause of sound crafts in America."[30] Although Philadelphia hosted neither exhibition, decades later the Museum was able to acquire works by a number of the designers who had been represented, among them Richard Riemerschmid (fig. 50), Peter Behrens (figs. 51, 205), and Thomas Theodor Heine.

Several of Dana's progressive programs did spread to Philadelphia. In 1913 he established a junior museum for children at Newark, and in 1918 a children's museum opened on the ground floor of Memorial Hall during Warner's leave of absence. Dana believed that museums needed to advertise, and in 1915 John D. McIlhenny actively endorsed that view, proposing for the first time in the Museum's history that someone should be employed "to promote publicity in the newspapers."[31] To further his populist goals, in 1921 Dana advocated storefront branch museums for various city neighborhoods;[32] in 1931, with funding from the Carnegie Corporation, the Museum opened an experimental branch west of the city on Sixty-ninth Street, exhibiting contemporary American and other work designed to engage the interest of the surrounding suburban, middle-class community.

Although the Metropolitan Museum of Art in New York had refused Dana's German applied-arts exhibition in 1912 on the grounds that it was commercial, in 1917 the Metropolitan changed its policy, establishing an annual series (1917–40) of exhibitions of American factory products under the direction of Richard F. Bach, associate in industrial arts, and permitting the acquisition of objects from the exhibitions. Also in 1917 Joseph Breck was appointed the Metropolitan's curator of decorative arts and assistant director. Together Bach and Breck (until the latter's death in 1933) led the museum's active program of modern-design exhibitions and acquisitions. As in Philadelphia, a number of the New York exhibitions involved the AFA; others, like the annuals, were organized in-house. In 1922 Edward C. Moore, Jr., gave funds to the Metropolitan for the purchase of contemporary decorative arts, enabling Breck in 1923 and 1925 to purchase objects in Europe by contemporary designers Simon Gate, Georg Jensen, André Mare, Jean Puiforcat, Jacques-Émile Ruhlmann, Louis Süe, and Paul Véra. Although the Pennsylvania Museum had no funds dedicated to the purchase of modern objects, through gifts and purchases it was later able to acquire work by some of these important designers, including Gate, Puiforcat (fig. 113), and Ruhlmann (fig. 280).

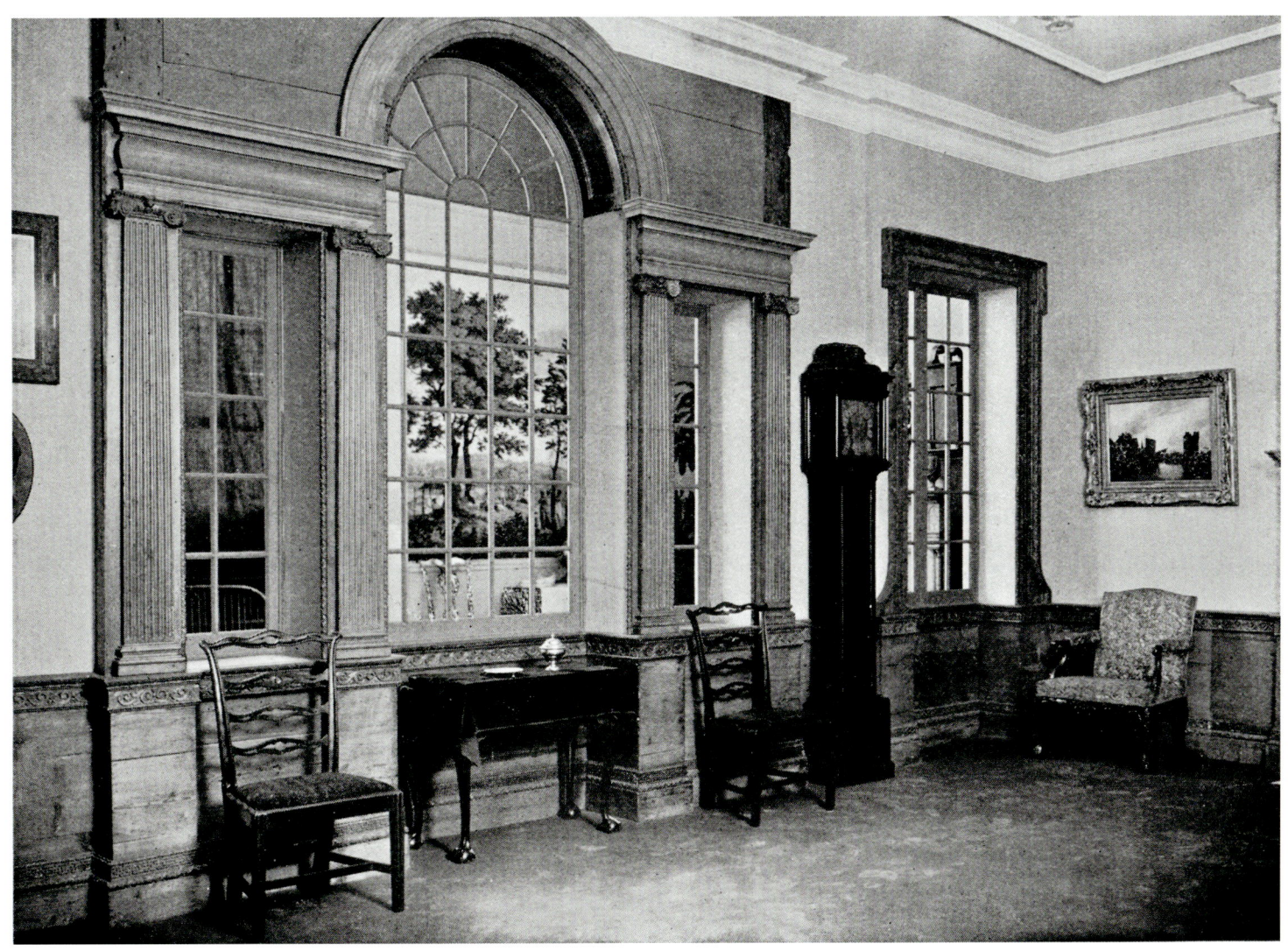

THE MUSEUM'S PERIOD ROOMS

As the Newark Museum and the Metropolitan were actively pursuing avant-garde decorative arts for their exhibition programs and collections, in Philadelphia Langdon Warner was wrestling with problems related to the physical plant at Memorial Hall and the display of art therein. He followed Barber's interest in simulating historic environments through period installations, proposing to the board as early as May 1920 that Samuel Woodhouse (then still a volunteer member of the staff) travel to Europe to acquire "proper decorative materials which will be exhibition, background, and atmosphere for the other objects,"[33] both in Memorial Hall and in the new building on Fairmount—already under construction since July of the previous year. Warner also endeavored to build up the staff; Arthur Edwin Bye became in 1922 curator of paintings, and Horace H. F. Jayne, who would soon become the Museum's curator of Oriental art, was named assistant.[34] Of critical importance "in our present stage," Warner stated,

62. **Artist/maker unknown** (England) : Room from Tower Hill : originally London : c. 1763–66 : wood : 1922-8-1 (cat. 9) : photographed at the Pennsylvania Museum and School of Industrial Art, Memorial Hall, 1923

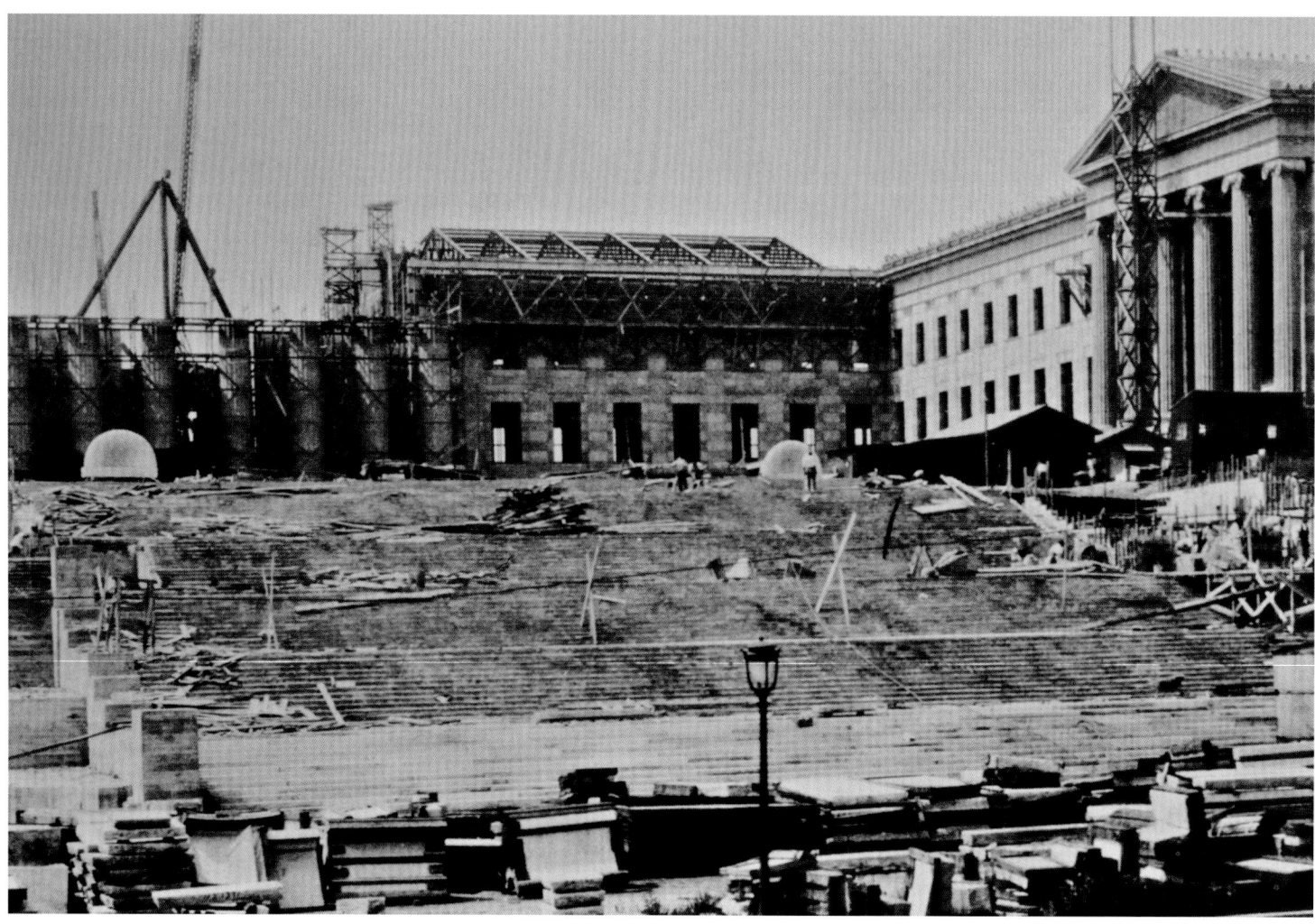

"is the addition to our staff of a man trained in the field of decorative arts to attract collections to us, serve local collectors with his advice and seriously to take up the problems which have been developed during the last three years beyond a point where they can be added to the burdens of the present staff."[35] However, Warner was not to fill the decorative arts position during his tenure, suddenly announcing his resignation as the Museum's director in February 1923, to return to academia at Harvard and to undertake fieldwork in China, although McIlhenny persuaded him to remain advisor in Oriental art.[36]

Other board and staff changes followed. In April 1923 McIlhenny asked Woodhouse to become acting director of the Museum.[37] When John Story Jenks died the same month, his nephew, also John Story Jenks, took his place as chair of the Museum's finance committee. School principal Huger Elliott announced his resignation in the spring of 1924 to become director of the department of educational work at the Metropolitan Museum of Art. Under McIlhenny's tutelage Woodhouse pursued modern aspects of museum management, reporting in September 1923 that "we had some novel publicity the other afternoon when I broadcasted for the radio from Lits [department store]."[38] From late 1924 through the early spring of 1925, Woodhouse sought to hire a decorative arts curator for the Museum, trying unsuccessfully to lure Richard Bach from the Metropolitan with the promise of organizing an "art and industry" exhibition,[39] but finally recommending the appointment of Joseph Downs as assistant curator;[40] Downs was then working at the Museum of Fine Arts, Boston and additionally employed in the design departments of "leading furniture manufacturers" in New York.[41] During Woodhouse's two-year tenure, the Museum acquired a contemporary tapestry designed by Gustave Jaulmes for the Gobelins manufactory, representing American army units passing Independence Hall in Philadelphia, on their way to France, a gift from the republic of France to the city of Philadelphia. The Museum's new Print Room[42] hosted a sale exhibition, *Etchings and Engravings by Contemporary Artists of Holland*, which brought the Museum publicity and about $1,000 in revenue.[43]

Meanwhile, from the spring of 1924 to June 1925, McIlhenny sought a Museum director, courting Fiske Kimball (fig. 64), a Harvard-trained architect and architectural historian (B.A. and M.Arch., with a Ph.D. from the University of Michigan) who in 1923 had left the University of Virginia, where he headed the department of art and architecture, to create a graduate program at New York University's Institute of Fine Arts. As Kimball remembered a decade later, his first reaction on seeing the Museum in Philadelphia and its collections in 1924 was mixed:

> The Pennsylvania Museum . . . had occupied since 1876 the art building of the Centennial Exposition, Memorial Hall. . . . Few other American public buildings of that date held their own so well. In the public mind, however, it passed as a stuffy relic of an unfashionable era. . . .
>
> The Museum had stressed the industrial aspect, both in the reading of its title and in its collections. Indeed, naturally enough—as there were then no museums of industry in the United States—industrial products had been admitted which had little to do with industrial art in any aesthetic sense. . . . Much had been done to reform the Museum, although as a whole it still presented a forlorn and unpromising aspect.[44]

Kimball refused McIlhenny's initial offer, as he had only recently arrived at his position in New York: "It is indeed with great regret that I have to inform you that it seems best that I remain here. My associates and superiors seem to feel it would be disloyal for me to desert the ship after such a brief time at the helm."[45] When asked again a year later, however, Kimball accepted the post of director in Philadelphia, subsequently recalling: "This time the New York authorities gave me their blessing. . . . The new Museum building had meanwhile advanced notably [figs. 63, 65]. . . . [McIlhenny] had made it a condition that I should go abroad, where I had not been for a dozen years, before taking up my duties in September."[46]

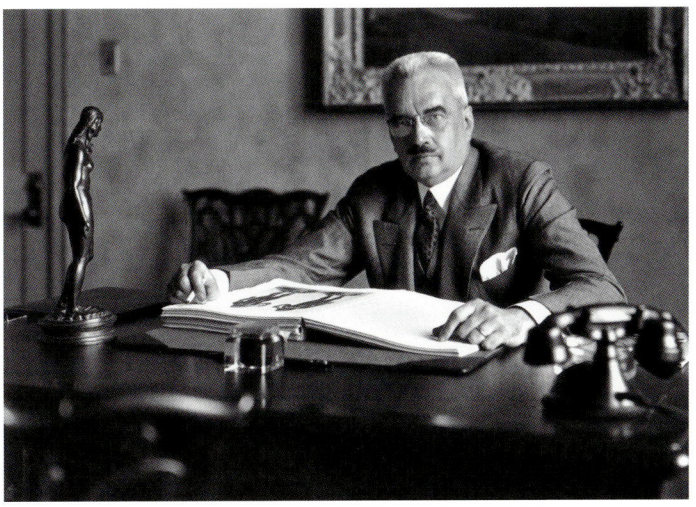

Like Edwin Atlee Barber's visit before him, Kimball's trip to Europe impressed the new director with the "antique architectural features" installed at German museums, which "added greatly to the effect and gave an idea of the ensemble in their periods."[47] Completing the new Museum building and fitting it with period architecture and objects in chronological and geographic sequence would be Kimball's life work as director over a thirty-year period. In addition, he became deeply involved with the restoration and furnishing of the eighteenth- and nineteenth-century houses in Fairmount Park that were under the custodianship of the Museum. Kimball regarded the park houses as Philadelphia's unique artistic resource, illustrating the

Opposite : **63.** The Museum under construction : July 11, 1926   Above : **64.** Fiske Kimball : Museum director, 1925–55

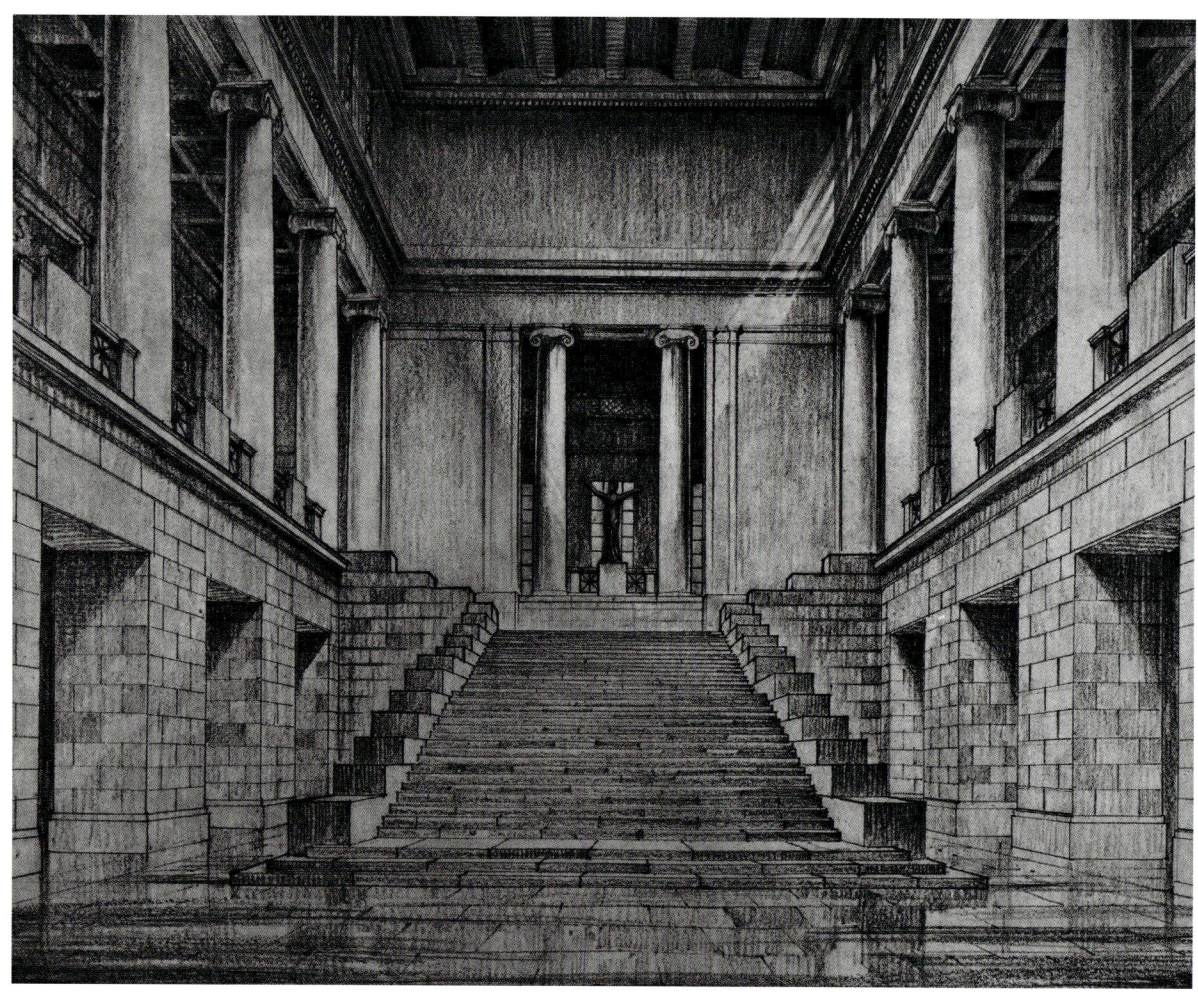

development of American architecture and decoration alongside the Museum's own collections. As a specialist in eighteenth-century American architecture, Kimball held the park houses, as well as the Museum's American period rooms, particularly dear to his heart. He also announced soon after his arrival that it was the Museum's "local duty . . . to buy fine examples of Philadelphia craftsmanship as they become available."[48]

John D. McIlhenny did not live to see the opening of the Museum's new building in 1928 (fig. 71), and died shortly after Kimball's return to Philadelphia from Europe in November 1925.[49] In McIlhenny's place, Eli Kirk Price became Museum president and John Story Jenks chair of the museum committee.

What Kimball must have seen in Europe, although curiously he made no mention of it, was the great International Exposition of Decorative and Industrial Arts, which also featured modern architecture, then being held in Paris. Woodhouse, however, had already written McIlhenny in March 1925 that "good old Mrs. Blankenburg broke into the Museum's proceedings to announce the many attractions of [the exposition] and that you were going to finance one professor going abroad, that Mrs. McFadden Brinton has financed another, that the Women's Committee were going to finance a third and that they greatly wished to send a fourth."[50] As had been the case for the late nineteenth-century international exhibitions, the board seemed to feel it most necessary to send abroad staff from the school, rather than from the Museum, to see contemporary international decorative arts. Moreover, the

Above and opposite, left to right : **65. Attributed to Julian Abele** : Perspective of the Museum's Stair Hall : c. 1927 : crayon on tracing paper : H 16" : PDP-1085 (cat. 000)   **66.** Catalogue for the American exhibition featuring selections from the Paris Exposition of 1925 (Washington, D.C.: American Association of Museums, 1925)   **67. Edgar Brandt** : Forged iron console table, mirror, and standing lamps, with bronze statuette by Max Blondat : from the Paris Exposition of 1925 : on view at the Museum in 1926

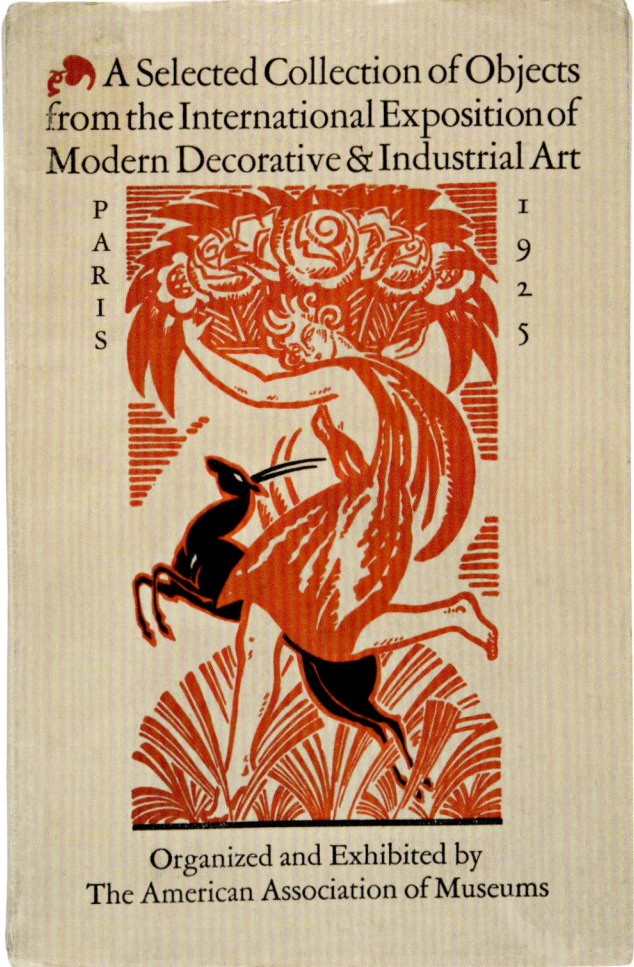
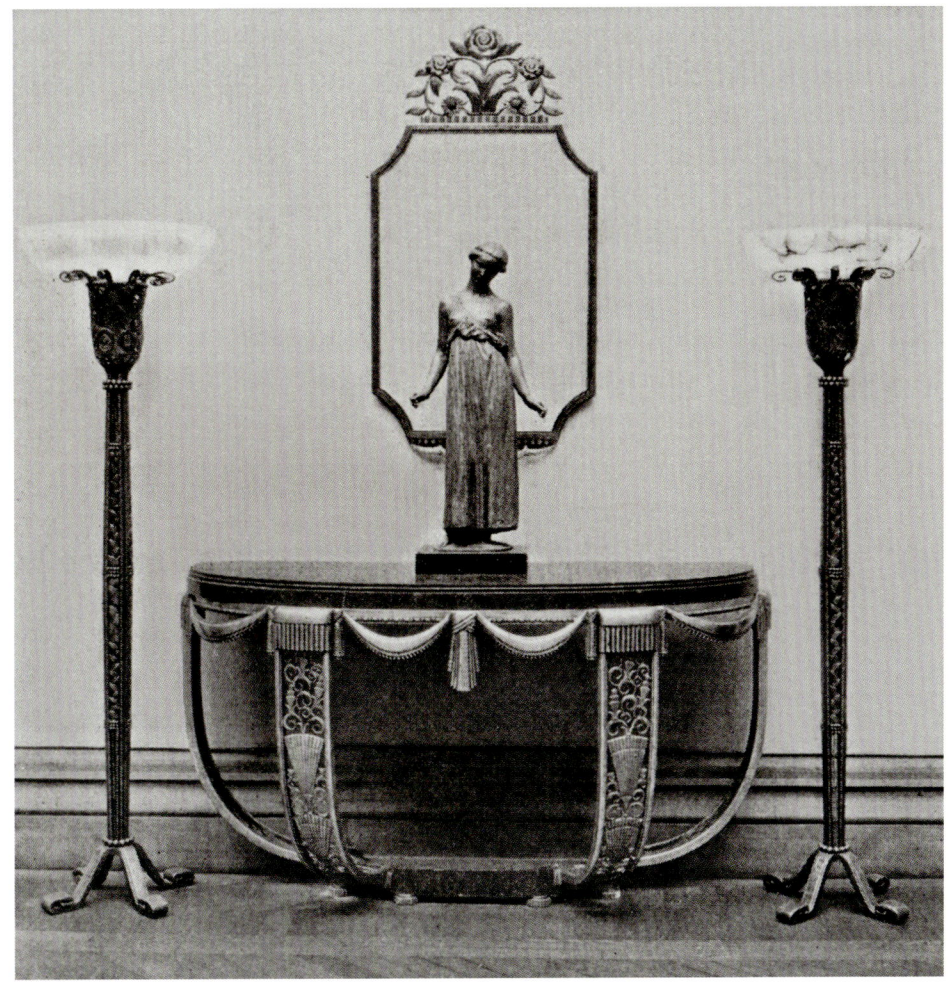

Museum acquired no objects from the exhibition for its collections, either by gift or by purchase, as it certainly would have if John T. Morris had still been alive. Board members and others might be forgiven, however, since the United States had officially declined to participate in the exhibition, a government commission determining that American manufacturers and craftsmen had "almost nothing to exhibit in the modern spirit."[51] Still, architect George Howe was among the Philadelphians who did visit the exposition, returning deeply impressed by Le Corbusier's Pavilion de l'Esprit Nouveau—a radical experiment in mass-production building and furnishing.

Although the curatorial staff of the Museum seems largely to have ignored the exhibition in Paris, a selection of its objects traveled to Philadelphia the following year (figs. 66, 67) and, as Kimball noted in his second annual report, "attracted much serious attention from students and designers."[52] The objects in the exhibition had been selected from those at the 1925 Paris venue by Charles Richards, former director of the Cooper Union in New York and at the time director of the American Association of Museums, which circulated the show to nine American cities. The show provided many Philadelphians with their first exposure to the new, international French Art Deco style as well as the opportunity to acquire examples of it, but apparently none did. However, Joseph Downs, who had taken up the position of assistant curator for decorative arts around the time that Kimball became director, wrote an article about the contemporary decorative arts exhibition in the November 1926 issue of the Museum's *Bulletin*, in which he argued: "It is perhaps to the designer and manufacturer that this exhibition will make the widest appeal, since a solution of the problems of industrial arts is presented in terms of modern life. In America, where architecture has advanced by leaps and bounds to meet logically the demands of the present day, little or no effort has been made to develop the decorative arts in a similar manner. Into diminutive apartments and office buildings . . . have gone the copies of the past."[53]

But three years later, in early 1929, Downs could boast of the Museum's first American acquisition "in the contemporary style," a buffet by the New York designer Eugene Schoen (fig. 68) that had been given that year by the Modern Club of Philadelphia, a women's service organization. Downs wrote that the buffet represented "the first link toward a collection of modern decorative arts and is particularly welcome owing to the lack of any example of this period in the Museum's collection."[54] The previous fall, the Museum had hosted the AFA's *International Exhibition of Ceramic Art* (funded by the General Education Board, a Rockefeller philanthropy), which comprised some four hundred pieces and was, Downs indicated, "the first of many [exhibitions] which the Museum plans in its programme of coordinating the problems of art with industry in Philadelphia."[55] Once again, no acquisitions for the Museum resulted from the exhibition, although Kimball observed that "public interest has been very considerable, as evidenced by attendance, by sale of catalogues and of objects."[56]

These exhibitions of contemporary decorative arts were only footnotes in the history of the Museum during the later 1920s, as the board and Kimball were galvanized in their efforts to complete and open the new city building—which was known at least from the winter of 1924–25 as the Philadelphia Museum of Art.[57] Despite reductions in state appropriations to the Museum, its president Eli Kirk Price proved himself a mighty fund-raiser. There were increases in revenue, gifts to the endowment, and special contributions encouraged by Kimball for the purchase of objects for the collections. An organized effort to raise approximately two million dollars was concluded in 1928 and covered "the cost of obtaining and erecting in the Museum an adequate number of original interiors of rooms, in which to display paintings, sculptures, furniture, curtains, china, silver and glass of the same period and country, and to create the nucleus of an endowment fund for the future operation of the Museum on the greatly extended scale required by the new building."[58] Price believed that an endowment of $15 million was vitally necessary to pay for installation of the architectural elements and objects Kimball was acquiring, as well as to complete construction of the Museum's still unfinished interior for study collections and administrative offices. However, it was only five decades later, in 1978, that the Museum's total endowment would reach Price's goal.[59]

The rate at which Kimball acquired period architecture during the later 1920s was nothing short of astonishing; in 1926 alone he obtained a room from the Powel House in Philadelphia, as well as architectural elements from the Derby House in Salem, Massachusetts; from the town of Millbach in Lebanon County, Pennsylvania; and from Treaty House (now known as "New Place") in Upminster, England. Two years later Kimball purchased thirteen major architectural elements, including a medieval stone portal from the abbey church of Saint-Laurent, in central France; a cloister from the abbey church of Saint-Génis-des Fontaines; a seventeenth-century Dutch interior; two eighteenth-century French rooms; four eighteenth-century English rooms; and a ceremonial teahouse of about 1917 from Tokyo. His plan for the new Museum building was revealed in the October 1927 issue of the *Bulletin* as

> a series of galleries ranged in historic order, a selection of masterpieces in painting and sculpture along with the furniture and other objects of their own time. By following only this "main street" of the Museum, the visitor will retrace the great historic pageant of the evolution of art. . . . The new building provides such

68. **Eugene Schoen** : for Schmieg, Hungate & Kotzian : Buffet : 1927 : Macassar ebony, rosewood, walnut, oak, and cherry woods and veneers, brass : W 6' : 1929-45-1a,b (cat. 174)

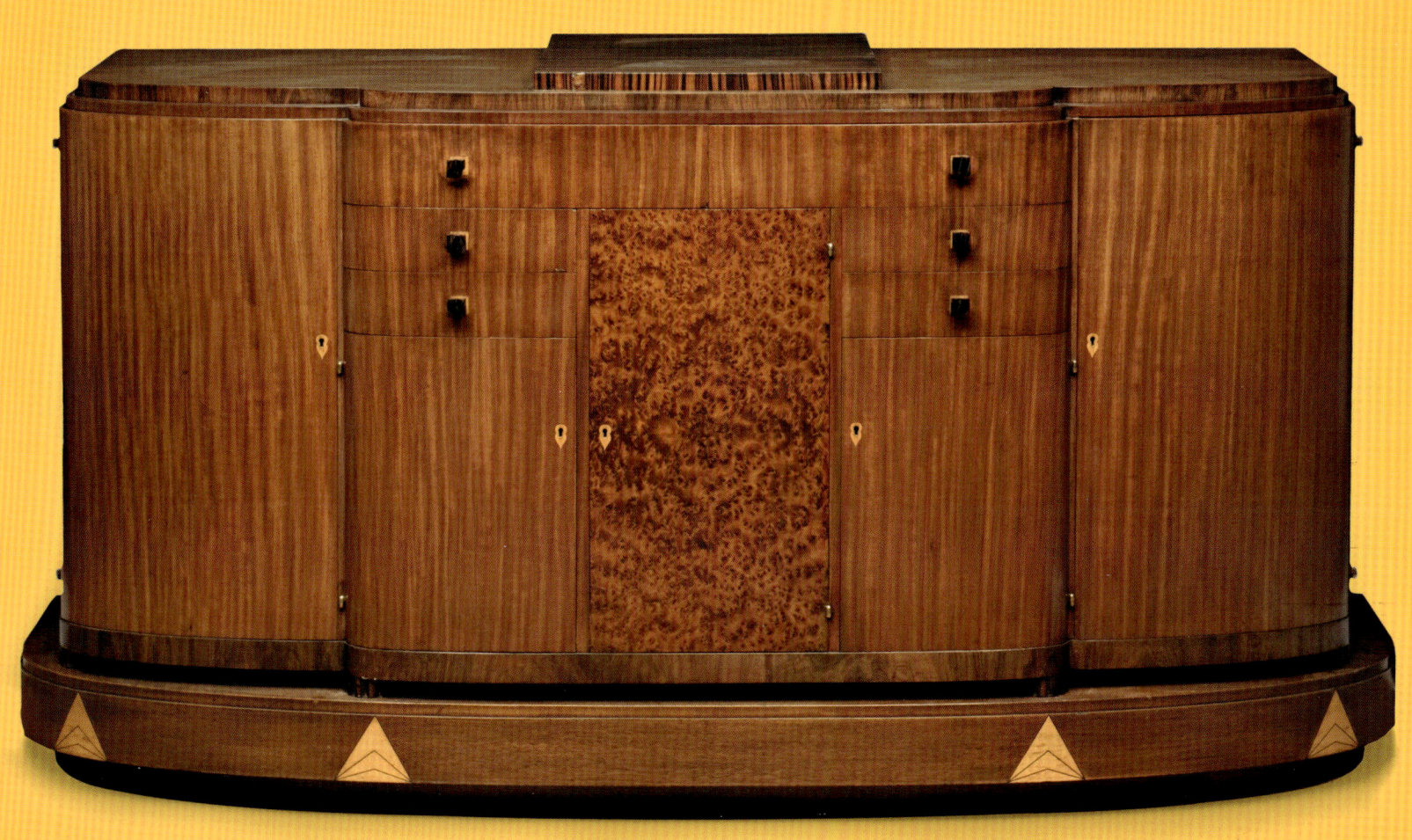

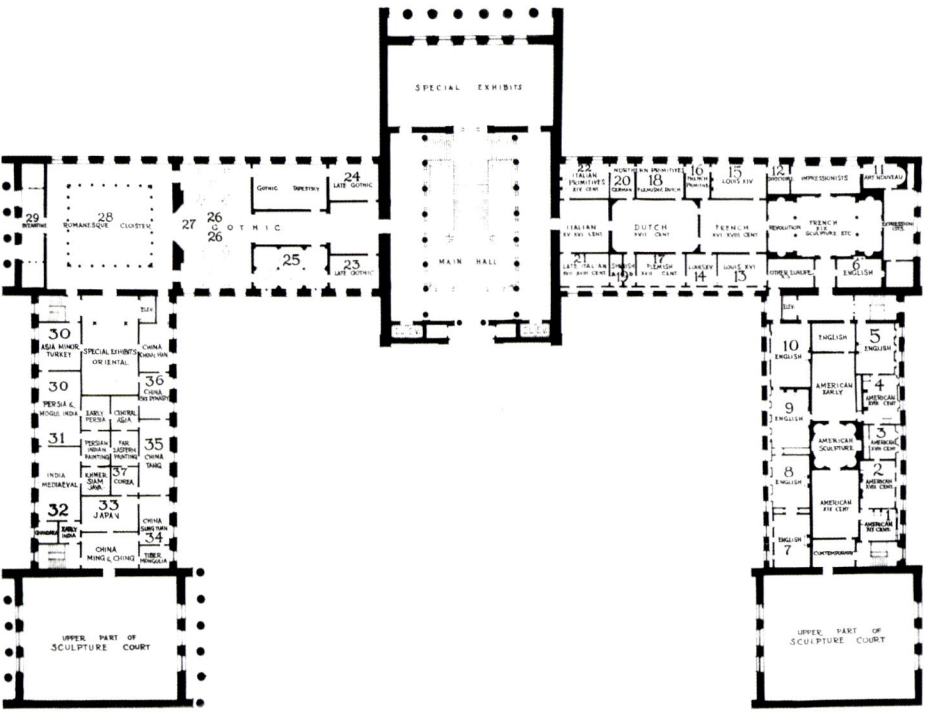

advantages of space, design and flexibility as hitherto have not been available, at one time, in an American museum. It will allow the devotion of the entire main floor to the masterpieces and period rooms which are of greatest popular interest, and of another floor to the multitude of objects constituting the study collections, which are of primary interest to the student, the manufacturer and the collector.[60]

These specialized study exhibits were to be arranged according to material and technique, as they had been in Memorial Hall under Barber's directorship. Kimball's proposed floor plan of the new building illustrated his historical chain of galleries and period rooms on the second floor (fig. 69).[61] Room 11, labeled Art Nouveau, was intended for French nineteenth-century objects, "style of Bing, glass of Lalique and Gallé, ceramics of Delaherche, etc."[62] The display of modern if not contemporary French decorative arts, along with Impressionist and Expressionist paintings and French nineteenth-century sculpture, thus concluded a suite of historic French rooms and galleries. Kimball's plan also indicated that the English and American exhibition galleries and period rooms would similarly culminate in a "contemporary" gallery, adjacent to nineteenth-century American woodwork and works of art. It is clear that Kimball intended this art historical sequence in the Museum to finish in the present, and he provided, even if not liberally, space to house contemporary works. In this spirit the Museum years later acquired by gift a twentieth-century American period room—a library (as well as a music room) from the home of Curtis and Nellie Lee Bok in Gulph Mills, Pennsylvania, with woodwork and furniture by Philadelphia artist-craftsman Wharton H. Esherick (fig. 70). Kimball had noted in 1926 that "compared to Museums in many smaller cities our income for purchases from Museum funds is still relatively small,"[63] and in the following year that "any active purchasing of portable objects has been suspended in favor of the acquisition of these major decorative and structural elements—carved doorways, ceilings and whole interiors."[64] He nevertheless successfully exploited the economic boom of the 1920s in Philadelphia and the nation, acquiring within five years all of the American, European, and Asian architectural elements, woodwork, and interiors necessary to realize his great historical plan for the second-floor galleries.

Above : **69.** Fiske Kimball's floor plan for the new Museum building on Fairmount : c. 1927   Opposite : **70. Wharton H. Esherick** : Fireplace and Doorway from the Library of the Curtis and Nellie Lee Bok House (Gulph Mills, Pennsylvania) : 1936 : oak, stone, copper : L 16' : 1989-1,2 (cat. 58)

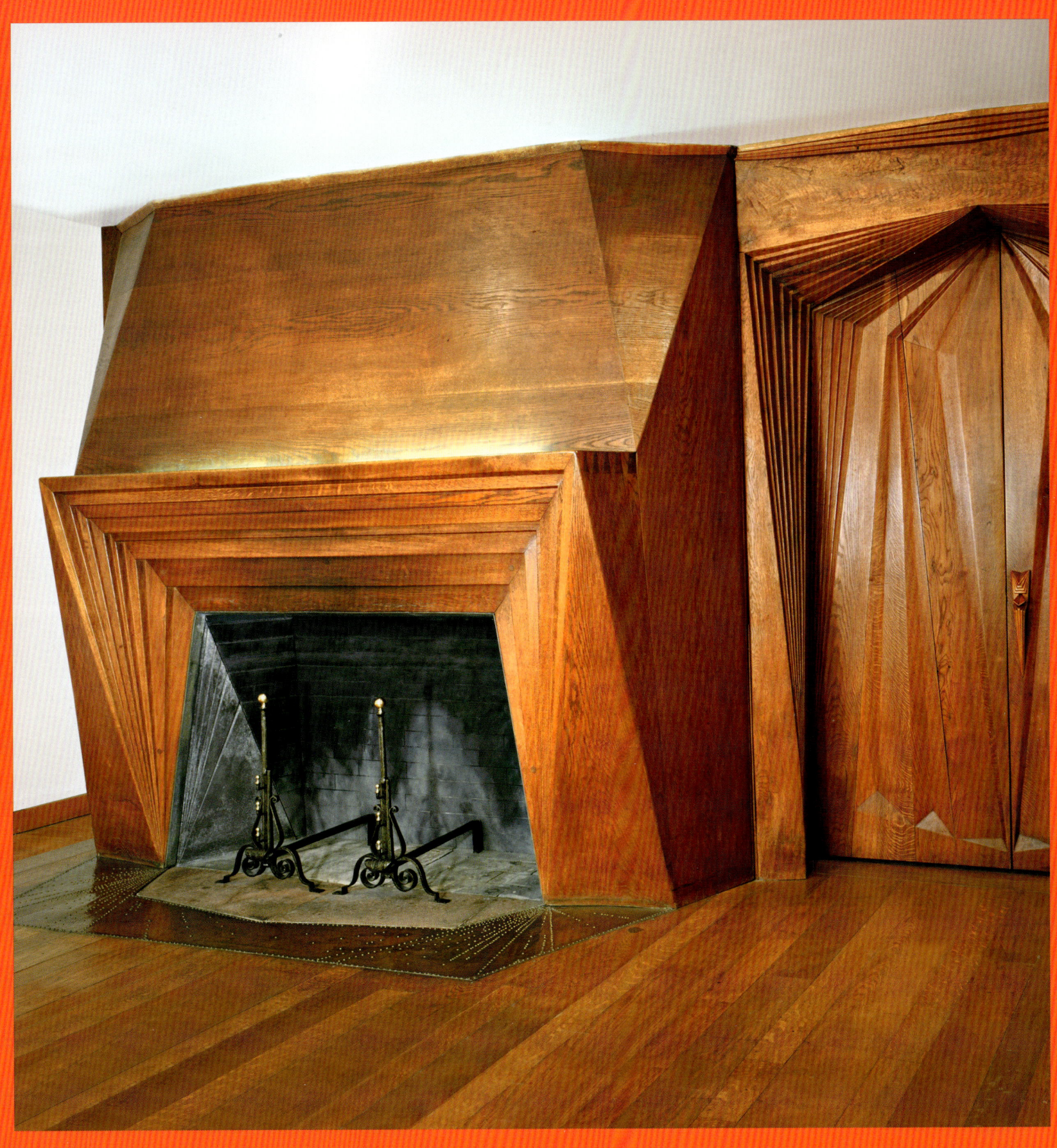

A MOVE TO FAIRMOUNT

The new Museum opened to the public on March 26, 1928, with ten eighteenth-century American and English period rooms on view in the northeast wing. For his "indefatigable and excellent work in connection with the installation of the collections at Fairmount," Joseph Downs was promoted to curator of decorative arts.[65] The building was described by Richard Bach of the Metropolitan Museum of Art as "a Philadelphian Acropolis" that required "a goodly assortment of superlatives," and as "a model of Greek Ionic architecture" that "should please any classicist."[66] A temple to the arts, Philadelphia's new museum, if not modern in style, was a grand summation of nineteenth-century nationalistic ideas and historicizing forms, consistently and broadly applied (fig. 71).

The taste for modernism in general was nonetheless advancing in Philadelphia and elsewhere during the 1920s, despite opposition by the Philadelphia Art Teachers Association and other reactionary groups.[67] Earl Horter was one of a group of avant-garde artists and collectors in Philadelphia, along with painters Arthur B. Carles, Henry McCarter, and Franklin Watkins, who promoted modern art to collectors—including Carroll S. Tyson, Jr., and Anna Warren Ingersoll (both of whom were also artists); R. Sturgis Ingersoll; Vera White (also an artist) and her husband, Samuel S. White III; Alexander Lieberman; and George Howe.[68] The inaugural exhibition at the new building on Fairmount included contemporary paintings by Georges Braque, Henri Matisse, Pablo Picasso, and others lent by Horter, Sturgis Ingersoll, Lieberman, Tyson, and the Whites (who later became trustees of the Museum).[69] Sturgis Ingersoll joined the museum committee in 1932 and Carroll Tyson the following year; Ingersoll was elected to the Museum's board in 1938. Descended from a distinguished family of well-born and well-educated Philadelphia lawyers, including Jared Ingersoll, a signer of the Constitution, Sturgis and his sister Anna were among the Museum's most important advocates for acquisitions of modern painting and sculpture (see fig. 73).

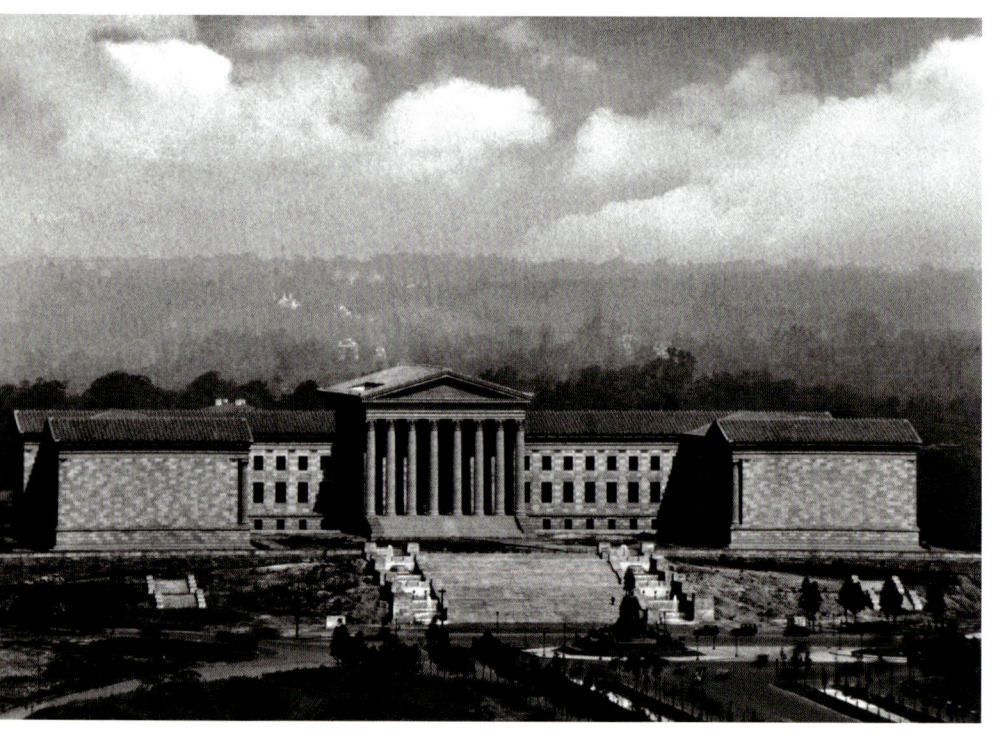

Fiske Kimball was certainly aware of developments in modern art beyond Philadelphia. His papers preserved at the Museum include the second annual report for the Harvard Society for Contemporary Art,[70] which had been formed at Harvard College in the winter of 1928–29 by three students—Lincoln Kirstein, John Walker, and Edward Warburg—to exhibit and sell contemporary works, a project that continued until 1934. The society's first exhibition, in February 1929, featured American paintings, sculptures, and works on paper, along with objects by American designer Donald Deskey and others;[71] the second exhibition, *The School of Paris*, also

Above : **71.** The Museum with unfinished courtyard and ramping walkways : c. 1928   Opposite : **72. Alphonse Mucha** : Boutique Fouquet : 1901 : Musée Carnavalet : Paris

held that year, included lacquers by Jean Dunand and glass by René Lalique and Maurice Marinot.[72] Nine months later, the Museum of Modern Art was founded in New York—modeled on the Harvard Society for Contemporary Art—by collectors Lillie P. Bliss and Abby Aldrich Rockefeller (both sustaining members of the society) and Mary Quinn Sullivan, with the cooperation of patrons, collectors, and dealers who had been enlisted in the Harvard experiment. The Modern's first director, Alfred H. Barr, Jr., was a former graduate student at Harvard University and member of and unofficial advisor to the Harvard Society for Contemporary Art. Linking the modernists of Cambridge, New York, and Philadelphia was Paul J. Sachs, member of the great New York banking family, professor of fine arts and assistant director of the Fogg Art Museum at Harvard, trustee of the Harvard Society, and founding trustee of the Museum of Modern Art. Sachs regularly brought his students to Philadelphia as part of his legendary course on museum methods, including a visit in 1930 after Kimball had advised him about "newer" collections of modern art, such as those of Sturgis Ingersoll, Carroll Tyson, and S. S. White.[73] Several of Sachs's students eventually joined the Museum staff, among them, Henry P. McIlhenny, only surviving son of the Museum's former president John D. McIlhenny. A student of fine arts at Harvard from 1929 to 1933, as well as an advisee of Sachs, Henry would become the curator of decorative arts at the Philadelphia Museum of Art, but he must have observed the Harvard Society for Contemporary Art from a distance, as he was more comfortable with the acceptably modern than the avant-garde or controversial. In 1934 Kimball reported that "John D. McIlhenny, in his day, bought old pictures, but his son Henry now buys nothing but moderns, and the same is true of everybody else."[74]

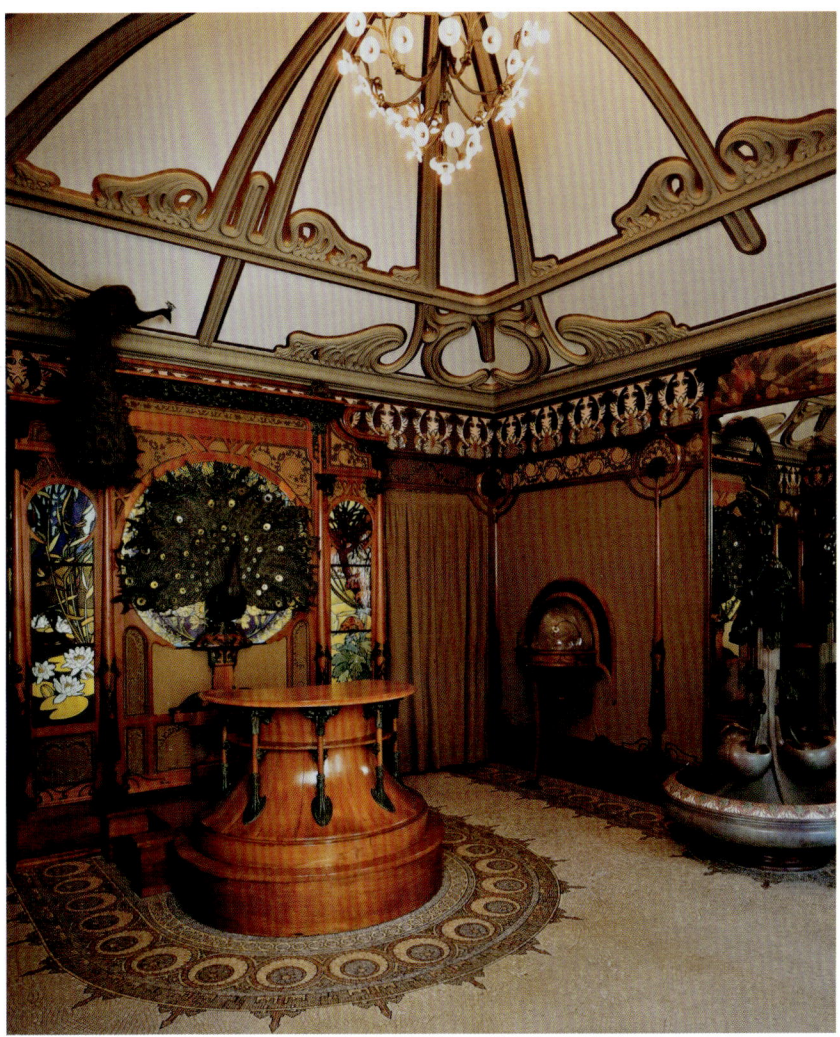

In March 1929 Kimball traveled to Europe to continue his search for period rooms and related elements, as the institution had received large specific subscriptions for three items: a French Gothic chapel, a Directoire or Adam interior, and a "modern French room."[75] After Kimball's departure, acting director Horace Jayne reported more precisely that Kimball would be taking steps "toward securing designs by one of the leading French decorative designers, for the room subscribed for by Mr. Louis Page, to be conceived as something similar to a shop interior, of refinement and dignity, so as to permit the display not only of furniture and painting, but in vitrines, of objects of minor art."[76] However, when Kimball revealed in September 1929 that he had been negotiating "the purchase of materials of a shop in the rue Royale, Paris, designed by Alphonse Mucha, 1900,"[77] he already knew that the museum committee would not readily approve the purchase, as he had earlier written the vendor:

> Since leaving Paris and arriving here I have had your shop very constantly in mind, and have worked more than you may imagine toward its acquisition by the Museum. Our friend [Charles] Richards, I am glad to say, joined with me in urging its importance and its desirability for us. It will scarcely surprise you however, to learn that he and I, in our enthusiasm for it, are more than a little in advance of the conservatism of a number of our Museum Trustees, and that it has not been easy to persuade them to favor it. The purchase would be one of those courageous, prophetic actions which are so difficult to take when a number of persons are concerned.[78]

As Kimball had feared, the matter was tabled by the committee, to be brought up later by the director at his discretion, and sadly disappeared thereafter from the records of the Museum. The shop in question had been designed by the Czech artist Alphonse Mucha for the Parisian jeweler Georges Fouquet, a unique commission of extravagantly rich carving, stained glass, mosaics, and bronze fittings that would have given the Museum the most important French Art Nouveau interior outside France. Instead, in 1941 the interior was acquired by the Musée Carnavalet in Paris, where it can be seen today (fig. 72).

Despite the conservatism of the museum committee, in November 1929 its chair, John Story Jenks, "presented certain considerations regarding the situation of the Museum in respect to works of modern art," and the committee "resolved to recommend to the Trustees the creation of a Committee on Modern Art to assist in securing for the Museum representative works."[79] The new committee included Jenks himself and Kimball, along with artists Adolphe Borie and Carroll Tyson, architect George Howe, Sturgis Ingersoll, and Charles Richards (recently appointed executive secretary of the New York Museum of Science and Industry and Kimball's supporter regarding the Mucha/Fouquet shop). Although the modern art committee had been established, according to Kimball, for the purpose of devoting "adequate space . . . to the work of contemporary artists"[80]—defined largely as painting and sculpture—Jenks, Howe, and Richards brought their own ideas about modern art and design into the mix. While studying art in Paris in the spring of 1928, Jenks's daughter, Ann, had met Alexey Brodovitch, the Russian-born art director of the Maison Blanche department store.[81] Convinced of Brodovitch's talent, Jenks persuaded the designer to give notice at Maison Blanche, uproot his family, and come to America to accept a teaching post in advertising design at the Pennsylvania Museum school. Brodovitch assumed the position in the fall of 1930,[82] bringing advanced European graphic approaches to the school and subsequently to *Harper's Bazaar* magazine,

73. Catalogue for an exhibition from the collections of Anna Ingersoll and Marion and Sturgis Ingersoll : November 4–December 6, 1933

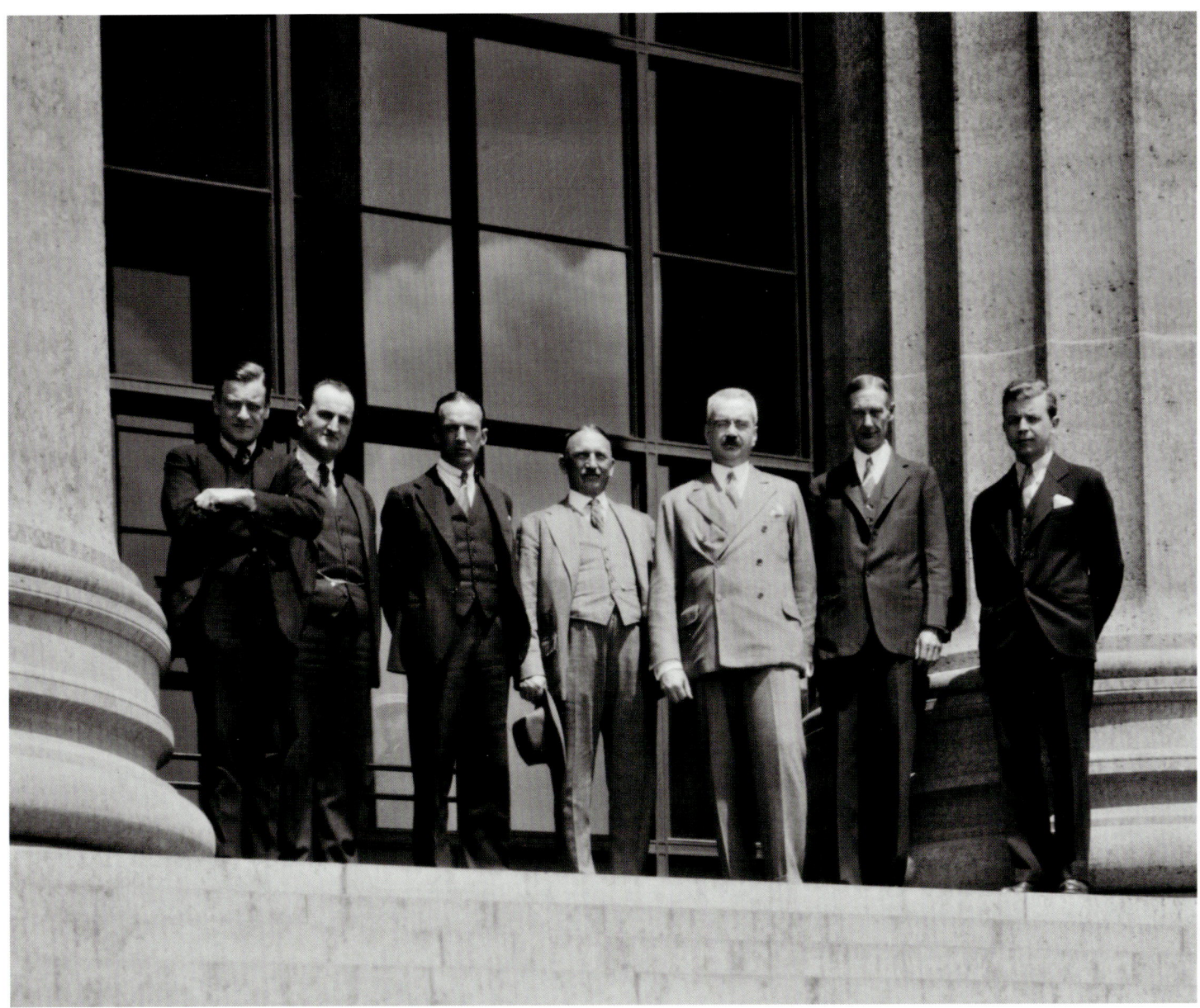

where his use of new typefaces, photography, subtle color combinations, and clear, open spaces revolutionized American advertising and editorial design. He was recognized as a gifted and generous teacher, assisting photographers Irving Penn and Ben Rose, among others.

As modernism began to gain a foothold at the Museum and school, Kimball struggled to complete the medieval section of the building, adding curatorial staff to help him develop and install collections there (fig. 74). New staff members included medievalist Francis Henry Taylor and Henri Marceau, who was named curator of fine arts in 1929, the same year he also succeeded Hamilton Bell as curator of the John G. Johnson Collection.[83] Affluent, Oxford-educated, and well-traveled, Henry Clifford arrived at the Museum in 1930 to become Marceau's assistant. Joseph Downs, meanwhile, heroically and intelligently carried on as curator of decorative arts, a position vital to Kimball's program of installing period architecture and interiors on Fairmount.

74. Senior staff at the Museum's East Entrance : June 4, 1929 : left to right : Horace H. F. Jayne, Francis Henry Taylor, Joseph Downs, J. Stogdell Stokes, Fiske Kimball, Paul H. Rea, and Erling Pedersen

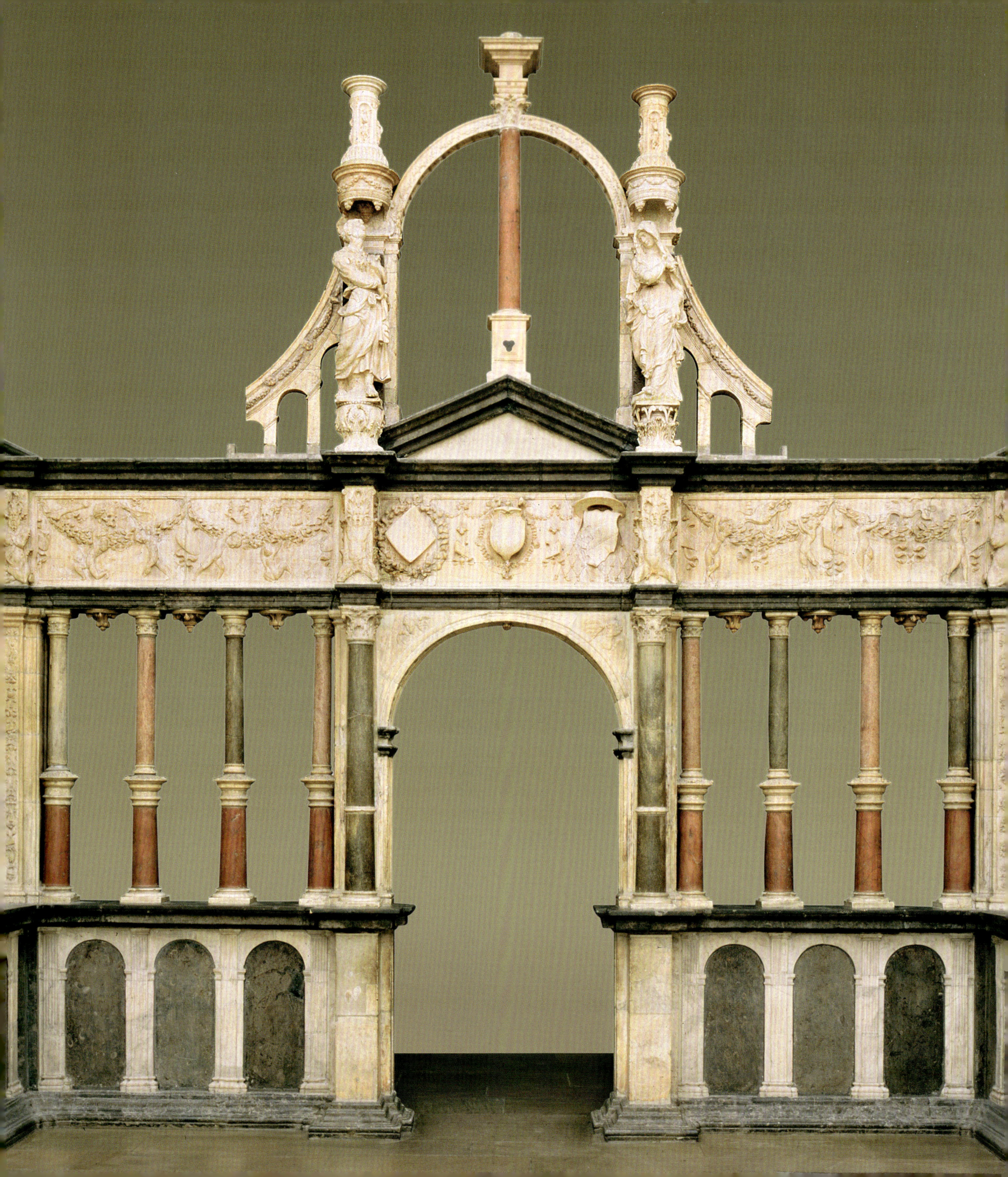

AN ECONOMIC CRISIS

The effects of the stock market crash in October 1929 and the ensuing Great Depression were not felt immediately at the Museum. In May 1930 the annual report provided an optimistic account of the most expensive acquisition in the institution's history: "During the year an opportunity occurred of securing the well-known Foulc Collection of late Gothic and early Renaissance objects of French and Italian art and the obtaining of the funds requisite to complete its purchase is going forward satisfactorily with every prospect of success."[84] It would take some twenty-two years to repay the several bank loans as well as a group of benefactors who had advanced the down payment on the purchase price of $1,100,000;[85] but by the close of the 1930 fiscal year, $654,412 had been subscribed by 353 donors toward the collection's purchase.[86] Individuals who wanted to make an impressive gift to the Museum could "buy" objects from the Foulc Collection, ranging from a seventeenth-century set of wrought-iron fireplace tools ($50) to a complete stone choir screen ($150,000; fig. 75), with each gift then transferred from storage to the exhibition galleries, where it was appropriately credited to the donor.[87] A number of objects from the collection were installed in the Museum's medieval section when it opened to the public less than a year later, in March 1931, Price proudly reporting that "this important period in the history of art has been so successfully done, that visitors to the Museum are unanimous in stating that a real atmosphere of the Middle Ages seems to have been created, which is far beyond anything hitherto achieved in other museums."[88] Preceding the Metropolitan Museum of Art's Cloisters building by seven years, Philadelphia's exhibition of Romanesque and Gothic architecture, interiors, and objects was then unmatched in the United States, reflecting "great credit" on the curator,

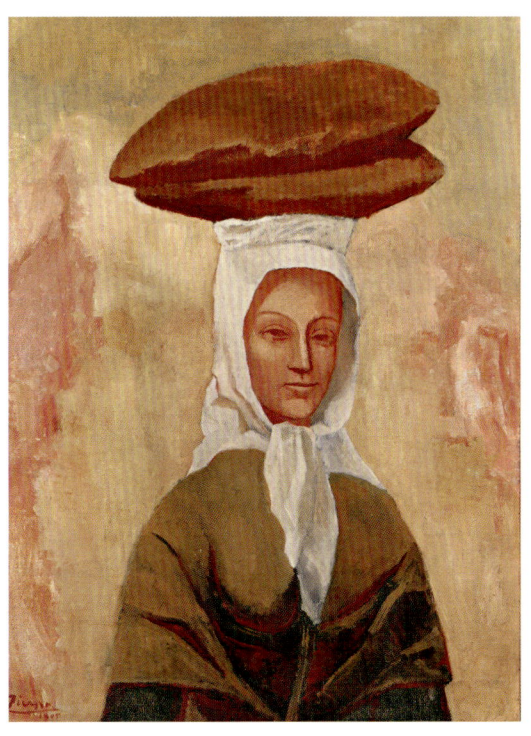

Francis Henry Taylor, according to Kimball.[89] Consequently, it came as no surprise when two months after the opening of the medieval section, Taylor resigned to assume the directorship of the Worcester Art Museum, in Massachusetts, later becoming director of the Metropolitan. That spring Kimball hired two young protégés of Paul Sachs, A.M. students at Harvard, to take on some of Taylor's responsibilities, including Calvin S. Hathaway, who became secretary to the director and editor of the *Bulletin*, and Beaumont Newhall, lecturer in education.

By early 1931 the museum committee was forced to acknowledge the severe economic downturn, although the momentum for modernism in general proceeded. Kimball described the acquisition of two paintings, Pierre-Auguste Renoir's portrait of Mme Renoir (1885; purchased with Elkins Fund income[90]) and the Museum's first Picasso, *Woman with Loaves* (1906; given by Charles E. Ingersoll at the behest of his son, Sturgis) as proof that the Museum was "alive to modern movements" (fig. 76).[91] In addition, Kimball applied to and received funding from the Carnegie Corporation of New York for an experimental branch museum to be located

Opposite : **75. Artist/maker unknown** (France) : Choir Screen from the Chapel of the Château of Pagny (detail) : 1536–38 : marble, alabaster : H 18' 9" : 1930-1-84a–d (cat. 10)   Above : **76. Pablo Ruiz y Picasso** : *Woman with Loaves* : 1906 : oil on canvas : H 39 3/16" : 1931-7-1 (cat. 150)

at the Sixty-ninth Street Arts and Crafts Community Center in Upper Darby, just west of Philadelphia, a site that would help to assess the value of branch museums, to be organized in a way similar to the existing system of branch libraries. In their letter to the corporation, Price and Kimball noted that the branch museum also should promote "the art interest of the local community" through exhibitions "specially adapted to the needs of the community" and visits by "outside personalities of a stimulating character."[92] Upon the recommendation of Frederick P. Keppel, president of the Carnegie Corporation, Kimball hired architect and educator Philip N. Youtz to run the suburban Sixty-ninth Street site as its curator (fig. 77). Among the exhibitions on view at the branch museum during its first year was a show on American industrial art, circulated by the AFA (see page 99).

Keppel and Carnegie were interested in industrial art, Keppel sharing with Kimball his outline for a report titled "The Arts and Recent Social Changes," in which he argued that "the substitution of the craftsman by the machine need not result, and as a matter of fact has not resulted, in lower standards of beauty in manufactured articles, but has undoubtedly changed the character of these standards."[93] In early 1931 Kimball too was thinking about contemporary industrial design, writing to the AFA that the Museum had been considering "an American manufacturer's exhibition, stressing Philadelphia products, not unlike the Manufacturers' show held annually at the Metropolitan Museum."[94] In fact, exhibitions held in the winter and spring of 1931–32 marked the Museum's greatest commitment to contemporary art and design during Kimball's long tenure as director, and members of the Museum's modern art committee assisted in all of them. The first exhibition, *Living Artists*,[95] opened in November 1931 and consisted of paintings and sculptures selected and installed by committee members Adolphe Borie, Sturgis Ingersoll, and Carroll Tyson, with Ingersoll lending paintings by Marc Chagall and Henri Matisse as well as a Matisse sculpture.

In February 1932 curator Joseph Downs opened his monumental exhibition of industrial design, *Design for the Machine: Contemporary Industrial Art*,[96] again with the help of modern art committee members, in this case Charles Richards and George Howe (who with his partner, William E. Lescaze, was also an exhibitor). Richards outlined

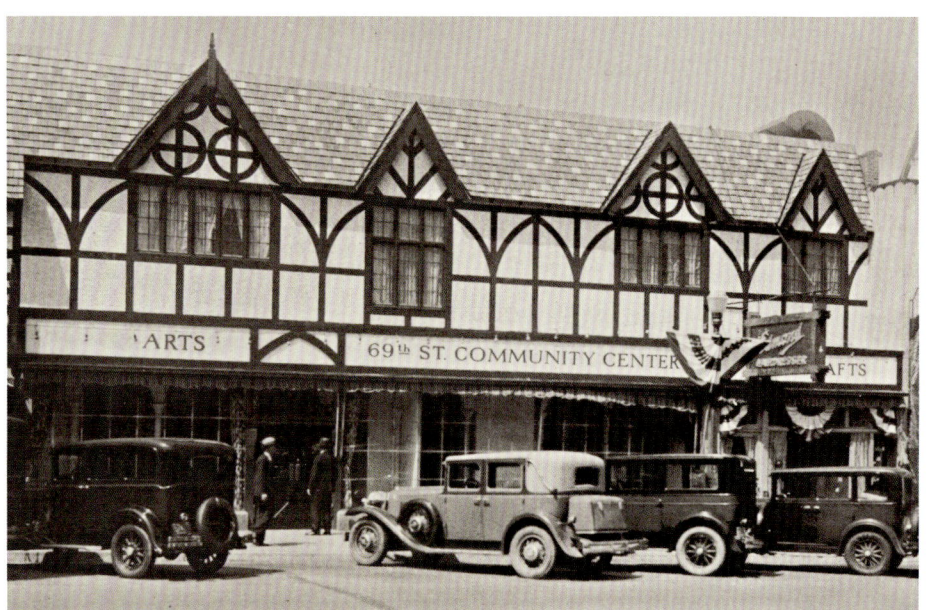

the exhibition program in a catalogue that had been designed by the Museum school's Alexey Brodovitch (fig. 78): "The special qualities of the machine as a tool are speed, accuracy and strength. . . . In consequence, the aesthetic problem facing the designer for the machine is twofold: first, to determine the limits beyond which the machine or process should not be required to function; second, to determine the artistic principles that should govern the design of repetitive production. Both of these considerations make for simplicity of form and the elimination of all but extremely reserved functional ornament."[97] To plan the exhibition Downs collaborated with the American Union of Decorative Artists and Craftsmen, established in 1928; Brodovitch and Howe were members of the group, as

Above and opposite, left to right : **77.** The Museum's Sixty-ninth Street branch : Upper Darby, Pennsylvania : 1931 **78.** *Design for the Machine* (Philadelphia: Philadelphia Museum of Art, 1932) : cover illustration by Alexey Brodovitch **79.** *Modern Architecture: International Exhibition* (New York: Museum of Modern Art, 1932)

were the well-known industrial designers Donald Deskey, Gilbert Rohde, Walter Dorwin Teague, Kem Weber, and Russel Wright. Rohde designed a man's study to display at the Museum and equipped it with a contemporary furniture line he had created for Heywood-Wakefield, the first modern furniture produced by the firm (fig. 82).98 Downs counted 225 designers, manufacturers, and distributors represented in the Philadelphia exhibition, and declared: "Whether it be the shop front designed by Walter

design, and lauded for the inclusion of models of large-scale machines, including an ocean liner, an automobile, a locomotive, and two airplanes.101 Another publication pointed out the advantages of displaying contemporary design in room settings, next to ensembles from earlier eras: "Immediately adjoining the galleries where this exhibition is held are the museum's historic period rooms where the visitor may observe and appreciate by contrast, the deathless elements of handcraftsmen of the past—their period furniture, ceramics, paintings, sculptures and metal-work."102

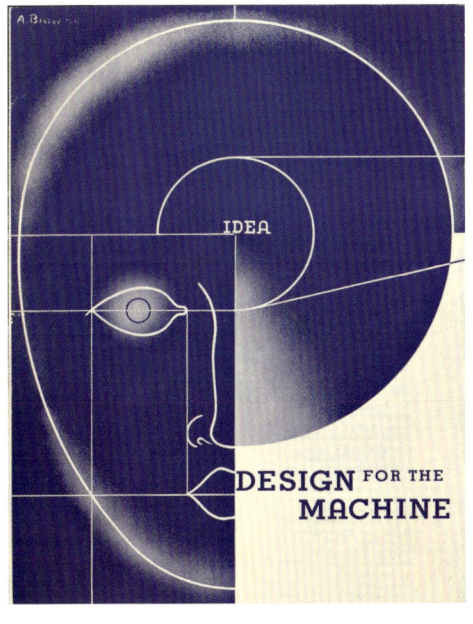
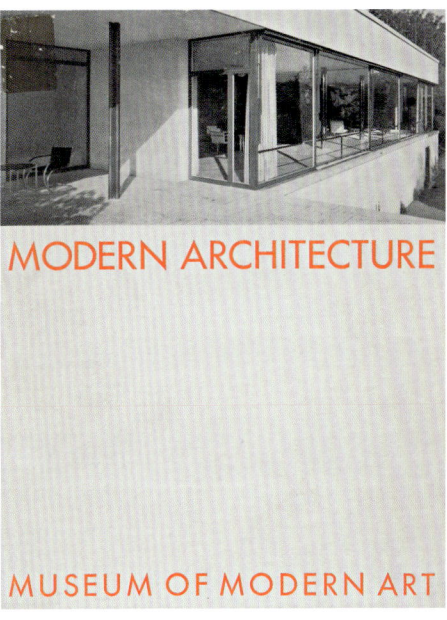

Dorwin Teague, at the beginning of the exhibition [fig. 80], the drawing room by Howe and Lescaze just beyond [fig. 81], or the eight rooms of a complete house devised by as many artists which follow, even the person who can see little of value in mass production should find much here to admire and remember."99 And so the public and press did, Kimball noting that the exhibition had attracted "a very large attendance and wide favorable comment."100 Reviews of the exhibition were carried in the local and national press, including the *San Francisco Chronicle,* the *Chicago Post,* and the *New York Times.* A large illustrated spread appeared in the *New York Times Magazine*, where the "comprehensive" exhibition was described as "graphically" demonstrating the aesthetic advances of contemporary

Ten days after the close of *Design for the Machine*, in March 1932 *Modern Architecture: International Exhibition* arrived at the Philadelphia Museum of Art directly from the newly founded department of architecture at the Museum of Modern Art in New York, where the show had introduced Americans to the radical European buildings of Le Corbusier, Walter Gropius, Ludwig Mies van der Rohe, and J. J. P. Oud that are now landmarks of twentieth-century modernism (fig. 79).103 Furniture and objects by these architects, among them Mies's tubular steel and cane chair (fig. 85) and works by Bauhaus designer Wilhelm Wagenfeld, would later enter the collection. Among the few Americans included in the exhibition were Howe and Lescaze, represented by their nearly completed Philadelphia Saving Fund Society Building—the first modern International Style skyscraper to be built in the United States, with its strip windows, thin curtain walls, and dependence on modern materials (fig. 83). Beyond this progressive architectural vocabulary, the tower was heralded for its pioneering mechanical and circulation systems, including escalators, high-rise elevators, and thermostatically controlled heat and air-conditioning. Howe and Lescaze designed every aspect of the building,

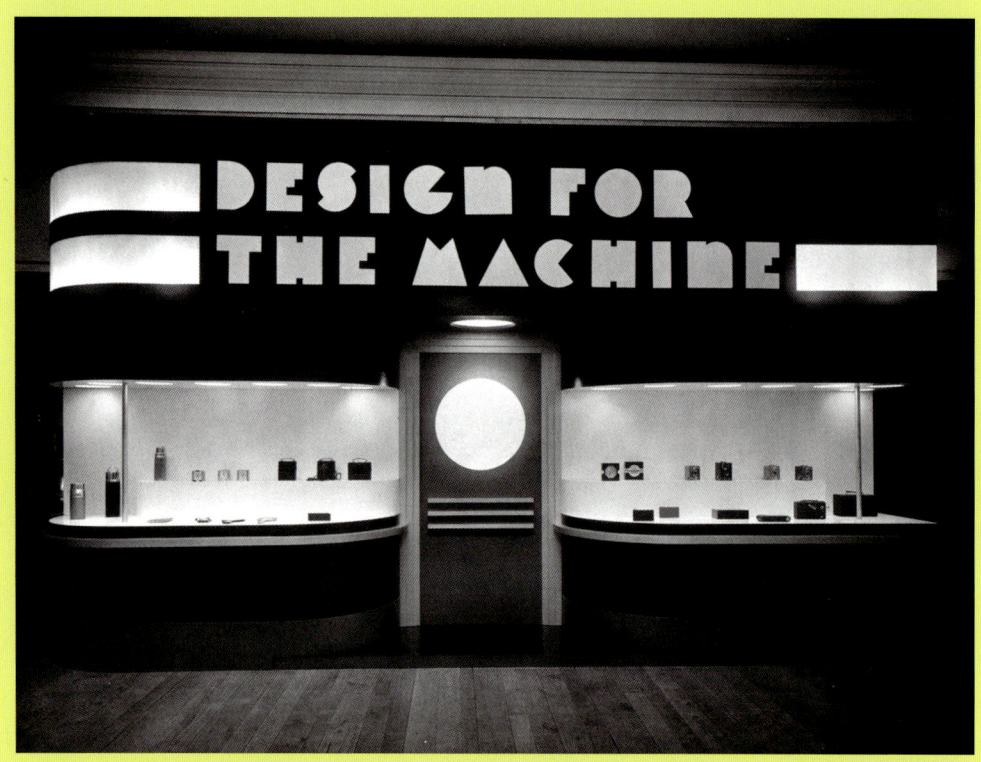

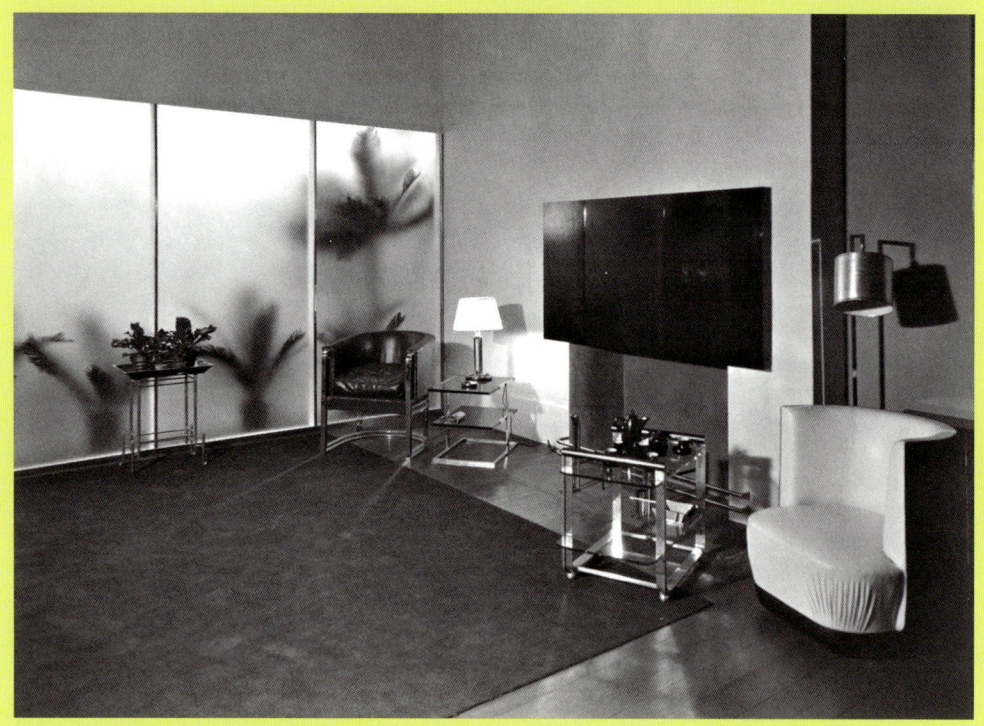

Design for the Machine : 1932

Above, top to bottom : **80. Walter Dorwin Teague** : Shop Front   **81. George Howe and William E. Lescaze** : Drawing Room
Opposite : **82. Gilbert Rohde** : Man's Study

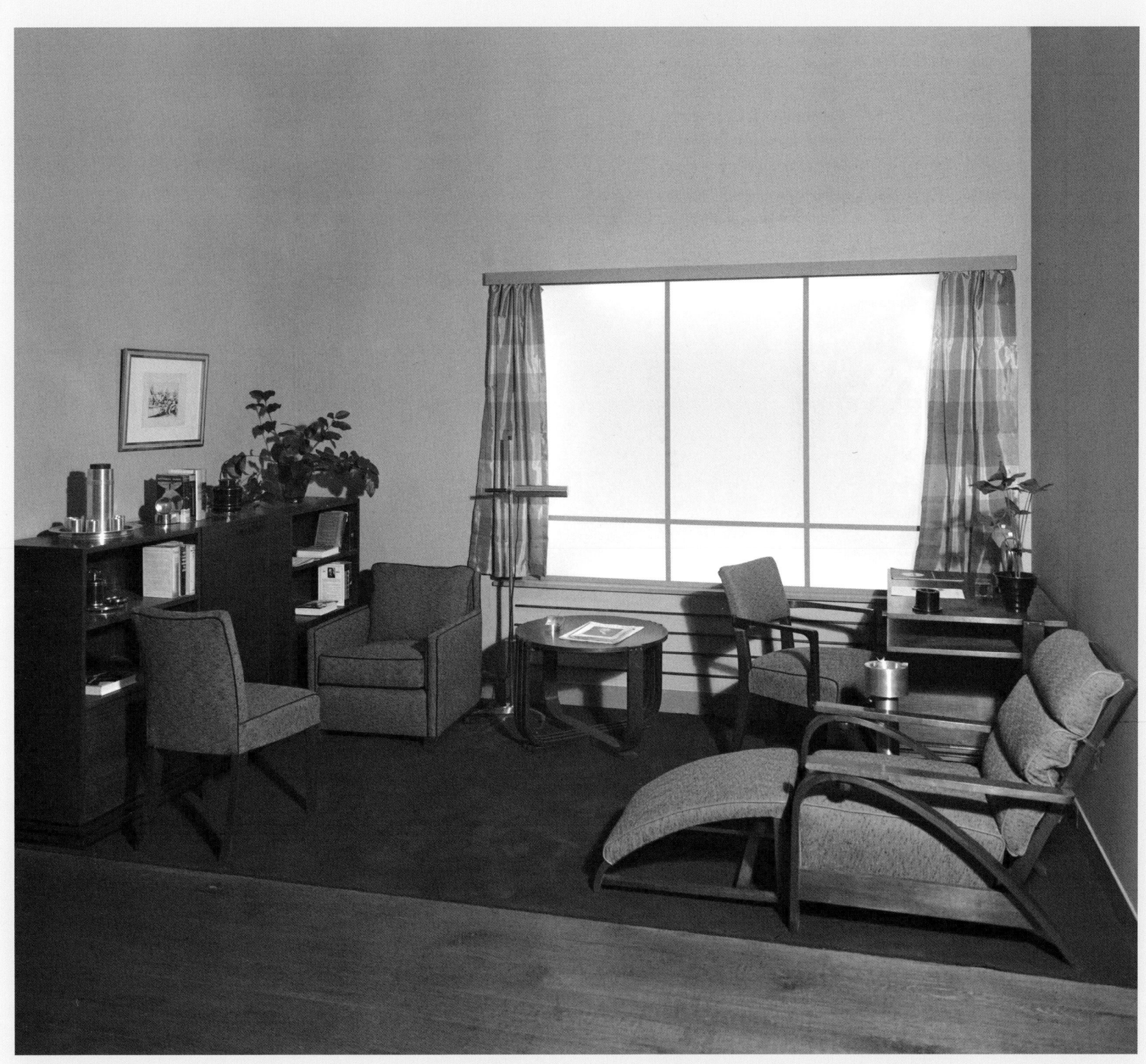

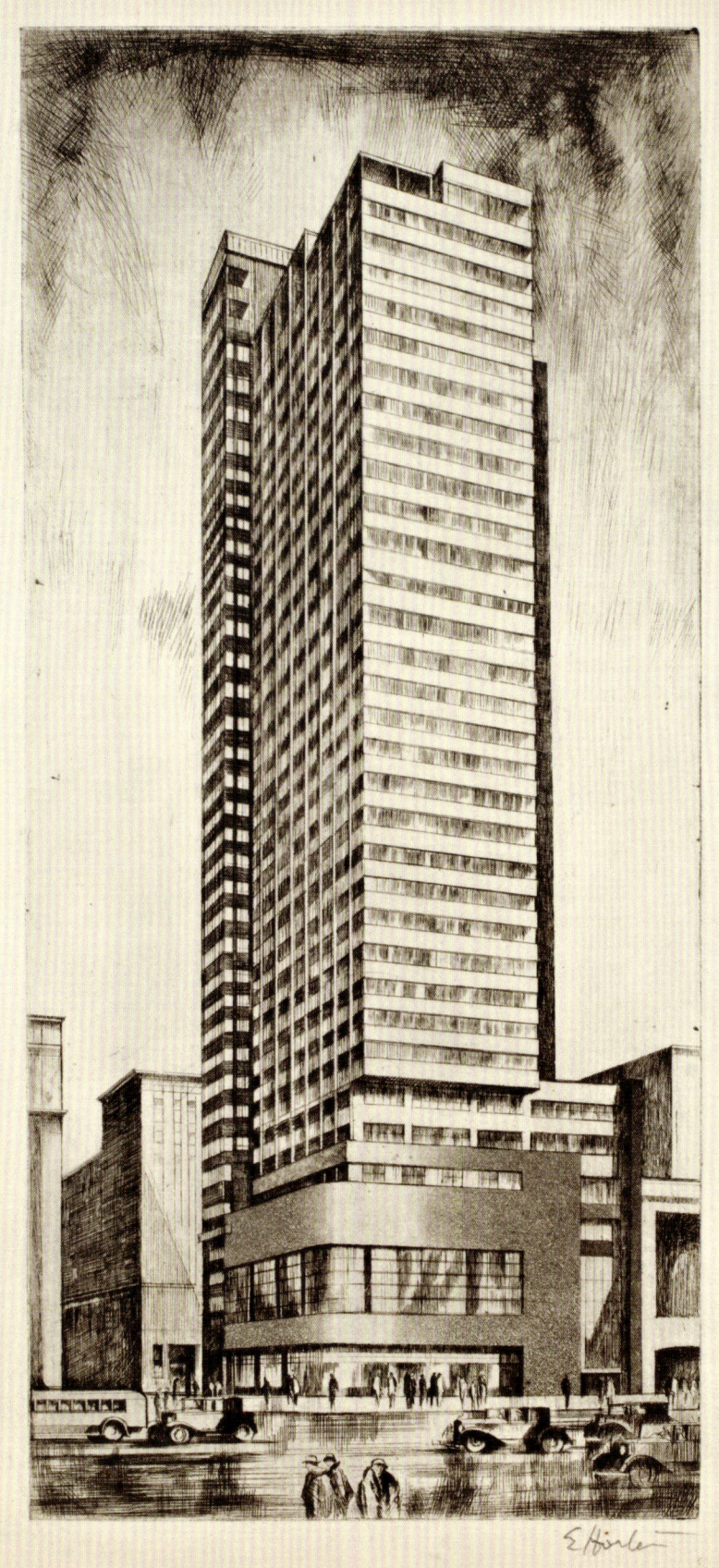

from its rooftop sign to the furniture, several pieces of which entered the Museum's collections many decades later, when the structure was converted into a hotel. Like the skyscraper itself, the bank's tubular metal furniture was informed by European modernist precedents (fig. 84).

Some months earlier, in 1929–30, Howe and Lescaze had completed a nursery school building, also in the new International Style, for the Oak Lane Country Day School, outside Philadelphia in Blue Bell, Pennsylvania. Kimball was so inspired by the building and its furnishings that he asked his assistant, Erling Pedersen, to inquire whether Howe and Lescaze would allow the Museum to reproduce the school's Oak Lane chairs and tables for new children's classrooms at the Museum. "I believe they are made of plywood," Pedersen wrote, "and have the distinct advantages of being inexpensive."[104] In reply Lescaze sent drawings—for chairs, as well as for a desk, tables, a wall counter, and a cabinet in birch wood with metal frames and legs—that have not survived, nor sadly was the modern children's furniture ever made, for lack of funding.[105]

In May 1932 an exhibition of some 260 American industrial arts objects opened at the Sixty-ninth Street branch. Circulated by the AFA, the show had been organized originally for the Metropolitan Museum of Art by Richard Bach, as the twelfth in its annual series of modern industrial arts exhibitions. Although advertisements for the show mentioned the inclusion of pieces that were reasonably priced and available from stock in any part of the country, the Philadelphia Museum of Art acquired nothing.

In fact, while these exhibitions of modern art, architecture, and design were going on, Fiske Kimball was facing financial crisis at the Museum, due to the Depression and the drastic curtailment of the Museum's usual appropriation from the city. By 1933 the main building on Fairmount was closed three days a week, the Rodin Museum—which had opened in 1929 under the administration of the Museum—six days a week, and Memorial Hall closed entirely, while construction on Fairmount came to a "standstill."[106] To reduce administrative costs, salaries and wages were cut and staff were let go. Those curators who could afford to work without pay did so, among them, Boies Penrose, the Museum's recently appointed curator of prints, and Henry Clifford.

Kimball scrambled to find new positions for other staff members, writing museum directors in Cincinnati, Detroit, Pittsburgh, and elsewhere, as well as Paul Sachs at Harvard: "We shall have to let go a number of very well trained and valuable members of our staff, whose loss we greatly deplore. I feel the availability of these persons presents a real opportunity to executives of other museums."[107] In a separate letter to Sachs, Kimball had special words of praise for Calvin Hathaway, who decades later would become the Museum's curator of decorative arts: "I want your help in finding some fine post for Calvin Hathaway, for whose work I have the highest admiration. . . . As you know, he formerly volunteered in our department of decorative arts, and in this field he is thus already experienced. . . . He has the faculty of absorbing rapidly what a task requires."[108] In April 1932 Joseph Downs, invaluable curator of decorative arts, was one of the first to leave Philadelphia, for the Metropolitan Museum of Art.[109] By February 1933 Hathaway, who had been given responsibility for the Museum's collections of decorative arts after Downs's departure, had resigned to accept the position of assistant to the curator of decorative arts at the Cooper Union Museum in New York (later becoming its director).[110] At the same time, Philip Youtz left the Sixty-ninth Street branch to become assistant director (and later director) of the Brooklyn Museum.[111] The branch museum itself fell victim to the Depression in October 1932, some eighteen months after it opened, when developer John H. McClatchy—who had provided the funding necessary to supplement the Carnegie grant as well as the building used by the Museum—had to withdraw his pledge. The corporation, however, permitted the staff and exhibition programs of the branch museum to be transferred to the

83. **Earl Horter** : *The PSFS Building* : c. 1932 : etching, aquatint, drypoint : H (image) 14 7/8" : 1962-82-63 (cat. 84)

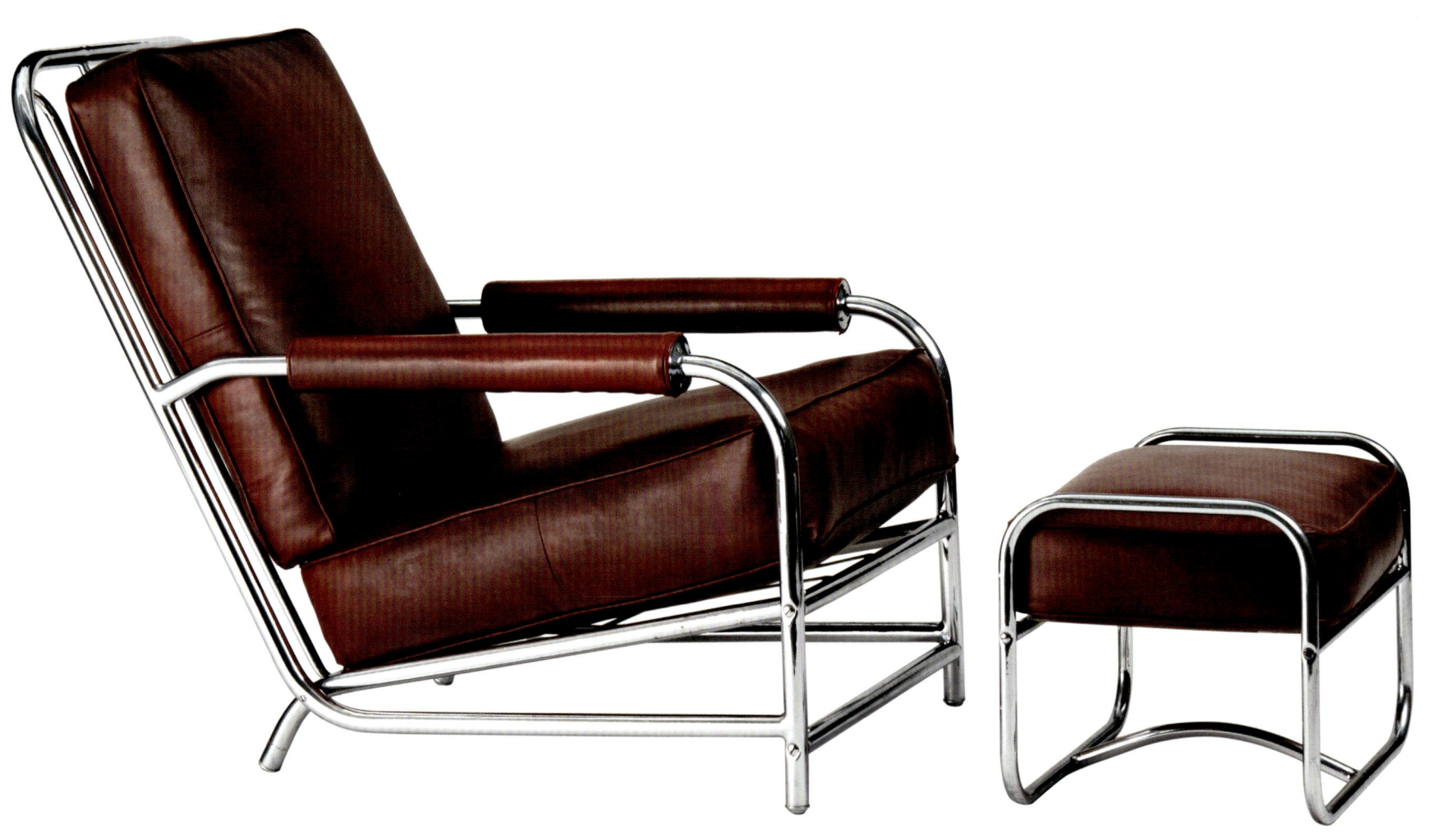

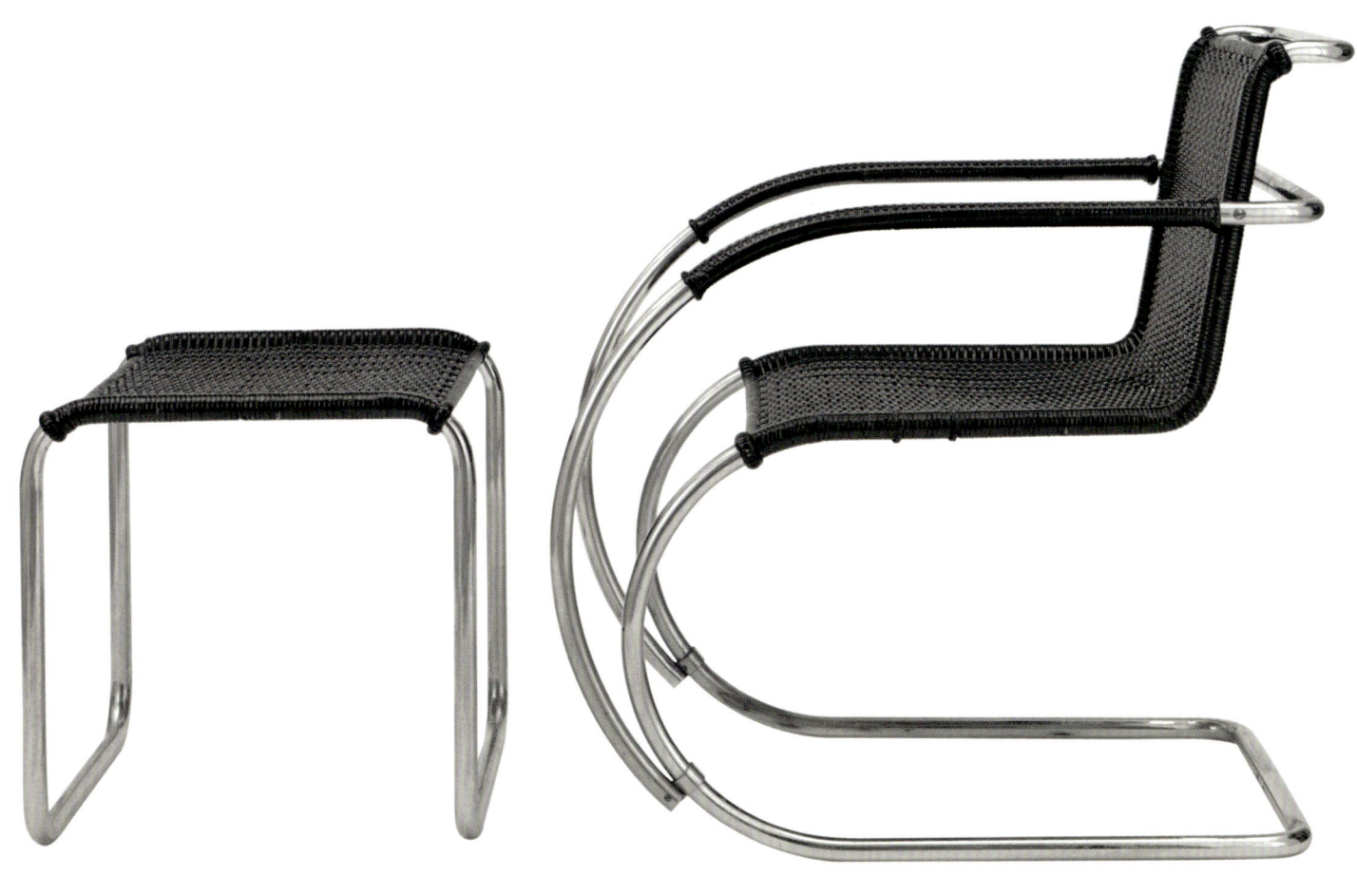

Opposite : **84. George Howe and William E. Lescaze** : for Lloyd Manufacturing : Lounge Chair and Ottoman : 1932 : chromed steel, imitation leather : H (chair) 34 1/2" : H (ottoman) 14 1/2" : 2004-13-1,3 (cat. 85)   Above : **85. Ludwig Mies van der Rohe** : for Berliner Metallgewerbe Joseph Muller : *MR20* Armchair and Stool : 1927 : chrome-plated steel, caning : H (armchair) 32 1/2" : H (stool) 18 1/2" : 1978-116-1,2 (cat. 129)

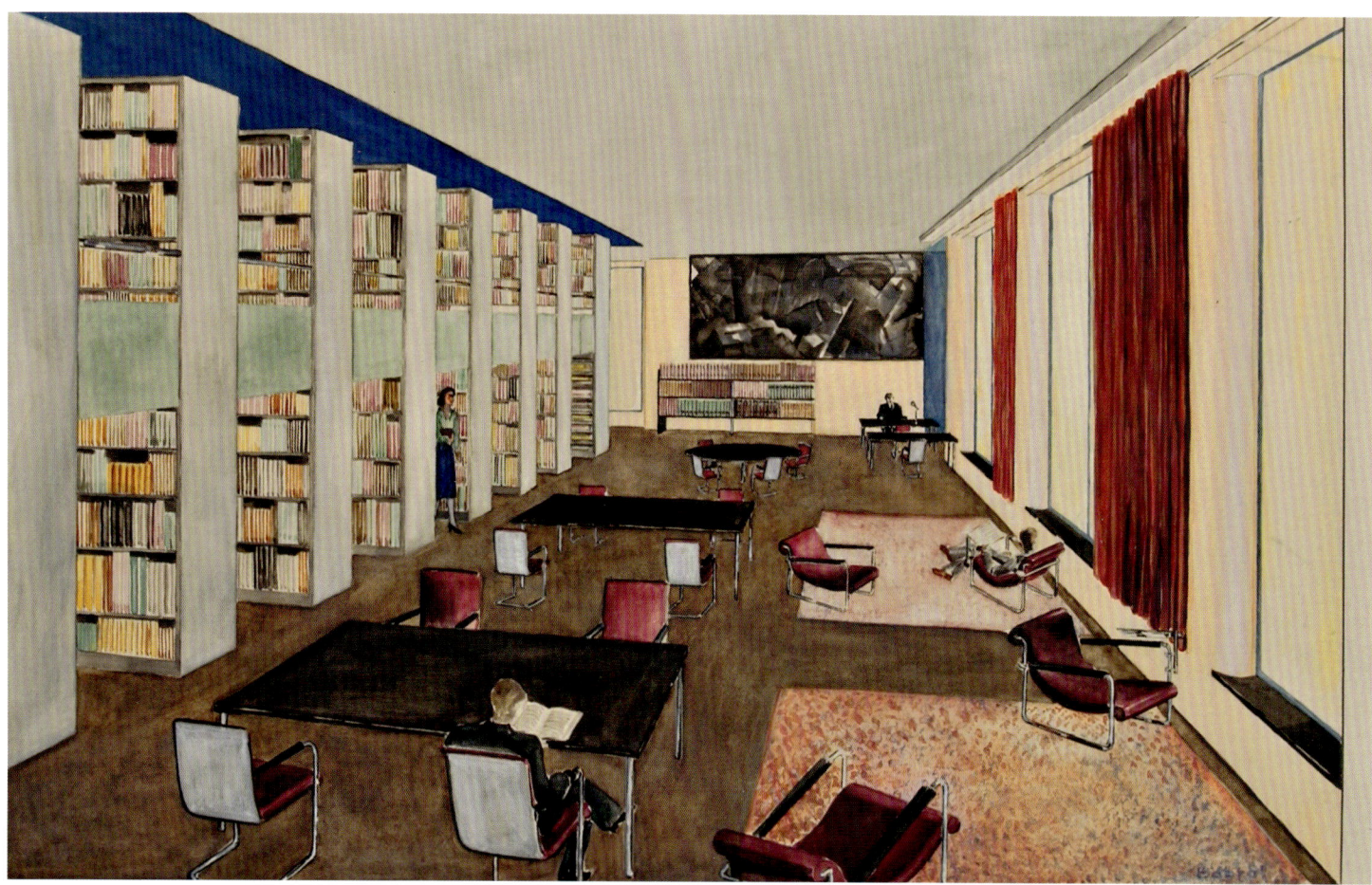

main Museum, with the understanding that the branch would reopen when conditions were more favorable.[112] Conditions were not soon favorable, and the experiment lapsed, one of a number of programs in adult education and the arts initiated by the Carnegie and Keppel to which resources were committed on a short-term basis.

Another loss for the Museum came in January 1933 with the death of Museum president Eli Kirk Price.[113] Named by the Museum board to take Price's place as president, J. Stogdell Stokes was, like his predecessor, a member of a prominent Quaker family; but whereas Price had practiced law, Stokes was a manufacturer, founder of Stokes & Smith, a pioneer in the production of packaging machinery. Stokes had joined the board and the museum committee in 1923 and chaired the finance committee from 1928. In those capacities he was later credited by Kimball for identifying donors to fund most of the period rooms and architectural elements that "make ours a unique museum," and for courageously undertaking the purchase of the Foulc Collection "in the darkest days of 1929."[114] Stokes was also deeply interested in the arts of rural Pennsylvania and helped build the Museum's Pennsylvania German collection, which had been established by Edwin Atlee Barber and John T. Morris.

Immediately after taking office as president, Stokes confronted the Museum's difficulties with a purposeful declaration in the March 1933 issue of the *Bulletin*. He announced that the city's reduced appropriation to the Museum had resulted in a halt to construction, with only one-sixth of its interior space finished, and no purchases of works of art would be allowed until the Foulc Collection debt was reduced.[115] Although services were slashed and the Museum's physical plant languished, attendance at the Museum in 1933 increased (per open days), as visitors sought inexpensive entertainment and were drawn by such Carnegie-funded exhibitions as *Contemporary Sculpture*, and by paintings from the Johnson Collection that had been installed by Marceau for the first time at the Museum in temporary galleries. When the federal government created the Civil Works Administration in November 1933, followed by the Works Progress (later Work Projects) Administration (WPA) in April 1935, Stokes and Kimball immediately submitted proposals for the completion of the Museum building (including galleries for modern art),[116] as well as improvements at Memorial Hall—all of which were granted. The Museum library was among the interiors studied (but never built) under these programs, Kimball remarking on the Howe-and-Lescaze-inspired design that "certain phases of the modern style are particularly well suited to the purposes of a library" (fig. 86).[117] The institution was the first, and over the course of the next seven and a half years, the largest museum recipient of WPA funds,[118] initially using the collections (referred to in the proposals as "antique materials") that were to be incorporated in the construction work to match, dollar for dollar, the government allotment, as required.[119] By November 1935, thanks to WPA funds that supplemented the diminished city appropriation, the Museum on Fairmount, Memorial Hall, and the Rodin Museum were again open seven days a week.[120]

In order to maintain or expand the Museum's programs in a period of general economic depression that was aggravated by a slender endowment and operating budget, Kimball had to find well-trained, devoted staff who would work hard for small pay. Accordingly, in the spring of 1934 he wrote Henry McIlhenny at Harvard: "Before you go away anywhere, & the sooner the better, I want to talk with you seriously about an appointment to the staff of the Museum."[121] Kimball's relationships with the McIlhennys had remained close after the death of Henry's father, John D. McIlhenny, who had served as the Museum's president from 1918 until his death in 1925 and had bequeathed his art collection to the Museum.[122] Henry, meanwhile, was preparing to follow in his father's footsteps as a collector, hoping to become the kind of serious art professional his parents admired and to join the ranks of the important art historians, curators, and dealers to whom his parents had introduced him. In 1933 he wrote his mother from Harvard about a recent dinner party in Worcester, Massachusetts: "I felt in my element. Of course there was lots of gossip, the cynosure of all eyes being Lord Duveen who asked how you were and said he was shortly going to Philadelphia. . . . I met Gordon Washburn, head of the Buffalo Museum, who said that he had been at our house with Sachs. . . . Everybody, of course, gave me

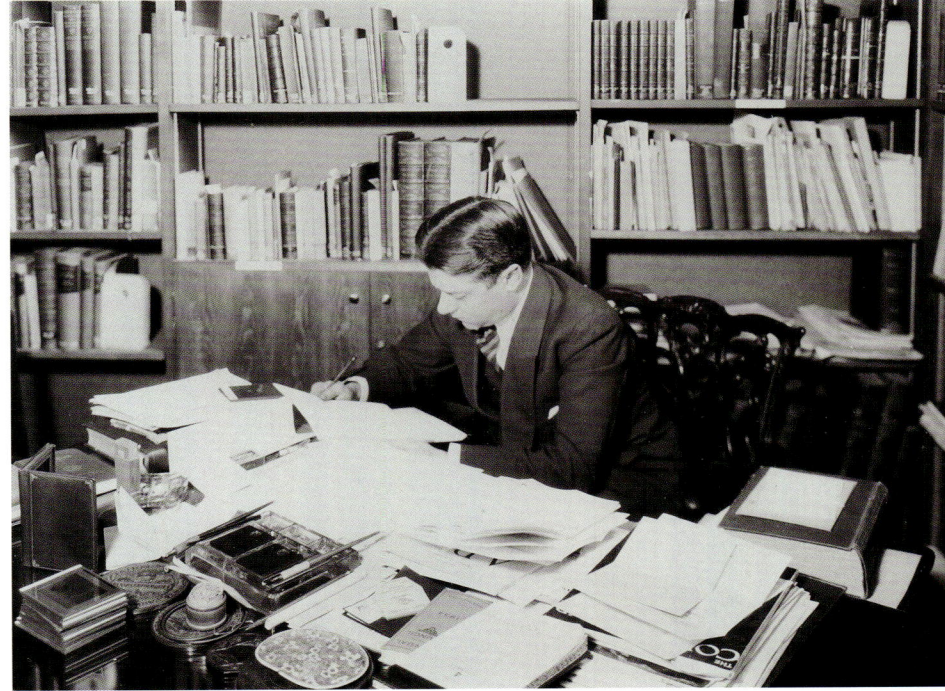

advice as to what to do to be a perfect museum man."[123] Although McIlhenny's personal interests lay in French paintings—in 1930 he purchased Jean-Baptiste-Siméon Chardin's *Still Life with a Hare* (c. 1730), which he presented to the Museum in 1958, and with his mother the following year Henri de Toulouse-Lautrec's *At the Moulin Rouge: The Dance* (1890; bequeathed to the Museum at

Opposite : **86.** Ludwig Babral : proposed design for the Museum library interior on Fairmount : c. 1935 : Civil Works Administration Project
Above : **87.** Henri Gabriel Marceau : appointed assistant curator in 1926 : Museum director, 1955–64

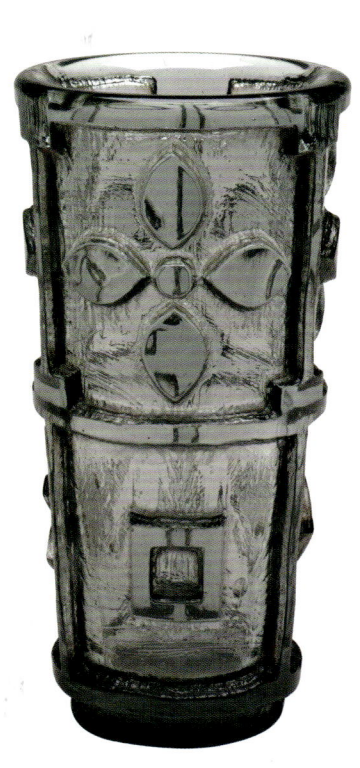 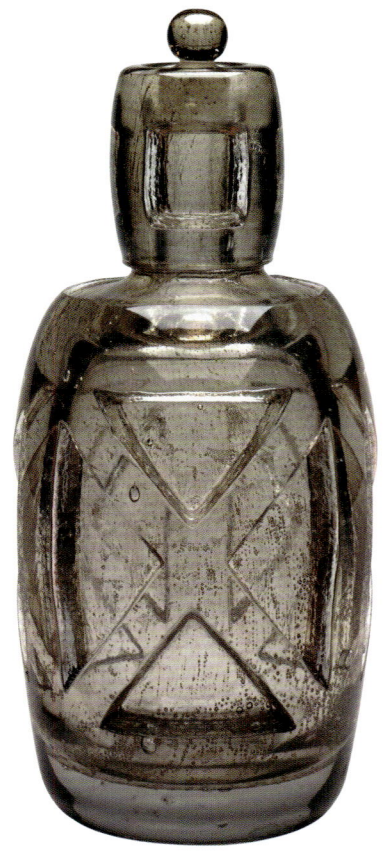 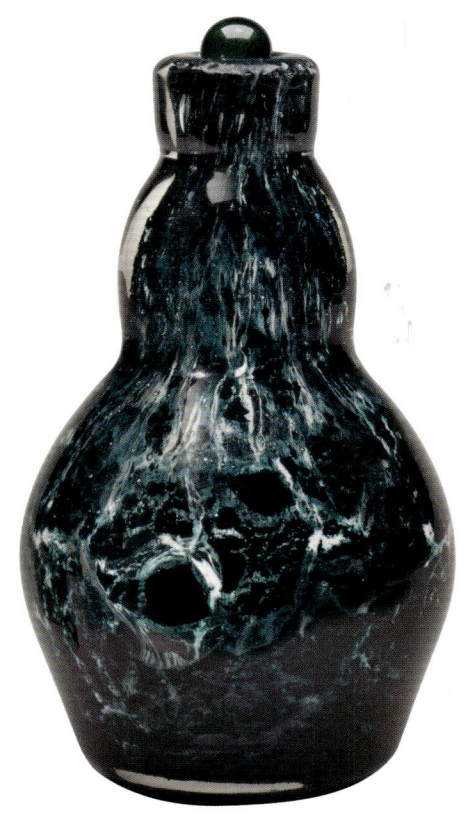

his death)—Kimball needed the young man in what was then the unstaffed department of decorative arts. In 1934 McIlhenny (fig. 92) was named the Museum's assistant curator of decorative arts (at the time an unsalaried position), where he would remain for thirty years, until his retirement as curator in 1963.[124]

With the staff still much reduced (curatorial and administrative personnel had numbered over thirty persons in 1931–32, but only twelve in 1935–36),[125] McIlhenny joined Henry Clifford, recently promoted to associate curator of painting, and Henri Marceau (fig. 87), now the Museum's assistant director as well as curator of painting and sculpture, to plan and produce the general program of exhibitions regardless of subject. In 1936, for example, McIlhenny was largely responsible for an important Degas exhibition ("the most comprehensive showing . . . ever attempted in America," according to Kimball)[126] to which he and Clifford lent works from their private collections and which McIlhenny's mother financed. In 1936–37 eleven new galleries were completed and opened under the first WPA grant, among them a series of French galleries and period rooms, for which Kimball gave McIlhenny credit. "The great inaugural installation of the

Above, left to right : **88. Maurice Marinot** : Vase : 1923 : acid-etched glass : H 7" : 1967-98-13 (cat. 112)   **89. Maurice Marinot** : Bottle : 1924 : acid-etched glass : H (bottle) 10" : 1967-98-16a,b (cat. 113)   **90. Maurice Marinot** : Bottle : 1923 : glass with encased enamel : H (bottle) 7 3/16" : 1967-98-10a,b (cat. 111)

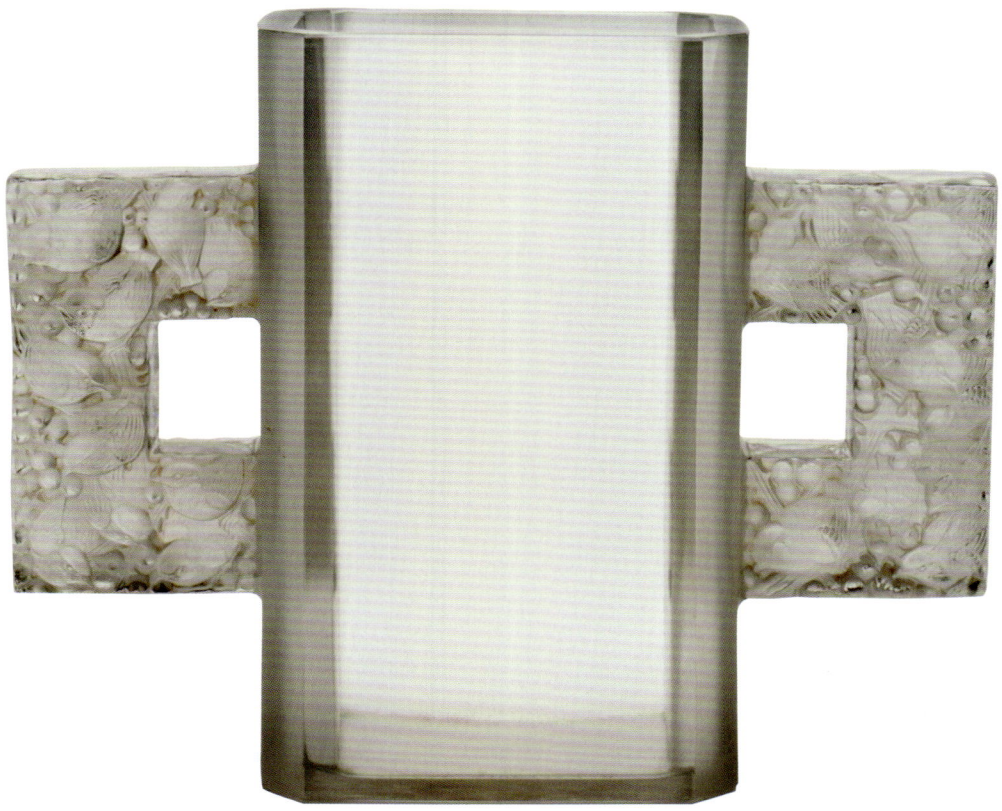

French galleries is over, and we know what a success it was," Kimball wrote him, ". . . due above all to you."[127] At the same time Kimball expressed his appreciation more concretely by promoting McIlhenny from assistant to associate curator.

Over the long course of his curatorship and connection with the Museum, McIlhenny displayed little regard for modern and contemporary decorative arts. However, his mother and their cosmopolitan friends, among them Williamina and Rodolphe Meyer de Schauensee, began in the 1930s to purchase—for their homes in Philadelphia and abroad—distinguished contemporary objects and tableware that were later given to the Museum. Frances McIlhenny acquired Lalique's masterful *Tourbillons* vase (fig. 95), its faceted edges painted with shiny black enamel, and other molded glasswares from the Lalique shop in Paris. The de Schauensees bought French glass by Lalique too, such as the *Margaret* vase (fig. 91), as well as Italian glass by Paolo Venini (fig. 126) and Gio Ponti's *Four Seasons* porcelain plates for Richard Ginori (fig. 93).[128] Other French glass of the period was subsequently added to the Museum's collections, most importantly, twenty pieces by Maurice Marinot, one of the most celebrated

Above : **91. René Lalique** : for Lalique, Paris : *Margaret* Vase : 1929 : patinated glass : H 9 1/8" : 1960-70-1 (cat. 105)

105

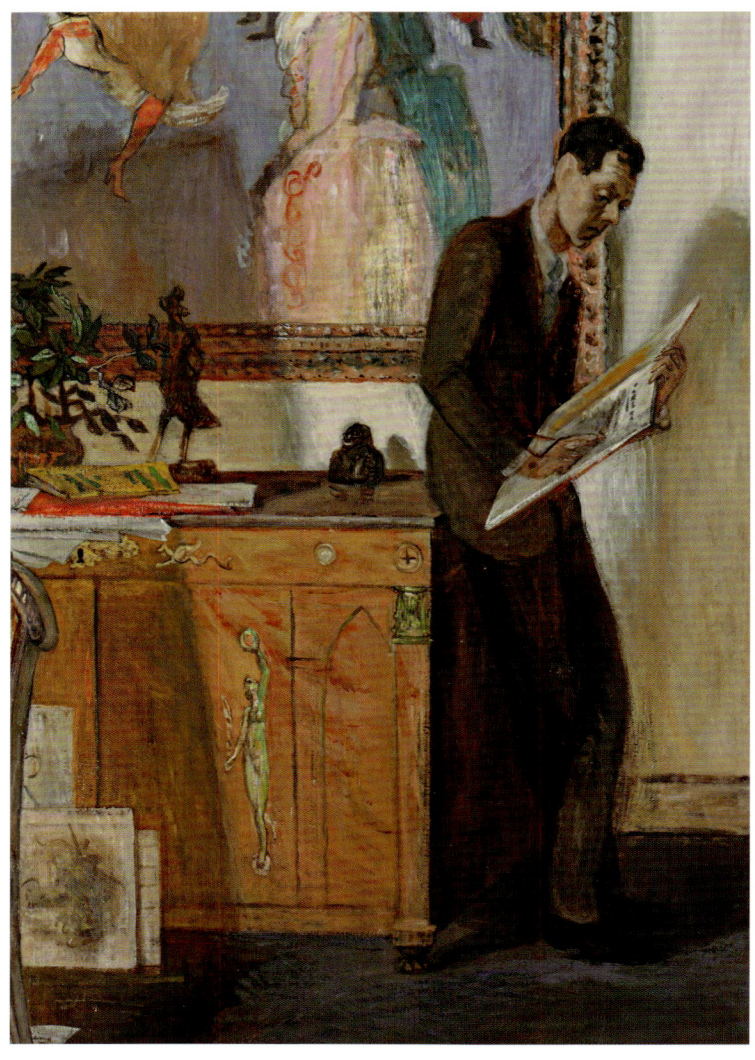

artist-glassmakers of the twentieth century (figs. 88–90, 129). In 1936 Louis V. Placé, Jr., vice president of W. V. McCahan Sugar Refining and Molasses Company in Philadelphia, gave the Museum a handsome silver dish designed and made by Georg Jensen (fig. 94).[129]

Museum president Stokes again made use of the *Bulletin* in February 1937, announcing a ten-year development campaign to raise $15.5 million, in part to fund the completion of the Museum's interior, permanent curatorial and administrative staff for care of the collections, and cataloguing and installation of additional works[130]—a bold but necessary step during what Kimball described, at nearly the same time, as a period of "poverty and retrenchment."[131] The death of publisher Arthur H. Lea in 1938 brought the Museum a bequest of $50,000, as well as a collection of paintings, "conditioned upon the official designation . . . of said museum as 'Philadelphia Museum of Art,' its right and proper name."[132] The board readily acquiesced to the nomenclature, which was already in unofficial use, and the legal title of the Museum corporation was duly changed with little fanfare on April 15 of that year.[133]

Above : **92. Franklin Chenault Watkins** : *Portrait of Henry P. McIlhenny* : 1941 : oil on canvas : H 47" : 1986-26-38 (cat. 207)   Opposite : **93. Gio Ponti** : for Richard Ginori : *Inverno (Winter)* Plate from *Four Seasons* : c. 1923–30 : enameled porcelain : D 9" : 1990-102-1 (cat. 151)

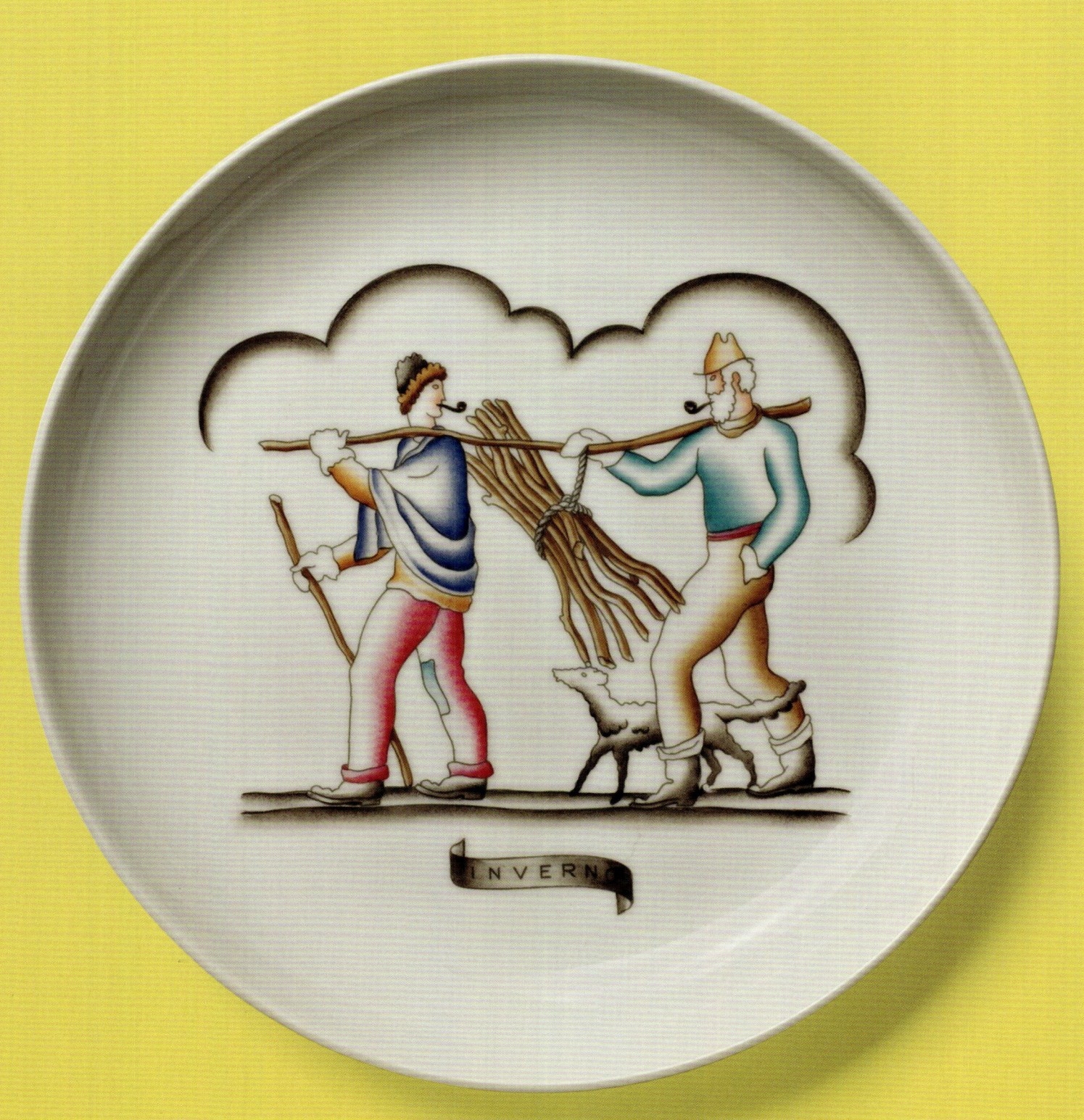

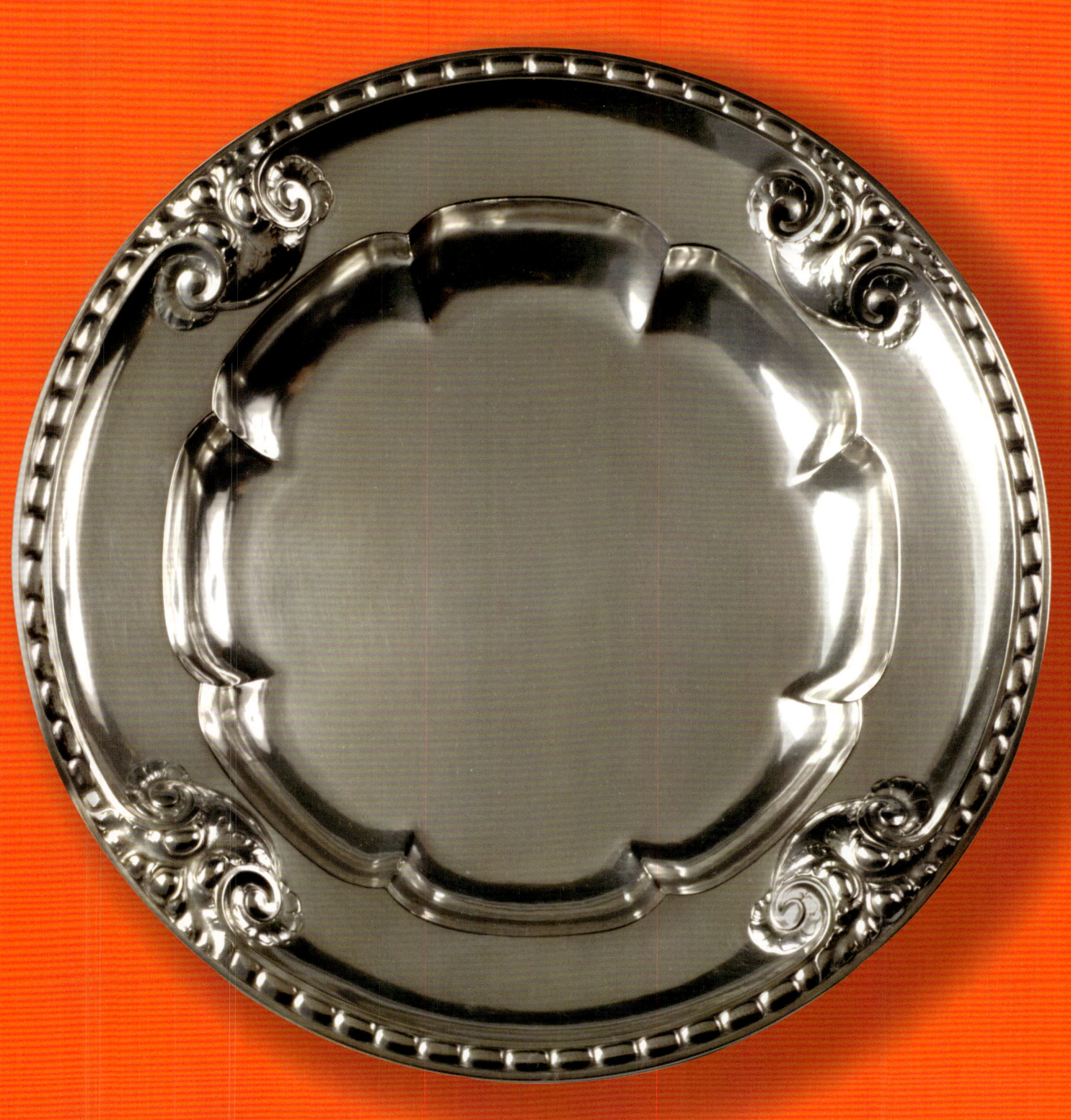

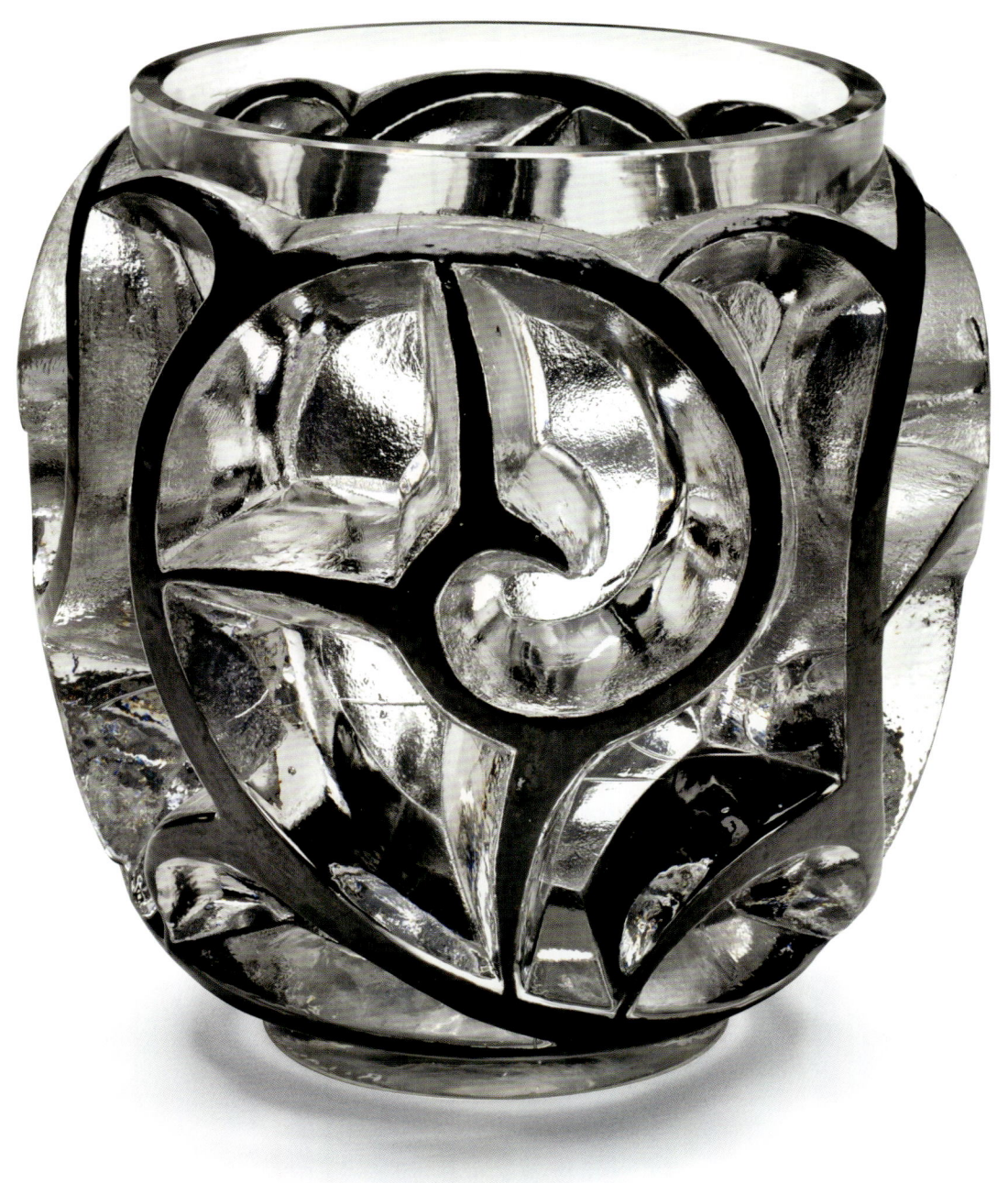

Opposite : **94. Georg Jensen** : for Georg Jensen Sølvsmedie : Dish : 1919 : silver : D 14 7/16" : 1936-33-1 (cat. 93)   Above : **95. René Lalique** : for Lalique, Paris : *Tourbillons (Whirlwinds)* Vase : 1926 : enameled glass : H 8" : 1986-26-146 (cat. 104)

109

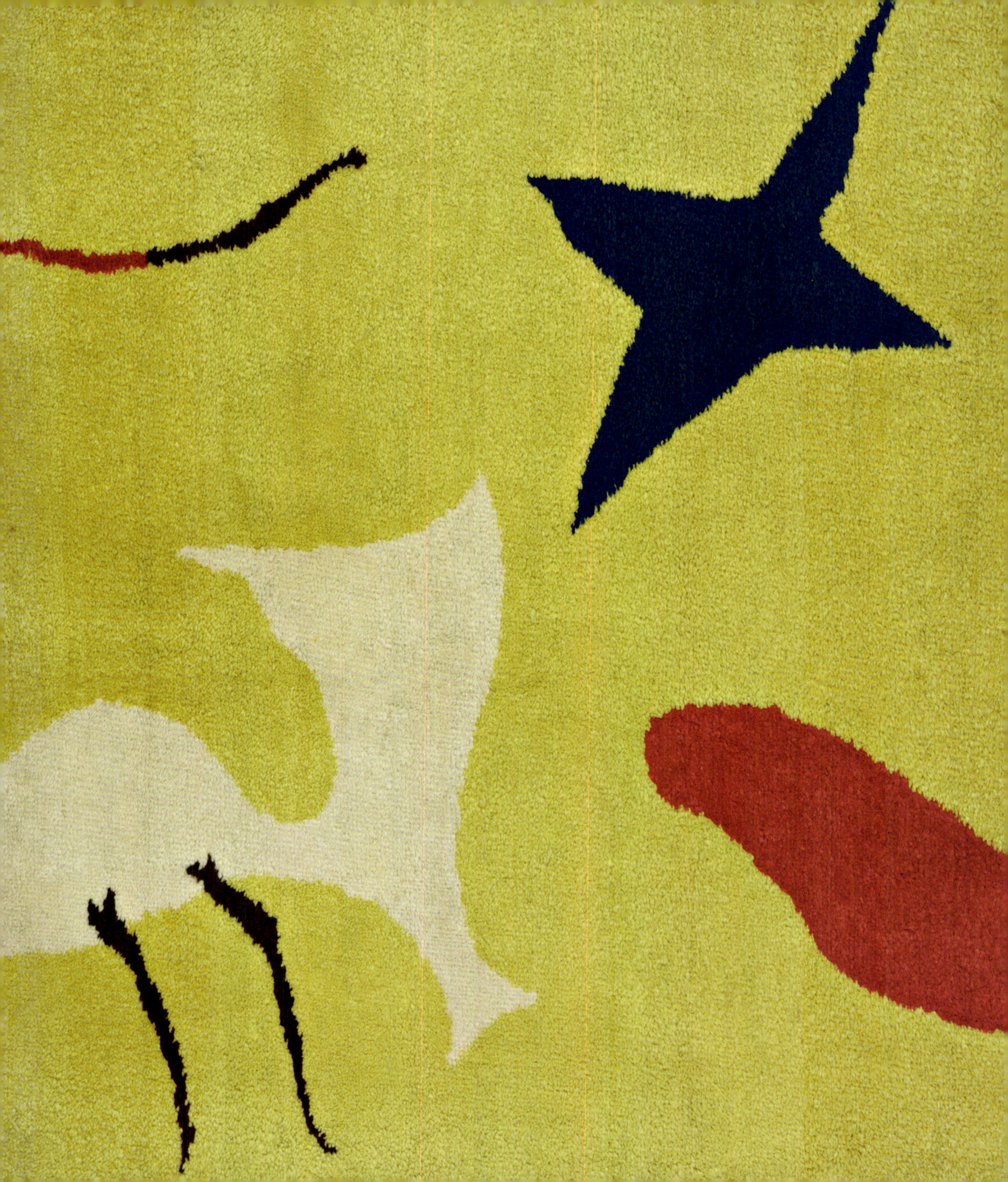

THE MUSEUM IS REDEFINED

Kimball also took a hard look at the collections, as new galleries were opening in the Museum that redefined the collecting parameters of the institution. He further refined the collections through loans and exchanges, and ultimately sold off objects that the staff considered to be superfluous or undesirable. This deaccessioning was undertaken not only as a housekeeping measure when the burden of maintaining collections at three separate locations was proving difficult (in 1944 the Samuel S. Fleisher Art Memorial would be added by the bequest of its founder, offering tuition-free neighborhood art classes and housing Fleisher's personal collection of paintings and sculpture), but also for whatever income those objects might bring. Kimball had earlier pointed out that, lacking current funds for new purchases, the Museum hoped to acquire desirable objects by exchange, or by the exchange of loans. Noting at the time that the "few Egyptian exhibits, in the basement of Memorial Hall, have long been an anomaly," he negotiated an exchange of these objects with the University of Pennsylvania and its museum, within whose scope they more suitably fell; in return the Philadelphia Museum of Art received Persian pottery of high quality for its division of Eastern art.[134]

From about 1940 until he left the Museum in 1955, Kimball presided over a series of transfers, exchanges, and sales of objects as authorized by the board: first, duplicates or undesired minor examples of surplus objects that were in storage, some acquired by the Museum through purchase and others through abandonment by the exhibitors at the Centennial Exhibition,[135] and next surplus and duplicate objects that had been received without conditions or restrictions prior to 1900.[136] Motivated by considerations of the expense and labor that would be necessary to transfer these objects to the new building as well as the additional space required for storage, and with the support of the museum committee and decorative arts curator Henry McIlhenny, Kimball and his staff bravely, but in hindsight not always wisely, sifted through the great bulk of study material at Memorial Hall. Many of the roughly sixty-nine-thousand objects, according to Kimball, were "of relatively little value, at least to us, by Museum standards today."[137] The study collections so thoughtfully amassed by Barber and Morris were thus dispersed, among them the Elkington electrotypes acquired in 1876 (sold in 1944); Rookwood pottery (1941–54); Castellani jewelry (1944 and 1945); French ceramics by Henri Cros and Clement Massier purchased by John T. Morris in 1900 at the Paris Universal Exposition (1945 and 1949); and Tiffany glass also purchased in 1900 (1940 and 1949). However, Kimball was able to place objects "excellent of their kind but of classes not within the scope of the Philadelphia Museum of Art"[138] on deposit with other Philadelphia institutions, including the University Museum (archaeological and ethnological objects), the Franklin Institute (industrial objects), the Commercial Museum (commercial products), and the Atwater Kent Museum (historical objects). Also transferred were objects that did not meet the standards of the Philadelphia Museum of Art but were welcomed by other Pennsylvania institutions, including materials that would be useful to schools and furnishings for historic houses.[139]

In 1941 Kimball defined the scope and areas of collecting for the University Museum and the Philadelphia Museum of Art, in collaboration with the museum committee and Horace Jayne—who had recently resigned his concurrent posts as director of the University Museum and as the Philadelphia Museum of Art's chief of the division of Eastern art and curator of Chinese

96. Joan Miró : woven by unknown atelier (Aubusson, France) : Rug (detail) : c. 1934 : wool and cotton : W 6' 9 7/8" : 1940-2-1 (cat. 130)

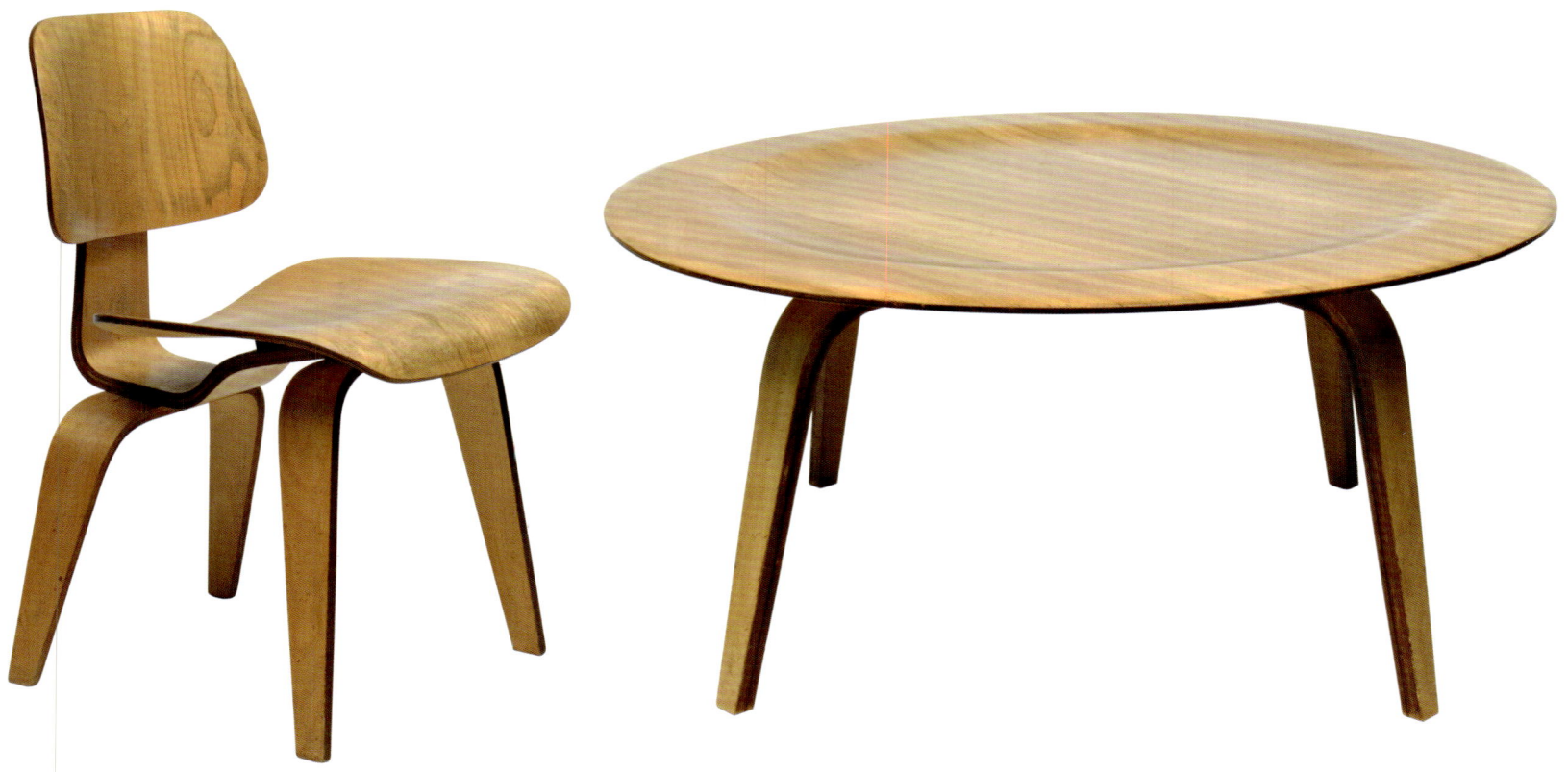

art—to become vice director of the Metropolitan Museum of Art. To avoid competition in acquisitions and exhibitions between two museums in the same city, the agreement divided the institutional collections between archaeology and the history of art.[140] In terms of the Western world, the University Museum would collect and exhibit objects dated up to the end of the Roman empire, while the Philadelphia Museum of Art would focus on works dated from the beginning of "Christian civilization" and forward, with the geographical parameters in North and South America, Africa, and Polynesia to be determined by contact with European civilization. In the Americas, Pre-Columbian and American Indian art would be the field of the University Museum, while the Philadelphia Museum of Art would cover colonial and national arts since the European conquest. Accordingly, the Museum's board of trustees transferred ownership of American Indian, Mexican, and other precolonial American objects, receiving in exchange the Sasanian and Islamic stuccos excavated at Rayy in Persia that Kimball needed for his new Oriental wing, which had opened in April 1940.[141]

Many of the WPA construction workers responsible for building and installing the new galleries and the white-collar "educational" workers who served as guards and gallery guides, as well as engineers, draftsmen, librarians, registrars, and conservators, were recalled to war work when the United States entered World War II after the bombing of Pearl Harbor in December 1941. Kimball stated that "with the outbreak of war we face conditions which will no doubt get worse and not better."[142] At the same time the Museum took measures regarding air-raid protection, including plans to store the Museum's most precious objects in a special vault, among them, only one twentieth-century object, Paul Cézanne's *The Large Bathers* of 1906.[143] As Kimball had hoped, the installation

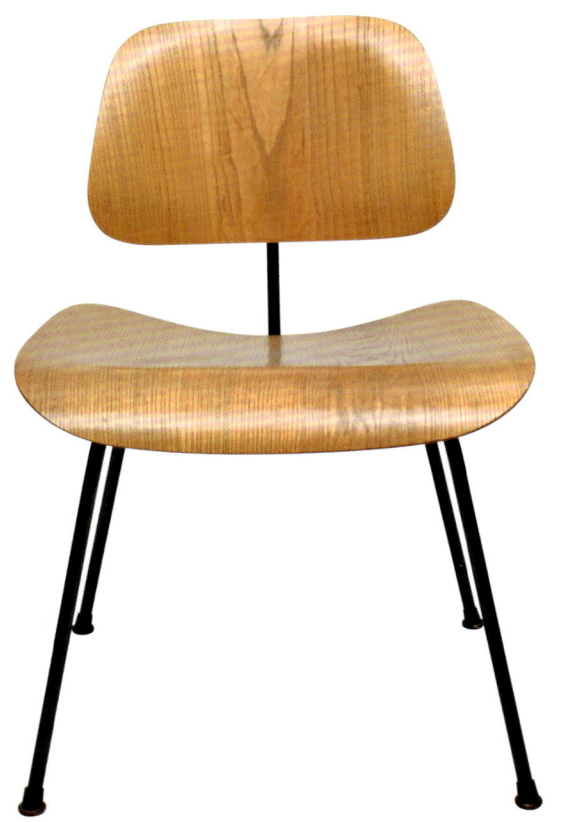 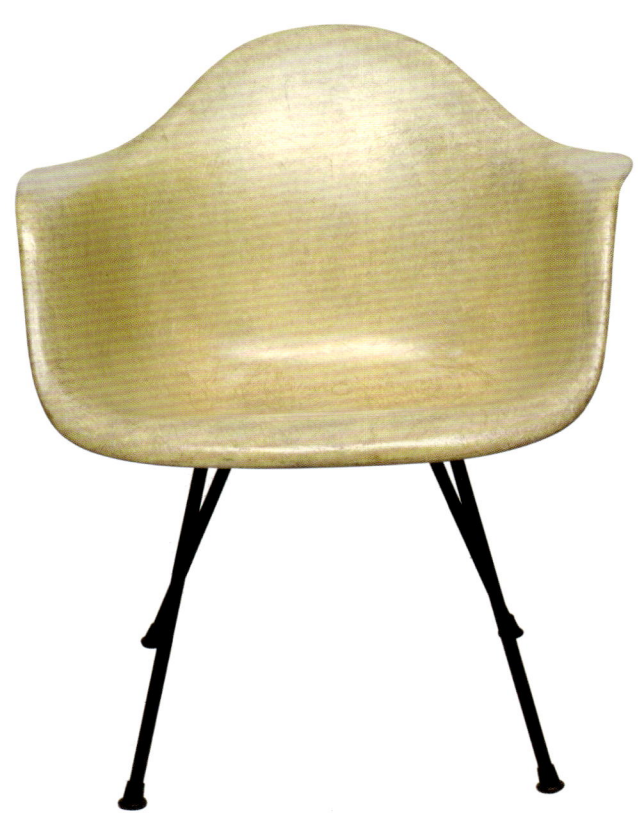

of newly available galleries continued, and the Museum staged various exhibitions within its limited means.[144] By coincidence, in 1942 modern and contemporary design had its best year for exhibitions at the Museum in a decade. In January the ground-breaking show *Organic Design in Home Furnishings*,[145] which originated at the Museum of Modern Art, came to the Philadelphia Museum of Art in a smaller format, thanks to the sponsorship of Gimbel Brothers department store in Philadelphia. The exhibition was based on a furniture competition organized by architect Eliot Noyes, who had become the first director of the Museum of Modern Art's new department of industrial design in 1940. Henry McIlhenny encouraged the Philadelphia Museum of Art to take the show, arguing: "The weakest part of our corporation is the lack of cooperation between the Museum and its School of Industrial Art. This show would be of great benefit to our pupils, and I suggest that it be held . . . in collaboration with the school."[146]

However, McIlhenny suggested that before proceeding, the material should be examined in New York; it was easy enough to arrange a visit, as he knew Noyes personally—both men had lived in the same dormitory at Harvard. When the exhibition opened, some of the designs for furniture, which featured the experiments in molded-plywood seat shells by Eero Saarinen and Charles and Ray Eames, among others, were then in production and for sale at various department stores,[147] but the Museum acquired nothing from or related to the show. Nevertheless, over the succeeding decades, the progeny of the *Organic Design* experiments—the Eames's molded-plywood and fiberglass-reinforced furniture first produced by and for Herman Miller in the 1940s (figs. 97–100), and Saarinen's 1940s molded-plywood furniture for Knoll (fig. 101)—were eventually acquired by gift and purchase, as was Saarinen's molded-fiberglass and fiberglass-reinforced plastic *Pedestal* chair and table series of the 1950s (fig. 102).

Opposite and above, left to right : **97. Charles Eames and Ray Eames** : for Herman Miller : *DCW* Chair : 1945 : plywood, rubber, metal : H 28 1/4" : 1999-106-3 (cat. 50)   **98. Charles Eames and Ray Eames** : for Herman Miller : *CTW* Coffee Table : 1945 : plywood : D 34 1/2" : 1999-106-1 (cat. 49)
99: Charles Eames and Ray Eames : for Herman Miller : *DCM* Chair : 1946 : ash-faced plywood, steel, rubber : H 29" : 1972-37-2 (cat. 51)
100. Charles Eames and Ray Eames : for Herman Miller : Chair : 1948–50 : fiberglass-reinforced plastic, steel : H 26" : 1972-37-1 (cat. 52)

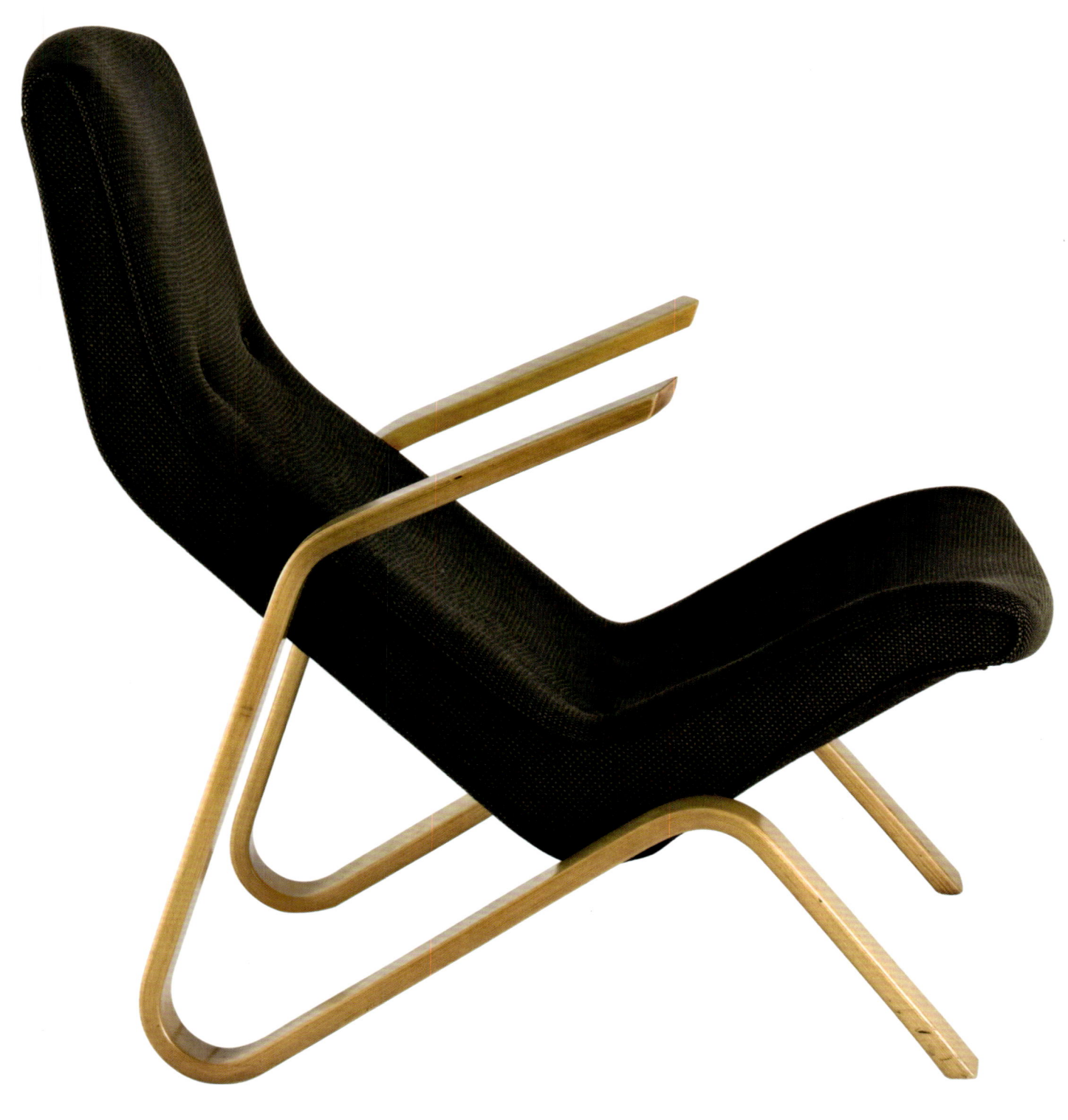

Above : **101. Eero Saarinen** : for Knoll : *Grasshopper* Chair : 1946 : birch, fabric : H 34" : 1984-34-1 (cat. 166)   Opposite : **102. Eero Saarinen** : for Knoll : *Pedestal* Chair : 1955–57 : fiberglass-reinforced plastic, lacquered aluminum, wool : H 31" : 1973-96-1 (cat. 167)

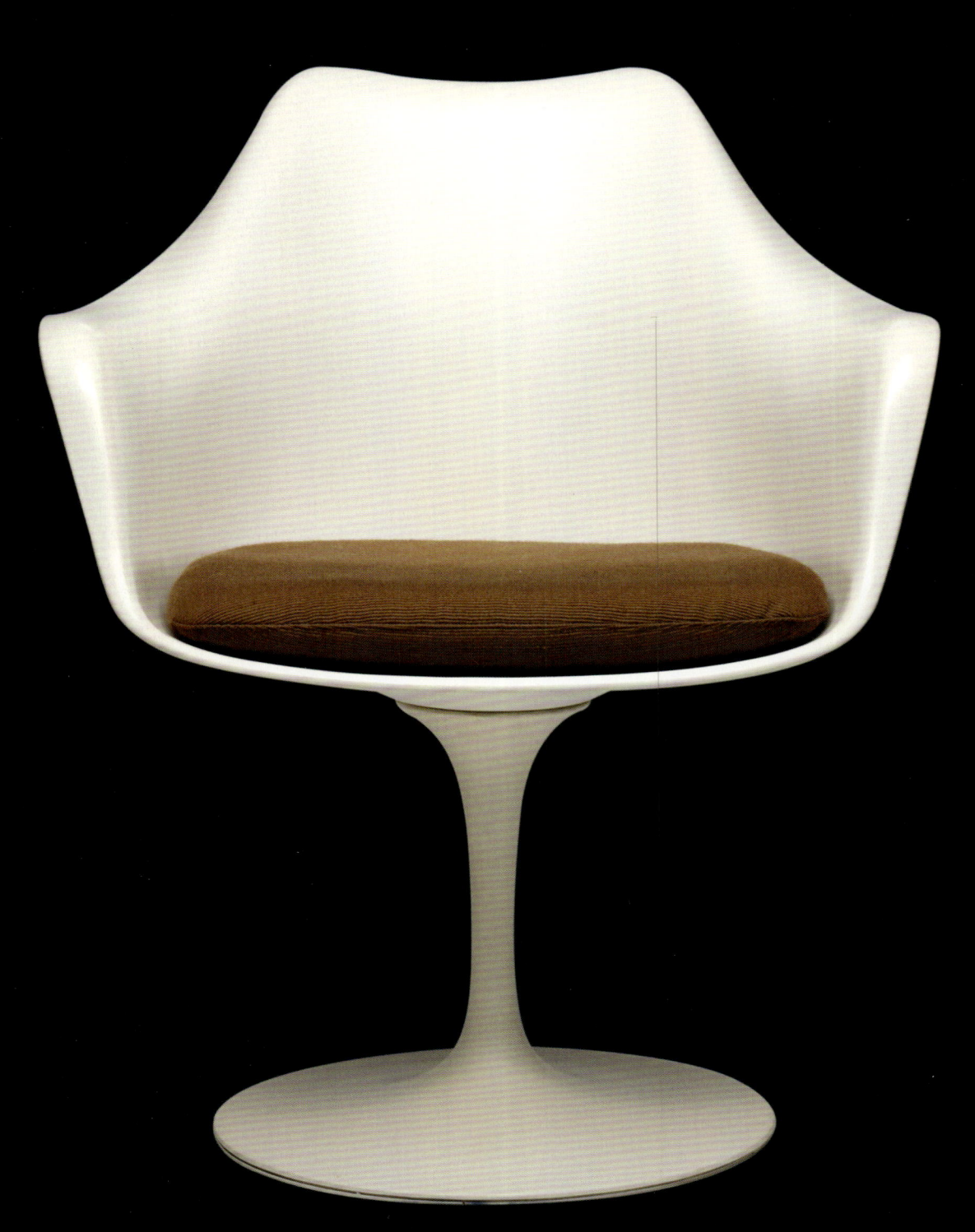

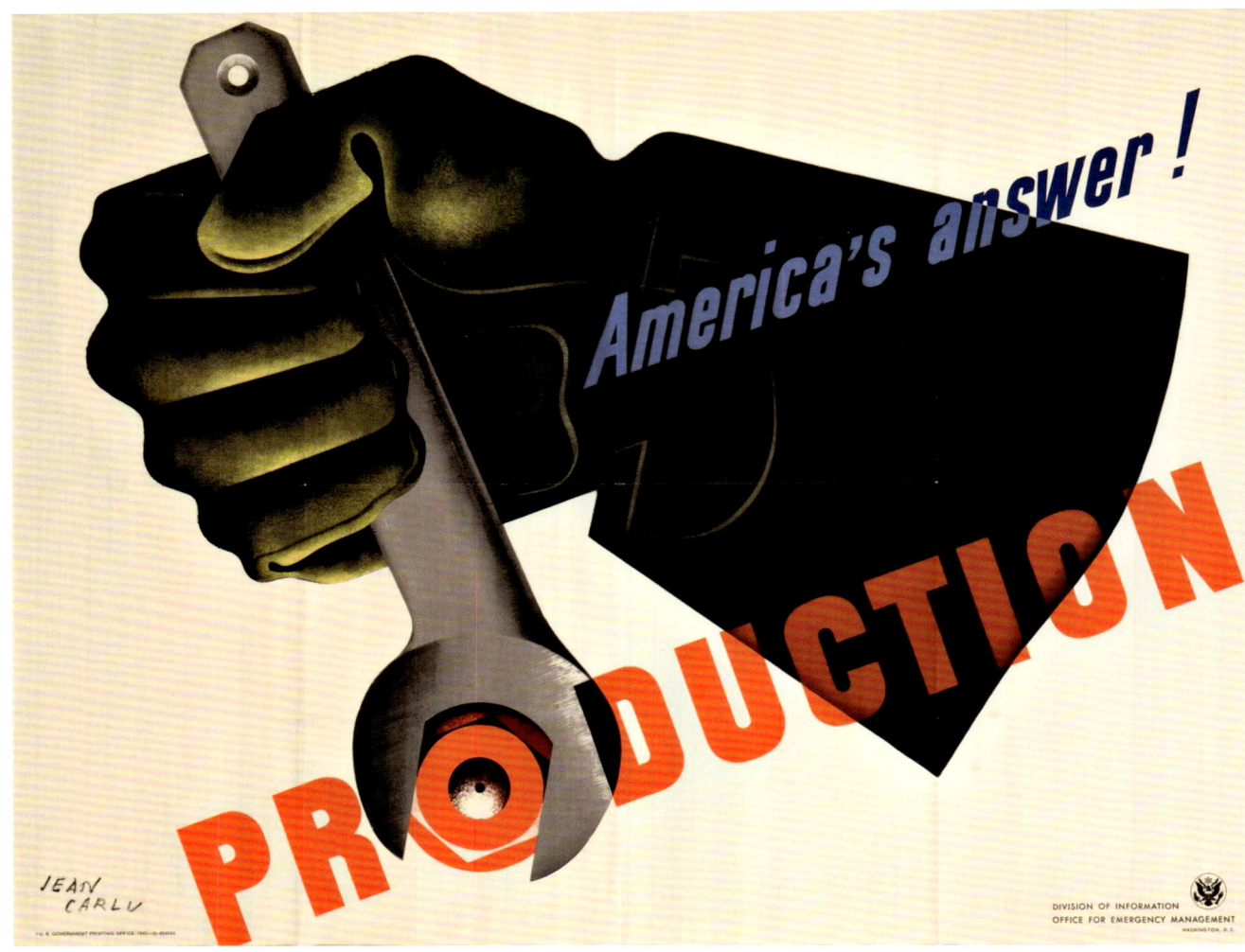

Shortly after *Organic Design* closed at the Museum, *Art in Advertising* opened, the second such exhibition held at the Museum and sponsored by the Art Directors Club of Philadelphia.[148] Museum president Stokes commented in a news release that, "while quite naturally one of the dominant notes of the show this year will be the vital role the artists of America are playing in the war effort, we believe the exhibition demonstrates convincingly a rapidly narrowing margin between the fine arts and the work of commercial artists whose works hitherto have been seen only in reproduction in the newspapers and magazines of the country and seldom in original on the walls of our important museums."[149] Kimball remarked on the addition of "a patriotic note" to the exhibition by a large group of war posters and "the handsome decoration with flags."[150]

Again, the Museum acquired nothing directly from *Art in Advertising*, but Jean Carlu's now well-known *America's Answer! Production* poster, which was featured in the exhibition, came to the Museum years later as a gift (fig. 103). Philadelphia graphic designer Matthew Leibowitz, formerly a student of Alexey Brodovitch at the Museum school, was also included in the exhibition (winning a prize for design and lettering in this, his first year of independent practice), and examples of his work were also eventually acquired by the Museum (fig. 104).

Following *Art in Advertising*, the Museum showed a group of modern French tapestries designed by Georges Braque, Raoul Dufy, Fernand Léger, Jean Lurçat, Henri Matisse, Joan Miró, and Georges Rouault. Commissioned

Above : **103. Jean Carlu** : for the U.S. Government Printing Office, Office for Emergency Management : *America's Answer! Production* Poster : 1942 : offset lithograph : H 29 7/8" : 2003-70-1 (cat. 27)   Opposite : **104. Matthew Leibowitz** : for Caedmon Records : *H. L. Mencken: Speaking* Album Cover : 1958 : letterpress on Lustro Gloss paper : H 12 1/2" : 2007-103-4 (cat. 108)

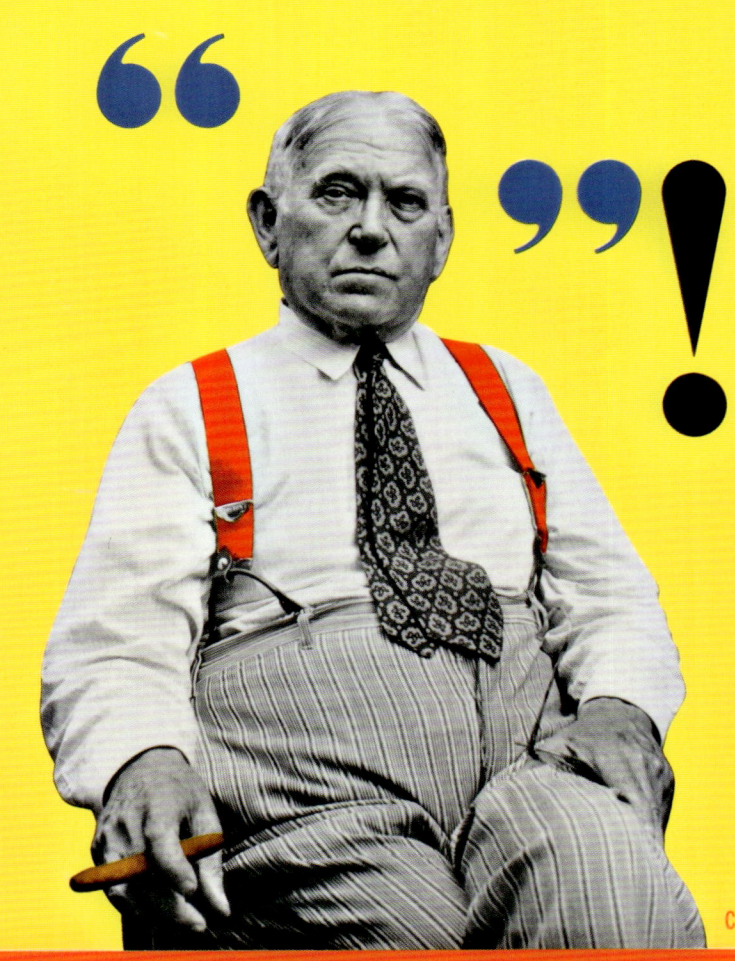

by Marie Cuttoli, wife of a French senator from Algeria, the tapestry designs had been woven in workshops in Aubusson, and then offered for sale at Cuttoli's Paris boutique and through the Bignou Gallery in New York. Kimball was circumspect in describing the exhibition, whether because many of the works were abstract or surreal or because the painted cartoon originals had been produced as woven hangings, noting that if one liked the work of these artists, one would like the tapestries, "otherwise not—though a case can be made for such designs in this decorative medium even with those who regard painting as purely representative."[151] For once the Museum could claim prescience, having acquired in 1940 a Cuttoli tapestry designed by Joan Miró as the gift of Henry McIlhenny's sister, Bernice (Mrs. John) Wintersteen (fig. 96). Henry McIlhenny must have encouraged his sister's purchase, as he had been in contact with both Mme Cuttoli and the Bignou Gallery for a number of years. In December 1942, *Design This Day: Industrial Design*, prepared in collaboration with Walter Dorwin Teague, opened at the Museum, and Teague and George Howe gave accompanying lectures.[152] The exhibition (about which we know little) was based on Teague's book, *Design This Day: The Technique of Order in the Machine Age*, published in 1940. Teague would return to Philadelphia in 1958 for a symposium on the same subject at the Museum school (fig. 105).

In the spring of 1942 Bernice, known as Bonnie, Wintersteen, was invited to join the museum committee. At the same time Henry McIlhenny, like other members of the staff, was called for military service, leaving the department of decorative arts in the capable hands of his assistant, Joan Prentice. Following Kimball's plan, Prentice and her colleague Rachel Randolph completed the Museum's first study galleries, designated for American and European ceramics and divided by medium into porcelains, pottery, and stoneware. "Great beauty of display, combined with well-prepared labels of historical and technical information," declared Kimball, "make this at once the most effective and the most delightful of facilities for the study of such material."[153]

The WPA was closed in 1943 by the United States government, ending seven and a half years of federal contributions to the interior construction of the Museum building. When the program had begun in 1935, only 35 finished units of the Museum had been completed; with WPA help over 170 additional units were finished, increasing sixfold the usable space for galleries, offices, and other services. Stokes announced that the Philadelphia city council would make special appropriations to the Museum to counter the withdrawal of the WPA workforce, allowing all of the galleries in the Museum to remain fully open to the public.[154] According to Kimball's calculation (and his calculations tended to vary), only a third of the building was left "unassigned,"[155] that is, empty of art and support services.

The Museum's most important acquisition of the war years was the purchase in 1945 of the George Grey Barnard collection of medieval art, which would furnish the Museum's medieval section with many distinguished

Above : **105.** Symposium at the Museum school with Walter Dorwin Teague : 1958   Opposite, top to bottom : **106. Marion Dorn** : Scarf : screen-printed silk : c. 1941–44 : W 36" : 1971-42-1 (cat. 47)   **107. Edward McKnight Kauffer** : for the U.S. Government Printing Office for C.A.A. War Training Service, Department of Commerce : *Watch Out for Fire* Poster : 1943 : lithograph : H 44 1/4" : 1963-84-56 (cat. 97)

objects.[156] Yet as Kimball had observed only a few months earlier, the Museum's twentieth-century collections of decorative arts, were "almost totally lacking."[157] There was little interest among board members or staff in filling that gap in any important way during the balance of Kimball's tenure, even though he was quick to point out that the Museum's unassigned spaces were highly attractive to would-be donors and for future acquisitions. During the later years of the decade, modern and contemporary decorative arts were acquired gradually as isolated gifts. In 1945 Williamina de Schauensee recognized the Museum's need "for distinguished examples of contemporary decorative art," and made it possible for the Museum to acquire a vase of Orrefors glass by Simon Gate,[158] to which additional Swedish glass would be added in later decades, as well as a pair of pewter vases by Laurits C. Eichner (fig. 108). The Eichner vases were early examples of the revival of American craft, although the Museum, through its school, had never really lost touch with handcraft activity. The school's metalwork and jewelry instructor, Virginia Wireman Cute (later Curtin), herself became a nationally known silversmith and advocate of contemporary American craft. A descendant of eighteenth-century Philadelphia silversmith Joseph Richardson, Cute later gave the Museum an example of her own work of the 1940s (fig. 125) along with silver made by her ancestor. At this time few museums were collecting such work.

In 1946 two groups of "modern design"—the Museum's first use of the term—by Russel Wright and Gertrud and Otto Natzler were given by Mrs. Herbert Cameron Morris, a member of the museum committee, and Joan Prentice.[159] Textile designer Marion Dorn (fig. 106) also later gave the Museum posters and printed ephemera designed by her husband, Edward McKnight Kauffer, from the 1940s (fig. 107). Wright, already a nationally known industrial designer, created handsome, inexpensive, mass-produced tablewares from the later 1920s (figs. 109–12). The Natzlers, who had immigrated to the United States after the annexation of Austria by Germany in 1938, were

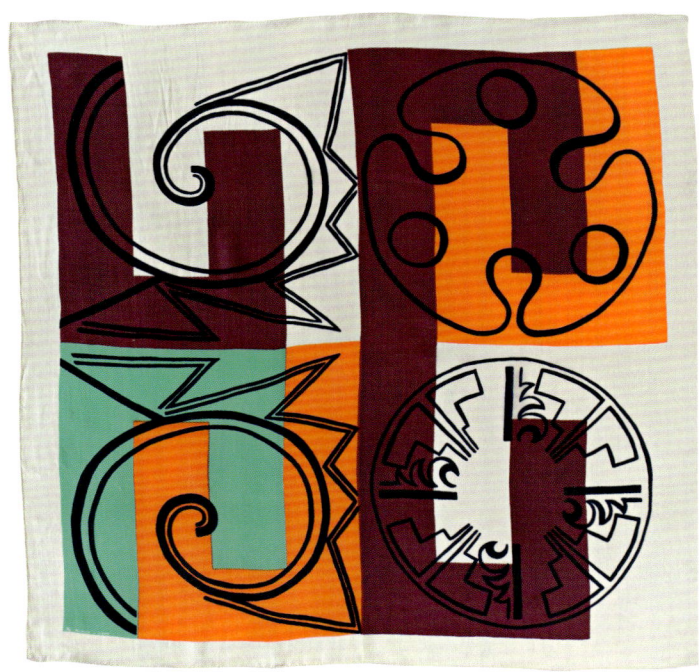

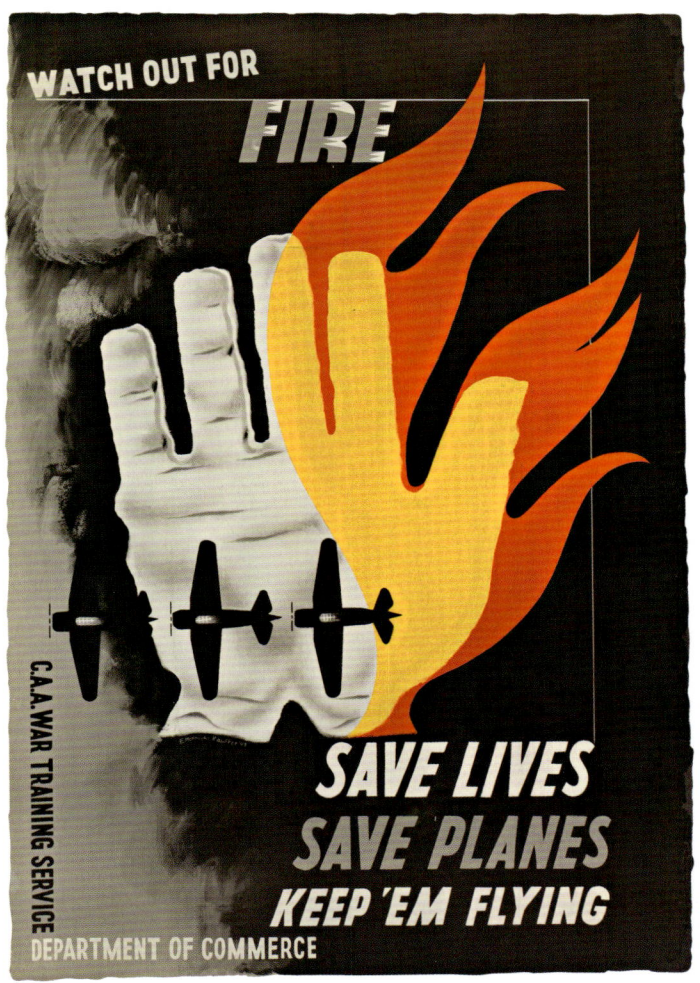

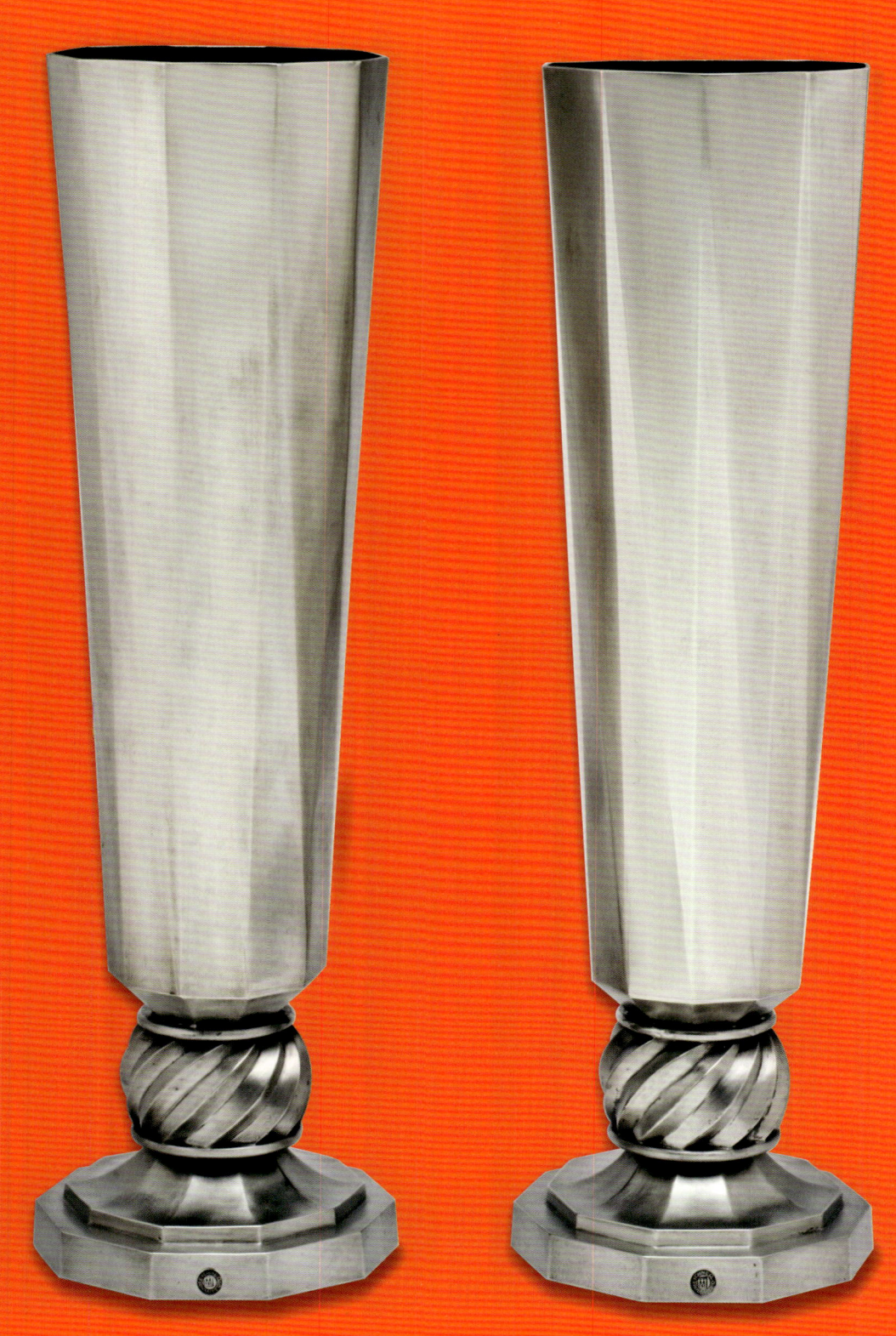

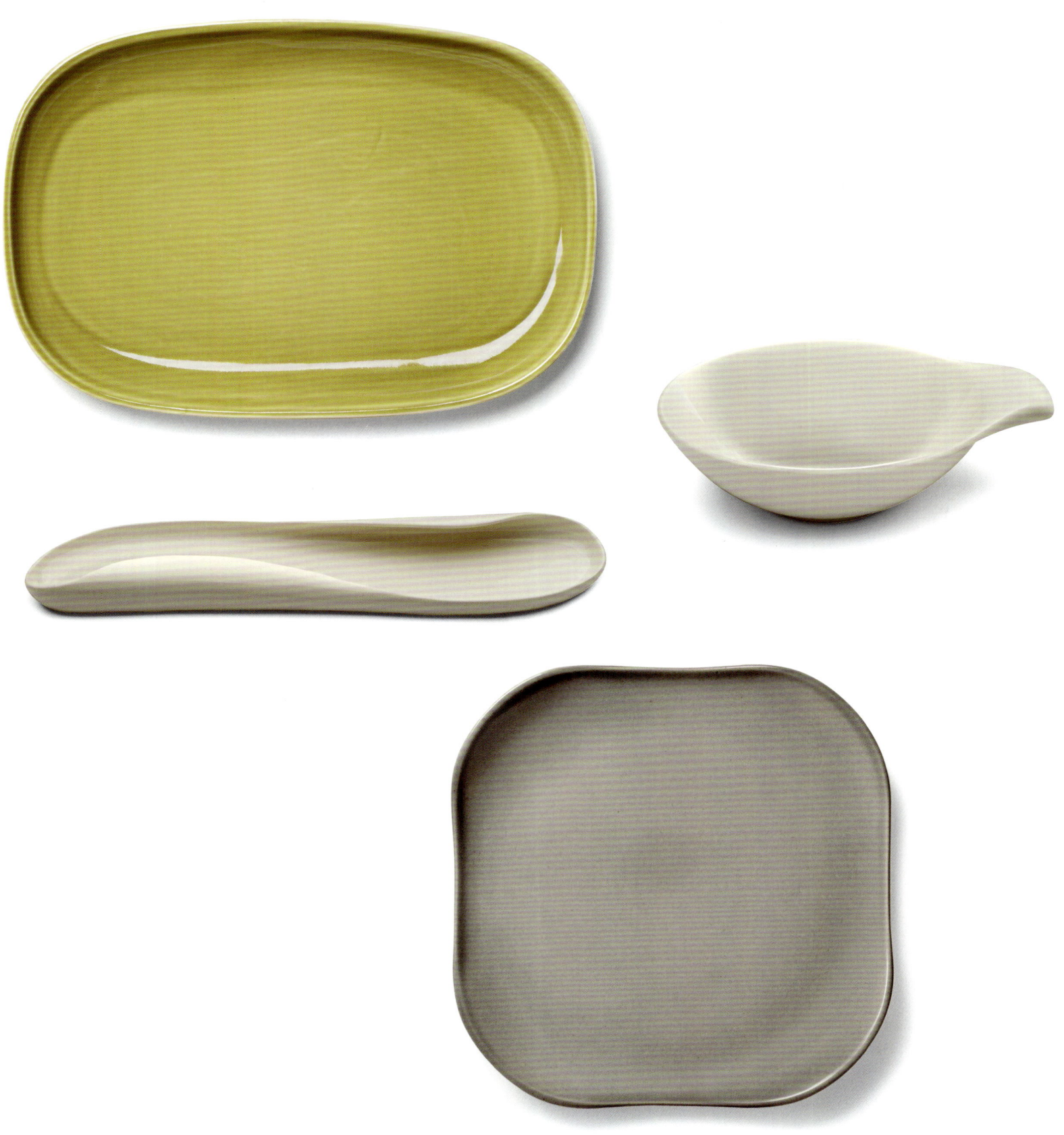

Opposite : **108. Laurits C. Eichner** : Pair of Vases : 1937 : pewter : H 24" : 1944-92-1a,b (cat. 55)   Above : **109–12. Russel Wright** : for Steubenville : *American Modern* Dinnerware : c. 1937–39 : glazed earthenware : W (chop plate, bottom) 12⅝" : 1945-66-1,3,4,8 (cats. 215–18)

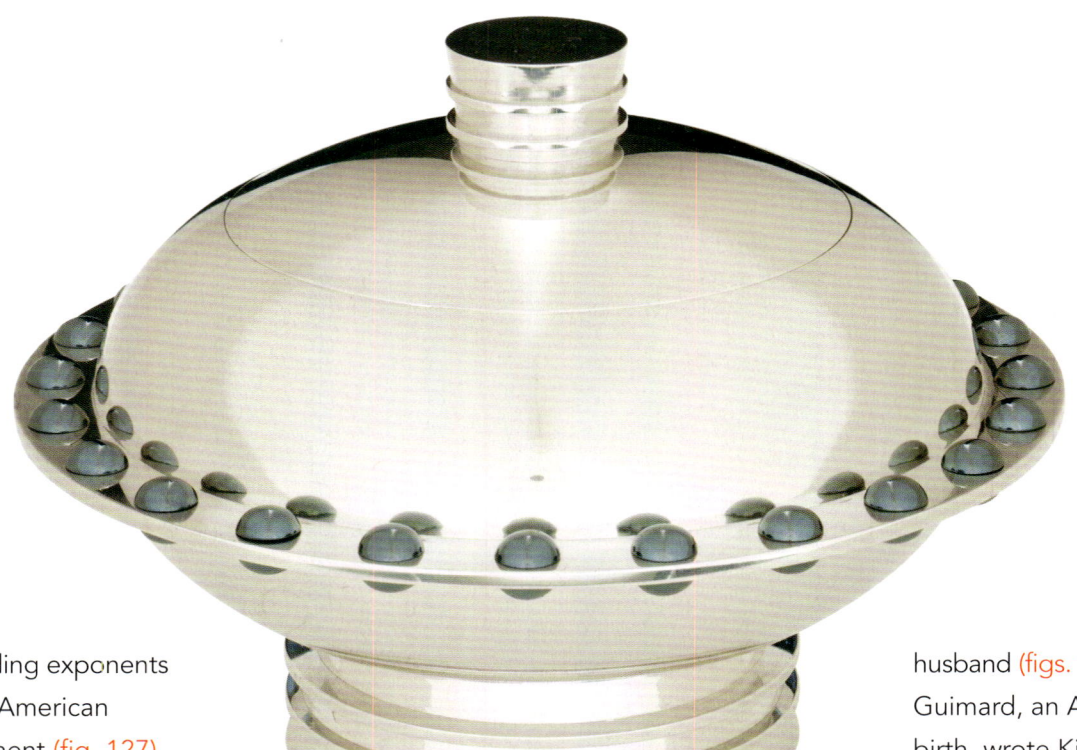

among the leading exponents of the modern American ceramic movement (fig. 127). In 1946 curator Joan Prentice organized *Styles in Silver: Period Silver in Period Settings*, an exhibition of silverware from the seventeenth to the twentieth centuries, the latest piece being a tureen of 1945 made by the Parisian firm of Jean Puiforcat. As Kimball explained, the show was designed to present pieces that had not previously been on view and to feature styles that were not generally emphasized, including modern silver "of creative design."[160] Inspired by the exhibition, in 1948 the Museum purchased its own Puiforcat tureen of silver and hematite, which had been shown at the New York World's Fair of 1939 (fig. 113).

In 1948 and 1949 the widow of French architect Hector Guimard (who had died in New York during the war) dispersed his collection among several museums, including the Philadelphia Museum of Art, which received an armchair, metalwork, and Mme Guimard's framed, embroidered wedding handkerchief, designed by her husband (figs. 114, 124). Mme Guimard, an American by birth, wrote Kimball in April 1949 that she had recently begun to distribute "the *portable* objects created by Mr. Guimard" that she had brought with her from France: "Appreciating the interest you have manifested for his career—I would very much like to reserve for your museum a few choice objects."[161] When a gilt bronze platter and the handkerchief were presented for approval to the museum committee, however, "Mrs. [William M.] Elkins and three others were recorded in the negative"—fortunately for the Museum, a minority vote.[162]

The Museum's department of decorative arts, which was at less than full strength during the war, in the short term never quite recovered its former momentum. When the war was finally over, curator Henry McIlhenny rejoined the department but found it difficult to take up once again his peacetime profession, writing Paul Sachs at Harvard in December 1946: "I have returned to the Museum but am not completely content. It was a great temptation to stay in Ireland where I had a truly wonderful summer."[163] Less than a year later, in 1948, McIlhenny was granted a one-year leave of absence to assume the post of visiting art historian at the American Academy in Rome. The following spring he was again granted leave to spend from mid-May to November in Ireland and elsewhere, a pattern that would be followed regularly during his curatorship and extended to a sabbatical leave during 1959–60. To keep the department of decorative arts afloat during the long absences of its curator, Fiske Kimball had named himself chief of the division of decorative arts in 1941 (Henri Marceau was chief of the division of painting and sculpture), a title he maintained until his resignation in 1955. Joan Prentice, curator of ceramics and silver, resigned suddenly in the spring of 1947. Louis C. Madeira, member of a wealthy, upper-class Philadelphia family and son-in-law of artist and collector Carroll Tyson, took up the slack as a departmental volunteer, a service that was warmly appreciated by Kimball: "Your readiness to help in any capacity has placed everyone in your debt, and we admire the ability with which you have handled such varied matters. As I told you when you were good enough to say you would volunteer again next year, we

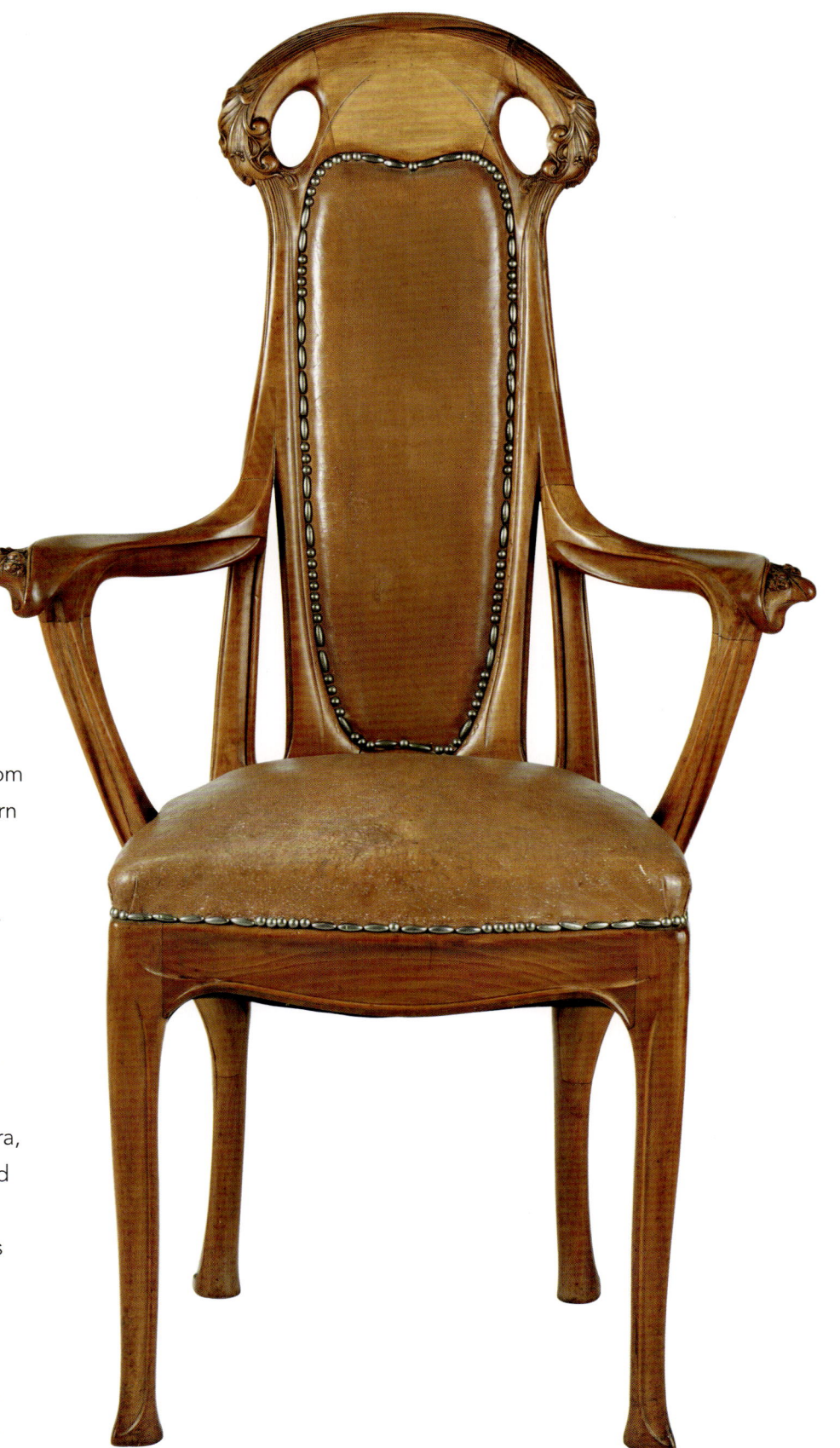

Opposite : **113. Jean Puiforcat** : for Puiforcat : Tureen : 1937 : silver, hematite : D 11¾" : 1948-70-1a,b (cat. 153)   Above : **114. Hector Guimard** : Chair : c. 1912 : cherry wood, leather : H 44" : 1948-64-1 (cat. 81)

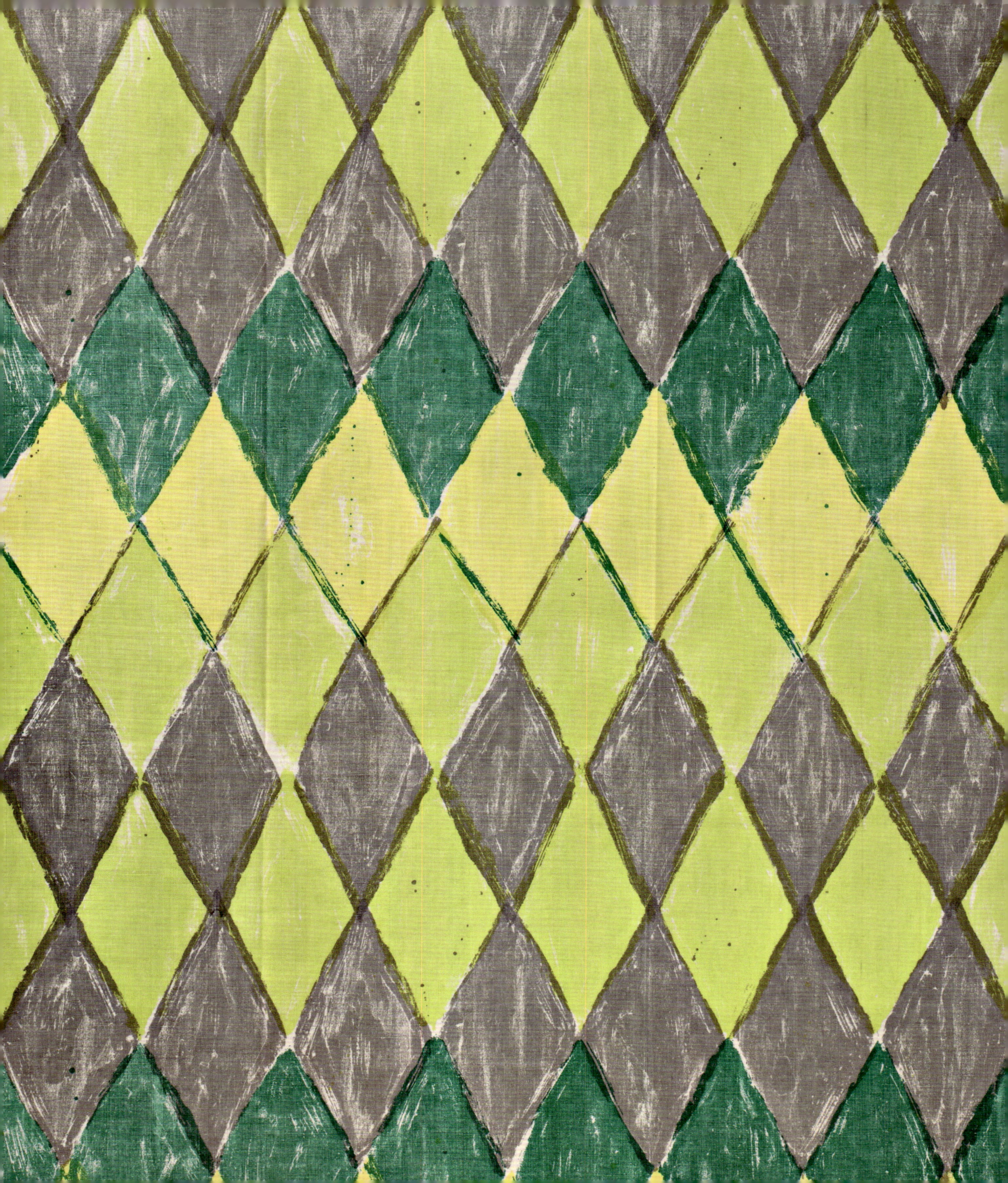

now appoint you regularly on the staff as assistant in Decorative Arts. . . . I know you understand, what we deeply regret, that we cannot compensate you for your services, but no doubt in good time promotion in rank and some honorarium will follow."[164]

There were additional staff, as well as board, changes at the Museum. Henry's mother, Frances McIlhenny, died during the war in 1943 and was replaced on the Museum board in 1948 by her daughter, Bonnie Wintersteen. John Story Jenks, chair of the museum committee for more than twenty years and credited by the board for building up the collections of Chinese art, his particular interest, died in 1946; and Museum president J. Stogdell Stokes died in 1947.[165] Sturgis Ingersoll, a committed collector of and advocate for modern art, in 1947 was named chair of the museum committee—at this time retitled the board of governors of the Museum—and the following year, president of the Museum (fig. 116). In a message to the Museum membership published in January 1948, Ingersoll wrote of his ambition "to create a focal point of inspiration and encouragement to the contemporary artist, since without contemporary art, the art of the past dies. In our great manufacturing city we must establish ideals of beautiful utility for the products of our looms and other manufactures [sic]."[166] Ingersoll saw Kimball bring three important modern art collections to the Museum: in 1943 that of Pennsylvania-born A. E. Gallatin (acquired permanently on Gallatin's death in 1952), a collection of largely geometric abstractions, including Léger's *The City* (1919) and Picasso's *Three Musicians* (1921); in 1949 photographs, paintings, and works on paper by the celebrated New York photographer and gallery owner Alfred Stieglitz;[167] and finally the collection of Louise and Walter Arensberg, which Kimball secured in 1949 but which came to the Museum only with the deaths of the Arensbergs in 1953 and 1954, respectively. The Arensbergs' gift included paintings by Georges Braque, Marcel Duchamp, and Francis Picabia as well as an outstanding group of sculptures by Constantin Brancusi and an

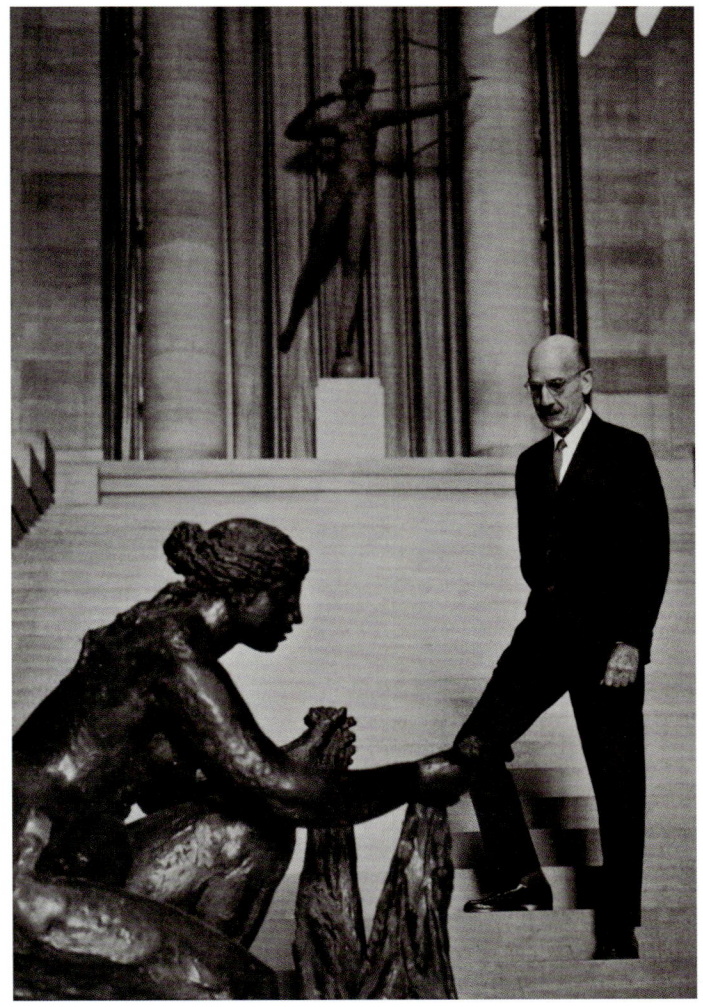

important collection of Pre-Columbian sculpture. Kimball had only recently ceded the field of Pre-Columbian art to the University Museum, but he made a necessary exception of the Arensberg gift.[168]

Kimball's skill in acquiring gifts of such magnitude was needed in the postwar years, as the Museum once again became dependent on city appropriations for capital projects, including completion of unassigned spaces and, in particular, construction of galleries to house the new collections of modern art. In 1947 an organization of professionals concerned with the fashion industry, known as the Fashion Group, assumed the task of securing financial support for the permanent installation and maintenance of galleries that would constitute a Fashion Wing, including in 1951 a contribution from one of its members for a twentieth-century fashion gallery that

Opposite : **115. June Groff** : Fabric (detail) : 1947 : screen-printed linen : W 54" : 1948-13-1 (cat. 78)   Above : **116.** R. Sturgis Ingersoll : Museum president, 1948–64

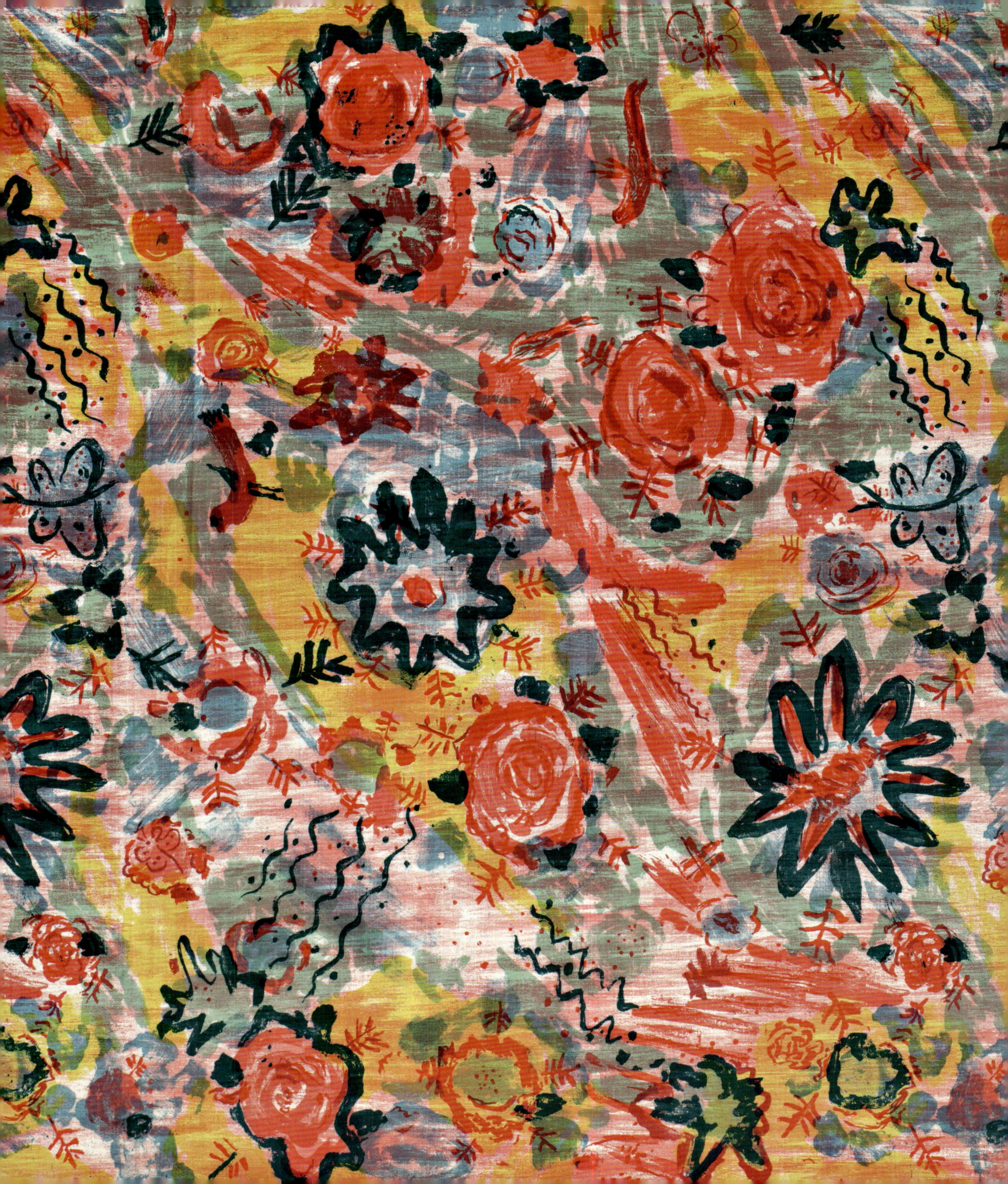

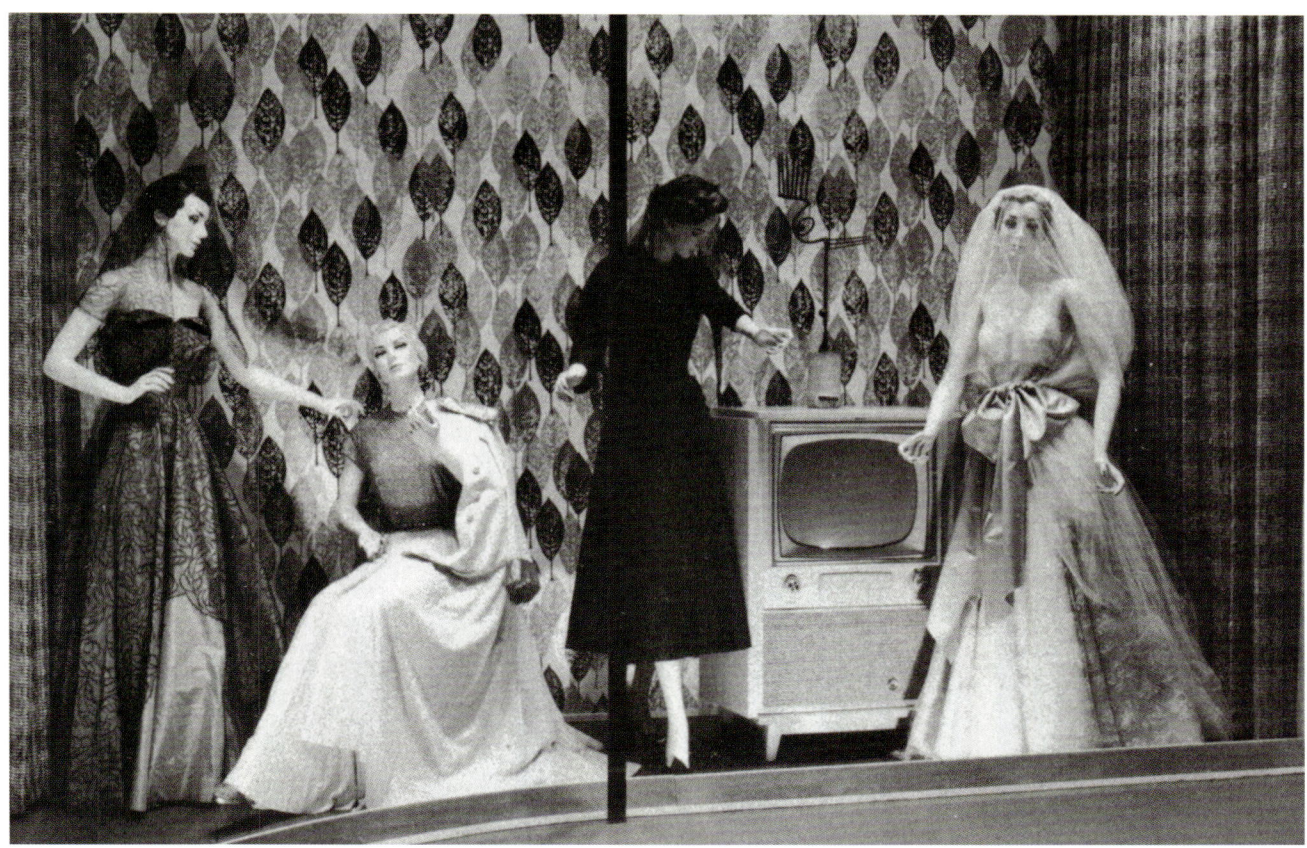

opened in 1953 (fig. 118) decorated with fabrics by June Groff (figs. 115, 117).[169] In fact, the Museum's first Eames chair and first television set were given for the new fashion gallery by the Herman Miller Furniture Company and the Radio Corporation of America, respectively.

While not a significant presence at the Museum during this period, modern industrial design made notable gains in the 1950s and 1960s at the Museum's schools, which had grown rapidly during the war. In 1941 the School of Textiles had been granted authority to award baccalaureate degrees and change its name to the Philadelphia Textile Institute. Lack of studio space and inadequate teaching facilities at its Broad and Pine location became increasingly critical; by 1948 the Textile Institute had broken ground for a new building and taken steps to re-create itself as a legally independent corporation. When the Textile Institute moved in 1950 to its new building on Henry Avenue in the East Falls section of Philadelphia, the Museum and its remaining school—known from 1949 as the Philadelphia Museum School of Art (and after accreditation in 1959 as the Philadelphia Museum College of Art)—were still required to share their city appropriations with the Textile Institute, to assume all of the operating costs of the building at Broad and Pine, and to pay the expenses of retrofitting the old building for single-occupancy use. In little more than a decade, however, the Museum school itself would cite the need to expand its buildings and facilities as one of its most compelling problems,[170] and by 1960 the Philadelphia Museum College of Art (later the Philadelphia College of Art, now the University of the Arts) would consider its own separation from the Museum as a corporate entity.[171]

Pioneering industrial designer Harold Van Doren (who had opened an office in Philadelphia to better serve his clients at Philco, leaders in the radio industry) joined the Museum school's board of governors in 1950 and thereafter acted as advisor to the institution's department of industrial design. In 1953 designer Paul McCobb was appointed coordinating director of the school's interior and industrial

Opposite : **117. June Groff** : Fabric (detail) : 1947 : screen-printed cotton : W 41¼"" : 1948-13-4 (cat. 79)   Above : **118.** 20th-Century Fashion Gallery : Philadelphia Museum of Art : 1953

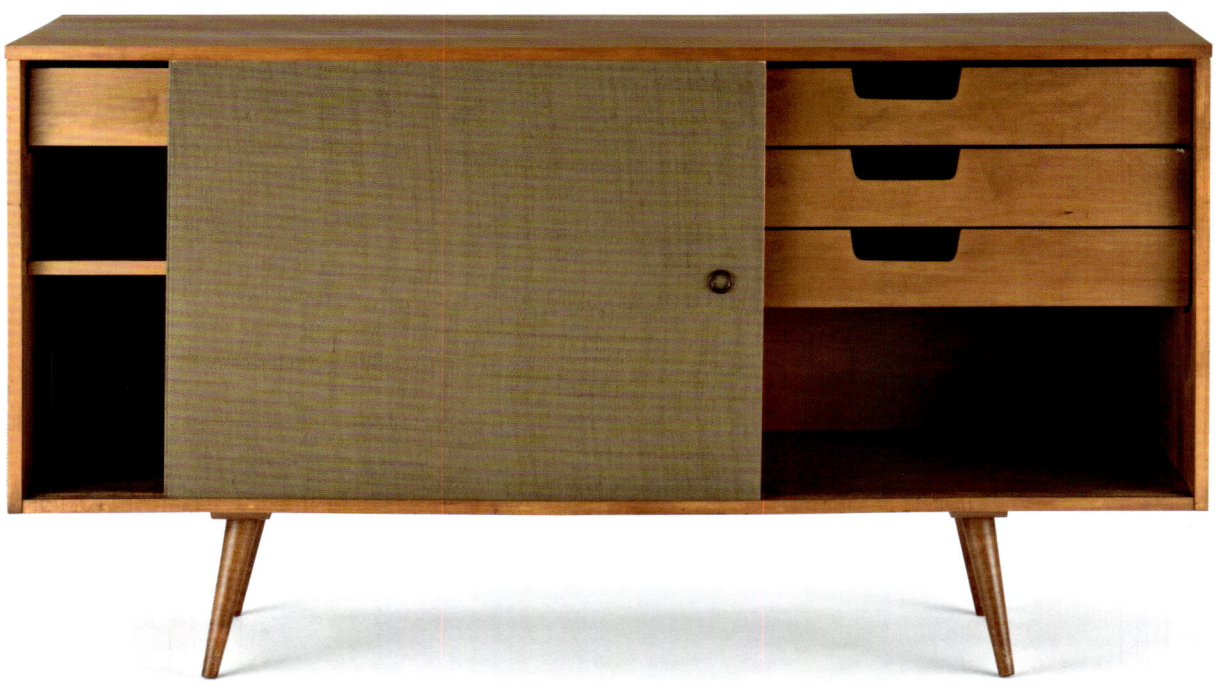

design departments and renovated several interiors on the Broad Street side of the school building. The Museum's annual report noted that he had furnished these spaces with pieces "from the greatest names in contemporary design," providing students "with a healthy, stimulating new look—to live with and learn from."[172] While none of the contemporary furnishings was found worthy of acquisition by the Museum—or perhaps they were simply considered the domain of the school—decades later a number of pieces by McCobb and his contemporaries were acquired (figs. 119, 120), including furniture designed by Marcel Breuer before the war for the James E. Rhoads Residence Hall at Bryn Mawr College outside Philadelphia (fig. 123).

The school also initiated a program of annual design awards for nationally recognized artists and designers, given first to McCobb in 1954 "for his contribution of good design in mass production";[173] followed by photographer Edward Steichen, who delivered the school's commencement address in 1955; the Ford Motor Company in 1956 for its design of the Thunderbird and the Continental Mark II; and designers Walter Dorwin Teague in 1958, Eliot Noyes in 1959, Charles Eames in 1960 ("for making a fine art of furniture and the film"[174]), and George Nelson in 1961.

Meanwhile, after the war Ingersoll and Kimball had expanded the Museum's program of special exhibitions, a particular concern of the board of governors, charging admission fees for some shows and discovering in them additional sources of revenue—most notably the great Vincent van Gogh exhibition held in 1954 and also, less successful but nonetheless significant in a history of the decorative arts at the Museum, an exhibition of jewelry by Salvador Dalí in 1955.[175] Self-supporting special exhibitions

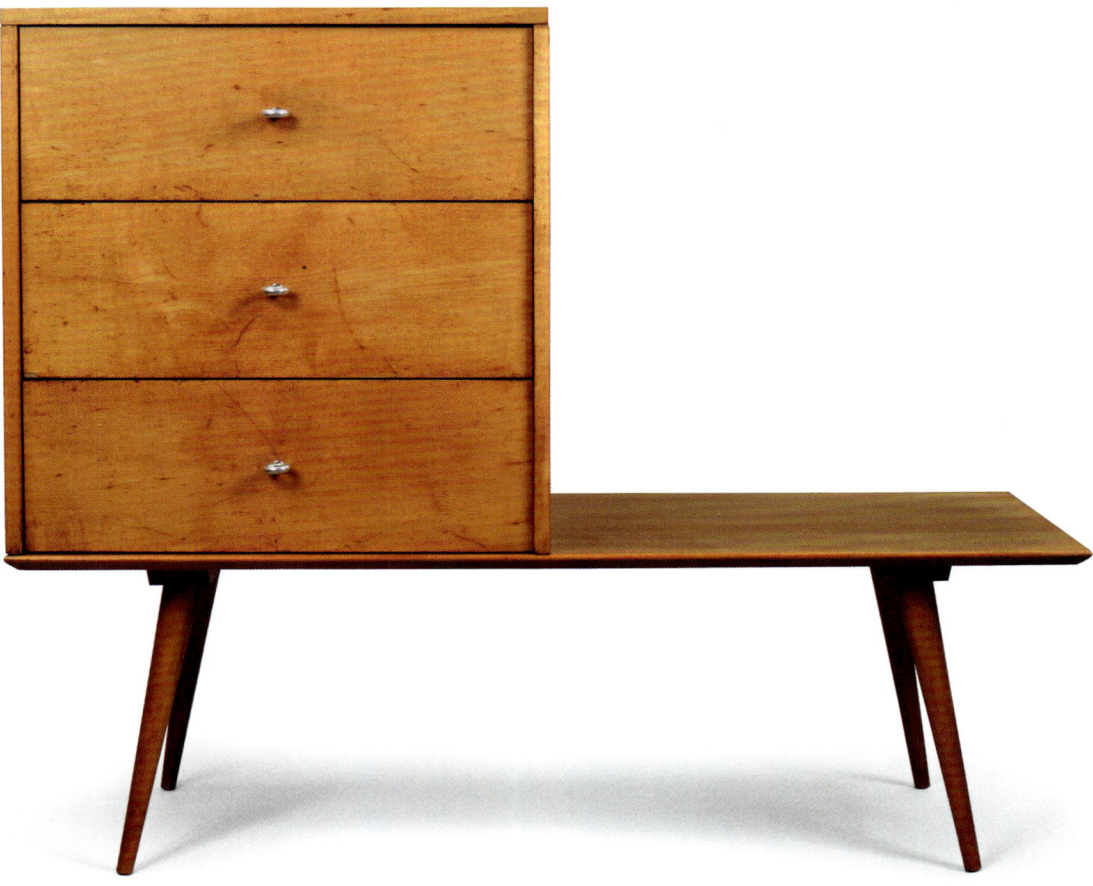

ensured the continuation of the Museum's programs and drew large paying audiences, but in the years after the war Ingersoll nevertheless initiated additional cost-saving and income-producing measures, which included charging rental fees for traveling exhibitions, abandoning separate publication of the annual report in 1948 (it was included until 1980 in the Museum's *Bulletin*), liquidating purchase loans related to the Barnard and Foulc collections (1950 and 1952), and continuing the disposal of "excess" objects from Memorial Hall under pressure from the Fairmount Park Commission to vacate the building "expeditiously."[176] The final sales of works of art from the Museum's collections at Memorial Hall—the largest sales in the institution's history—were held there over several days in October 1954; net proceeds from the decorative arts were $44,925.01.[177] Still, in the same month the Museum succeeded in opening on Fairmount twenty-eight new galleries for modern art to house the Gallatin and Arensberg collections (figs. 121, 122). "There are two schools of thought as to the ultimate distinction of twentieth-century art," Ingersoll commented. "If it be great art, as we believe it is, the fame of our museum will be unequalled with respect to the period."[178]

In January 1955 Ingersoll officially announced to the board of trustees that Fiske Kimball would take a leave of absence, to be followed by his resignation. Elected director emeritus, Kimball was replaced by his longtime associate, Henri Marceau, first as acting director, then as director. Kimball had been behaving erratically for many months, a condition culminating in the strokes and heart attack that would cause his death the following summer. In addition, Kimball's wife and closest supporter, Marie, in failing health, would die two months after Kimball's resignation. In the news release announcing Kimball's departure, Ingersoll described the modern wing of the Museum housing the Arensberg and Gallatin collections

Opposite : **119. Paul McCobb** : for Winchendon Furniture : *Planner Group* Buffet : 1949 : birch, *Madagaska* plastic-coated cloth : L 60" : 1999-106-4 (cat. 125)   Above : **120. Paul McCobb** : for Winchendon Furniture : *Planner Group* Bench and Chest of Drawers : 1949 : maple : L (bench) 48" : H (chest) 24" : 1983-5-2,3 (cat. 124)

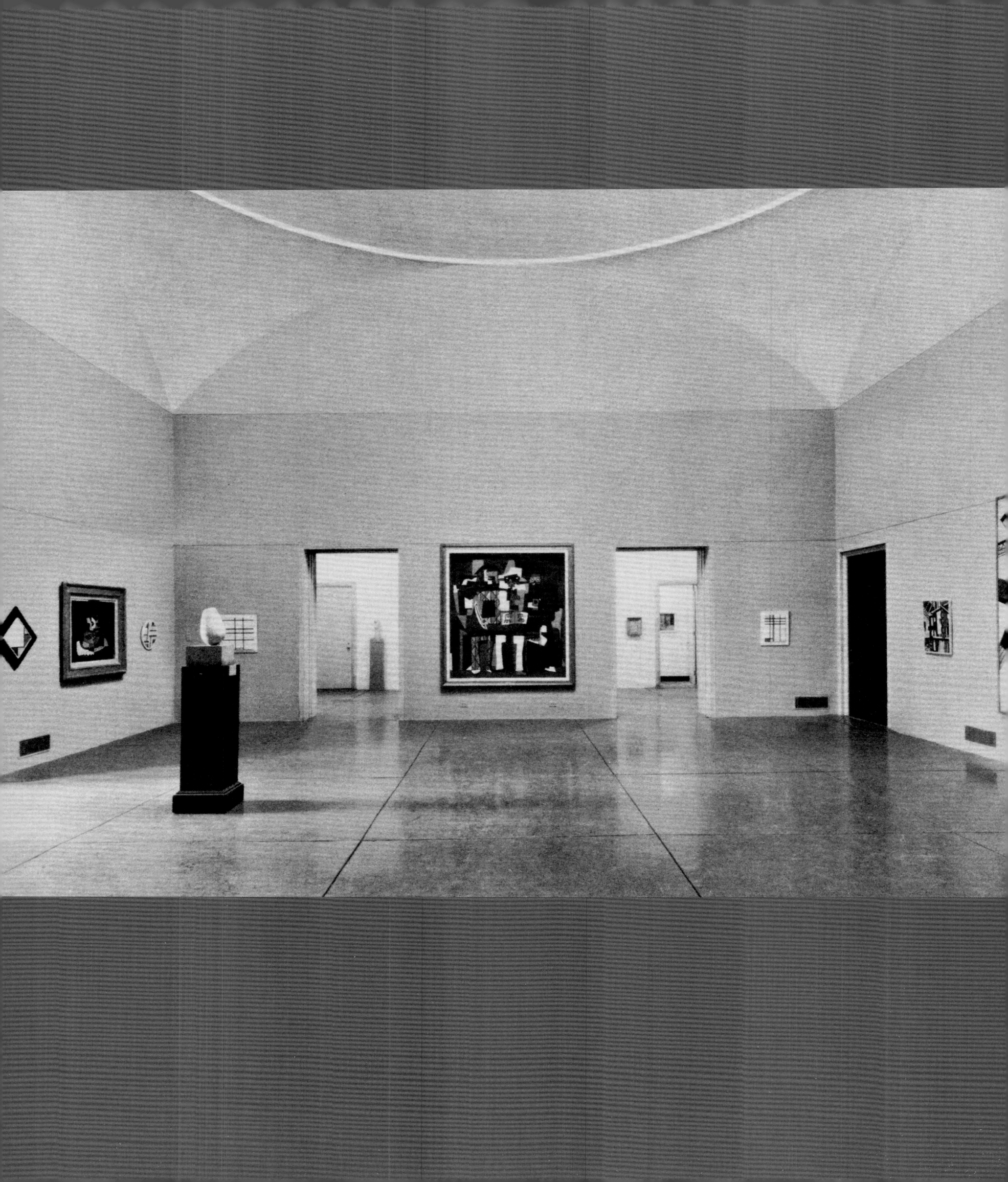

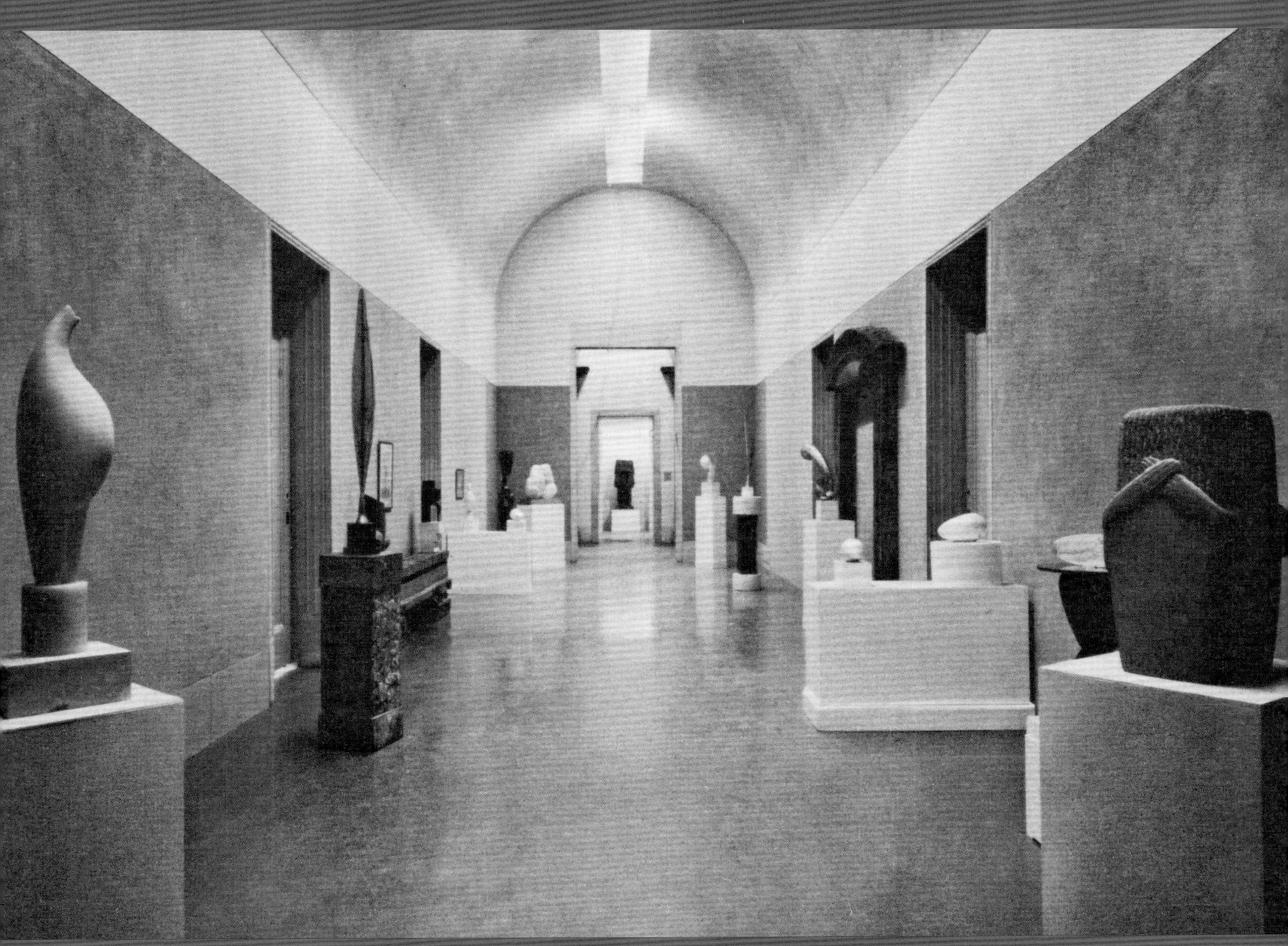

Opposite : **121.** Gallatin Collection : Philadelphia Museum of Art : 1954   Above : **122.** Arensberg Collection : Philadelphia Museum of Art : 1954

as "the culmination of Mr. Kimball's distinguished accomplishment."[179] In one of his last letters, Kimball seemed to agree with that assessment, writing Marceau from Florence: "My first reaction, in the great Botticelli room [of the Uffizi], was how right Sturgis is in saying we can never buck the European museums. . . . All this is why we have a chance, scooping everyone but Basel on the 20th century."[180] It would take another half-century before the design collections could share in the Museum's modernist reputation. Kimball died in Munich in August 1955. A memorial tribute, written by Horace Jayne and Henri Marceau, stressed not only his heroic accomplishment in "making a museum out of a mole hill,"[181] but that he remained (like Edwin Atlee Barber) a publishing scholar of great distinction until his death.[182]

Marceau was a trained architect, like Kimball, and had been closely involved with the completion of the Museum's interior spaces, while remaining chief of the division of painting and sculpture and curator of the Johnson Collection. Continuing Kimball's building program throughout his tenure as director, Marceau began in the Museum's south wing with the installation of the Japanese temple, Japanese tea house and garden, Chinese temple, and Chinese scholar's study, all acquired decades earlier. He also oversaw completion of the Great Stair Hall, the auditorium underneath it, and an area at the head of the stairs reserved for the arms and armor collection of Otto von Kienbusch, secured by Kimball in 1951–52 and bequeathed to the Museum by Kienbusch in 1977.

Curator Henry McIlhenny, long encouraged by the board to organize a major exhibition,[183] chose to concentrate his later career on eighteenth- and nineteenth-century Philadelphia subjects, with shows in 1952–53 on the furniture makers Henry Connelly and Ephraim Haines, in 1956 on Philadelphia silver (assisted by board of governors member and collector Walter Jeffords), and in 1957 on Tucker porcelain, as well as an exhibition on Shaker arts and crafts in 1962.[184] McIlhenny also was responsible for the installation of a wing of American decorative arts, which opened in November 1958 and included American and European silver, eighteenth-century Philadelphia furniture, and the arts of rural Pennsylvania. In his last annual departmental report before retiring at the end of 1963, he made clear the collecting priorities he had pursued: "It has long been the policy of the Department that Philadelphiana must be given especial attention, and the retiring curators have long felt that Philadelphia furniture, silver and other works of art of local origin must be acquired, even to the neglect of European objects that sorely tempted their acquisitive desires."[185]

The years 1963 and 1964 represented a watershed period in the history of the Museum's staffing.[186] Not only did McIlhenny retire as curator of decorative arts after a thirty-year tenure—"his enduring monument," noted Ingersoll, "is our Collection of Decorative Arts and its installation"[187]—but Louis C. Madeira, the department's associate curator, retired as well; McIlhenny was then elected to the board of trustees, and Madeira to the board of governors. Most notably, Henri Marceau asked to be retired as director; cited by the Museum as "Fiske Kimball's right arm" and successor, he "had endeared himself to multitudes, from charwomen to mayors . . . [and] played an important role in substantially every artistic activity in his adopted city of Philadelphia."[188]

While the administration of the Museum underwent major changes, the committee structure of the board was reorganized in 1964. Sturgis Ingersoll retired as president of the Museum to serve as chair of the board of trustees, and his place as principal officer of the corporation and board was taken by Bonnie Wintersteen. The corporation's bylaws were amended to include standing committees focused on specific executive and administrative concerns as well as curatorial areas. According to the bylaws of 1964–65, new curatorial departmental committees, including a committee for decorative arts, would function in an advisory capacity to the president and director with respect to the Museum's programs and projects pertaining to their

123. **Marcel Breuer** : Desk and Chair for Bryn Mawr College : 1938 : maple plywood : L (desk) 50" : H (chair) 33 1/2" : 1999-11-1–3 (cat. 24)

respective fields.[189] Although as early as 1941 the museum committee had agreed in principle to subdivide into additional committees organized by discipline—paintings, prints, Eastern art, and decorative arts[190]—and some of these subcommittees subsequently met, it was only with the amended bylaws that the departmental committees became officially recognized.[191] The first chair of the new decorative arts committee was trustee Fitz Eugene Dixon, Jr., nephew of (and later heir to) George D. Widener, the Museum's outgoing chair of the board of trustees, both of whom supported the department's tapestry-conservation program.[192] Other members of the committee included Louis Madeira, Henry McIlhenny, Williamina de Schauensee, and two distinguished collectors of American art, H. Richard Dietrich, Jr., and Robert L. McNeil, Jr.

In 1964 the board of governors and the board of trustees were consolidated into a single, fifty-seven-member board,[193] with an executive committee empowered to act for the board, resulting in a more efficient division of labor, and in essence ushering the Museum into the modern age and its present corporate structure. That same year the school, now college, received independent corporate status, separating from the Museum to which it had been attached since 1876. At a special meeting of the board to consider and act upon the division of the college and the Museum, it was pointed out that "persons interested in supporting the school . . . often have little interest in supporting the Museum; just as those interested in the Museum often have little interest in the College."[194] Separated from the activities of the college, the Museum would soon become a center for all modern and contemporary arts in its own right.

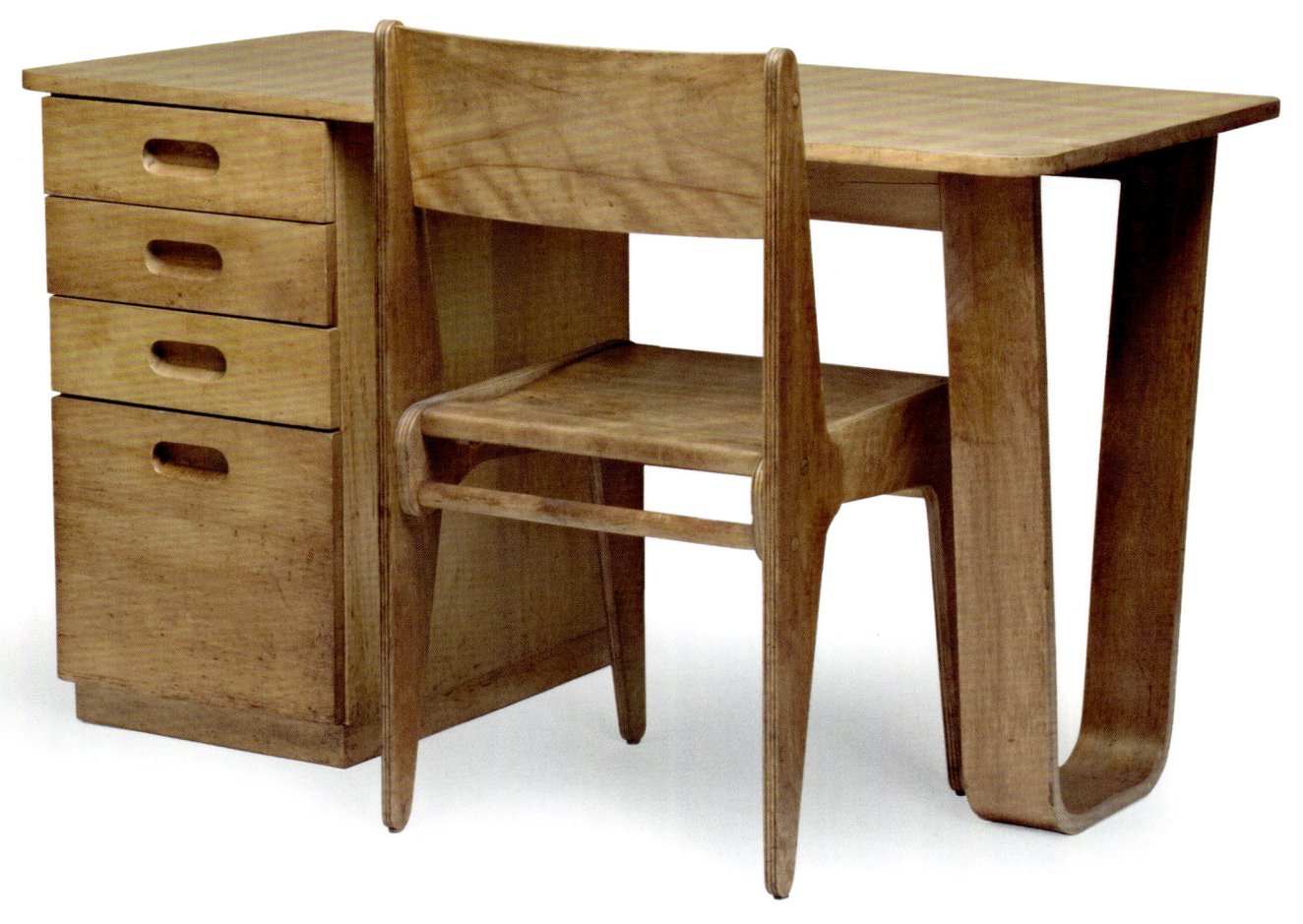

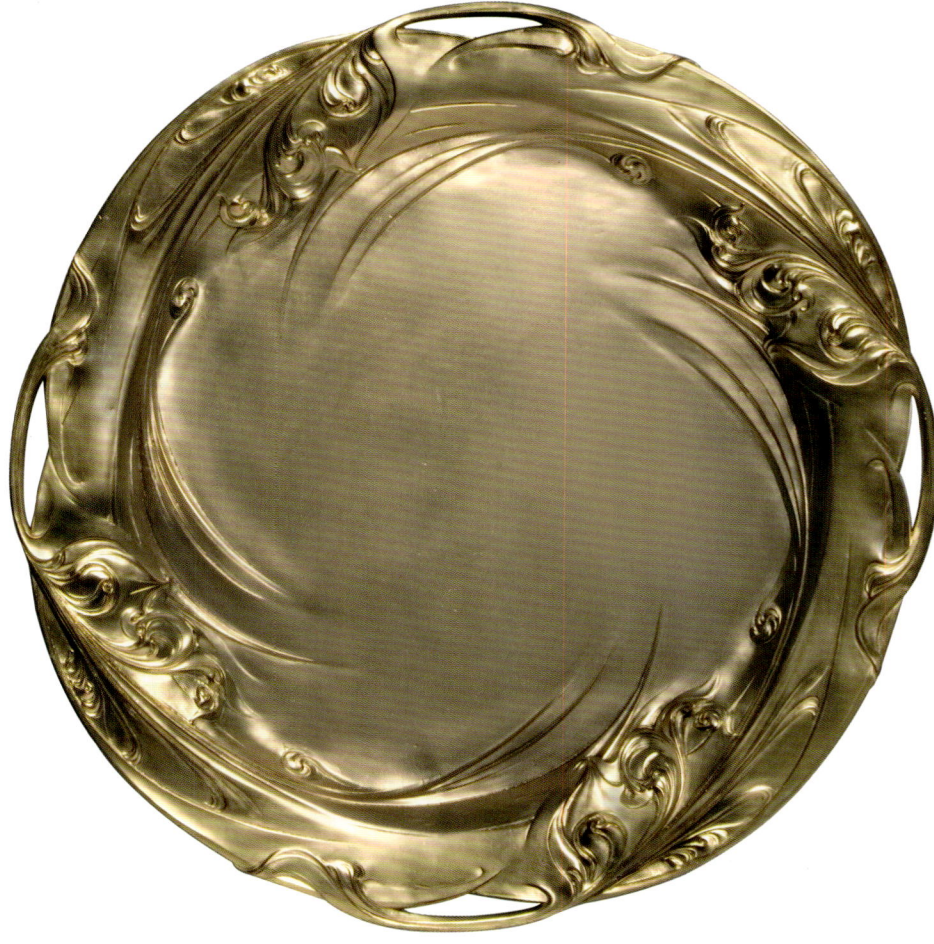

1. In 1911 plans for the new parkway were exhibited to the board of trustees by the Museum's president Theodore Search, and a motion to apply for a site on the parkway was approved; Board of Trustees Records, Minutes, January 12, 1911.

2. Leslie W. Miller, "Removal to the Parkway," *Bulletin of the Pennsylvania Museum*, vol. 15, no. 57 (January 1917): pp. 12–13. As administrator of Fairmount Park, the commission oversaw all construction and was also responsible for the new museum's public funding, as well as for covering the expenses and wages of certain employees, including guards, engineers, and electricians. As the secretary of the Fairmount Park Art Association, which had supported the design of the parkway, and a member of Philadelphia's Art Jury that eventually approved the design of the Museum, Miller was well placed to lobby for a new, larger building, as were a number of Museum board and committee members who served variously and sometimes simultaneously as park commissioners and members of the Fairmount Park Art Association, the Art Jury, and the City Parks Association—public and private organizations concerned with Philadelphia city planning and the arts. In addition, lawyer Eli Kirk Price, member of one of Philadelphia's oldest Quaker families, was elected in 1917 to the Museum's board of trustees while serving as vice president and commissioner of Fairmount Park, member of the City Parks Association, and member of the Art Jury. At the same time Stotesbury was president of the Park Commission, appointed to represent the commissioners on the Museum board of trustees.

3. The Wilstach bequest to the city of some 150 paintings (administered by the commissioners of Fairmount Park) in 1893, and later by pictures added through purchases from the Wilstach Fund, first raised issues of crowding. As a commissioner of Fairmount Park, lawyer John G. Johnson had responsibility for the Wilstach Collection and wrote the Museum more than once about obtaining wall space for it in Memorial Hall; see, for example, Board of Trustees Records, Museum Committee, Minutes, February 1, 1904, and December 27, 1906. Johnson's own important art collection was bequeathed to the city at his death in 1917.

4. R. Sturgis Ingersoll, "Writings on Sculpture," undated typescript, pp. 16, 17; R. Sturgis Ingersoll Records.

5. Thanks are owed to Perry Benson, Jr., grandson of Sturgis Ingersoll, for sharing his photographic record of the Ingersoll residences.

6. "Announcement," *Bulletin of the Pennsylvania Museum*, vol. 15, no. 59 (October 1917): p. 33.

7. "Report of the Museum," in *Annual Report, The Pennsylvania Museum and School of Industrial Art* [year ending May 31, 1919] (Philadelphia, 1919), p. 18.

8. Board of Trustees Records, Museum Committee, Minutes, December 3, 1917.

9. Board of Trustees Records, Museum Committee, Minutes, February 3, 1919. Warner traveled to Siberia and Japan on behalf of the United States Department of State.

10. Ibid., January 7, 1918. On Hamilton Bell and the Johnson Collection, see Carl Brandon Strehlke, *Italian Paintings, 1250–1450, in the John G. Johnson Collection and the Philadelphia Museum of Art* (Philadelphia: Philadelphia Museum of Art in association with Pennsylvania State University Press, 2004), p. 19n39.

11. Board of Trustees Records, Museum Committee, Minutes, January 7, 1918.

12. Board of Trustees Records, Museum Committee, Minutes, March 5, 1918.

13. Morris to Barber, December 9, 1914, Edwin Atlee Barber Records, Correspondence with Morris, Jenks, Miller, and Allan; emphasis in the original.

14. Board of Trustees Records, Museum Committee, Minutes, February 3, 1919. As a condition of his leave, Warner had been charged by the board with the acquisition of objects for the collections, and he reported that while abroad he had secured "one of the finest stone Chinese heads that is known and a rare and early Korean painting of the first quarter of the XV century"; ibid.

15. Board of Trustees Records, Museum Committee, Minutes, March 3, 1919. The Museum also announced that the "process of elimination is to go on until the South entrance no longer blocks the visitor and gives him a first impression of clutter and baulked [sic] vision," and that it hoped to present the collections at Memorial Hall "in as orderly manner as possible," after retiring "several thousand objects" from public view. "Report of the Museum," in *Annual Report* [1919], p. 15.

16. "Report of the Museum" [1919], pp. 15–16.

17. Board of Trustees Records, Museum Committee, Minutes, April 7, 1919.

18. "Report of the Museum," in *Annual Report, Pennsylvania Museum and School of Industrial Art* [year ending May 31, 1920] (Philadelphia, 1920), p. 14. "At a single stroke [the gift] made us pre-eminent in America and Europe for Indian architecture"; ibid.

19. Ibid, p. 13.

20. Board of Trustees Records, Minutes, May 12, 1921.

21. H.H.F.J. [Horace Jayne], "The Georgian Room," *Bulletin of the Pennsylvania Museum*, vol. 17, no. 71 (May 1922): p. 9.

22. Langdon Warner, "Standard in the Museum," *Bulletin of the Pennsylvania Museum*, vol. 17, no. 65 (February 1920): pp. 24–25.

23. The Museum had lobbied with the AFA in 1913 to remove tariffs on art entering the United States, Barber serving as the Museum's delegate to the convention held in Washington, D.C., for that purpose; Board of Trustees Records, Minutes, April 10, 1913.

24. Elihu Root, United States Secretary of State, convention proceedings, May 11–13, 1909, Washington, D.C., quoted in American Federation of Arts, overview, www.afaweb.org/about. It was at this convention that the American Federation of Arts was formed.

25. "American Handicrafts Exhibition," *Bulletin of the Pennsylvania Museum*, vol. 18, no. 73 (January 1923): p. 15. *Exhibition of American Handicrafts Assembled and Circulated by the American Federation of Arts* was on view at the Museum December 5–25, 1922.

26. Board of Trustees Records, Museum Committee, Minutes, December 4, 1922. The Museum supplemented

the AFA exhibition with works from Philadelphia craftsmen, according to Langdon Warner, "increasing the size of the exhibition by more than a third, and its quality very considerably.... A space of twenty linear feet, 10 feet high, was allotted to the ironwork lent by Mr. Yellin ... and the city may well be proud of his showing and that of Mr. [Nicola] D'Ascenzo and Mrs. [Anne Lee] Willett [sic] in stained glass."

27. Ibid.

28. "John Cotton Dana Dies in 73d Year," obituary, *New York Times*, July 22, 1929, p. 18. "Beauty," Dana once wrote, "has no relation to age, rarity, or price" (sounding like Langdon Warner, although approaching modernism from the other direction); quoted in H. M., "Art for the People's Sake: The Newark Museum's Idea," *New York Times*, April 20, 1924, p. xx12.

29. The Deutsches Museum had been founded in 1910 by Karl Ernst Osthaus in association with the Deutscher Werkbund. *German Applied Arts* was shown at at the Saint Louis Art Museum, the Art Institute of Chicago, and the Carnegie Institute in Pittsburgh before opening in New York at the National Arts Club. The *New York Times* reported that "wherever it was shown it aroused great interest, and the criticisms in all cities were highly complimentary to the excellence shown in the production of the objects"; "German Art Exhibit Here," *New York Times*, March 7, 1913, p. 11.

30. Warner to A. W. Kendall, October 13, 1922, Langdon Warner Records, Correspondence.

31. Board of Trustees Records, Executive Committee, Minutes, November 11, 1915.

32. John Cotton Dana, *Newark, N.J., the Industrial City, Has Her Own Museums* (Newark, NJ: The Newark Museum Association, 1921).

33. Board of Trustees Records, Museum Committee, Minutes, May 3, 1920. Warner reported that he hoped to make "an interesting and in fact unique Oriental room," to purchase French scenic wallpapers as interiors for the exhibition of American furniture, and to obtain a "fine wooden paneled American interior." Board of Trustees Records, Museum Committee, Minutes, June 7, 1920.

34. Board of Trustees Records, Museum Committee, Minutes, June 5, 1922. Privately, Warner wrote to McIlhenny, "I need to emphasize to you the pressing need of such a person"; Warner to John D. McIlhenny, Warner Records, Correspondence, September 27, 1922.

35. Board of Trustees Records, Museum Committee, Minutes, February 5, 1923. Warner told the board that his regret was "tempered by ... the really extraordinary advances that have taken place under Mr. McIlhenny's chairmanship [of the Museum Committee] and [which under his] Presidency will be even more marked and rapid in the future. I like to think that it was during my directorship that we have inaugurated one of the great Oriental departments of the country, having procured an invaluable collection of the textiles of the Nearer East, have brought the Museum Bulletin from obscurity to a high rank among such publications and have carried on Dr. Barber's reputation for scholarship in fields, which, with his limited means, he had no chance to enter."

36. Board of Trustees Records, Museum Committee Minutes, March 5, 1923. McIlhenny praised Warner's "excellent rearrangement of [the Museum's] collections and ... the high standard of taste and quality which actuated him"; *Annual Report, Pennsylvania Museum and School of Industrial Art* [year ending May 31, 1923] (Philadelphia, 1923), p. 11.

37. John D. McIlhenny to Samuel W. Woodhouse, April 3, 1923, Samuel W. Woodhouse, Jr., Records, Director Correspondence.

38. Woodhouse to McIlhenny, September 22, 1923, Woodhouse Records, Director Correspondence.

39. Woodhouse to Richard Bach, January 23, 1925; April 17, 1925; and May 28, 1925; Woodhouse Records, Director Correspondence.

40. Board of Trustees Records, Museum Committee, Minutes, April 6, 1925.

41. Ibid.

42. See *Annual Report, Pennsylvania Museum and School of Industrial Art* [year ending May 31, 1923] (Philadelphia, 1923), p. 15.

43. See *Annual Report, Pennsylvania Museum and School of Industrial Art* [year ending May 31, 1925] (Philadelphia, 1925), p. 17. Paintings curator Arthur Edwin Bye organized this and other exhibitions of prints, prior to the arrival of Boies Penrose as the Museum's first curator of prints.

44. Fiske Kimball, "Opportunity Knocks," manuscript dated October 24, 1933, pp. b–c, Fiske Kimball Papers, Writings and Research, Memoirs.

45. Kimball to McIlhenny, April 24, 1924, Kimball Papers, Writings and Research, Memoirs.

46. Kimball, untitled and undated manuscript, pp. a, d; Kimball Papers, Writings and Research, Memoirs.

47. Ibid.

48. Board of Trustees Records, Museum Committee, Minutes, November 2, 1925.

49. McIlhenny was eulogized in the Museum's *Bulletin* for his "taste which had made him internationally known as a collector" as well as "the ability and judgment which had made him prominent in the world of business," qualities that "bore their fruits in the skill and success with which he administered the affairs of the institution"; "In Memoriam: John D. McIlhenny," *Bulletin of the Pennsylvania Museum*, vol. 21, no. 99 (January 1926): p. 67.

50. Woodhouse to McIlhenny, March 3, 1925, Woodhouse Records, Director Correspondence.

51. International Exposition of Modern Decorative and Industrial Art, *Report of Commission* (Washington, D.C., 1925), p. 16.

52. "Report of the Director of the Museum," in *Annual Report, The Pennsylvania Museum and School of Industrial Art* [year ending May 31, 1927] (Philadelphia, 1927), p. 22.

53. Joseph Downs, "Loan Exhibition of Modern Decorative Arts," *Bulletin of the Pennsylvania Museum*, vol. 22, no. 107 (November 1926): p. 253.

54. Joseph Downs, "A Buffet in the Contemporary Style," *Bulletin of the Pennsylvania Museum*, vol. 24, no. 126 (March 1929): p. 19.

55. Joseph Downs, "The International Exhibition of Ceramic Art," *Bulletin of the Pennsylvania Museum*, vol. 24, no. 122 (October–November 1928): p. 9. The exhibition was on view November 14–December 12, 1928.

56. Board of Trustees Records, Museum Committee, Minutes, December 4, 1928.

57. It was at this time that paintings from the William L. Elkins collection, together with suitable furniture, ceramics, and textiles from Memorial Hall, were installed in temporary galleries in the "Philadelphia Museum of Art." *Annual Report, Pennsylvania Museum and School of Industrial Art* [year ending May 31, 1925] (Philadelphia, 1925), p. 16. These works were later joined by paintings from the collection of George W. Elkins, William's son and heir, fulfilling the terms of his will and bringing the title of these collections to the Museum through his specific legatee, the city of Philadelphia.

58. "Report of the Board of Trustees," in *Annual Report, Pennsylvania Museum and School of Industrial Art* [year ending May 31, 1928] (Philadelphia, 1928), p. 15.

59. "Annual Report, July 1, 1977–June 30, 1978," *Philadelphia Museum of Art Bulletin*, vol. 74, no. 323 (December 1978): p. 20.

60. Fiske Kimball, "An Opportunity and an Obligation," *Bulletin of the Pennsylvania Museum*, vol. 23, no. 115 (October 1927): p. 3. Kimball elaborated his programmatic theories of museum planning in several articles, among them: Fiske Kimball, "The Museum of the Future," *Creative Art*, vol. 4 (April 1929): pp. xxxvi–xliii; "Planning the Art Museum," *Architectural Record*, vol. 66 (December 1929): pp. 582–90; and "The Modern Museum of Art," *Architectural Record*, vol. 66 (December 1929): pp. 559–80.

61. *Bulletin of the Pennsylvania Museum*, vol. 23, no. 117 (December 1927–January 1928): pp. 4–5.

62. Ibid, p. 6.

63. Board of Trustees Records, Museum Committee, Minutes, September 14, 1926.

64. Board of Trustees Records, Museum Committee, Minutes, November 1, 1927.

65. Board of Trustees Records, Museum Committee, Minutes, April 3, 1928.

66. Richard F. Bach, "A Philadelphian Acropolis: The New Building of the Pennsylvania Museum," *Bulletin of the*

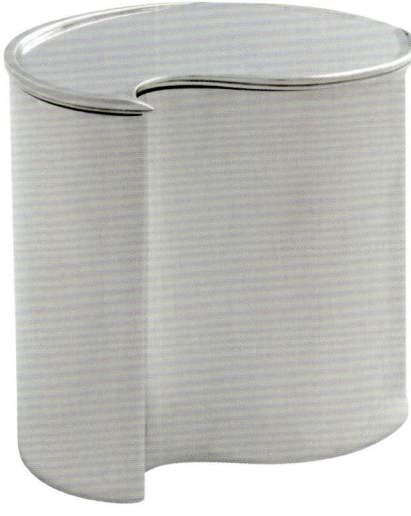

Opposite : **124. Hector Guimard** : Tray : 1909 : gilt copper : D 18 1/2" : 1949-43-1 (cat. 80)   Above : **125. Virginia Wireman Cute** : Cigarette Box : 1949 : silver : W 3 5/16" : 1970-202-1 (cat. 41)

Metropolitan Museum of Art, vol. 23, no. 6 (June 1926): pp. 160, 162.

67. Katharine Martinez and Page Talbott, eds., *Philadelphia's Cultural Landscape: The Sartain Family Legacy* (Philadelphia: Temple University Press, 2000), p. 181.

68. See Innis Howe Shoemaker, *Mad for Modernism: Earl Horter and His Collection* (Philadelphia: Philadelphia Museum of Art, 1999).

69. Many of these contemporary works were subsequently acquired from the lenders by gift, bequest, or purchase.

70. Fiske Kimball Records, General Correspondence, 1929–30, Fogg Art Museum, Philadelphia Museum of Art, Archives. A copy (not completed) of the Harvard society's membership application is preserved with Kimball's papers in the archives of the Philadelphia Museum of Art.

71. Nicholas Fox Weber, *Patron Saints: Five Rebels Who Opened America to a New Art, 1928–1943* (New York: Knopf, 1992), p. 41.

72. Sybil Gordon Kantor, *Alfred H. Barr, Jr. and the Intellectual Origins of the Museum of Modern Art* (Cambridge, MA: MIT Press, 2002), p. 206.

73. Kimball to Paul J. Sachs, February 10, 1930, Kimball Records, General Correspondence, 1929–30, Fogg Art Museum, Philadelphia Museum of Art, Archives.

74. Kimball to George Howe, June 22, 1934, Kimball Records, General Correspondence, 1933–37.

75. Board of Trustees Records, Museum Committee, Minutes, January 8, 1929.

76. Board of Trustees Records, Museum Committee, Minutes, April 2, 1929. The installation of the Louis Rodman Page Gallery of Miniatures at the Museum later recognized Mr. Page's subscription; see *Annual Report, Philadelphia Museum of Art* [year ending May 31, 1942] (Philadelphia, 1942), p. 15.

77. Board of Trustees Records, Museum Committee Minutes, September 10, 1929.

78. Kimball to Georges Fouquet, July 6, 1929, Kimball Records, General Correspondence, 1929–30.

79. Board of Trustees Records, Museum Committee, Minutes, November 5, 1929.

80. Kimball to Earl Horter, June 12, 1930, Kimball Records, General Correspondence, 1929–30.

81. As Brodovitch later recalled, "All three Jenks came to see me in Paris in 1928, and asked me to take Ann to museums, exhibits, lectures, etc., etc. connected with art. Ann was sixteen at the time. She studied in Philadelphia with Henry McCart[er]"; Alexey Brodovitch to Charles Coiner, October 5, 1962, Charles T. Coiner Collection, Correspondence 1962 (July–December), II, Syracuse University Library, Syracuse, New York.

82. "I was very closely associated with the school and the family Jenks all this time," wrote Brodovitch of his career in Philadelphia, ". . . and Ann Jenks participated in many projects"; ibid.

83. Marceau replaced Arthur Edwin Bye as curator of paintings, who had left to pursue his more lucrative outside interests in art dealing and painting conservation. Bye also taught at the Museum school. As concurrent curator of the Johnson collection, Marceau would oversee the collection's move to the Museum in 1933.

84. "Report of the Board of Trustees," in *Annual Report, Pennsylvania Museum of Art* [year ending May 31, 1930] (Philadelphia, 1930), p. 15. On the acquisition of the Foulc Collection, see Kathryn B. Hiesinger, "Fiske Kimball and the Collection of Edmond Foulc," *Hommage à Hubert Landais. Art, objets d'art, collections* (Paris: Blanchard, 1987), pp. 238–42.

85. *Annual Report, Philadelphia Museum of Art* [year ending May 31, 1948] (Philadelphia, 1948), p. 14: "It was a proud moment for the Museum . . . last fall when J. Stogdell Stokes . . . could announce that the last payment on our purchase of the Foulc collection had been made to banks." The balance due to underwriters of the loan was liquidated in 1952; Board of Trustees Records, Minutes, October 1, 1952.

86. "Report of the Director of the Museum," in *Annual Report* [1930], p. 17.

87. "Estimated Cost of Objects in the Edmond Foulc Collection," February 26, 1930, Fiske Kimball Records, Writings and Research: Memoirs.

88. "Report of the Board of Trustees," in *Annual Report, Pennsylvania Museum of Art* [year ending May 31, 1931] (Philadelphia, 1931), p. 15.

89. "Report of the Director of the Museum," in ibid., p. 28.

90. The painting (acc. no.1957-1-1) is now credited as a Wilstach Fund acquisition of 1957, at which time it was "sold" to the Wilstach Collection so that another work of art could be purchased with Elkins Fund income.

91. Board of Trustees Records, Museum Committee, Minutes, January 26, 1931.

92. Eli Kirk Price and Fiske Kimball to the Carnegie Corporation, March 16, 1931, Kimball Records, General Correspondence, 1929–30. Support was also provided by John H. McClatchy, a major developer of Upper Darby.

93. Frederick P. Keppel to Kimball, p. 6 of enclosed memorandum, August 20, 1930, Kimball Records, General Correspondence, 1929–30.

94. Kimball to Helen Plumb, American Federation of Arts, February 5, 1931, Kimball Records, General Correspondence, 1931–32.

95. *Living Artists*, November 20, 1931–January 1, 1932.

96. *Design for the Machine: Contemporary Industrial Art*, February 20–March 20, 1932.

97. C. R. Richards, "Introduction," *Design for the Machine*, exh. cat. (Philadelphia: Pennsylvania Museum of Art, 1932), unpaginated.

98. Steven Rouland and Roger W. Rouland, *Heywood-

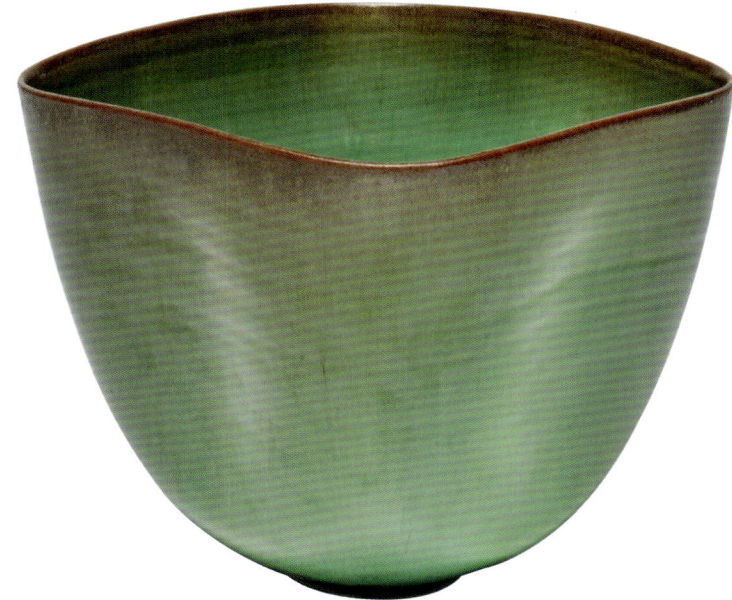

Wakefield Modern Furniture (Paducah, KY: Collector Books), pp. 18–21.

99. Joseph Downs, "Design for the Machine," *Bulletin of the Pennsylvania Museum*, vol. 27, no. 147 (March 1932): p. 166.

100. Board of Trustees Records, Museum Committee, Minutes, March 28, 1932.

101. Walter Rendell Storey, "Linking Beauty to Machine Products," *New York Times Magazine*, March 6, 1932, p. 14.

102. "Art of the Machine to Have 'Fair Show,'" *Springfield* (MA) *Republican*, February 21, 1932.

103. At the Philadelphia Museum of Art the exhibition was titled *Museum of Modern Art: Modern Architectural Exhibition*, on view March 20–April 30, 1932. Shortly after the show closed in Philadelphia, an exhibition titled *Philadelphia International Salon of Photography*, organized by Philip Youtz, opened at the Museum's Sixty-ninth Street branch. In the Museum *Bulletin*, Youtz noted that photography had become an art in its own right, and that although no such salon had taken place in Philadelphia for thirty years, the city had played an important part in the development of American photography, with the oldest camera organization in the country (the Philadelphia Photographic Society) and the first photographic publications; Philip N. Youtz, "The Philadelphia International Salon of Photography," *Bulletin of the Pennsylvania Museum*, vol. 27, no. 148 (April 1932): p. 139.

104. Erling H. Pedersen to George Howe, July 28, 1931, Kimball Records, General Correspondence, 1931–32.

105. Kimball to Howe, October 6, 1931, Kimball Records, General Correspondence, 1931–32: "When I returned in early September, I found how extremely kind you and Lescaze had been in the matter of designing furniture for our children's room. . . . Naturally we are very much embarrassed, after all the trouble Lescaze went to in the matter, not to make good with the execution, which would have delighted us so much."

106. Fiske Kimball, "The Task of the Museum," *Bulletin of the Pennsylvania Museum*, vol. 28, no. 154 (March 1933): p. 59.

107. Kimball to Paul J. Sachs, January 7, 1932, Kimball Records, General Correspondence, 1931–32.

108. Kimball to Sachs, January 2, 1932, Kimball Records, General Correspondence, 1931–32. Sachs condoled, "I can imagine how you must feel that as a result of the drastic economic program of the City Council you are forced to discharge so many excellent people from your staff. The same mail . . . brought me a letter with similar news from my good friend, Beaumont Newhall. I shall try to be helpful in both cases." Sachs to Kimball, January 4, 1932, Kimball Records, General Correspondence, 1931–32. Newhall moved to the Museum of Modern Art in 1935, becoming its first curator of photography in 1940.

109. At the Metropolitan Museum of Art, Downs became the first curator of the newly established American Wing in 1934, and remained at the museum until 1949, when he was hired by Henry Francis duPont as curator of the Winterthur Museum.

110. The Cooper-Hewitt Museum, a branch of the Smithsonian Institution since 1967, is now known as the Cooper-Hewitt, National Design Museum.

111. Kimball noted in the Museum *Bulletin* that "the Pennsylvania Museum is proud to have been the training school in museum work of these and so many other high museum officials"; "Notes," *Bulletin of the Pennsylvania Museum*, vol. 28, no. 153 (February 1933): p. 53. Privately, however, Kimball had warned the museum committee that "economies by reduction of staff cannot be carried much further without threatening grave detriment to the institution"; Board of Trustees Records, Museum Committee, Minutes, February 29, 1932.

112. Board of Trustees Records, Museum Committee, Minutes, October 24, 1932; and *Annual Report, Pennsylvania Museum of Art* [year ending May 31, 1933] (Philadelphia, 1933), p. 25.

113. He was eulogized in the Museum's *Bulletin*: "Scholar, lover of the arts, civic leader of rare courage and foresight, he has built his own immortality by a life of selfless devotion to Philadelphia. Our city is permanently enriched by his achievements; at their head, perhaps, stands the great Museum of Art at Fairmount." "Eli Kirk Price," *Bulletin of the Pennsylvania Museum*, vol. 28, no. 152 (January 1933): unpaginated. It was as Museum builder that Price had been recognized four years earlier with the Philadelphia Award, given to a citizen who served the best interests of the community during the preceding year: "This man has done more, by intelligent, patient and persistent effort, than any other man to make possible in 1928 an event which will always loom large in the perspective of the history of this city . . . the great Gallery of Art upon the Parkway"; George Wharton Pepper in "Report of the Proceedings of the Philadelphia Award," Academy of Music, February 13, 1929, pp. 20–21, Kimball Papers, Writings and Research.

114. Fiske Kimball, "The Task of the Museum," *Philadelphia Museum Bulletin*, vol. 43, no. 216 (January 1948): p. 23.

115. J. Stodgell Stokes, "The Task of the Museum," *Bulletin of the Pennsylvania Museum*, vol. 28, no. 154 (March 1933): pp. 59–60.

116. Proposals were also submitted for funds related to clerical work in the library and the registrar's office and assistance for the educational staff; see Board of Trustees Records, Museum Committee, Minutes, April 22, May 27, September 30, and October 28, 1935.

117. Fiske Kimball, "The Library," *Bulletin of the Pennsylvania Museum*, vol. 30, no. 166 (March 1935): p. 55. Thanks are owed to my colleague C. Danial Elliott, the Museum's Arcadia Director of the Library and Archives, for pointing out the drawing and the issue of the *Bulletin* in which it was published.

118. "Philadelphia's Museum," *Time*, April 8, 1940; see also Board of Trustees Records, Museum Committee, Minutes, April 26, 1943.

119. *Annual Report, Pennsylvania Museum of Art* [year ending May 31, 1936] (Philadelphia, 1936), p. 18.

120. "Museums Back on Full Week," *Christian Science Monitor*, November 20, 1935, p. 12.

121. Kimball to Henry P. McIlhenny, April 27, 1934, Kimball Records, Curatorial Issues, Personnel.

122. In May 1932 Kimball wrote Henry's mother, Frances McIlhenny, longtime museum committee member and soon to be trustee, that he would be in Cambridge, Massachusetts, to preside at the meetings of the American Association of Museums (which Kimball headed from 1929 to 1932), "and where I trust I shall have the pleasure of seeing Henry more than once." Kimball to Frances P. McIlhenny, May 10, 1932, Kimball Records, General Correspondence, 1931–32.

123. Henry P. McIlhenny to Frances P. McIlhenny, undated, postmarked January 8, 1933, Henry P. McIlhenny Papers, Family Papers, Correspondence, 1927–75.

124. Board of Trustees Records, Museum Committee, Minutes, January 28, 1935. For a discussion of McIlhenny's career as collector and curator, see Joseph J. Rishel, *The Henry P. McIlhenny Collection: An Illustrated History* (Philadelphia: Philadelphia Museum of Art, 1987).

Opposite : **126. Paolo Venini** : for Venini S.p.A. : Glasses (4) : c. 1921–25 : glass with enamel decoration : H 6 3/16" : 1990-22-2–5 (cat. 198)
Above : **127. Gertrud Natzler and Otto Natzler** : Bowl : 1945 : glazed earthenware : H 5 7/8" : 1945-68-1 (cat. 133)

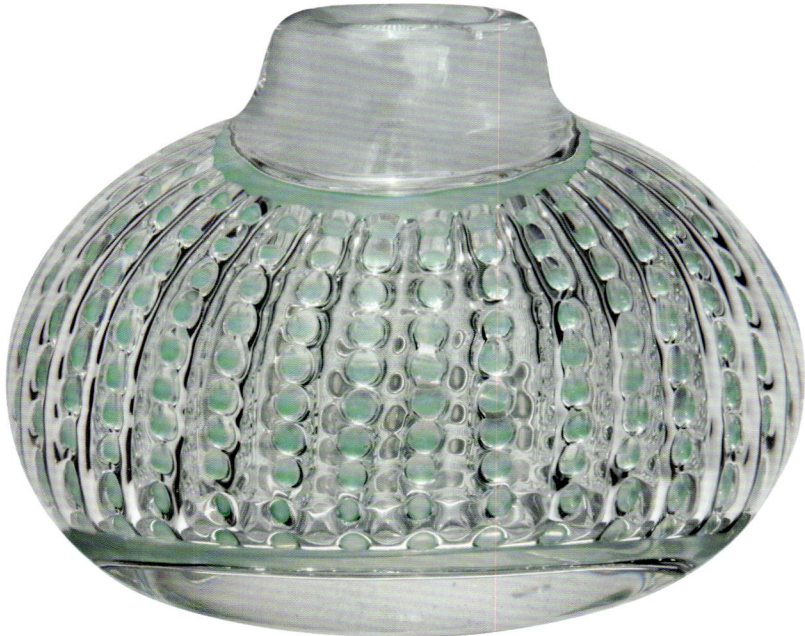

125. "Report of the Director of the Museum," in *Annual Report* [1936], p. 18.

126. "Report of the Director of the Museum," in *Annual Report* [year ending May 31, 1937], *Pennsylvania Museum of Art* (Philadelphia, 1937), p. 14.

127. Kimball to Henry P. McIlhenny, April 26, 1937, McIlhenny Papers, Family Papers, Correspondence, 1927–75.

128. Like Henry McIlhenny, the de Schauensees collected important modern French paintings, and Williamina de Schauensee—who would later become a member of the museum committee and board of trustees—additionally provided funds in 1933 to purchase Brancusi's *Mademoiselle Pogany I* (1912) for the Museum from Earl Horter. Mrs. de Schauensee wore clothes by contemporary designers Jeanne Lanvin, Elsa Schiaparelli, and Cristóbal Balenciaga that she eventually also gave to the Museum.

129. Board of Trustees Records, Museum Committee, Minutes, April 27, 1936: "The Chairman reported negotiations on an offer of a piece of Jensen silver, the matter being left to him and the Director with power."

130. J. Stogdell Stokes, "A Statement by the President," *Bulletin of the Pennsylvania Museum*, vol. 32, no. 173 (February 1937): p. 4.

131. Board of Trustees Records, Museum Committee, Minutes, March 22, 1937.

132. Board of Trustees Records, Museum Committee, Minutes, January 24, 1938.

133. Board of Trustees Records, Museum Committee, Minutes, April 25, 1938.

134. Board of Trustees Records, Museum Committee, Minutes, September 24, 1934.

135. Board of Trustees Records, Minutes, March 6, 1940.

136. Board of Trustees Records, Museum Committee, Minutes, June 4, 1941.

137. Board of Trustees Records, Museum Committee, Minutes, May 26, 1941.

138. Ibid.

139. Ibid.

140. Board of Trustees Records, Minutes, October 1, 1941.

141. Ibid. Acquisition of the Persian stuccos followed an earlier exchange between the museums of "Greek and Italian Vases" for "Islamic pottery and other objects"; Board of Trustees Records, Museum Committee, Minutes, March 25, 1935. Opened officially in April 1940, the Oriental wing occasioned a long article in *Time* magazine that described the Museum, Kimball, Stokes, the staff, and the institution's impressive successes despite lack of adequate city support and private endowments; "Philadelphia's Museum," *Time*, April 8, 1940, p. 63. The board gave credit for the installation of the fourth-century Sasanian palace hall, the Indian temple, the Chinese palace hall, and the other galleries in the new wing to Horace Jayne, who with "beauty and taste . . . planned and guided the installations"; Board of Trustees Records, Minutes, April 3, 1940.

142. Board of Trustees Records, Museum Committee, Minutes, December 23, 1941.

143. Board of Trustees Records, Museum Committee, Minutes, February 24, 1942. Cézanne's painting had been purchased in 1937 with Wilstach funds.

144. Ibid.

145. *Organic Design in Home Furnishings*, January 10–February 16, 1942.

146. Henry P. McIlhenny, undated handwritten note, Exhibition Records, *Organic Design* (Museum of Modern Art), Records of the Directors.

147. Board of Trustees Records, Museum Committee, Minutes, January 26, 1942.

148. *Art in Advertising in Collaboration with the Art Director's Club of Philadelphia*, February 28–March 29, 1942. The first exhibition at the Museum by the Art Directors Club was held in 1941.

149. J. Stogdell Stokes quoted in Philadelphia Museum of Art, "Art Directors Club of Philadelphia 11th Annual Exhibition of Advertising Art," undated news release, Exhibition Records, Records of the Directors.

150. Board of Trustees Records, Museum Committee, Minutes, February 24, 1942.

151. Board of Trustees Records, Museum Committee, Minutes, April 27, 1942. *Tapestries by Contemporary French Painters Lent by Madame Marie Cuttoli* was on view at the *Museum* April 18–June 14, 1942.

152. Board of Trustees Records, Museum Committee, Minutes, December 28, 1942. *Design This Day* was held December 26, 1942–April 18, 1943.

153. "Report of the Director of the Museum," in *Annual Report, Philadelphia Museum of Art* [year ending May 31, 1942] (Philadelphia, 1942), p. 15.

154. *Annual Report, Philadelphia Museum of Art* [year ending May 31, 1943] (Philadelphia, 1943), p. 11.

155. *Annual Report, Philadelphia Museum of Art* [year ending May 31, 1944] (Philadelphia, 1944), p. 19.

156. The offer of $75,000 was reported in the Board of Trustees Records, Minutes, October 4, 1944; and acceptance of the purchase offer was reported in the Board of Trustees Records, Minutes, February 7, 1945.

157. Board of Trustees Records, Minutes, February 7, 1945, p. 17.

158. *Annual Report, Philadelphia Museum of Art* [year ending May 31, 1945] (Philadelphia, 1945), p. 21.

159. *Annual Report, Philadelphia Museum of Art* [year ending May 31, 1946] (Philadelphia, 1946), p. 20.

160. Board of Trustees Records, Museum Committee, Minutes, February 25, 1946. *Styles in Silver: Period Silver in Period Settings* was on view April 13–May 19, 1946.

161. Adeline Hector Guimard to Fiske Kimball, April 26, 1949, European Decorative Arts after 1700 Files; emphasis in the original.

162. Board of Trustees Records, Museum Committee, Minutes, May 23, 1949.

163. McIlhenny to Sachs, December 13, 1946, McIlhenny Papers, Family Papers, Correspondence, 1927–75.

164. Kimball to Louis C. Madeira, June 16, 1948, Kimball Records, Curatorial Issues, Personnel. For the next decade and a half, Madeira served as the Museum's assistant curator and then associate curator of decorative arts.

165. Stokes was eulogized by the board for his service "during the years of trial and of triumph since 1933. . . . It was he who led in securing for the Museum the generous support of notable benefactors, on a scale commensurate with the large contributions of the public treasury. To him primarily the Museum thus owes its wonderful series of ensembles from so many ages and climes. . . . He lived to see his work fulfilled, and the Museum transformed from a bright promise to a noble realization—in the front rank of the museums of America"; Board of Trustees Records, Minutes, October 1, 1947. Stokes's political acumen was acknowledged; he had initiated, among other practices, dinners at the Museum for city council members and other elected officials. He was also praised for financing the acquisition of the Foulc and Barnard collections.

166. R. Sturgis Ingersoll, "A Personal Message," *Philadelphia Museum Bulletin*, vol. 43, no. 216 (January 1948): p. 21.

167. Part of Stieglitz's collection had been shown at the

Museum in 1944 by Carl Zigrosser, the Museum's new curator of prints (he succeeded Boies Penrose in 1941).

168. Walter Arensberg was remembered by the board for "leaving to the Art Museum of his native state what has been called the greatest collection of art of the 20th century, as well as the greatest private collection of pre-Columbian sculpture. Poet, critic, scholar and inspired collector of choice examples of the art of our time, he has placed the Museum first among its peers in this field"; Board of Trustees Records, Minutes, February 3, 1954.

169. Fiske Kimball, "A Fashion Wing in the Museum," *Philadelphia Museum Bulletin*, vol. 43, no. 215 (November 1947): p. 3; see also Board of Trustees Records, Minutes, November 17, 1951.

170. "Philadelphia Museum College of Art" [annual report, 1961–62], *Philadelphia Museum Bulletin*, vol. 57, no. 274 (Summer 1962): p. 145.

171. Records of the Schools, Minutes of the Board of Governors, School of Industrial Art, February 19, 1960. In 1964 the Museum college separated from the Museum, becoming the Philadelphia College of Art. In 1985 it merged with the Philadelphia College of Performing Arts and became the Philadelphia Colleges of the Arts. Granted university status in 1987, the colleges were renamed the University of the Arts.

172. "Annual Report [year ending May 31, 1954]," *Philadelphia Museum Bulletin*, vol. 49, no. 242 (Summer 1954): p. 59.

173. Records of the Schools, School of Industrial Art, Board of Govenors, Minutes, February 24, 1954.

174. Records of the Schools, School of Industrial Art, Board of Govenors, Minutes, May 20, 1960.

175. *Paintings and Drawings by Vincent van Gogh*, January 13–Febuary 28, 1954; *Dali Jewels*, January 15–February 13, 1955. As works of art in Europe were returned to their homes after the war, and during the reconstruction of many museum buildings that had suffered war damage, opportunities for exhibitions presented themselves, including paintings belonging to the Kaiser Friedrich Museum in Berlin in 1948 and *Vienna Art Treasures* in 1952. To celebrate the Diamond Jubilee of the Philadelphia Museum of Art in 1951, ticketed exhibitions of masterworks of paintings and works on paper in American collections were assembled and a campaign to secure gifts and funds to purchase works of art was launched. Combining income from the Wilstach and Elkins funds, in 1950 Kimball purchased Peter Paul Rubens's *Prometheus Bound* (begun c. 1611–12, completed by 1618) to celebrate the occasion.

176. Board of Trustees Records, Minutes, November 5, 1952. John B. Kelly, commissioner of Fairmount Park, led the lobby for converting Memorial Hall to public recreational use; Board of Trustees Records, Museum Committee, Minutes, March 24, 1947, and February 23, 1948. In the fall of 1956 the Museum finally turned over the key to Memorial Hall to the commissioners of Fairmount Park and vacated the building.

177. Board of Trustees Records, Minutes, January 5, 1955.

178. "Annual Report," *Philadelphia Museum Bulletin*, vol. 49, no. 242 (Summer 1954): p. 51.

179. Philadelphia Museum of Art, untitled news release, January 25, 1955.

180. Kimball to Marceau, July 1, 1955, Henri Gabriel Marceau Director Records, Correspondence.

181. Horace H. F. Jayne and Henri Marceau, "Fiske Kimball (1888–1955)," in American Philosophical Society, *Yearbook* (Philadelphia: American Philosophical Society, 1955), p. 469. On Kimball and the Philadelphia Museum of Art, the authors wrote: "His preeminence is conclusively attested by the Philadelphia Museum of Art. It stands today in the very forefront of great museums of this country. Thirty years Fiske Kimball devoted to the fashioning of it. . . . Coming to Philadelphia first in 1925 . . . funds were almost non-existent: where other institutions had thousands to play with, Fiske Kimball had shoestrings." Ibid., pp. 446–47 passim.

182. "It is the world of art museums that must particularly mark and lament the death of Fiske Kimball," wrote Jayne and Marceau, "yet the wide range of his scholarship and his extraordinary productivity will be missed in many diverse fields. For the mind of the man was voltaic, his enthusiasms many, and his influences positive and widespread. A score of learned publications will be less learned without his provocative contributions. . . . As a museum man he knew that objects as diverse as a Gothic capital and a Picasso have value and meaning in a museum of the history of art. . . . His busy pen found time to turn out several books and a host of effective articles. . . . Of the books, Kimball's *Creation of the Rococo* will long stand as the authoritative work on the subject"; ibid., pp. 446–69, passim.

183. Board of Trustees Records, Museum Committee, Minutes, June 28, 1948.

184. *Connelly & Haines, Cabinetmakers: Philadelphia Sheraton Furniture*, March 20–April 19, 1953; *Philadelphia Silver*, April 14–September 9, 1956; *Tucker China*, May 3–September 9, 1957; and *The Shakers: Their Arts and Crafts*, April–May 20, 1962.

185. "Annual Report [year ending May 31, 1964]," *Philadelphia Museum of Art Bulletin*, vol. 59, no. 282 (Summer 1964): p. 138.

186. Other members of the staff also departed. Carl Zigrosser retired as curator of prints, hailed by the board of trustees for creating "one of the most important cabinets of prints in this country," as did Julius Zieget, the Museum corporation's secretary and treasurer since 1928. Henry Clifford, the Museum's curator of painting and sculpture, retired at the end of 1964 (soon after to join the board) following "thirty-two years of brilliant service to this department. . . . [His] connoisseurship and knowledge have unquestionably contributed to the significance of the exhibitions and acquisitions of the Museum." Board of Trustees Records, Minutes, October 7, 1964.

187. "Annual Report [year ending May 31, 1963]," *Philadelphia Museum of Art Bulletin*, vol. 58, no. 278 (Summer 1963): p. 249.

188. Ibid. Following Marceau's death in 1964, he was remembered by the board as having made, "with the possible exception of Fiske Kimball . . . a greater contribution to the growth and management of the Museum than did anyone else. He was a stupendous worker, accepting every responsibility as it was thrown at him. It was often said that Henri could accomplish more in one hour than most men could in a day"; Board of Trustees Records, Minutes, October 8, 1969.

189. "By-Laws of the Philadelphia Museum of Art" [1964–65], unpaginated.

190. Board of Trustees Records, Museum Committee, Minutes, November 24, 1941.

191. Initially, a committee on acquisitions was also envisioned, to concern itself with gifts, acquisitions by purchase, and loans; R. Sturgis Ingersoll to Bonnie Wintersteen, March 9, 1964, Marceau Director Records, Correspondence. However, the committee was never formed, and it fell instead to the departmental committees to recommend purchases for presentation to the board and assist in fund-raising for particularly important acquisitions, but not to carry responsibility for the professional functions of the department; "A Policy Program for Curatorial Departmental Committees," Marceau Director Records, Correspondence.

192. George Widener's mother had earlier given the Museum an eighteenth-century French period room and the woodwork and furnishings of her own eighteenth-century-French-style drawing room in New York.

193. Ingersoll considered the structure "unwieldy" but believed it would be tempered by the creation of an executive committee of board members, who would have wide powers to act for the board; R. Sturgis Ingersoll to Bonnie Wintersteen, March 9, 1964, Marceau Director Records, Correspondence.

194. Board of Trustees Records, Minutes, special meeting, March 4, 1964: "The further growth and progress of the College is jeopardized by its subordinate status as a division of the Museum corporation, and the Museum corporation, with its collections of art and other assets, is in no position to commit itself to the financing and other obligations which the College is virtually obliged to undertake."

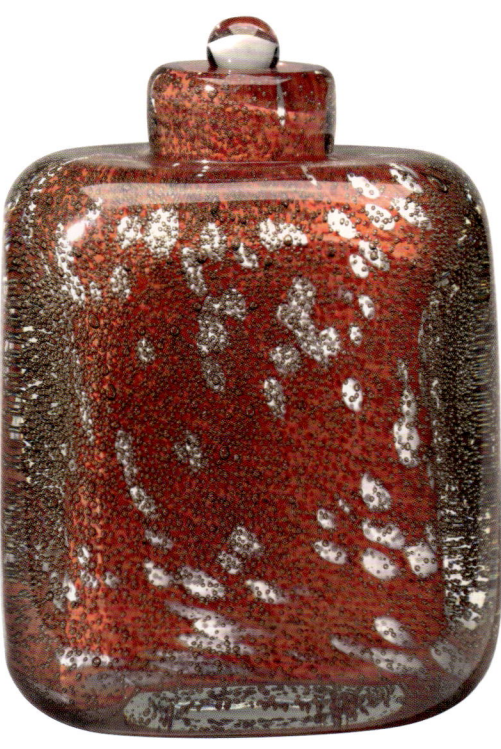

Opposite : **128. Edvin Öhrström** : for Orrefors Glassbruk : Vase : 1948 : glass with trapped-air decoration : H 4⁷⁄₁₆" : 1967-17-8 (cat. 140)
Above : **129. Maurice Marinot** : Bottle : 1932 : glass with encased enamel and bubbles : H (bottle) 4⁷⁄₁₆" : 1967-98-28a,b (cat. 114)

1965-2010

A NEW ERA FOR CONTEMPORARY ARTS

Even as the Museum witnessed the retirement of its curators of decorative arts and its director, two appointments in 1963 heralded a new era focused on contemporary art. Calvin S. Hathaway was named the R. Wistar Harvey Curator of Decorative Arts, a title created by the board of trustees in memory of and in gratitude to the donor, a collector of furniture and decorative arts who had left his collection and considerable funds to the Museum.[1] Within a few years, however, Hathaway was renamed curator of decorative arts after 1700, when the department was split along chronological lines, using the eighteenth century as the point of division.[2] Thirty years earlier, when he had left Philadelphia for the Cooper Union Museum (now the Smithsonian's Cooper-Hewitt, National Design Museum), Hathaway had been a favorite of Fiske Kimball; he was now director of the museum, which its trustees were considering closing.[3] Delighted at the prospect of returning to the Philadelphia Museum of Art and to the city itself, Hathaway wrote to Sturgis Ingersoll, chair of the Museum's board, that "after so many years at a museum director's desk it will please me more than I can say to enjoy once again work carried on more immediately with the collections of a museum."[4]

That same year the Museum also appointed a new director. Previously director of the Montreal Museum of Fine Arts (from 1959), Harvard-educated Evan H. Turner (A.B., A.M., Ph.D.) was heartily endorsed for the position at the Philadelphia Museum of Art by John Coolidge, professor of fine arts at Harvard University and director of its Fogg Art Museum, as "a most promising younger man.... He has done an outstanding job.... He has a first-rate eye and boundless energy."[5] Henry McIlhenny also lobbied for a young candidate, writing Ingersoll, "I am hoping for a really young live wire, not from the Philadelphia area."[6] At the age of thirty-six Turner (fig. 130) was the youngest of all the candidates considered.

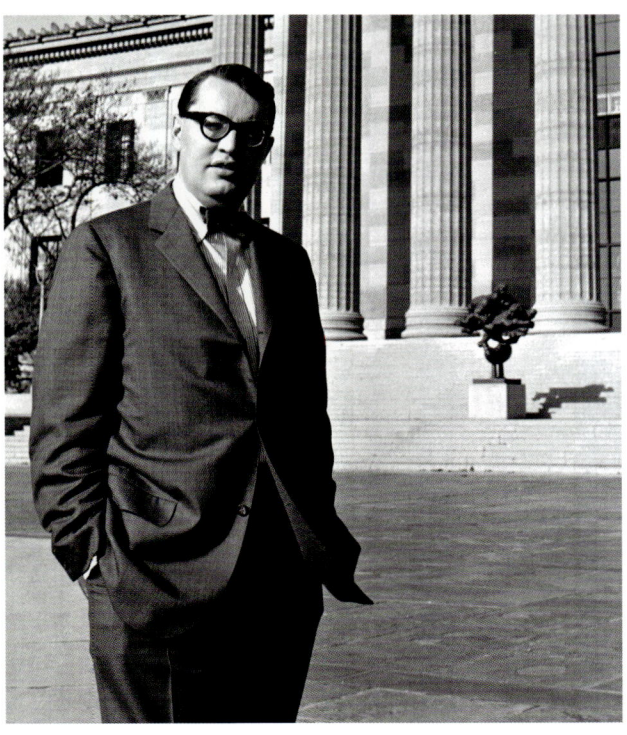

130 : Evan H. Turner : Museum director, 1964–77

He would have his work cut out for him, according to Charles Cunningham, director of the Wadsworth Atheneum in Hartford, who in a letter to Ingersoll noted the Museum's greatest needs, foremost among them, a professional staff and a clear division of responsibilities with the city.[7] In fact, within a few months of his appointment, Turner requested funds for additional curatorial staff and an increase in city funds, drawing attention to the number of galleries that were closed each day for lack of sufficient security guards.[8]

Ingersoll, Turner, and Hathaway shared a strong interest in modern and contemporary arts. In a tribute to Ingersoll as outgoing president, Claire McLean, a member of the board of governors, wrote, "Because of Mr. Ingersoll, Philadelphia is known today as the city that has opened its gates to modern American sculpture. What a comfort he has been to artists!"[9] Turner's first message to the Museum membership, written in 1965, urged that the institution address "integration of the most up-to-date achievements of contemporary art into the over-all program of the Museum,"[10] while noting the need for endowment funds to assure the growth of the collections. He repeated his commitment to contemporary art in his first annual report, declaring that "the art of today is one of our leading problems since we have a duty to see that Philadelphians have a sound chance to study international achievements."[11] That same annual report recorded the first major contemporary art acquisition of Turner's tenure, Alexander Calder's *Ghost* mobile (1964), which, as Museum president Bonnie Wintersteen had envisioned two years earlier, would be suspended from the ceiling of the Great Stair Hall—a "logical climax and focal point for a masterpiece by this third generation of Philadelphia sculptors."[12]

For Calvin Hathaway collecting and exhibiting contemporary decorative arts was just as important as building the historic collections. Outlining his departmental collections policy in 1965, he wrote: "The continued acquisition of representative masterpieces should be pursued; in developing the collections, their present weaknesses in both historic and contemporary material should not be entirely overlooked in favor of amplifying their present strengths."[13] Recalling that "the Museum was one of the first in this country to organize a display of contemporary domestic furnishings," with its 1932 exhibition *Design for the Machine*, he argued:

> Surely the time is ripe for another survey of the good work of our own day—an exhibition that ideally, like the majority of the Department's efforts, would encourage visitors to say, "What a good idea! I'd like to have one of those in my living room," rather than, "Didn't we . . . have one like that in the attic?"
>
> . . . In all its programs, the Department of Decorative Arts should help the Museum to maintain contact with those of its public who for one reason or another are as interested in the future as in the past, and to occupy a position of leadership in the forming of that future.[14]

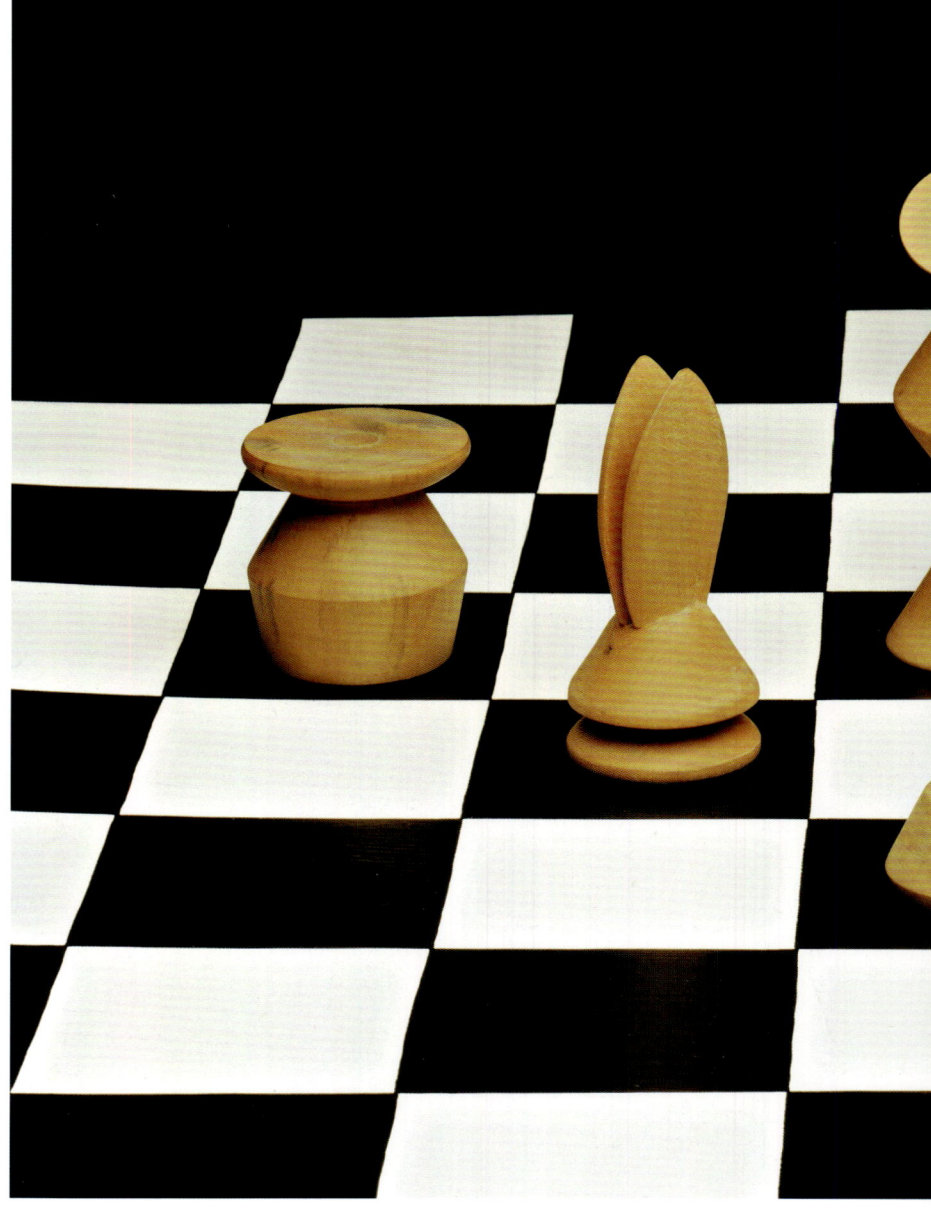

Hathaway also advocated strengthening the department's study collection (a decade after it had largely been dispersed) to "improve its capacity to serve its audience through the development of depth as well as breadth."[15] His intentions to acquire the modern when new, and in depth, echoed those of Edwin Atlee Barber and John T. Morris a half-century earlier.

In 1965 Hathaway was able to announce a gift, from Philadelphia architect and collector John F. Harbeson, of chessmen and chessboards ranging in date from the

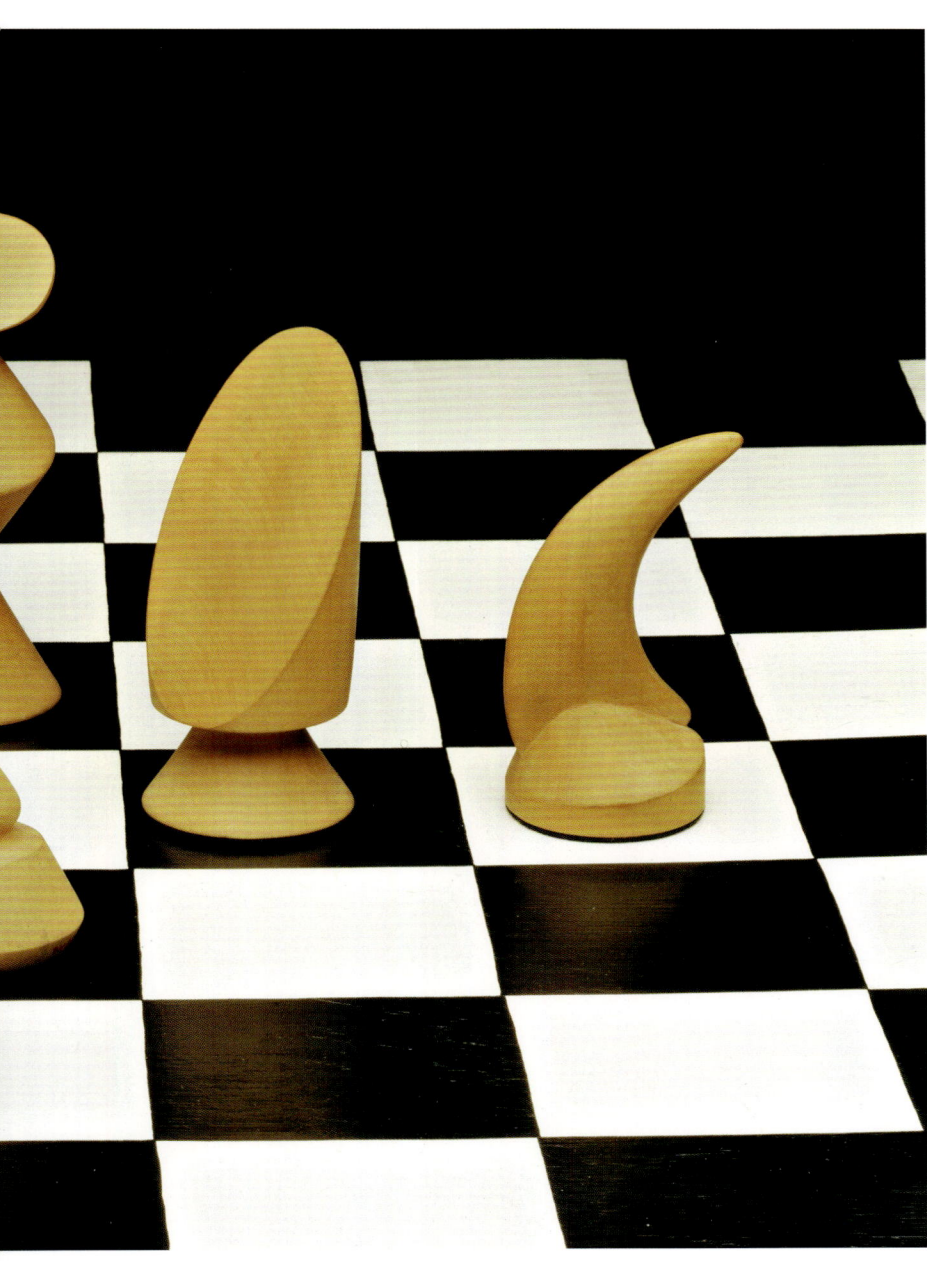

gifts ranged from Bohemian glass to Chinese theatrical costumes, presented Swedish glass designed and made by Orrefors after designs by Vicke Lindstrand and Edvin Öhrström (fig. 128). In 1967 Florence Marinot gave the Museum twenty pieces of French glass made by her father (figs. 88–90, 129), a magnificent gift that was due to Hathaway's diplomatic skills, excellent French, and the previous absence of the designer's glass in the collection, despite the curator's efforts to acquire examples.[16]

Hathaway was also deeply interested in rebuilding and developing the department's nineteenth-century collections. He began by purchasing three pieces of early Tiffany glass while encouraging gifts of other Tiffany pieces. Hathaway's greatest purchases in this regard were twelve bentwood chairs made largely from the 1840s to the 1890s after designs by Michael Thonet and his successors (figs. 9, 10). The chairs were part of a collection belonging to John Sailer of Vienna that had been exhibited in 1967 at Harvard's Carpenter Center for the Visual Arts, where Hathaway had seen them. Presenting the chairs to the decorative arts committee in 1969, Hathaway wrote: "The unique achievement of Michael Thonet, in devising unprecedented techniques for the production of chairs and in developing a design expressive of the materials and means employed, was a characteristic manifestation of nineteenth-century progress that continues to be admired and applied in the twentieth."[17] Like architects Le Corbusier (designer of the Carpenter Center) and Philadelphian Robert Venturi, who deemed Thonet's creations still among the best and most progressive designs many decades after their initial manufacture, Hathaway saw Thonet as a pioneering "modern" industrial designer for mass production. Turner reported the acquisition of the chairs as assuaging, in at least one area, "Hathaway's proper concern that the achievements of fine design postdating the beginning of the machine age should be as well represented in the collection as the quality of the finest work deserves."[18]

sixteenth to the twentieth century. The gift notably included three sets designed by Max Ernst (fig. 131), Man Ray, and Richard Filipowski that had been exhibited at the avant-garde Julien Levy Gallery in New York in 1944. In the years that followed this acquisition, Hathaway reported other modern and contemporary gifts, among them the Museum's first piece of furniture by Philadelphia craftsman Wharton Esherick, a radio cabinet made for the Armstrong Cork Company of Lancaster, Pennsylvania. Mrs. Henry Breyer (member of the Breyers Ice Cream family and later Museum trustee), whose numerous other

131. **Max Ernst** : Chess Set : 1944 : boxwood : H (queen) 4 15/16" : 1964-91-35(1–32) (cat. 56)

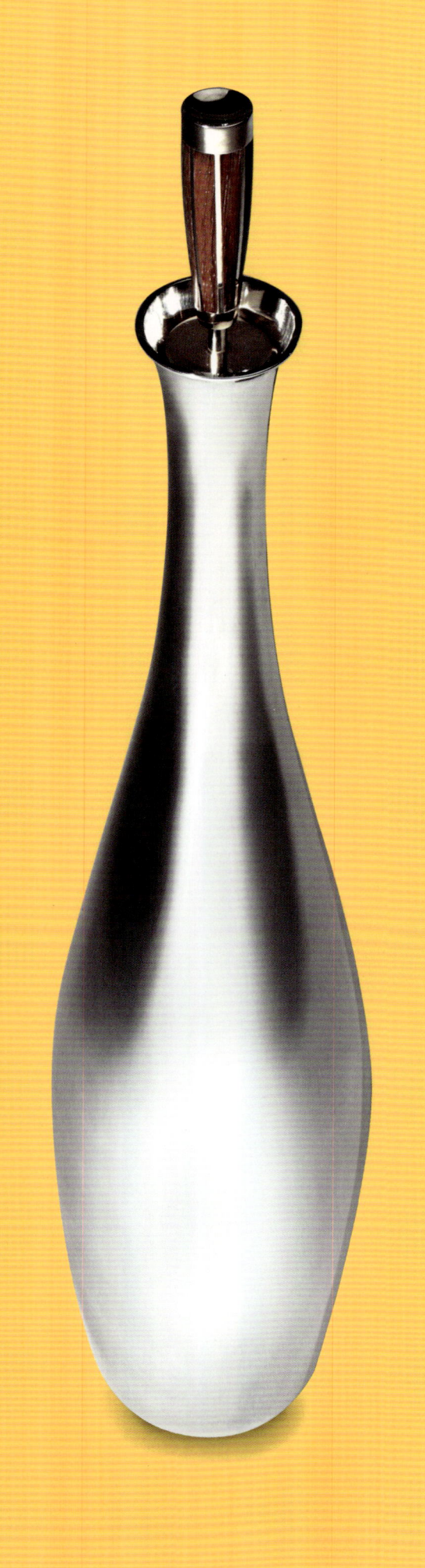

NEW SUPPORT FOR DESIGN

In 1970 Turner and Hathaway welcomed the opportunity to campaign for modern design with the formation of the Inter-Society Committee for Twentieth-Century Decorative Arts and Design (fig. 133), a volunteer group of professional architects and designers who wished to raise funds for design acquisitions and programs at the Museum, much as the Fashion Group had done earlier for the department of costume and textiles. The new organization was initially comprised of representatives from the Philadelphia chapters of various design societies[19] and from the Friends of the Philadelphia Museum of Art (the latter group had been founded in 1964 to provide funds for acquisitions—particularly contemporary—and to stimulate interest in the Museum). The Inter-Society was the brainchild of Cynthia Drayton in collaboration with Evan Turner; she was a former vice chair of the Friends, a current member of the women's and decorative arts departmental committees, and a practicing interior designer. In 1968 Drayton had helped Hathaway acquire a silver decanter made by Olaf Skoogfors (fig. 132), the first piece by this distinguished Philadelphia silversmith to enter the collections. Puzzled that the Museum was not more actively acquiring contemporary furniture and decorative arts, she met with Turner, who enthusiastically supported the idea of developing the Museum's collections, "heretofore," as Hathaway remarked separately (echoing Fiske Kimball's comment two decades earlier; see page 13), "nearly totally lacking."[20] Together Drayton and Turner contacted various design organizations

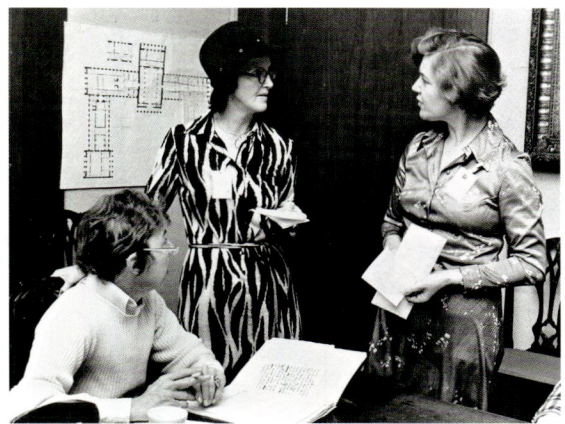

to solicit their help, and in March 1970 a "launching party" for the Inter-Society and its campaign of acquisitions was held at the Museum (fig. 134). The event was successful, Hathaway wrote Francis L. Rodebaugh, treasurer of the American Institute of Interior Design: "Already I have had several calls from people who wonder whether we wished to receive their early twentieth-century furniture."[21] Known as Collab (short for "collaboration") since 1975 after the title of their fund-raising events, the group remains to this day a singular Museum organization, composed largely of designers who support the collections from the vantage point of their professions.

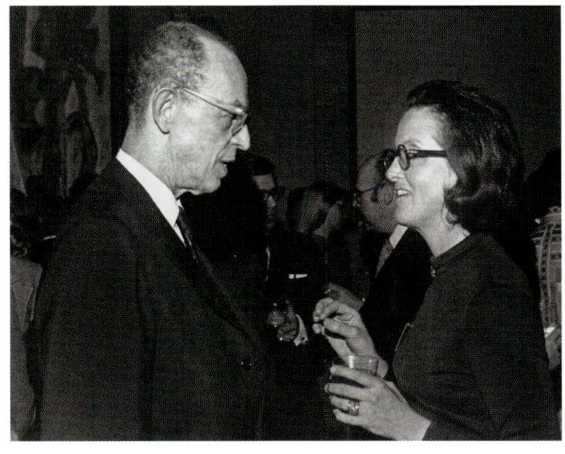

After the group's inauguration, participating societies led the way in making gifts to the Museum. From the National Home Fashions League came contemporary crafts made by artists working in Philadelphia, including ceramists Paula Winokur and Rudolf Staffel and glassmaker Roland Jahn; the American Institute of Architects gave the Museum a lounge chair by Charles and Ray Eames (fig. 135); and the Pennsylvania chapter of the National Society of Interior Design presented Danish architect Arne Jacobsen's *3107* stacking chair and *Egg* armchair and ottoman (fig. 136). Members of the Inter-Society also gave objects in their own names, among them Helen Drutt, who in 1974 would found an internationally recognized contemporary craft gallery in Philadelphia;

Opposite : **132. Olaf Skoogfors** : Decanter : 1966 : silver, rosewood : H (with stopper) 13 3/16" : 1968-2-1a,b (cat. 177)   Above, top to bottom :
133. Elisabeth Fraser (left), Cynthia Drayton (center), and Hava Gelblum (right) at an Inter-Society meeting at the Museum   **134.** Calvin Hathaway, the R. Wistar Harvey Curator of Decorative Arts after 1700, and Cynthia Drayton

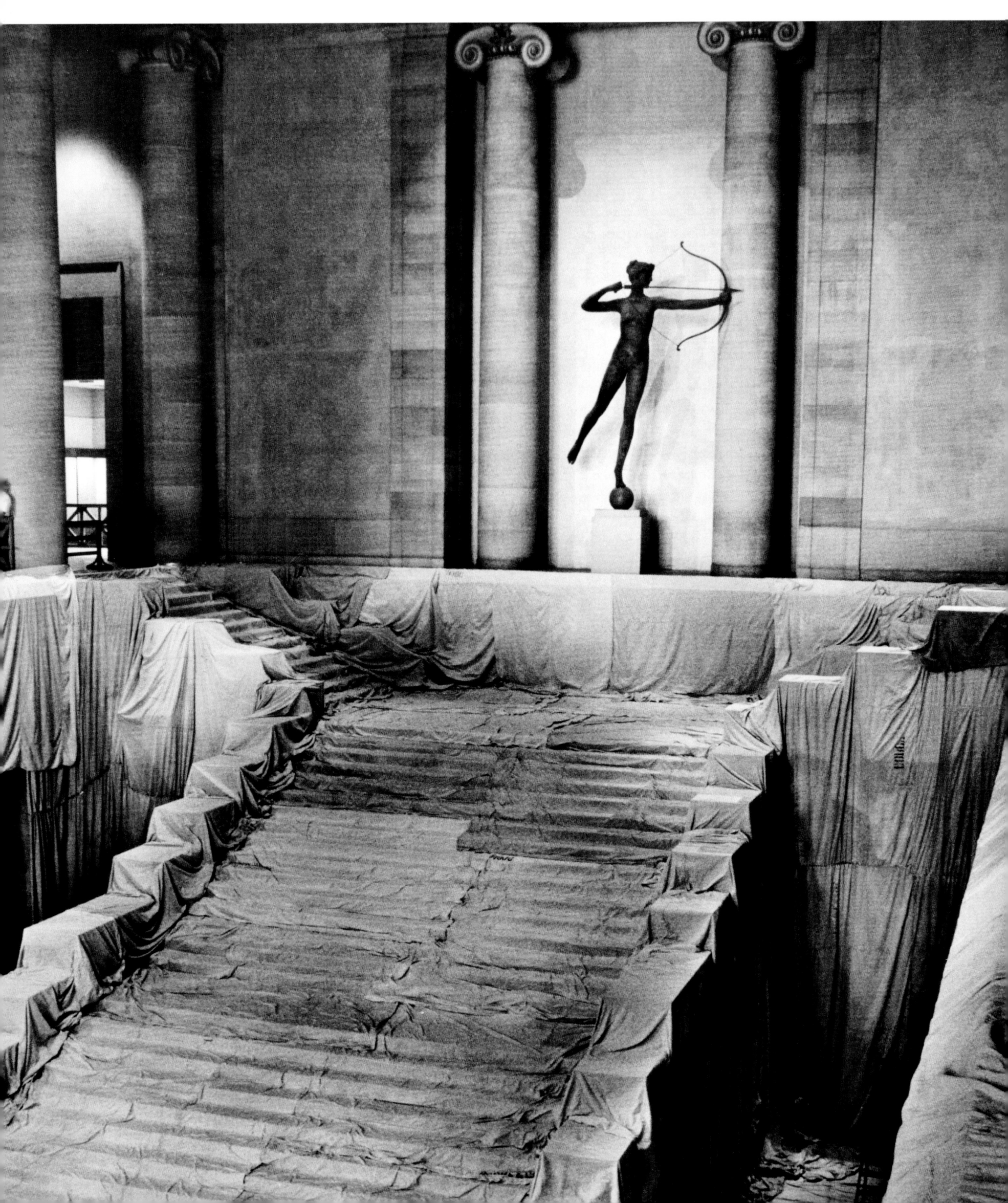

NEW SUPPORT FOR DESIGN

In 1970 Turner and Hathaway welcomed the opportunity to campaign for modern design with the formation of the Inter-Society Committee for Twentieth-Century Decorative Arts and Design (fig. 133), a volunteer group of professional architects and designers who wished to raise funds for design acquisitions and programs at the Museum, much as the Fashion Group had done earlier for the department of costume and textiles. The new organization was initially comprised of representatives from the Philadelphia chapters of various design societies[19] and from the Friends of the Philadelphia Museum of Art (the latter group had been founded in 1964 to provide funds for acquisitions—particularly contemporary—and to stimulate interest in the Museum). The Inter-Society was the brainchild of Cynthia Drayton in collaboration with Evan Turner; she was a former vice chair of the Friends, a current member of the women's and decorative arts departmental committees, and a practicing interior designer. In 1968 Drayton had helped Hathaway acquire a silver decanter made by Olaf Skoogfors (fig. 132), the first piece by this distinguished Philadelphia silversmith to enter the collections. Puzzled that the Museum was not more actively acquiring contemporary furniture and decorative arts, she met with Turner, who enthusiastically supported the idea of developing the Museum's collections, "heretofore," as Hathaway remarked separately (echoing Fiske Kimball's comment two decades earlier; see page 13), "nearly totally lacking."[20] Together Drayton and Turner contacted various design organizations

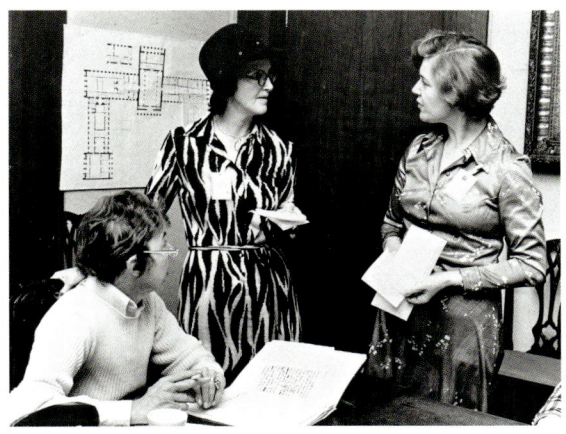

to solicit their help, and in March 1970 a "launching party" for the Inter-Society and its campaign of acquisitions was held at the Museum (fig. 134). The event was successful, Hathaway wrote Francis L. Rodebaugh, treasurer of the American Institute of Interior Design: "Already I have had several calls from people who wonder whether we wished to receive their early twentieth-century furniture."[21] Known as Collab (short for "collaboration") since 1975 after the title of their fund-raising events, the group remains to this day a singular Museum organization, composed largely of designers who support the collections from the vantage point of their professions.

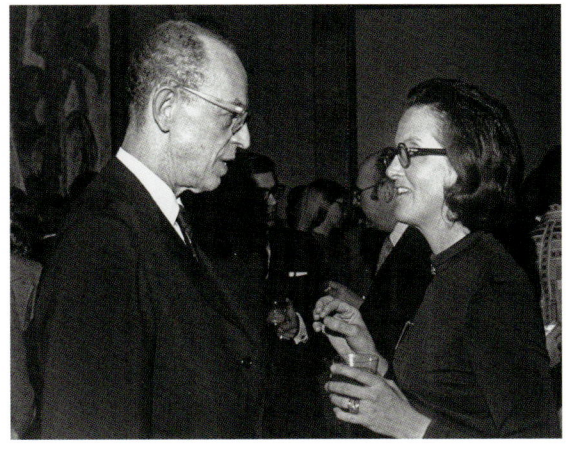

After the group's inauguration, participating societies led the way in making gifts to the Museum. From the National Home Fashions League came contemporary crafts made by artists working in Philadelphia, including ceramists Paula Winokur and Rudolf Staffel and glassmaker Roland Jahn; the American Institute of Architects gave the Museum a lounge chair by Charles and Ray Eames (fig. 135); and the Pennsylvania chapter of the National Society of Interior Design presented Danish architect Arne Jacobsen's *3107* stacking chair and *Egg* armchair and ottoman (fig. 136). Members of the Inter-Society also gave objects in their own names, among them Helen Drutt, who in 1974 would found an internationally recognized contemporary craft gallery in Philadelphia;

Opposite : **132. Olaf Skoogfors** : Decanter : 1966 : silver, rosewood : H (with stopper) 13 3/16" : 1968-2-1a,b (cat. 177)   Above, top to bottom : **133.** Elisabeth Fraser (left), Cynthia Drayton (center), and Hava Gelblum (right) at an Inter-Society meeting at the Museum   **134.** Calvin Hathaway, the R. Wistar Harvey Curator of Decorative Arts after 1700, and Cynthia Drayton

145

they also used their influence to help acquire twentieth-century objects for the Museum from nonmembers, including Orrefors glass given by the local firm of Fisher, Bruce and Company, an importer of ceramics and glassware. A year later, hailing the activities of the Inter-Society as "the most impressive single impetus for acquisitions in decorative arts," Turner noted that the

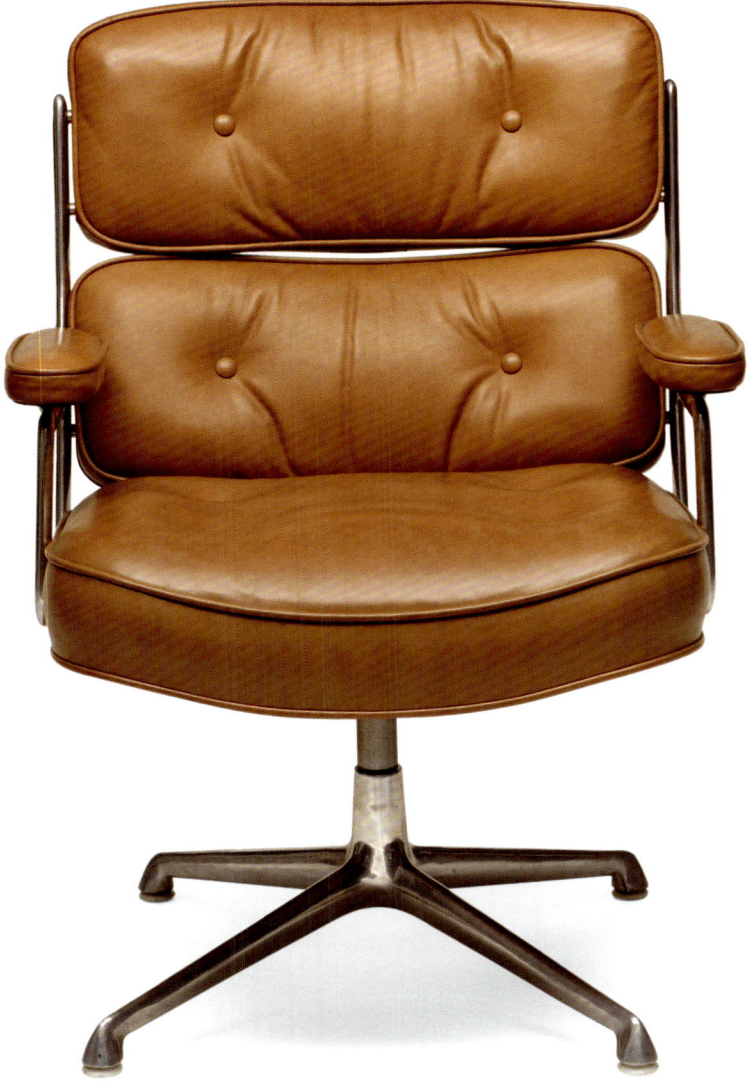

group's efforts to add fine objects of contemporary design to the collection had revived a tradition that originated in the Museum in the years following the Centennial Exhibition.[22] Gallery space for the rapidly growing collection was an early concern of Turner's, and in the fall of 1970 he promised permanent exhibition space for contemporary decorative arts within a gallery adjacent to the Arensberg collection.[23] However, it was not until 1976—when the Museum's scheduled installation of air-conditioning was completed—that he was able to fulfill that pledge.

The Inter-Society was born in a turbulent era of political and social activism—from antiwar protests to city labor strikes—through which the Museum was deftly steered by Turner and Museum president George M. Cheston, a patrician Harvard-trained lawyer who succeeded Bonnie Wintersteen in 1968. Following another successful van Gogh exhibition,[24] in 1970, in which attendance figures exceeded all expectations and improved the Museum's financial situation, students from the Philadelphia College of Art and other local art schools were permitted to hold a "peace exhibition" at the Museum in May and June 1970,[25] selecting sometimes challenging works by contemporary American artists such as Jasper Johns, Ellsworth Kelly, and James Rosenquist along with ceramics, jewelry, and other decorative arts. The show was considered a constructive way to express a concern for peace, its focal point the Museum's Great Stair Hall "wrapped" by the artist Christo (figs. 137, 138).

Deeply committed to ensuring the Museum's accessibility and relevance to the broadest possible audience, in the fall of 1970 Turner created the department of urban outreach, headed by David Katzive (formerly director of the Museum of Contemporary Art in Chicago), to develop the Museum's activities beyond its walls. The next year Turner, Katzive, and architect Richard Saul Wurman (a principal of the Philadelphia firm Murphy, Levy, Wurman), organized *City/2*, on view in the Museum's vacant Armory galleries.[26] This exhibition of photographs, films, drawings, and architectural models proposed that half of the city of Philadelphia (including the Museum) belonged to its citizens, who should consequently assume responsibility for its appearance. Turner further suggested to the board

Above : **135. Charles Eames and Ray Eames** : for Herman Miller : Lounge Chair : 1965 : aluminum, steel, leather, latex foam, Dacron, plywood : H 35" : 1970-113-1 (cat. 54)   Opposite : **136. Arne Jacobsen** : for Fritz Hansen : *Egg* Armchair and Ottoman : 1957 : plastic, leather, chromed steel : H (armchair) 42½" : H (ottoman) 17½" : 1971-30-1,2 (cat. 88)

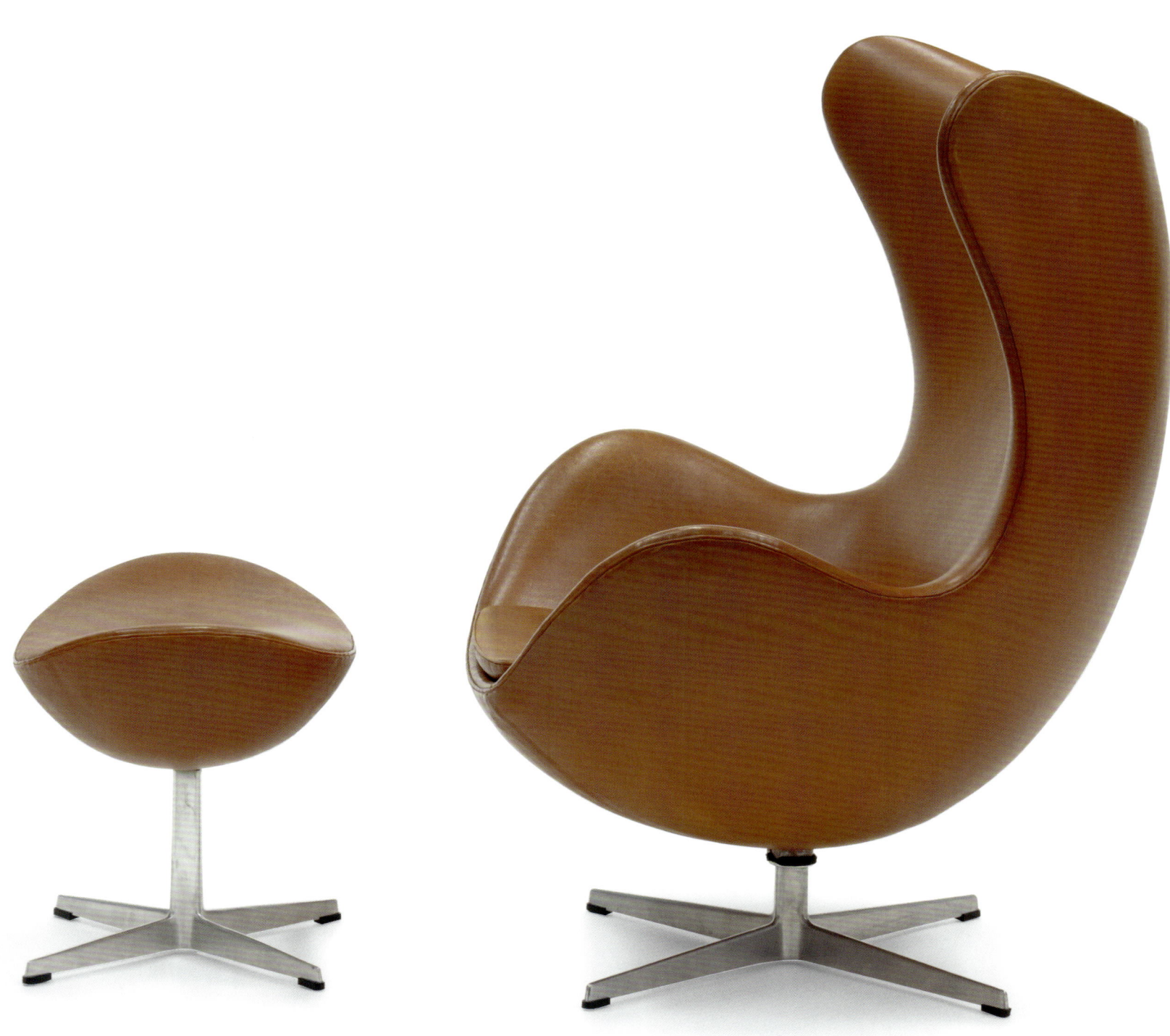

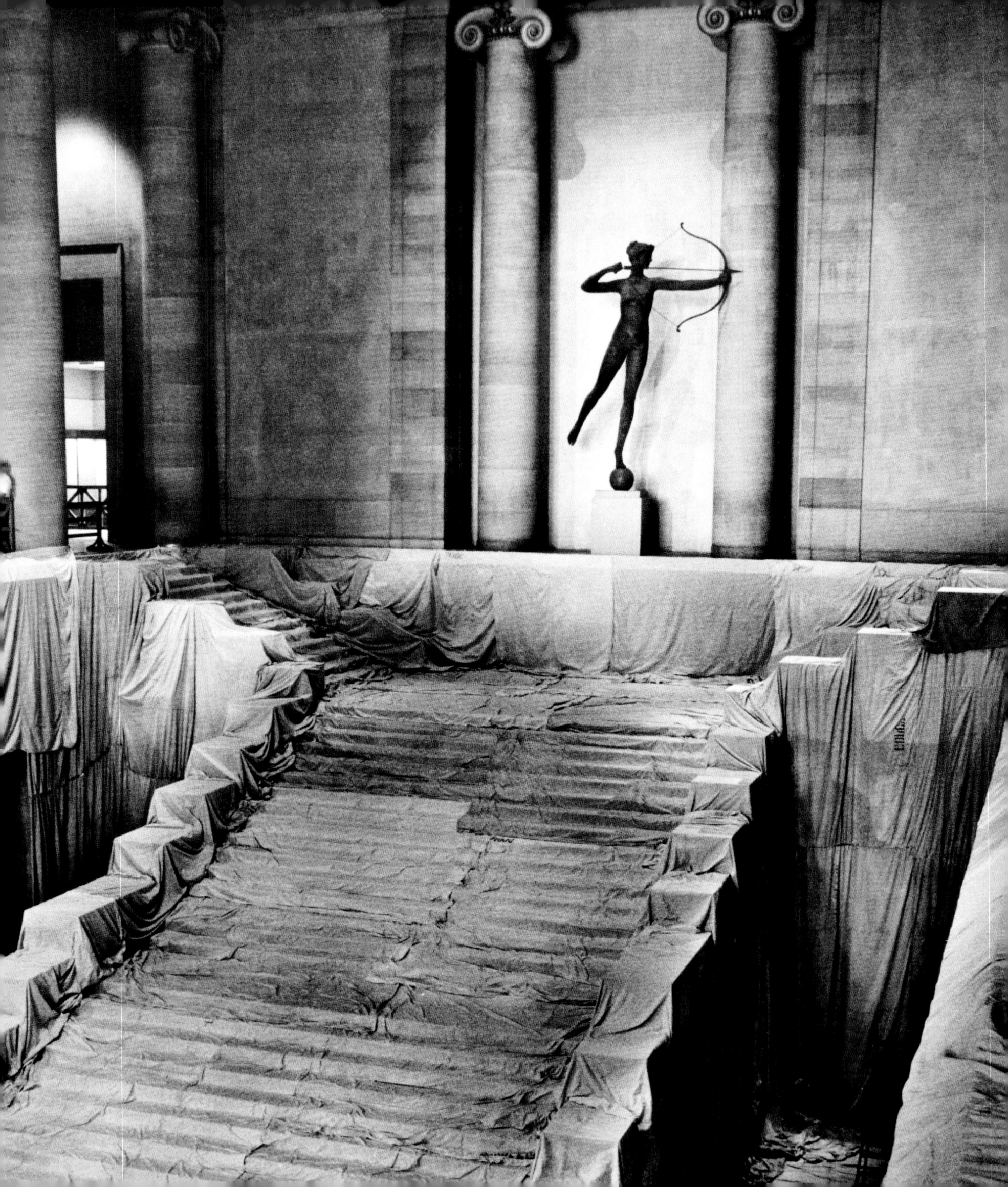

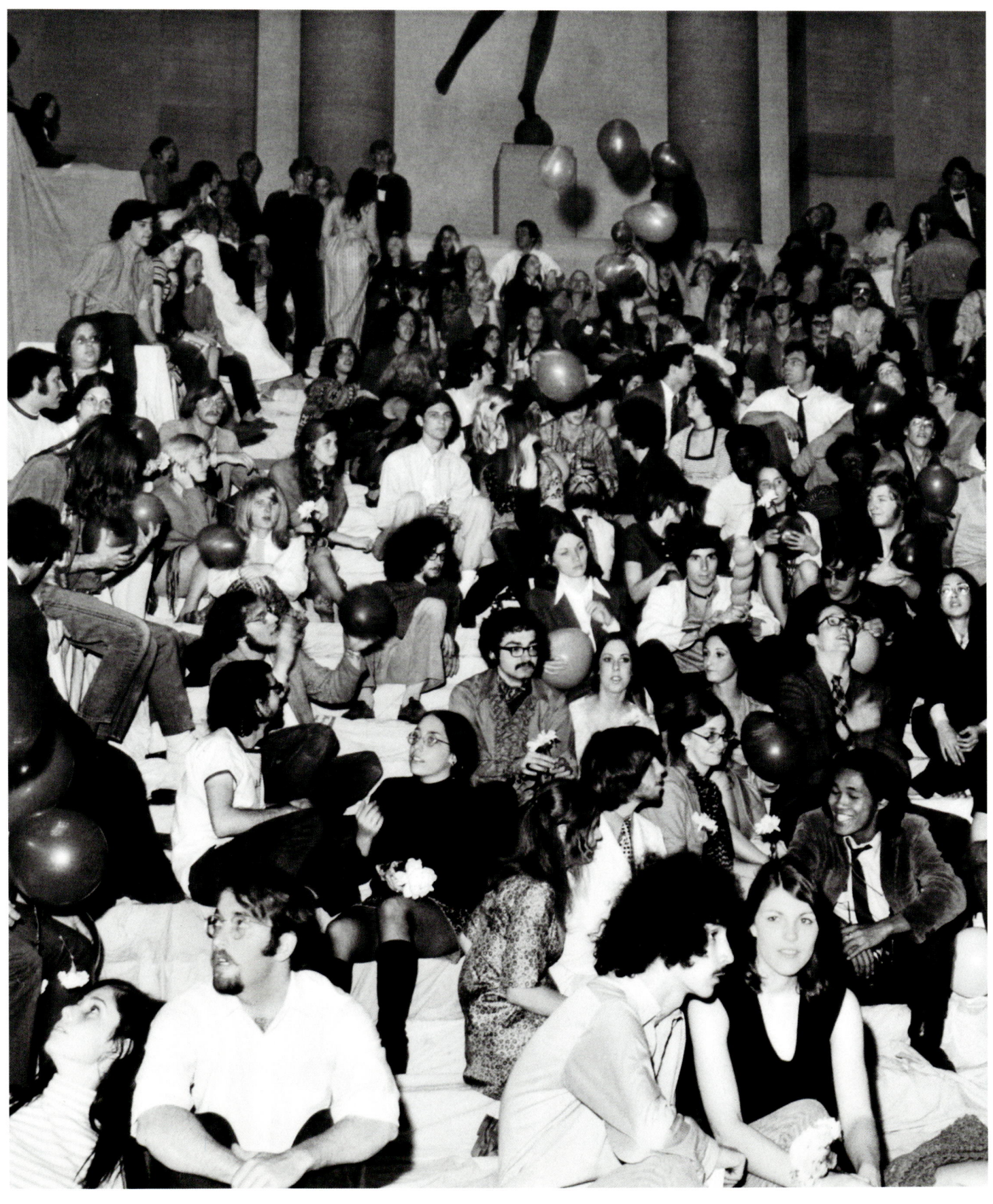

Opposite : **137.** The Museum's Great Stair Hall "wrapped" by the artist Christo : 1970   Above : **138.** A celebration of Christo's installation at the Museum

149

Product Environment: New Furniture arrived at the Museum at the end of September 1970 from the City Art Museum of Saint Louis (now known as the Saint Louis Art Museum), displaying the kind of innovative domestic furnishings favored by Hathaway and Inter-Society members. In connection with the exhibition, New York manufacturing firm Habitat gave the Museum a group of polished aluminum and steel objects in undecorated geometric shapes by the firm's president, industrial designer Paul Mayen (fig. 141). Setting a precedent for acquiring contemporary designs related to exhibitions, *Product Environment* also met Turner's goal of introducing new work to Philadelphians. "'Product Environment' is off—and from all evidence it is off to a flying start," he wrote to Bartine Stoner at the advertising firm of N. W. Ayer and Son. "It is one of those rare exhibitions that not only delights visitors but seems to attract families in considerable numbers, the happiest sort of exhibition for this Museum."[27]

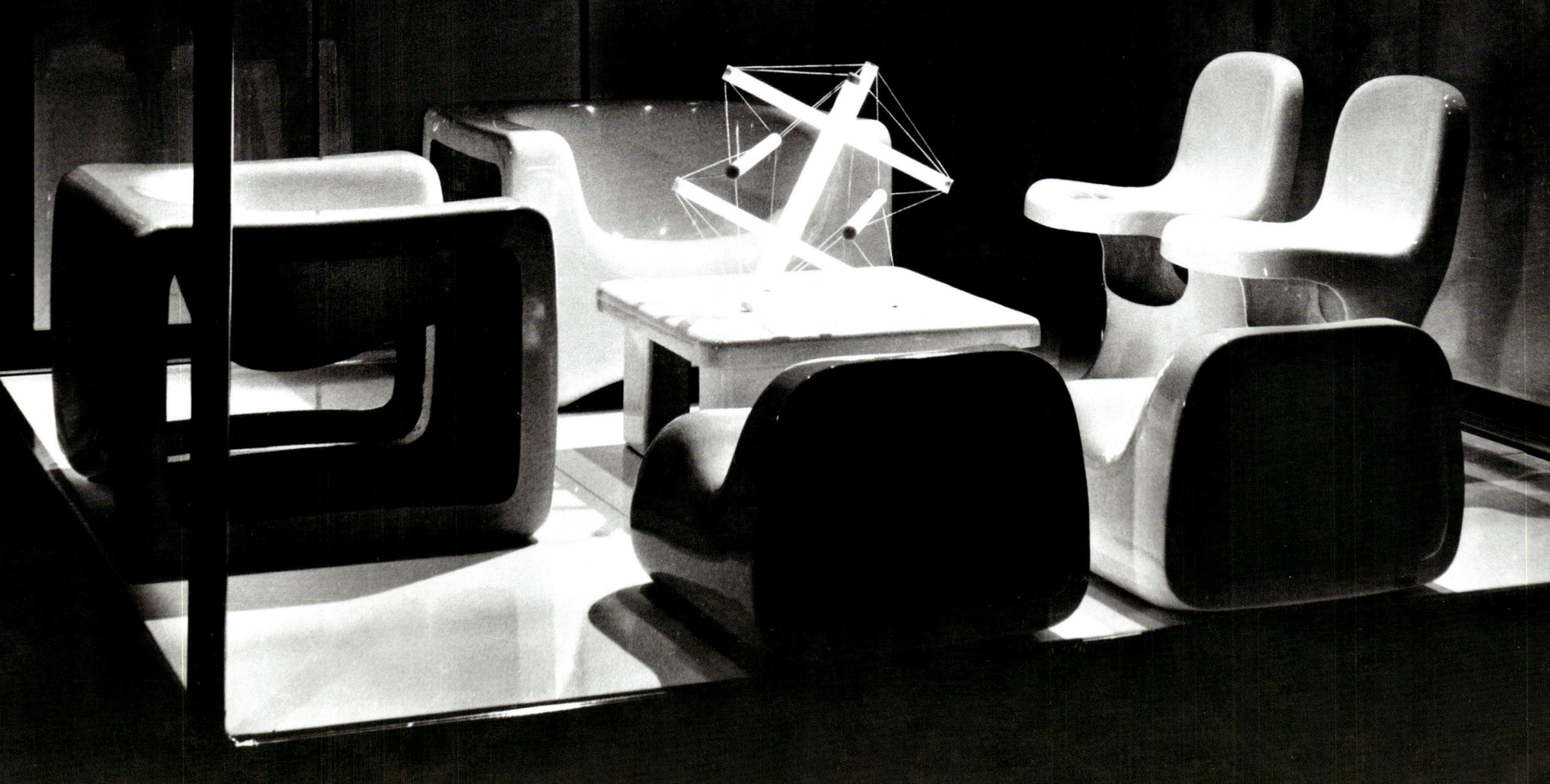

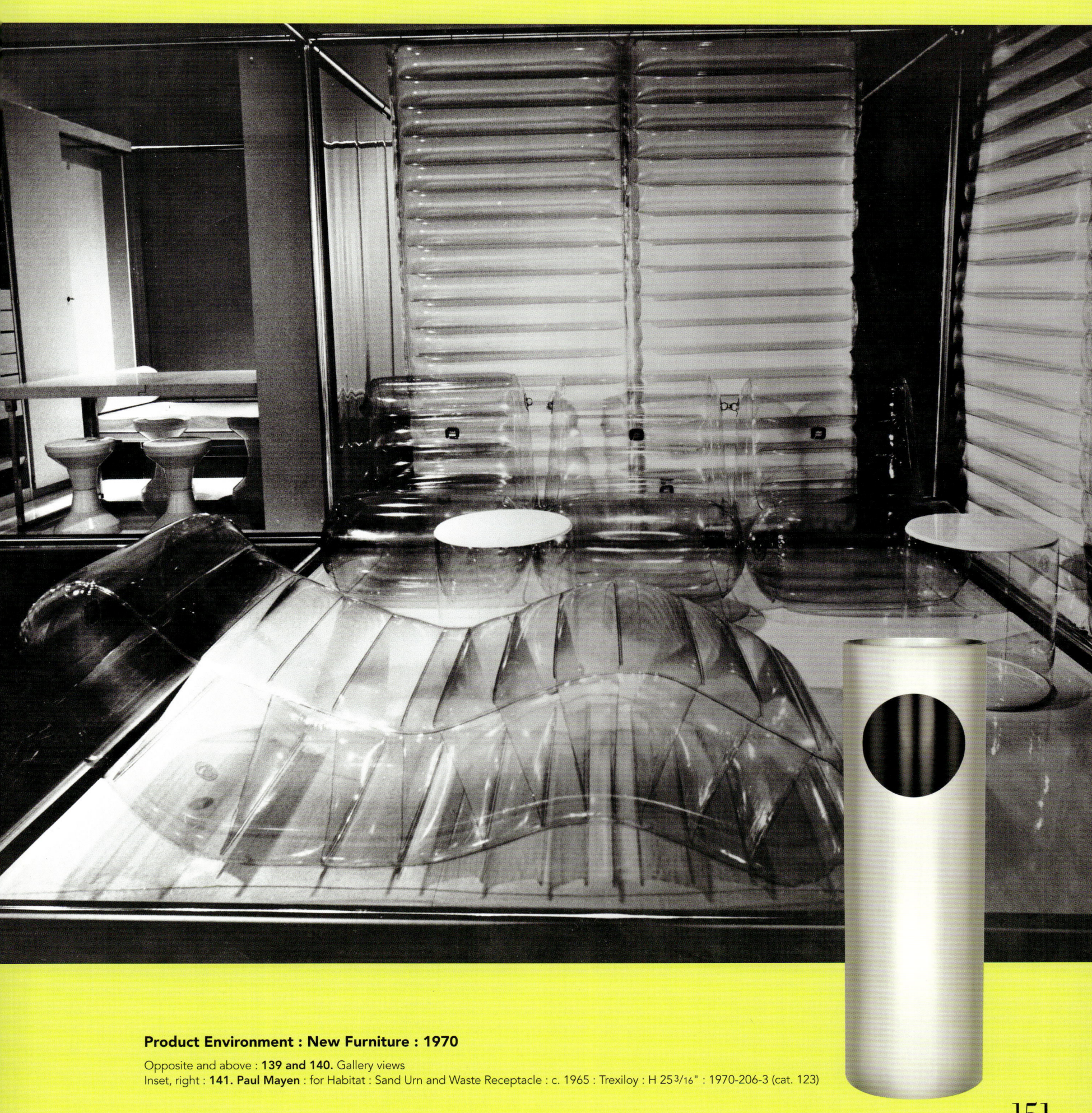

Product Environment : New Furniture : 1970

Opposite and above : **139 and 140.** Gallery views
Inset, right : **141. Paul Mayen** : for Habitat : Sand Urn and Waste Receptacle : c. 1965 : Trexiloy : H 25³/₁₆" : 1970-206-3 (cat. 123)

of trustees that since the Museum functioned in a world where an increasing number of young people were interested in their environment, the Museum should take the lead in improving the aesthetic quality of their lives.28 In late 1971 the department of urban outreach commissioned from Washington, D.C. artist Gene Davis a monumental stripe painting (of traffic paint and fast-drying, durable, high-gloss enamel) titled *Franklin's Footpath*, in front of the Museum on the asphalt surface of the Benjamin Franklin Parkway. Hailed as the largest painting in the world—it was the size of a football field—the work was executed by staff artists from the department of urban outreach and high school students in an extraordinary community effort using street-painting equipment lent by the city (fig. 142).

At the same time, the Museum began preparations for the coinciding celebrations of the nation's bicentennial and the Museum's centennial in 1976. Philadelphia would be an obvious center of the national celebration, and Museum staff were charged by the board to organize a major exhibition of American art. Led by pharmaceutical manufacturer and Museum trustee Robert L. McNeil, Jr., the board in 1969 had previously created a new committee for American art, with responsibility for the Museum's strong collections of American paintings, sculptures, and decorative arts;29 however, it was only with the appointment in 1973 of a curator, Darrel Sewell, that the committee acquired a department.30 Building on the important collections acquired by Fiske Kimball, a new department of twentieth-century art was also established for that area in 1972; its curator of painting, Anne d'Harnoncourt, later the Museum's director, returned to the Museum from the Art Institute of Chicago to fill the post.31

Henry McIlhenny had originally opposed the creation of a department of contemporary art, arguing to the executive committee that the painting and sculpture committee, which he headed, should not be divided: "This Museum aims to represent the history of art, starting with Christ. If

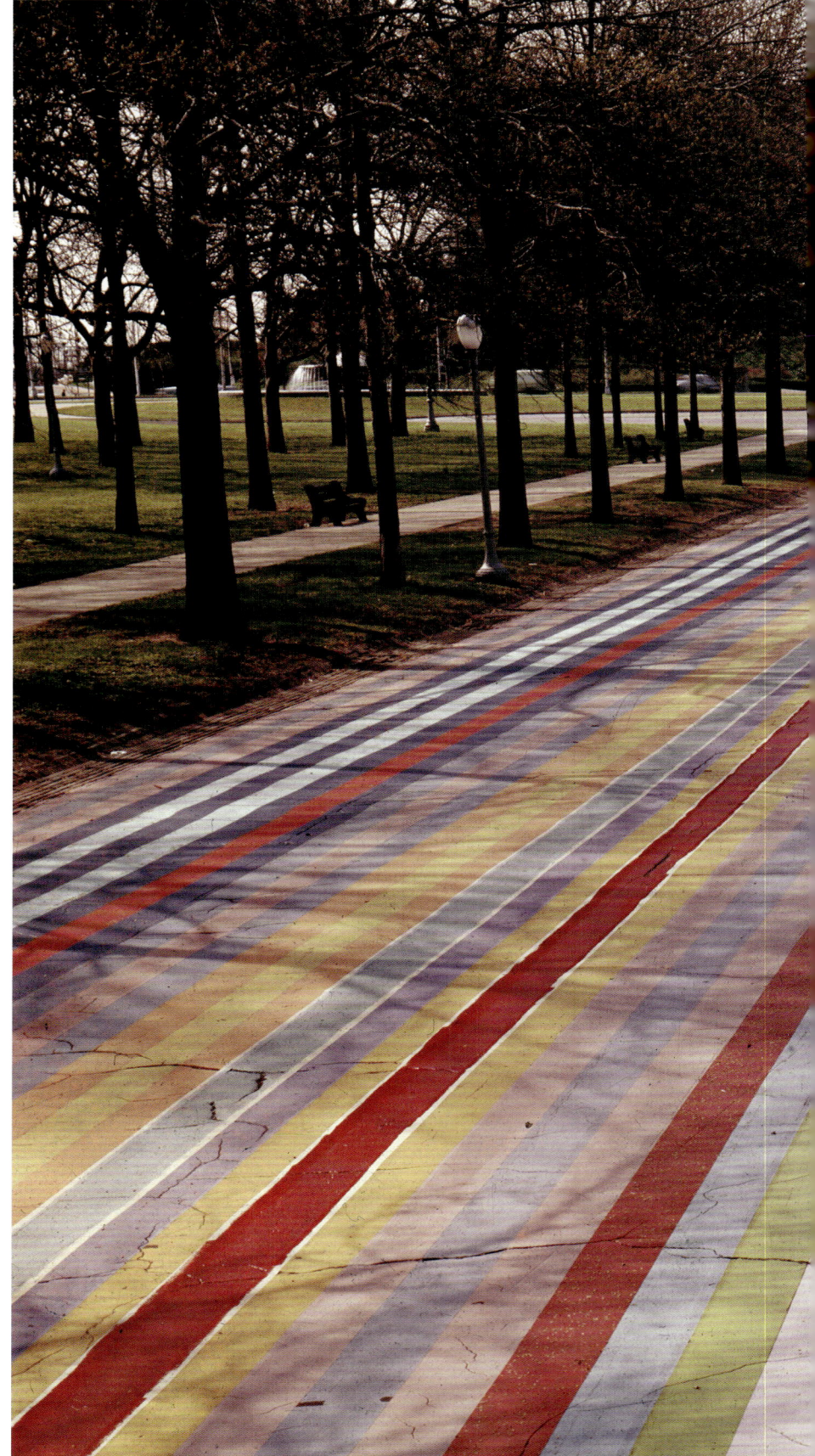

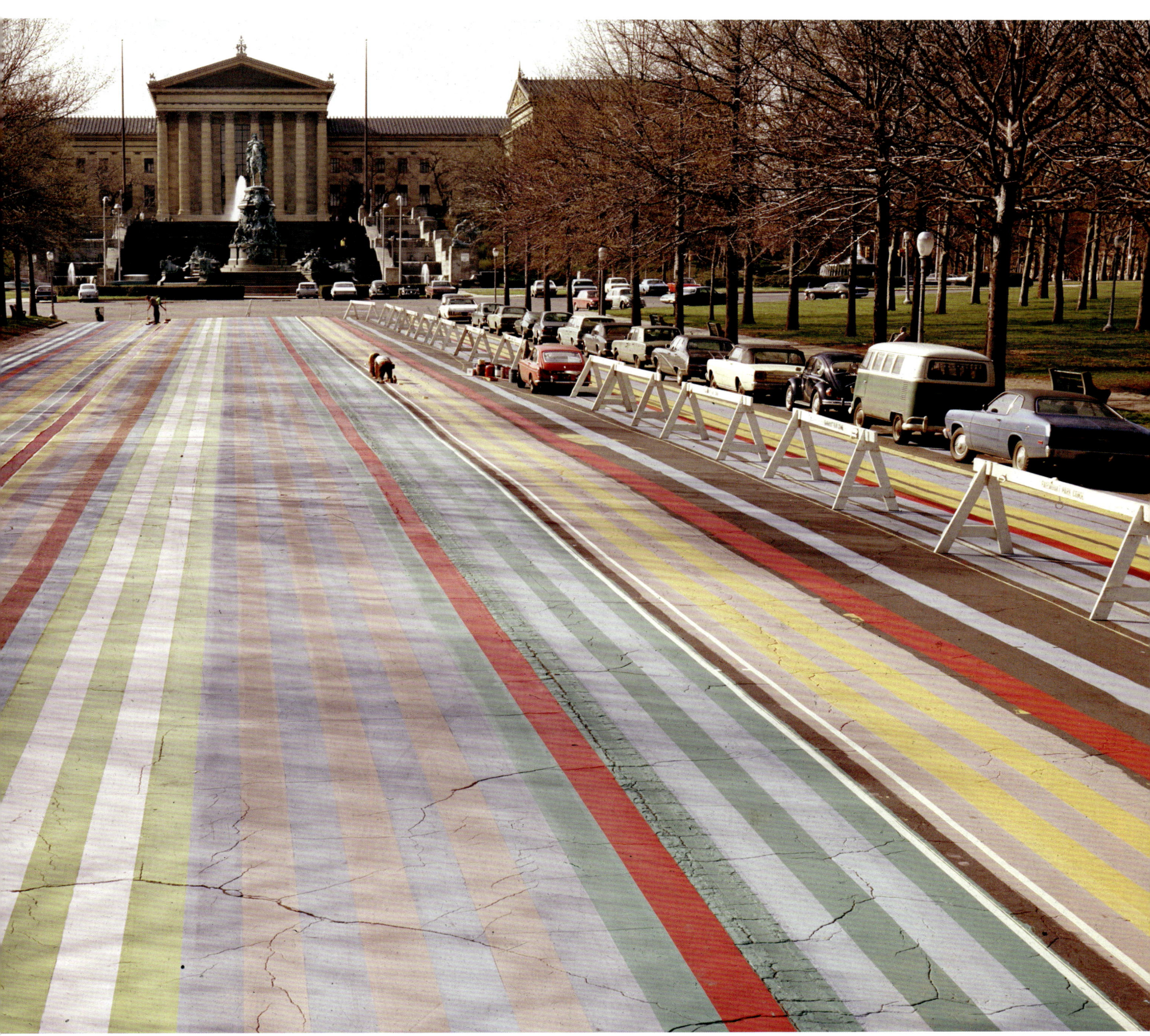

142. **Gene Davis** : *Franklin's Footpath* : Benjamin Franklin Parkway : Philadelphia : 1971 (cat. 42)

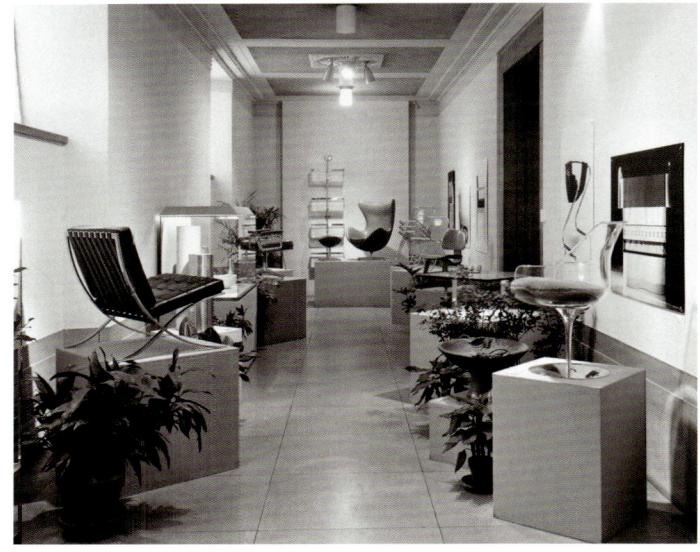

the modern-minded members are bored or unable to be interested in art before 1950, they are ignorant of the functions of this Museum and the point of the collection. This is not a gallery solely of contemporary art. The balance now of interests seems to me healthy, and it has been stimulating for the conservatives and should have been instructive for the firebrands."[32] Curiously, at the same time McIlhenny had no objection to creating a department of American art,[33] which would separate that collection from European painting, sculpture, and decorative arts and affect the responsibilities of both the painting and decorative arts committees. In the spring of 1971, as the board of trustees considered the new departments and their committees, it was decided that the two decorative arts staff members specializing in American works of art, Beatrice B. Garvan and Raymond Shepheard, would be transferred to the American art department to work under Sewell. Hathaway, scheduled for retirement within a year, became with board approval "Curator of European Decorative Arts since 1700 and all twentieth-century decorative arts,"[34] an assignment of responsibility that exists to the present.[35]

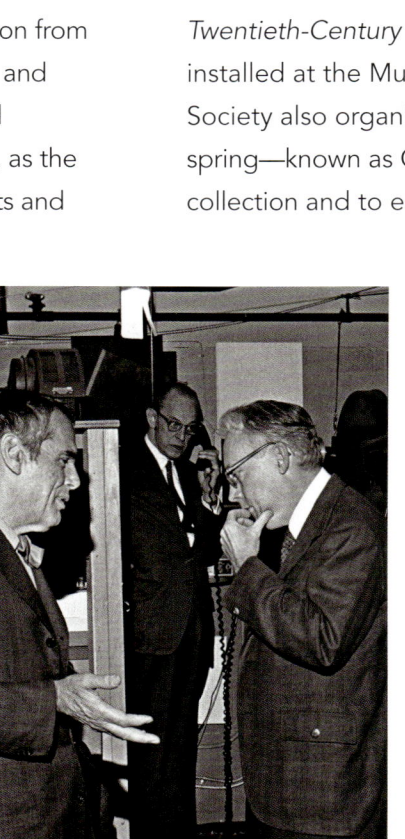

At this point the Museum story becomes autobiographical. In 1970 I moved to Philadelphia and a position at the Philadelphia Museum of Art. Trained as an art historian at Wellesley College (B.A.) and Harvard University (A.M., Ph.D.) specializing in Italian Renaissance studies, in 1971 I was given a joint appointment by Evan Turner as assistant curator in the department of medieval and Renaissance decorative arts and the department of painting and sculpture. When Calvin Hathaway retired in 1972 as scheduled, to become curator emeritus, Turner asked me to assume responsibility for the department of European decorative arts after 1700. Pleading total ignorance of the field, I was reluctant to take the position, but Turner was persuasive, promising that I could return to either or both of my previous assignments if I so chose after a year. At the time of this writing, nearly forty years later, I remain curator of European decorative arts after 1700, still fascinated and energized by the variety of material within the department's responsibility, and most particularly by modern and contemporary design. My first exposure to the material had been the exhibition *Recent Acquisitions: Twentieth-Century Decorative Arts*,[36] which Hathaway had installed at the Museum in 1971 (fig. 143). The Inter-Society also organized its first fund-raising event that spring—known as Collab '71—to acquire objects for the collection and to educate the community about design. A roundtable discussion, moderated by Evan Turner, included architect Robert Venturi, designer George Nelson, ceramist William Daley, and *House Beautiful* magazine editor (and subsequently interior designer) Sarah Tomerlin Lee. The event was so successful and informative, due particularly to Nelson's dominant voice,[37] that the fund-raiser has continued annually. The following year, in the spring of 1972, Hathaway invited Charles Eames to lecture for the Inter-Society benefit.

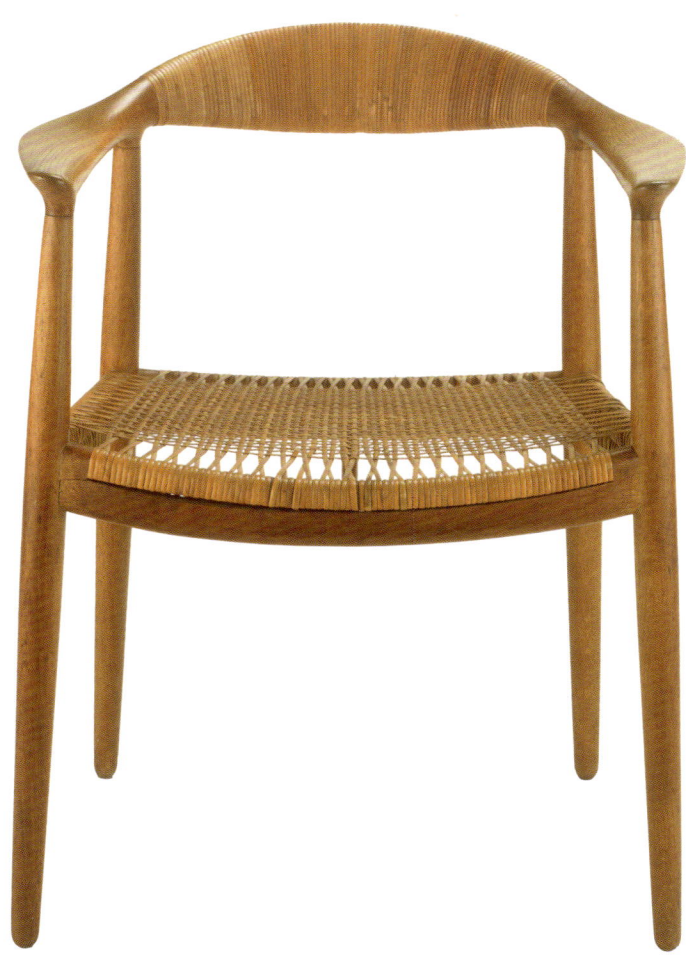

Eames gave a dazzling visual presentation, showing some of his recent films and projecting multiple images simultaneously (fig. 144); afterward Hathaway thanked him for "the nuggets of pure gold that you gave to your Philadelphia auditors."[38]

As Hathaway neared the date of his official retirement, the Inter-Society honored him by purchasing for the collection two pieces of contemporary glass that he had selected. Made by glass artist and sculptor Karel Mikolas, the works were given in appreciation of the curator's devotion to the cause and work of the group. Hathaway continued to collaborate with the Inter-Society until his resignation from the committee in October 1973, soliciting gifts from manufacturers and committee members, among them interior designer Carl Steele, who donated the Museum's first piece of furniture by Hans Wegner (fig. 145). In November 1972 Hathaway was involved in preparing the Inter-Society's first "Rules of Organization," drafted by committee president and interior designer Charles Agnew, which specified that the committee had been

> created for the purpose of acquiring items for a permanent collection of Twentieth-Century Decorative Arts and Design. When approved by the Museum Curator, such items will be given to and housed by the Philadelphia Museum of Art. When gallery space is made available by the Museum the collection will be given permanent display space. . . . Money raising programs shall be planned, at least one each year. Profits are to be used for the purchase of items not available through gifts. . . . The collection is to be representative of the era primarily from the turn of the twentieth-century to the present. The furniture and decorative arts may be hand-crafted or mass-produced items. . . . The collection is intended to further the awareness of contemporary design and education to the general public and students.[39]

This founding statement, soon after described as the Inter-Society's bylaws, still articulates the committee's mission today, although after the debut of the Philadelphia Craft Show in 1977 by the Museum's Women's Committee to generate funds for American crafts, Collab and the design collections have been focused largely on manufactured products. Turner also subsequently reminded the committee that objects acquired for the collections must also be approved by the director and the board of trustees.[40]

The fund-raising event in 1973 was the last in which Hathaway actively participated. "Masterpieces of Mass-Production: Good Design and How It Happens" included presentations by furniture craftsman Wendell Castle, textile designer Jack Lenor Larsen, furniture designer Richard Schultz, and industrial designer Russel Wright. Wright nearly stole the show with photos of the sell-out crowds at the 1939 launch of his *American Modern* dinnerware at Macy's Herald Square in New York. From Collab '73

Opposite, top to bottom : **143.** *Recent Acquisitions: Twentieth-Century Decorative Arts* : 1971 : gallery view   **144.** Charles Eames (left), before his lecture to the Inter-Society : 1972   Above : **145. Hans Wegner** : for Johannes Hansen and Knoll : *Round* Armchair, *Model No. JH5* : 1949 : oak, caning : H 30" : 1972-5-2 (cat. 208)

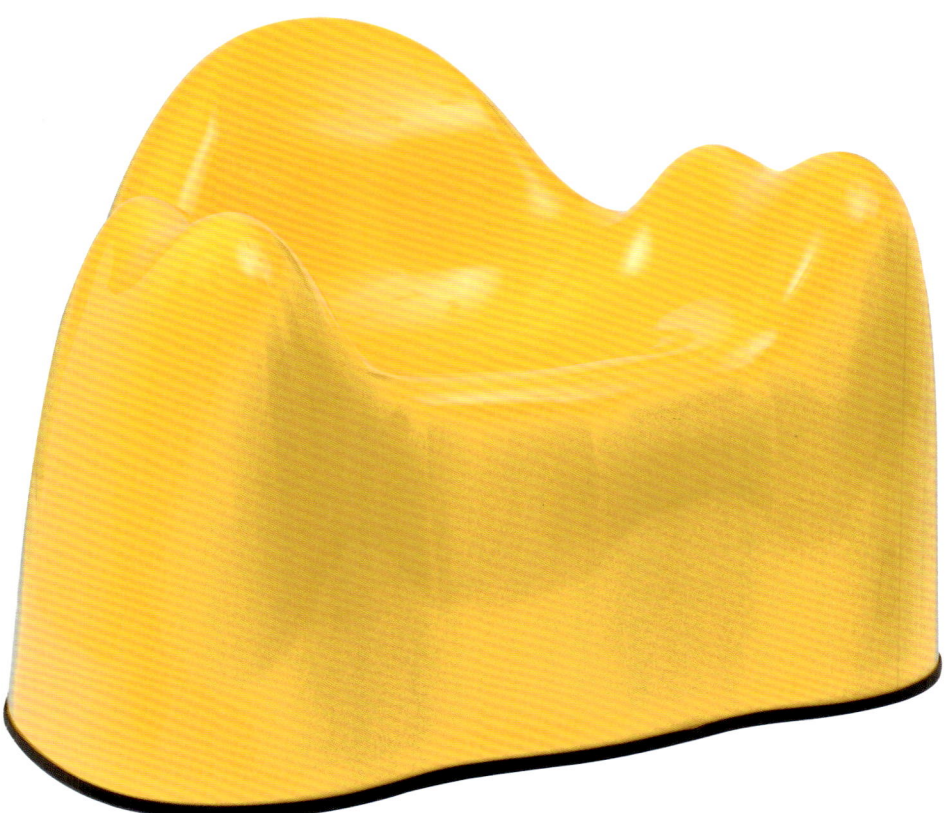

the Museum also acquired Wendell Castle's yellow plastic *Molar* chair (fig. 146), as a gift of the artist, along with his cherry-wood music stand. The first Inter-Society meeting that I attended as the Museum's representative, along with Evan Turner, was in November 1972 when discussions of Collab '73 were ongoing. In the tradition of Calvin Hathaway, I proposed that the Museum should organize a major twentieth-century design exhibition for the spring of 1974, little realizing, having never before undertaken such a project, what that might entail.[41]

It quickly became evident that the Museum could build its collections of modern and contemporary design without making a significant impact on the institution's limited endowments for acquisitions. With Collab's support we slowly began to expand the collections, simultaneously filling in historical gaps and adding obvious classics. The Museum funded acquisitions beyond Collab's means, design being relatively affordable compared to other fields in which the Museum collects. While the Museum's founders in 1876 optimistically believed that the collections could provide moral and commercial benefit by their good example, we value design differently today, separating moral improvement from aesthetics. Our criteria for collecting are still based primarily on aesthetic considerations, but we are also concerned, like Edwin Atlee Barber, with the historical, cultural, and technological significance of objects, and following the pioneering path of John Cotton Dana at the Newark Museum Association, we include household equipment.

Today the Museum collects a wide range of well-designed and well-made products that inspire our admiration and interest based on a variety of factors. It is hoped that by making fine modern and contemporary achievements such as these widely accessible they will provide fresh, sometimes surprising insights to the Museum's audience. For example, when first manufactured, a toilet designed by architect Gio Ponti and acquired by the Museum in 1983 (fig. 147) was compared to the Winged Victory of Samothrace,[42] a famously beautiful ancient Greek sculpture now at the Louvre, known—like the toilet—for the elegant forward thrust of its composition.

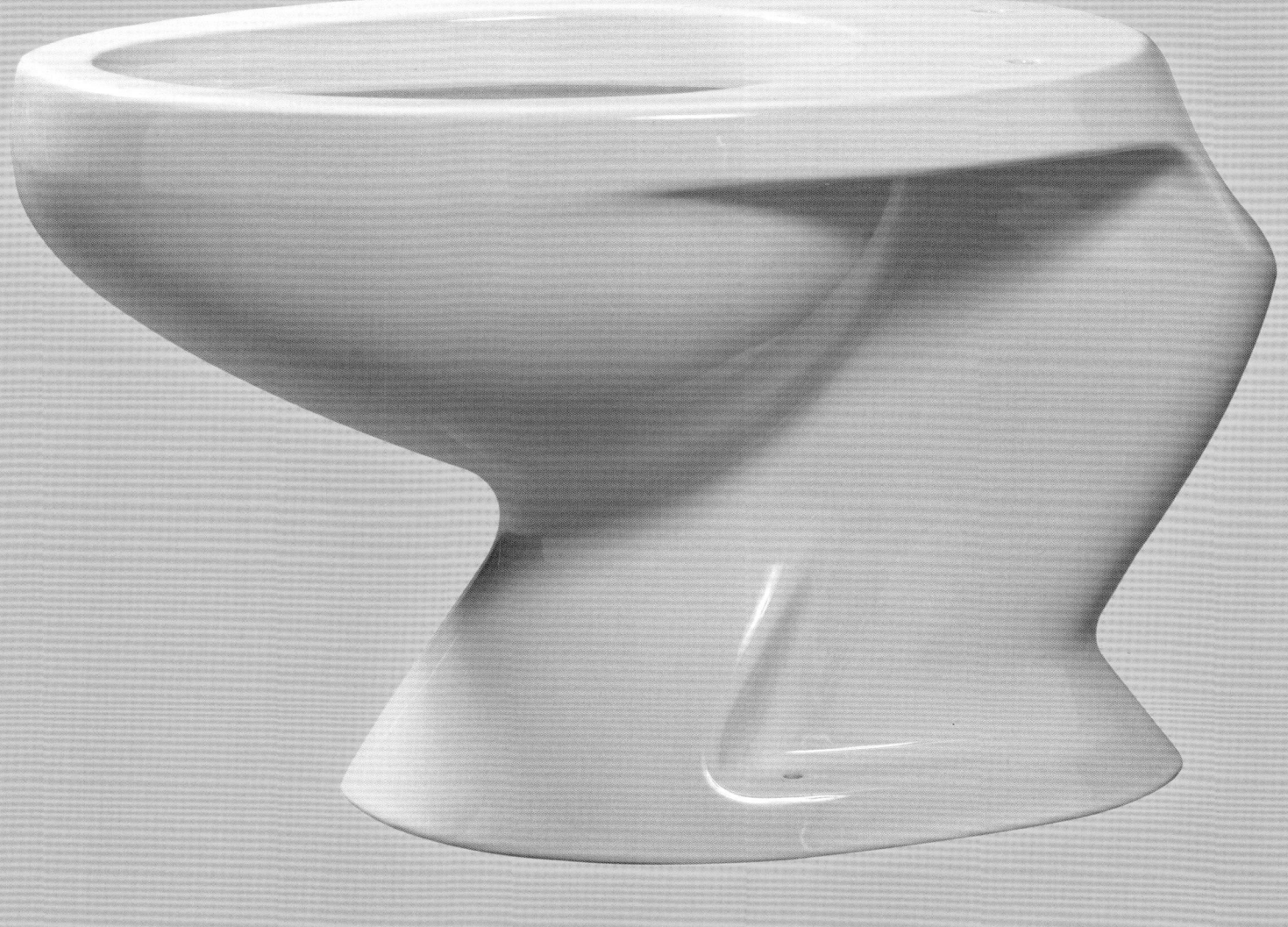

Opposite : **146. Wendell Castle** : *Molar* Chair : 1973 : fiberglass-reinforced polyester : H 26" : 1973-99-1 (cat. 30)   Above : **147. Gio Ponti** : for Ideal Standard : Toilet : 1953 : porcelain : H 15¹/₈" : 1983-52-2 (cat. 152)

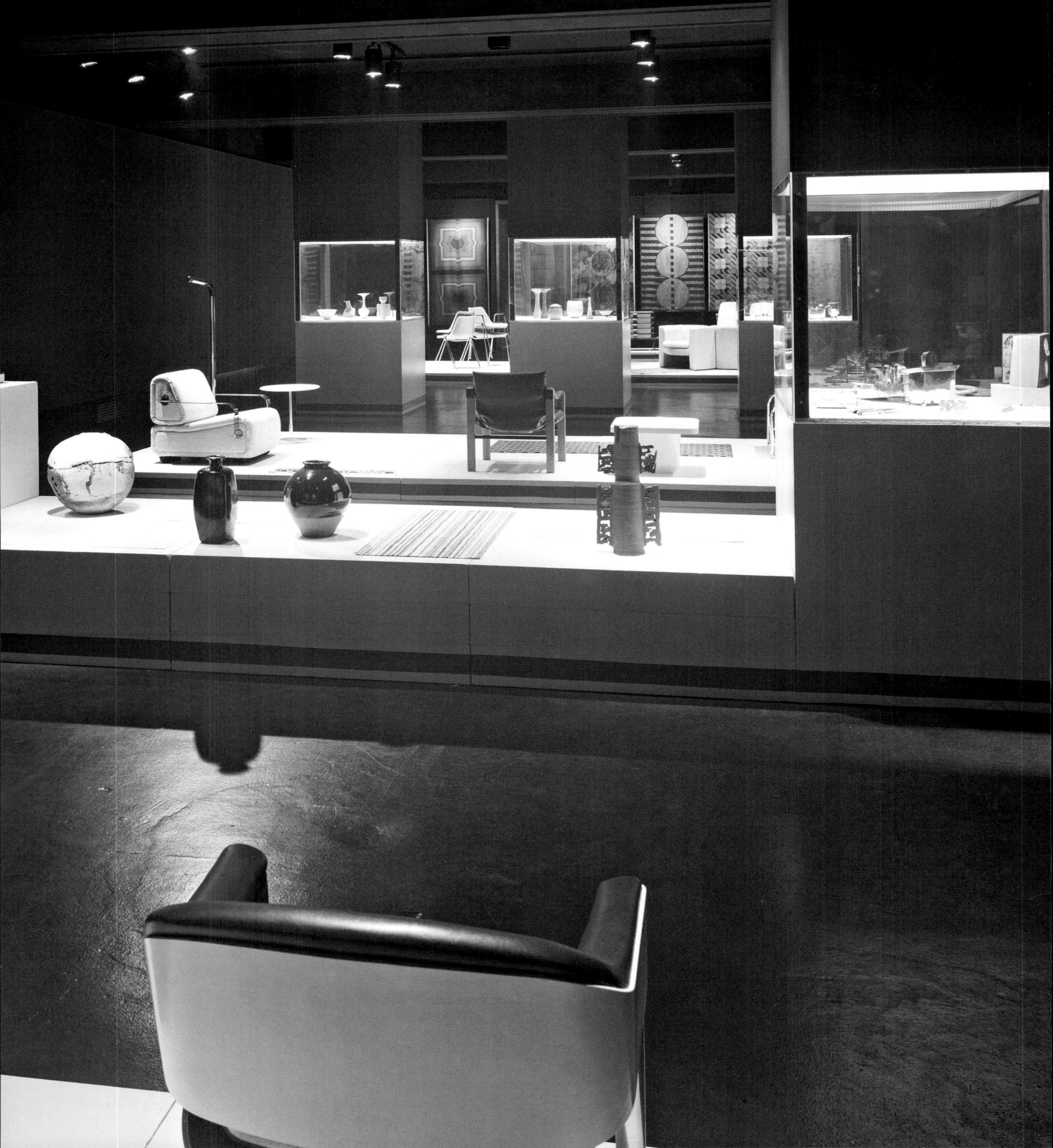

A SERIES OF DESIGN EXHIBITIONS

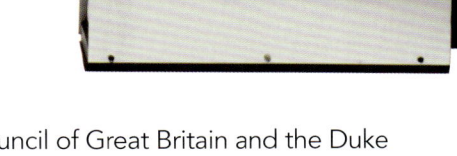

In early 1973 architect Richard Saul Wurman joined the Inter-Society; he would later become internationally known as a pioneer of "information architecture" as well as creator of the popular *Access* guidebooks. Wurman developed a number of strategies that have since guided the growth of the Museum's design collections, particularly his insistence on the need to contact manufacturers directly when trying to acquire objects by donation.[43] He also assumed responsibility for investigating themes that could shape Collab '74. With Helen Drutt and architect and Inter-Society chair Roland Gallimore, Wurman proposed sponsoring an international-design trade fair to present each country's leading products, although it soon became apparent that instead of inviting many countries at once, it would be more practical (and economical) to feature a single country each year. Thus the exhibition of crafts and industrial objects *British Contemporary Design*[44] was conceived for Collab '74, and it fell to the department of European decorative arts after 1700 to realize what became the first in a long series of design exhibitions produced for the committee and the Museum.

Britain represented a well-calculated theme for the initial exhibition because the Design Council of Great Britain and the Duke of Edinburgh, through their respective programs of national design awards granted to industry, could provide a ready-made short list of exhibition objects from which to select. In addition, the Crafts Advisory Committee of Great Britain helped us to identify handcrafted objects and to contact the country's most prominent craftspersons for their recent, best work. As we discovered, British manufacturers not only wanted to lend their award-winning pieces, but also to donate them to the Museum.

In order to cover the exhibition expenses (Evan Turner had made it clear that the Museum had no space in its own budget to finance the show),[45] and guided by the Museum's development office, the Inter-Society launched a fund-raising campaign that netted not only contributions but also a new audience. Ninety percent of the individuals and design-trade firms that helped support the exhibition had no prior history of contribution to the Museum or Museum-sponsored events.[46] This was an important moment for the Museum and the Inter-Society, as it revealed that modern and contemporary design had its own audience.

British Contemporary Design, a small, elegant exhibition, was designed and installed by Inter-Society members in collaboration with Museum staff. It consisted of thirty-six manufactured objects lent by British firms, thirty-two handmade objects lent by the Crafts Advisory Committee, and eleven objects lent to the exhibition from private collections and the Museum, all displayed on white modular platforms banded in red and framed by walls painted deep blue (fig. 148). Three hundred guests attended the subscription opening of the exhibition, where Sir Peter Shepheard, dean of the Graduate School of Fine Arts at the University of Pennsylvania and member of the Duke of Edinburgh's prize committee in 1971 and 1972, delivered a lecture. The exhibition and opening event accomplished the Inter-Society's core mission of adding works to the collection—twenty-nine in all—and generating substantial new support for and interest in the Museum's collections of modern and contemporary design.

British Contemporary Design : 1974

Opposite : **148.** Gallery view : 1974   Above : **149. Gerald Abramovitz** : for Best & Lloyd : *Cantilever* Desk Lamp : 1961 : aluminum, steel : H 20" : 1974-58-1 (cat. 4)

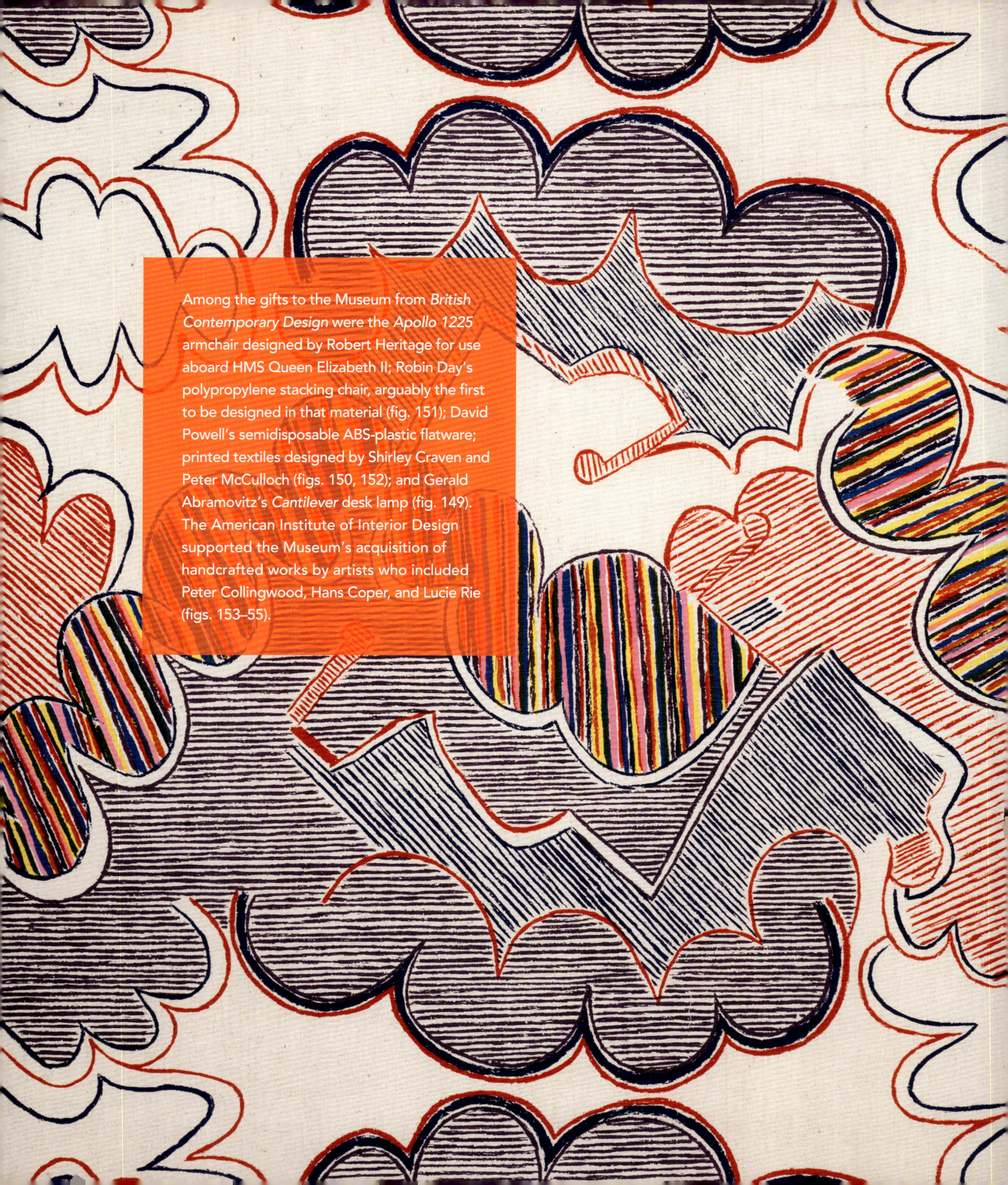

Among the gifts to the Museum from *British Contemporary Design* were the *Apollo 1225* armchair designed by Robert Heritage for use aboard HMS Queen Elizabeth II; Robin Day's polypropylene stacking chair, arguably the first to be designed in that material (fig. 151); David Powell's semidisposable ABS-plastic flatware; printed textiles designed by Shirley Craven and Peter McCulloch (figs. 150, 152); and Gerald Abramovitz's *Cantilever* desk lamp (fig. 149). The American Institute of Interior Design supported the Museum's acquisition of handcrafted works by artists who included Peter Collingwood, Hans Coper, and Lucie Rie (figs. 153–55).

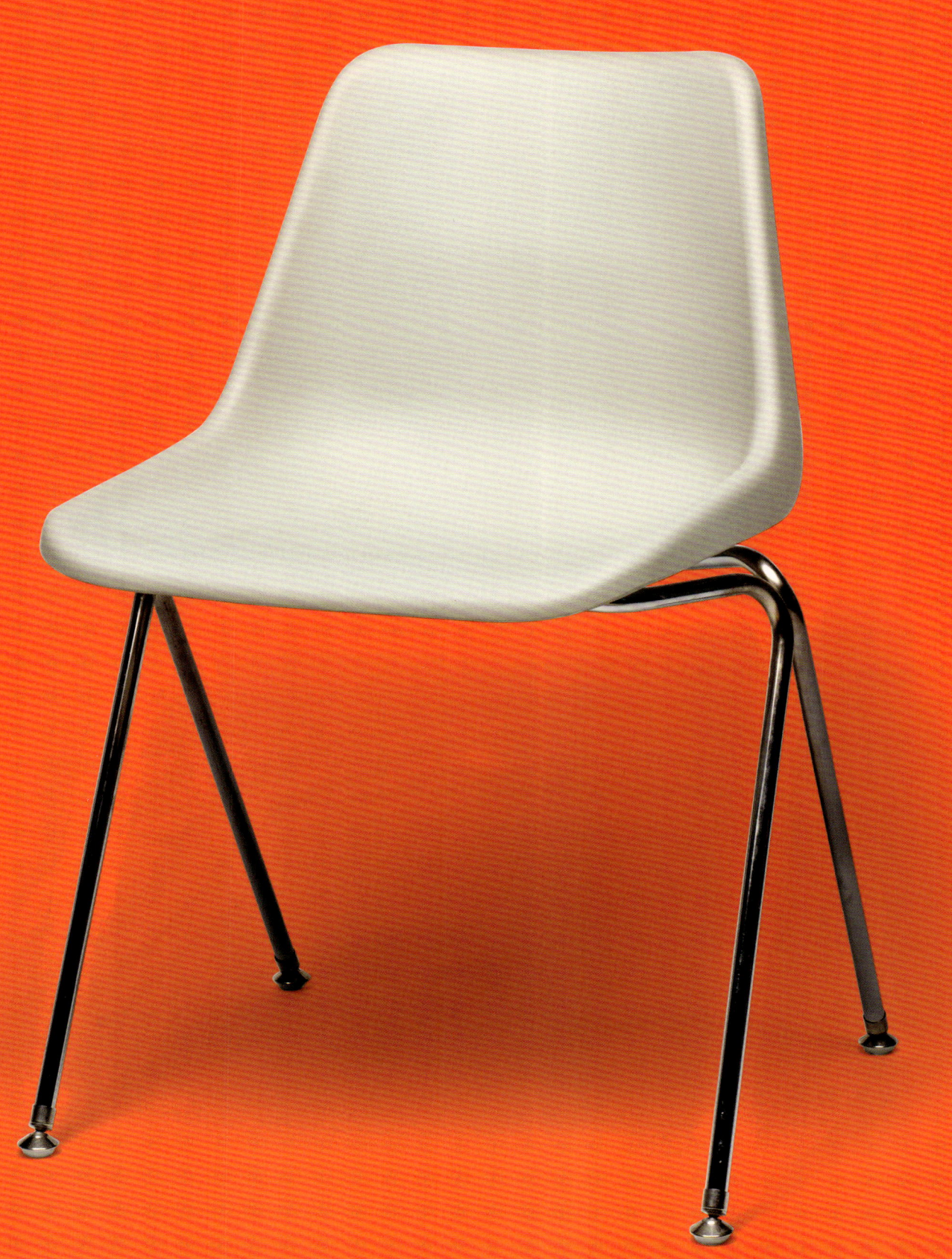

British Contemporary Design : 1974
Opposite : **150. Shirley Craven** : for Hull Traders : *Five* Fabric (detail) : 1967 : screen-printed linen and cotton : W 50" : 1975-8-1a–c (cat. 40)
Above : **151. Robin Day** : for Hille : *Polyprop* Stacking Chair : 1963 : steel, polypropylene : H 29¾" : 1974-150-1 (cat. 43)

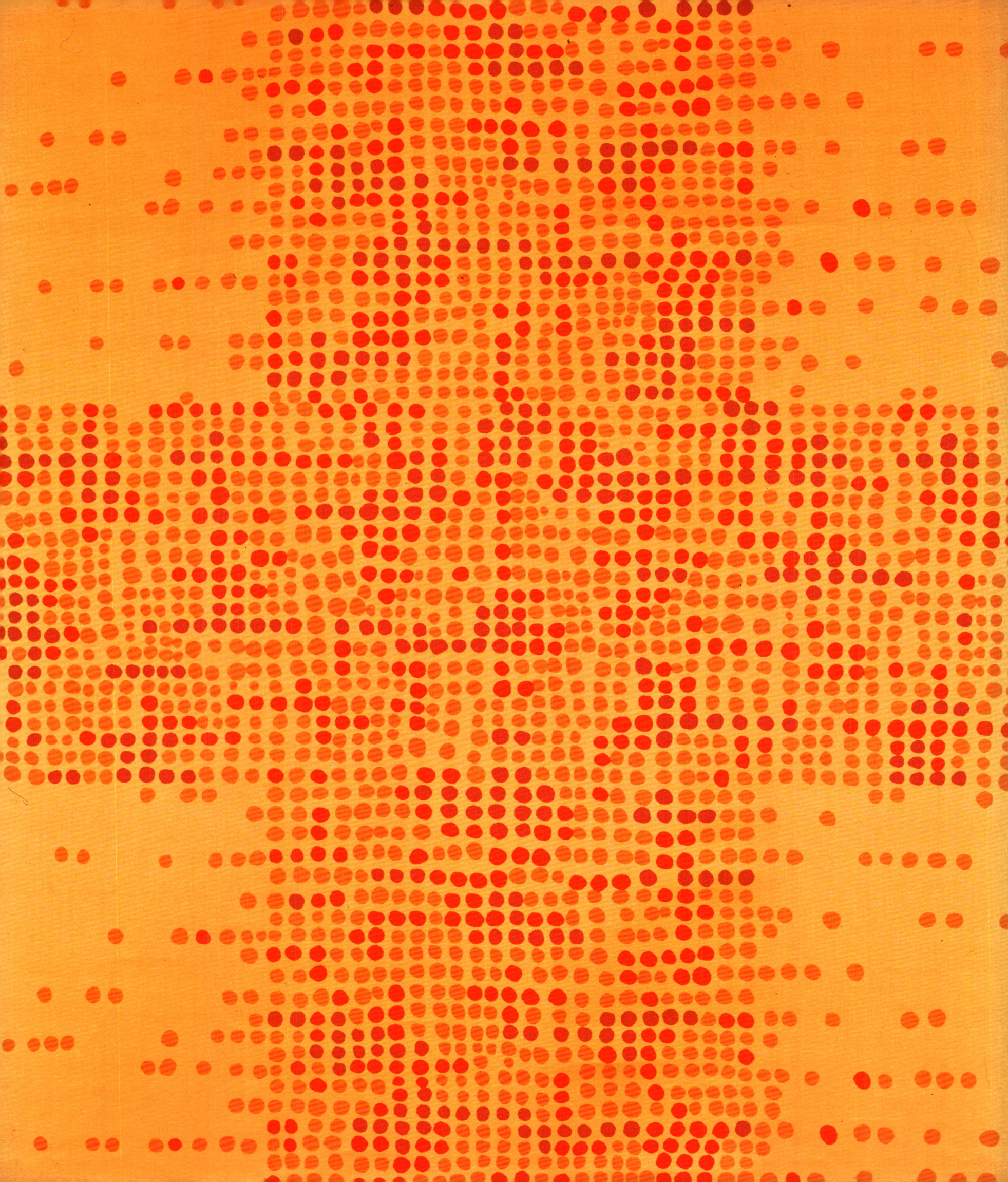

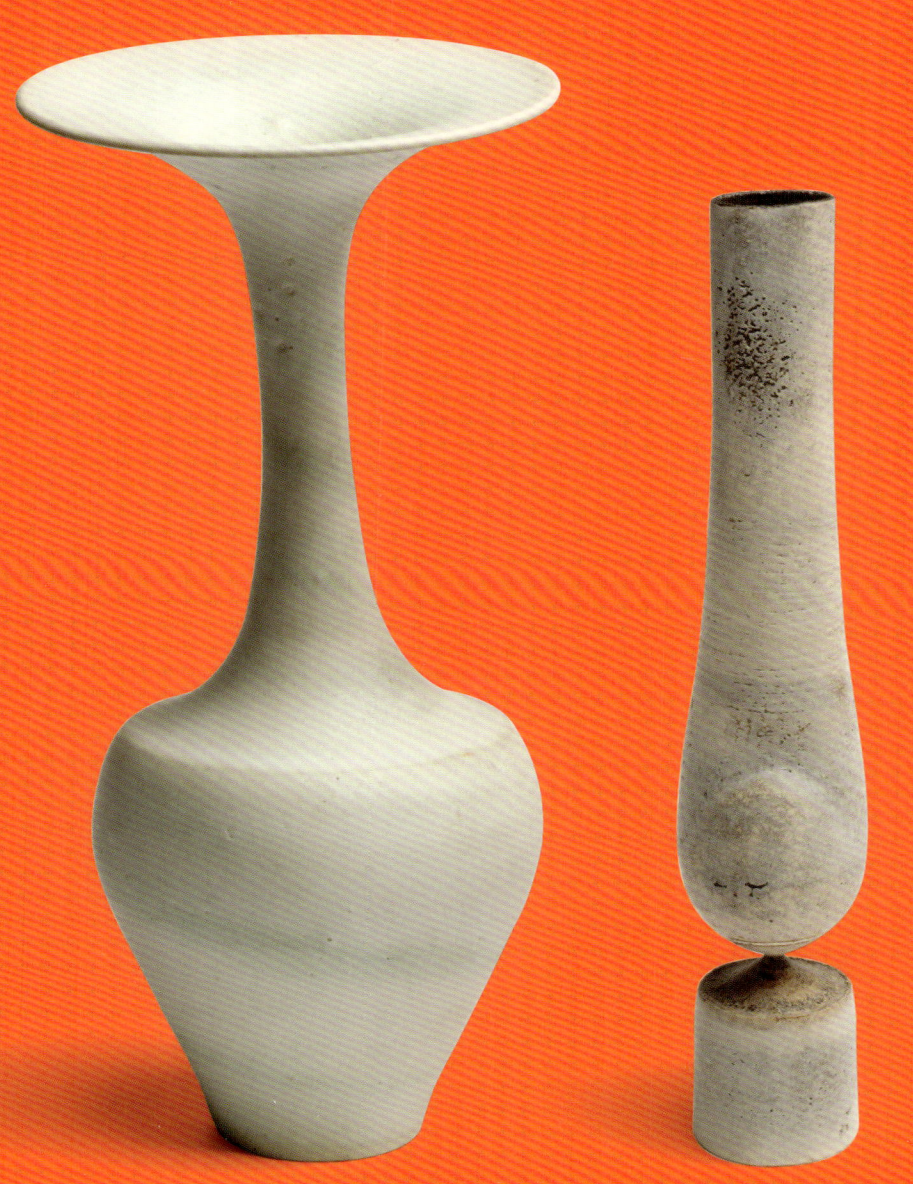
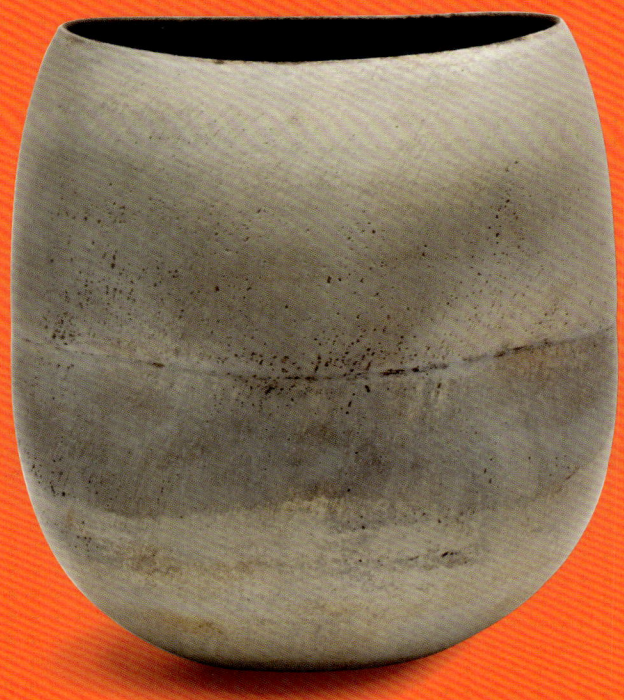

British Contemporary Design : 1974
Opposite : **152. Peter McCulloch** : for Hull Traders : *Cruachan* Fabric (detail) : 1963 : screen-printed cotton : W 48" : 1975-8-2a,b (cat. 126)
Above, left to right : **153. Lucie Rie** : Bottle : 1974 : glazed porcelain : H 11" : 1975-46-6 (cat. 158)   **154. Hans Coper** : Vase : 1974 : stoneware : H 9 1/8" : 1975-46-3 (cat. 39)   **155. Hans Coper** : Vase : 1974 : stoneware : H 7 3/4" : 1975-46-2 (cat. 38)

Just days after the opening of *British Contemporary Design*, another, smaller design exhibition was installed. Organized by the Women's Committee of the Museum, *A Touch of Gold*[47] displayed handcrafted contemporary jewelry, chiefly by Philadelphia artists, to celebrate the tenth anniversary of the Museum's Art Sales and Rental Gallery, a small gallery within the Museum that featured orginal crafts and works of art for sale. The works on view were available for purchase, and the exhibition thus forecast the much larger and more diverse Philadelphia Craft Show that the Women's Committee would initiate three years later. Both exhibition projects were modest of necessity, as they took place during the installation of the Museum's air-conditioning system. In fact, the two shows were shoehorned into an almost overwhelming schedule of construction and activity as the Museum prepared for its own centennial and the nation's bicentennial celebrations in 1976.

Under Turner's direction and the leadership of trustee Lewine Russell, indomitable chair of the Museum's building committee, so many significant construction projects were accomplished between 1969 and 1978 (when Russell resigned as chair)—notably climate control for the entire building, new special-exhibition galleries, and the creation of the new American wing—that the trustees jubilantly acknowledged: "The fifty year process of finishing the interior of the Museum building has been virtually completed and the Museum faces its second fifty years with a building which for the first time is properly equipped to function as a modern museum facility."[48] Even as the Museum's interior was being concluded, however, the board was already seriously considering the purchase of the former Fidelity Mutual Life Insurance building opposite the Museum at Fairmount and Pennsylvania avenues,[49] to provide space for its ever increasing collections and programs. This prospect would become a reality in 1999 when the support of the city of Philadelphia and Ruth and Raymond G. Perelman, the latter then chair of the Museum's board of trustees, made it possible for the institution to acquire the landmark building.

The many improvements made to the Museum could be carried out only by closing the building to the public from April 1975 through February 1976, while the staff moved and ultimately reinstalled nearly every one of some 450,000 objects in renovated galleries or new storage areas. With the help of my colleague Suzanne F. Wells, our department moved thousands of ceramics, including modern and contemporary works, to a new study-storage space, piece by piece in padded carts; we also inventoried, planned, and supervised the transfer of the Museum's furniture collection to its new storage areas. Following *British Contemporary Design*, Collab had envisioned a series of exhibitions that would explore design by country of origin, but other departmental concerns took priority, including the United States bicentennial exhibition *Philadelphia: Three Centuries of American Art*;[50] the Museum's centennial anniversary celebration; and development of a major international exhibition, *The Second Empire: Art in France under Napoleon III*.[51] Organized with my colleague Joseph J. Rishel, the Museum's curator of European paintings before 1900, and a team of French curators, *The Second Empire* opened in October 1978, before traveling to Detroit and then Paris, and occupied all 13,000 square feet of the Museum's new special exhibition galleries. It was described in the *New York Times* as "the single most outstanding exhibition of the year,"[52] representing "a

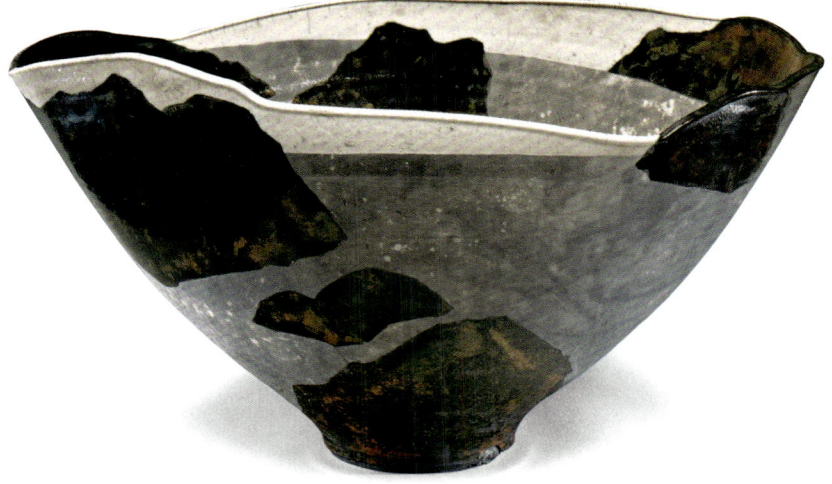

major challenge to established artistic opinion,"⁵³ an assessment shared by the *Washington Post*: "deliciously subversive . . . it pokes a hundred holes in that agreed-on fable called The Origin of Modern Art."⁵⁴ A number of the decorative arts objects arrived in Philadelphia from France in need of treatment, and in 1979, for the first time in the Museum's history, an objects conservator was added to the staff: P. Andrew Lins would eventually take responsibility for the conservation, preservation, and treatment of all the Museum's collections of decorative arts and sculpture.⁵⁵ However, throughout the project modern design remained on my mind, and during a research trip to Paris, I found an elegant French Art Deco writing desk made by Jacques-Émile Ruhlmann. Collab subsequently purchased the desk as a gift to honor the Museum's centennial (fig. 280), and in 1977 it was displayed at the Museum in *Gifts to Mark a Century: An Exhibition Celebrating the Centennial of the Philadelphia Museum of Art*.⁵⁶

During the 1970s the heavy demand placed on the Museum's staff and interior spaces—by the construction of an air-conditioning system, the bicentennial exhibition, and the installation and reinstallation of the American wing as well as other permanent galleries—made it virtually impossible for Collab to plan fund-raising projects within the Museum building. Collab '75, a public auction of modern and contemporary designs, was thus held in Memorial Hall, the first of a long series of fund-raising auctions that took place at different locations and finally at the Museum. Under the remarkably efficient direction of chair and interior designer Elisabeth Fraser, friends and business associates of Collab members (including manufacturers and their sales representatives) donated some 140 contemporary manufactured and handcrafted objects, a model followed at succeeding auctions. George Freeman, of the Philadelphia auctioneers Samuel T. Freeman and Company, advised the group on charity-auction procedures and served as auctioneer to some 500 guests. The proceeds of the Collab '75 and Collab '76 auctions were used to purchase the Ruhlmann writing desk,

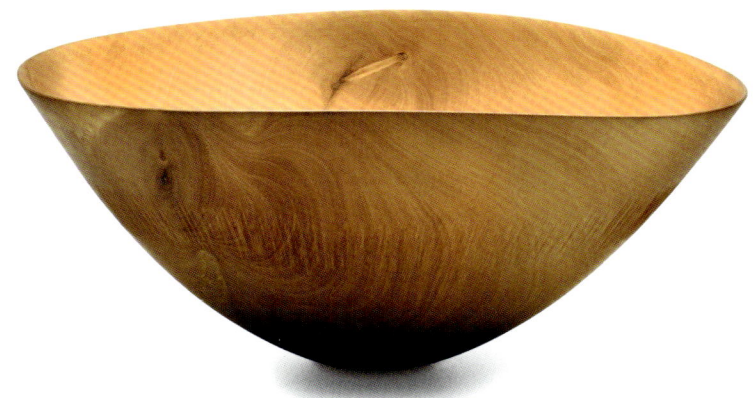

the group's most expensive acquisition to date. From the 1975 auction an executive lounge chair and ottoman designed by Charles Eames was purchased with funds contributed by Mr. and Mrs. Adolph G. Rosengarten, Jr., in memory of Calvin S. Hathaway, who had died in 1974. Through Helen Drutt, Collab was also able to sponsor the acquisition of additional fine contemporary crafts for the collections, including a raku-glazed earthenware vessel by Wayne Higby (fig. 156) and an Indonesian boxwood bowl carved by Robert Stocksdale (fig. 157).

When the newly reinstalled and air-conditioned Museum reopened in February 1976, modern and contemporary design was given its own small gallery within the section of the building devoted to modern art, fulfilling Turner's earlier promise to Collab. Our display of Marinot glass, Scandinavian ceramics, and a Puiforcat tureen, juxtaposed with Amécée Ozenfant's similarly composed still-life painting *Nacres No. 2* (1923–26), was a particular favorite with the press. The *New York Times* celebrated the Museum's reopening as a great victory over the challenges posed by the monumental building: "The museum is already bursting with new energy and sparkling with a combination of face-lifting and genuine rejuvenation. . . . a worthy habitation for its great collections."⁵⁷ Museum president George Cheston described the reopening as "one of the most exciting and personally satisfying events" during his tenure of eight years and gave fulsome credit to Turner for achieving it.⁵⁸

Opposite : **156. Wayne Higby** : *Many Rocks Pass* : 1976 : glazed and unglazed earthenware : H 12" : 1976-106-1 (cat. 82)
Above : **157. Robert Stocksdale** : Bowl : 1975 : Indonesian boxwood : D 8 1/4" : 1976-107-1 (cat. 184)

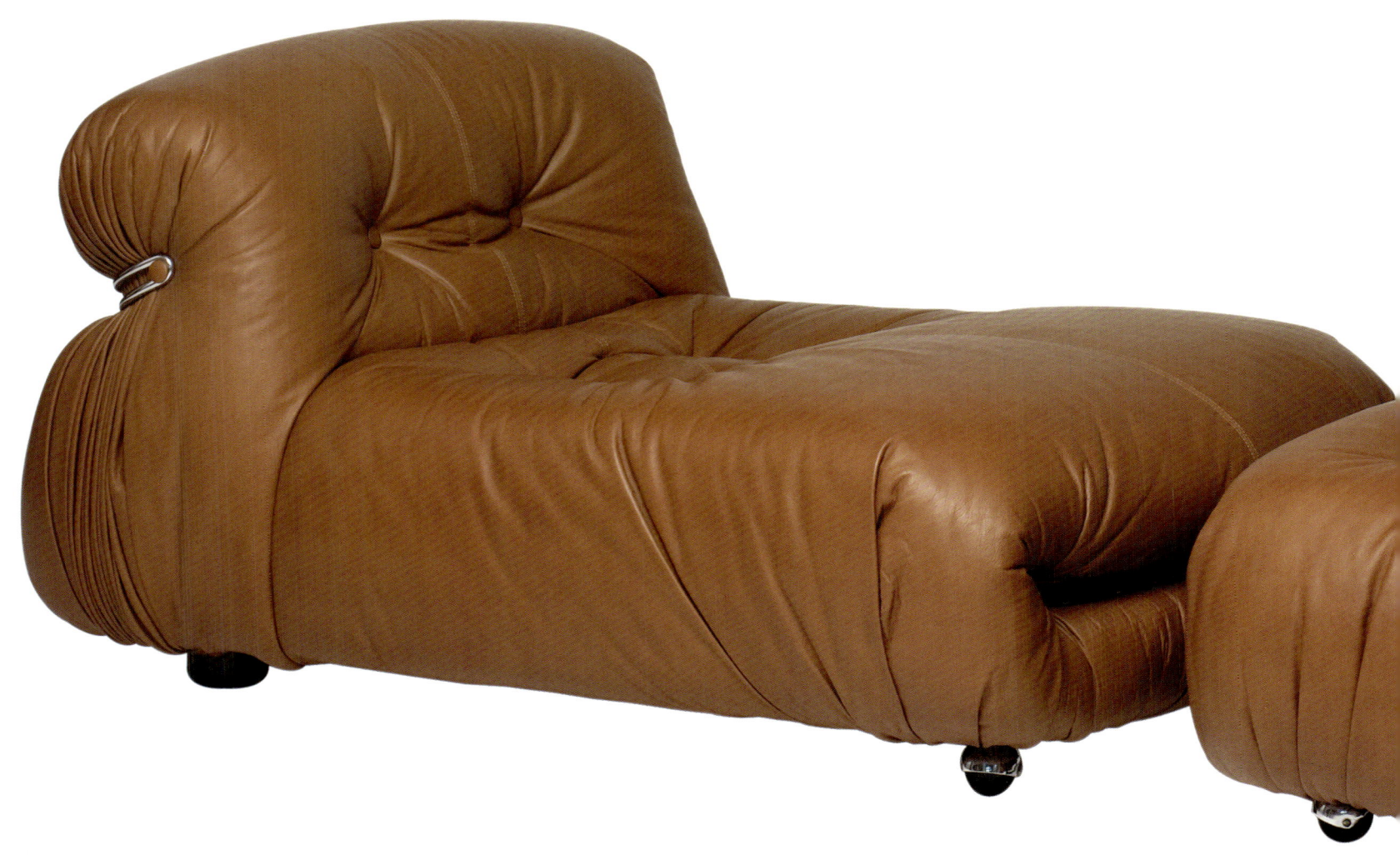

The Museum staff was therefore taken by complete surprise when only a year later Turner announced his resignation as director, just after the inauguration of the new American wing in April 1977. In his letter of resignation Turner acknowledged that the Museum was "at a major turning point in its history," and noted his "great satisfaction" in the "realization of our programs leading up to the Centennial." However, he concluded, "it is proper that someone else should undertake the challenges of the Directorship and bring different energies to bear as the Museum faces its second century."[59] Turner's resignation was accepted with regret by William P. Wood, the Harvard-trained lawyer and collector of Indian paintings who in 1976 had succeeded George Cheston as Museum president. Wood further recognized the "magnitude of Dr. Turner's contribution" to the Museum's board of trustees and cited a long list of his accomplishments.[60] Comparing Turner to "the cowboy hero who rides off into the sunset after he's cleaned up the town," the *Christian Science Monitor* cited the Museum's "massive renovation and reinstallation . . . ushering the museum into the twentieth-century."[61] In his last annual report as director, Turner summarized what he felt were the most important achievements of his directorship, among them developing a professional Museum staff, creating order in the collections with new galleries and study-storage areas, and making the Museum more accessible to the public through the activities of the division of education and department of urban outreach. Collab chair Elisabeth Fraser expressed the group's appreciation for Turner, "its staunchest

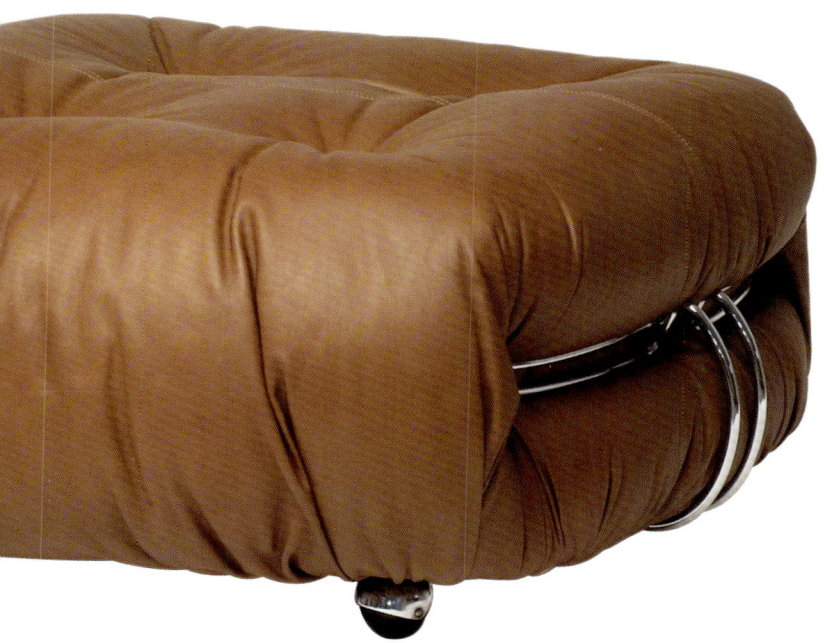

supporter . . . through [whose] efforts Collab has been able to reach its capabilities."[62] To find a successor to Evan Turner, the board appointed a search committee,[63] on which I served as staff representative along with Arnold Jolles, who since 1974 had been the Museum's assistant director for art and would serve as acting director in the interim.

Despite the Museum's impressive achievements under the direction of Turner, and the city of Philadelphia's major contributions to the Museum's capital budget for air-conditioning, renovation, and construction, the institution faced tremendous pressures due to eroding financial support from the city for other services. Of particular importance was the gradual depletion of municipal personnel—including guards, art handlers, the individual responsible for packing and shipping art, and craft technicians such as carpenters, painters, and plasterers. The city's bleak financial outlook reflected the effects of a global recession and inflation triggered in 1973 by the oil embargo and subsequent energy crisis. In the winter of 1977 the Museum took its own steps to address the energy crisis by closing the Fairmount Park Houses and the Rodin Museum, and by turning off lights and hot water at night in the building on Fairmount. Heated by steam rather than gas, the Museum remained open during regular visitor hours, although a number of galleries were closed for lack of guards; in addition, the Museum was forced temporarily to discontinue programs such as studio art classes and to cut public services, among them visitors' use of the library and slide library.

There were no funds for acquisitions in fiscal 1977, but among other gifts the Museum received a lamp and six pieces of twentieth-century furniture from Atelier International—constituting the most substantial gift from a manufacturer in many years—including lighting and furniture by Tobia and Afra Scarpa (fig. 158), Achille and Pier Giacomo Castiglioni (fig. 159), and Vico Magistretti. A small exhibition of these and other pieces was organized in the Director's Corridor of the Museum during the spring of 1979 by Suzanne Wells, soon to be named assistant curator, who also published an exhibition checklist that was distributed without charge in the gallery. Against the background of preparations for the Museum's *Second Empire* exhibition, Collab presented its annual fund-raising auction in 1977 at the Marketplace Design Center, and in 1978 at the Academy of Music Rehearsal Hall, both in Philadelphia. In memory of Roland Gallimore, architect and former Collab chair who had died recently, Collab used the proceeds from Collab '78 to support the Museum's purchase of a tubular-steel and cane chair and stool designed by Mies van der Rohe (fig. 85). This gift inaugurated a tradition of donating objects in honor of Collab chairs that has continued to the present.

158. **Tobia Scarpa and Afra Scarpa** : for Atelier International and Cassina : *Soriana* Lounge Chair and Ottoman : 1970 : chromed metal, polyurethane, Dacron, leather : H (chair) 27" : H (ottoman) 15 3/4" : 1978-21-1a,b (cat. 172)

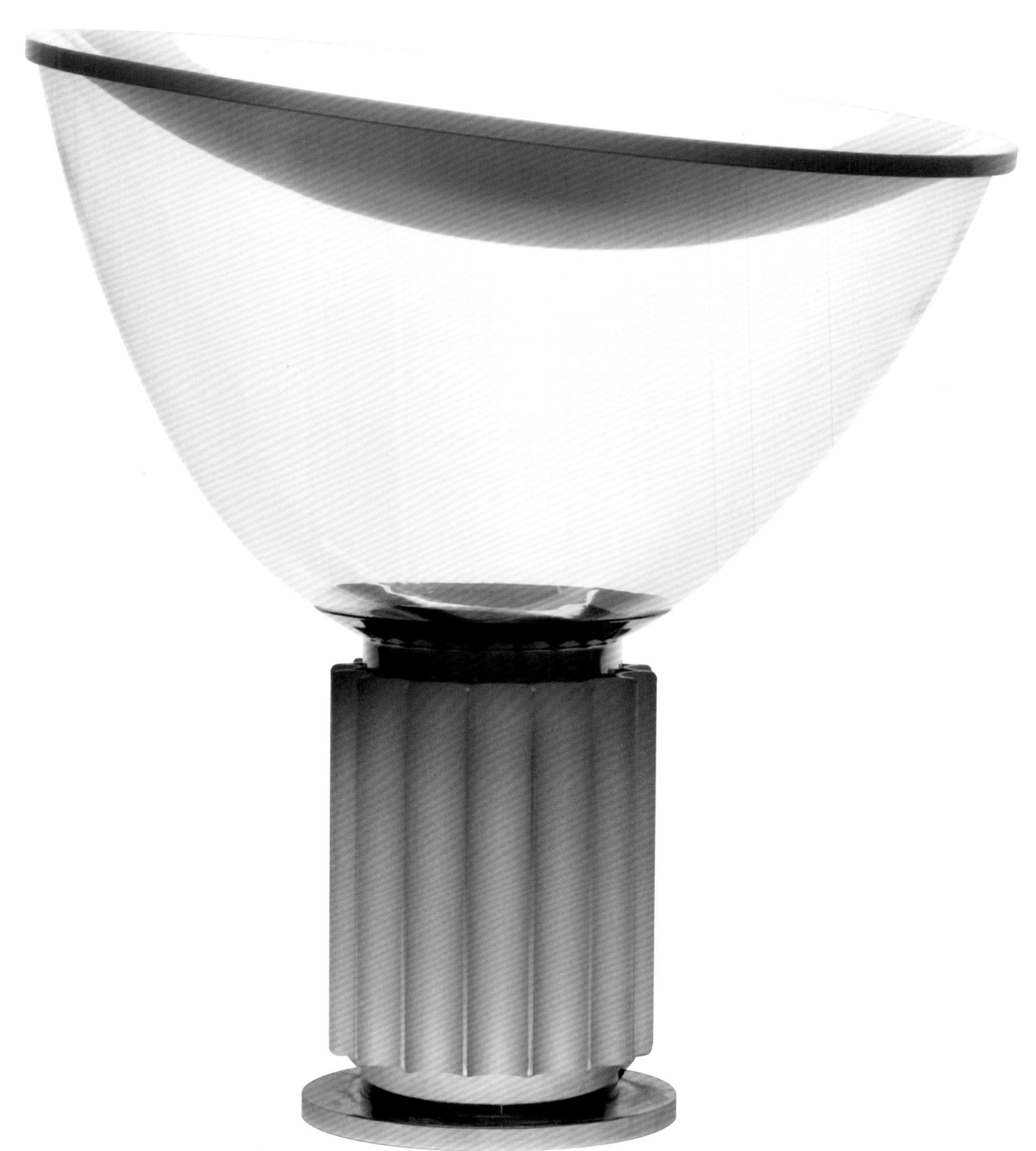

In July 1978 the Museum's nominating and search committees unanimously recommended fifty-six-year-old Jean Sutherland Boggs, then professor of fine arts at Harvard—where she had received A.M. and Ph.D. degrees in art history from Radcliffe College—as director, to assume her duties in March 1979 (fig. 160). Boggs was the first woman director of the Philadelphia Museum of Art and, as such, the first to direct one of the country's largest museums, a fact little remarked by the Museum's trustees in the face of her formidable accomplishments as a scholar, an educator, and a museum director.[64] Boggs's aesthetic interests extended well beyond her chosen field of modern painting. In a typescript preserved in the Museum's archives, Boggs, who grew up in Canada, described her first visit to the Museum of Modern Art in New York in 1939, at the age of seventeen, to see an exhibition of Italian works that had been on view at the San Francisco World's Fair: "For the first time in my life I saw, pristinely installed, Botticelli's *Birth of Venus*, Verrocchio's *David*, Titian's *Paul III*. A taste for the old within the new was born within me. I enjoyed feeling that the predictable inhabitants of the Museum of Modern Art essentially belonged with Botticelli's *Venus*."[65]

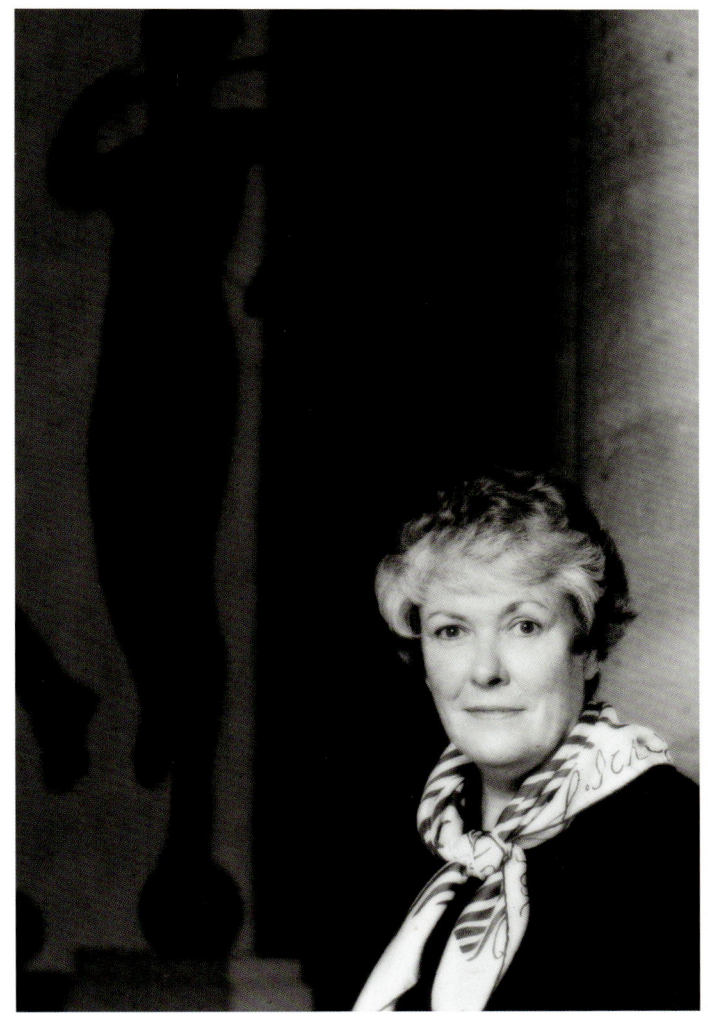

Boggs's broad interests led her to support Collab's goals and programs. She proposed, for example, that the group sponsor a lecture by Isamu Noguchi and help develop a small, auxiliary exhibition of his commercial designs to accompany the major exhibition *Noguchi's Imaginary Landscapes*, which would open at the Museum in October 1979.[66] As a result, a group of Noguchi's mulberry-bark-paper *Akari* lamps was shown in conjunction with the exhibition and given to the Museum by the artist (fig. 161). Noguchi's lecture for Collab filled the Museum's auditorium and "enchanted everyone."[67] Collab '79, an auction held that September (once again at the Marketplace), was as successful as its predecessors. In the following two years Collab again sponsored auctions, as well as illustrated lectures in 1980 by Mies van der Rohe's daughter, Georgia van der Rohe (who presented a film about her father), and in 1981 by architect Michael Graves. Boggs wrote me to say how successful she thought the last auction had been: "I do hope you thoroughly enjoy the fruits of the endeavor—major new acquisitions for the collection."[68] In fact, the proceeds made possible the purchase of an important silver cup by Josef Hoffmann (fig. 310),[69] and a chair designed by Peter Behrens presented in honor of Collab chair Elisabeth Fraser. Building on Hathaway's earlier acquisition of the collection of Thonet chairs, the Museum thus began to assemble a core group of objects representing the important turn-of-the-century modern reform styles of Secession and Jugendstil, to which it would continue to add works in the years to come. At the end of 1981 Boggs wrote to Collab: "We cannot thank you enough for all you are doing. . . . You have been very busy and very generous."[70]

Opposite : **159. Achille Castiglioni and Pier Giacomo Castiglioni** : for Flos : *Taccia* Table Lamp : 1962 : aluminum, glass : H 21" : 1977-199-1 (cat. 29)
Above : **160.** Jean Sutherland Boggs : Museum director, 1979–82

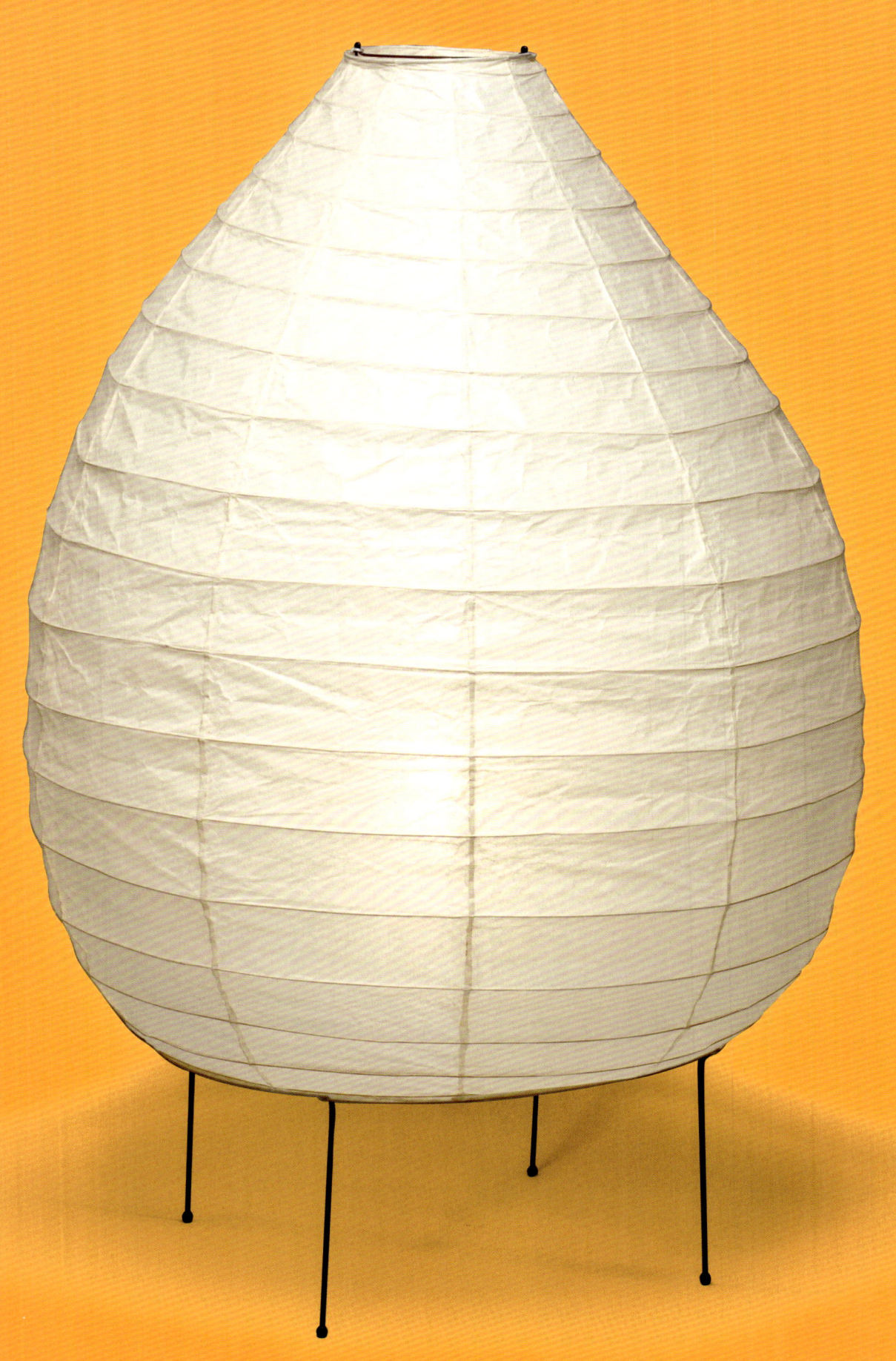

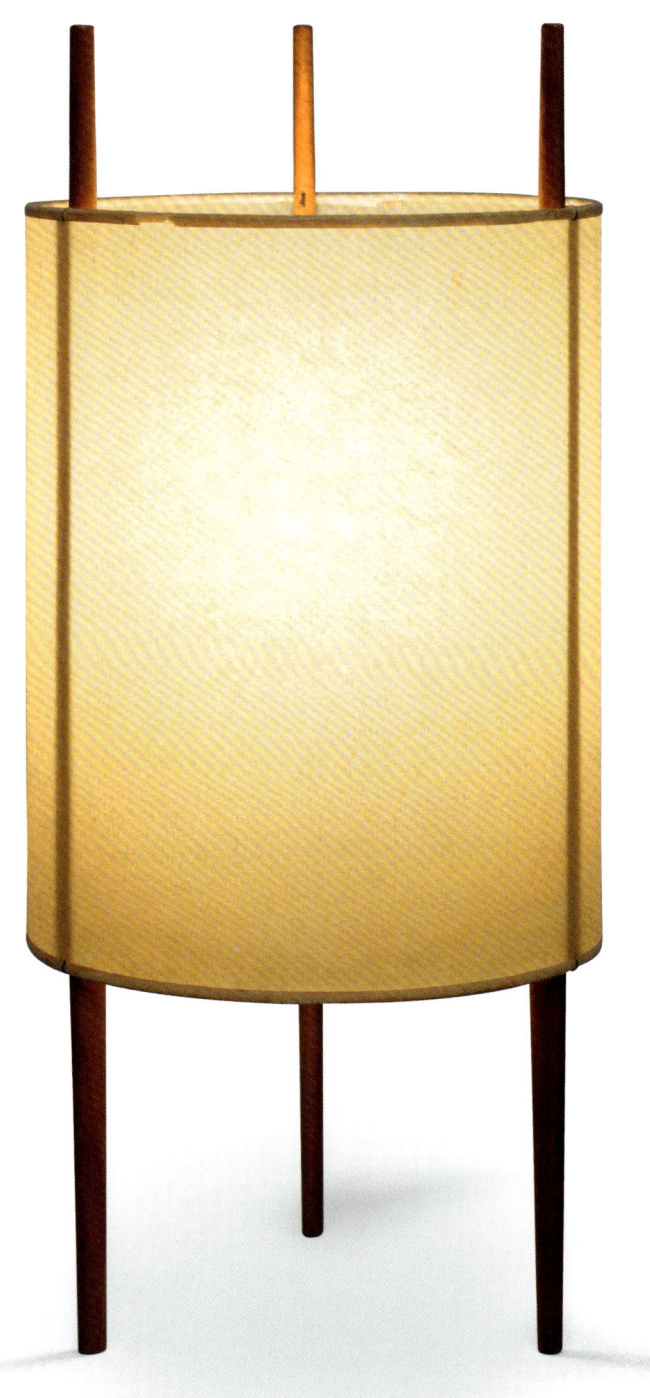

Opposite : **161. Isamu Noguchi** : for George Kovacs : *Akari* Floor Lamp : 1975 : mulberry-bark paper, bamboo, metal : H 45" : 1979-87-1a–d (cat. 139)
Above : **162. Isamu Noguchi** : for Knoll : Table Lamp : 1948 : plastic, wood : H 15 3/4" : 1977-85-1 (cat. 138)

In early 1979 I began discussing with Collab the organization of a major exhibition of modern and contemporary design. It was difficult to define the scope of the project, but with the encouragement of Collab chair Hava Gelblum and others it was concluded that material postdating World War II offered the most exciting and novel possibilities for exhibition, with a focus on objects of aesthetic distinction that were innovative in their forms, manufacturing techniques, and materials. Envisioned as a kind of sequel to the Museum's 1932 exhibition *Design for the Machine*, the show would include some four hundred objects made for household use, from appliances to armchairs, reflecting changing tastes, lifestyles, and technology. By 1980 I had prepared a tentative exhibition list and begun to contact manufacturers for help in assembling *Design Since 1945*, the first comprehensive survey in this country of recent decorative arts and designs. Over the next three years funding for the exhibition and its accompanying publication was provided not only by Collab, but by grants from corporations and public and private foundations.

Design Since 1945 was on view at the Museum from October 1983 to January 1984.[71] George Nelson (fig. 164) designed the exhibition to allow controlled circulation among various groups of objects that were generally arranged by medium and in chronological order (figs. 165–71, 173–96). Throughout, video programs, didactic labels, and objects from the larger world of design helped to acquaint visitors with manufacturing processes and the effects of technology on style and products. Seven "designer profiles"—of Charles Eames, Arne Jacobsen, George Nelson himself, Dieter Rams, Ettore Sottsass, Tapio Wirkkala, and Marco Zanuso—consisting of photographs, objects, chronologies, and quotations, underscored the impact of creative individuals on the field and conveyed a sense of their personal style, achievements, and attitudes toward design as a whole. A section devoted to ergonomics invited visitors to test various examples of office chairs, and included a video program in which Niels Diffrient discussed his own ergonomically designed chair.

To introduce discussions of molding and miniaturization, a fiberglass Corvette shell was suspended over a group of molded plastic furniture, while Explorer 1 and other communication satellites (borrowed from the National Air and Space Museum in Washington, D.C.) hung above the appliances section. The exhibition included a number of audiovisual programs. Period commercials were shown on Philco Predicta (1958) and Sony Profeel (1979) televisions, marking the wide distance in taste, lifestyle, and technology within two decades of design.

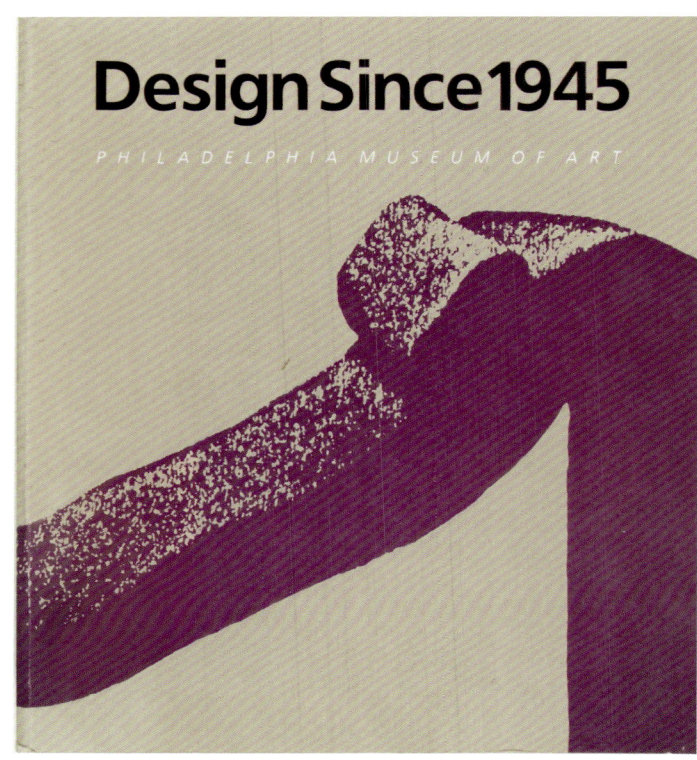

A continuous, two-hour program took place in a small theater, screening short videos on individual designers. Nelson was circumspect on the subject of the audiovisual programs: "I am fearful of any 20-minute show on the main path through the exhibit," he wrote. "Bottlenecks for sure. . . . It should be possible to show the range of Eames's activities in 2–3 minutes. After all, the standard TV commercial is 30 seconds, and some of them seem interminable!"[72] A 251-page, fully illustrated catalogue provided the theoretical basis for the exhibition and

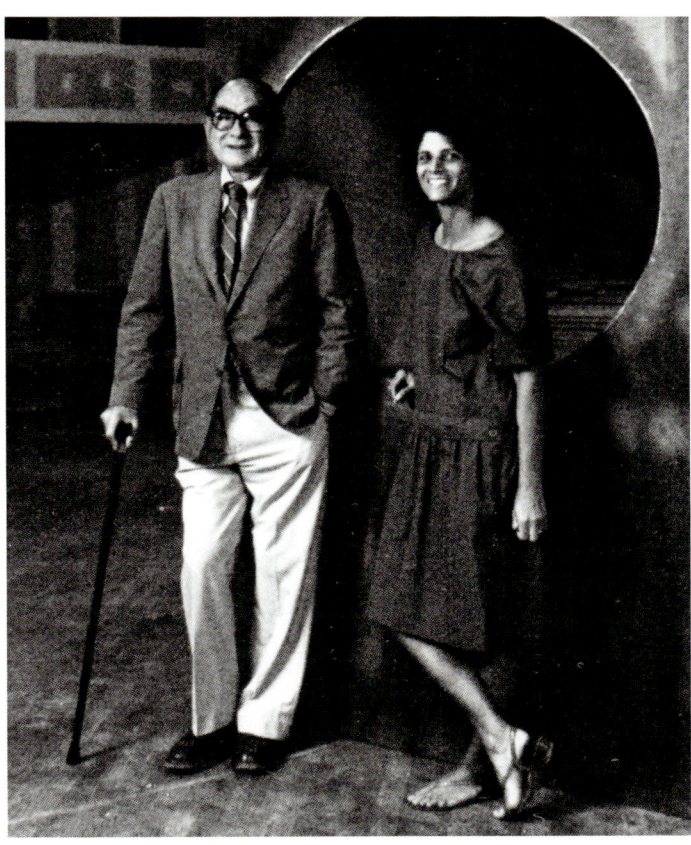

included the essays of sociologist Herbert Gans and sixteen internationally known designers and manufacturers who had helped shape the history they described, along with biographies and bibliographies of the designers and manufacturers (fig. 163).[73]

Like *Design for the Machine* a half-century earlier, the exhibition attracted a remarkable amount of press coverage. The *New York Times* called the show "brilliant" and named the catalogue "the design reference handbook of the decade."[74] This critical acclaim was reaffirmed by the *Washington Post*, the *Christian Science Monitor*, the *Boston Globe*, *Time* magazine, scholarly journals such as the *New Criterion*, and foreign publications, including *Svenska Dagbladet*, Sweden's largest daily newspaper, and the *Sunday Press* of London.[75]

Jean Boggs believed that it was important for programmatic activities to be developed around special exhibitions, in order to strengthen their impact and reach larger audiences.

Accordingly, a wide range of programs was organized: Philadelphia's first intercollegiate design course, taught at the Museum cooperatively by faculty members from Drexel University, Moore College of Art, Philadelphia College of Art, and Philadelphia College of Textiles and Science; "Objects and Objectives," a symposium featuring six internationally recognized designers and theorists—among them, Nicholas Negroponte, founder of the Media Lab at the Massachusetts Institute of Technology, who talked about the future of human-computer interaction; a lecture series that included presentations by NASA astronaut James Bagian and consumer advocate Ralph Nader; and a panel discussion, supported by Collab and the Friends of the Museum, with architects Charles Gwathmey and Robert Stern and other designers on the influence of product design on contemporary interiors.

By the time the exhibition and these programs took place, however, Boggs was no longer director of the Museum, having been asked in 1982 by the Canadian government to head a specially designated Crown Corporation that would supervise the design and construction of two new national museums and recommend architects and sites for them.[76] Before she left the Philadelphia Museum of Art, however, Boggs initiated an extensive study of programming and planning to evaluate the uses and shortages of space within the Museum building, and asked Collab to suggest architects who might carry out the project.[77] Led by architect and trustee James Nelson Kise, the Museum's building committee interviewed ten Philadelphia firms. In February 1980 the firm of Venturi, Rauch and Scott Brown was appointed to conduct the architectural study; a year later the firm addressed the board with its plan and goals, which included improving public perception of the collections and their relationship to the spatial sequence of the Museum, particularly with regard to the Johnson Collection. Integrating the Johnson Collection and other galleries containing European art, reinstalling the Museum's European collections, and renovating the galleries of modern and contemporary art were among

Design Since 1945 : 1983–84

Opposite : **163.** Exhibition catalogue : edited by Kathryn B. Hiesinger and George H. Marcus (Philadelphia: Philadelphia Museum of Art, 1983)
Above : **164.** Designer George Nelson and Kathryn Hiesinger amid construction for the exhibition

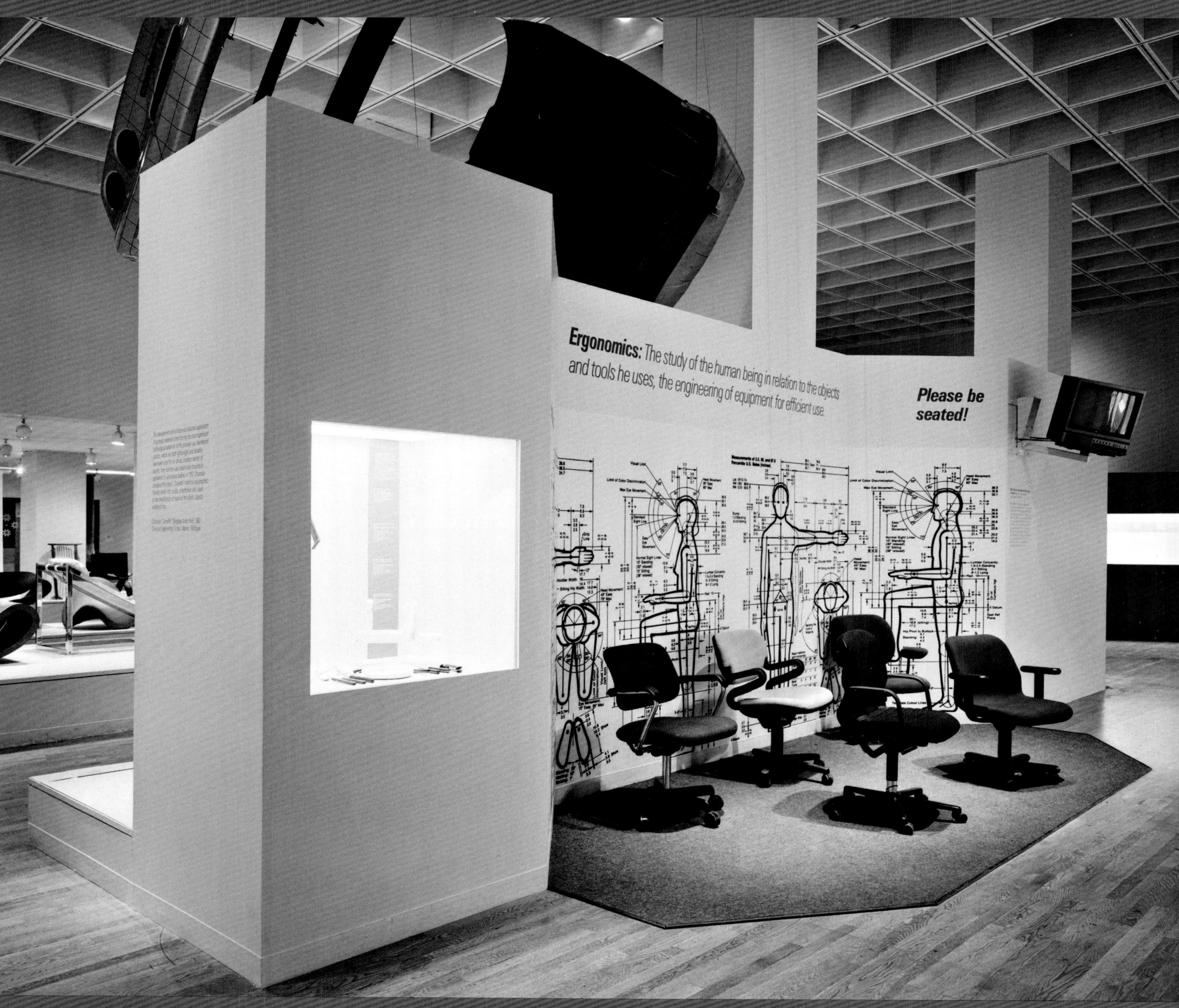

Design Since 1945 : 1983–84
165 and 166. Gallery views

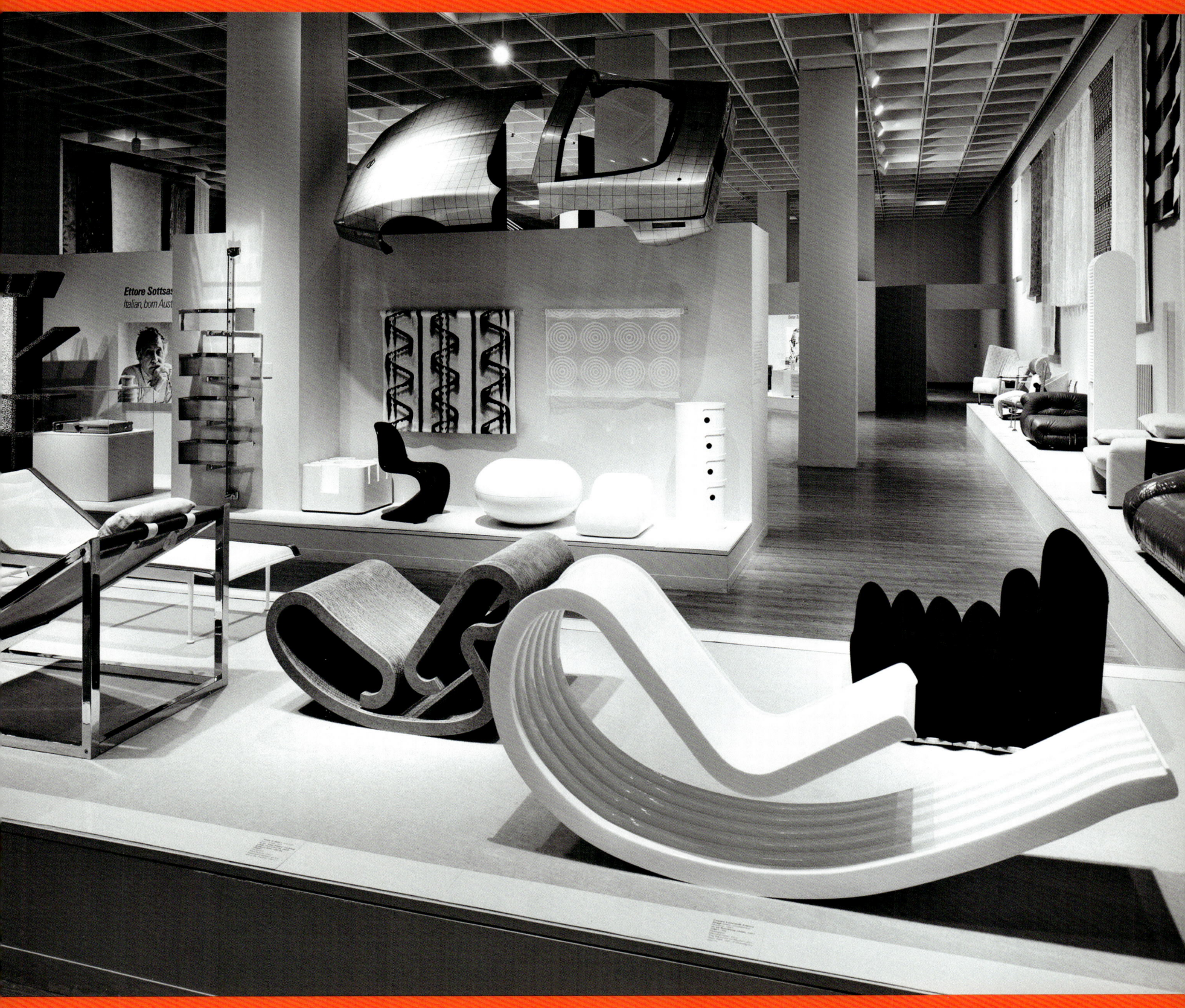

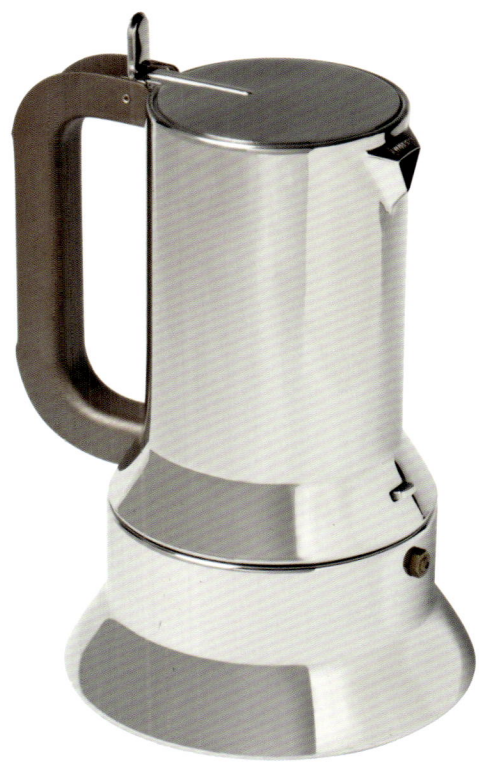
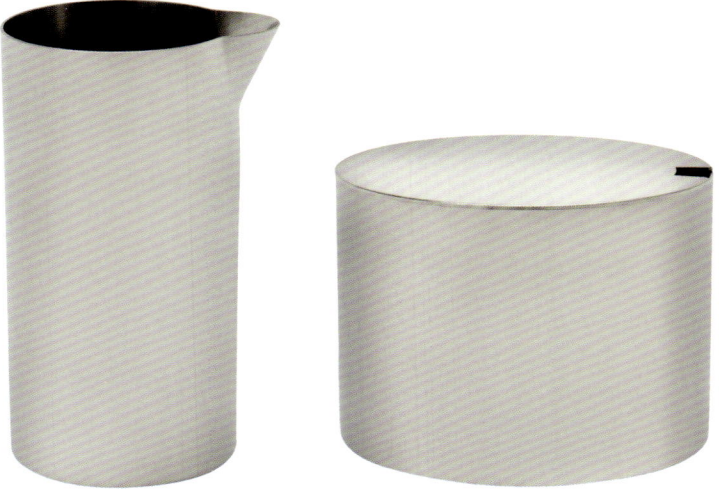

the most important projects carried out by Boggs's successor, thirty-nine-year-old Anne d'Harnoncourt, who had previously been the Museum's curator of twentieth-century art (fig. 172). At the June 1982 meeting of the board of trustees, d'Harnoncourt was elected director of the Museum while trustee Robert Montgomery Scott[78] was elected paid president and chief executive officer.[79] Following Scott's retirement in 1996, d'Harnoncourt was named both chief executive officer and director: that same year the board also created the new position of chief operating officer, appointing Gail M. Harrity to the position, which she still retains; in 2009 she was also named president of the Museum.

D'Harnoncourt's early years as director saw the disappearance of trustees who had served the Museum in leadership positions for decades. In 1986 Bernice McIlhenny Wintersteen, former Museum president, and her brother Henry P. McIlhenny, formerly curator of decorative arts, died within fifteen days of each other. Under his will McIlhenny gave the Museum an endowment as well as his extraordinary collection. At the final board meeting he attended, McIlhenny voiced reservations about the proposed acquisition of a twentieth-century American period room, with woodwork made by Wharton Esherick for the Curtis and Nellie Lee Bok House (fig. 70). While d'Harnoncourt argued that Esherick was "a regional figure of national importance," McIlhenny suggested that "the Museum's policy on period rooms be reviewed with consideration given to space utilization and to the historical periods to be emphasized;"[80] he had privately admitted to trustee and former University of Pennsylvania president Martin Meyerson that, while he supported the acquisition, "if we were to have a 20th century room, Frank Lloyd Wright would outweigh Wharton Esherick."[81]

Several long-serving members of the curatorial staff also retired or died in the late 1980s, among them Louis Madeira, who, like McIlhenny, served on the curatorial staff of the decorative arts department and subsequently as a trustee; he was cited on the occasion of his retirement in 1986 as an active trustee for his "unfailing discernment,

Design Since 1945 : 1983–84

Above and opposite, left to right : **167. Richard Sapper** : for Alessi : *9090* Espresso Coffeemaker : 1978 : stainless steel, cast iron : H 8 1/16" : 1983-41-1 (cat. 170) **168–71. Arne Jacobsen** : for Stelton : *Cylinda-line* Service : 1967 : stainless steel, nylon (coffeepot, teapot) : H (coffeepot) 7 1/2" : 1982-53–5a,b–8a,b (cat. 89–92)

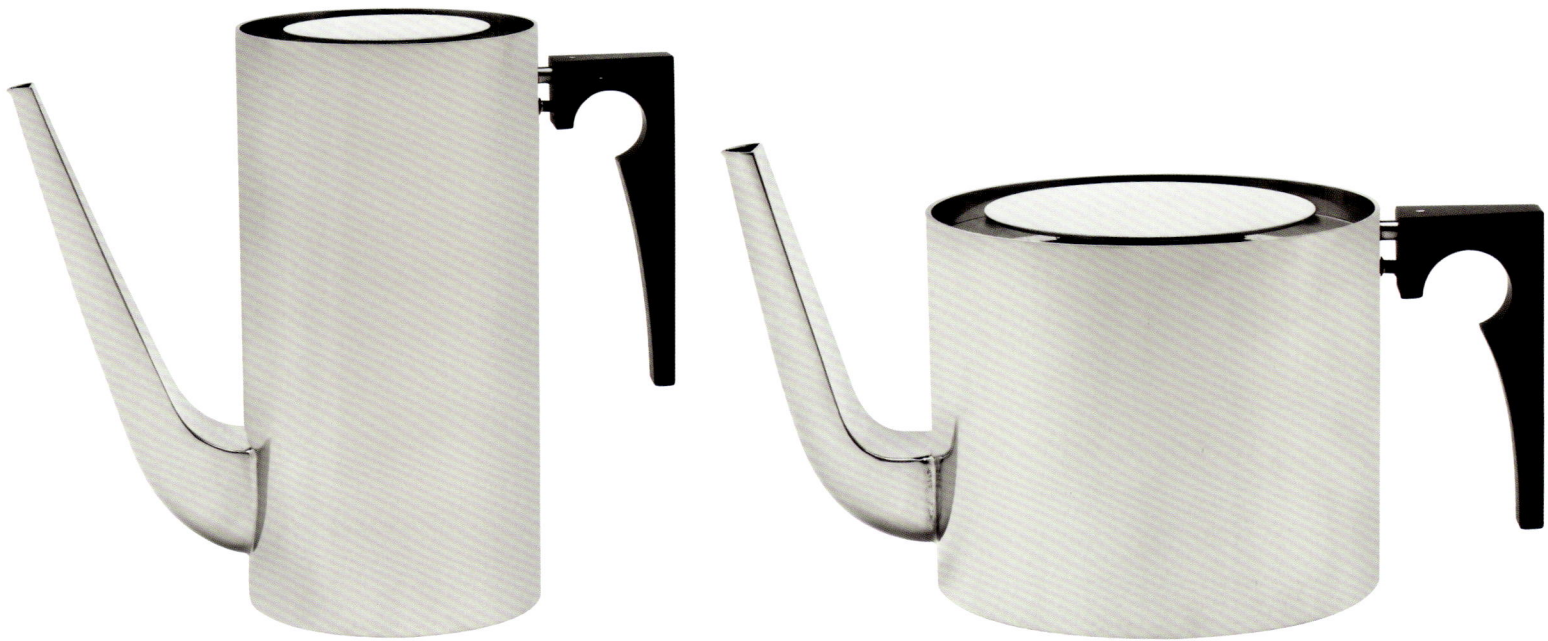

his judgment and his humane and wise participation in the counsels of the Museum."[82] Madeira was chairman of the advisory committee on European Decorative Arts when I joined the department in 1972 and served in that capacity until his death in 1993. A staunch and often witty supporter of our department whatever the issue or acquisition, he tried to resign from the committee (and the board) on more than one occasion, pleading health, age, and hearing in a letter to Scott in 1987: "You must admit that I am the last of the so-called 'old guard' and I feel unsupportable as a relic 'hanging on' stubbornly."[83] Jean Gordon Lee, curator of Far Eastern art, also retired in 1986;[84] she had begun her career at the Museum as assistant to Horace Jayne in 1939 and witnessed the creation of the Museum's Asian wing, period room by period room, object by object. Thus the last remaining links to the Kimball years were broken, just as Anne d'Harnoncourt began her tenure.

Educated at Harvard (A.B., Radcliffe College) and the Courtauld Institute of Art in London (M.A.), Anne was the only child of René d'Harnoncourt, director of the Museum of Modern Art from 1949 until 1968; she was therefore in close contact with art, artists, and museum professionals from her earliest years. A specialist in modern art—particularly the work of Marcel Duchamp—Anne d'Harnoncourt, like her father, was deeply interested in the exhibition of objects. She approached the reinstallation and renovation of the Museum's spaces with unwavering

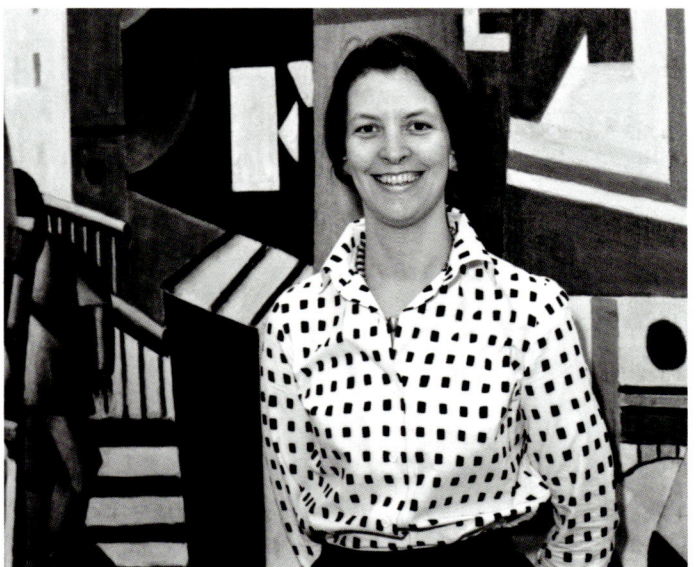

172. Anne d'Harnoncourt in 1982 : Museum director, 1982–2008

commitment from 1986, when the board first undertook to increase the Museum's endowment to support the project, to 1995, when the third and final phase of the renovation was completed, incorporating European art from 1500 to 1850. What distinguished d'Harnoncourt from her predecessors was her assumption of responsibility for fundraising, sometimes on a massive scale, whether joining Robert Montgomery Scott in the major Landmark Renewal capital campaign of 1986–93, in which the two were considered "essential to securing larger gifts,"[85] leading a second successful campaign from 2001–4, or rallying support in 2006 to keep the peerless Thomas Eakins painting *The Gross Clinic* in Philadelphia when Thomas Jefferson University announced the painting would be sold. In addition, in 1991 d'Harnoncourt reported to the executive committee that "a substantial portion of her time [was] spent on exhibition fundraising."[86] As Fiske Kimball and Sturgis Ingersoll had earlier discovered, it was expensive to organize and produce the special exhibitions that drew high attendance and thus brought income that raised the Museum's annual revenues above expenditures; *Masterpieces of Impressionism and Post-Impressionism: The Annenberg Collection*,[87] proved itself at the end of fiscal year 1990 to be a significant financial success despite a recessionary economy.

D'Harnoncourt championed the acquisition of modern and contemporary art, including works by Anselm Kiefer and Cy Twombly, and expressed her appreciation of Collab's contributions to the life of the Museum in her preface to the Collab '82 auction catalogue: "Thanks in large part to the energy and initiative of Collab, the Philadelphia Museum of Art has enjoyed a lively association with the community of architects and designers in this city for many years. Providing support for exhibitions and installations, purchasing important objects such as Josef Hoffmann's silver footed cup for the 20th-century design collection, Collab has made a significant contribution to the Museum's mission of heightening people's awareness of the contemporary visual environment."[88]

A number of pieces on view in *Design Since 1945* were already in the Museum's collections, but the exhibition also offered the opportunity to acquire additional objects in various mediums and by numerous designers. By the time *Design Since 1945* closed in January 1984, over 175 objects had been added to the Museum's collections by donations. Thus, through gifts and purchases, an extraordinary number of distinguished objects entered the collections in a very short time, as d'Harnoncourt noted with restraint: "Thanks to the generosity of many designers and manufacturers, as well as to Collab, the Museum's collection of modern design has been substantially augmented."[89]

Following the numerous acquisitions, events, and publications sponsored by Collab in connection with *Design Since 1945*—among them, the Design Dazzle preview reception—the organization reduced its pace and presented fewer public programs over the next two years. Collab marked its fifteenth anniversary in 1985, and to celebrate the occasion and honor founding member Cynthia Drayton it funded the largest and most important acquisition in its history: three pieces of furniture by Alvar Aalto, including a tea cart and a rare high-back armchair, a variant of the designer's "standard" armchair (figs. 199, 200). I discovered the furniture in the collection of German dealer Alexander von Vegesack, later director of the Vitra Design Museum in Weil am Rhein, Germany, who would express his regret for selling such a rarity as the high-back chair when he needed money.[90]

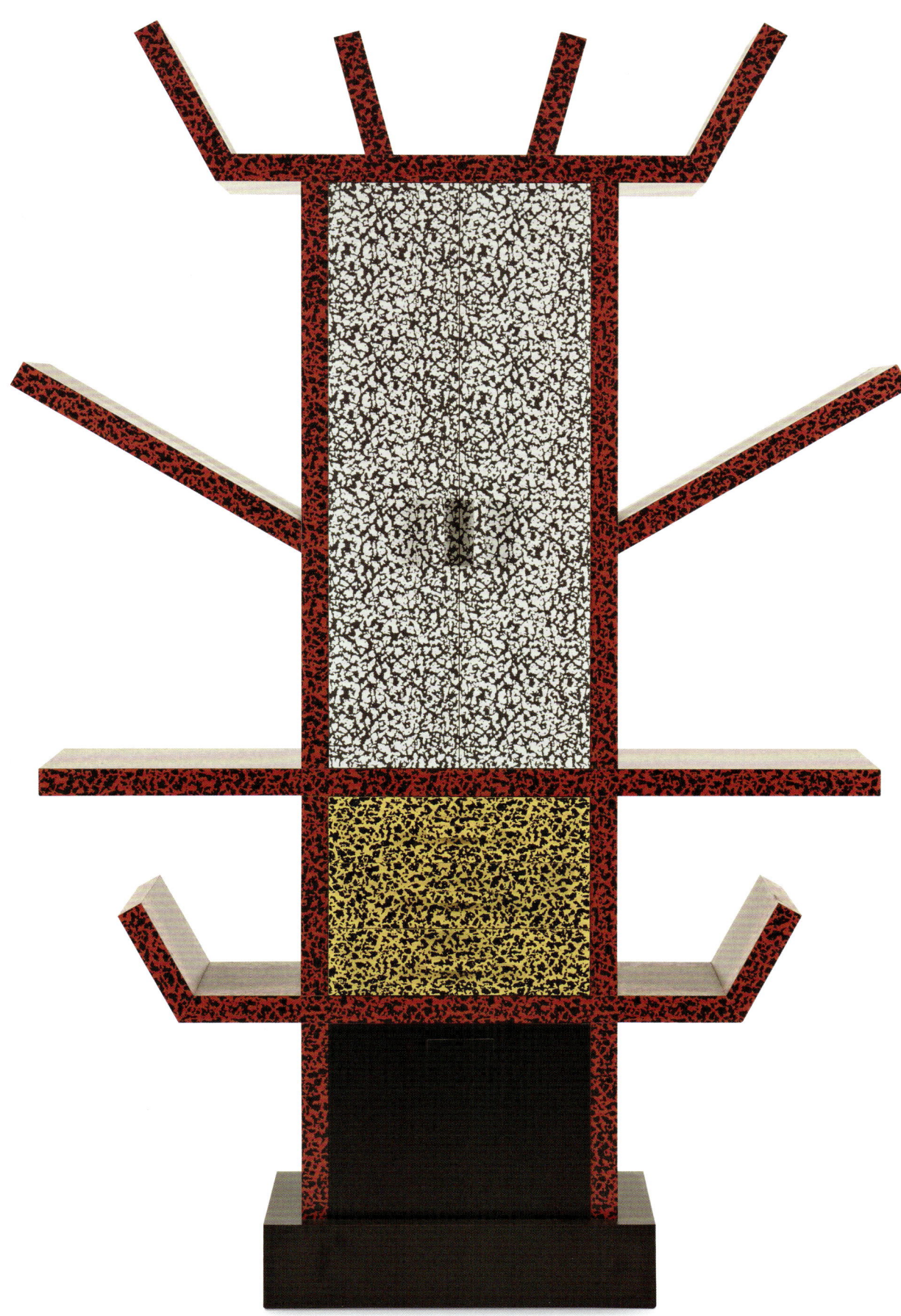

Design Since 1945 : 1983–84
173. **Ettore Sottsass** : fcr Abet Laminati and Memphis : *Casablanca* Sideboard : 1981 : plastic laminate, wood, chipboard : H 7' 6½" : 1983-113-1 (cat. 181)

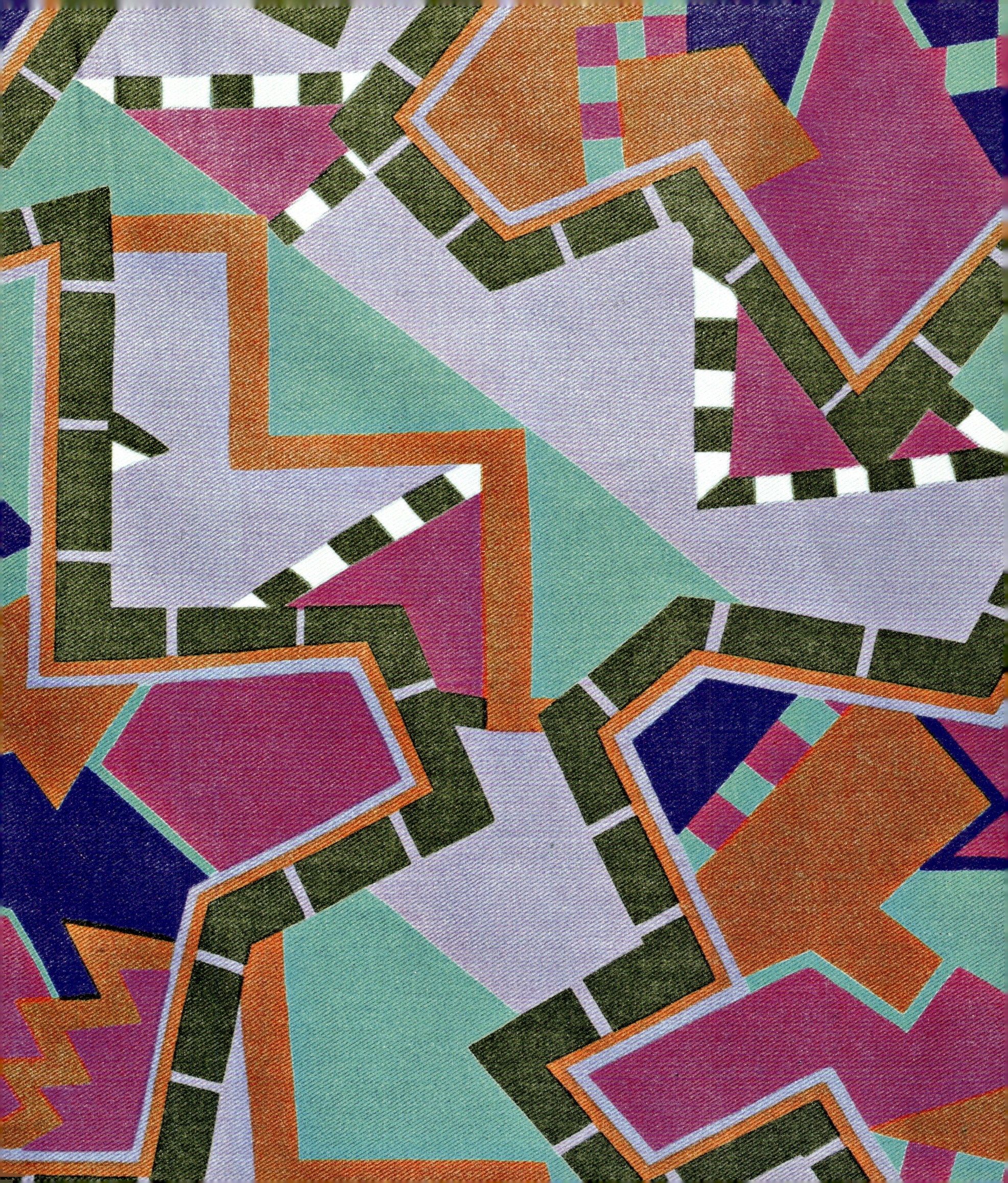

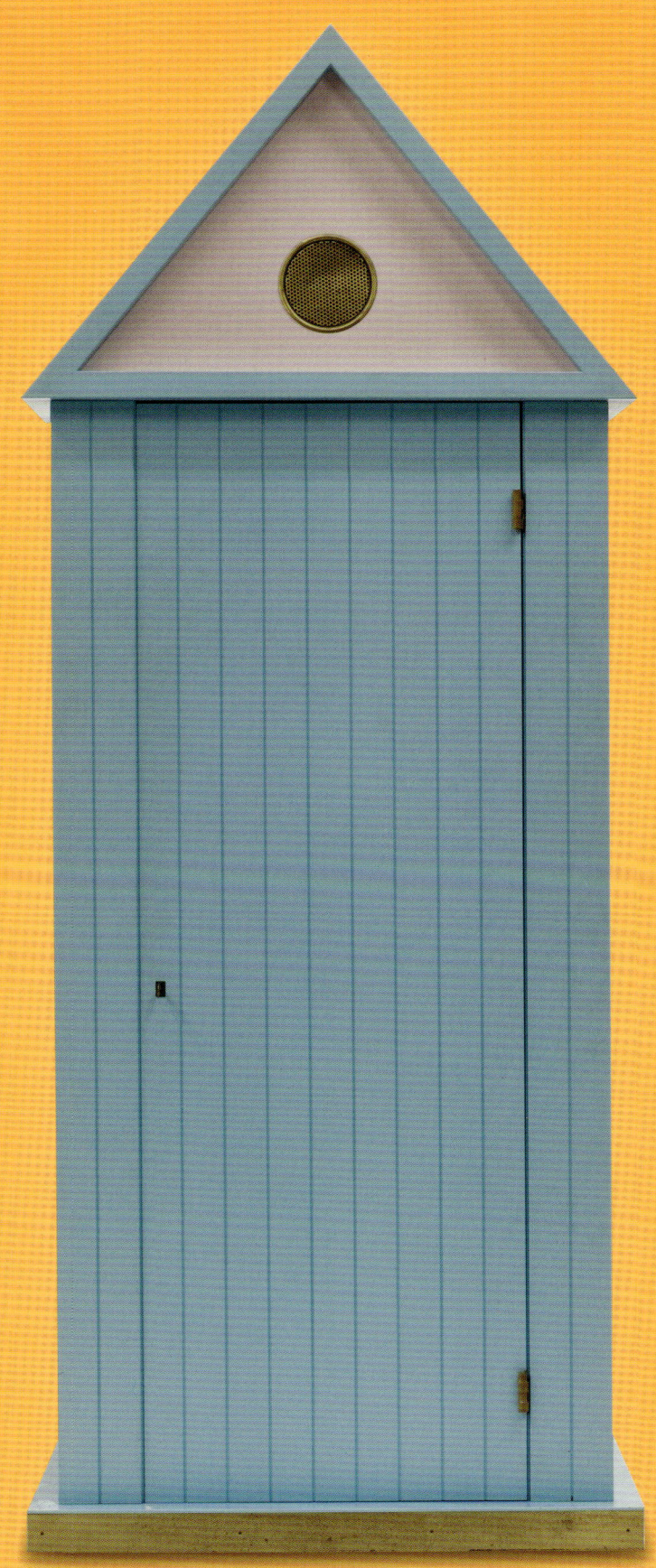

Design Since 1945 : 1983–84

Opposite : 174. Nathalie du Pasquier : for Rainbow : *Gabon* Fabric (detail) : 1982 : screen-printed cotton : W 60" : 1983-119-1 (cat. 143)
Above : 175. Aldo Rossi : for Molteni : *Cabina dell'Elba* Wardrobe : 1980 : particle board, plastic laminate, brass : H 7' 6 1/4" : 2000-70-2 (cat. 163)

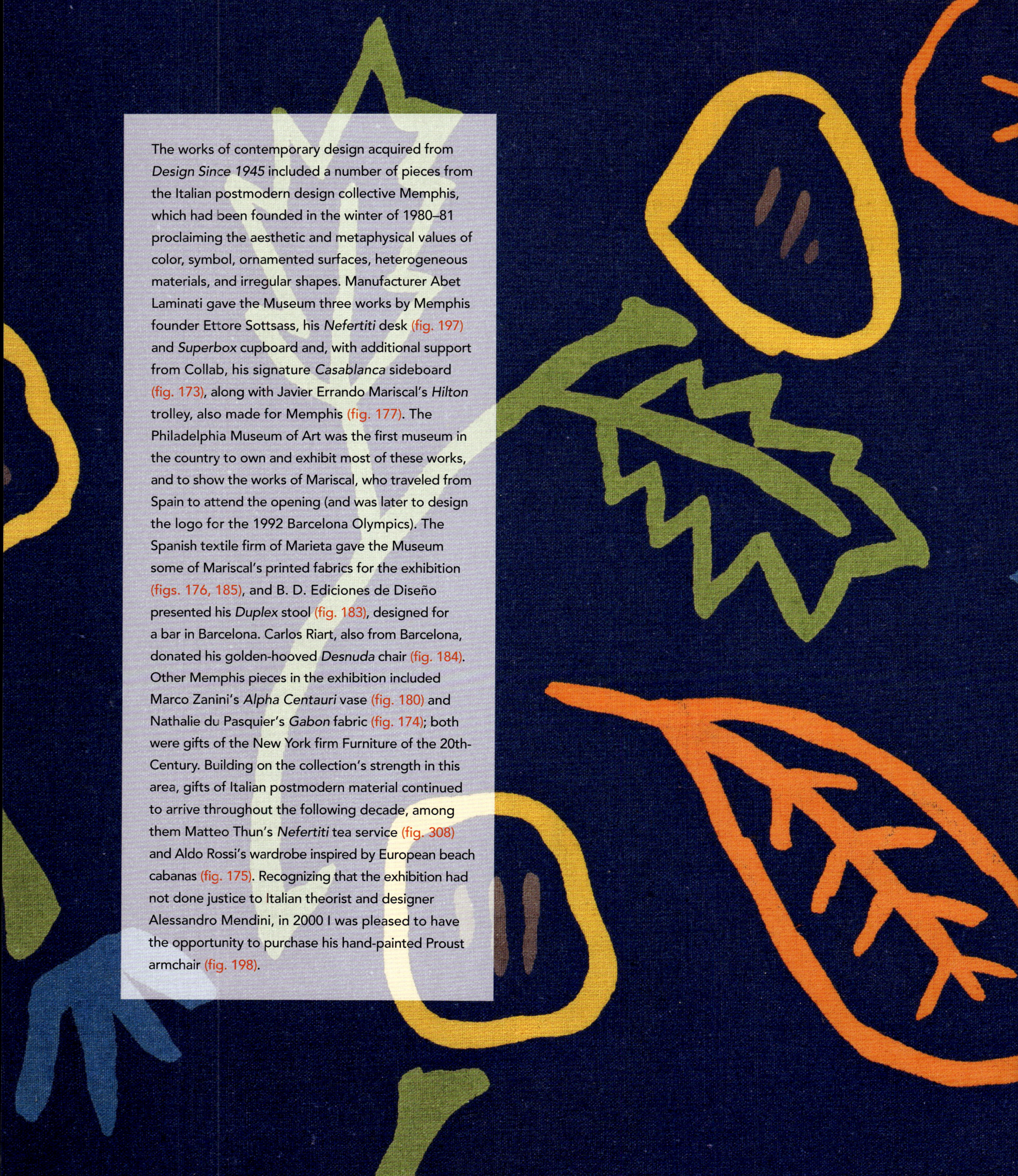

The works of contemporary design acquired from *Design Since 1945* included a number of pieces from the Italian postmodern design collective Memphis, which had been founded in the winter of 1980–81 proclaiming the aesthetic and metaphysical values of color, symbol, ornamented surfaces, heterogeneous materials, and irregular shapes. Manufacturer Abet Laminati gave the Museum three works by Memphis founder Ettore Sottsass, his *Nefertiti* desk (fig. 197) and *Superbox* cupboard and, with additional support from Collab, his signature *Casablanca* sideboard (fig. 173), along with Javier Errando Mariscal's *Hilton* trolley, also made for Memphis (fig. 177). The Philadelphia Museum of Art was the first museum in the country to own and exhibit most of these works, and to show the works of Mariscal, who traveled from Spain to attend the opening (and was later to design the logo for the 1992 Barcelona Olympics). The Spanish textile firm of Marieta gave the Museum some of Mariscal's printed fabrics for the exhibition (figs. 176, 185), and B. D. Ediciones de Diseño presented his *Duplex* stool (fig. 183), designed for a bar in Barcelona. Carlos Riart, also from Barcelona, donated his golden-hooved *Desnuda* chair (fig. 184). Other Memphis pieces in the exhibition included Marco Zanini's *Alpha Centauri* vase (fig. 180) and Nathalie du Pasquier's *Gabon* fabric (fig. 174); both were gifts of the New York firm Furniture of the 20th-Century. Building on the collection's strength in this area, gifts of Italian postmodern material continued to arrive throughout the following decade, among them Matteo Thun's *Nefertiti* tea service (fig. 308) and Aldo Rossi's wardrobe inspired by European beach cabanas (fig. 175). Recognizing that the exhibition had not done justice to Italian theorist and designer Alessandro Mendini, in 2000 I was pleased to have the opportunity to purchase his hand-painted Proust armchair (fig. 198).

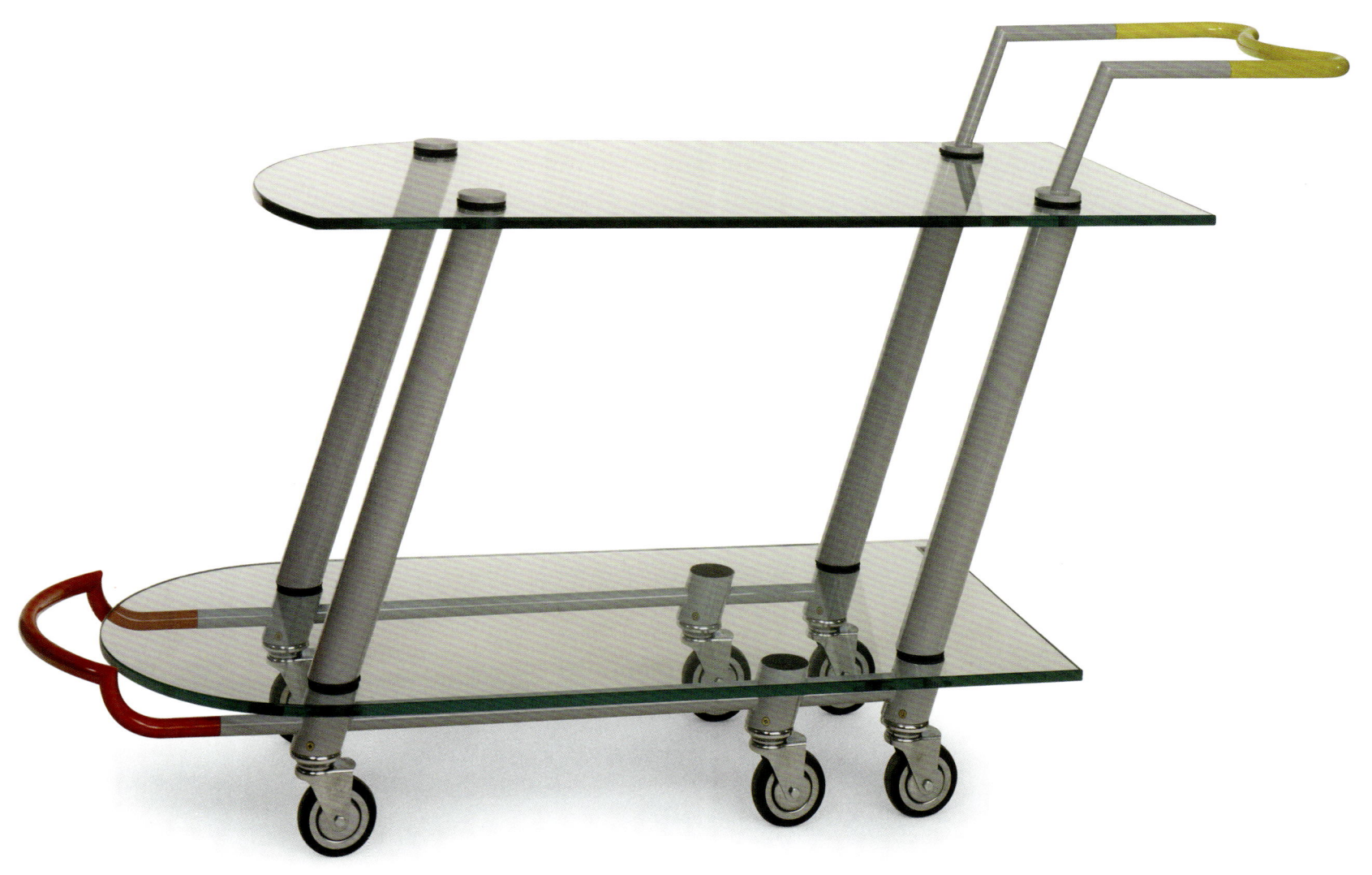

Design Since 1945 : 1983–84

Opposite : **176. Javier Errando Mariscal** : for Marieta Textil : *Floresta* Fabric (detail) : 1981 : screen-printed cotton : W 63" : 1983-8-2 (cat. 117)
Above : **177. Javier Errando Mariscal** : for Memphis : *Hilton* Trolley : 1980 : enameled metal, glass : H 31¾" : 1983-104-1 (cat. 116)

183

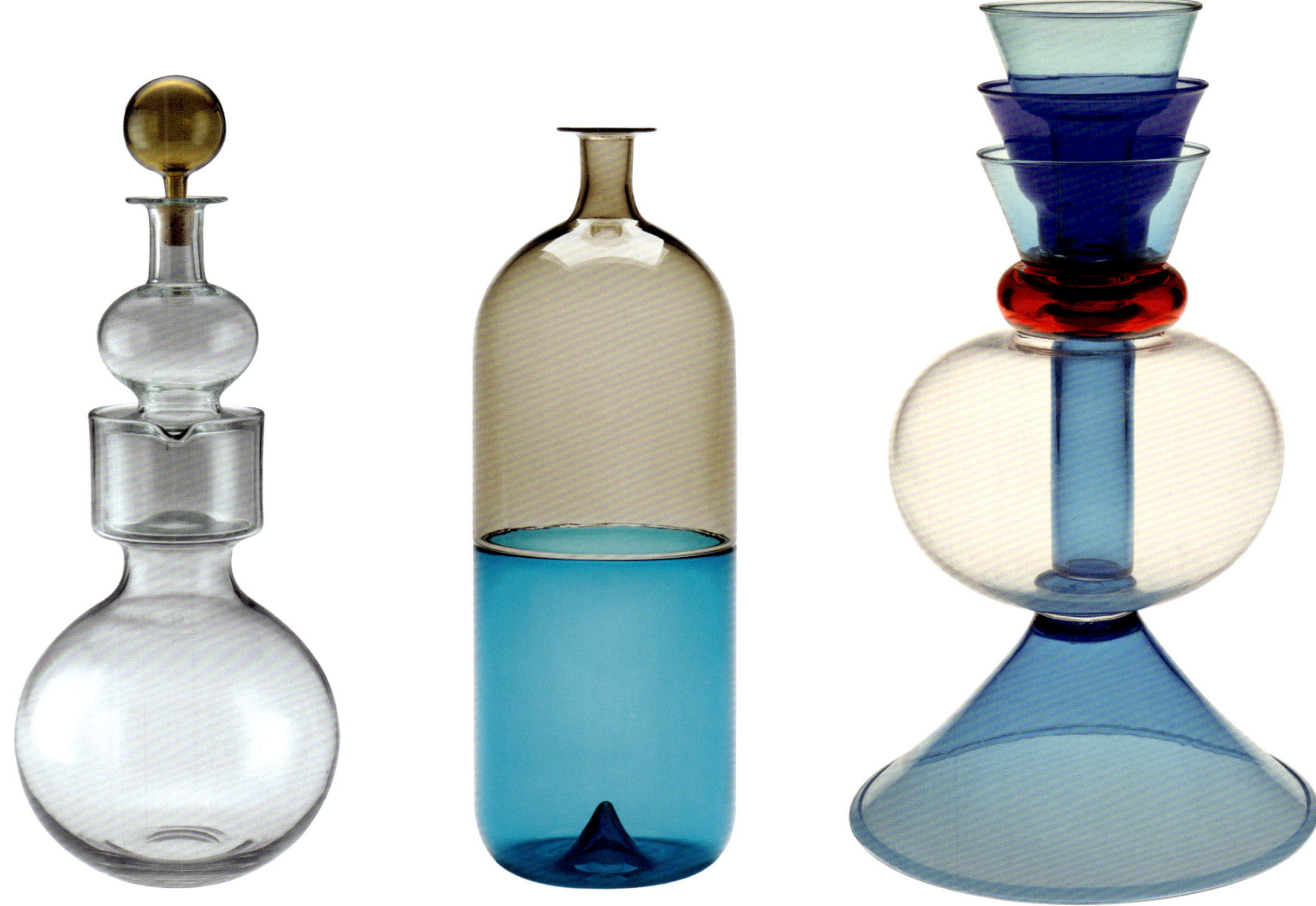

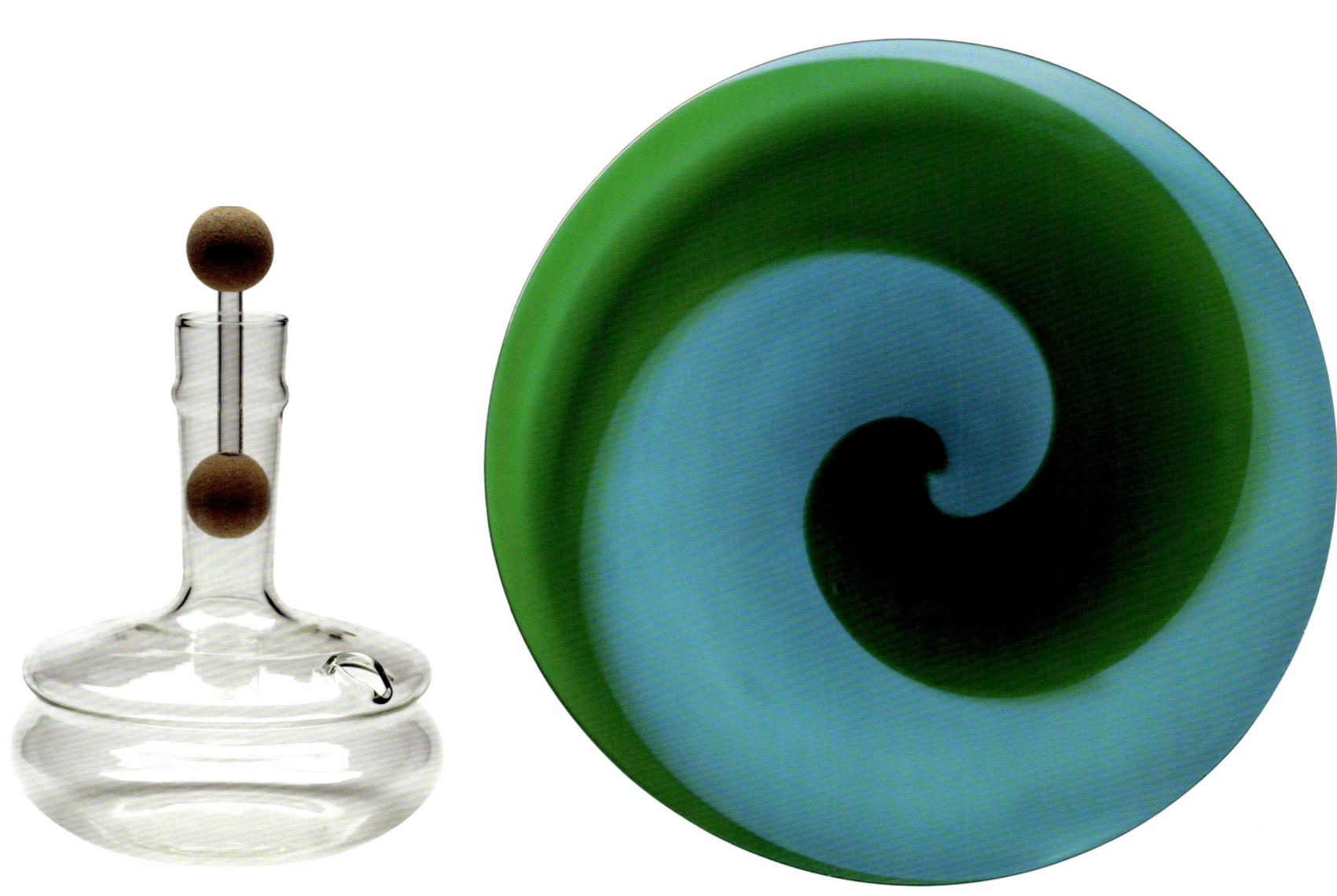

Design Since 1945 : 1983–84

Opposite and above, left to right : **178. Kaj Franck** : for Nuutajärvi : *Kremlin Bells* Double Decanter : 1957 : glass : H 13 3/4" : 1982-33-1a–c (cat. 60)
179. Tapio Wirkkala : for Venini : *Bolla* Vase : 1970 : glass : H 13 3/8" : 1983-151-4 (cat. 214)   **180. Marco Zanini** : for Toso and Memphis :
Alpha Centauri Vase : 1982 : glass : H 15 5/8" : 1983-112-5 (cat. 222)   **181. Peter Schlumbohm** : for Chemex : Water Kettle : 1949 : Pyrex glass, cork :
H 12 5/16" : 1983-4-2a,b (cat. 173)   **182. Tapio Wirkkala** : for Venini : *Coreano* Dish : 1970 : glass : D 15 3/4" : 1983-151-3 (cat. 213)

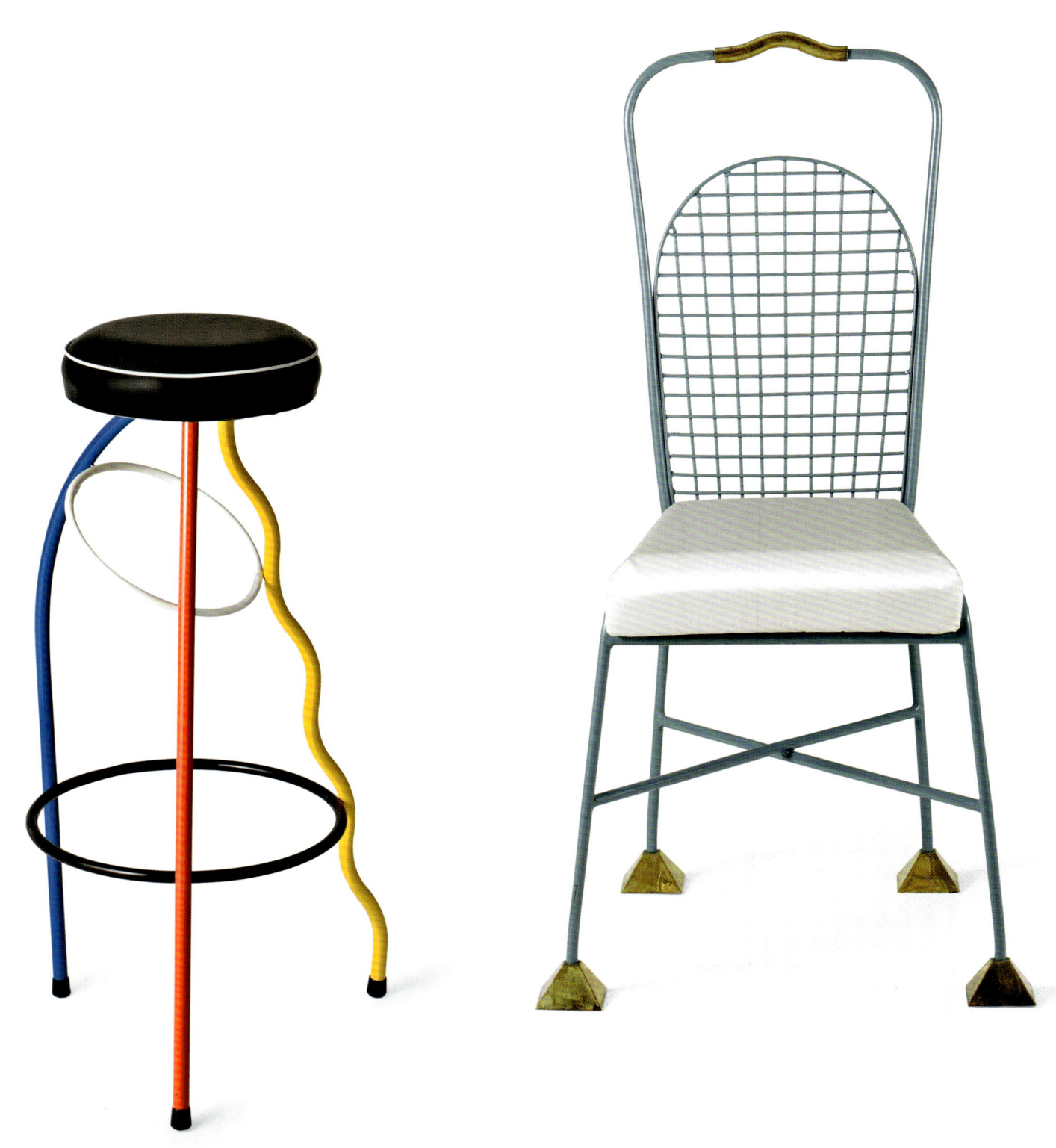

Design Since 1945 : 1983–84

Above, left to right : **183. Javier Errando Mariscal** : for B. D. Ediciones de Diseño : *Duplex* Stool : 1981 : metal, leather : H 32 1/2" : 1983-44-1 (cat. 118)
184. Carlos Riart : for Temco : *Desnuda* Chair : 1973 : enameled iron, brass, upholstery : H 39 3/8" : 1983-136-1 (cat. 157)
Opposite : **185. Javier Errando Mariscal** : for Marieta Textil : *Ensaladilla* Fabric (detail) : 1978 : screen-printed cotton : W 63" : 1983-8-1 (cat 115)

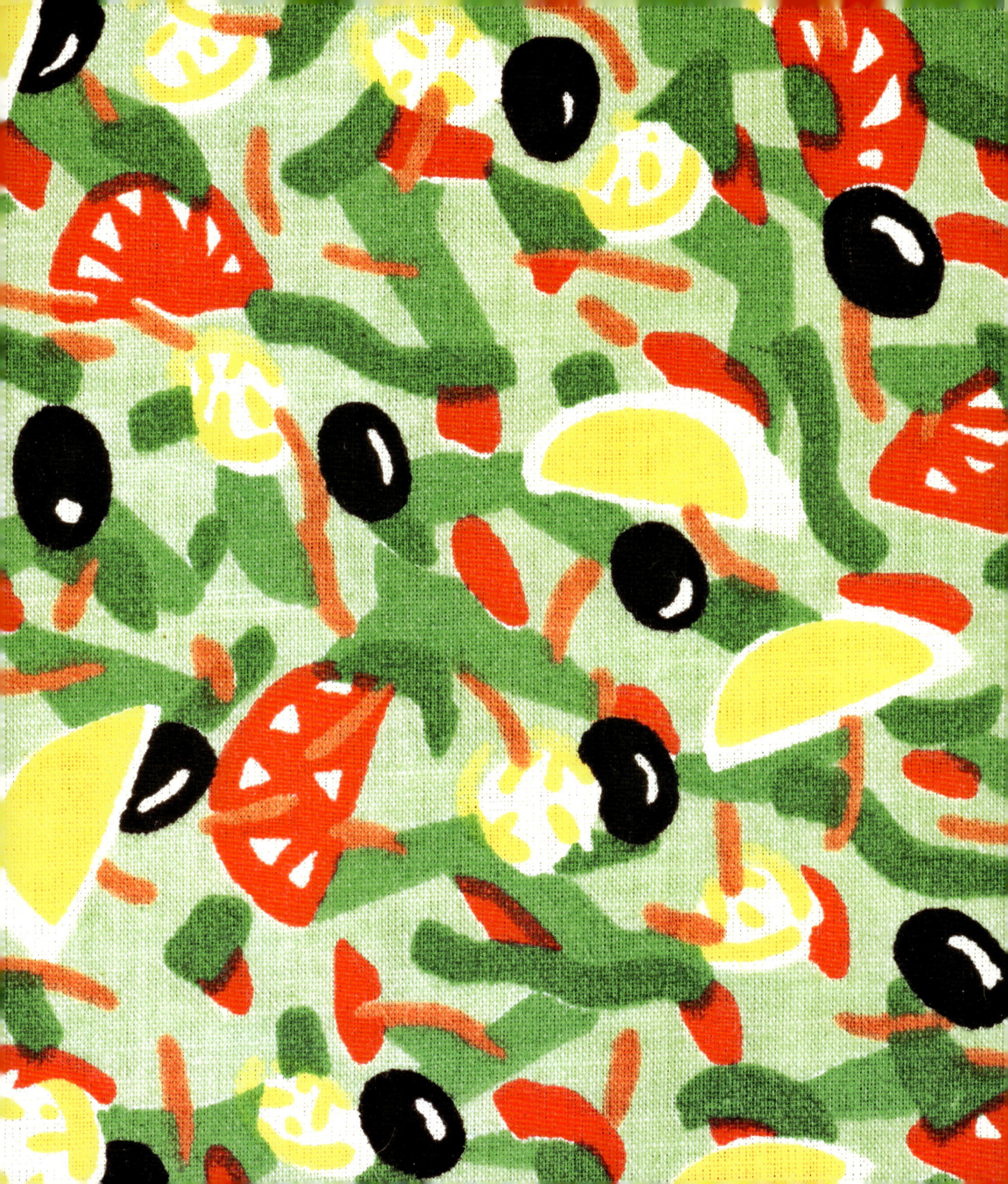

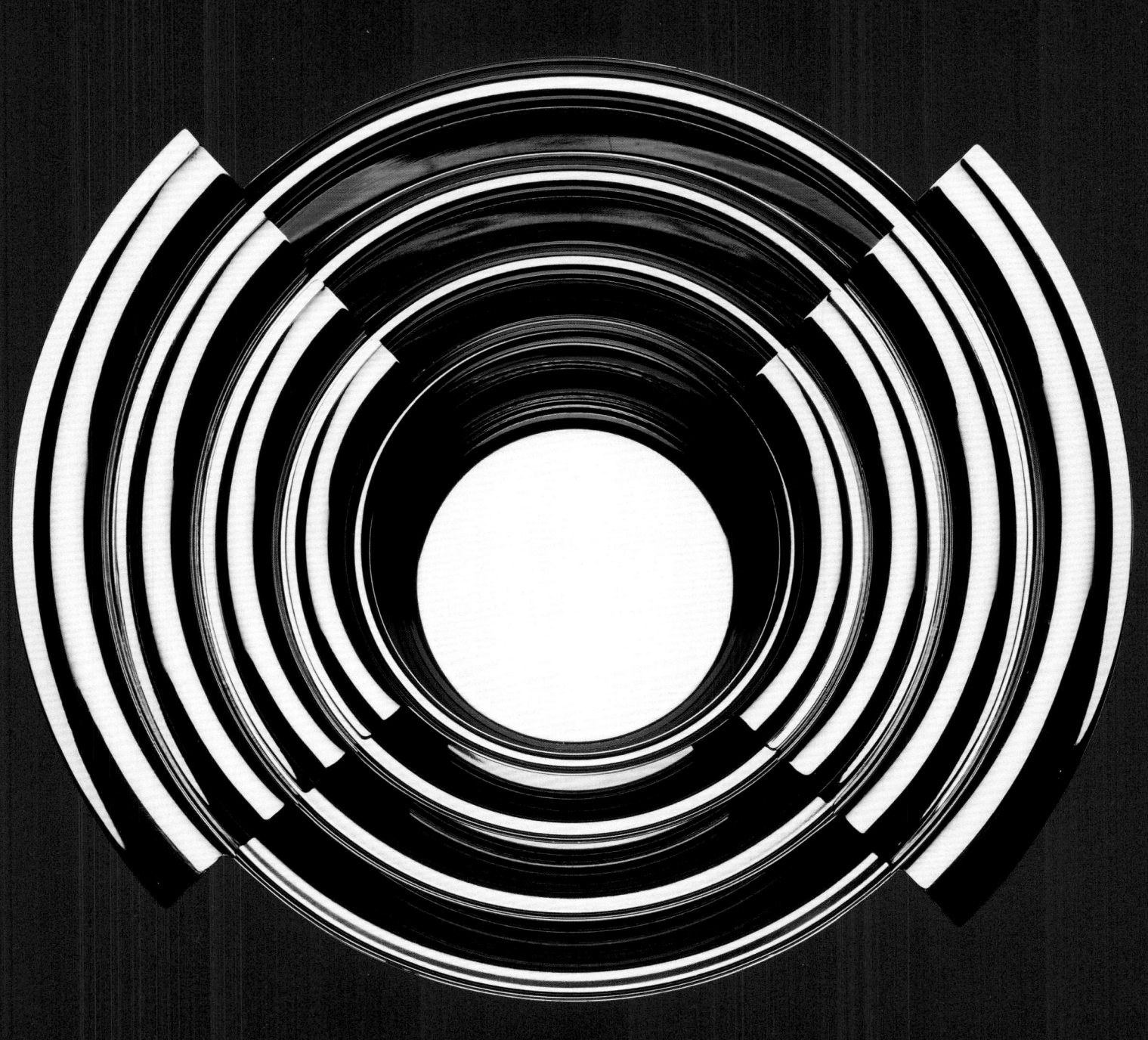

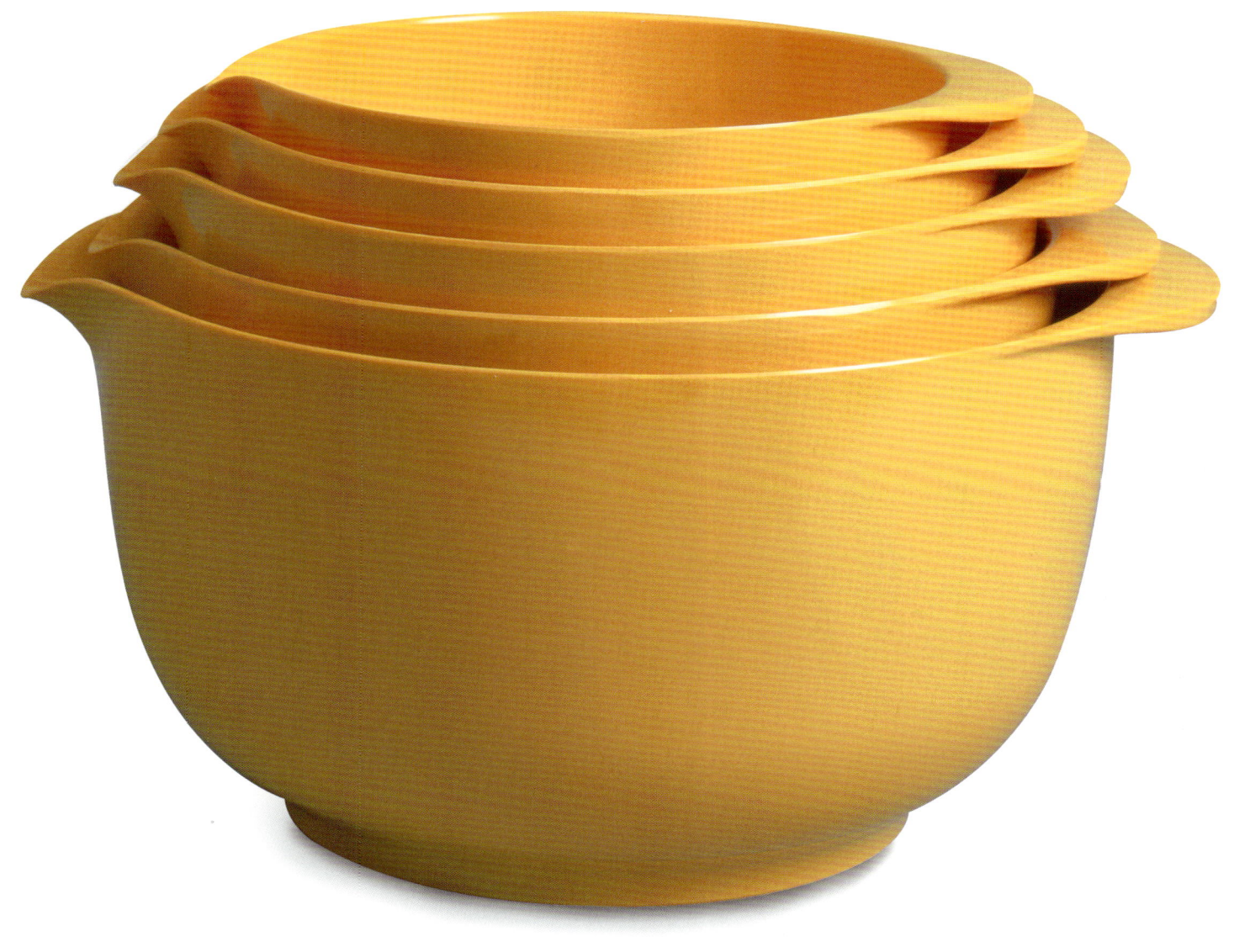

Design Since 1945 : 1983–84

Opposite : **186. Roberto Sambonet** : for Sambonet : *Center Line* Cooking Set (8) : 1964 : stainless steel : D (largest pot) 9 1/2" : 1983-141-1–8 (cat. 168)
Above : **187. Acton Bjørn and Sigvard Bernadotte** : for Rosti : *Margrethe* Bowls (5) : 1950 : melamine : D (largest bowl) 9 7/16" : 1983-56-1–5 (cat. 20)

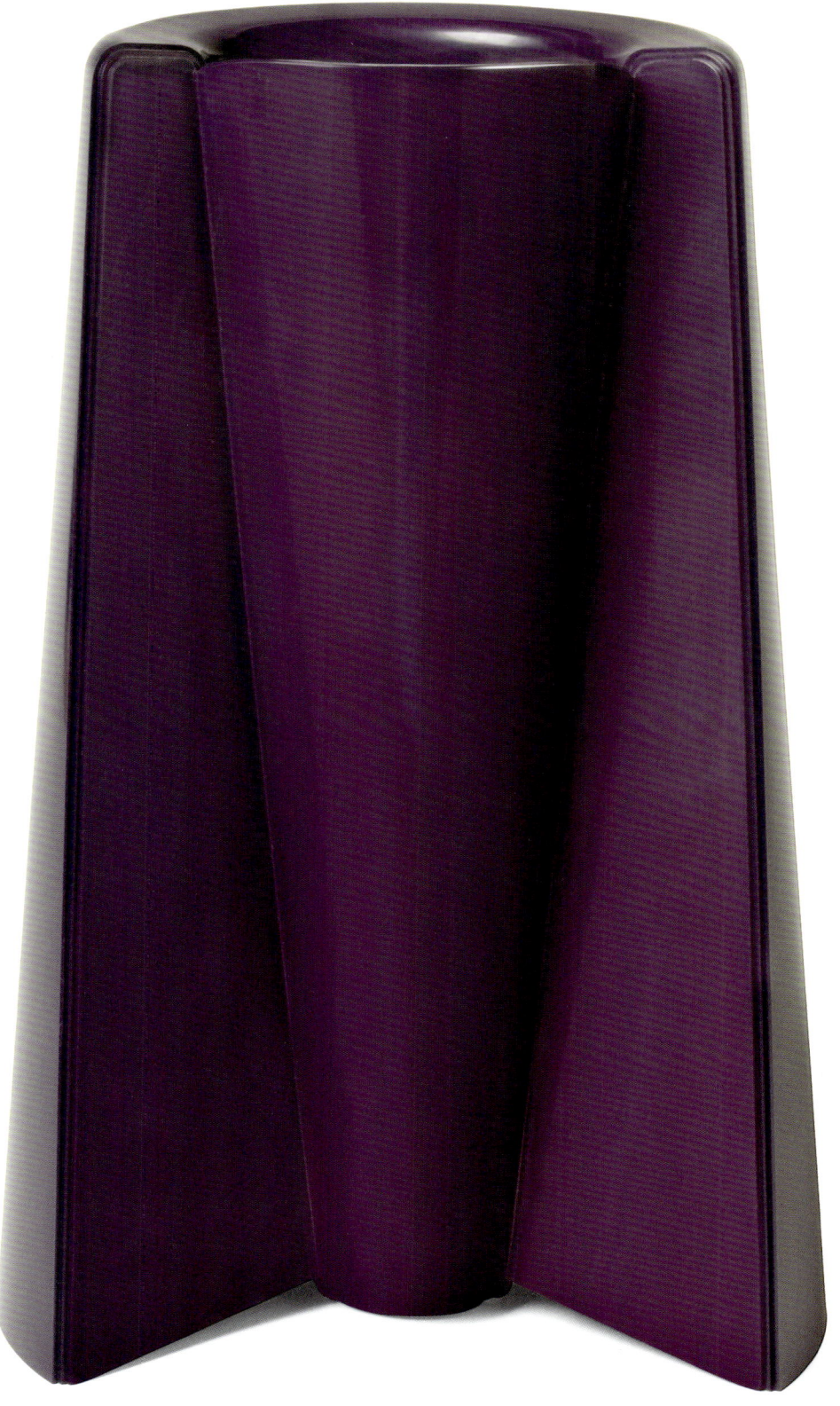

Design Since 1945 : 1983–84

Opposite : **188. Evelyn Hill Anselevicius** : for Knoll : Fabric (detail) : 1951 : wool, viscose, rayon, synthetic raffia : W 35" : 1983-42-2 (cat. 5)
Above : **189. Enzo Mari** : for Danese : *Pago-Pago* Vase : 1969 : ABS plastic : H 11$^{13}/_{16}$" : 1983-115-1 (cat. 110)

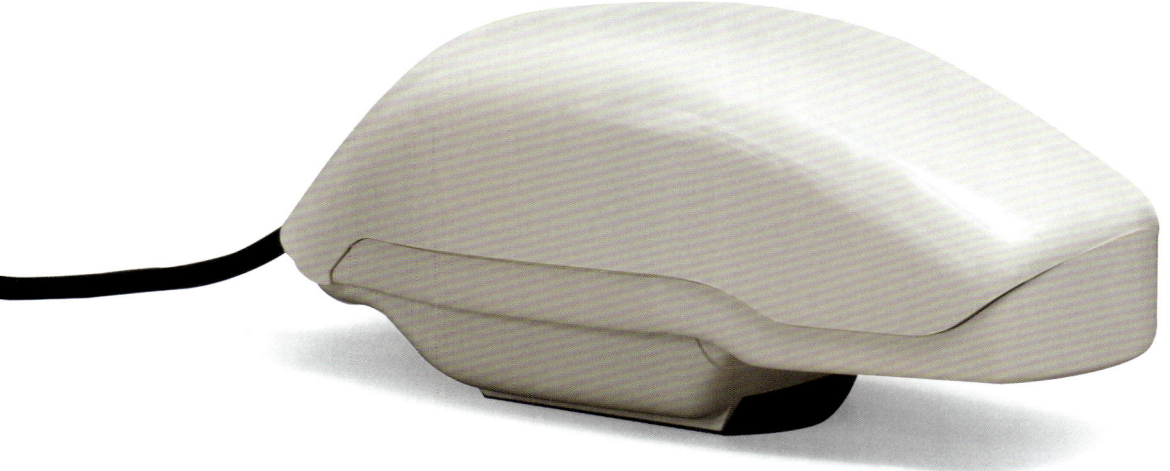

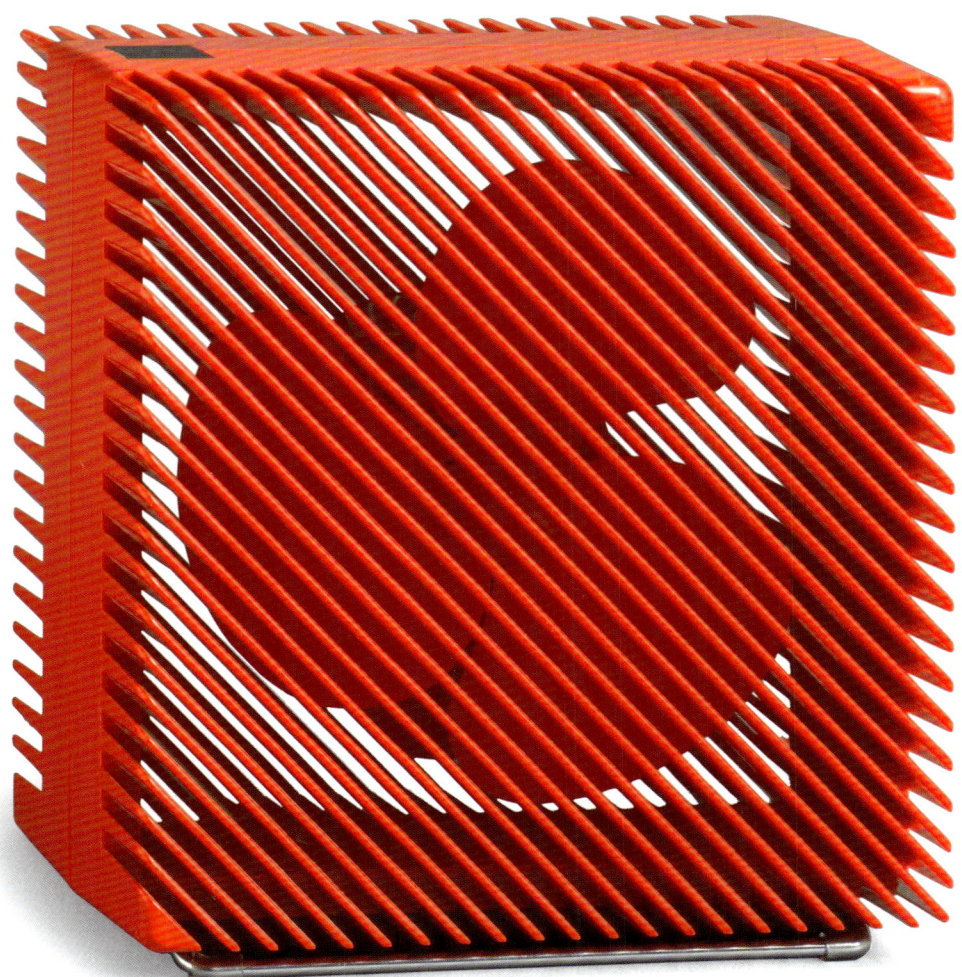

Design Since 1945 : 1983–84

Above, top to bottom : **190. Marco Zanuso and Richard Sapper** : for Italtel : *Grillo* Telephone : 1965 : ABS plastic : L 6⁵⁄₁₆" : 1982-54-1 (cat. 224)
191. Marco Zanuso : for Vortice Elettrosociali : *Ariante* Fan : 1973 : ABS plastic : H 7³⁄₁₆" : 1983-13-1 (cat. 223)   Opposite : **192. Richard Sapper** : for Artemide : *Tizio* Table Lamp : 1972 : ABS plastic, aluminum metal alloy : H 46¹⁄₂" : 1983-105-2 (cat. 169)

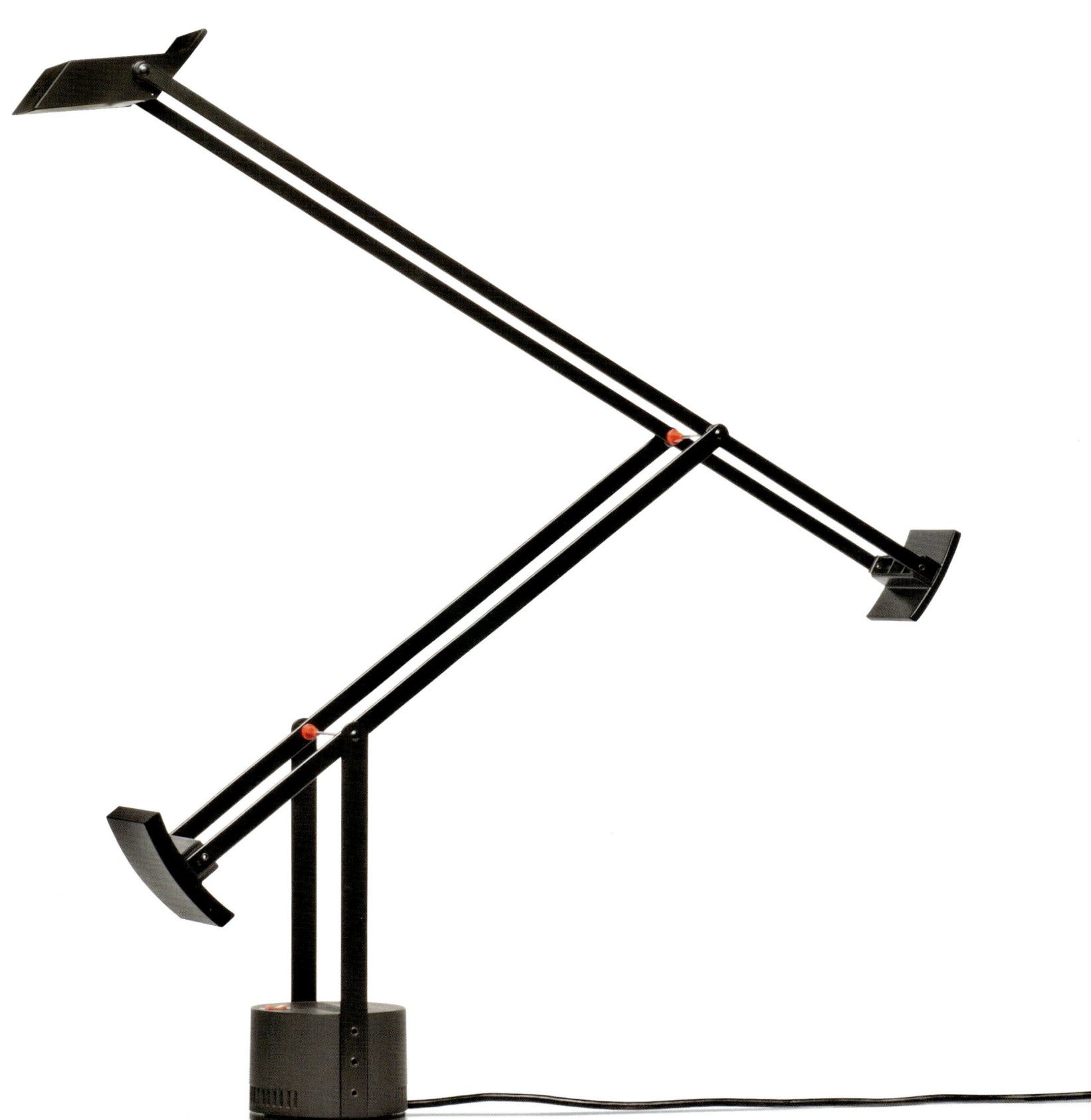

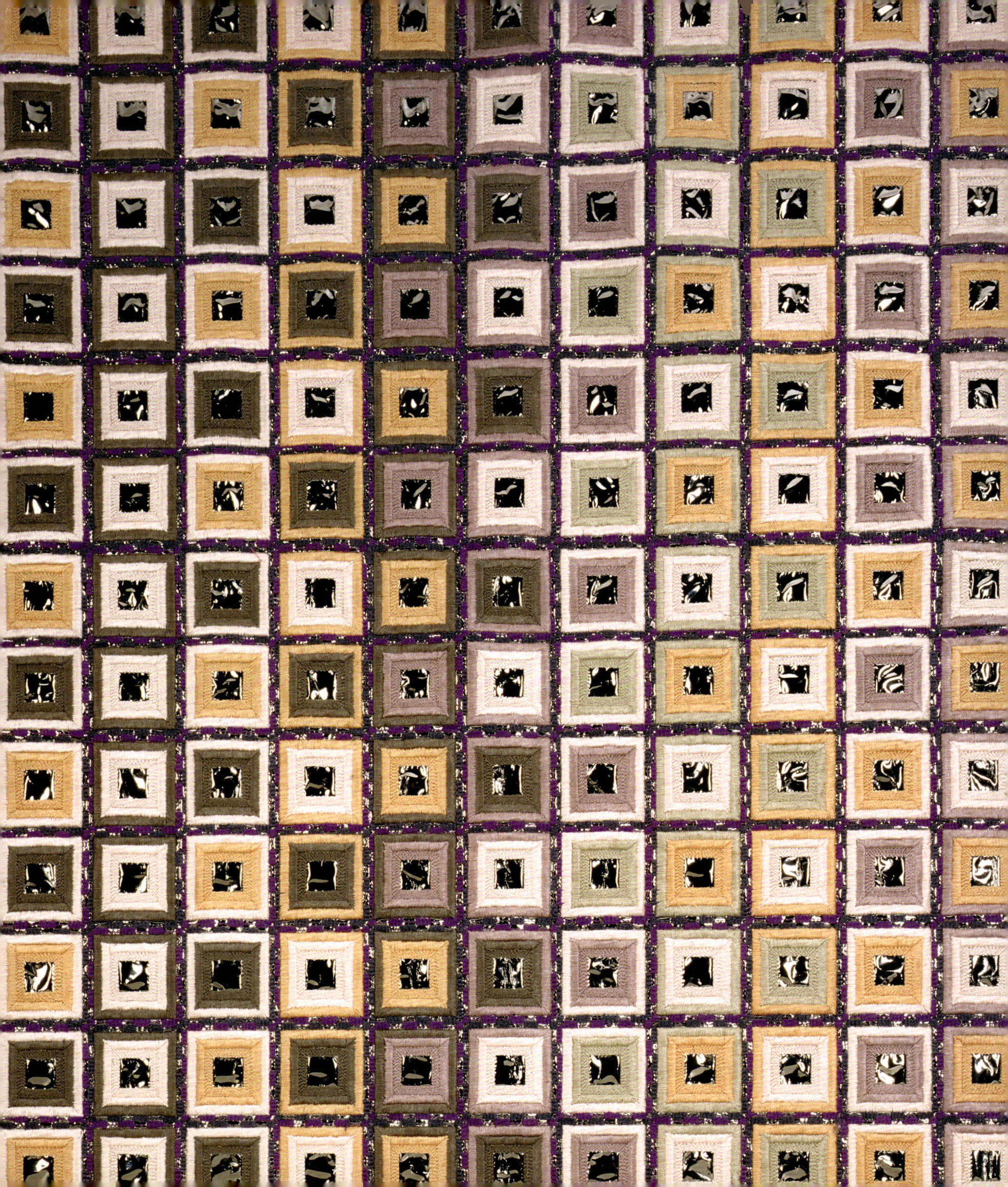

Design Since 1945 : 1983–84

Opposite : **193. Jack Lenor Larsen** : for Jack Lenor Larsen, Inc. : *Magnum* Fabric (detail) : 1970 : cotton, vinyl, nylon, polyamide, polyester : W 48" : 1983-186-2 (cat. 107)   Above : **194. Maija Isola** : for Marimekko Oy : *Kivet* Fabric (detail) : 1956 : screen-printed cotton : W 54" : 1983-131-3 (cat. 86)

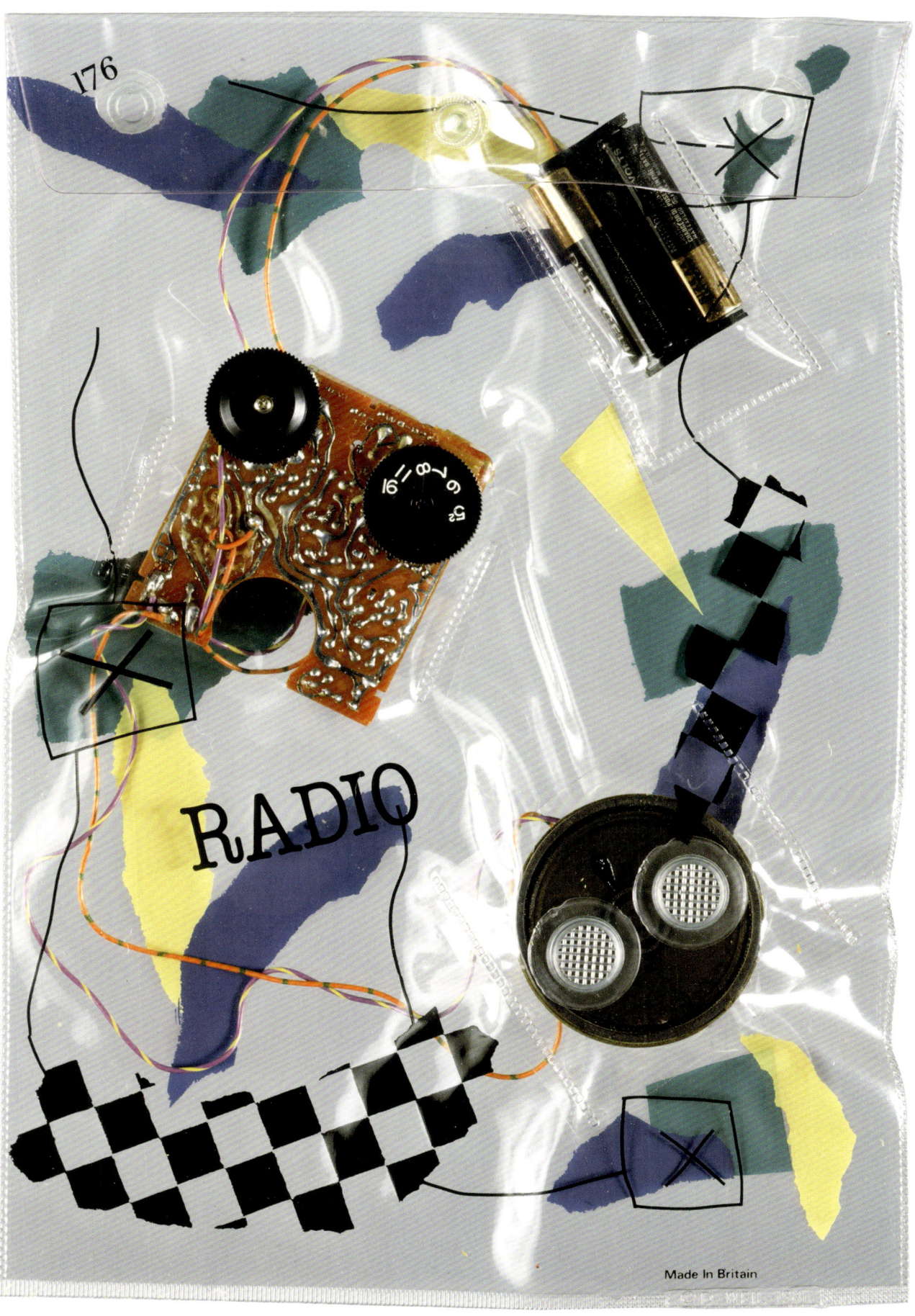

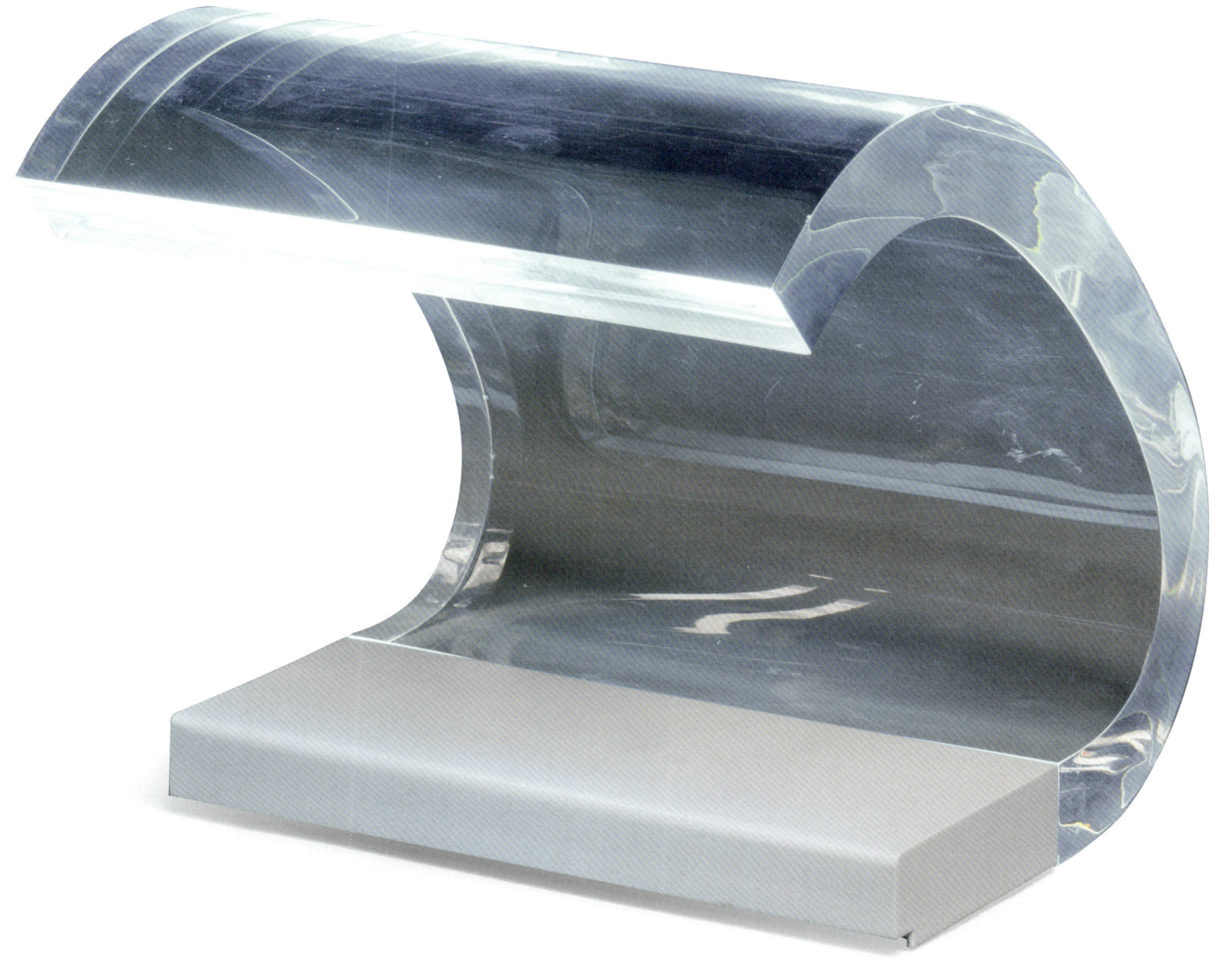

Design Since 1945 : 1983–84

Opposite : **195. Daniel Weil** : for Parenthesis : *Bag* Radio : 1981 : PVC plastic : H 11 11/16" : 1983-58-1 (cat. 209)   Above : **196. Joe Colombo with Gianni Colombo** : for O-Luce : *Acrilica* Table Lamp : 1962 : brass, Perspex : H 9 7/16" : 1983-134-1 (cat. 36)

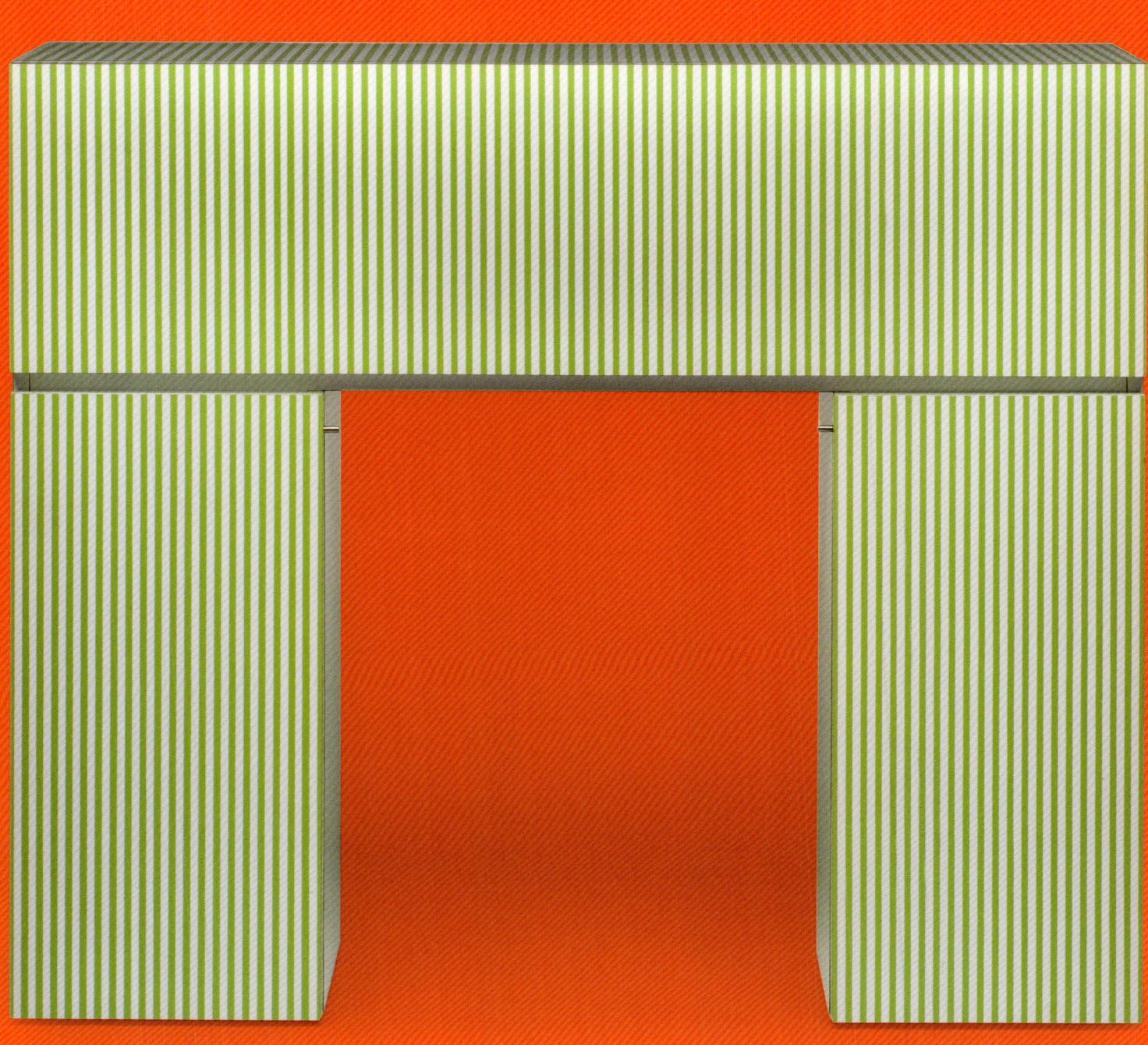

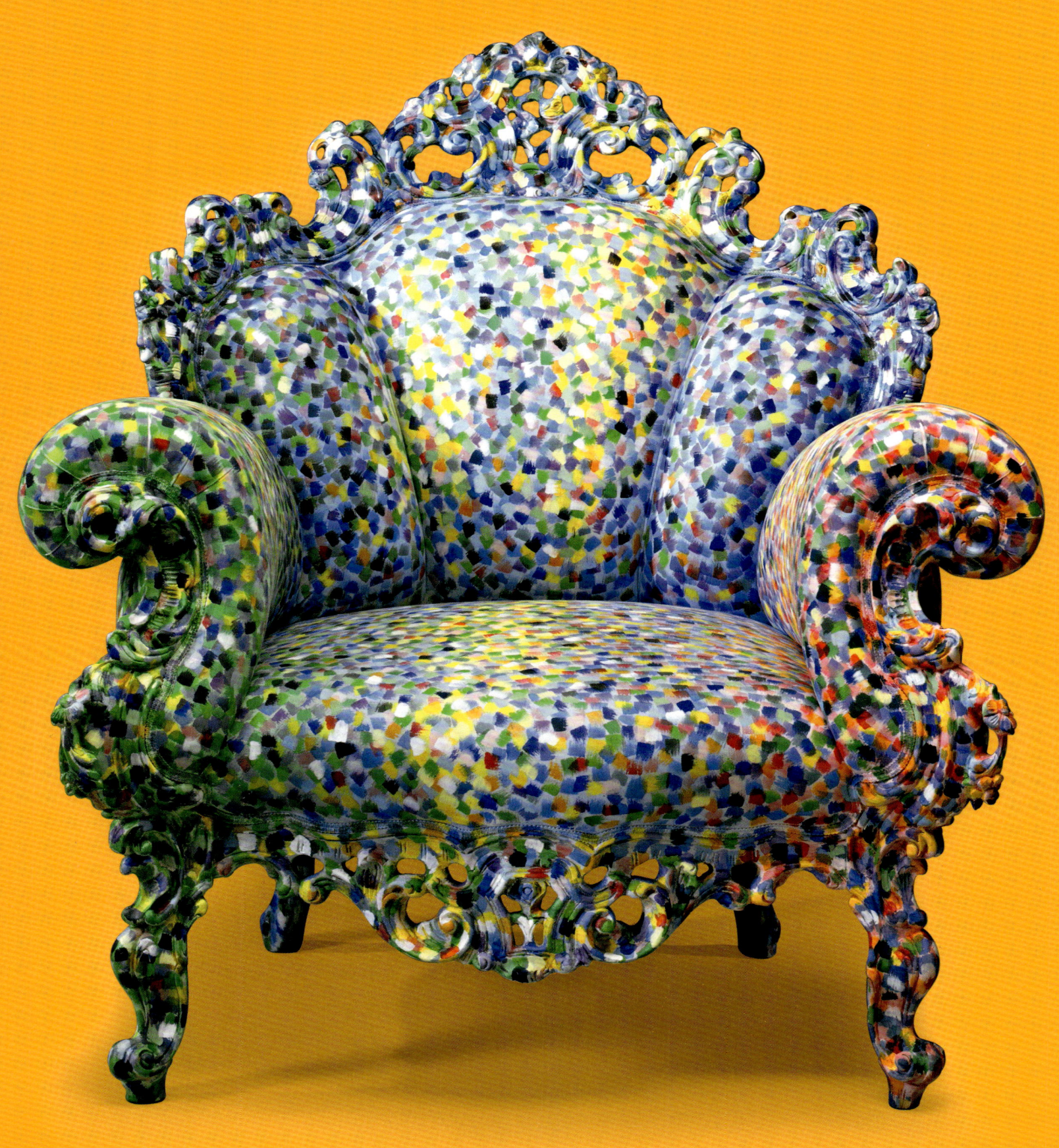

Opposite : **197. Ettore Sottsass** : for Abet Laminati : *Nefertiti* Desk : 1969 : chipboard, plastic laminate : H 43½" : 1983-40-1 (cat. 180)
Above : **198. Alessandro Mendini** : for Atelier Mendini : *Proust* Armchair : 1978 : painted wood and fabric upholstery : H 42½" : 2000-118-1 (cat. 128)

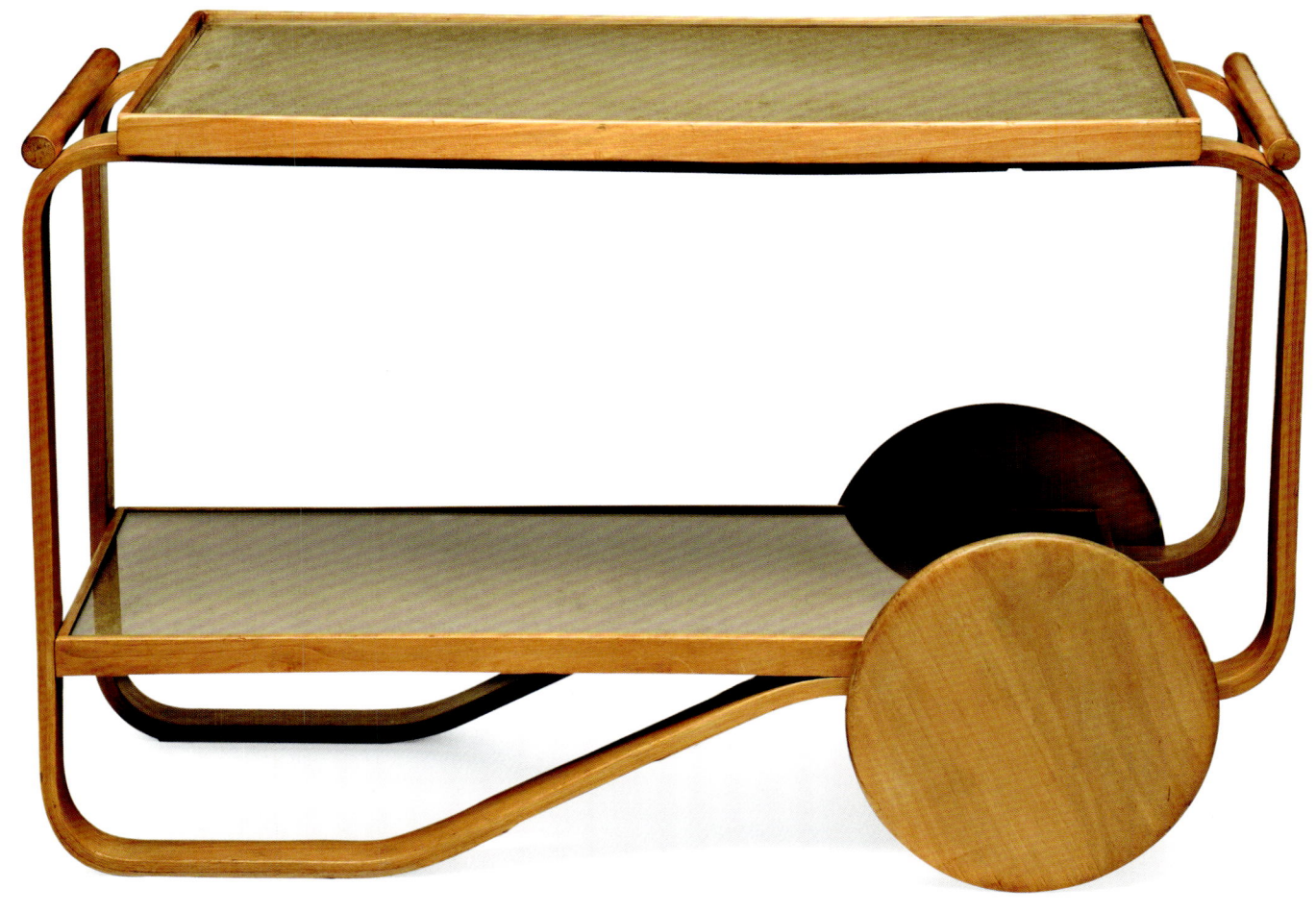

Above : **199. Alvar Aalto** : for Huonekalu-ja Rakennustyötehdas and Artek : Tea Cart : 1936 : cork, laminated birch : H 23 1/2" : 1985-67-3 (cat. 2)
Opposite : **200. Alvar Aalto** : for Huonekalu-ja Rakennustyötehdas : Armchair : c. 1931–32 : birch-faced plywood, laminated birch, leather : H 37 1/2" : 1985-67-1 (cat. 1)

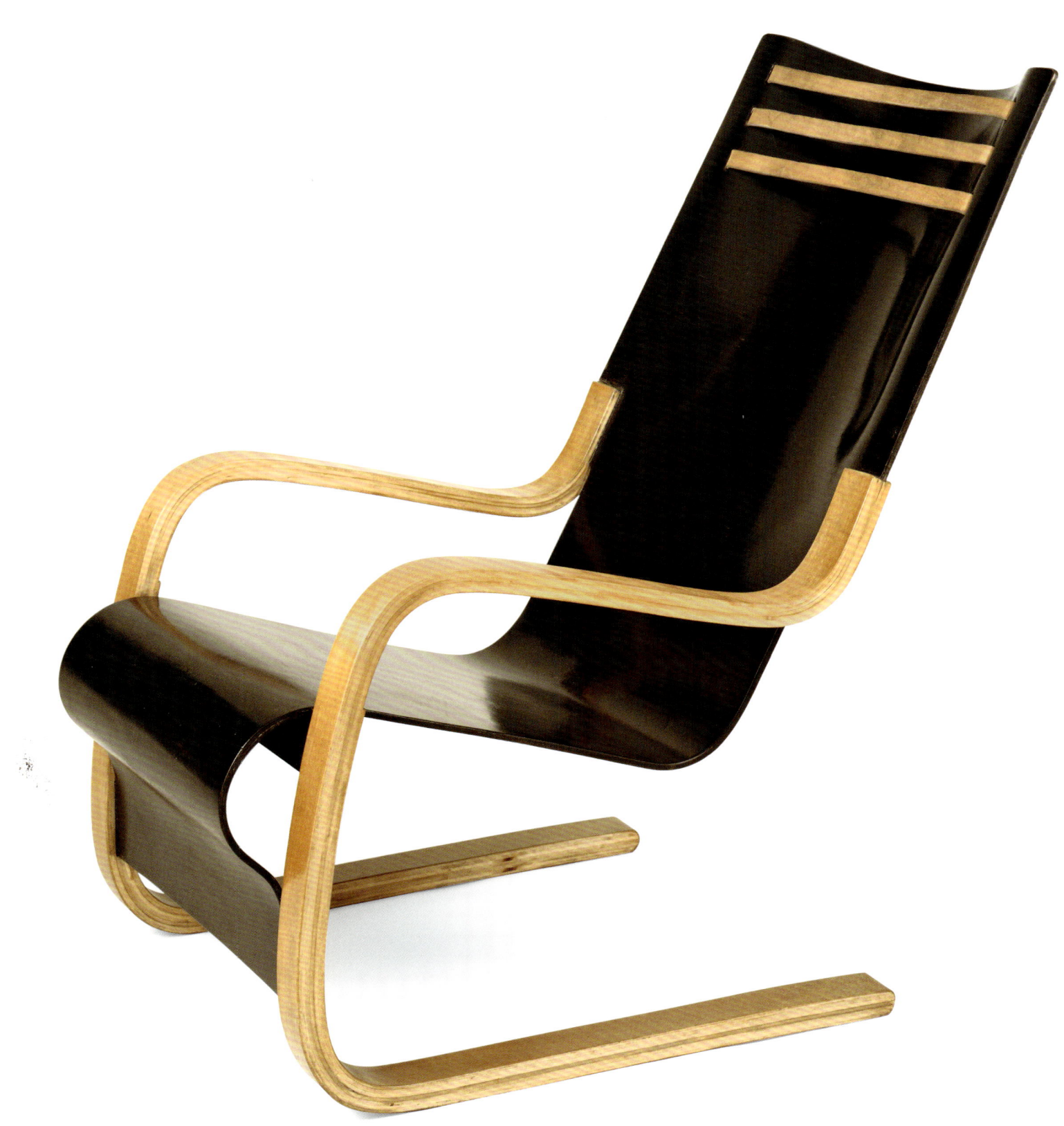

THE COLLAB DESIGN EXCELLENCE AWARD

In recognition of the committee's fifteenth anniversary, Collab's award for excellence in design was inaugurated at the Collab '86 auction and has continued to the present. The first recipient, furniture craftsman George Nakashima, was extolled by Collab cochairmen James L. Crowell and Grant Greapentrog as "one of this country's greatest craftsmen, whose achievements summarize all the goals of good design which Collab seeks to encourage."[91] Collab's second Design Excellence Award was presented to Massimo and Lella Vignelli in April 1988, again on the occasion of the benefit auction. "From the very familiar plastic stacking Heller dinnerware to furniture produced by Knoll to packaging," commented Crowell, " . . . the Vignellis have left their spare and elegant stamp on American life."[92]

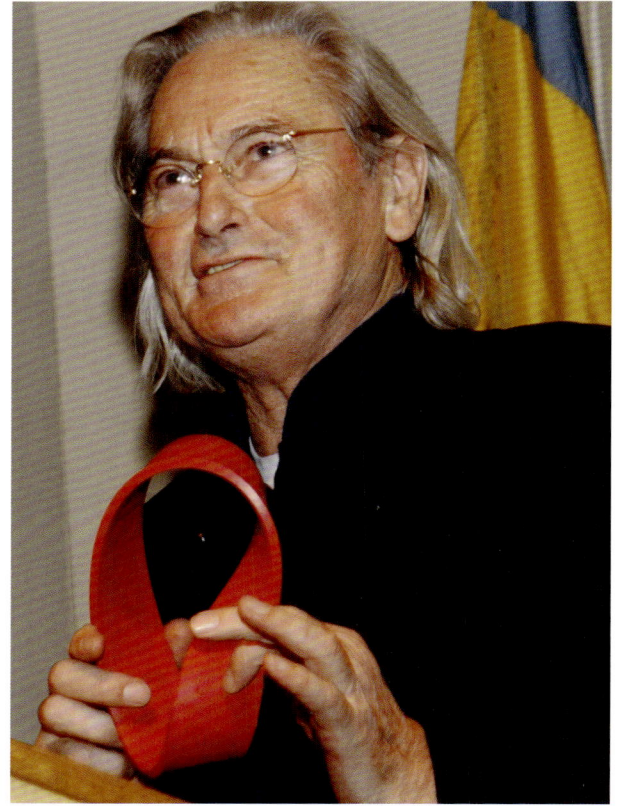

In 1989 Collab's fund-raising event returned to the Museum, perhaps particularly in response to a letter from Massimo Vignelli, who noted that he and Lella had been delighted to receive the award but strongly recommended that "future award ceremonies take place in your beautiful museum instead. Even the Museum's basement will always be better than any other place."[93] Under the leadership of cochairs Edward O. Eisen and Mary Ellen Weber, Collab presented its Design Excellence Award that year to Niels Diffrient for his lifetime achievements in the field of human-factors engineering. When asked by Collab's former chair Ralph Melick which of his designs might be most appropriate for donation to the Museum, Diffrient proposed his *Jefferson* chair, which was then given to the Museum by Sunar Hauserman, its manufacturer.[94] That same fall Collab helped support a symposium in conjunction with a small exhibition, *Building the City Beautiful: The Benjamin Franklin Parkway and the Philadelphia Museum of Art*,[95] which traced the historic design of the Benjamin Franklin Parkway and highlighted plans for the Museum building that would be enthroned atop Fairmount at the end of the parkway.

Flying on the momentum generated by *Design Since 1945*, the department of European decorative arts after 1700 initiated additional modern and contemporary design publications, acquisitions, installations, and exhibitions, beginning with the Museum's publication in 1984 of four guides to European decorative arts. With publication supported by grants from the J. E. Caldwell Company and the Women's Committee of the Museum, I wrote two of the four guides, *Porcelain* and *Styles, 1850–1900*, the latter illustrating some of the Museum's earliest "modern" acquisitions, ranging from the Worcester porcelain ewer and stand purchased in 1876 at the Centennial (fig. 4) to Gallé glass acquired by John T. Morris at the Paris Universal Exposition of 1900 (fig. 41).[96]

Above : **201.** Designer Ingo Maurer accepting his Collab Award : 2002   Opposite : **202.** *Design, 1900–1940* : by Kathryn B. Hiesinger and George H. Marcus (Philadelphia: Philadelphia Museum of Art, 1986)

202

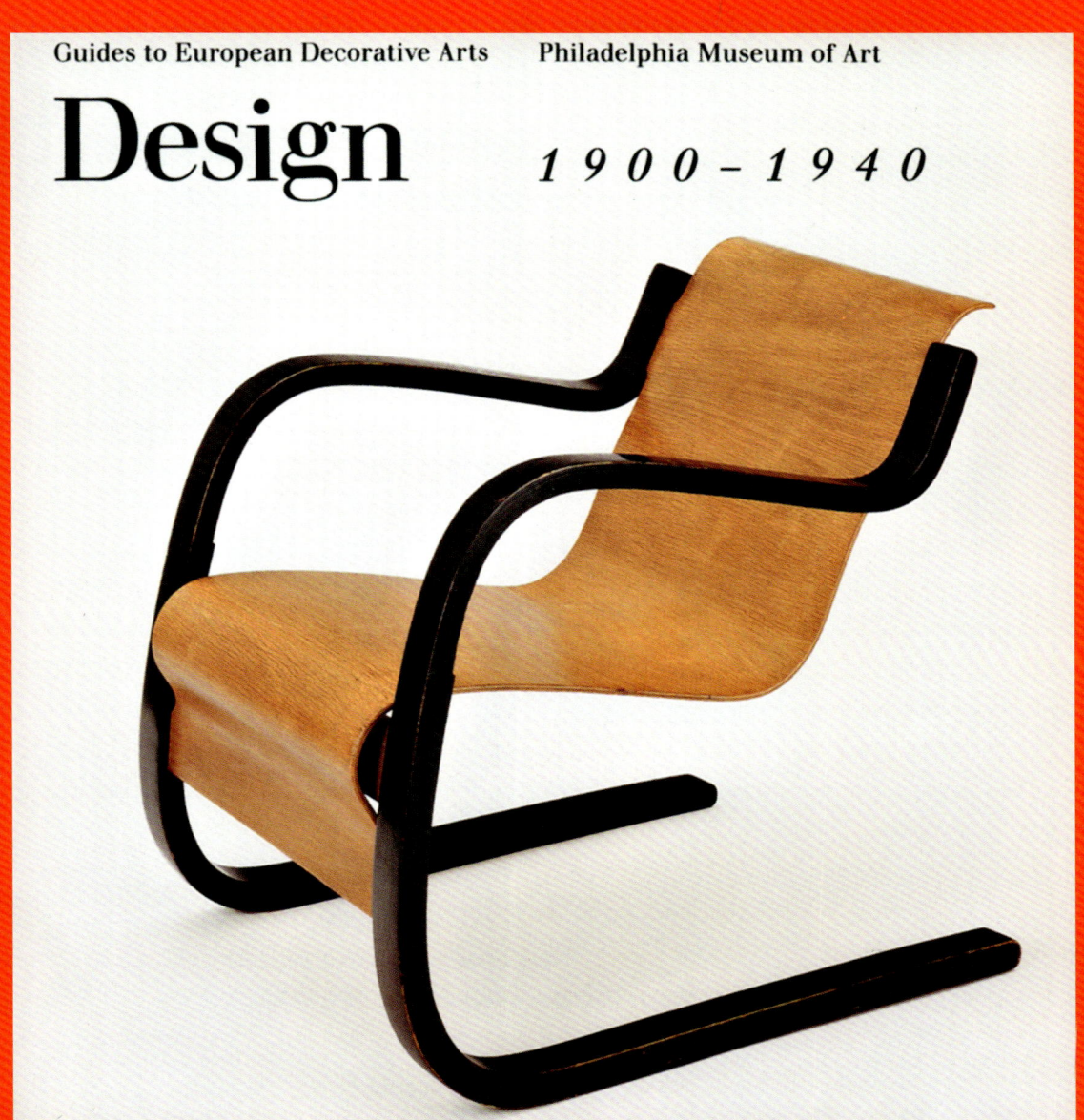

Guides to European Decorative Arts   Philadelphia Museum of Art

Design

1 9 0 0 - 1 9 4 0

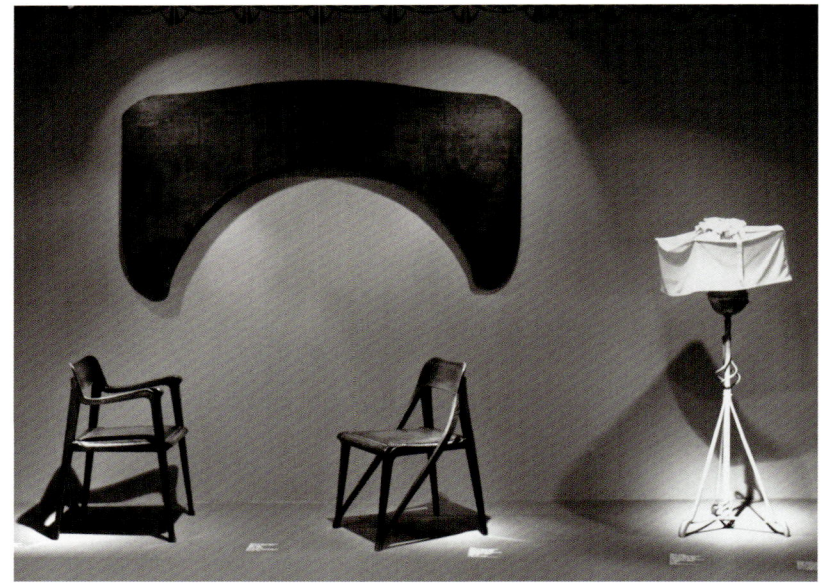
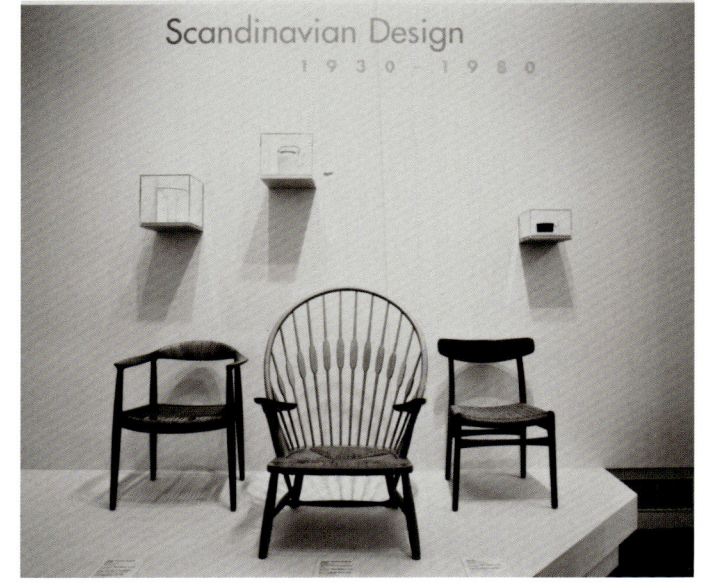

A fifth guide in the series, *Design, 1900–1940* (fig. 202), which I cowrote with my colleague George H. Marcus, head of publications at the Museum, was published in 1986 with the support of Collab. The book was celebrated in January 1987 with a reception honoring Collab and an installation of more than fifty modern and contemporary objects from the collections,[97] organized by Donna Corbin, who had joined the department to assist with *Design Since 1945*. She would take responsibility over the following years for organizing a number of thematic installations from the Museum's design collections in the Design Gallery we had maintained since 1976 as well as, on occasion, the larger Auditorium Gallery.

In 1985 I had begun organizing the major exhibition *Art Nouveau in Munich* following a year-long discussion with Hans Ottomeyer, curator of the furniture collection at the Münchner Stadtmuseum, which would provide the show with its greatest number of loans. Comprising furniture, decorative arts, textiles, graphic designs, and paintings made in Munich between 1895 and 1910, the exhibition demonstrated the importance of the city not only as a great cultural center, but also as the birthplace of a progressive new artistic style—Jugendstil—that became a foundation stone of modern design (fig. 203). The exhibition was held in the Museum's special exhibition galleries from September to November 1988, and traveled to the Los Angeles County Museum of Art, the Saint Louis Art Museum, and the Münchner Stadtmuseum.[98] The *New York Times* headlined the show as "Innovations from Munich's Masters of Art Nouveau" and reported that "most of the material shown . . . will probably be new even to enthusiasts of the movement,"[99] while the *Philadelphia Inquirer* described it as "the kind of exhibition that museums should be willing to risk more often," exemplary for its ability to "break new ground, stimulate discussion, and further scholarship, and bring to public attention a group of objects that deserves to be seen."[100] The *Frankfurter Allgemeine Zeitung* applauded the show as a "towering occurrence" and the catalogue's "inspiring, thesis-rich" essay "as a duty to read," adding that it revealed "a supreme knowledge of the German art literature of that time."[101] The Museum purchased

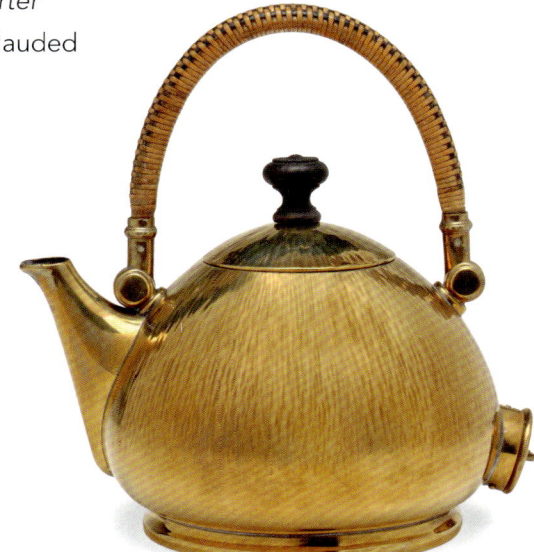

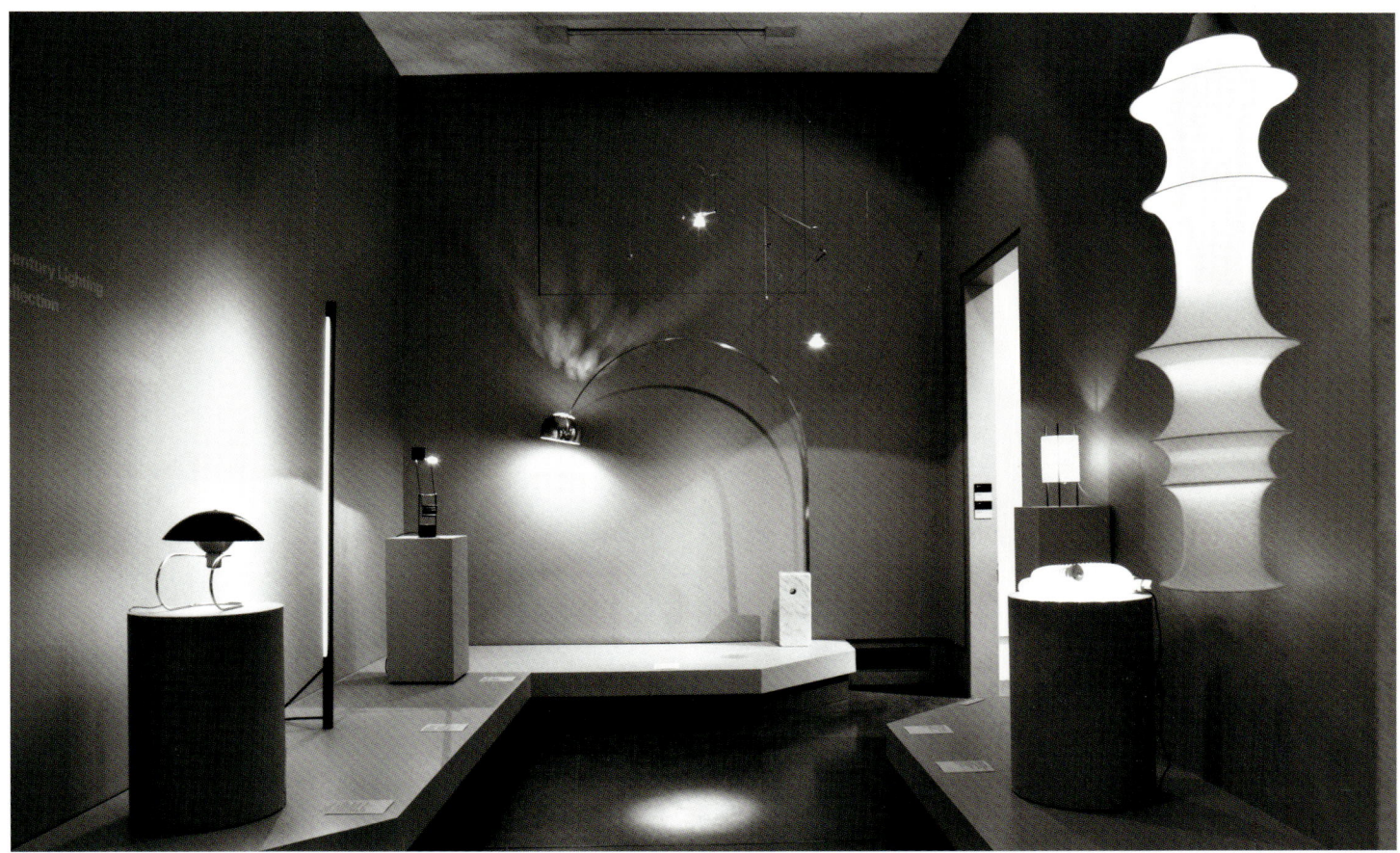

several objects from the exhibition, including a chair (fig. 50) and a salt-glazed stoneware jug by Richard Riemerschmid, along with an electric kettle by Peter Behrens (fig. 205).

Following the closing of *Art Nouveau in Munich*, the department continued to assert a strong presence at the museum in the 1990s through in-house modern and contemporary design installations, among them *Designs of the 1950s* (1990), *Twentieth-Century Lighting* (1991) (fig. 206), *Timeline of Twentieth-Century Chairs* (1995), and *Scandinavian Design, 1930–1980* (1997) (fig. 204), all organized by Donna Corbin, who became the department's assistant curator in 1992 and associate curator in 2004.[102] Recent acquisitions, such as the *YaYaHo* lighting system by Ingo Maurer, the *Arco* lamp by Achille and Pier Giacomo Castiglioni, and the *Kubus* containers and glass tea service by Wilhelm Wagenfeld given by Collab in honor of chair Mary Ellen Weber, were exhibited for the first time. In conjunction with *Designs of the 1950s*, John and Marilyn Neuhart (co-authors with Ray Eames of the recently published comprehensive catalogue *Eames Design*) gave a well-attended public lecture sponsored by Collab. In 1991–92, with the help of University of Pennsylvania professors David B. Brownlee and David G. De Long, Corbin coordinated the Philadelphia premiere of the major traveling exhibition *Louis I. Kahn: In the Realm of Architecture*, organized by the Museum of Contemporary Art, Los Angeles.[103] Arata Isozaki's exhibition design was inspired by Kahn's plans (1961–72) for the unbuilt Mikveh Israel Synagogue in Philadelphia, and was reconfigured at each of the show's venues.

While the development and realization of these exhibitions were underway, I had begun the organization of another major exhibition, *Japanese Design: A Survey Since 1950*, with my colleague Felice Fischer, the Museum's curator of East Asian art. Although *Design Since 1945* had included

Opposite, clockwise from top left : **203.** *Art Nouveau in Munich* : 1988 : gallery view   **204.** *Scandinavian Design : 1930–1980* : 1997 : gallery view   **205. Peter Behrens** : for AEG : Electric Kettle : 1909 : brass, cane : H (with handle) 8 5/16" : 1987-12-1a,b (cat. 17)   Above : **206.** *Twentieth-Century Lighting* : 1997 : gallery view

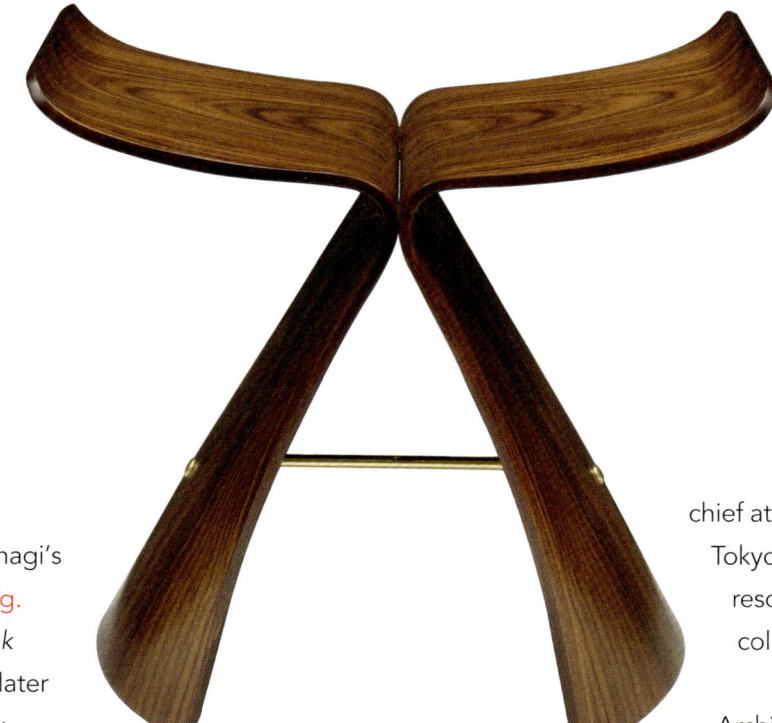

several works by Japanese designers—including Sori Yanagi's well-known *Butterfly* stool (fig. 207) and Toshiyuki Kita's *Wink* chair (fig. 208), which Collab later gave to the Museum—I knew there was much to discover about a field so little known outside Japan. Correspondence with Japanese designers, manufacturers, and design organizations, and a review of the critical literature, culminated in a list of some 250 objects selected for their aesthetic quality and historical significance, ranging from furniture, housewares, and consumer electronics to crafts, toys, and clothing. The aim of the exhibition was to define and record for the first time Japan's extensive and original contributions to modern design, bringing to the public a greater awareness of the variety and quality of Japanese design and a historical context in which to assess its development. Fischer and I traveled to Japan in the spring of 1991 to review the exhibition checklist with Shukuro Habara, secretary general of the Japan Industrial Designers Association, who had provided assistance to *Design Since 1945*, and with his colleague, Shutaro Mukai, professor in chief at Musashino Art University in Tokyo, who gave us access to the resources of his university collections and library.

Architect and theorist Kisho Kurakawa designed the exhibition, which was on view in the fall of 1994 (figs. 207–21).[104] Loosely organized by chronology and medium, *Japanese Design* included a wealth of interpretive and didactic materials, among them, two cultural and historical vignettes: a tatami room (c. 1960) with a television and other electrical appliances, to suggest the juxtaposition of traditional culture with new industrial technology; and a "one-room mansion" studio apartment, complete with kitchen and bathroom units, to demonstrate Japan's response to modern urban high-rise living in the mid-1970s. Videos on monitors mounted throughout the exhibition illustrated production processes and craft techniques, commercial advertisements, and concepts for future products. Five tenets of Japanese design—compactness, asymmetry, craftsmanship, simplicity, and humor—were reflected in text printed on screens, and

Japanese Design : A Survey Since 1950 : 1994

Above : **207. Sori Yanagi** : for Tendo Mokko : *Butterfly* Stool : 1954 : plywood, metal : H 15 3/8" : 1983-11-1 (cat. 220)   Opposite : **208. Toshiyuki Kita** : for Cassina : *Wink* Chair : 1980 : steel, Dacron-covered polyurethane-foam upholstery : L (extended) 6' 6 3/4" : 1994-132-1 (cat. 99)

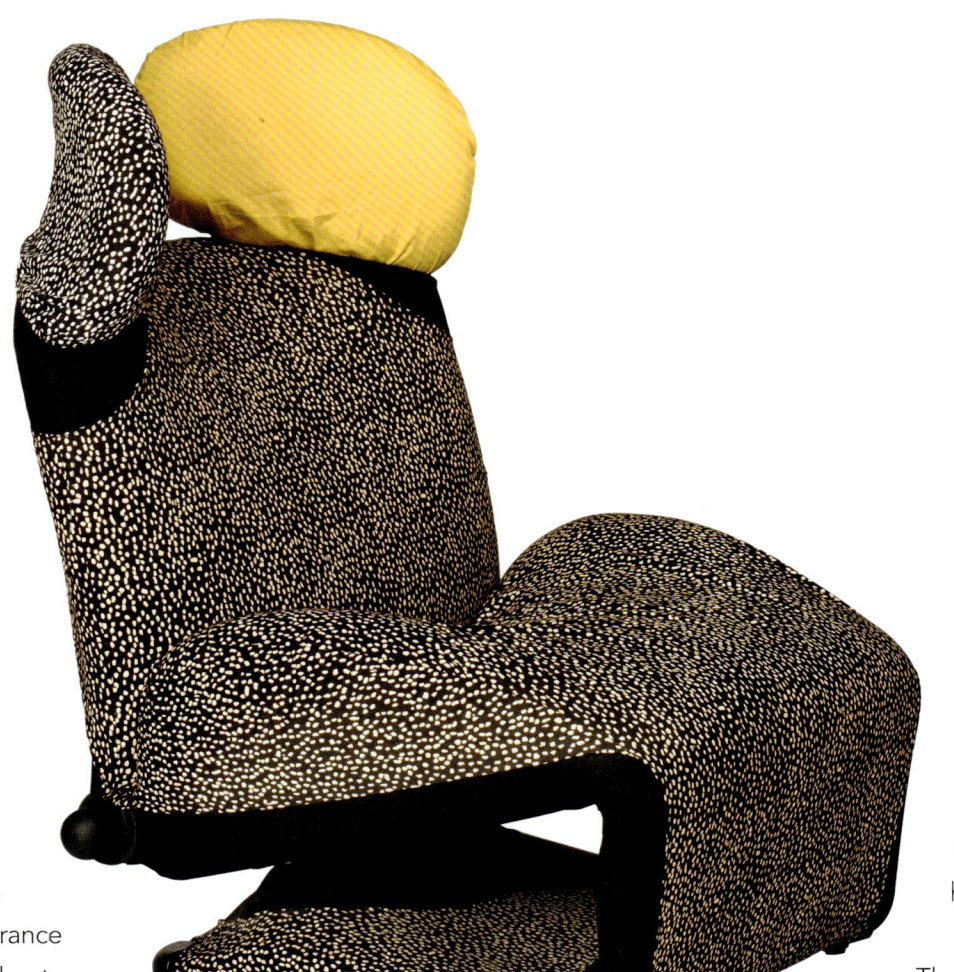

the themes were also discussed on informational cards available at the entrance to the galleries. A theater with cushions for seating was built into the exhibition and presented continuous films about Japanese designers and companies, including an award-winning video that the Museum produced for the occasion, titled *Japanese Design: The Spirit in the Thing*. The exhibition was enthusiastically reviewed by *Time* magazine as "a vibrant outpouring of talent and enterprise that pays homage to the past while striding boldly into the present,"[105] and the *Philadelphia Inquirer* declared that "anyone with an interest in materialism—from couture dresses to lacquered soy-sauce pitchers to in-line roller skates—will want to see this landmark show."[106] When *Japanese Design* opened at the Museum in September 1994, Philadelphia Mayor Edward G. Rendell and Masako Kuriyama, wife of Japan's ambassador to the United States, delivered speeches, Rendell commenting (without knowing the prohibitive cost) that the ultra-compact Japanese studio apartment might provide a model for housing Philadelphia's homeless.

The striking catalogue was designed by well-known artist Mitsuo Katsui, recognized in Japan for his use of computer-graphics technology (fig. 211). The publication served as an important scholarly record of the exhibition and defined the field of modern Japanese design through introductory essays by Fischer and myself, along with essays by seventeen Japanese critics, historians, and designers, a fully illustrated chronology, critical biographies of the designers and design firms whose works were included in the exhibition, and a selected bibliography.[107] The catalogue received numerous awards in the United States as well as in Japan, and was translated into Italian, German, French, and Japanese for the exhibition's international tour to the Triennale in Milan, the Kunsthalle Düsseldorf, the Centre Georges Pompidou in Paris, and the Suntory Museum in Osaka.

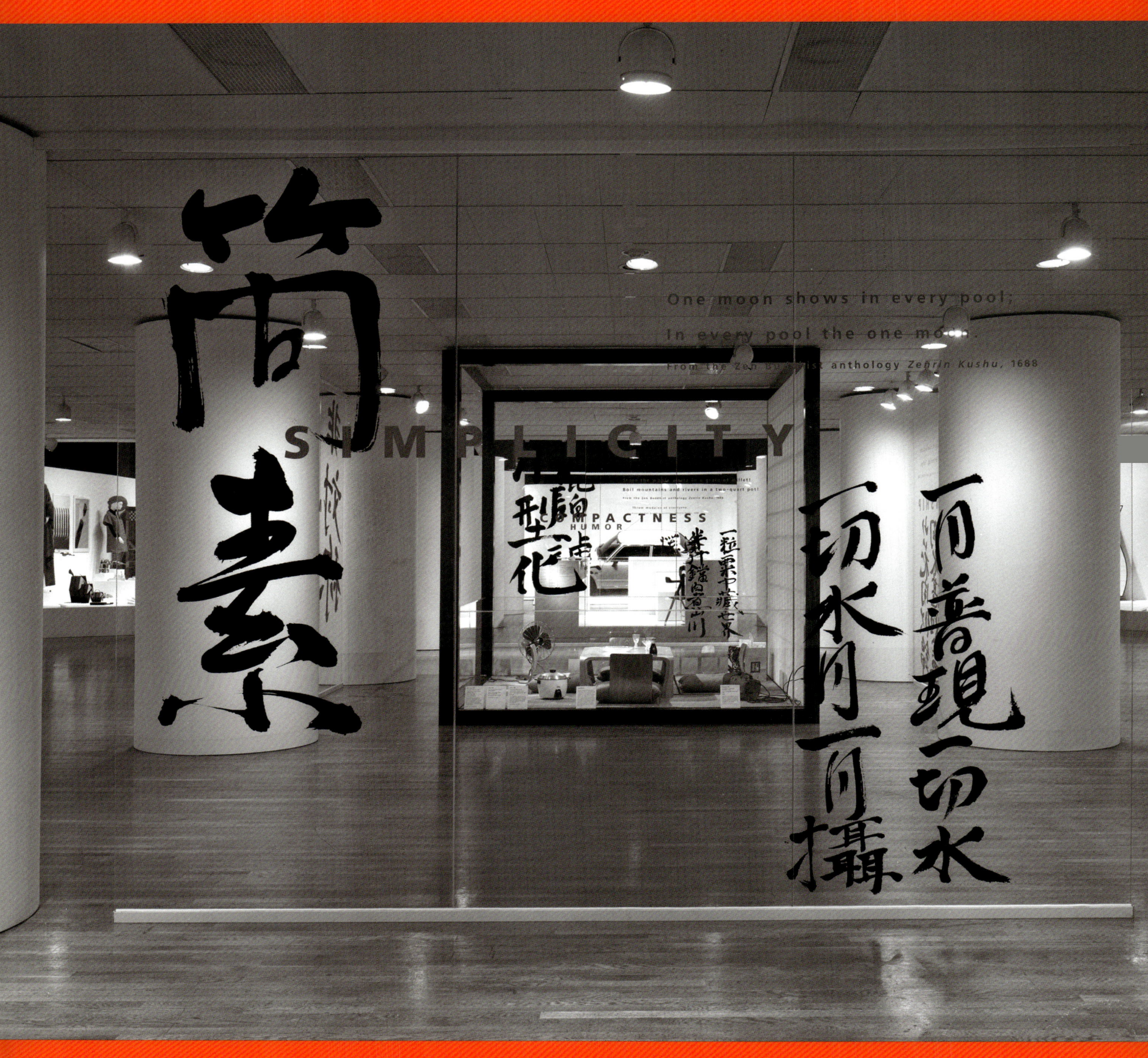

Japanese Design : A Survey Since 1950 : 1994
209 and 210. Gallery views

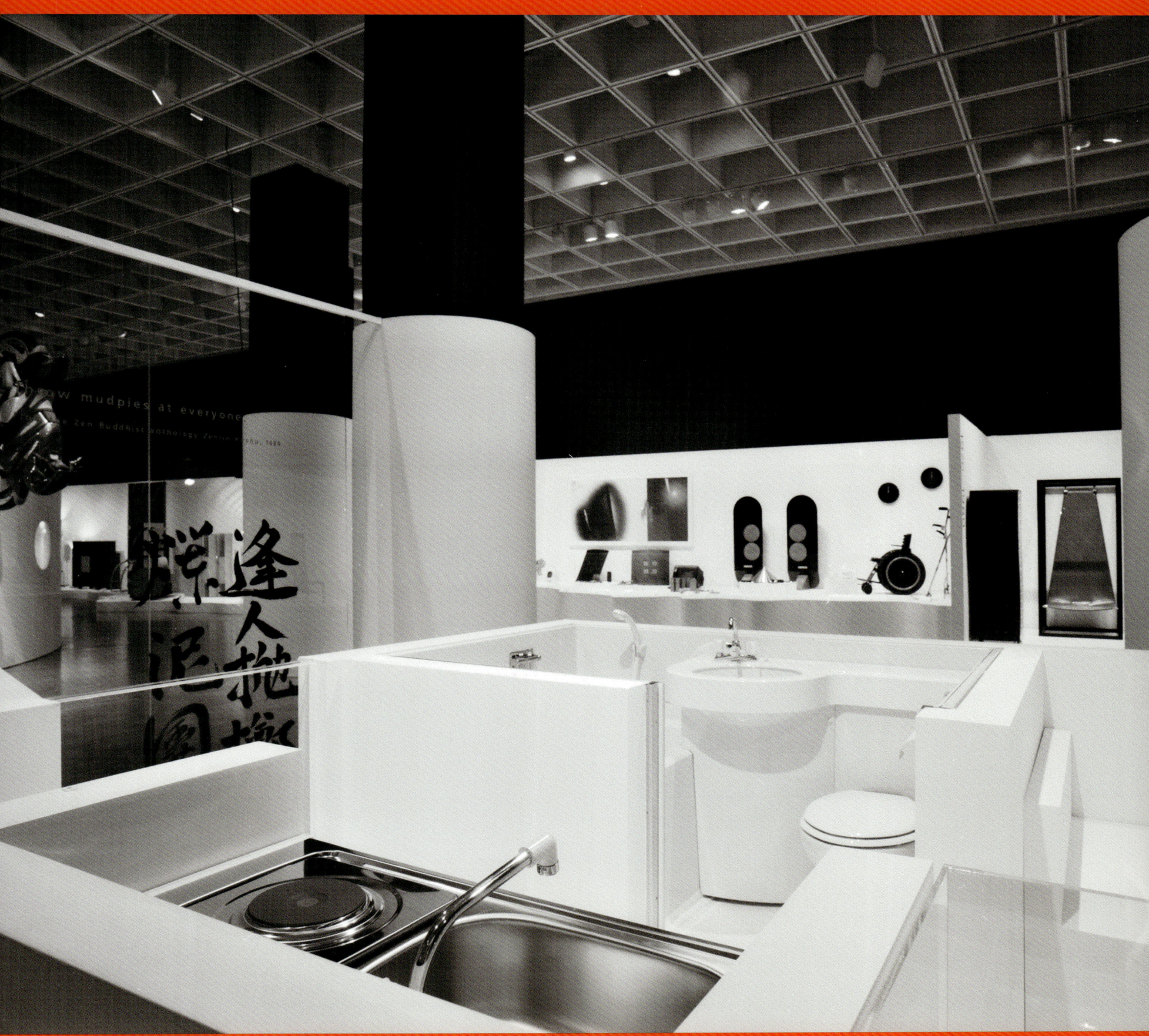

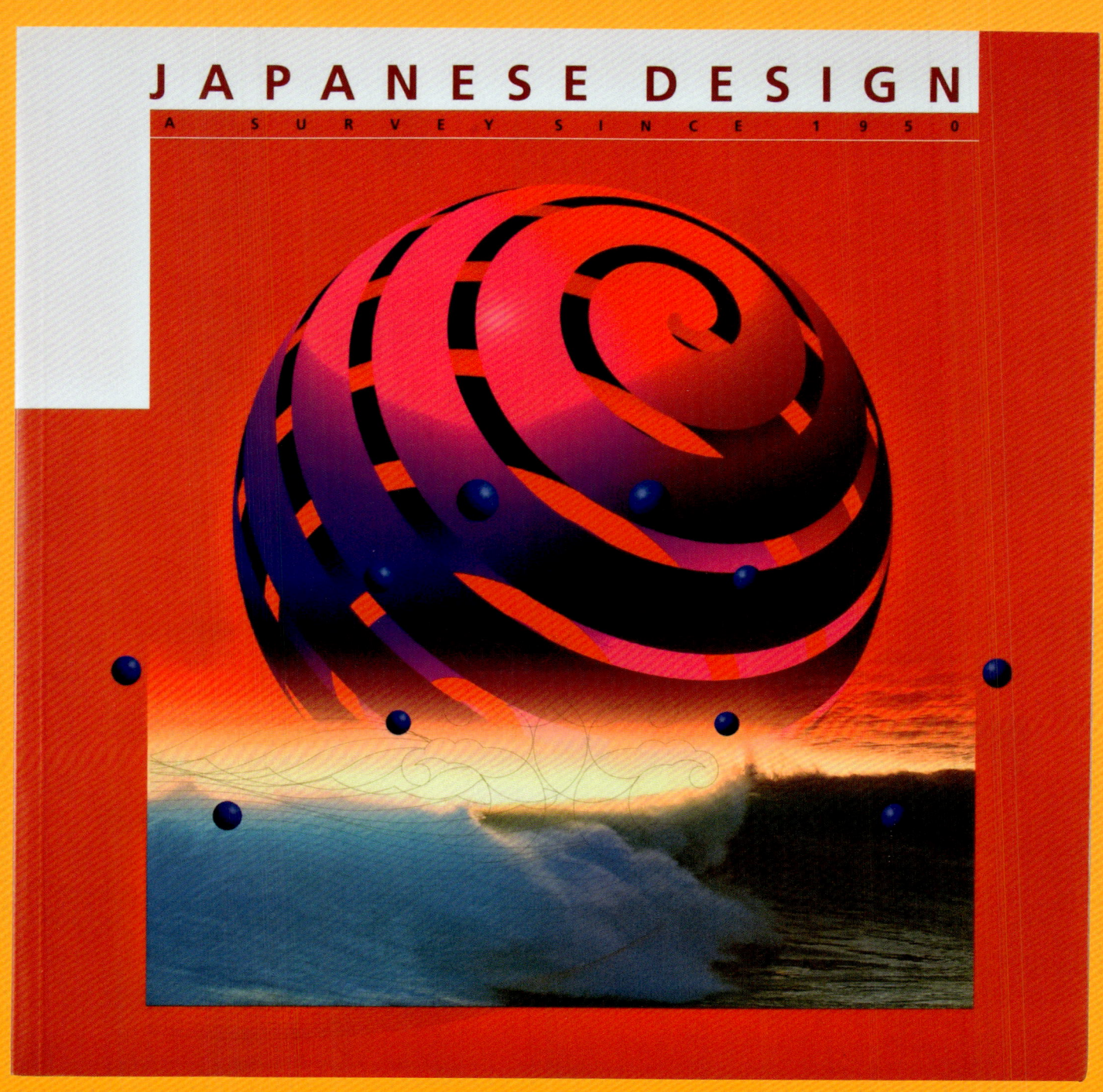

Japanese Design : A Survey Since 1950 : 1994

Above : **211.** Exhibition catalogue : edited by Kathryn B. Hiesinger and Felice Fischer (Philadelphia: Philadelphia Museum of Art, 1994)
Opposite : **212.** Hiroshi Awatsuji : for Fujie Textile : *Jitensha* Art Screen (detail) : 1982 : screen-printed cotton : W 5' 10⅞":1983-118-1 (cat. 15)

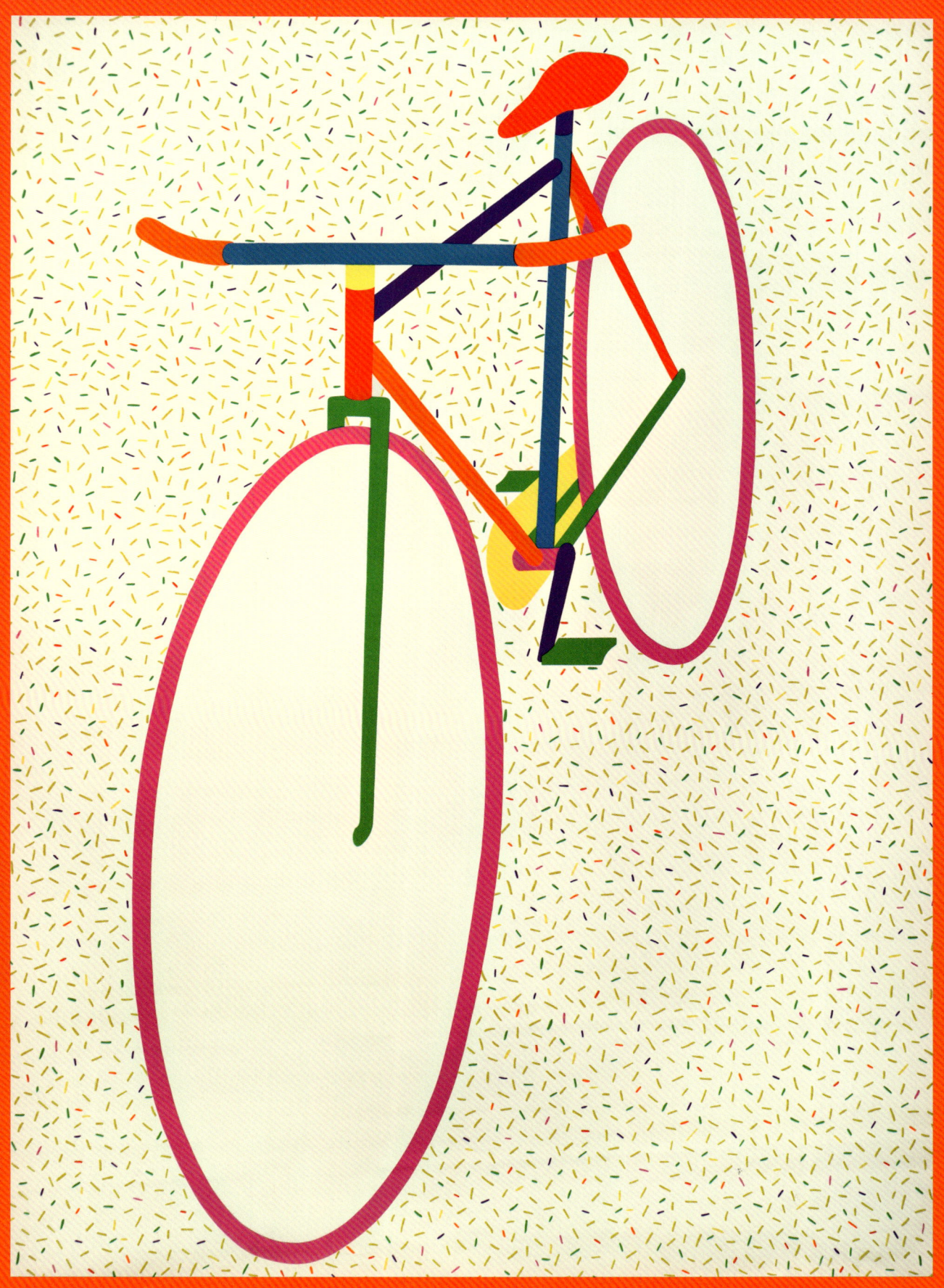

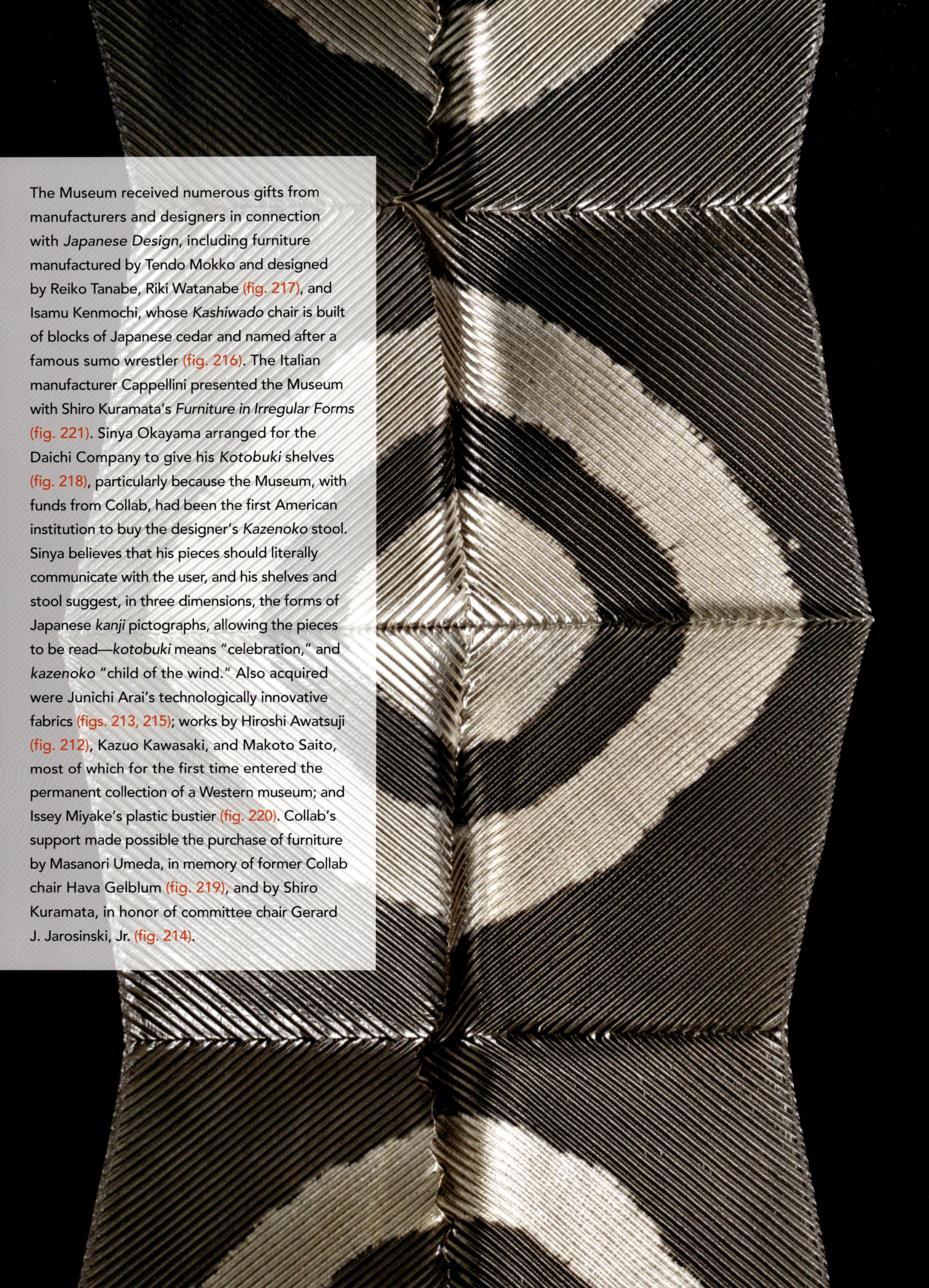

The Museum received numerous gifts from manufacturers and designers in connection with *Japanese Design*, including furniture manufactured by Tendo Mokko and designed by Reiko Tanabe, Riki Watanabe (fig. 217), and Isamu Kenmochi, whose *Kashiwado* chair is built of blocks of Japanese cedar and named after a famous sumo wrestler (fig. 216). The Italian manufacturer Cappellini presented the Museum with Shiro Kuramata's *Furniture in Irregular Forms* (fig. 221). Sinya Okayama arranged for the Daichi Company to give his *Kotobuki* shelves (fig. 218), particularly because the Museum, with funds from Collab, had been the first American institution to buy the designer's *Kazenoko* stool. Sinya believes that his pieces should literally communicate with the user, and his shelves and stool suggest, in three dimensions, the forms of Japanese *kanji* pictographs, allowing the pieces to be read—*kotobuki* means "celebration," and *kazenoko* "child of the wind." Also acquired were Junichi Arai's technologically innovative fabrics (figs. 213, 215); works by Hiroshi Awatsuji (fig. 212), Kazuo Kawasaki, and Makoto Saito, most of which for the first time entered the permanent collection of a Western museum; and Issey Miyake's plastic bustier (fig. 220). Collab's support made possible the purchase of furniture by Masanori Umeda, in memory of former Collab chair Hava Gelblum (fig. 219), and by Shiro Kuramata, in honor of committee chair Gerard J. Jarosinski, Jr. (fig. 214).

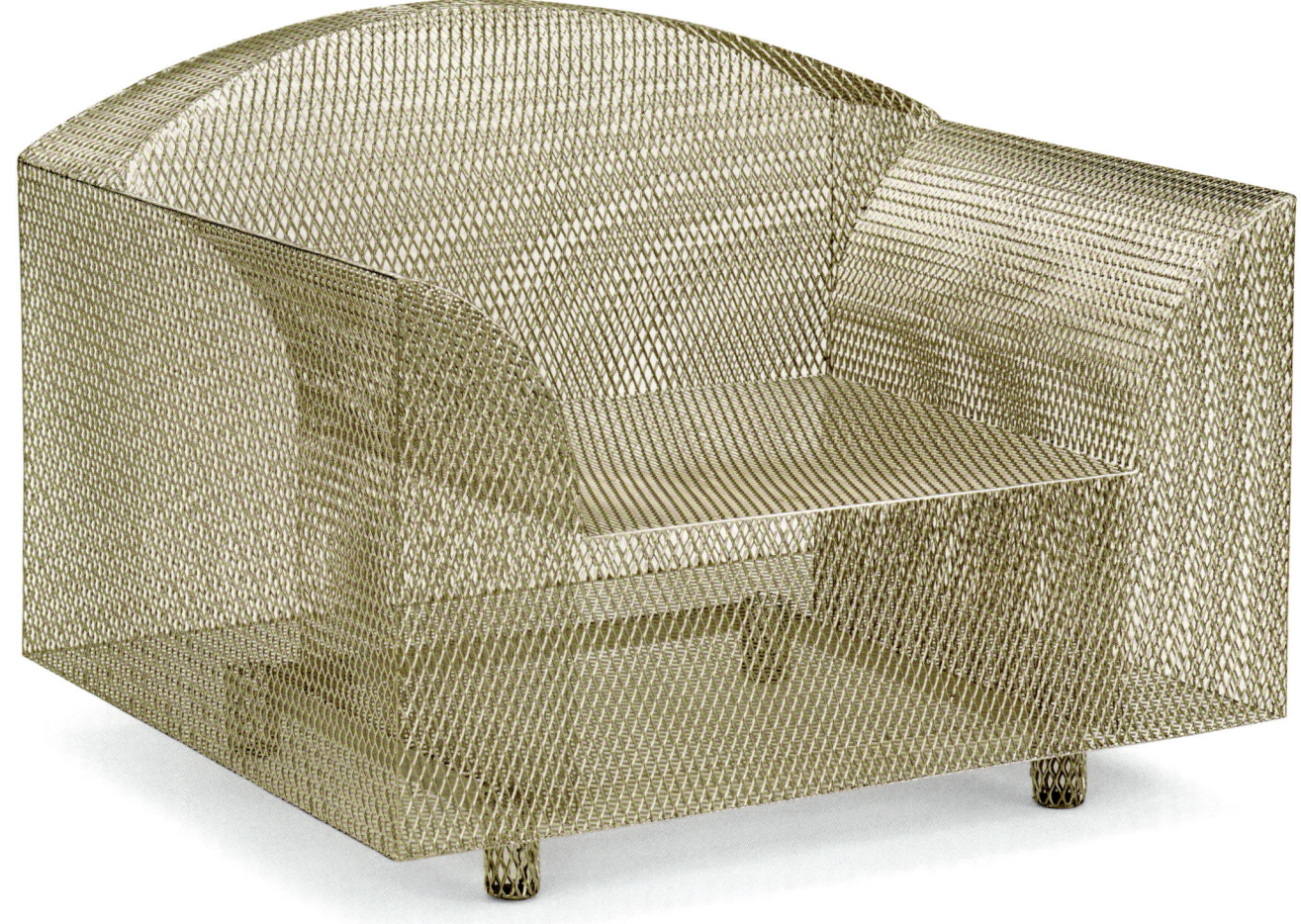

Japanese Design : A Survey Since 1950 : 1994

Opposite : **213. Junichi Arai** : for K. K. Arai Creation System : *Ojo de Dios* Fabric (detail) : c. 1990 : dyed, pleated polyester : W 38" : 1996-102-5 (cat. 7)   Above : **214. Shiro Kuramata** : for Vitra : *How High the Moon* Armchair : 1986 : nickel-plated steel : H 28¼" : 1993-1-1 (cat. 103)

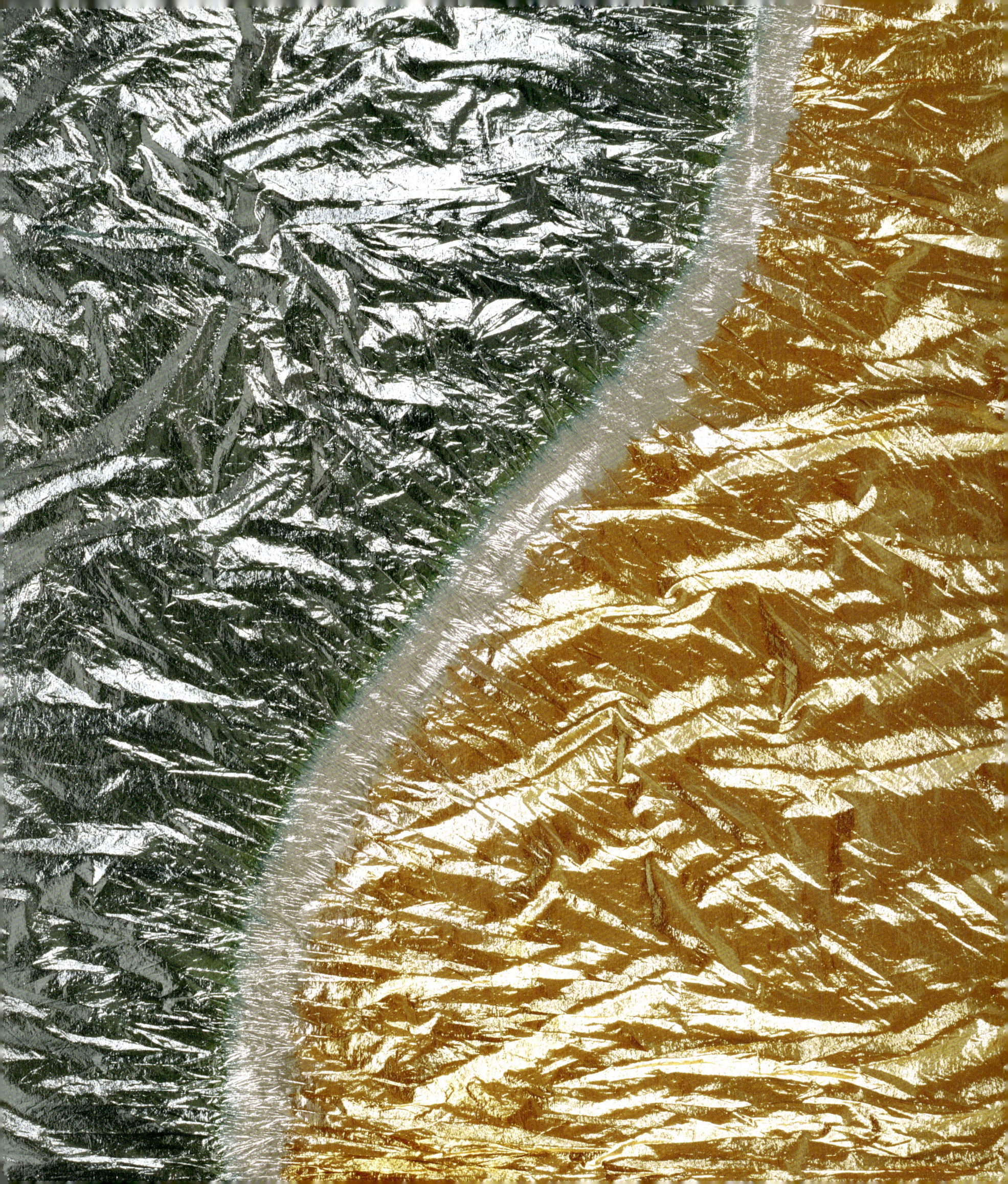

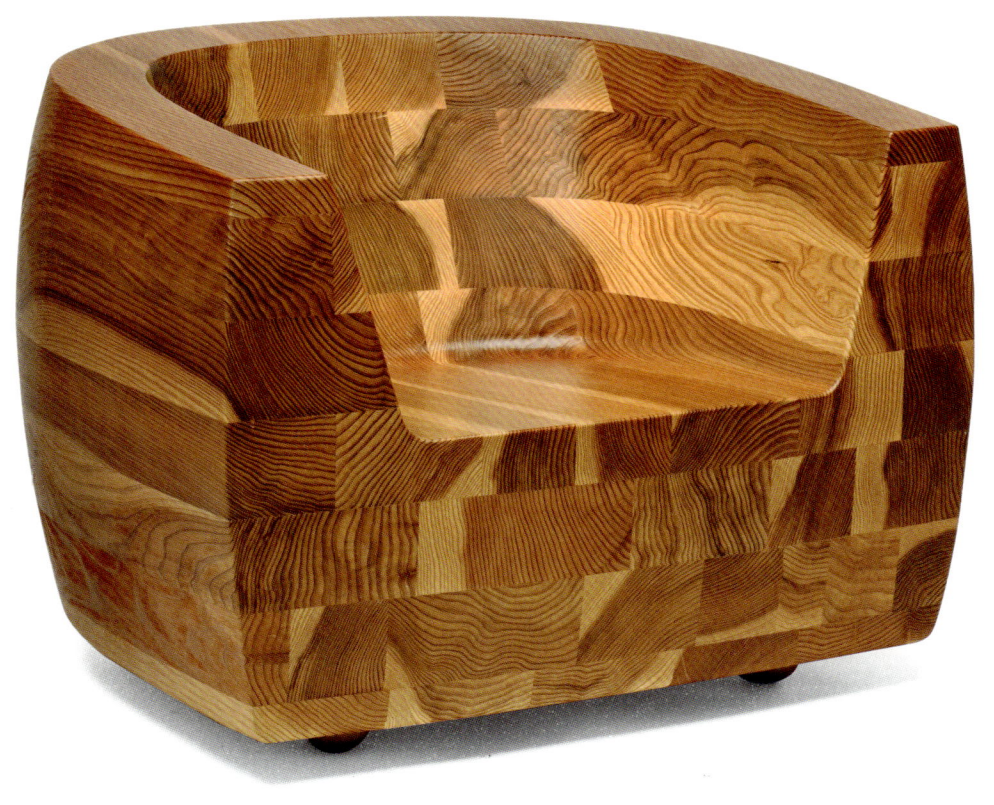

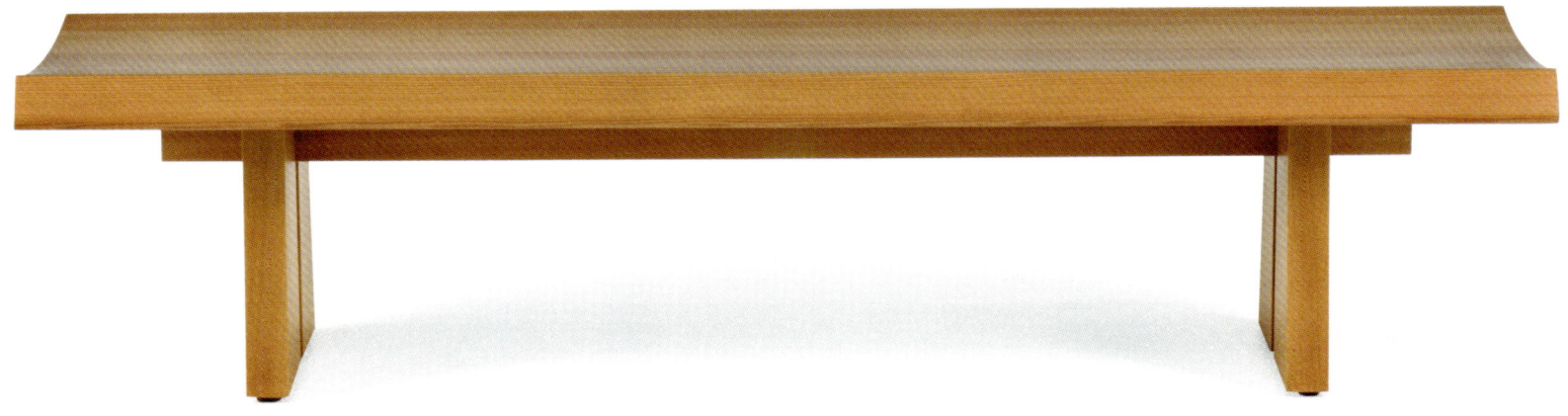

Japanese Design : A Survey Since 1950 : 1994

Opposite : **215. Junichi Arai** : for Nuno : *Big Wave* Fabric (detail) : 1988 : tie-resist dyed aluminum and polyester : W 50" : 1991-125-1 (cat. 6)
Above, top to bottom : **216. Isamu Kenmochi** : for Tendo Mokko : *Kashiwado* Chair : 1961 : lacquered Japanese cedar : H 24 3/4" : 1996-90-1 (cat. 98)
217. Riki Watanabe : for Tendo Mokko : Bench : 1960 : Douglas fir : L 5' 9 3/4" : 1996-90-2 (cat. 206)

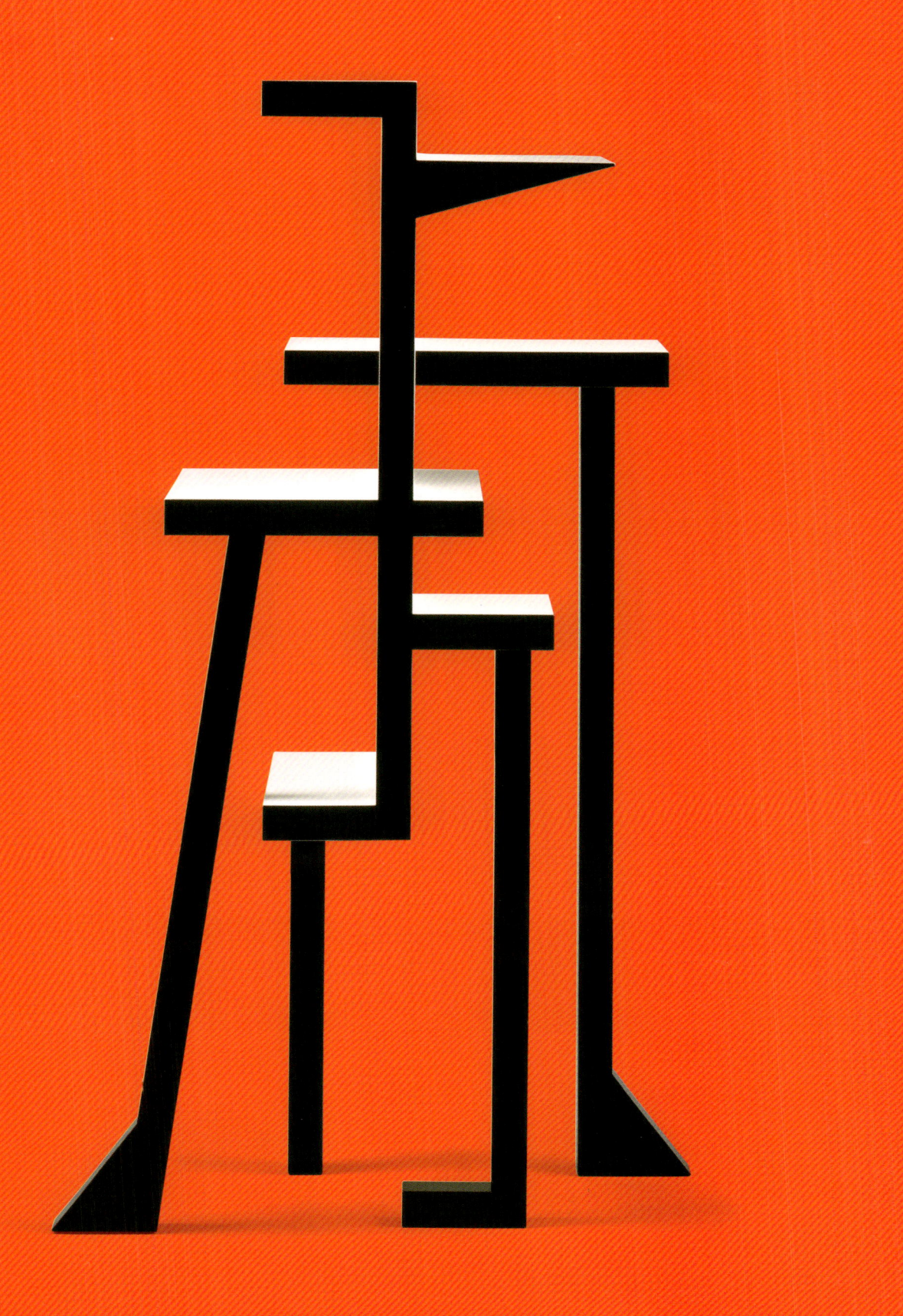

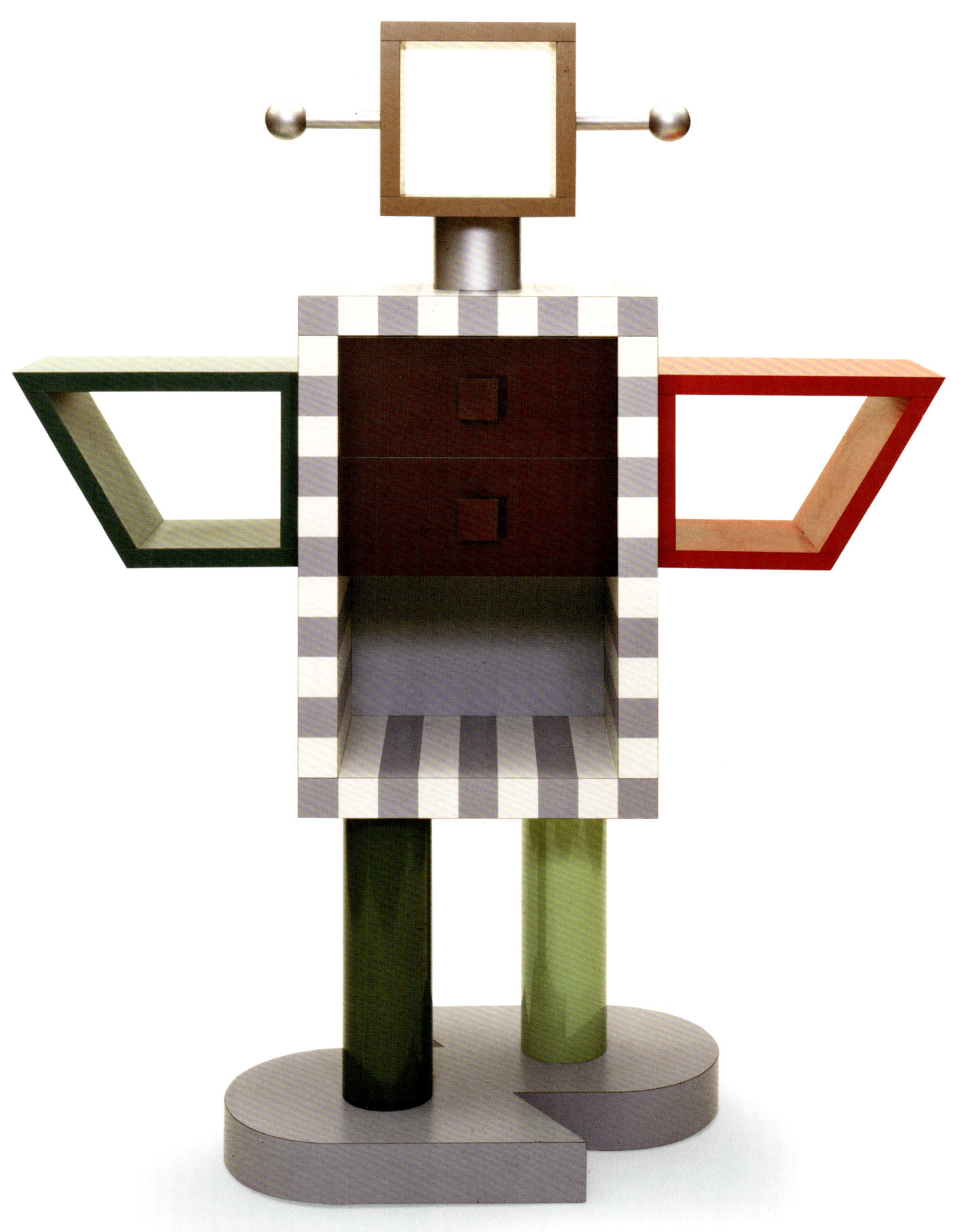

Japanese Design : A Survey Since 1950 : 1994

Opposite : **218. Sinya Okayama** : for Daichi : *Kotobuki* Shelves : 1989 : lacquered wood : H 5' 4 1/8" : 1990-25-1 (cat. 141)   Above : **219. Masanori Umeda** : for Memphis : *Ginza Robot* Cabinet : 1982 : plastic laminate, wood, chipboard : H 5' 8 7/8" : 1994-131-1 (cat. 195)

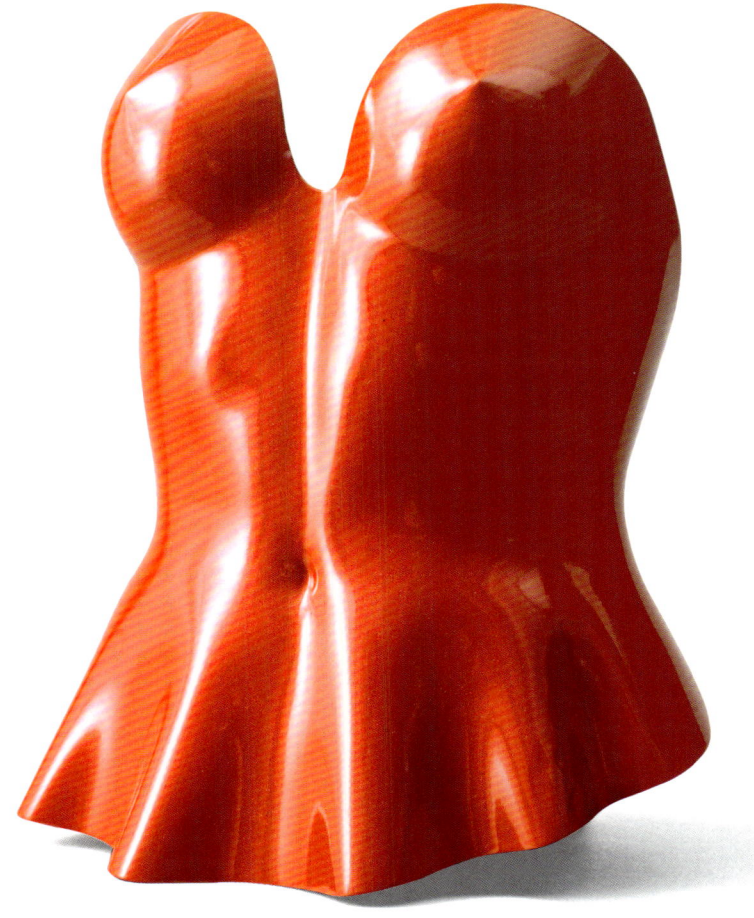

Japanese Design : A Survey Since 1950 : 1994

Above : **220. Issey Miyake** : for Issey Miyake, Inc. : Bustier : 1980 : plastic : H 15" : 1992-136-1 (cat. 131)   Opposite : **221. Shiro Kuramata** : for Cappellini : *Furniture in Irregular Forms: Side 2* Chest of Drawers : 1970 : lacquered wood : H 5' 6 15/16" : 1994-130-1 (cat. 102)

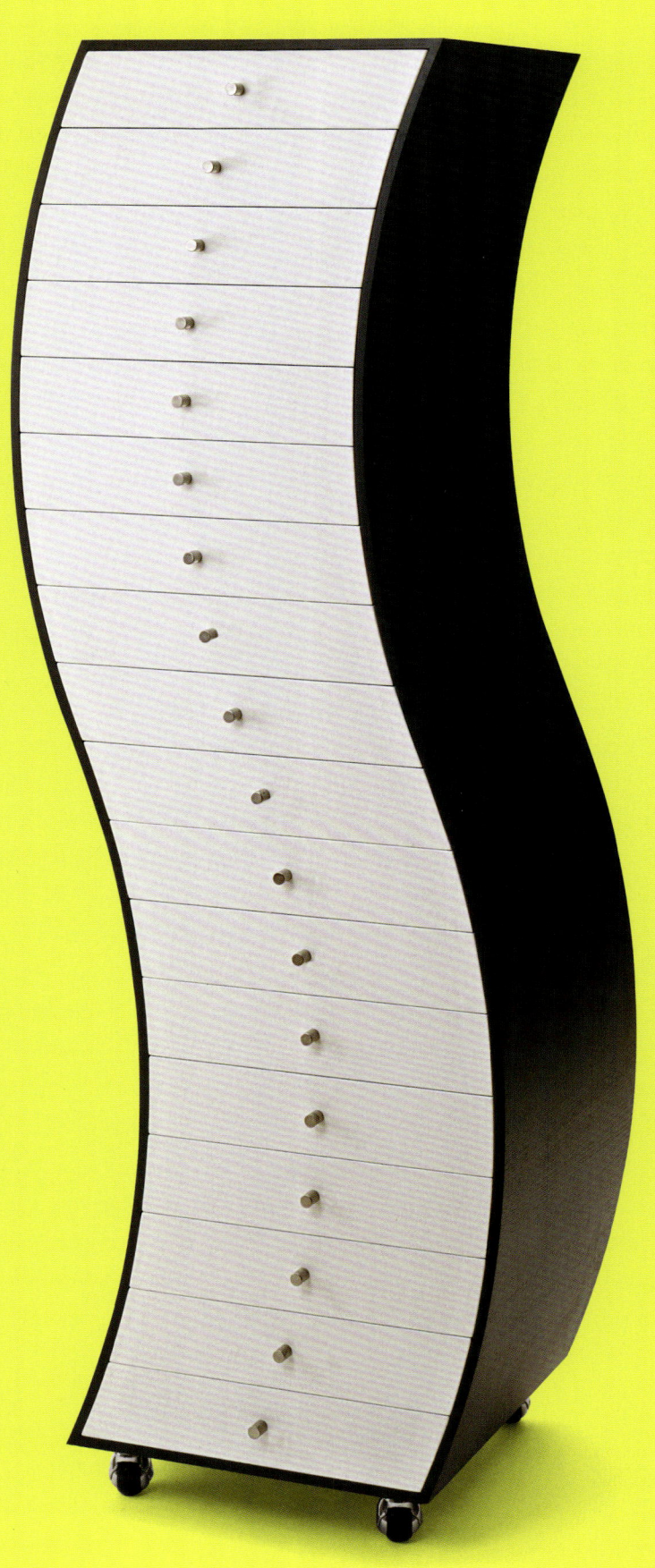

Mayor Rendell had been the object of close attention by the Museum's administration since his election in 1991. Inheriting massive fiscal problems, he confronted a $250-million deficit with stringent cost-cutting policies (such as privatizing city functions) and revenue-generating initiatives that directly affected the Museum's operations.[108] Under threat of closure the Museum's president, Robert Montgomery Scott, heroically battled Rendell and the city council to compel Philadelphia to honor its obligation to provide security, maintenance, and custodial staff at the Museum.[109] In 1993 Scott and the trustees privately recognized that it would be necessary for the Museum to operate within the city's five-year financial plan, even though it eliminated all municipal funding with the exception of utility costs and support for the Museum's essential capital improvements.[110] Seeking alternative strategies, Wharton School professor and Museum trustee Yoram (Jerry) Wind surveyed, for the first time in the Museum's history, the significant annual economic impact of its activities on the city.[111] The results of his study provided leverage to the Museum in its ongoing negotiations, positioning it as an institution that generates substantial income for the city and the region through cultural tourism—a strategy that successfully tied the Museum to the mayor's own economic development initiatives. Subsequently, the Museum developed a strong sense of partnership with the city in building an audience. Scott reported in 1996 that "in his fifteen years of attending City Capital Budget Meetings, [he] had never experienced such cooperation between the City and the Museum."[112]

During the 1990s Collab, too, sought to better promote its activities, and endeavored to build an audience for modern and contemporary design at the Museum, led by its committee chairs: Gabriele Windeck Lee, Gerard J. Jarosinski, Jr., and Eric Rymshaw, all three of whom practiced architecture and interior design; Lisa S. Roberts, a product designer trained as an architect; and Joan Doyle, a retail consultant to museums and cultural institutions. Together they began to strengthen the committee's activities despite continued frustration at the lack of exhibition space for expanding programs. In the fall of 1993, in conjunction with Collab's Design Excellence Award to the table- and giftware firm Swid Powell, Collab sponsored a citywide college-level student design competition, the first of its kind in Philadelphia. This enormously successful, ongoing event was created by Roberts, who assembled a jury comprised of Marc Hacker of Swid Powell, Steven Izenour of Venturi, Scott Brown and Associates, and collector Suzanne Cohn to judge designs for a dinnerware place setting and to present cash prizes. In conjunction with the Design Excellence Award and the Student Design Competition, I organized a small exhibition, *Design for the Table Top*,[113] comprised of objects given to the Museum for the show by Swid Powell, including Robert Venturi's *Flowers* dinner service (fig. 222) and (with support from Reed and Barton) his stainless-steel flatware with handles based on the architectural orders of columns.

The combination of the design award, the student competition, and a Museum exhibition related to the awardee became, and remains to this day, Collab's principal fundraising vehicle as well as an opportune means of building the Museum's collections of modern and contemporary design. In some cases award recipients have chosen to curate and design their own exhibitions; in others the projects have been left almost entirely to the Museum, with various degrees of participation by awardees.

In 1994, during the Museum's major *Japanese Design* exhibition, Collab presented its Design Excellence Award to Robert Venturi and Denise Scott Brown, who spoke about their experiences working in Japan and exhibited their collection of popular Japanese market objects in our design gallery, under a title borrowed from their 1991 book, *Architecture and Decorative Arts: Two Naifs in Japan* (figs. 223, 224).[114] Students competing for a prize were asked to design a lighting fixture inspired by Japanese arts and crafts.

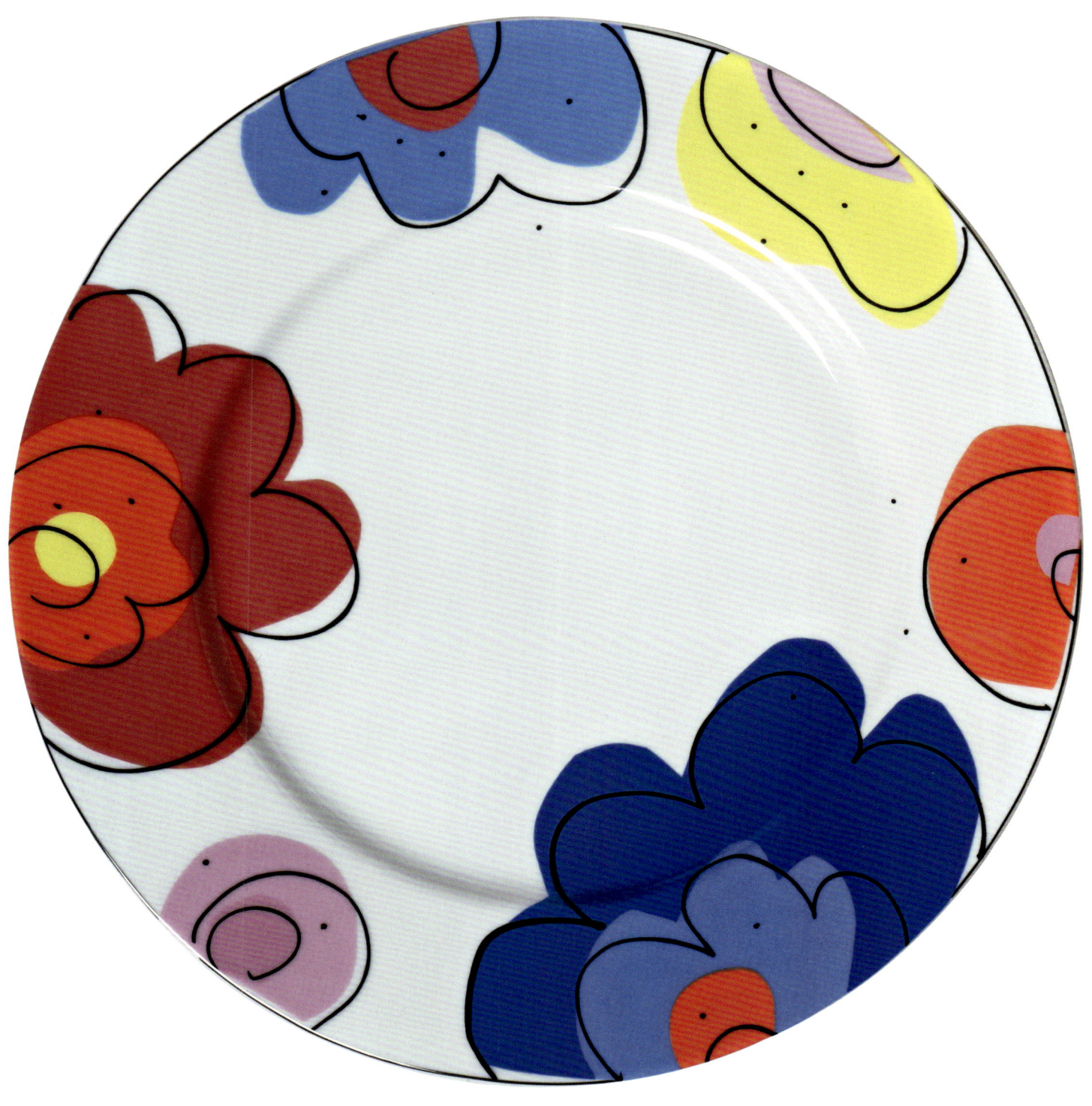

Design for the Tabletop : 1993

222. **Robert Venturi** : for Swid Powell : Dinner Plate from *Flowers* : c. 1993 : glazed, printed porcelain : D 12¼" : 1993-140-2 (cat. 203)

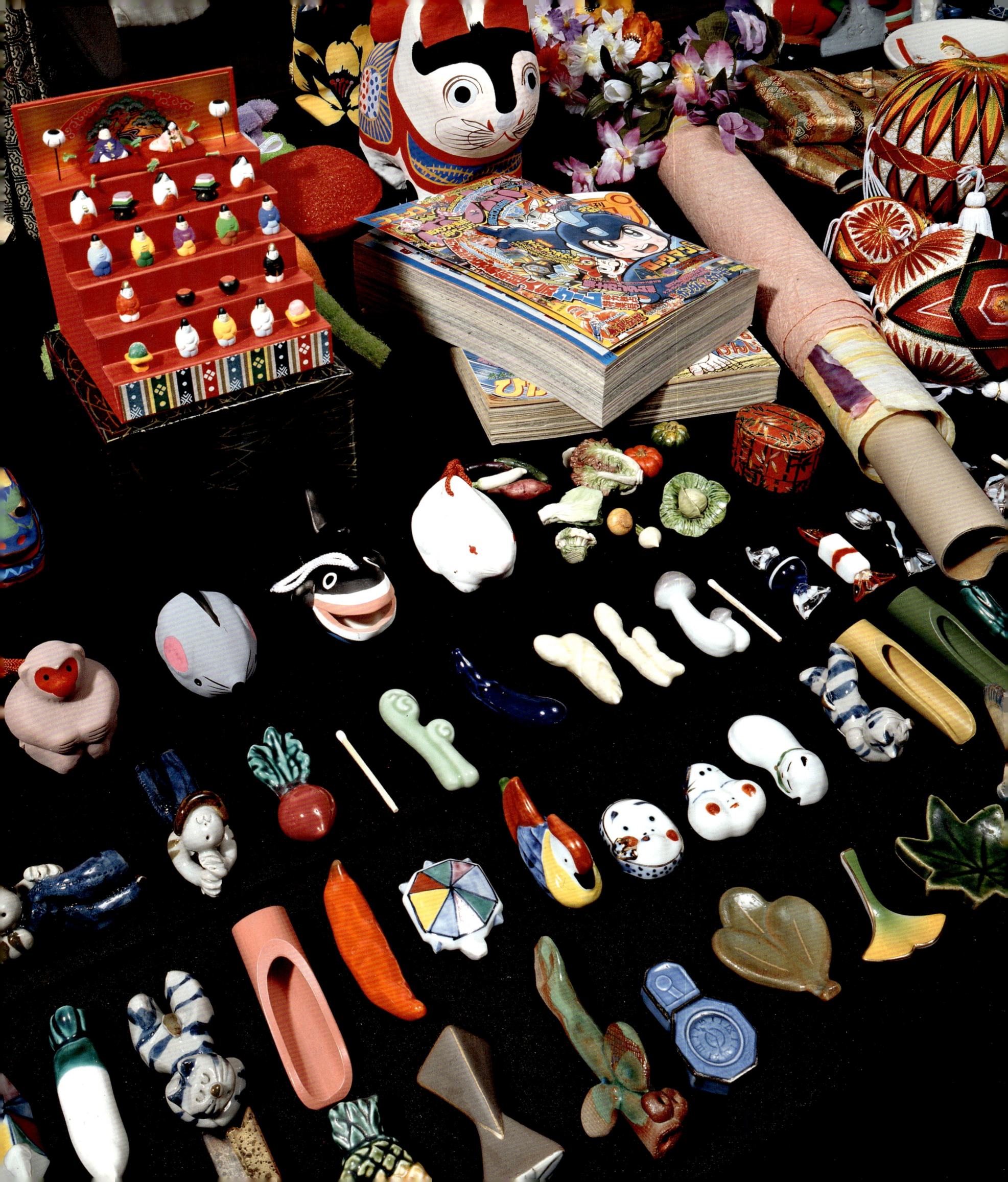

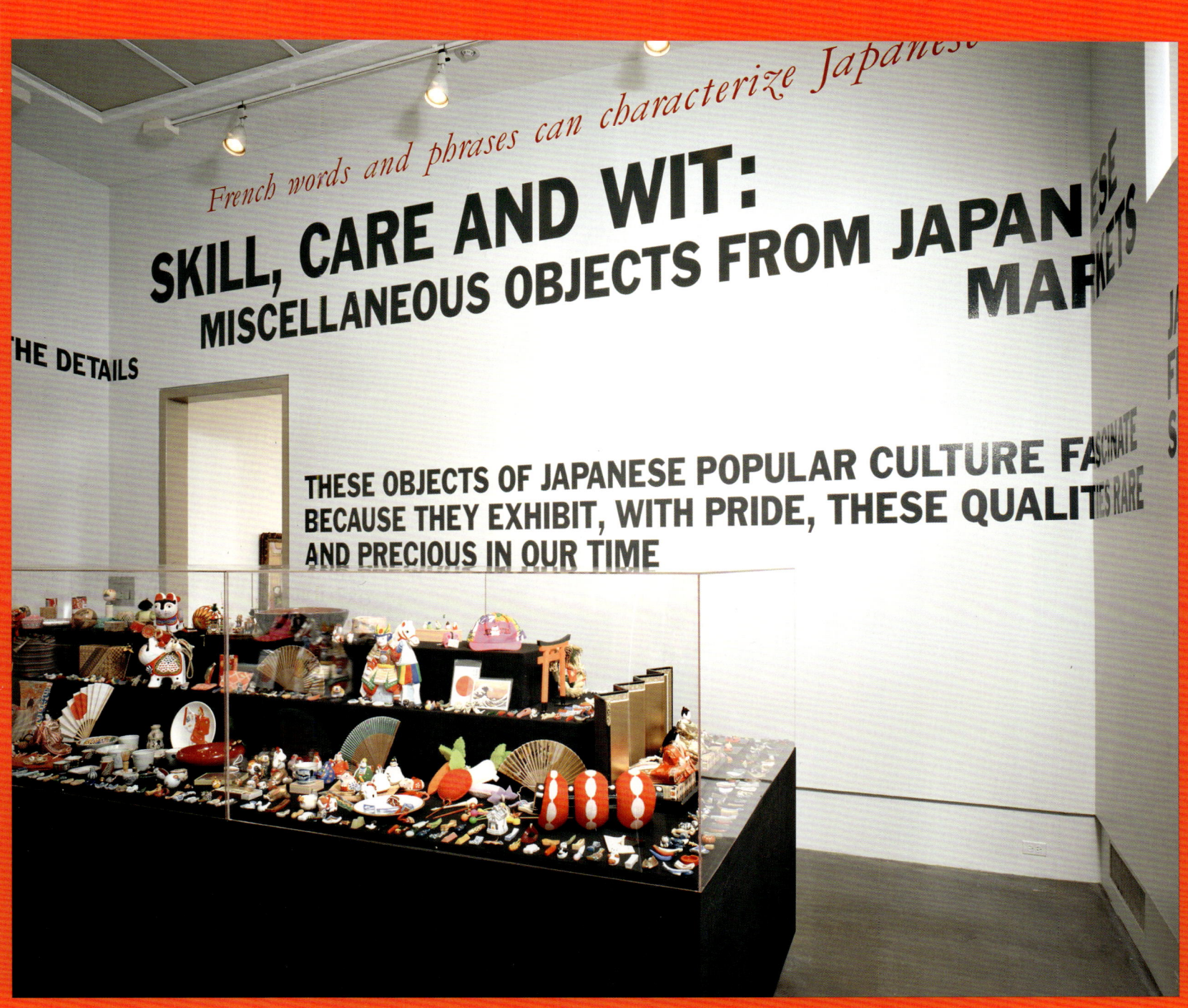

Two Naifs in Japan : Robert Venturi and Denise Scott Brown : 1994

Opposite : **223.** Detail of objects on display   Above : **224.** Gallery view

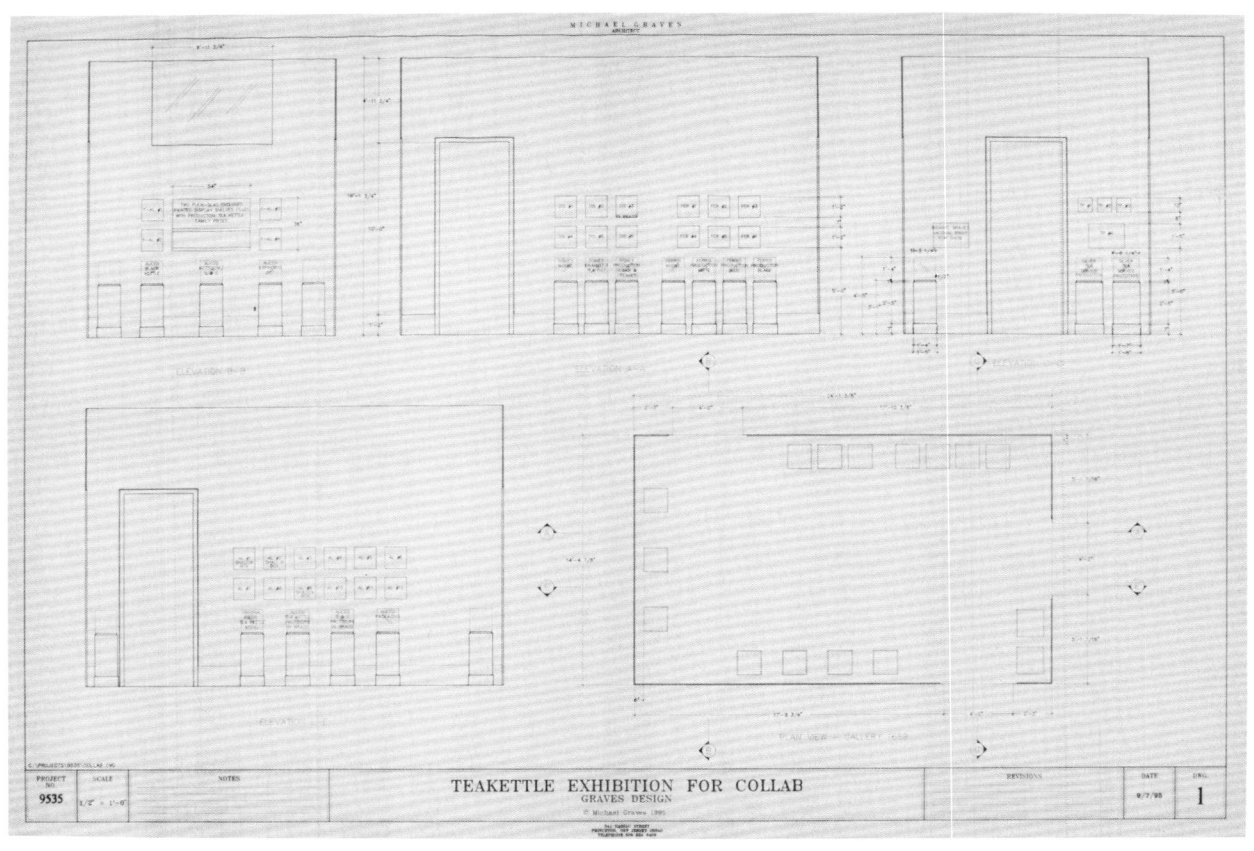

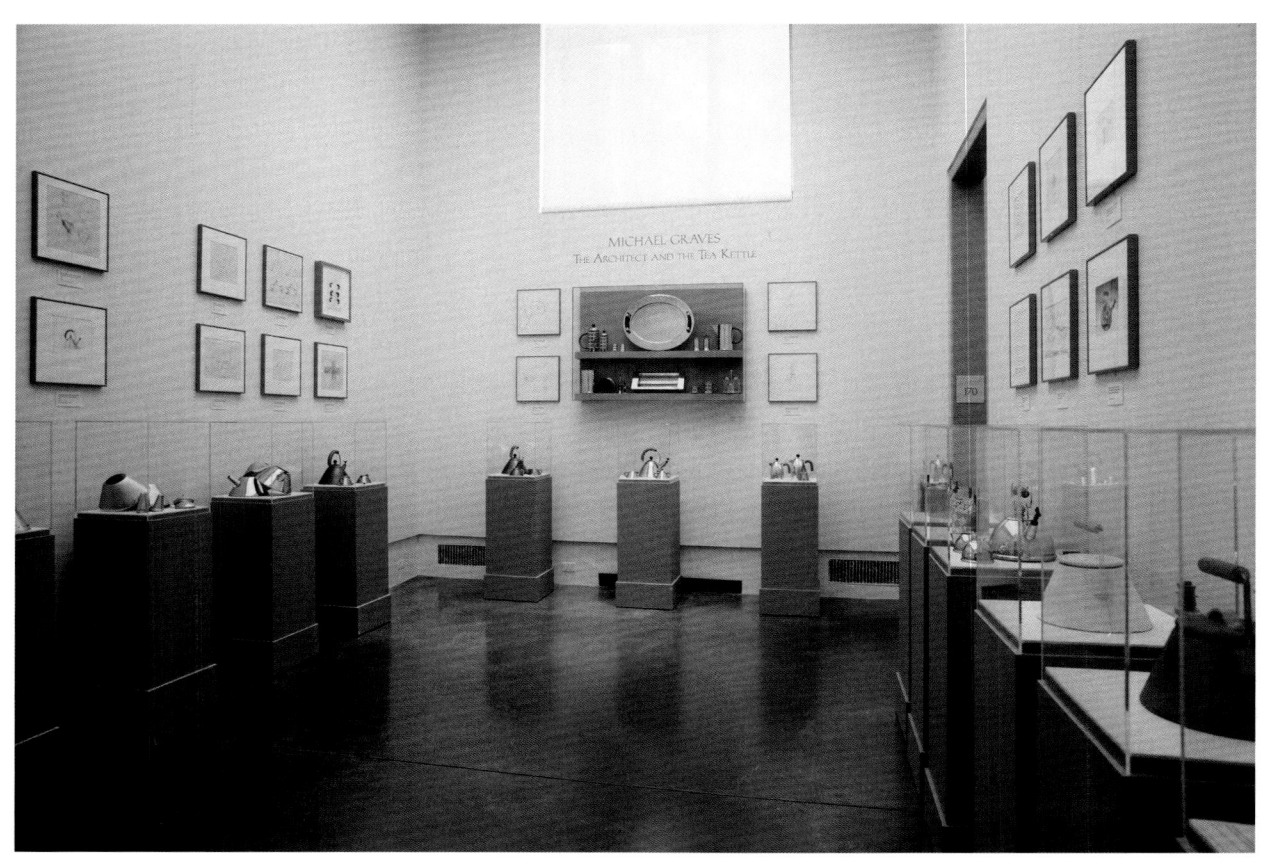

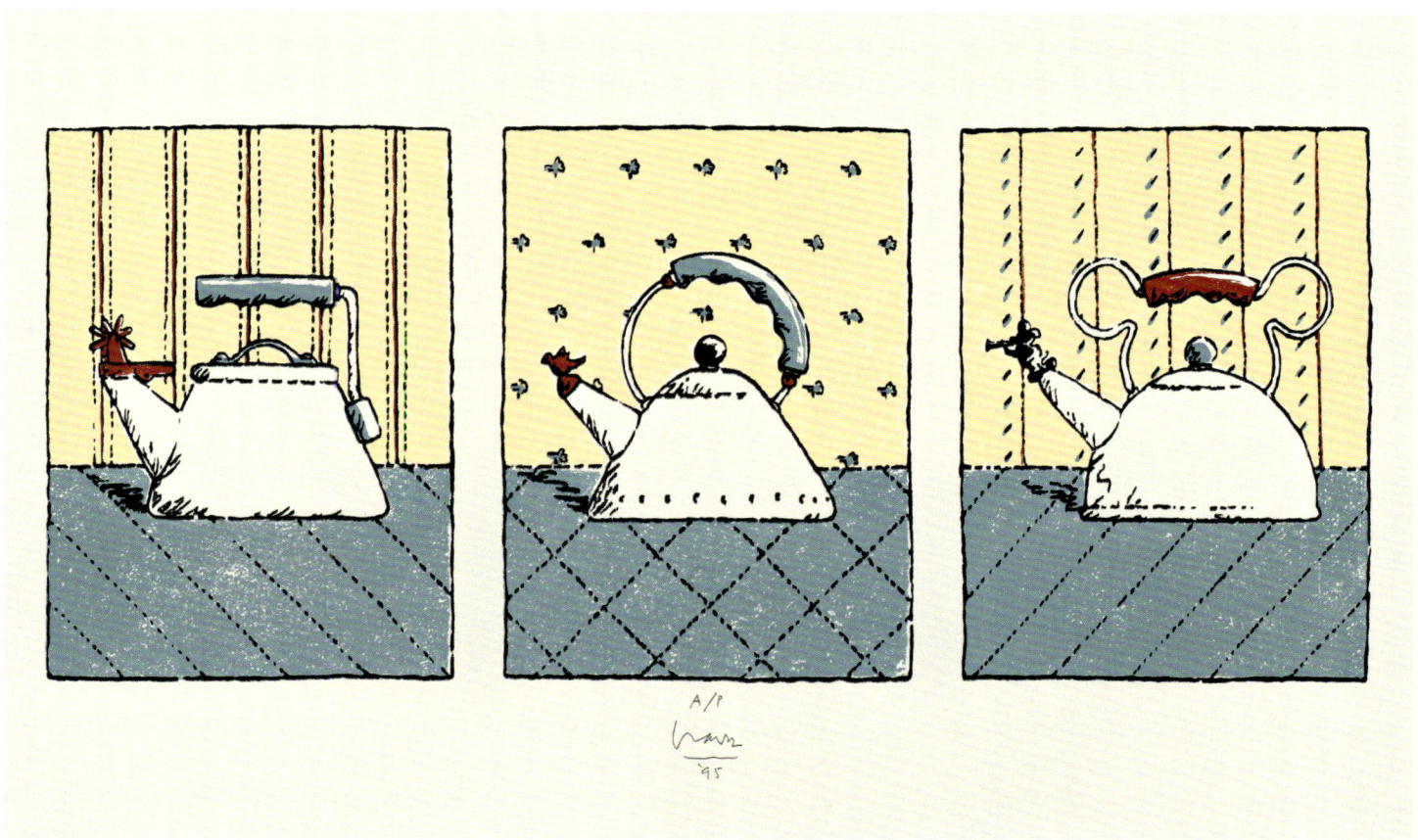

Michael Graves received Collab's 1995 Design Excellence Award. Like Venturi and Scott Brown, Graves organized and designed his own exhibition, *Michael Graves: The Architect and the Tea Kettle*,[115] which followed his design process from original concept to production of three of his teakettles; the show included sketchbooks, drawings, various kettle details and study models, prototypes, and production pieces (figs. 225, 226). Graves gave the Museum his *Whistling Bird* teakettle for Alessi (fig. 228), and Collab donated the *Tea for Three* four-color screenprint that Graves had designed to be sold in the Museum store for the benefit of Collab (fig. 227). Students were asked to design a teakettle for the organization's competition. Collab made two other gifts at about the same time, Gerrit Rietveld's *Zigzag* chair (fig. 229) in honor of committee chair Eric Rymshaw and Sony's *TR610* radio, a version of which had been shown in the *Japanese Design* exhibition.

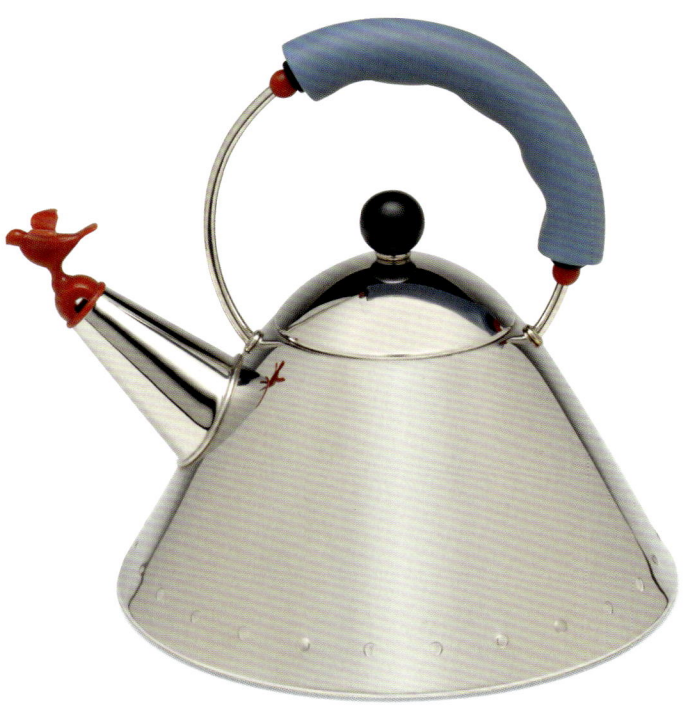

Michael Graves : The Architect and the Tea Kettle : 1995–96

Opposite, top to bottom : **225.** Michael Graves's exhibition plan   **226.** Gallery view   Above, top to bottom : **227. Michael Graves** : *Tea for Three* : 1995 : four-color screenprint : H 15" : 1995-154-1 (cat. 76)   **228. Michael Graves** : for Alessi : *Whistling Bird* Teakettle : 1985 : stainless steel, polyamide : H 8⅞" : 1996-27-1a,b (cat. 75)

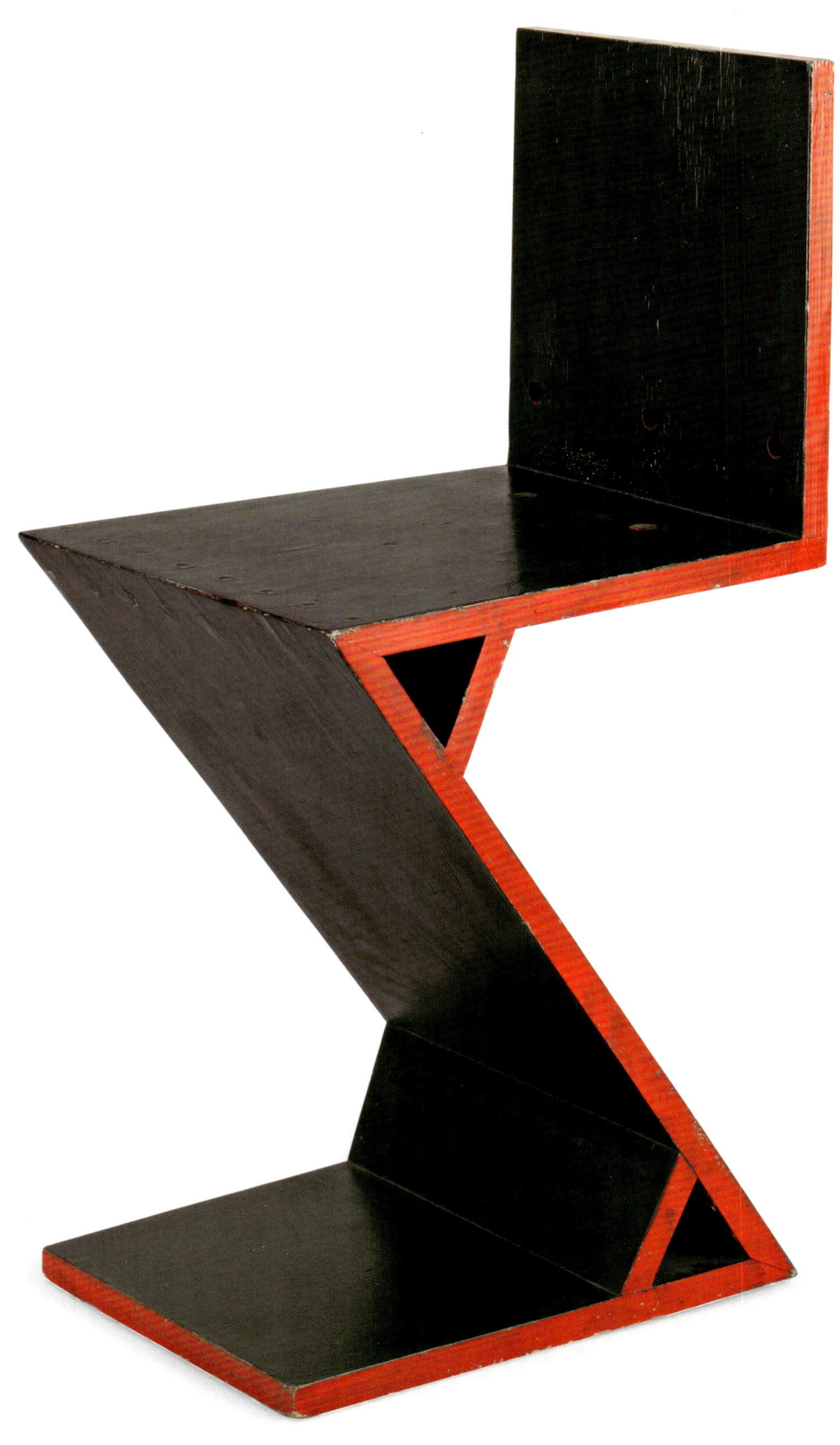

229. Gerrit Thomas Rietveld : for Gerard van de Groenekan : *Zigzag Chair* : 1932–33 : painted plywood : H 31 9/16" : 1995-65-1 (cat. 160)

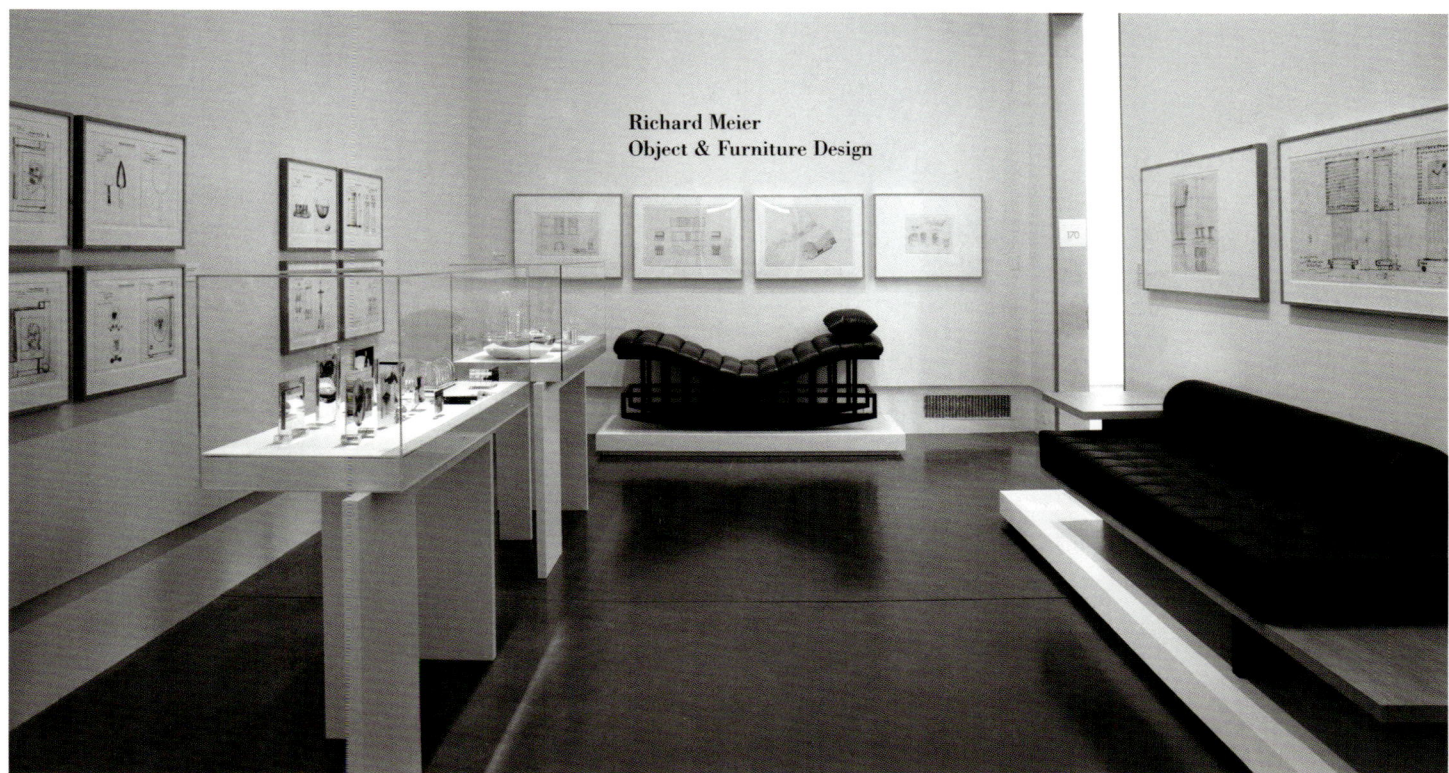

Continuing the run of programs devoted to architects who also design furniture and decorative arts, in 1996 Richard Meier received Collab's Design Excellence Award, spoke about his recent work at the Getty Center in Los Angeles, and organized an exhibition of his own work, *Richard Meier: Object and Furniture Design* (fig. 230).[116] The student competition required entrants to design a seating unit for an interior space in Meier's 1993 Stadthaus in Ulm, Germany, and the winning projects were placed on view in the Museum store's front window. The Museum acquired Meier's chaise lounge designed for Knoll in 1982 and featured in the exhibition.

In 1997 the department initiated an original exhibition project for Collab, "Philippe Starck and Ian Schrager: Reinventing the American Hotel." Borrowing the gallery adjacent to our small design space, we planned to exhibit some forty examples of Starck's work, ranging from a toothbrush to a motorcycle, and to re-create a model hotel interior with the help of Schrager, for whom Starck had designed four successful boutique hotels between 1990 and 1996. Although it ultimately proved impossible for Schrager's office to provide the hotel interior, he accepted Collab's 1997 award on behalf of Starck and himself; at the opening event Schrager spoke about the problems associated with renovating his properties, and the ways in which he and Starck had worked together to define the interior spaces.[117] A number of manufacturers, including Alessi, Modern Age, and Vitra International, gave the Museum objects designed by Starck that were included in the exhibition *Philippe Starck Designs* (figs. 231, 232).[118] For the Museum's design collection and presentation in the exhibition, Collab purchased Starck's *Lola Mundo* table/chair and *J. (Série Lang)* armchair (fig. 231), the latter presented in honor of chair Lisa Roberts. In conjunction with the exhibition and award presentation, Collab's student competition invited designs for an ice bucket for the new Starck-Schrager Mondrian Hotel in Los Angeles. The resulting projects ranged from a container that doubled as a planter (using recycled water from the melted ice) to another concealed in a velvet cushion.

Richard Meier : Object and Furniture Design : 1996–97

230. Gallery view

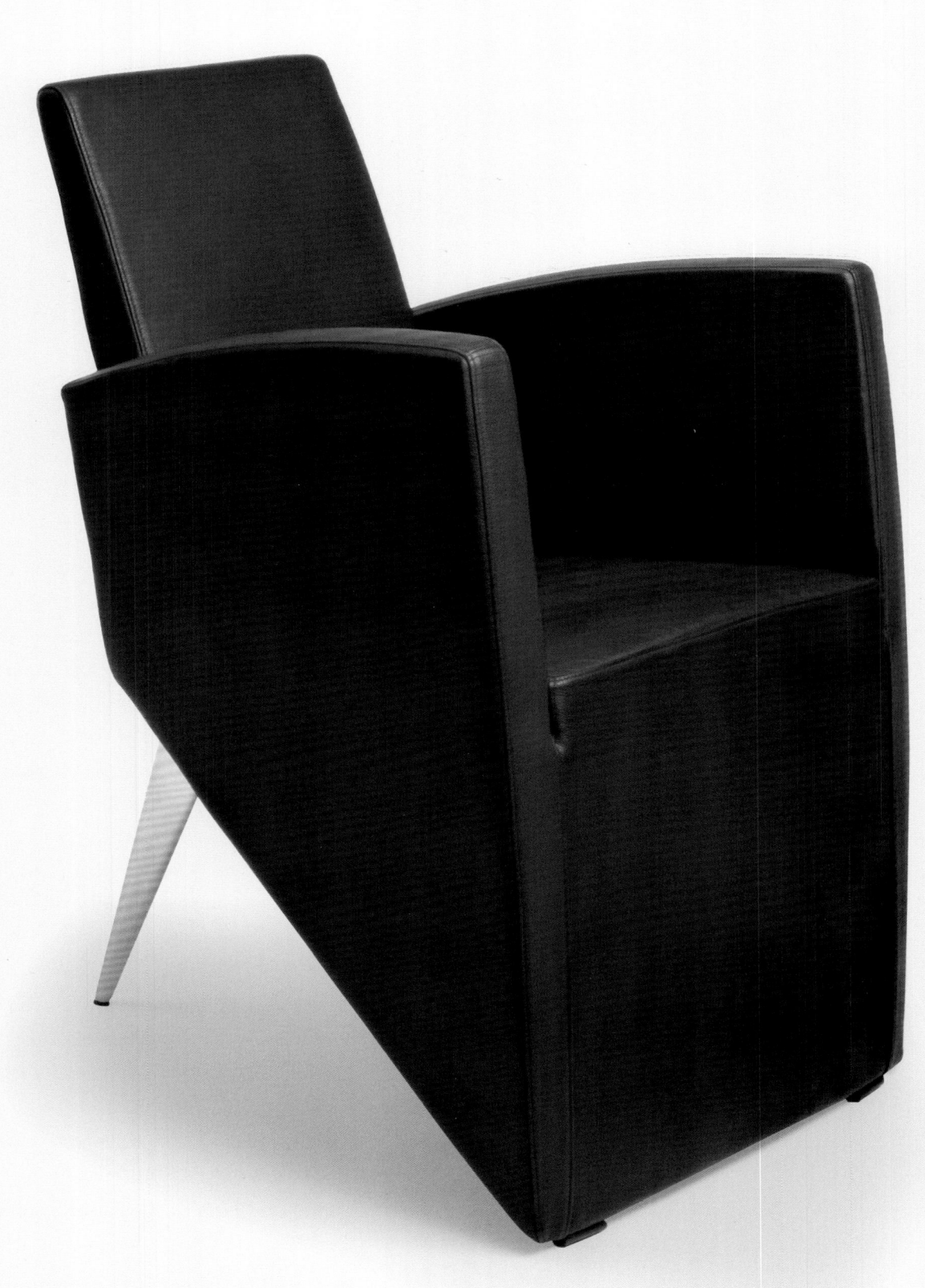

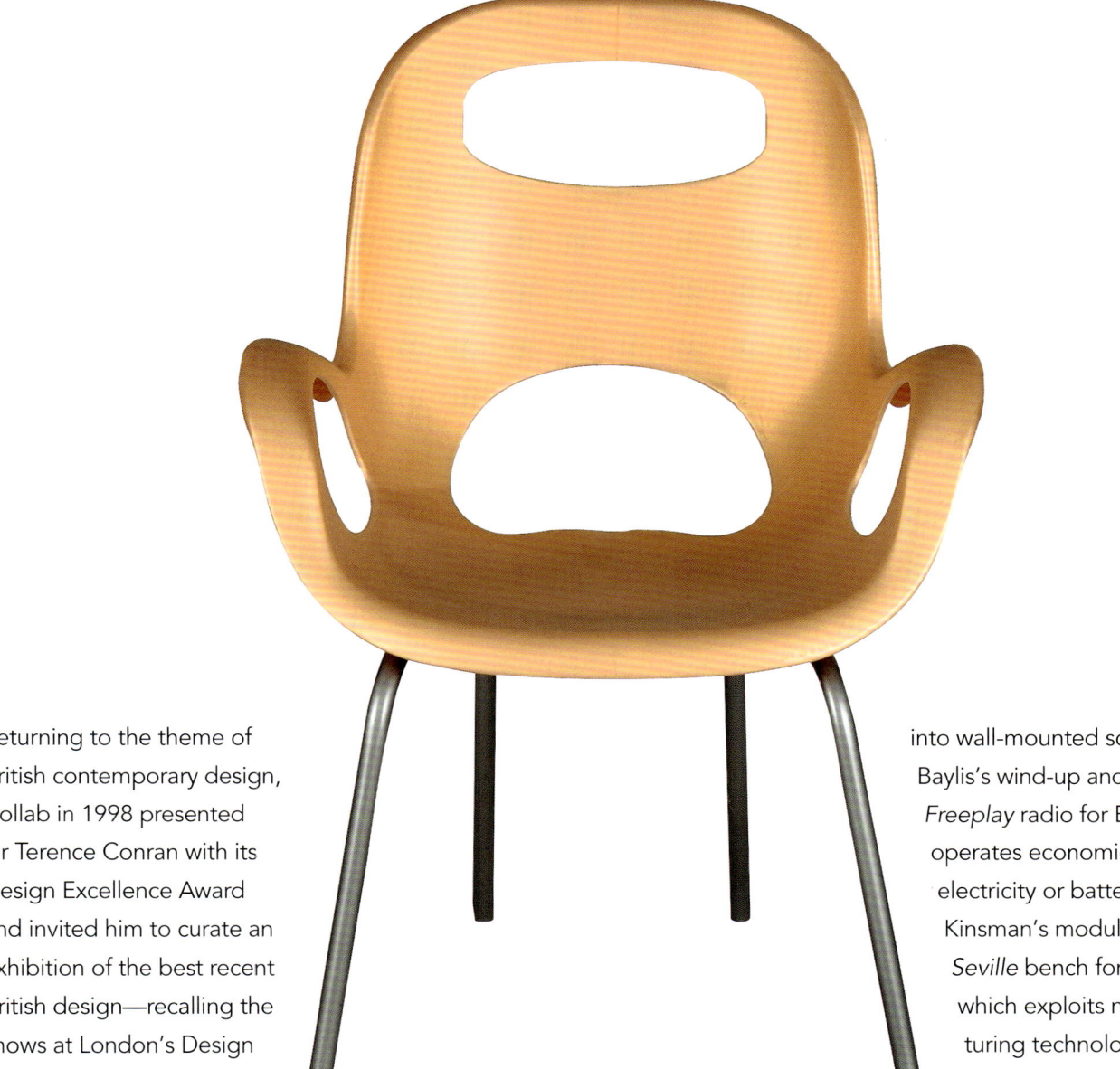

Returning to the theme of British contemporary design, Collab in 1998 presented Sir Terence Conran with its Design Excellence Award and invited him to curate an exhibition of the best recent British design—recalling the shows at London's Design Museum, founded by Conran in 1989. *Cool Britannia: Recent British Design Selected by Sir Terence Conran*[119] included nineteen objects—several of them already designated "millennium" products by the British government—that literally covered the walls and platforms of the small gallery. A number of the objects shown were offered to the Museum by their manufacturers as gifts, including Paul Priestman's *Hot Springs* radiators for Bisque, which transform energy-efficient hot-water heating into wall-mounted sculpture; Trevor Baylis's wind-up and solar-powered *Freeplay* radio for BayGen, which operates economically without electricity or batteries; Rodney Kinsman's modular aluminum *Seville* bench for OMK Design, which exploits new manufacturing technologies that strengthen construction without the need of intermediate support; and James Dyson's *Dual Cyclone* clear-canister vacuum cleaner for Dyson Appliances, which does away with dust bags (fig. 233). The Philadelphia Museum of Art was the first in the United States to acquire most of these well-made, functionalist objects. Collab's student competition, organized like the others by Lisa Roberts, received a record 230 designs for a shopping bag for the Conran Stores.

Designing the Future : Three Directions for the New Millennium : 1999–2000

234. **Karim Rashid** : for Umbra : *Oh* Chair Prototype : 1998 : polypropylene, powder-coated steel : H 34" : 2000-155-1 (cat. 156)

In 1999 I organized *Designing the Future: Three Directions for the New Millennium*,[120] an exhibition for Collab that celebrated the work of three young designers: Jonathan Ive, designer of the revolutionary iMac computer and other products for Apple Computers; Maya Lin, designer of the Vietnam Veterans Memorial in Washington, D.C., and a furniture collection for Knoll; and Karim Rashid, designer of housewares and furniture and former professor of industrial design at Philadelphia's University of the Arts. The accompanying student competition asked students to design a clock for the new millennium; the winning projects included a wristwatch, a crystal ball, and a nautilus clock. Collab provided funds to purchase from the exhibition an iMac—the first computer acquired by the Museum for the design collections—and Lin's *Stone* seats for Knoll, while manufacturers gave the Museum Rashid's prototype for his ubiquitous *Oh* chair (fig. 234), and *Garbo* and *Garbino* trash cans (fig. 235), among other objects.

Collab 2000 celebrated Milton Glaser, and I had the distinct pleasure of selecting some eighty of his works, including drawings, posters, book illustrations, prints, record jackets, and corporate-identity programs, so many, in fact, that it was necessary to hold the exhibition—titled *Milton Glaser Graphic Design: Design, Influence and Process*—not in our Design Gallery, but in the Director's Corridor.[121] As Glaser had instructed, finished works were displayed on one wall and connected by red cords to the genesis of each on the opposite wall, in order to organize the show along the principle of his design process. His appearance and lecture at the Museum drew a standing-room-only audience. Glaser also designed a poster for the exhibition that was sold in the Museum store, and I later found a version of his *Bob Dylan* poster that Collab was able to purchase for the collections (fig. 236). In recognition of Glaser's role in design for the music industry, the student competition required the creation of a box set of four CDs.

To celebrate Collab's thirtieth anniversary (one year after the fact), in 2001 the committee invited three Philadelphians influential in the field of design to lecture at the Museum: Karen Daroff, principal of Daroff Design; Laurie Olin, landscape architect and principal of the Olin Partnership; and restaurateur Stephen Starr. The student competition that year asked for designs of the Design Excellence Award itself. The winning project, submitted by a student in Philadelphia University's industrial design program, was a laser-etched rubber Möbius strip, symbolizing the endless continuity of design; the award, now embellished with a silver clasp, has been fabricated each year since for presentation to Collab's award recipient. The accompanying Museum exhibition extended the anniversary theme. *Collab Collects: Notable Acquisitions in Design, 1970–2000*,[122] was organized by Diane (Dee) L. Minnite, who in 1993 had joined the department as a research associate for the *Japanese Design* exhibition, which she accompanied on tour. She and Donna Corbin have continued to create exhibitions drawn from the Museum's design collections in addition to carrying out their other curatorial responsibilities.

Designing the Future : Three Directions for the New Millennium : 1999–2000
235. Karim Rashid : for Umbra : *Garbino* Can : 1996 : polypropylene : H 13" : 1999-107-4 (cat. 155)

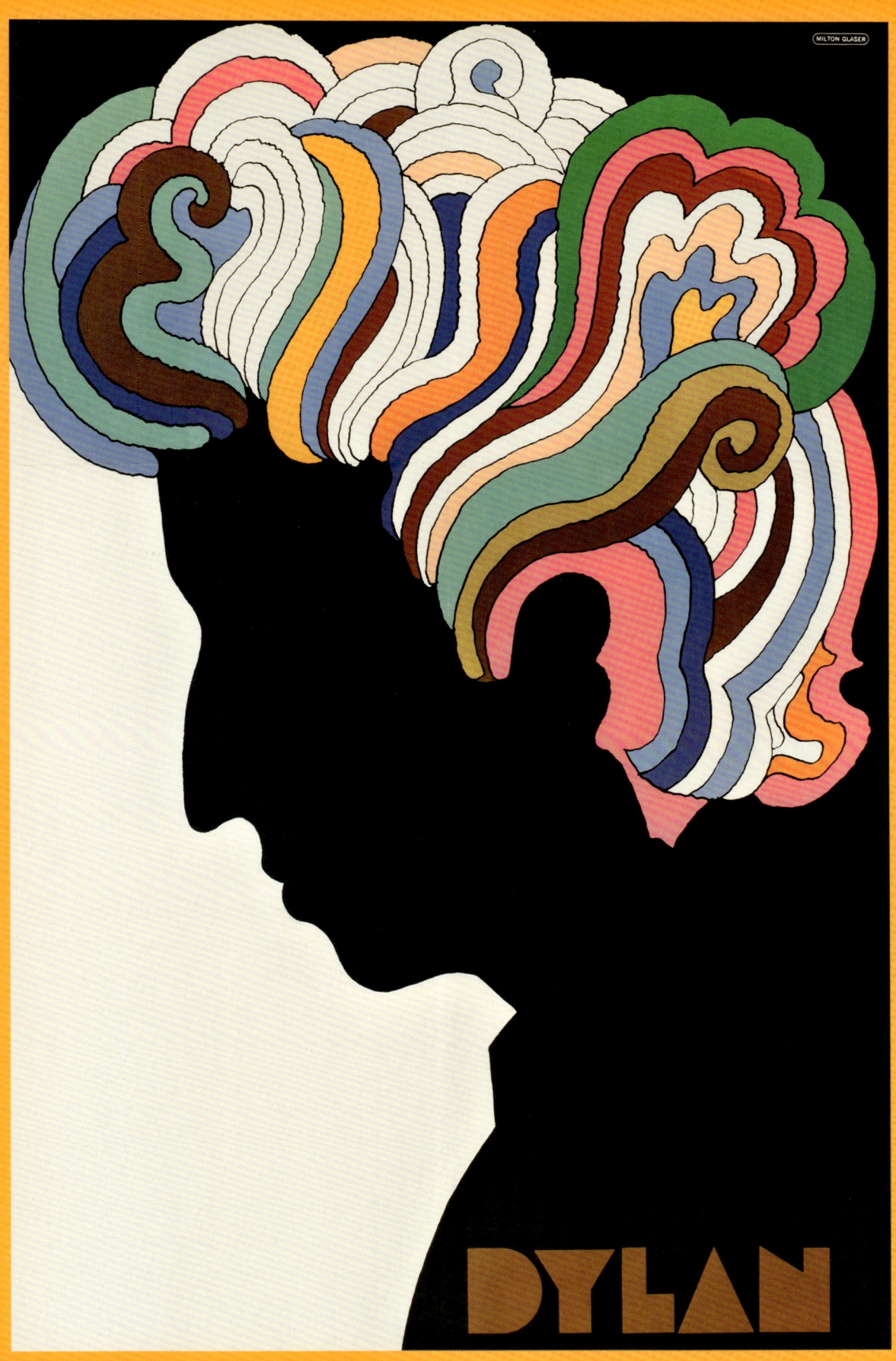

Milton Glaser Graphic Design : Design, Influence and Process : 2000–2001

236. Milton Glaser : for Columbia Records : *Bob Dylan* Poster : 1966 : offset lithograph : H 32⅝" : 2002-146-1 (cat. 72)

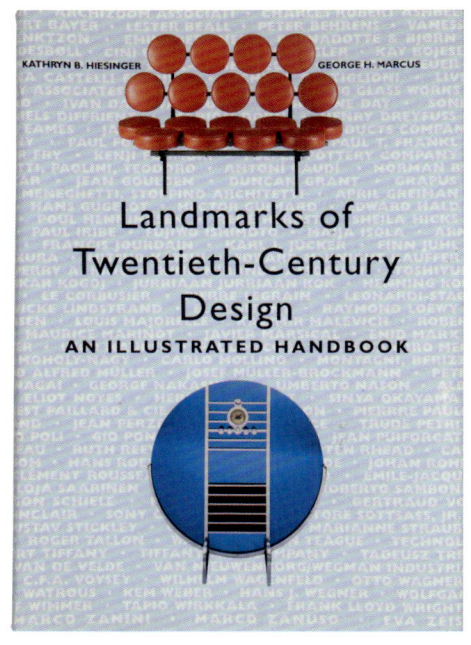 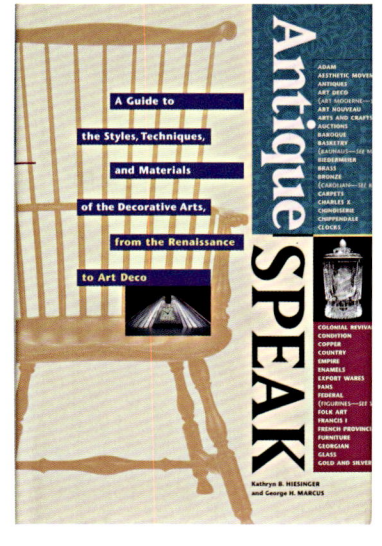 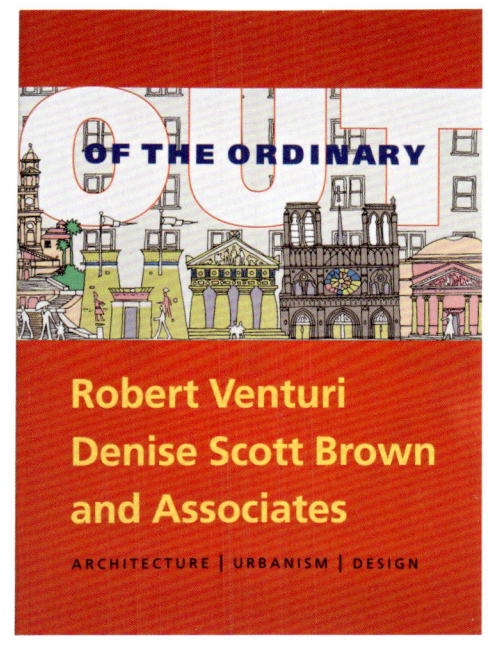

While organizing Collab's annual exhibitions, I cowrote with my colleague George Marcus two books, published by Abbeville Press, that featured objects from the Museum's design collections: *Landmarks of Twentieth-Century Design* (1993; fig. 237), widely used as a textbook, and *Antique Speak: A Guide to the Styles, Techniques, and Materials of the Decorative Arts, from the Renaissance to Art Deco* (1997; fig. 238).[123] Collaborating with architectural historians David Brownlee and David De Long, in 1997 I also began work on a major retrospective of buildings and decorative arts designed by the firm of Venturi, Scott Brown and Associates. Assisted by William Whitaker, collections manager of the University of Pennsylvania Architectural Archives, and Diane Minnite, we met regularly over many months at the Venturi archives to review the hundreds of thousands of drawings and models that comprised the work by Venturi and his firm, from his student days to the 1990s. I also embarked on the long process of reviewing correspondence records related to the firm's decorative arts projects, my particular area of scholarly responsibility for the exhibition. *Out of the Ordinary: The Architecture and Design of Robert Venturi, Denise Scott Brown and Associates*,[124] accompanied by a catalogue of the same name and written by the organizing team (fig. 239–46), opened at the Museum in the spring of 2001—one of a series of exhibitions showcasing artists who lived or worked in Philadelphia and held in celebration of the Museum's own 125th anniversary that year. The exhibition also traveled to the Museum of Contemporary Art San Diego and to the Heinz Architectural Center at the Carnegie Museum of Art, Pittsburgh.

Above, left to right : **237.** *Landmarks of Twentieth-Century Design* : by Kathryn B. Hiesinger and George H. Marcus (New York: Abbeville, 1993)
238. *Antique Speak* : by Kathryn B. Hiesinger and George H. Marcus (New York: Abbeville, 1997)   **239.** *Out of the Ordinary: Robert Venturi Denise Scott Brown and Associates* : by David B. Brownlee, David G. De Long, and Kathryn B. Hiesinger (Philadelphia: Philadelphia Museum of Art, 2001)

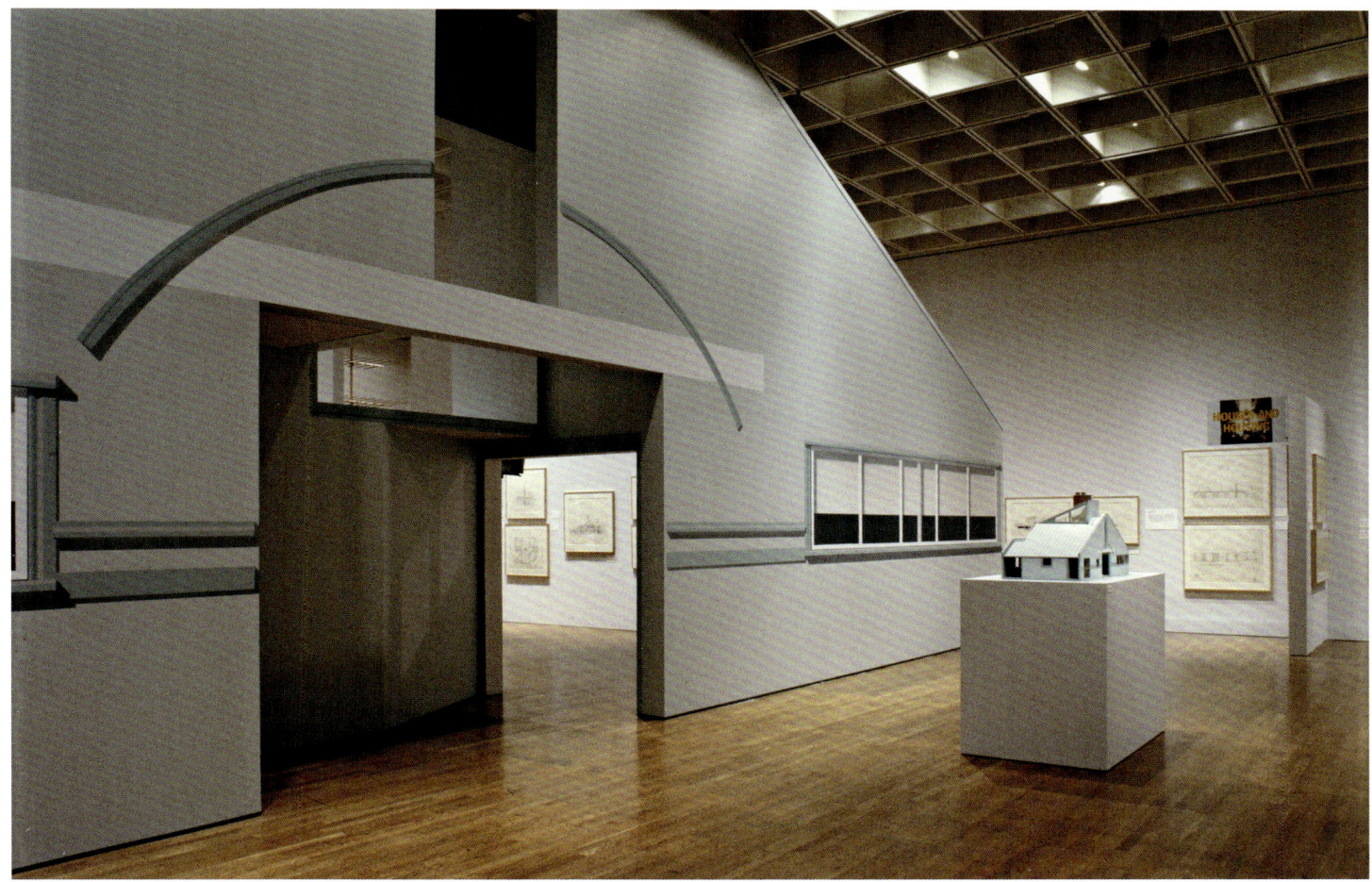

On view were some 250 drawings, scale models, decorative art objects, photographs, and videos, with a goal of redefining the historical position of this internationally celebrated Philadelphia firm and demonstrating the influence of its ideas and architecture over the last forty years. Designed by Tony Atkin of Atkin, Olshin, Lawson-Bell Associates, the installation also included a full-scale reproduction of the facade of the house Venturi designed for his mother, as well as his coffee-cup signboard for Grand's restaurant and a "period room" assemblage of decorative arts (figs. 240–42). The exhibition was accompanied by a lively schedule of programs, including tours, an architectural symposium, and a course on the art of architecture for schoolteachers. Reviewing the exhibition, New Yorker critic Paul Goldberger recognized its historical significance: "Venturi and Scott Brown's home city of Philadelphia has never given them a major commission . . . . Philadelphia is now making up for this with 'Out of the Ordinary,' an elaborate retrospective of the firm's work. . . . It is as important in its way, as the Mies exhibitions, or the huge retrospective of Frank O. Gehry's work now on view at the Guggenheim."[125] The New Republic declared, "There is much to love in 'Out of the Ordinary.'. . . One is overwhelmed . . . by the sheer inventiveness that has poured from these architects for more than forty years."[126] Interior Design magazine described the catalogue as an "authoritative and sympathetic summary of the work of one of the world's most distinguished, most adventurous, and most independent design firms."[127]

Out of the Ordinary : The Architecture and Design of Robert Venturi, Denise Scott Brown and Associates : 2001
240. Gallery view

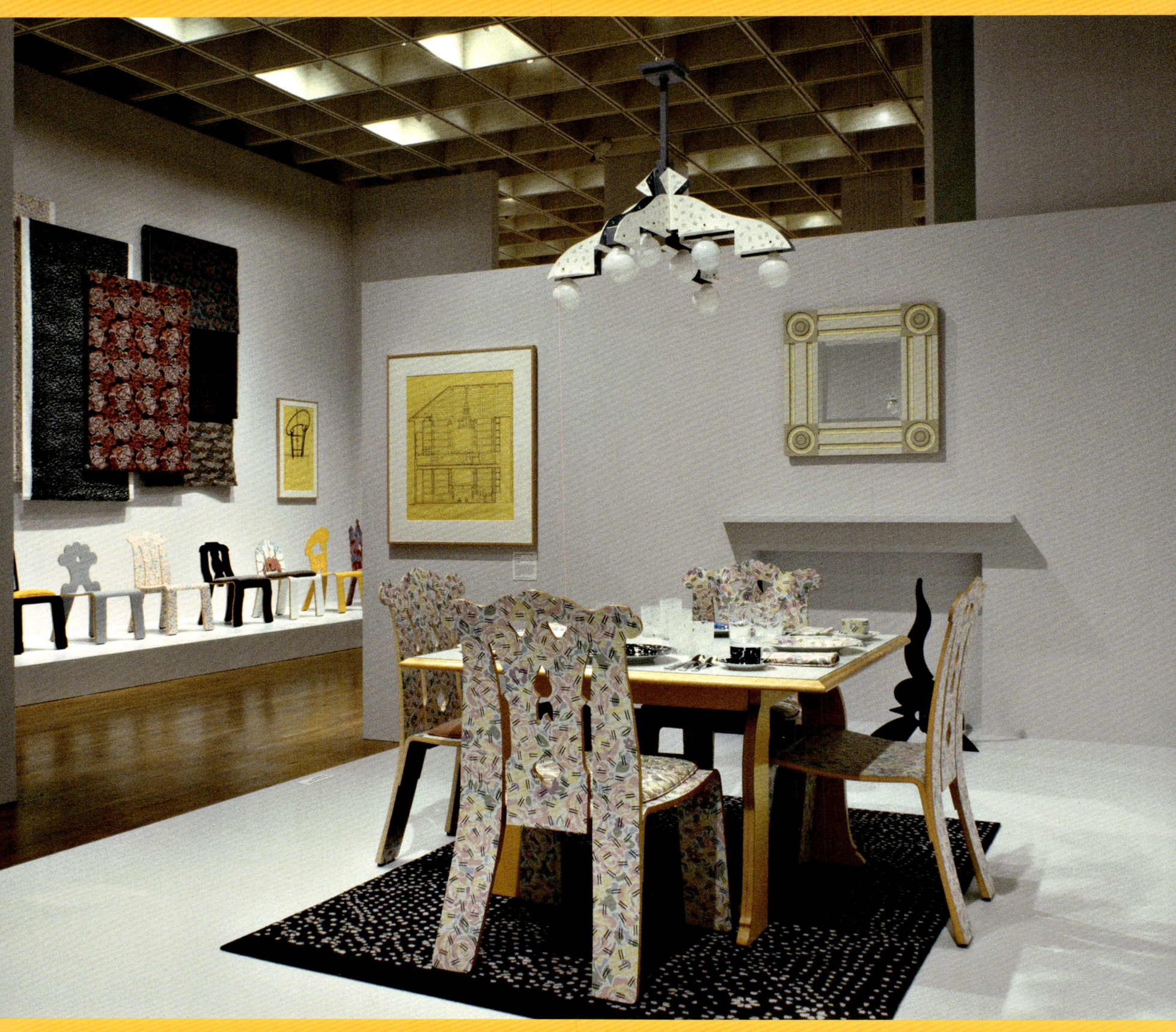

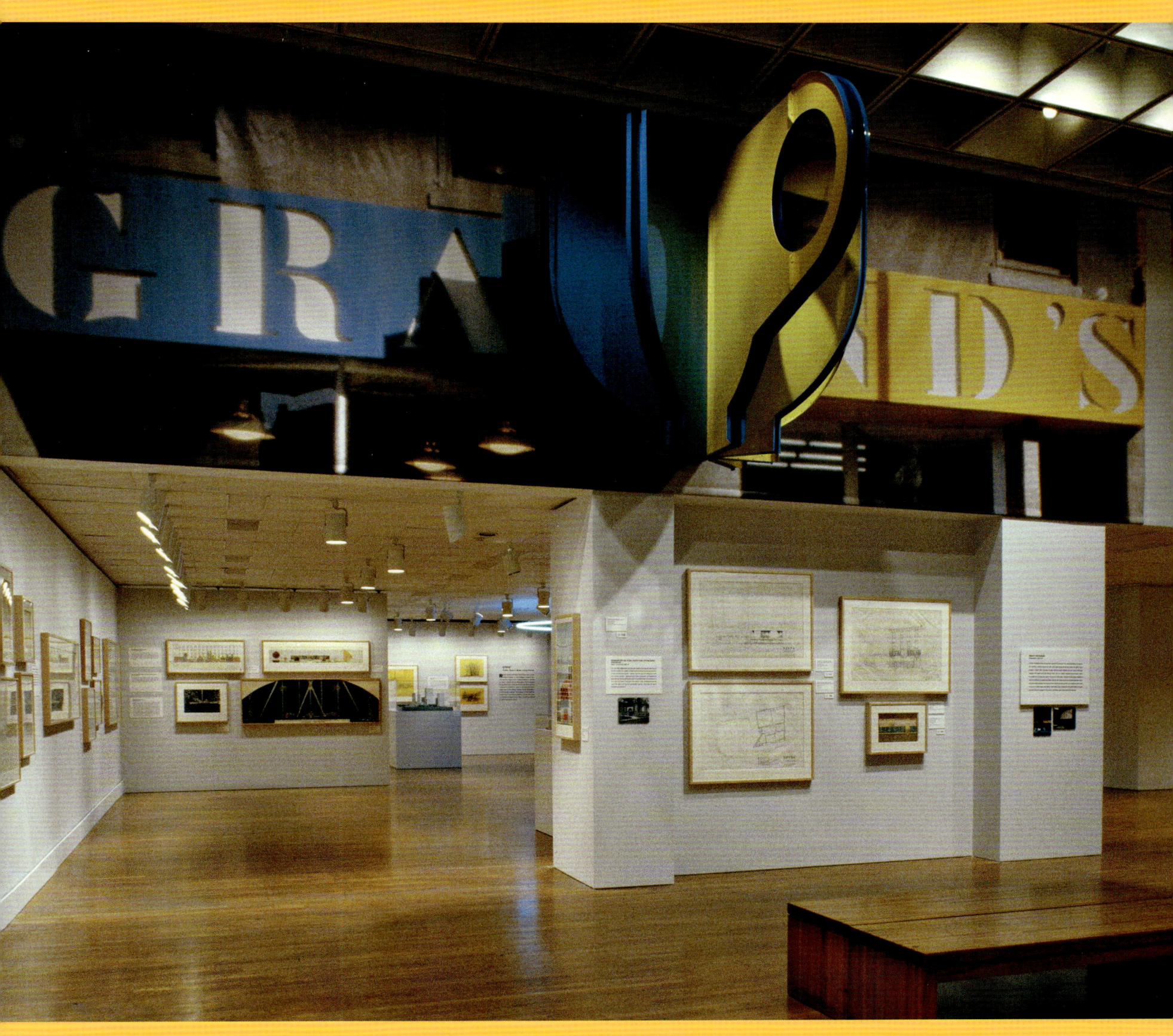

Out of the Ordinary : The Architecture and Design of Robert Venturi, Denise Scott Brown and Associates : 2001
241 and 242. Gallery views

Out of the Ordinary included pieces already in the Museum's collections as well as many that would be acquired when the show closed, among them Venturi's *Sheraton* and *Chippendale* chairs for Knoll, purchased with funds provided by Collab, and his "stylized traditional" tea and coffee service for Alessi, commissioned with a "PMA" monogram by my colleague Beatrice Garvan in the Museum's American art department (fig. 246). Collab also supported the purchase of Venturi's *Notebook* and *Grandmother* printed fabrics (figs. 243, 245), made by the Fabric Workshop and Museum in Philadelphia. Marion Boulton Stroud, Museum trustee and founder of the Fabric Workshop, gave the Museum Venturi's *Gothic Revival* chair (fig. 244); the Japanese Postal Savings Promotion Society presented the chairs and table Venturi designed for the Mielmonte Hotel in Nikko, Japan; and DesignTex donated his *Gingham Floral* and other fabrics. The Museum also acquired two objects specially commissioned for a house Venturi had designed on Long Island, New York: a pair of andirons, given by Collab in honor of its chair Neil Sandvold, and a cabriole-leg table, with flat legs set alternately in front and side elevations as if they could not determine the direction in which they should be oriented. Later, when Venturi's Best Products Company showroom in Langhorne, Pennsylvania, was sold and scheduled for renovation, the Museum received from Venturi, Scott Brown and Associates (through the new owners) a small grouping of the building's porcelain-enameled steel facade panels that had been shown in the exhibition in prototype.

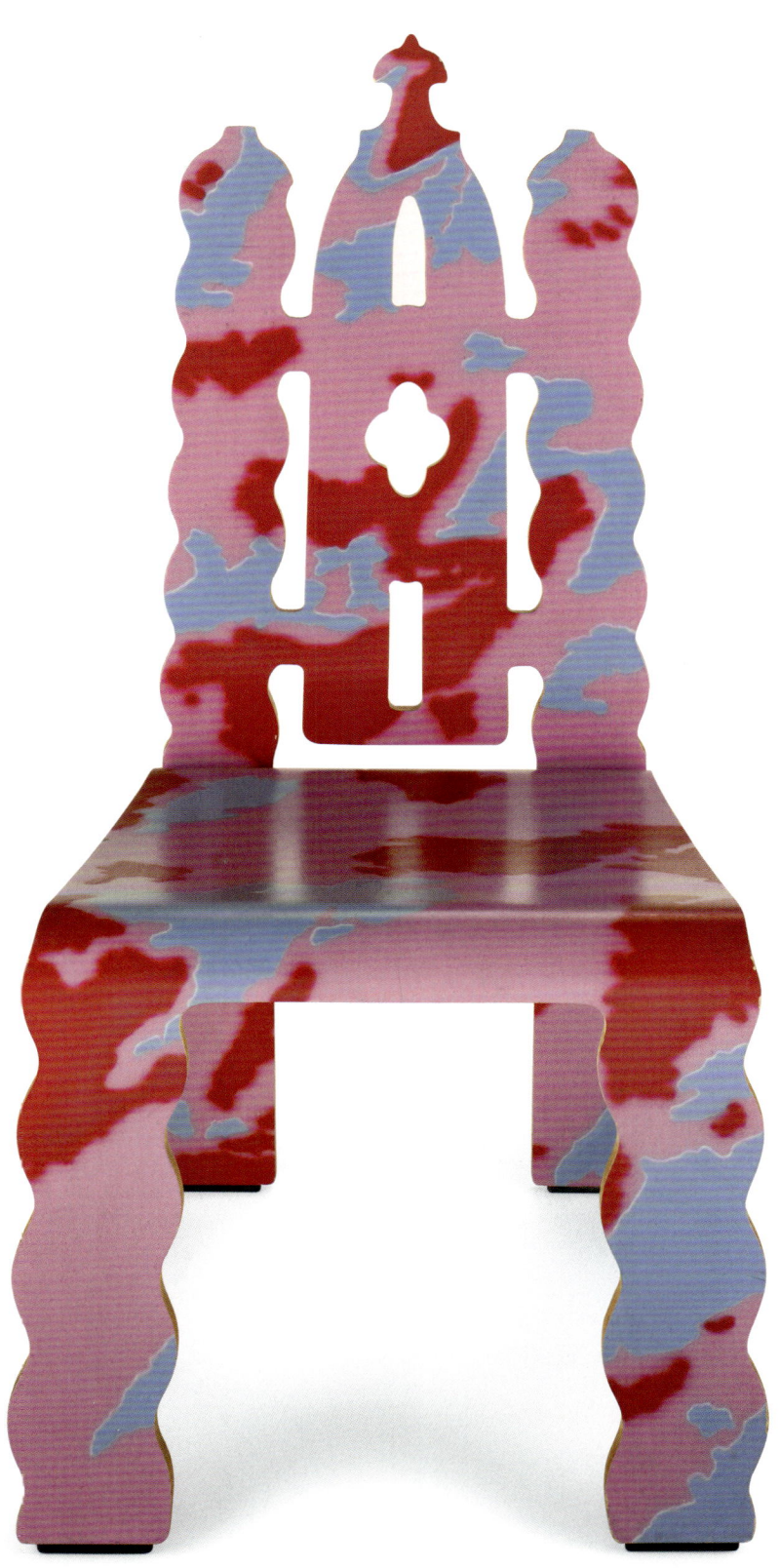

Out of the Ordinary : The Architecture and Design of Robert Venturi, Denise Scott Brown and Associates : 2001

Opposite : **243. Robert Venturi** : for The Fabric Workshop and Museum : *Notebook* Fabric (detail) : 1982–83 : screen-printed cotton : W 57" : 1987-99-1 (cat. 201) Above : **244. Robert Venturi** : for Knoll : *Gothic Revival* Chair : 1979–84 : laminated wood, painted plastic laminate : H 40¾" : 1999-158-1 (cat. 199)

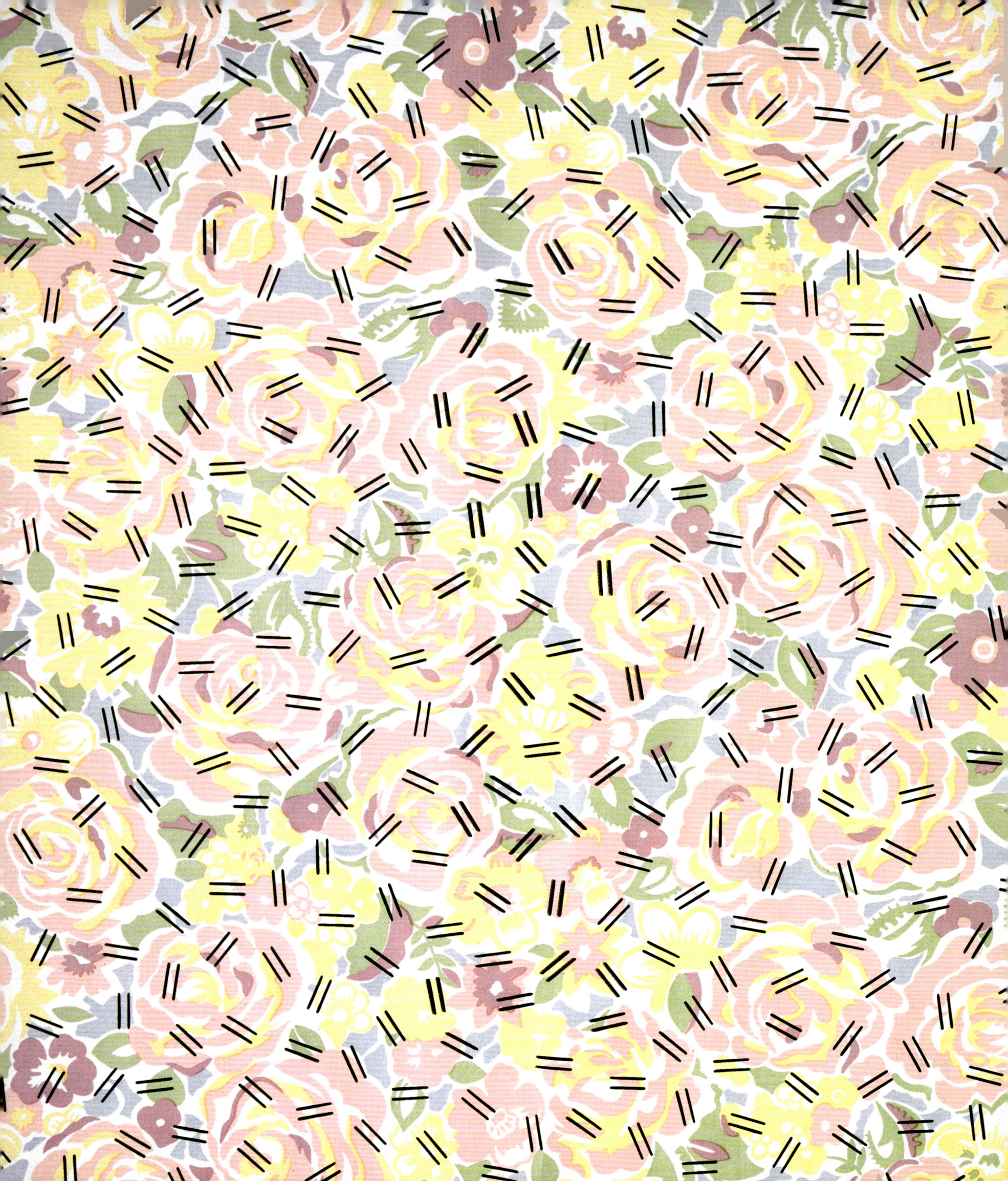

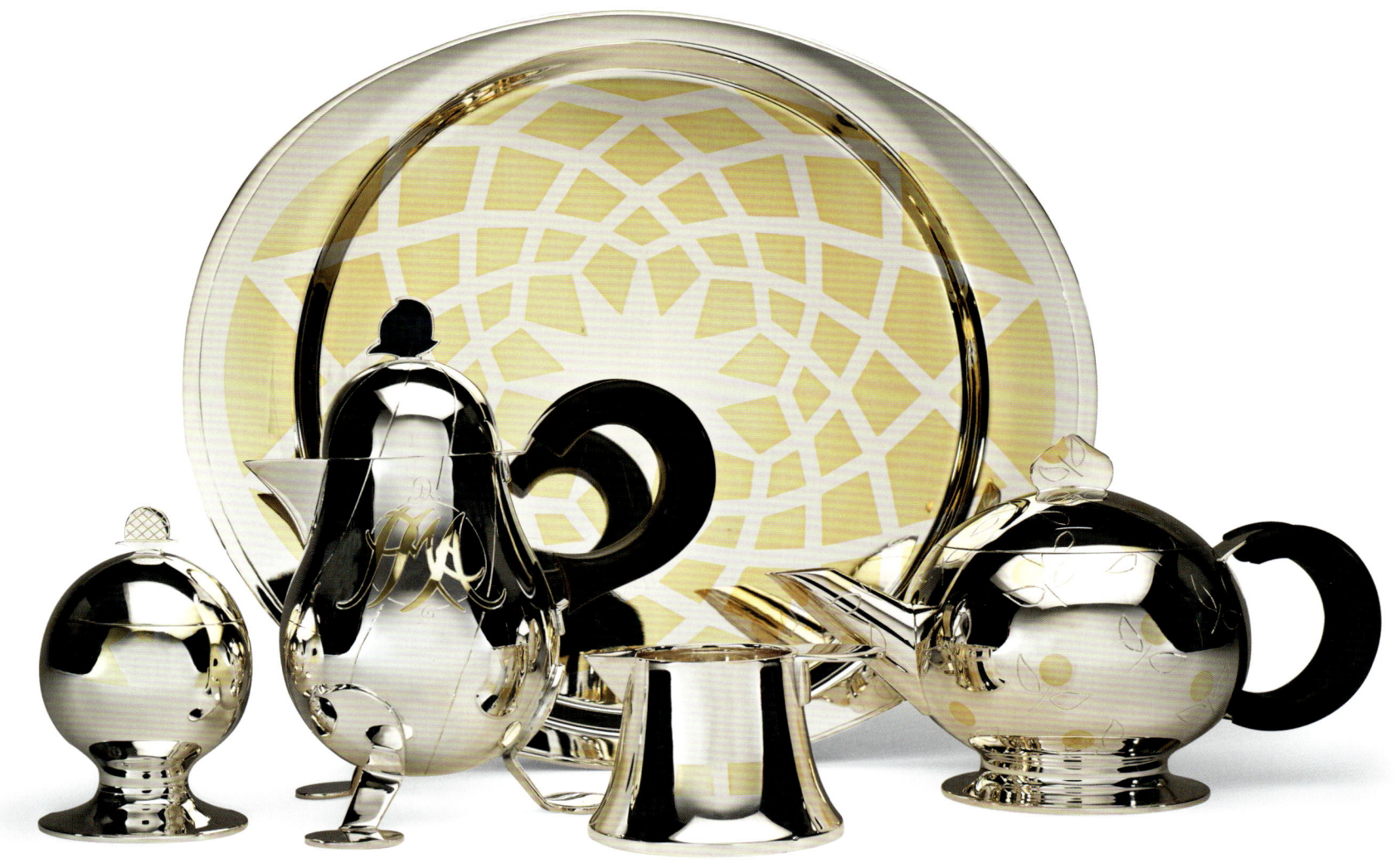

Out of the Ordinary : The Architecture and Design of Robert Venturi, Denise Scott Brown and Associates : 2001

Opposite : **245. Robert Venturi** : for The Fabric Workshop and Museum : *Grandmother* Fabric (detail) : 1982–83 : screen-printed cotton : W 57" : 1987-99-2 (cat. 202)   Above: **246. Robert Venturi** : for Alessi : Tea and Coffee Service : 1980–83 : partial gilt silver : H (teapot) 10¼" : 1986-15-1a,b–5 (cat. 200)

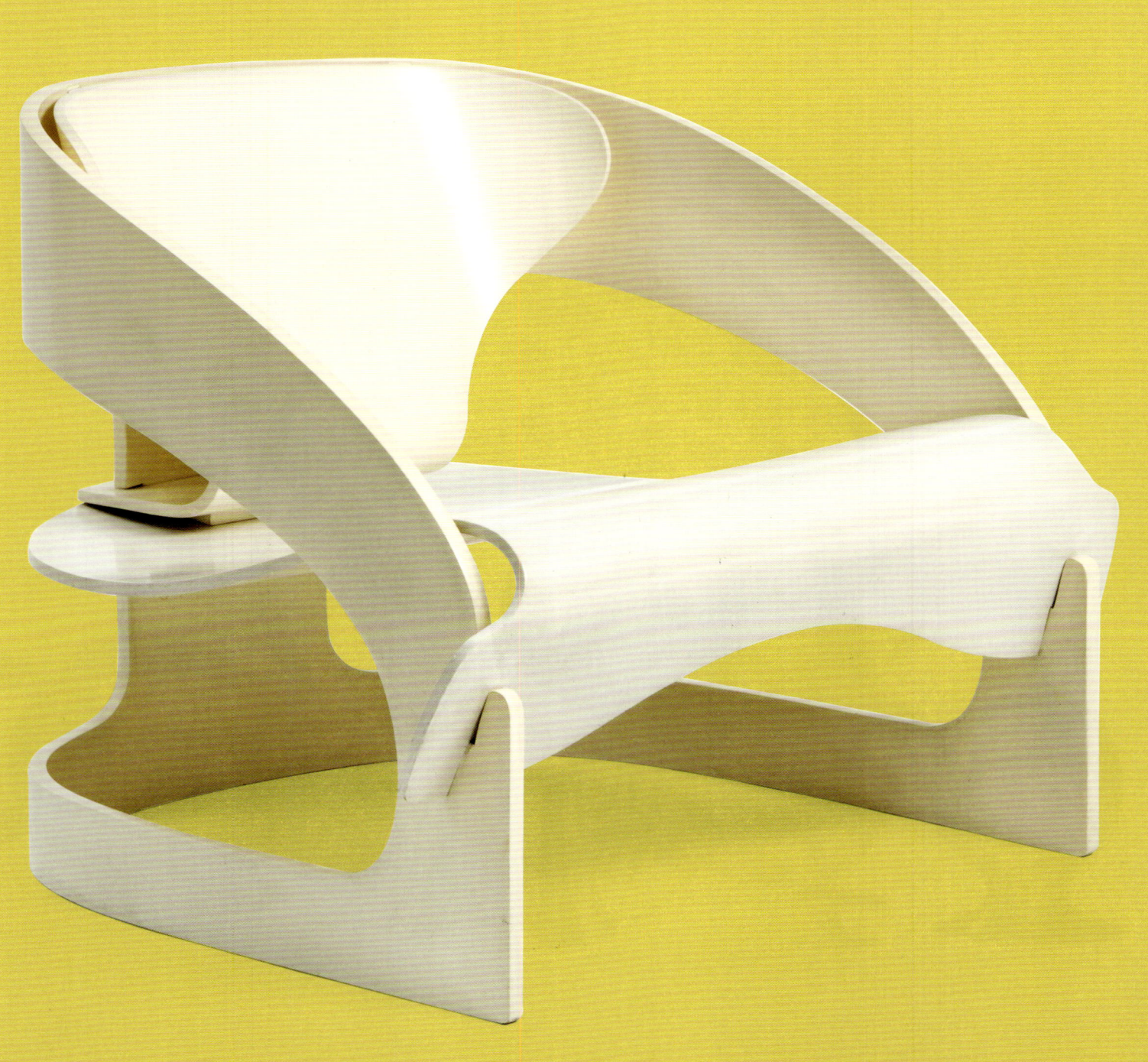

THE MUSEUM'S 125TH ANNIVERSARY

A centerpiece of the Museum's 125th anniversary initiatives was a campaign to acquire collection-transforming gifts of works of art, which culminated in 2002 in the exhibition *Gifts in Honor of the Museum's 125th Anniversary*.[128] Two important groups of modern furniture and decorative arts were added to the design collections and included in the exhibition. In recognition "of the strength of our modern design collection,"[129] the Museum in 1999 was offered fifteen pieces of artist-designed furniture from Lannan Foundation in Santa Fe, New Mexico. Surrealist in form and spirit, the furniture once decorated Four Winds, J. Patrick Lannan's Palm Beach estate; the gift included furniture by Diego Giacometti, Max Ernst (fig. 252), playwright Robert Wilson, and Pedro Friedeberg. Anne d'Harnoncourt wrote me. "I'm *thrilled* about the Giacomettis . . . and the Ernst bed sounds *wild—def.* worth going to see (*only* cautious given obvious size question). And if you go look maybe they have *even* more stuff?"[130]

The second group of furniture and objects acquired had been assembled by collectors of Joe Colombo's work,[131] who additionally arranged for Mr. and Mrs. Benjamin Thompson's gift of the designer's *Mini-Kitchen* on casters (fig. 249).[131] Collab funded the purchase of the Colombo collection as its 125th Anniversary gift to the Museum. The acquisition included a wide variety of Colombo's designs, including furniture, lighting, glassware, and his *Linea 72* in-flight service for Alitalia, with both first-class and disposable economy-class utensils (figs. 247, 248, 250, 251). All of these objects were designed to function in a variety of ways, underlining Colombo's deep-seated conviction that objects and their users interact in constantly changing patterns of relationship.

Planning the actual celebration of the Museum's anniversary had been a subject of much internal discussion beginning in the winter of 1998–99. With the support of Anne d'Harnoncourt and Gail Harrity, I proposed that the building itself should be the subject of our plans, and invited New York architects Elizabeth Diller and Ricardo Scofidio to design an installation project featuring the Museum.

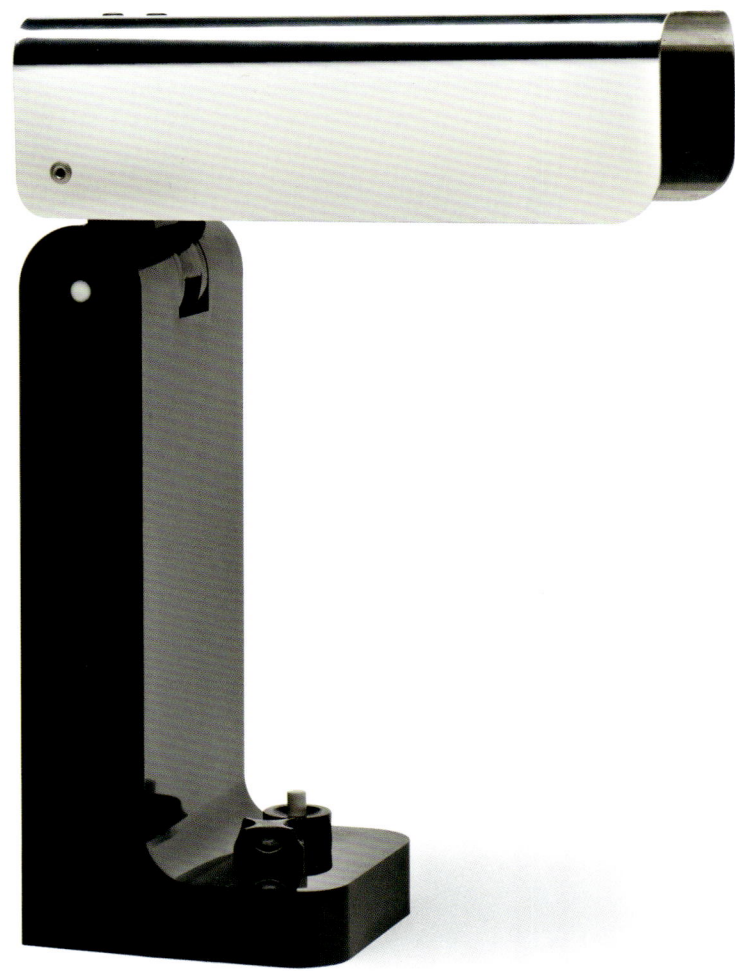

Gifts in Honor of the Museum's 125th Anniversary : 2002

Opposite : **247. Joe Colombo** : for Kartell : Armchair : 1964 : painted plywood : H 22 3/4" : 2001-42-2 (cat. 32)   Above : **248. Joe Colombo** : for Kartell : *Vademecum* Folding Lamp : 1986 : ABS plastic, stainless steel : H 9 7/8" : 2001-42-4 (cat. 33)

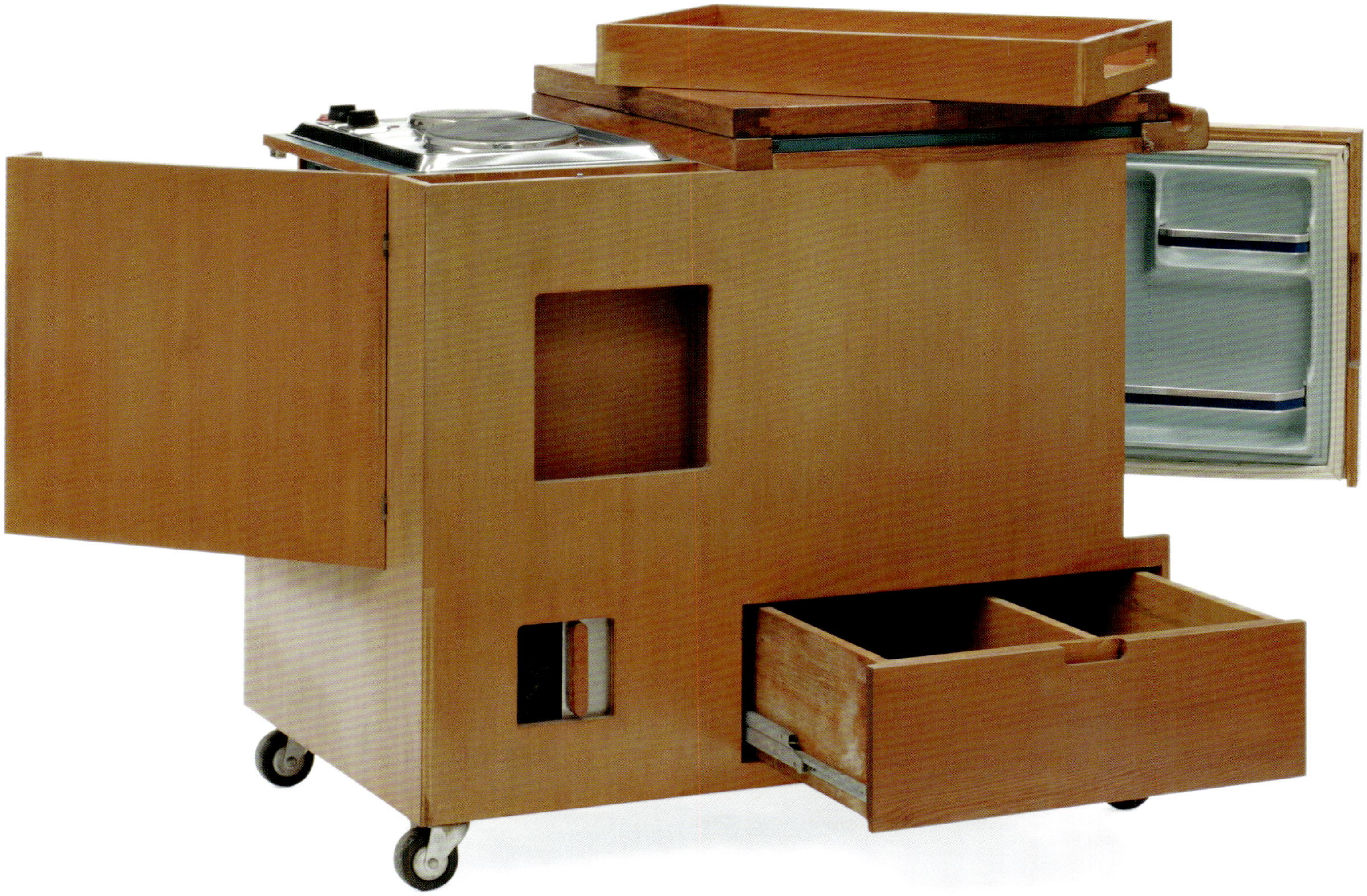

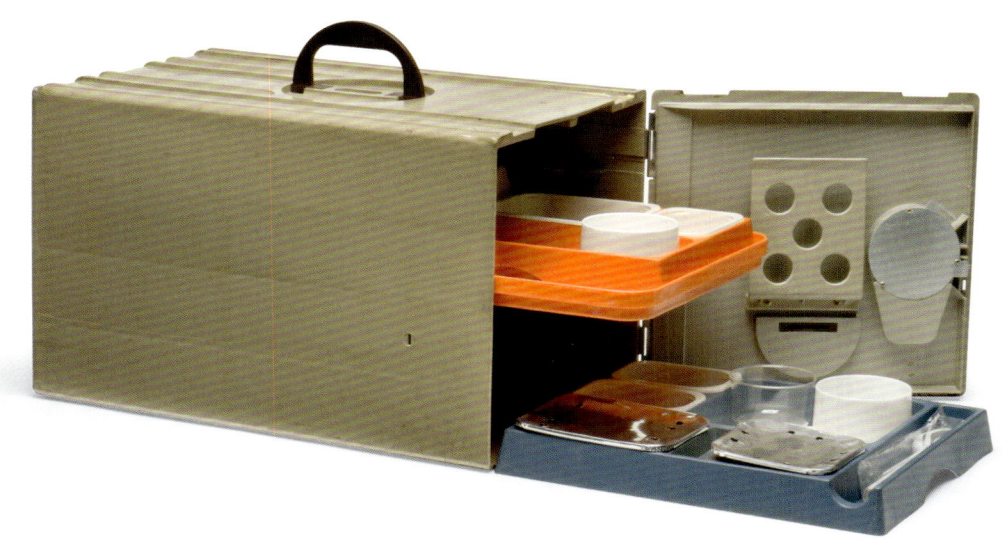

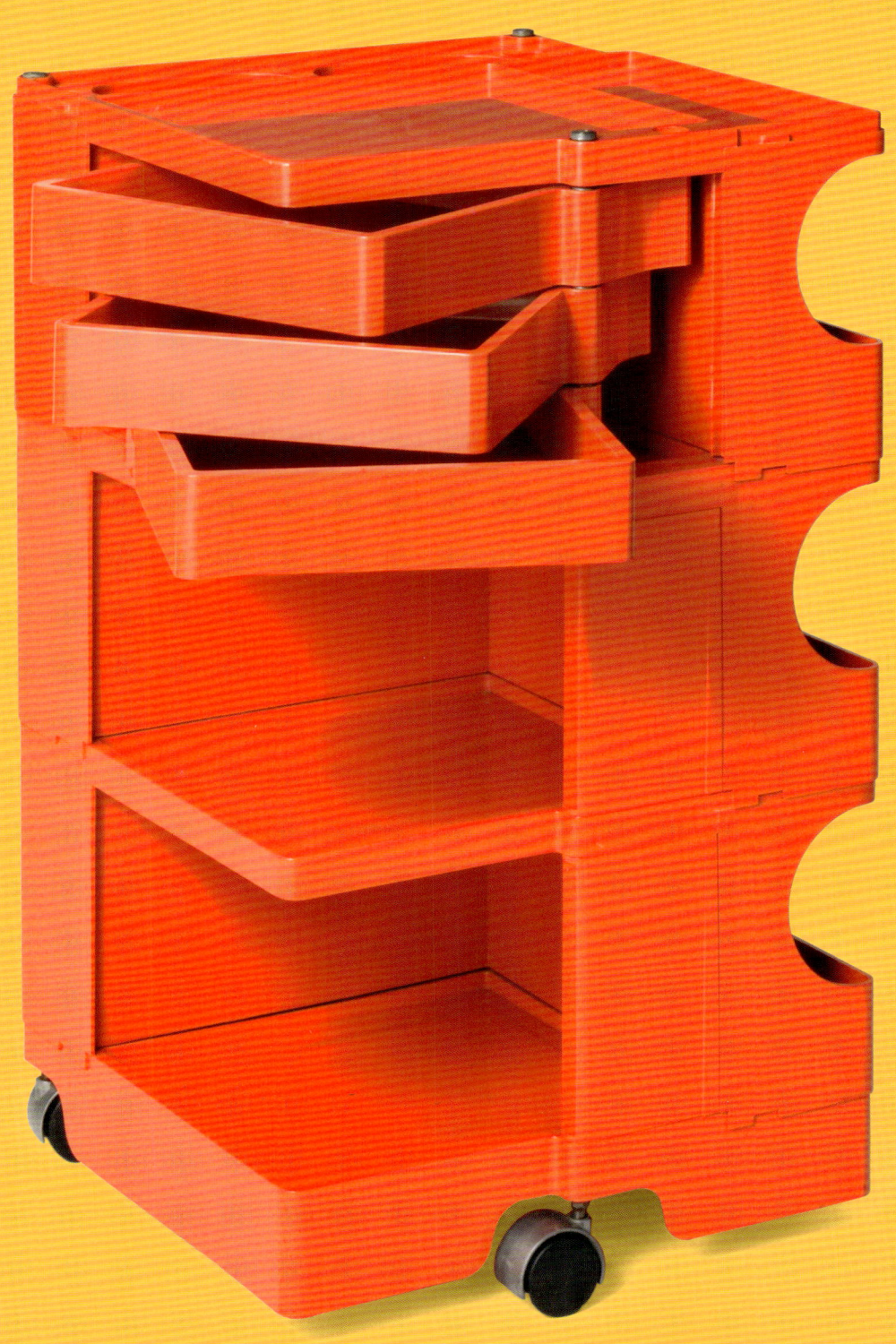

Gifts in Honor of the Museum's 125th Anniversary : 2002

Opposite, top to bottom : **249.** Joe Colombo : *Mini-Kitchen* : for Boffi : 1963 : plastic-coated wood, plastic, stainless steel : H 37¾" : 2000-89-1 (cat. 31)   **250.** Joe Colombo : for Richard Ginori : *Linea 72* In-Flight Service for Alitalia First Class : 1970 : porcelain, stainless steel, plastic, linen : L 7 1/16" : 2001-42-24a–r (cat. 35)   Above : **251.** Joe Colombo : for Bieffeplast : *Boby* Trolley : 1970 : ABS plastic : H 28¾" : 2001-42-7 (cat. 34)

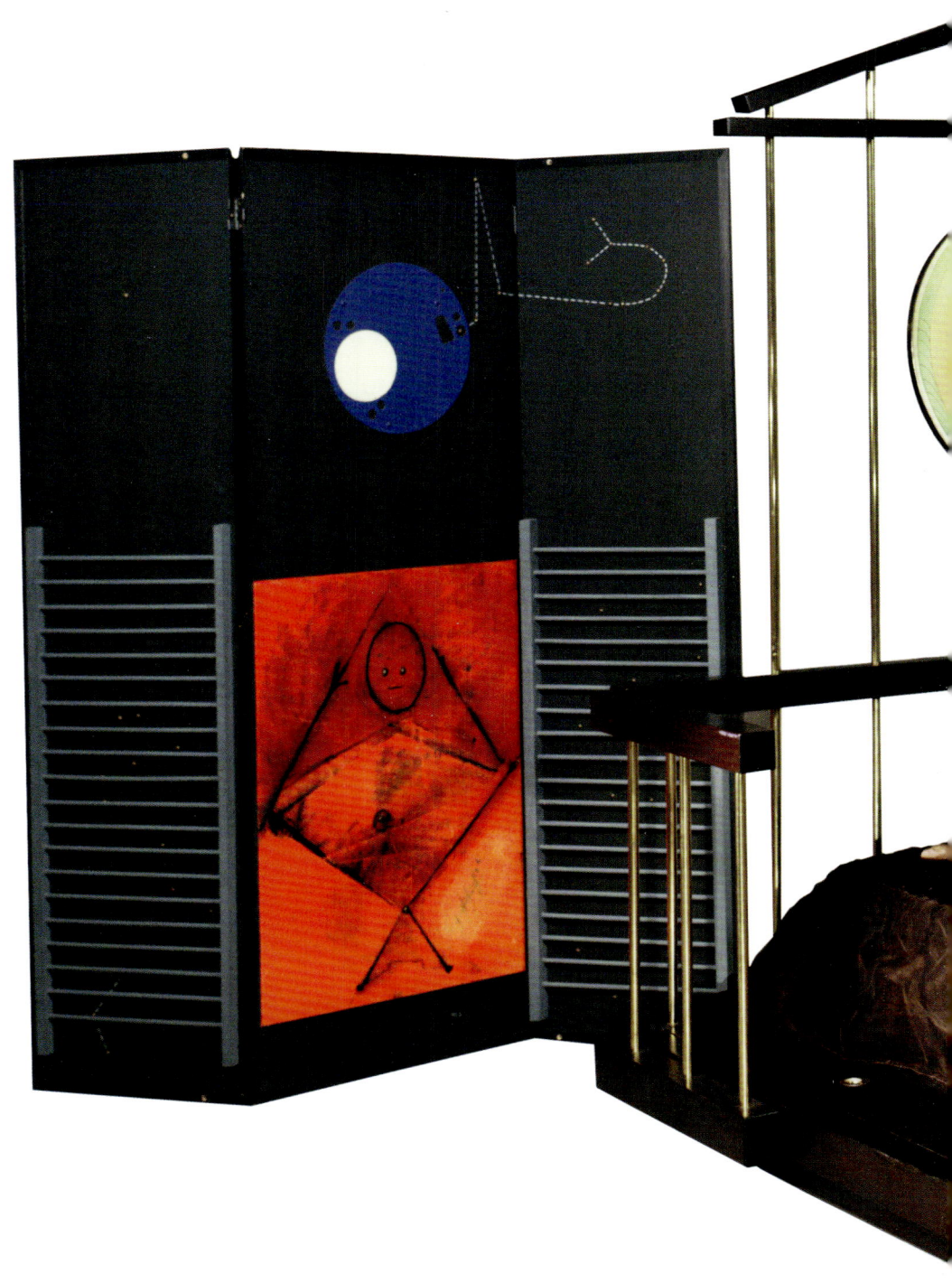

Gifts in Honor of the Museum's 125th Anniversary : 2002

252. Max Ernst : for Modern Art Associates : Bed-Cage, Screen, and Bedspread : 1974 : walnut, alder, brass, mirror, offset lithograph collage, mink : H (bed) 7' 4" : 1999-14-1a–c (cat. 57)

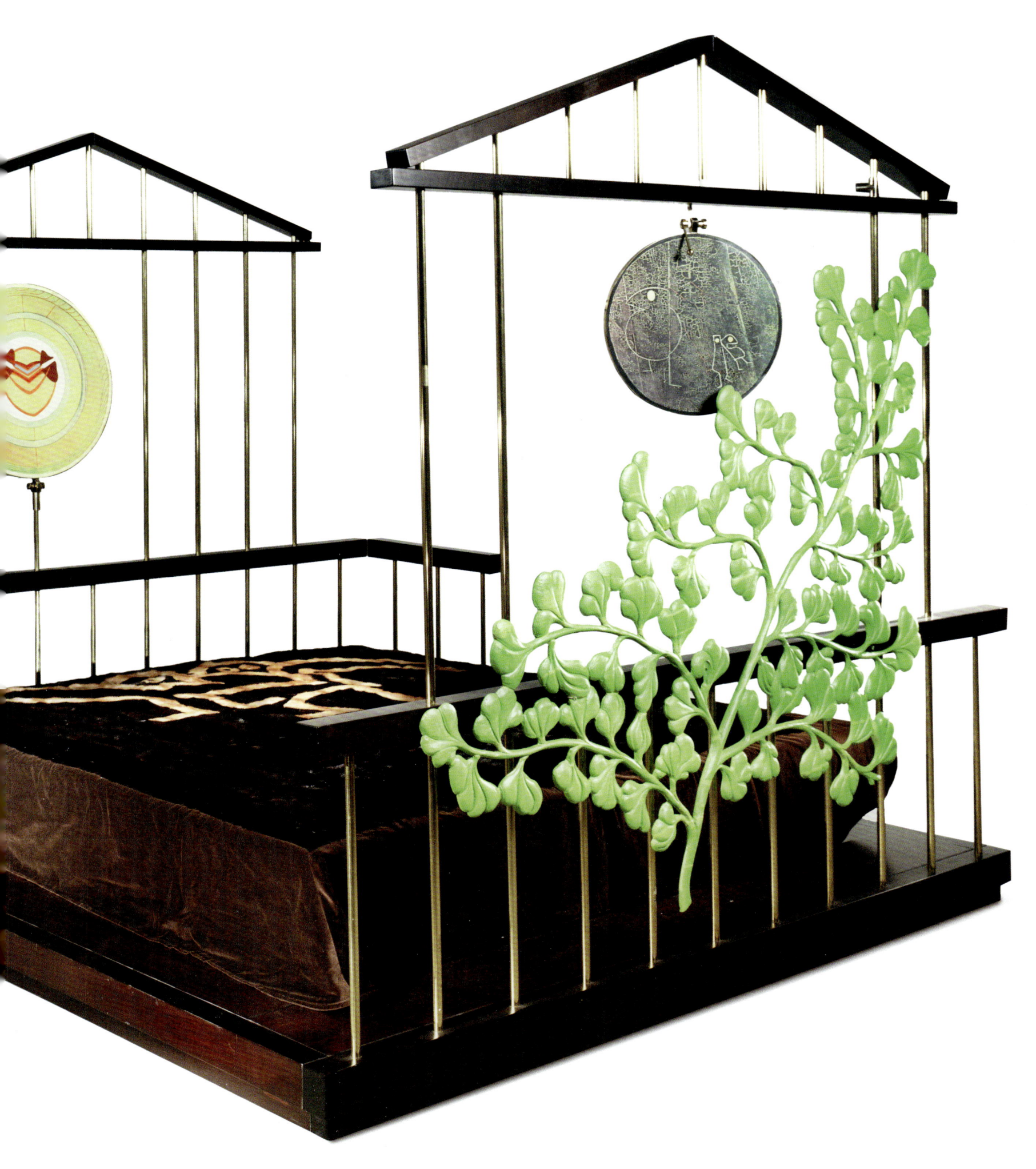

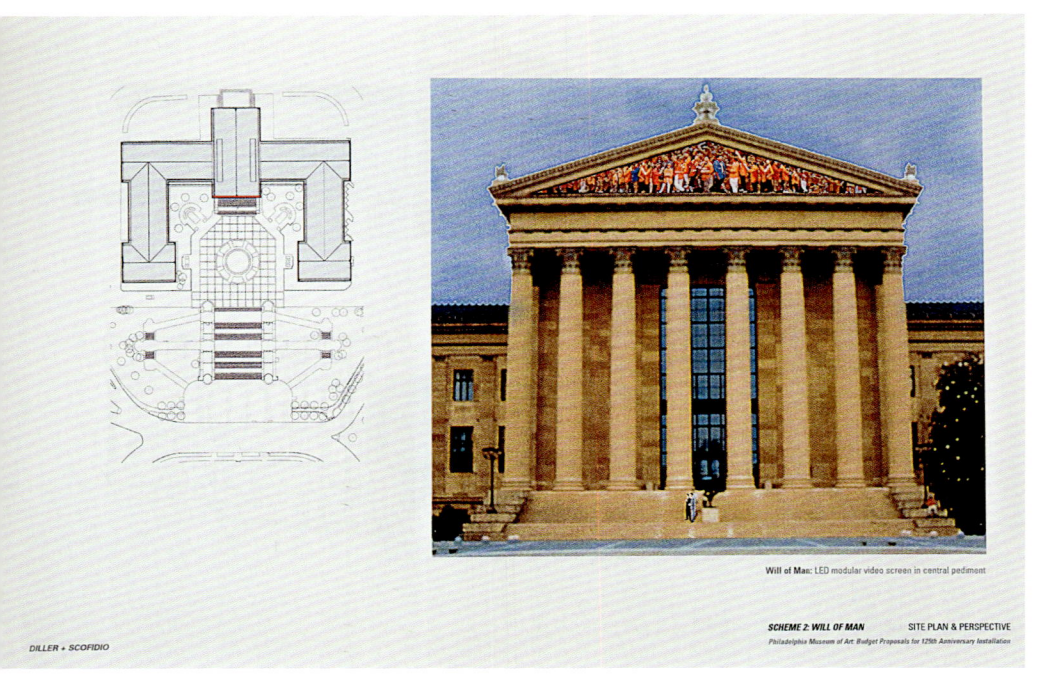
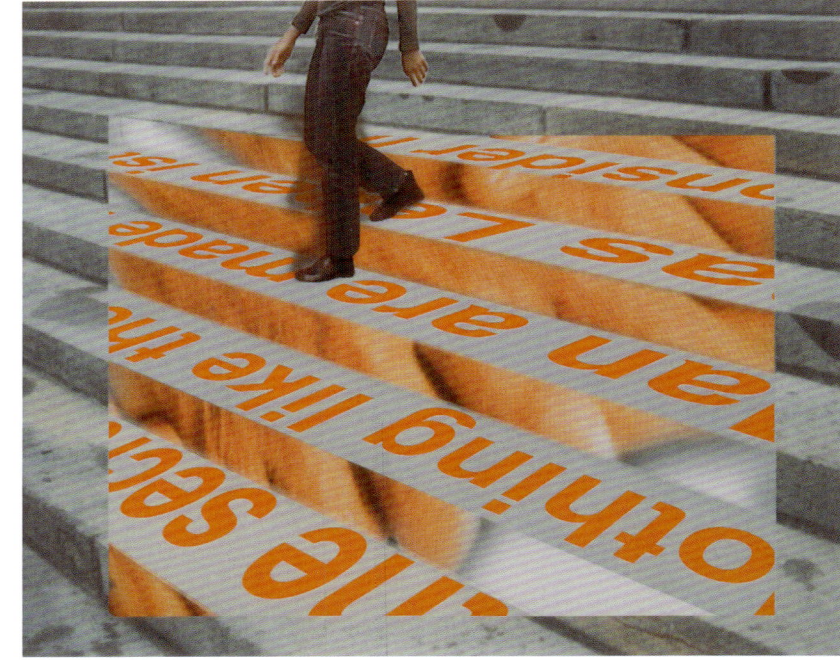

In June 2000 Diller and Scofidio presented four possible projects (figs. 253–56), all to be visible from the Benjamin Franklin Parkway and the Museum's adjacent neighborhoods: *Will of Man* proposed to install an LED video screen in the Museum's central pediment; in *Step Skin* a printed, molded-rubber carpet surfaced the main stair on the east side of the building; *Rapid Growth* featured motorized grass mounds with live trees that traveled slowly across the east plaza; and *Erase/Copy* consisted of back-to-back mirror walls stretched across the entry court, "erasing" the central section of the building so that it appeared still unbuilt between its wings as in 1925. There was great enthusiasm for all of the proposals, particularly *Rapid Growth*, but in the end it was not possible to proceed with the project due to lack of funding. A version of *Rapid Growth*, however, called *Arbores Laetae (Joyful Trees)* was created by the architects in 2008 for the Liverpool Biennial, happily giving life to a project originally conceived for Philadelphia.

The Museum had much to celebrate in its 125th anniversary year, particularly the acquisition of the former Fidelity Building (owned and occupied by the Reliance Standard Life Insurance Company since 1972), a purchase that the board had been considering off and on since the late 1960s. Just weeks after the Museum announced its acquisition of the building,[132] Collab member Lisa Roberts (a member of the Comcast cable television family) and her husband, David Seltzer, proposed endowing a Collab gallery for modern and contemporary design within the building's renovated and expanded interior, writing that they "would welcome this opportunity to participate in the Museum's exciting plans for the future."[133] This was the first of several important gifts Roberts and Seltzer would make to support modern and contemporary design at the Museum. Hailed by the board of trustees for her devotion to Collab and the design field,[134] Roberts was elected to the board the following year, becoming its greatest advocate for contemporary design since John T. Morris.

253–56. **Elizabeth Diller and Ricardo Scofidio** : installation proposals for the Museum : 2000 : (left to right) *Will of Man* : *Step Skin* : *Rapid Growth* : *Erase/Copy*

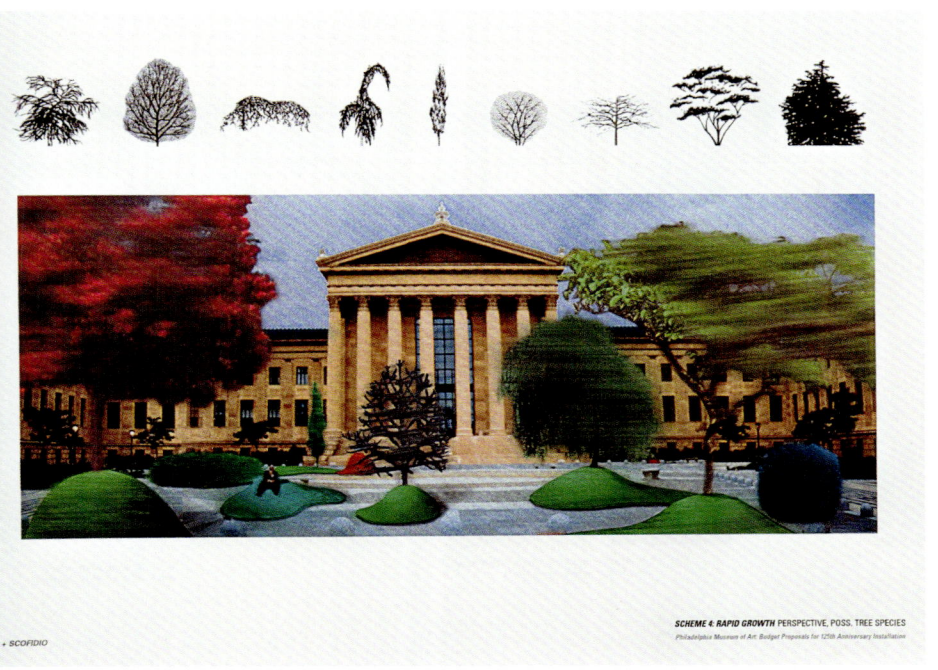
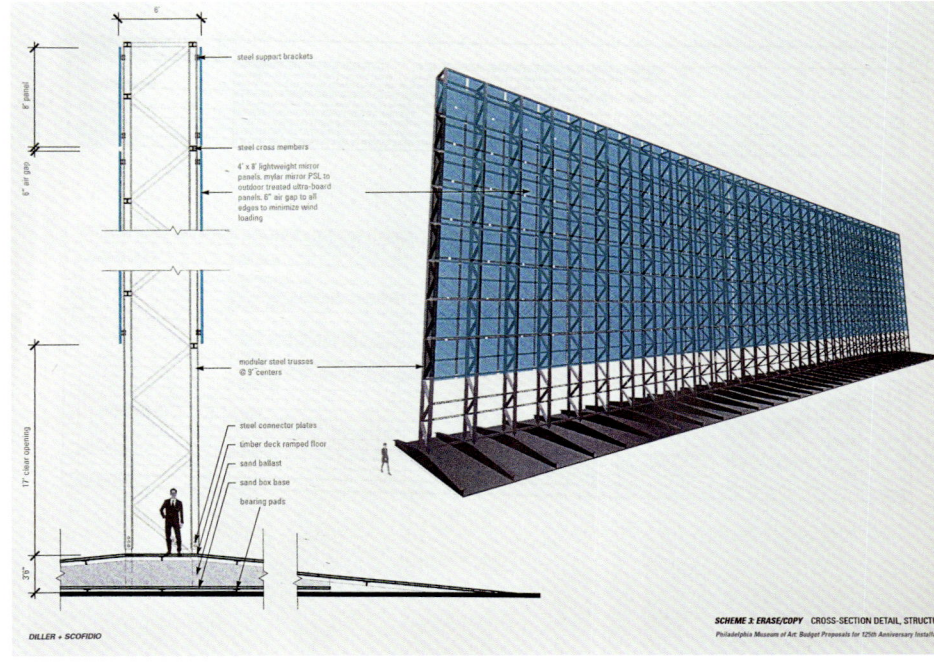

In 2005 she commissioned this history of the Museum's decorative arts and design collections, its publication originally intended to coincide with the opening of the Collab Gallery in the new building. Like Morris, Roberts was a passionate collector and her own book, *Antiques of the Future* (2006), described her personal collection: "I started collecting designer household products about 25 years ago. I had just changed careers from architecture to home furnishing design. . . . As part of the industry, I witnessed this explosion of extraordinary design of very ordinary objects."[135] In 2006 Roberts brought to Collab the services of an organizational consultant in order to improve the committee's governance, participation, and funding sources in preparation for the opening of the new gallery for modern and contemporary design.[136] She also underwrote the expenses of Collab's Student Design Competition and continues to do so to the present when other funding is unavailable. Finally, in 2009 Roberts and Seltzer (the latter elected a Museum trustee in 2007) established a fund to support exhibitions related to the work of Collab's Design Excellence Award recipients, beginning that same year with *Marcel Wanders: Daydreams*. In the wake of the global recession that followed the subprime mortgage crisis of 2008, the gift from Roberts and Seltzer took on added importance.

In the new millennium Collab chairs Neil Sandvold, James Fulton, Robert Aibel, and Lisa Benn left their individual marks on the committee and its mission and programmatic activities, as the collections of modern and contemporary design continued to grow around the Museum's exhibitions, large and small. Sandvold, an architect, Fulton, coprincipal of an architecture and interiors firm, Aibel, a gallery owner specializing in modern furniture and decorative arts, and Benn, a graphic designer who brought clarity and contemporaneity to Collab's graphic productions, supported increasingly ambitious projects. In addition to the Design Excellence Award, the committee initiated in 2005 a

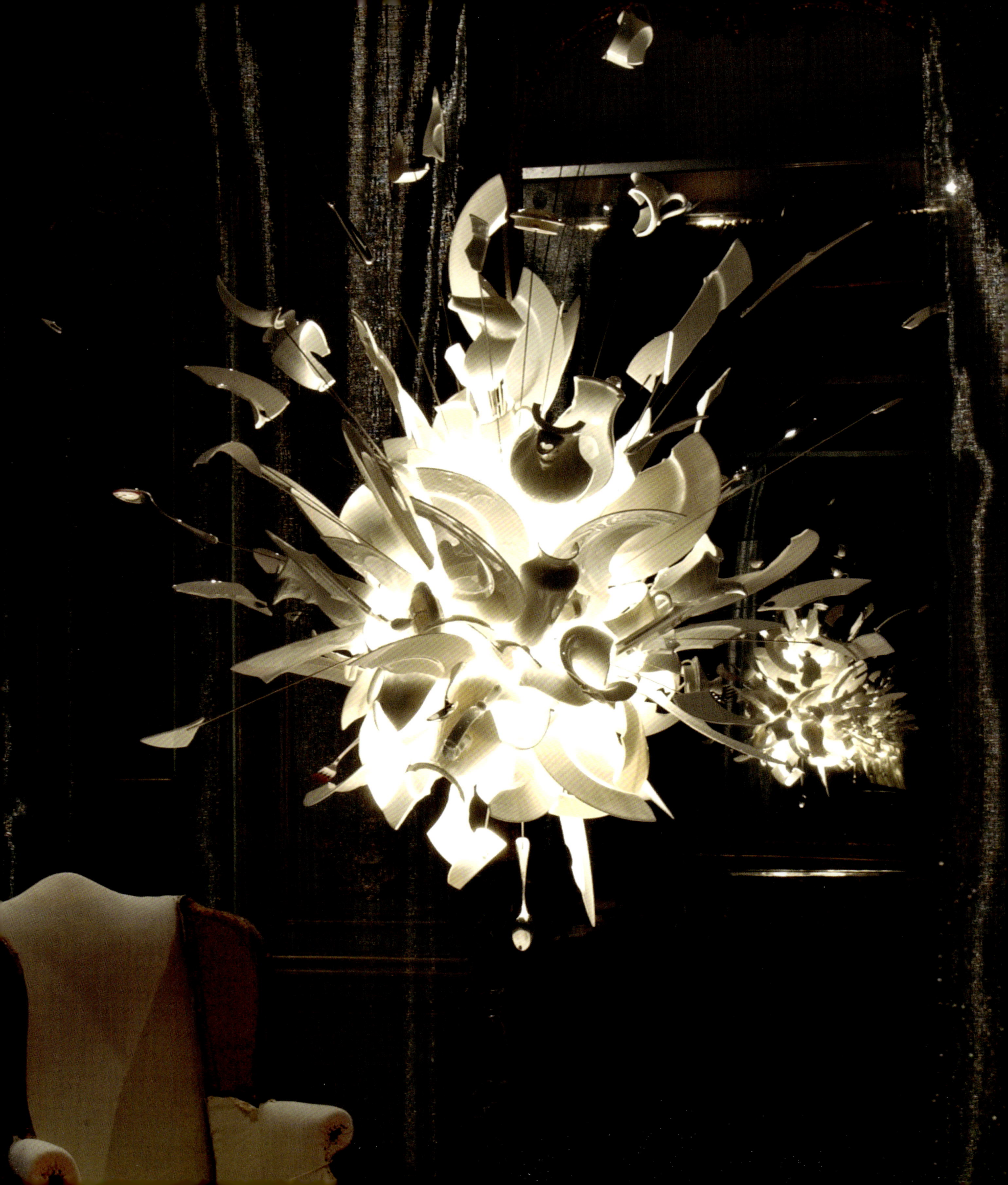

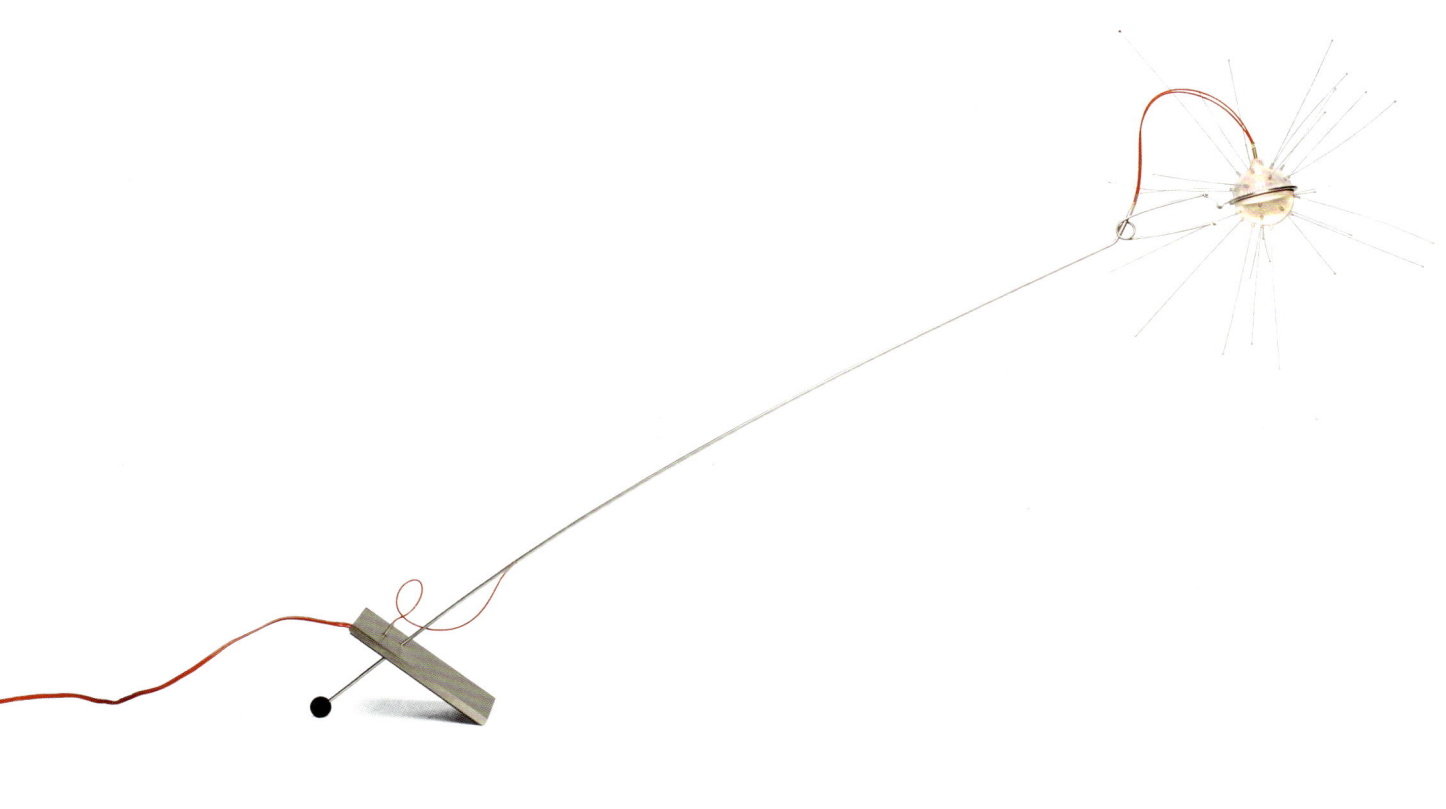

spring lecture series and a newsletter in an effort to build and inform Collab's audience. A regular feature of the publication has been a description of the Museum's recent acquisitions along with a "wish list" of desiderata, often happily marked "Donated—Thank You!"

Although few Collab members at the time knew the work of German lighting designer Ingo Maurer when I proposed his name in 2002, the committee supported not only his award for design excellence (fig. 201) but also the challenges of two separate Museum installations in dramatically different galleries, collectively referred to as *The Light Magic of Ingo Maurer*.[137] Over the years Maurer had generously donated his *YaYaHo* lighting system and *Bibibi*, *Mozzkito*, and *Kokoro* lamps to the Museum (figs. 258, 259). For one section of Collab 2002, I asked him to relight our eighteenth-century French period room from the Château of Draveil. Maurer hung his *Porca Miseria!* chandelier—a light sculpture made of broken porcelain dishes—from the central ceiling rosette and surrounded it with walls of wire mesh (fig. 257). The reflections were endlessly repeated in the room's large mirror glasses, leading Maurer to remark that "a room within a room is a room, is a room," in a playful allusion to poet Gertrude Stein.[138] As the second part of Collab 2002, Maurer installed in the design gallery his *aha SoSo* lighting system over a floor piece painted in DayGlo orange, white, and gray.[139] Maurer's dazzling installations were heralded by the *Philadelphia Inquirer* and illustrated in the *New York Times Magazine*.[140] In recognition of his recent pleated-paper lamps such as *Kokoro*, the student competition asked participants to design a table lamp made primarily of paper, a popular project that attracted over two hundred entries. In honor of Collab chair James Fulton, the committee gave the Museum Maurer's *Wo bist du, Edison?* lamp, which features a hologram of a lightbulb with a socket shaped like the silhouetted profile of Thomas Edison.

The Light Magic of Ingo Maurer : 2002–3

Opposite : **257.** Ingo Maurer's installation of *Porca Miseria!* in the Museum's eighteenth-century French period room from the Château of Draveil : 2002
Above : **258. Ingo Maurer** : for Ingo Maurer GmbH : *Mozzkito* Lamp : 1996 : metal, plastic, rubber : L 31 1/2" : 1999-12-1 (cat. 121)
Below : **259. Ingo Maurer and Dagmar Mombach** : for Ingo Maurer GmbH : *Kokoro* Lamp : 1998 : pleated paper, metal : H 30" : 2002-218-1 (cat. 122)

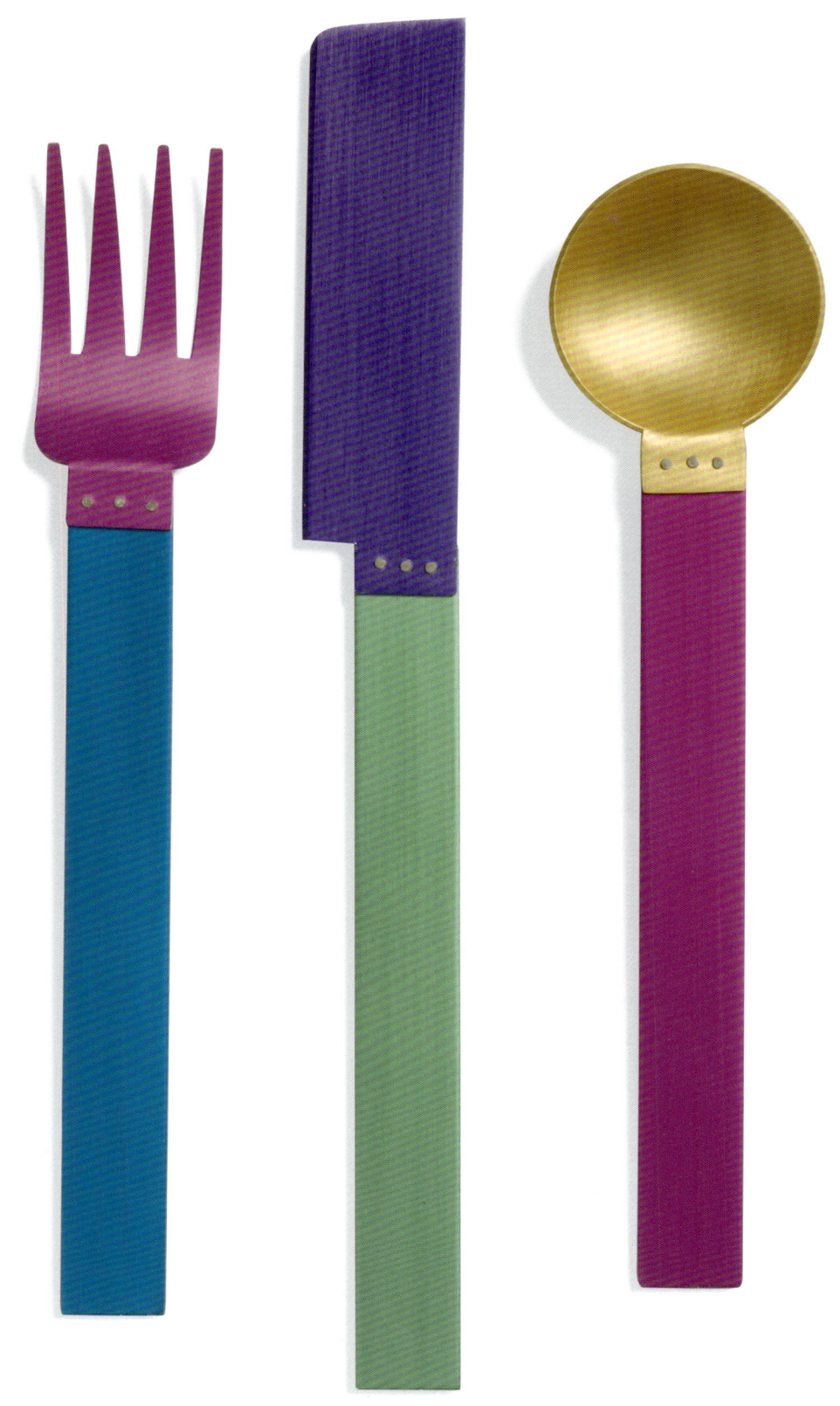

260. David Tisdale : for David Tisdale Design : *Picnic* Flatware : 1985 : anodized aluminum : L (knife) 8" : 2003-14-1–3 (cat. 194)

PLANS FOR EXPANSION

Collab 2003 celebrated the Museum's public announcement of the previous year that Gluckman Mayner Architects of New York would design the renovation of and addition to the former Fidelity Building (to be renamed the Ruth and Raymond G. Perelman Building in honor of its principal donors), which would house the Collab Gallery. Ahead of the groundbreaking celebration, which took place in 2004, the exhibition *Work in Progress: Gluckman Mayner Designs the Perelman Building*[141] illustrated the process of architectural planning and design through drawings, photographs, models, and samples of materials. The *Philadelphia Inquirer* applauded the exhibition's efforts to "demystify the profession" and demonstrate that "good architecture is as much about solving problems as it is about creating eye-popping sculpture."[142] In conjunction with the show, Richard Gluckman spoke about his work, while students in Collab's annual competition were asked to design the main exterior signage for the Perelman Building as it might appear after the renovation. The year 2003 also saw the decorative arts department collaborate with Philadelphia's Fabric Workshop and Museum for the exhibition *On the Wall: Wallpaper and Tableau*.[143] Diane Minnite coordinated the Museum's loans of historic papers, for which it received in exchange—as gifts of trustee Marion Boulton Stroud, the artists, and an anonymous donor—a group of contemporary wallpapers, ranging from Virgil Marti's *Bullies* in fluorescent ink and rayon flock on Tyvek to Francesco Simeti's *Arabian Nights* notations on the war in Afghanistan to Andy Warhol's *Cows*. Also in 2003, Donna Corbin organized an exhibition of twentieth-century flatware. *Have a Bite: 20th-Century Flatware from the Collection*,[144] included eleven newly acquired flatware services, among them David Tisdale's anodized aluminum *Picnic* set (fig. 260) and Michael Schneider's *Mono Tools* flatware, the latter inspired by prehistoric archaeology.

In 2004 we were able to coax eighty-seven-year-old Florence Knoll Bassett out of retirement to design and curate for Collab 2005 the first solo museum exhibition of her legendary work. *Florence Knoll Bassett: Defining Modern*,[145] which I organized, had repercussions far beyond its size. Publicity was extensive and international, appearing in the *New York Times* and *Philadelphia Inquirer* as well as the magazines *Architecture*, *House and Garden*, *Metropolis*, *Casamica* in Italy, and *SDQ Magazine* in Australia. Bassett had led an entirely private life since leaving Knoll, Inc., in 1965, but she had lost none of her considerable design skills or desire for perfection. She sent the Museum her model of the gallery as

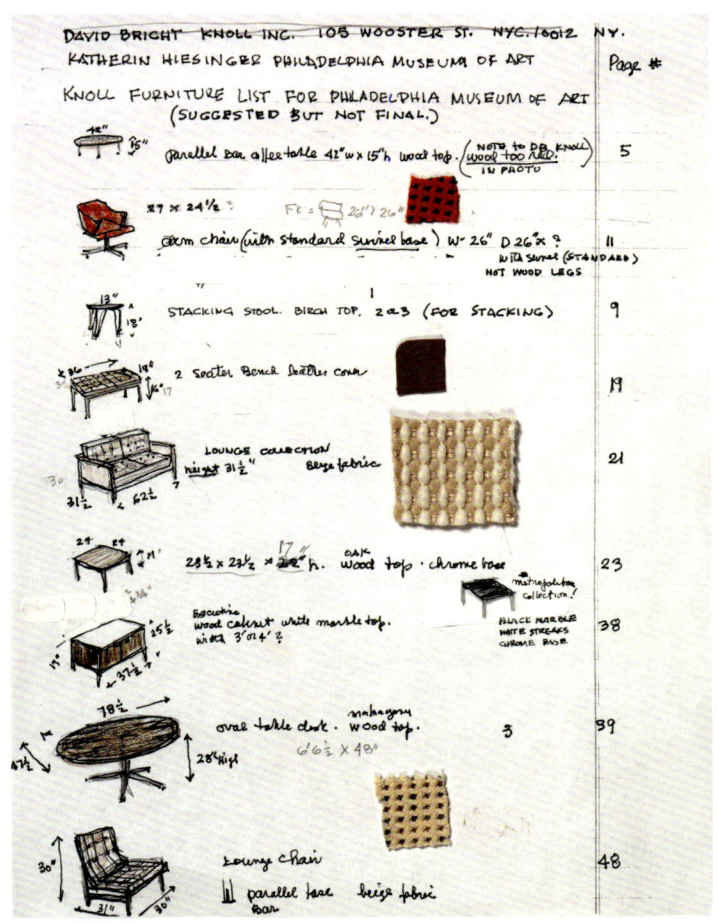

Florence Knoll Bassett : Defining Modern : 2004–5

261. Florence Knoll Bassett's exhibition list : 2004

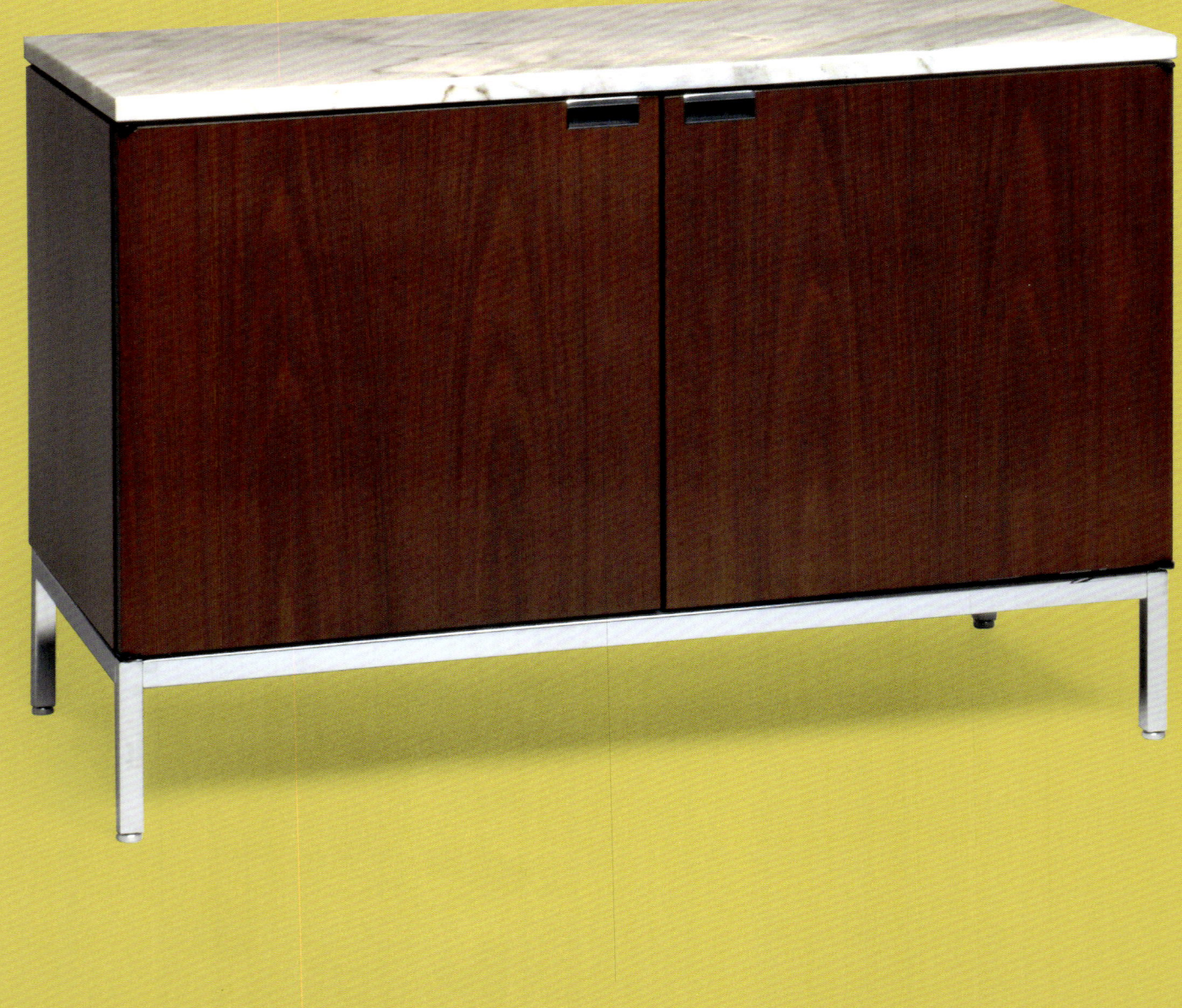

Florence Knoll Bassett : Defining Modern : 2004–5

Above : **262. Florence Knoll** : for Knoll : Credenza : 1955 : chromed steel, mahogany, marble : L 37" : 2005-20-1 (cat. 100)   Opposite : **263.** Gallery view

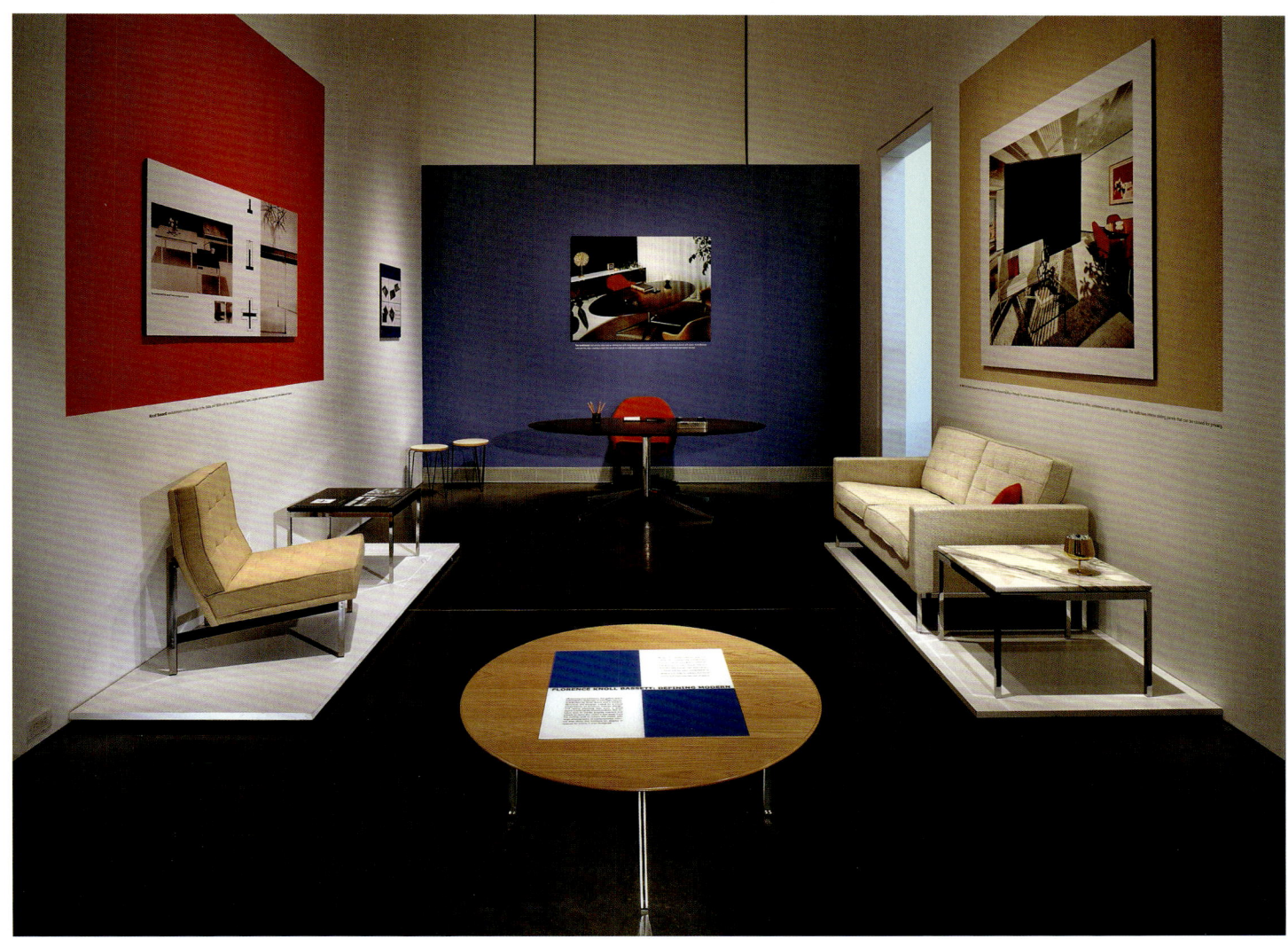

it should be installed and a hand-drawn illustrated exhibition list, complete with samples of fabric and veneer (fig. 261), following a presentation strategy she had begun while a student at the Architectural Association in London and had developed when the Planning Unit was formed at Knoll. Under the direction of David Bright, Knoll's vice-president of communications, the company produced furniture for the show to Bassett's specifications, while the Museum's installation design department, under the able direction of Jack Schlechter, helped realize her plans, resulting in one of the most perfect uses of the space to date (fig. 263). In conjunction with the exhibition, the Museum published an illustrated chronology of Florence Knoll's career and furniture designs, distributed as a gallery hand-out and funded by a generous grant from Elise Jaffe and Jeffrey Brown of New York. At the opening of the exhibition Bassett was presented with Collab's Design Excellence Award in absentia, and I delivered a lecture about her work that I had developed in close communication with the designer herself. Carl Magnusson, Knoll's design director, also spoke about Bassett's influence on the company she had cofounded. Collab's Student Design Competition asked for redesigns of a piece of Knoll's classic furniture, using new materials and new production technologies. A chair and table as well as a credenza designed by Bassett were made by the firm for the exhibition; the chair and table were donated to the Museum by Knoll, Inc., and the credenza by Collab to honor committee chair Robert Aibel (fig. 262).

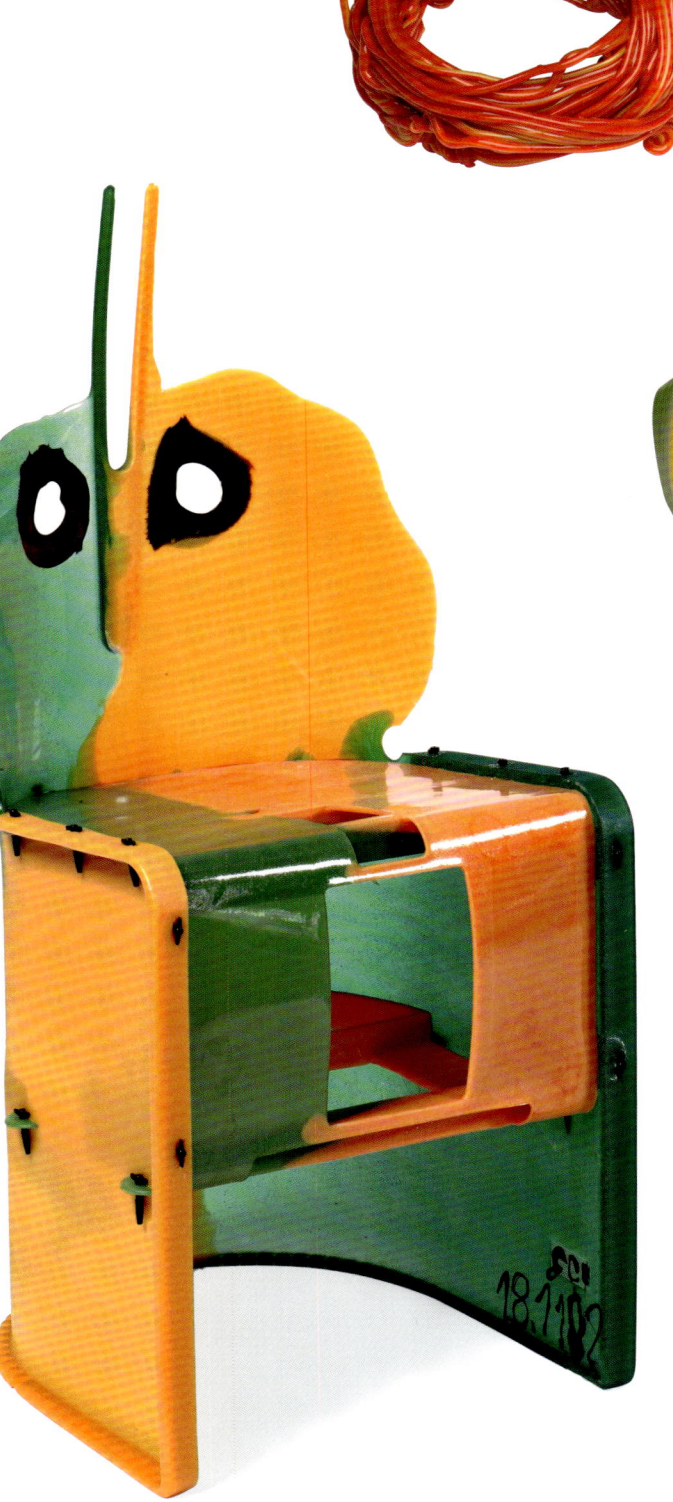

The Museum's design gallery was transformed again by Collab 2005, *Gaetano Pesce: Pushing the Limits*.[146] Few Italian designers have taken material and technological experimentation further than Pesce, who most recently has produced furniture and objects that vary in color and shape according to the chance flow of pigmented plastic resin in molds. For the opening of the exhibition, he designed a unique invitation in flexible resin. The show included a self-portrait with miniature chairs outlining Pesce's silhouette, an architectural model, chairs, lamps, and carpet prototypes. A number of the chairs were recent acquisitions by gift and purchase, among them, the *I Feltri* armchair (fig. 267) in low- and high-backed versions made of thick wool felt—soaked in resin at the bottom for support and flexible at the top so that the user can manipulate the shape—along with two chairs and a table from Pesce's *Nobody's Perfect* series (fig. 266). Several bracelets, also in flexible resin, were added to the collections after the exhibition (figs. 264, 265). The accompanying Student Design Competition was based on Pesce's use of nonstandard production processes, and asked for a full-scale functional prototype of a flower vase that reflected the designer's approach to variable production. Entries included a container molded out of soil and wax and others fashioned from pipe fittings, recycled concrete, and tree roots; first prize was awarded to a vase made of ice with flowers frozen into its surface. The "wildly varied" exhibition of the "always provocative" designer received front-page coverage in the "Home and Design" section of the *Philadelphia Inquirer*.[147]

Gaetano Pesce : Pushing the Limits : 2005–6

Above, clockwise from top : **264. Gaetano Pesce** : for Fish Design : *Spaghetti* Bracelet : 2005 : plastic resin : D 4 1/2" : 2005-183-1 (cat. 148)
265. Gaetano Pesce : for Fish Design : *Ribbon* Bracelet : 2005 : plastic resin : D 4" : 2005-102-2 (cat. 149)   **266. Gaetano Pesce** : for Zerodisegno : *Nobody's Perfect* Chair : 2002 : polyurethane-based resin, nylon : H (seat) 17 11/16" : 2003-136-1 (cat. 147)   Opposite : **267. Gaetano Pesce** : for Cassina : *I Feltri* Armchair (Lowback) : 1986 : wool felt with polyester resin, felt, cotton, hemp string, fabric : H 38 5/8" : 2006-32-1 (cat. 146)

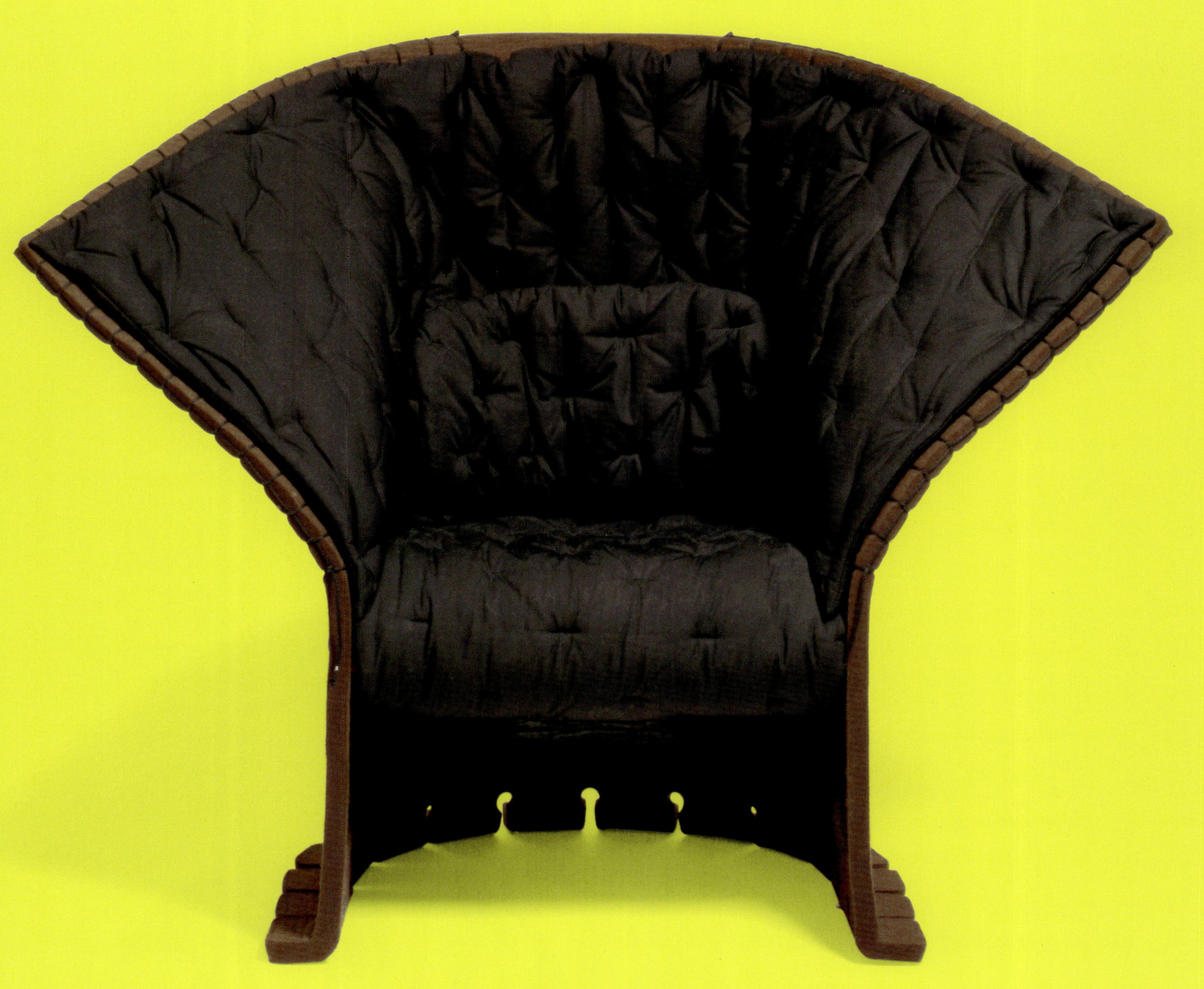

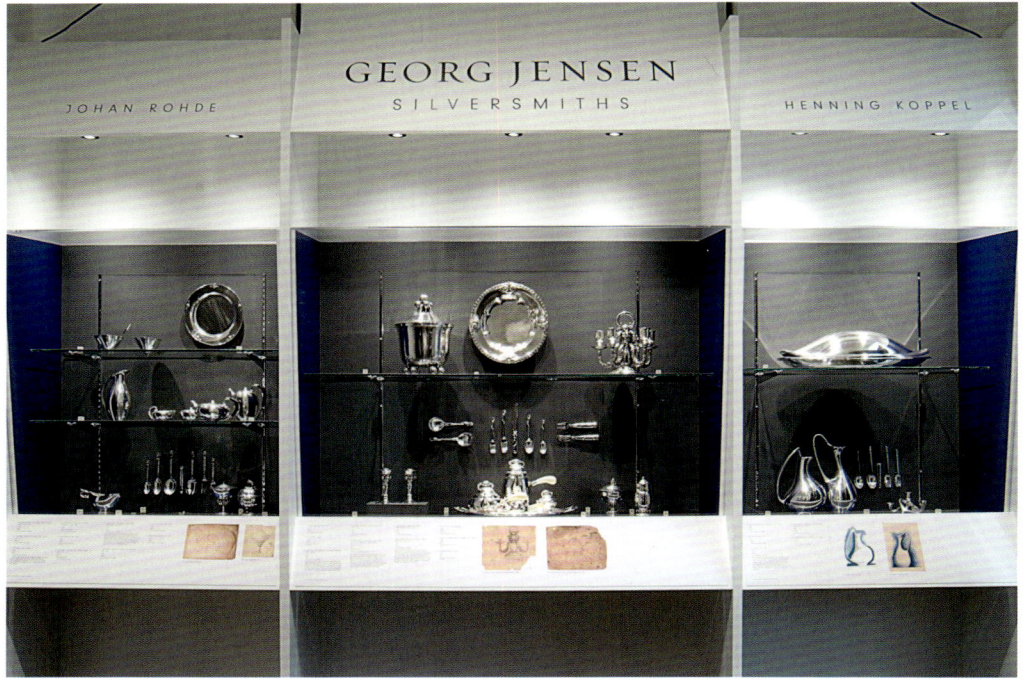

electrostatic coating applied to the interior, allowing bread to be kept warm long after it is moved from the oven to the table.

Georg Jensen Silversmiths was the last exhibition to be mounted by the department in the design gallery located in the heart of the Museum's modern and contemporary painting and sculpture collections. Design objects had occupied the gallery since 1976, but in anticipation of the opening of the Collab Gallery in the new building the small, 330-square-foot room reverted to painting and sculpture, d'Harnoncourt arguing the need for space as well as her conviction that the changing design exhibitions held there interrupted the overall Museum aesthetic. The decision left modern and contemporary painting and sculpture the only section of the Museum where works of art in all mediums are not exhibited together, as Fiske Kimball had conceived. James Nelson Kise, trustee and from 2001 to 2009 chair of the departmental advisory committee,[149] nevertheless advocated continuing Kimball's historical progression of decorative arts on Fairmount into the present.[150] Having given the Museum its first Olivetti typewriter—the classic *Lettera 22*, designed by Marcello Nizzoli (fig. 270)—Kise has continuously supported the Museum's acquisition and exhibition of modern and contemporary objects, particularly since 1994 when, with the promise that "it might be more fun"[151] than his previous trustee assignments, he joined the departmental committee. Nevertheless, as of this writing, modern and contemporary design (with the exception of contemporary American craft) continues to lack gallery space in the main Museum building.

In 2006 Collab gave its award for design excellence to the Danish silverware firm of Georg Jensen, bringing a different audience to the Museum and the exhibition that accompanied the award. With an installation design by Jack Schlechter, *Georg Jensen Silversmiths*[148] comprised over 120 objects from the Museum's permanent collection, the collections of Georg Jensen AS in Copenhagen, and private collections in Britain and the United States (figs. 268, 269) The exhibition was an exercise in installing a great many objects in a very small space without sacrificing aesthetic appeal or intelligibility. Grouped by designer, the silver was displayed along with facsimiles of the original design drawings for many of the pieces. Featured was the work of Georg Jensen, who founded the eponymous firm in 1904, Sigvard Bernadotte, Piet Hein, Søren Georg Jensen, Henning Koppel, Harald Nielsen, Verner Panton, Johan Rohde, Allan Scharff, and Magnus Stephensen. Hans-Kristian Højsgaard, president and chief executive officer of the Jensen firm, accepted Collab's Design Excellence Award on behalf of the company. Based on Georg Jensen's use of ornament, the student competition invited designs of an "intelligent ornament" that reflected the vernacular of the firm's founder and its enduring values. The winning project was a leafy, openwork breadbasket with an

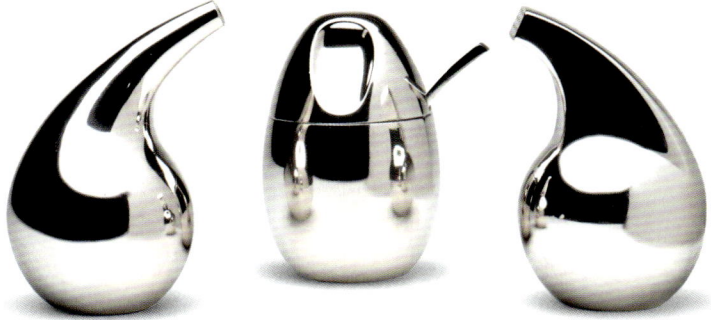

Georg Jensen Silversmiths : 2006–7

Top : **268.** Gallery view   Bottom : **269. Søren Georg Jensen** : for Georg Jensen Sølvsmedie : Condiment Set for Salt, Pepper, and Mustard, *no. 965* : 1951 : silver : H (pepper shaker) 3 1/8" : 1982-58-4a–c (cat. 94)

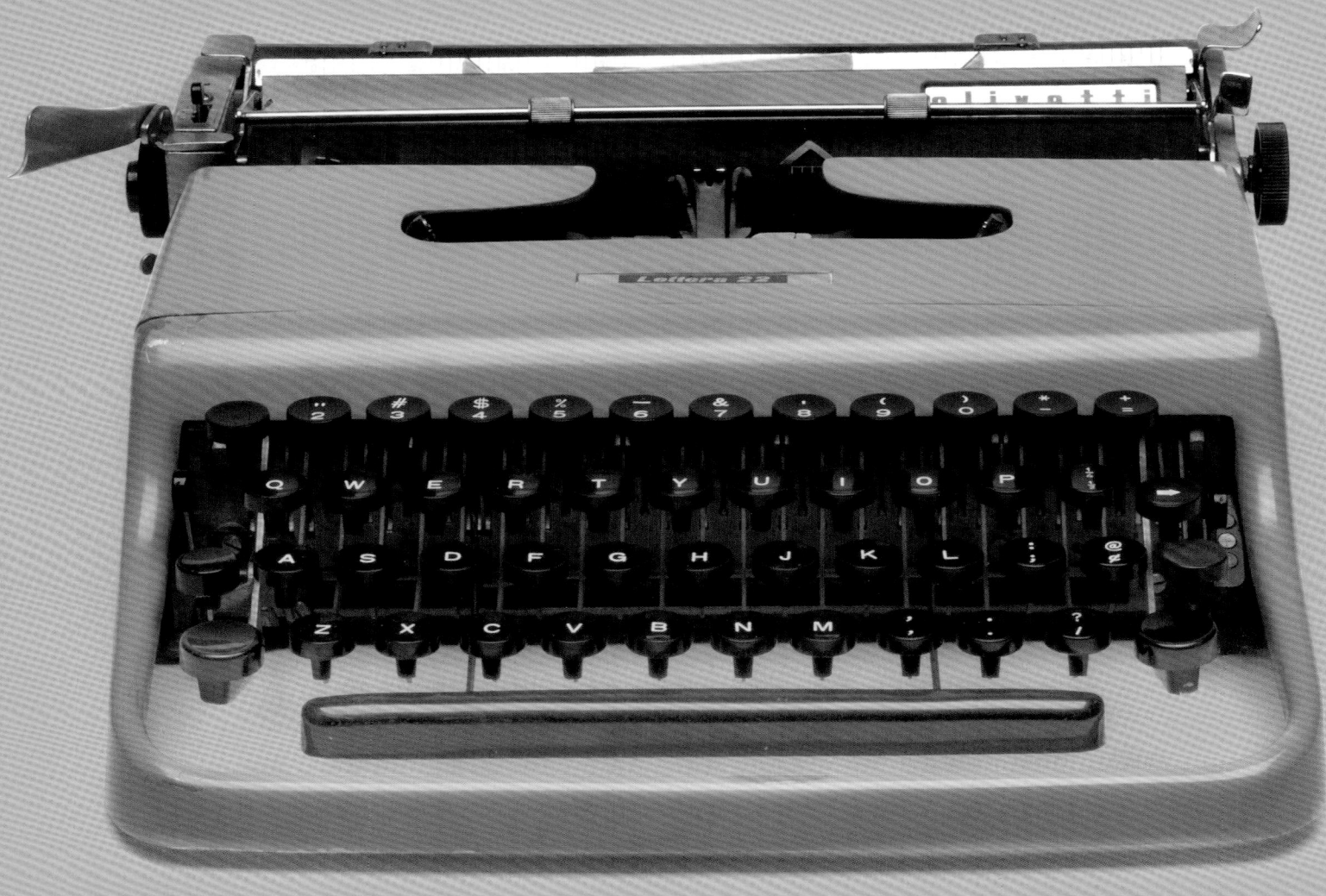

270. Marcello Nizzoli : for Olivetti : *Lettera 22* Typewriter : 1950 : enameled metal : W 11 3/8" : 1984-30-1 (cat. 137)

THE PERELMAN BUILDING OPENS

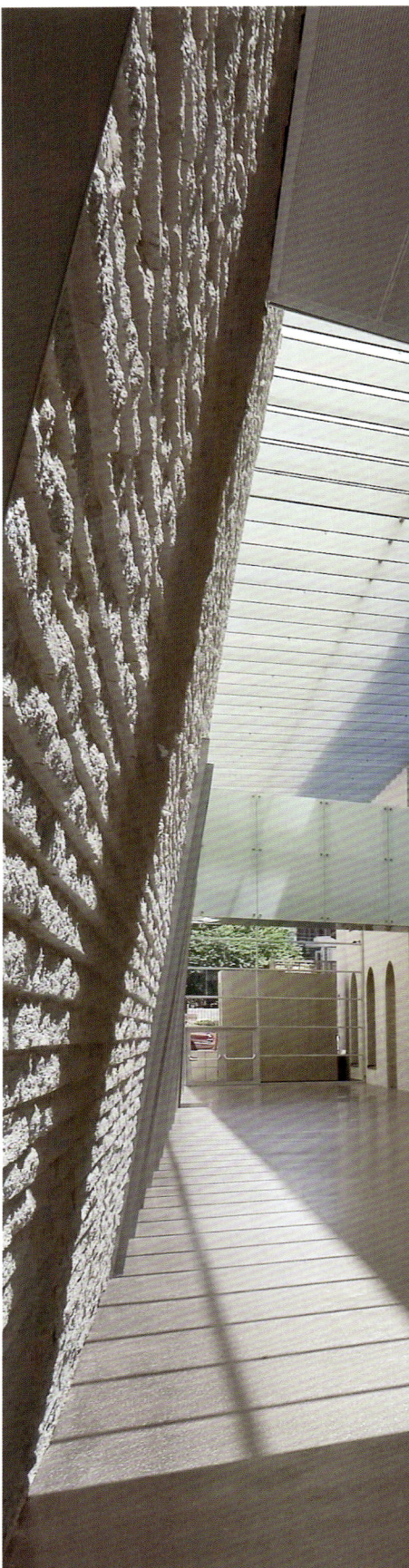

Gail Harrity's principal initiatives when she joined the Museum as chief operating officer in 1996 were to address, by means of a five-year strategic plan and multiyear building master plan, the Museum's chronic overcrowding and inadequate space for exhibition, storage, library collections, offices, and public amenities. These priorities were shared by Raymond G. Perelman, who became the Museum's chairman of the board in 1997. Assisted initially by the architectural firm of Jackson and Ryan in updating the Venturi building plan of 1981, and subsequently by architects and engineers specializing in historic renovation at the Vitetta Group, the board of trustees approved the purchase of the Fidelity Building in the fall of 1999.[152] Perelman's gift of $15 million, made jointly with his wife, Ruth, was announced in January 2000 and applied to the purchase costs of the building, which in June of the same year was officially dedicated and named the Ruth and Raymond G. Perelman Building (fig. 271).

The acquisition, renovation, and expansion of the Perelman Building was the first of several distinct but overlapping phases of a comprehensive architectural master plan developed by the Vitetta Group in 2001 to address the Museum's need for space and building improvements over the next ten to fifteen years. As the "Museum's chief fundraiser and most eloquent advocate," trustee and media entrepreneur H. F. (Gerry) Lenfest (who succeeded Perelman as chairman of the board in 2001) became a driving force in realizing the master plan—with the support of private foundations (including his own Lenfest Foundation), the city of Philadelphia, and the commonwealth of Pennsylvania.[153] Independently and through their philanthropic arm, Lenfest and his wife, Marguerite, have been the largest individual monetary donors in the history of the Museum, supporting with unbounded generosity projects that have included an urgently needed off-site art storage facility, which was completed in 2004 and presently houses all of the Museum's furniture collections, including its modern and contemporary pieces.

For the opening of the Perelman Building in September 2007, I organized *Designing Modern*,[154] a chronological exhibition of design since 1920 as told by the Museum's collections. Roughly 150 examples from pivotal movements in the history of design—Art Deco and Bauhaus (1920–40), American and Scandinavian modernism (1940–60), Italian design (1960–80), and postmodernism (1980 to the present)—filled all 2,300 square feet of the new Collab Gallery, the largest space in the Museum's history to be permanently devoted to modern and contemporary design (figs. 272–79). Located in Gluckman Mayner's modern addition to the Perelman Building, the Collab Gallery also provided the Museum's first contemporary setting for contemporary work.

271. **Gluckman Mayner Architects**: Skylit Atrium, The Ruth and Raymond G. Perelman Building, Philadelphia Museum of Art

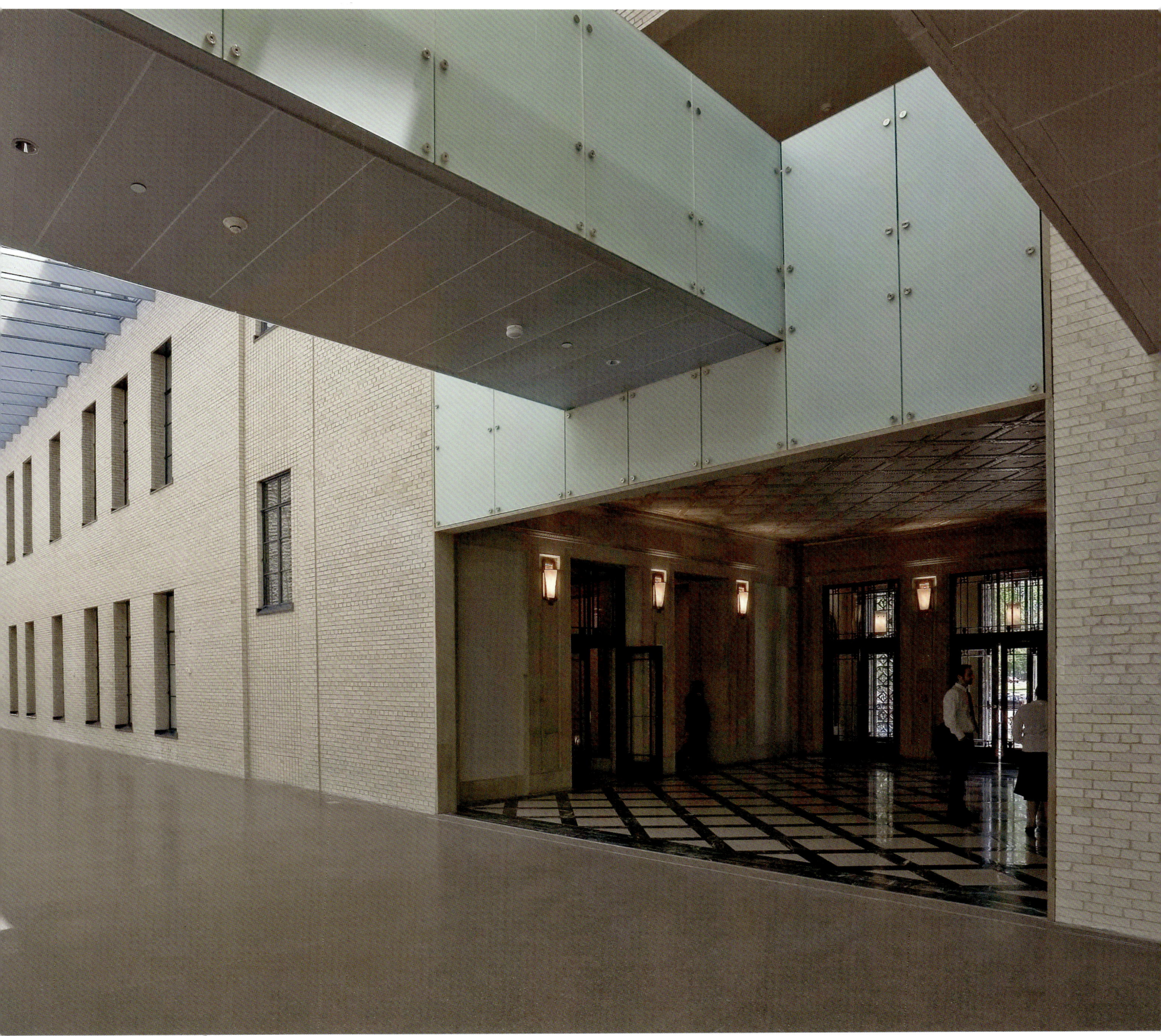

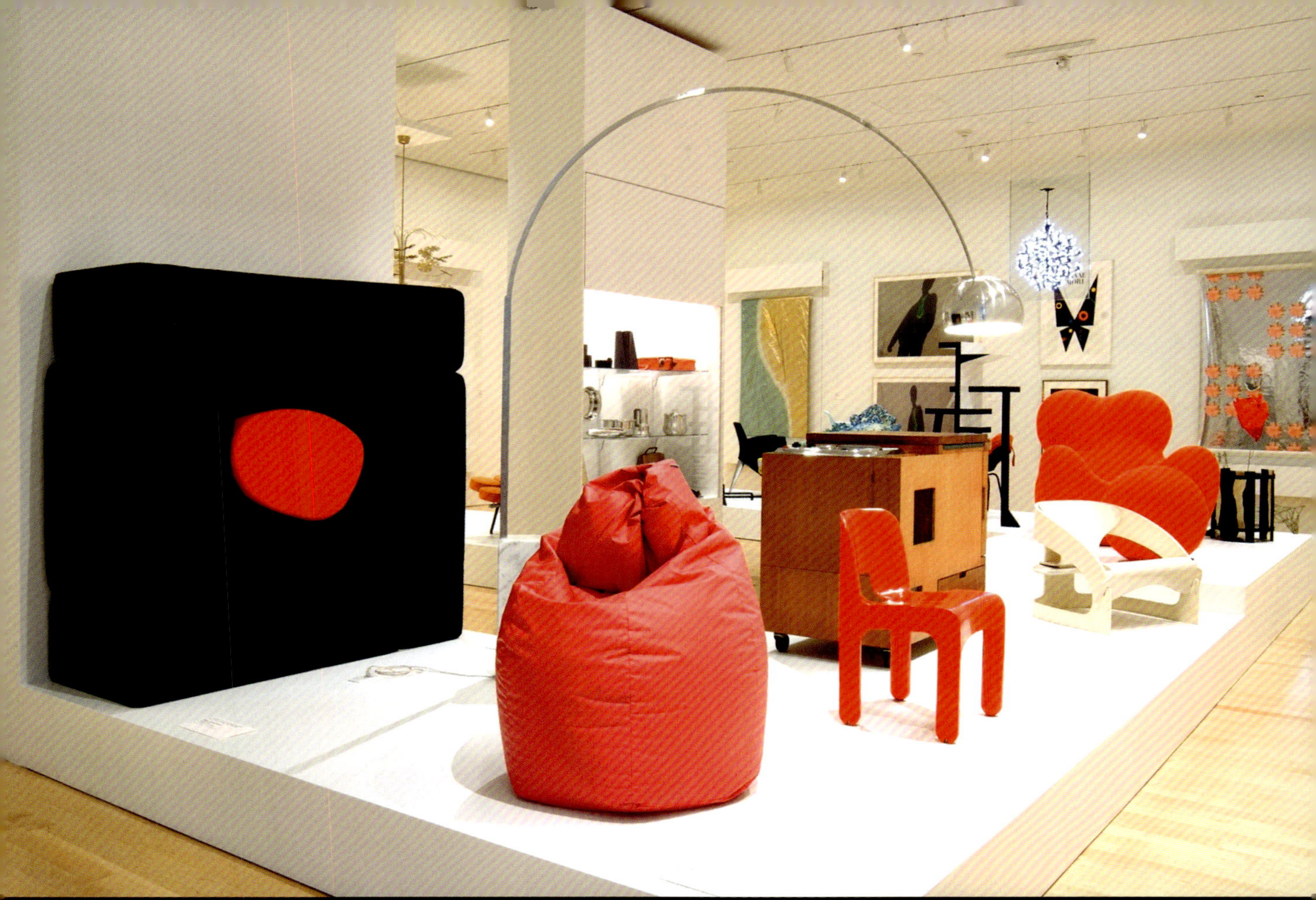

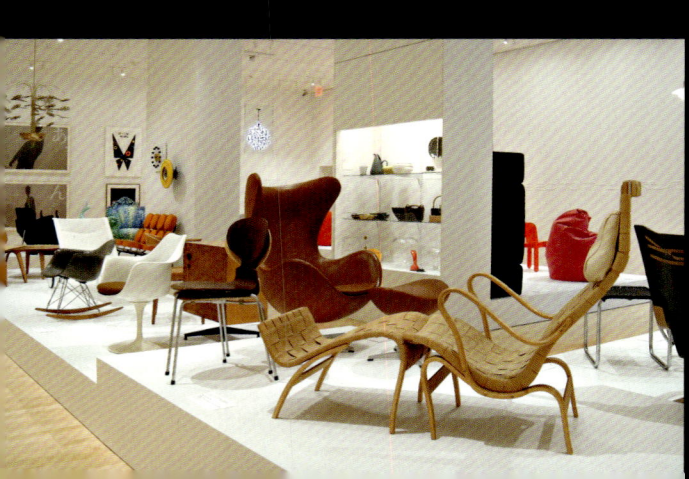
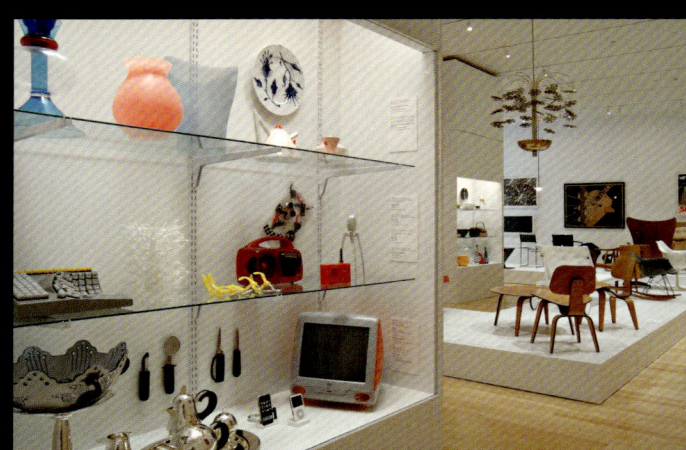

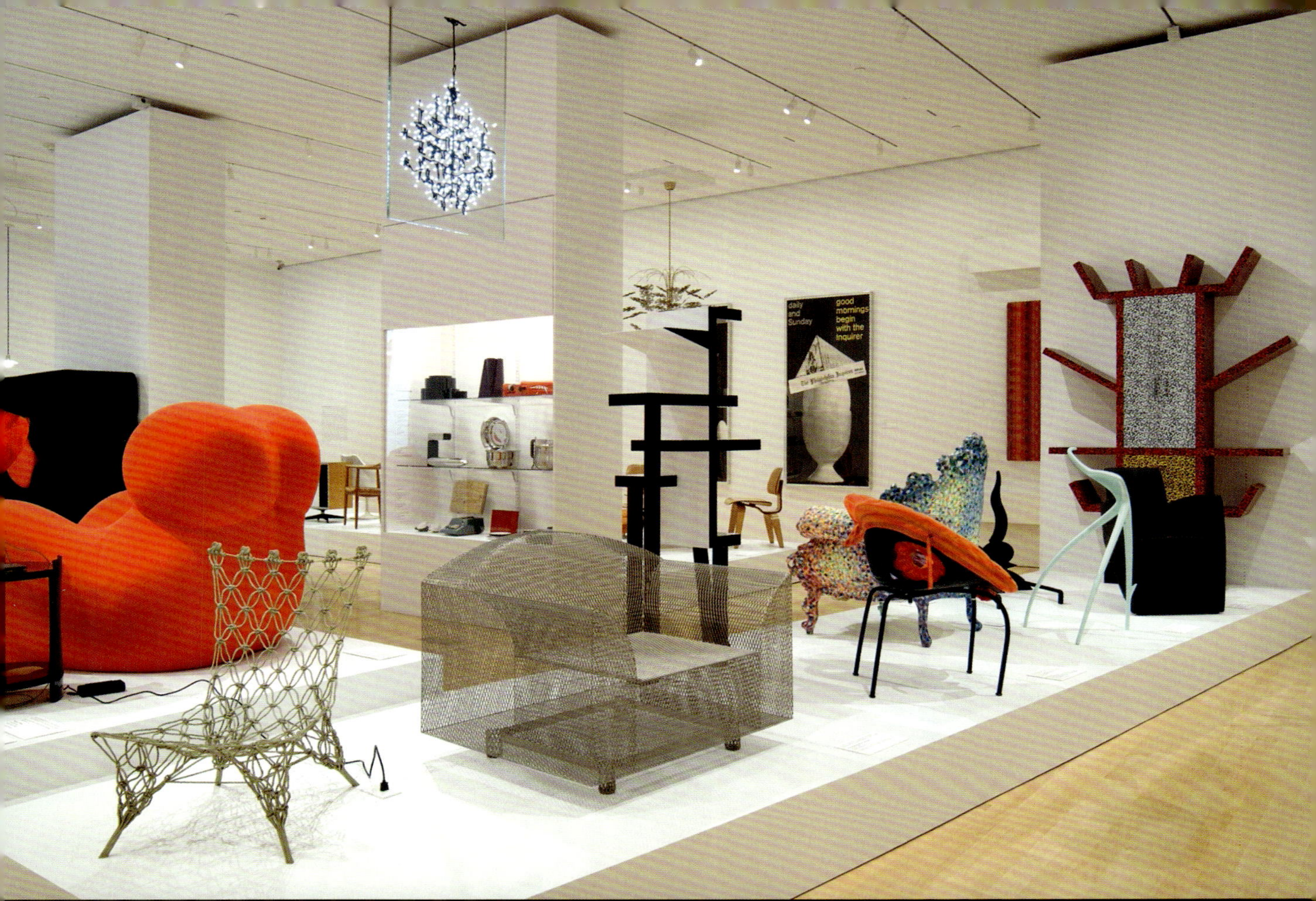

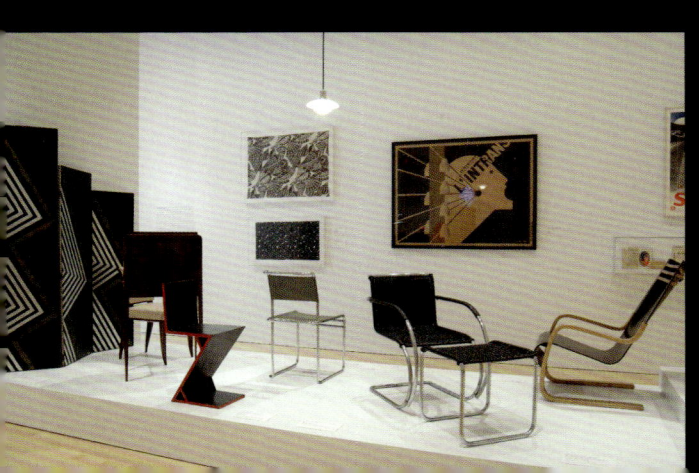
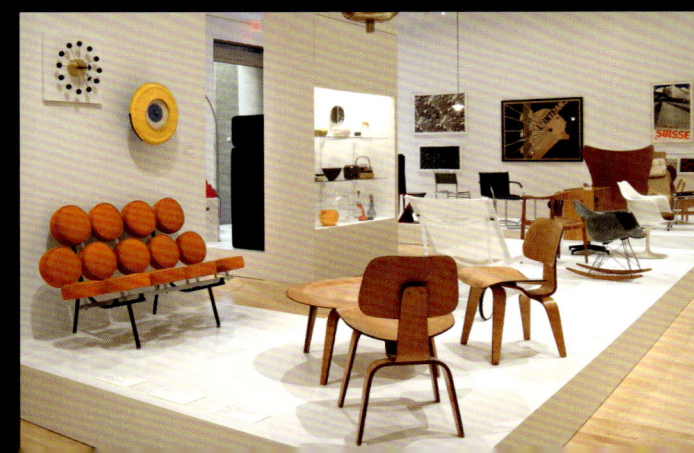

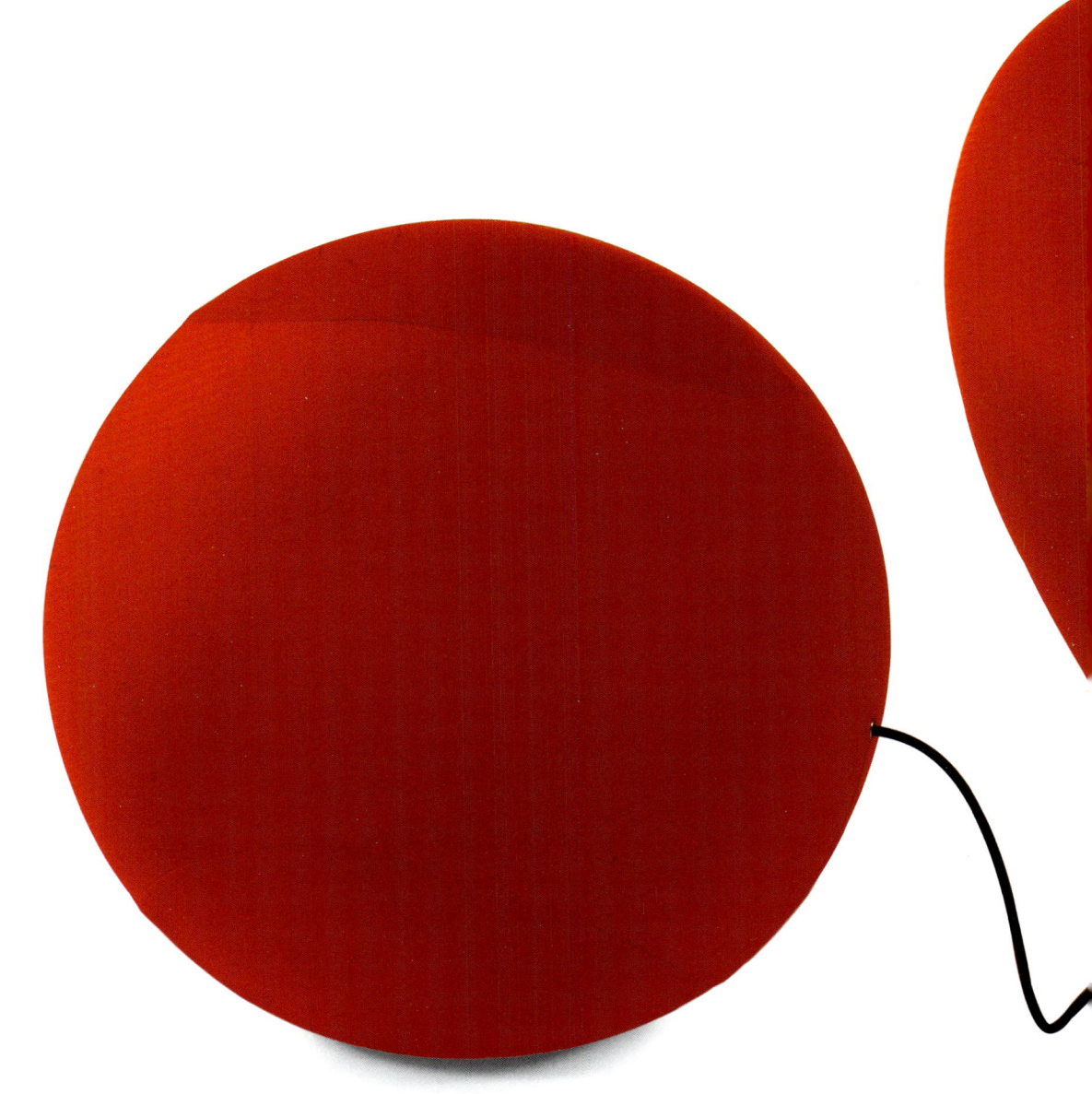

Designing Modern : 2007–8

278. Gaetano Pesce : for B & B Italia : *Up* 5 Chair and *Up* 6 Ottoman : 1969 : polyurethane foam, stretch jersey : H (chair) 40 1/2" : D (ottoman) 22 1/2" : 2000-151-1,2 (cat. 145)

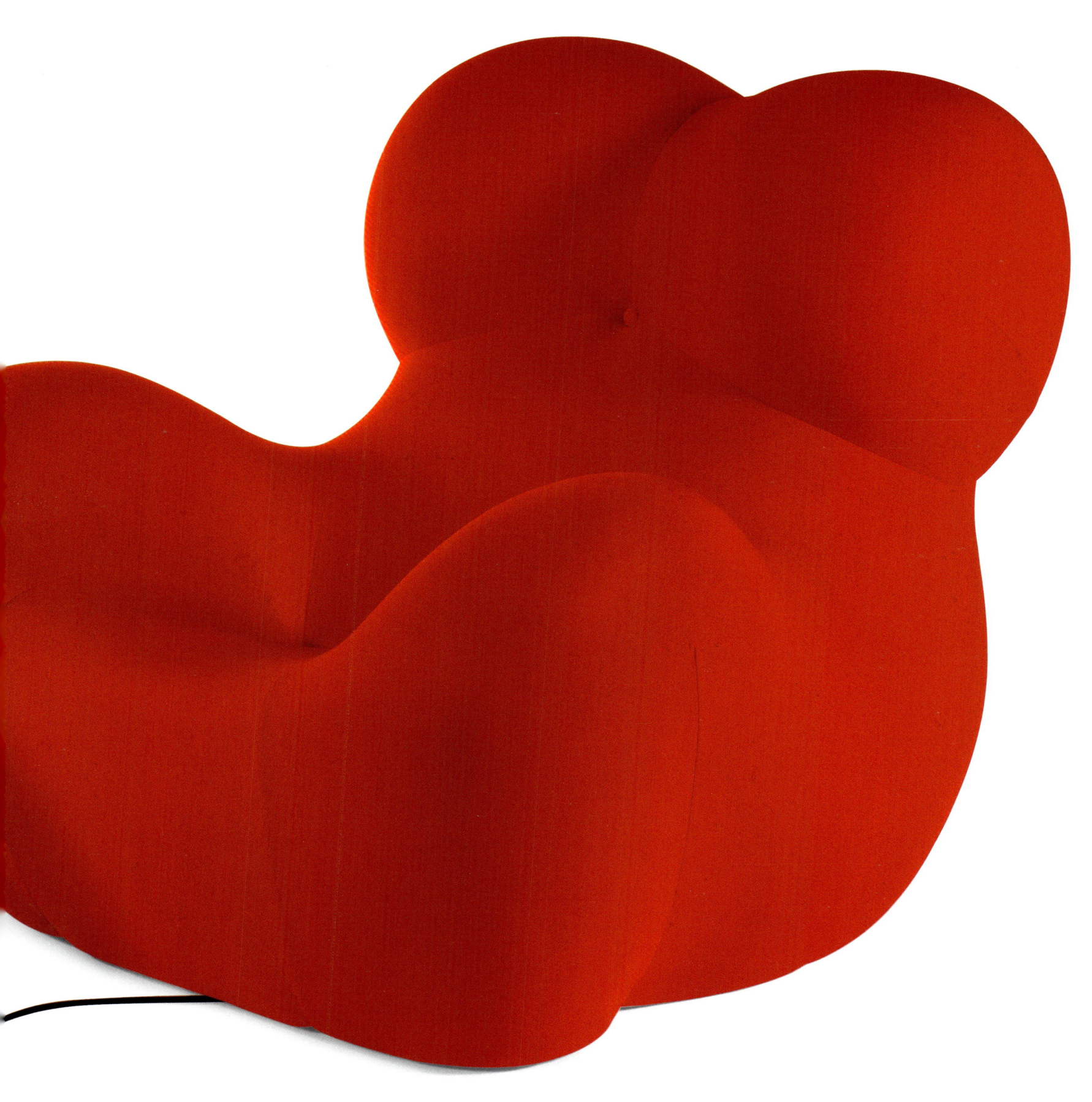

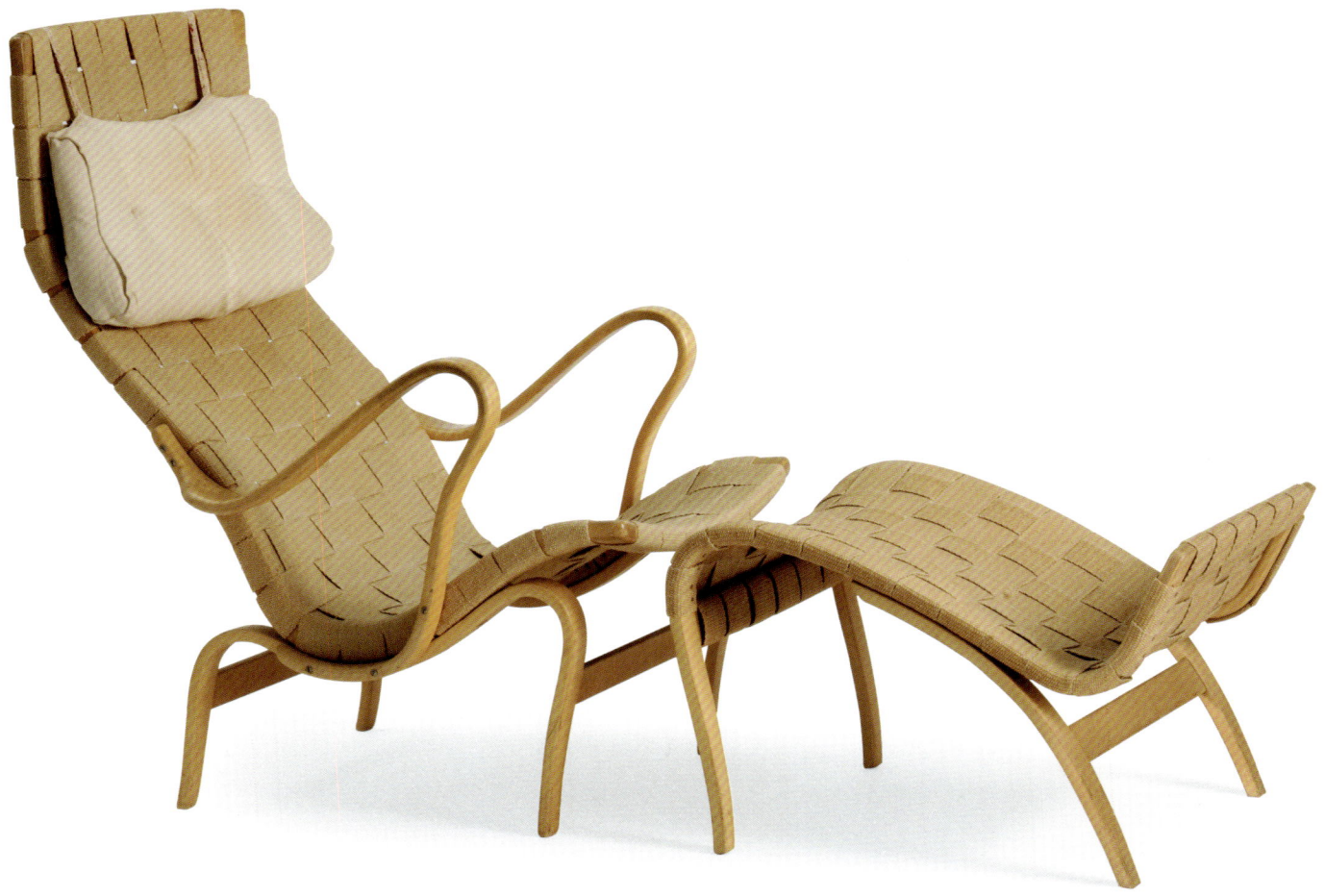

Most of the design objects on display had been acquired since 1970, providing visual evidence of Collab's role in fostering the rapid growth of the collections. The press was unanimously enthusiastic about the Museum's first public expansion since 1928, and about *Designing Modern* in particular. Calling it "the most variegated and visually energetic" of the exhibitions that inaugurated the building's opening, the *Philadelphia Inquirer* cited "a panoply of explosive color, seductive form and unconventional materials," offering "continuous enjoyment, especially for anyone old enough to remember when the more radical designs were introduced."[155] The *Wall Street Journal* discovered "the most excitement . . . among the furniture, kitchenware and gadgets at the Collab Gallery" and "a constant buzz of ecstatic exclamations, as visitors marveled that familiar everyday objects—from grandma's Eames chair, to mom's Chemex coffee carafe to sister's iPhone—were curator-certified treasures."[156] The exhibition displayed for the first time numerous recent acquisitions designed from the 1920s to the present, among them a Ruhlmann side chair (fig. 280) and vase, a travel poster by Herbert Matter (fig. 282), Bruno Mathsson's *Pernilla* chair and *Mifot* footstool (fig. 279), and Paul Rand's IBM rebus poster (fig. 283). The designs by Mathsson, Rand, and Maurer were gifts of Collab, the Rand poster in honor of Collab chair Lisa Benn. Collab 2007 was a celebration honoring Lisa Roberts, David Seltzer, and the new Collab Gallery (fig. 281). Honorary Design Excellence Awards were presented to Roberts and Seltzer, Cynthia Drayton (Collab's founder), and Gluckman Mayner Architects, represented by

Designing Modern : 2007–8

279. Bruno Mathsson : for Karl Mathsson : *Pernilla* Chair and *Mifot* Footstool : 1941–43 : laminated beech, bast fiber : H (chair) 39" : H (footstool) 17" : 2003-33-1,2 (cat. 119)

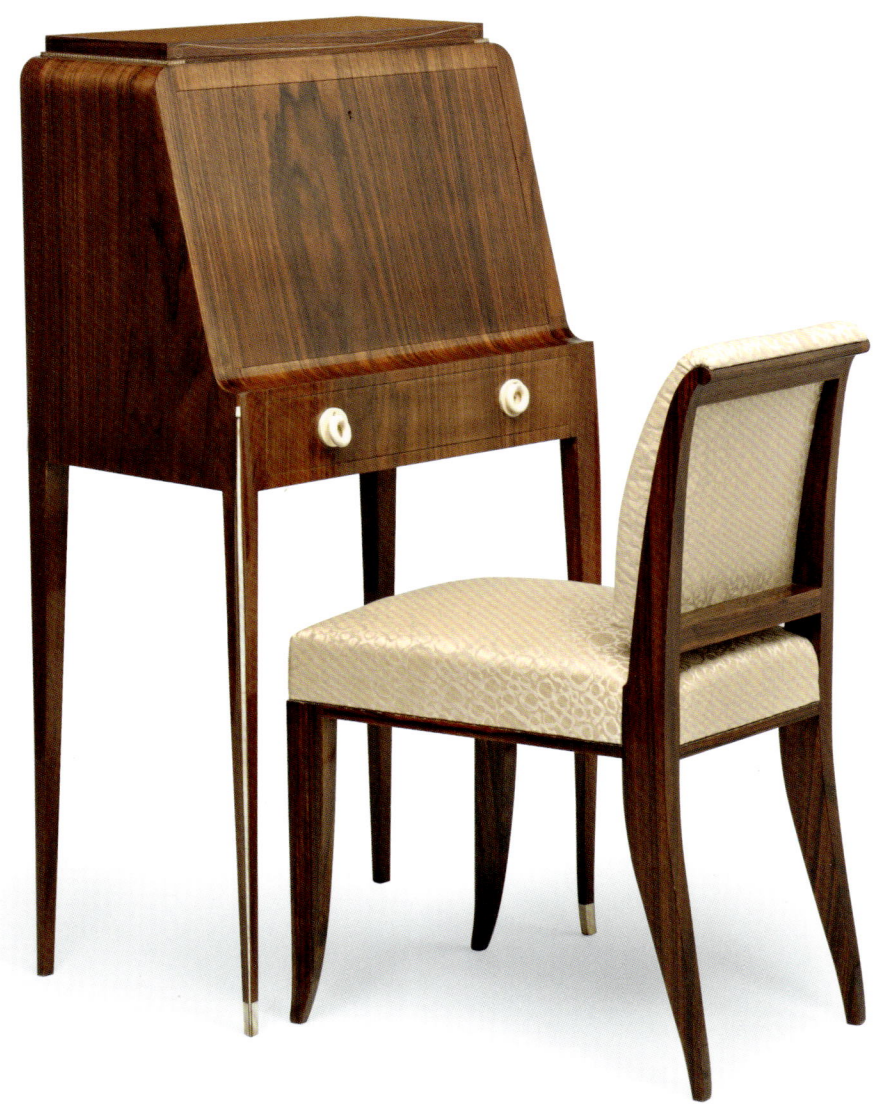

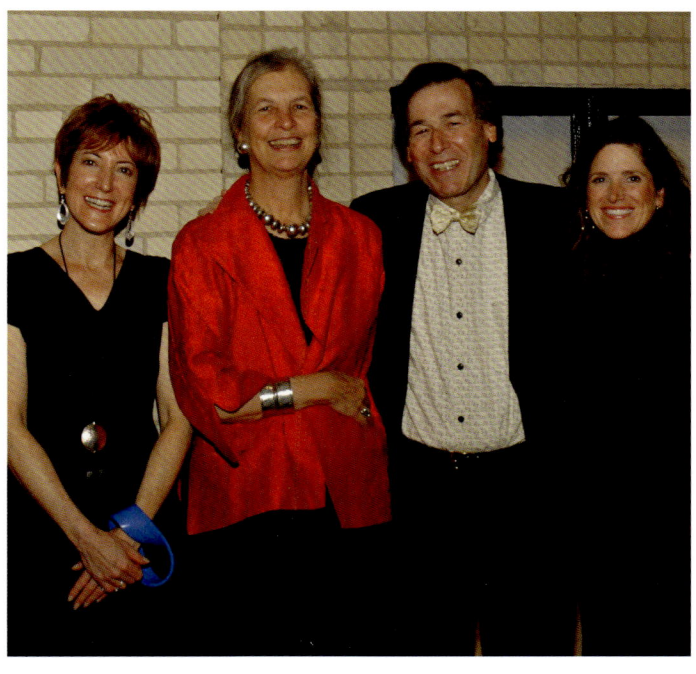

David Mayner. Afterward, Lisa Roberts wrote: "I'm just blown away. The building, the gallery, and the exhibit have all done our gift justice. . . . Your contribution, building modern and contemporary design at the [Museum] into a significant collection, will now have the opportunity to be seen, to be 'heard' and to make a difference. . . . Here's to our future together!"[157]

In conjunction with the opening of the Collab Gallery and the exhibition, information mapping was the theme of the Student Design Competition, which asked participants to map the history of modern design in the twentieth and twenty-first centuries. The winning project illustrated the development of modern chairs according to their formal characteristics.

Top : **280. Jacques-Émile Ruhlmann** : Chair : 1924 : rosewood, fabric upholstery : H 31⁷⁄₈" : 2006-77-1 (cat.164)   **Jacques-Émile Ruhlmann** : Writing Desk : c. 1925 : Macassar ebony, ivory, suede : H 44½" : 1976-227-1 (cat. 165)   Bottom : **281.** Left to right: Lisa Roberts, Anne d'Harnoncourt, David Seltzer, and Lisa Benn at Collab 2007

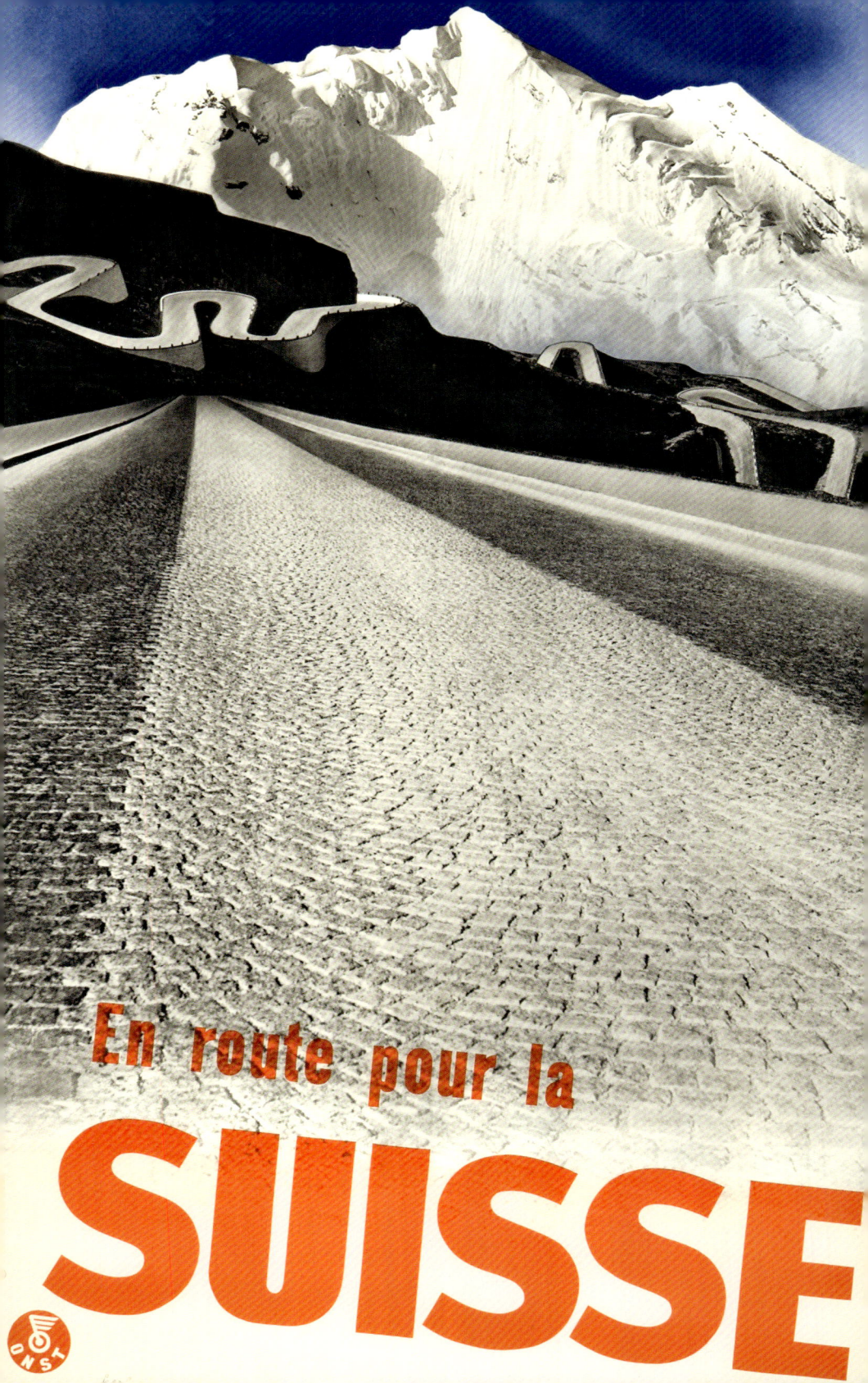

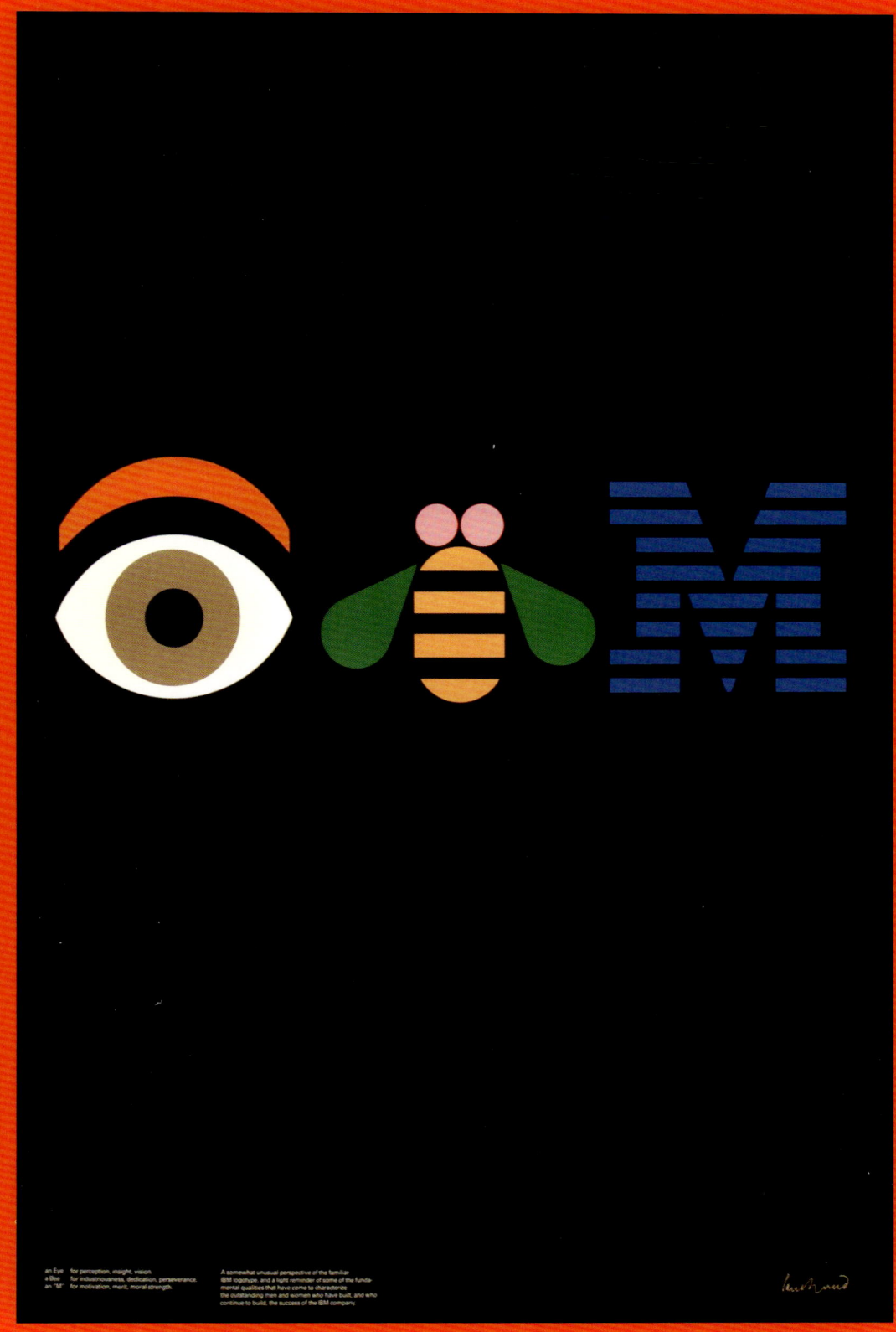

Designing Modern : 2007–8

Opposite : **282. Herbert Matter** : for Fretz Frères : *En route pour la Suisse (En Route to Switzerland)* Poster : 1935 : rotogravure : H 39 1/2" : 2003-71-1 (cat. 120)   Above : **283. Paul Rand** : for IBM : *IBM Rebus* Poster : 1981 : screenprint : H 36" : 2005-102-1 (cat. 154)

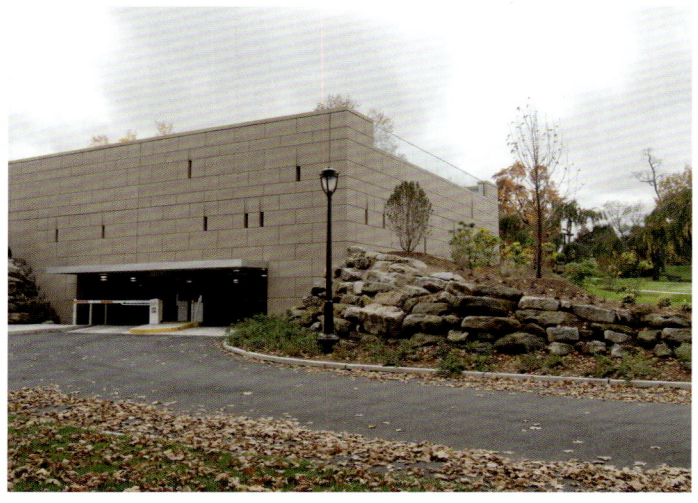
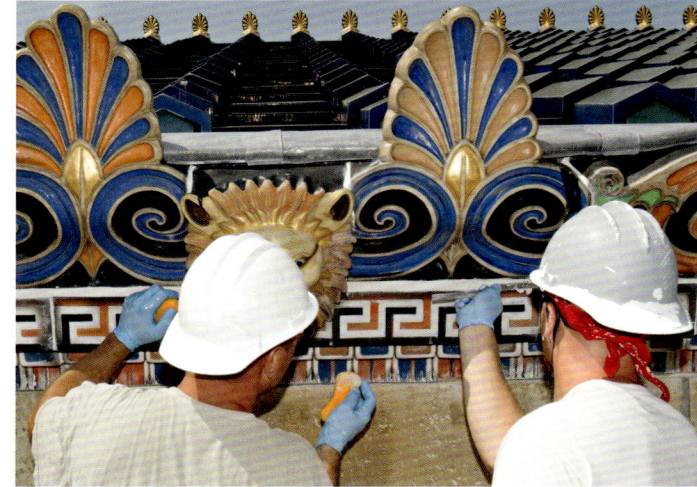

While the Museum scrambled to complete and open the Perelman Building, work on other phases of the master plan continued unabated, notably creation of a 400-car landscaped parking facility and sculpture garden (fig. 284) and restoration of the Museum's exterior facade and repair of the roof (fig. 285). In 2005 Gerry Lenfest had appointed trustees James Kise, Mark Rubenstein, Keith Sachs, and Marion Boulton Stroud to an ad hoc review committee for the selection of an architect who would undertake the crucial planning of the next phase of the master plan in the main building, including the creation of additional galleries and public spaces under the Museum's East Terrace, a new loading dock on the south facade of the building, and the expansion and upgrade of the Museum's central utility plant.[158] In September 2006, d'Harnoncourt reported to the trustees that the Museum would be actively and simultaneously managing four capital projects, each at a different stage of advancement.[159] A month later the Museum announced its selection of Frank O. Gehry as architect for the final phases of the master plan.[160]

Creating an exhibition around Gehry—to increase awareness of his work among Philadelphia and regional residents—seemed an obvious choice for Collab 2008. With the help of Jack Schlechter and his colleague Kathryn E. Higgins, I organized *Frank O. Gehry: Design Process and the Lewis House*,[161] an exhibition exploring a unique decade-long project (1985–95) in which the architect experimented with and ultimately achieved the formal and technological breakthroughs that characterized his later architectural and commercial work. Gehry tested many different materials through phases of this unbuilt project, constantly reevaluating his forms and compositions. Envisioning wood strips as a material that is both structural and flexible, in 1989–91 Gehry developed a series of bentwood chairs for Knoll that also were included in the exhibition: the *Cross Check* armchair, which had earlier been given to the Museum by Collab, and the *High Sticking* and *Power Play* chairs (figs. 287, 288). Gehry's abstract plastic-resin furniture for Heller and products for Alessi and Tiffany were also included in the show—his Heller pieces, *Pito* teakettle, and ceramic *Rock* and *Torque* vases as gifts of Collab. In conjunction with the exhibition Vitra gave the Museum Gehry's corrugated-cardboard *Beaver* armchair and ottoman, dyed red (fig. 289). From trustee Marion Boulton Stroud came the most important individual gift to the Museum's modern and contemporary design collections in recent history—Gehry's sculptural *Fish* lamp, fabricated of ColorCore, wood, and silicone (fig. 286). A popular and critical success, the exhibition was described as "a mini-retrospective illuminating Gehry's now familiar but no less pathbreaking design aesthetic,"[162] and as offering visitors "a compelling insight into the career and creativity of a highly gifted man."[163]

Above, left to right : **284.** The Museum's landscaped parking facility : 2009   **285.** Restoration of the Museum's building on Fairmount : 2008

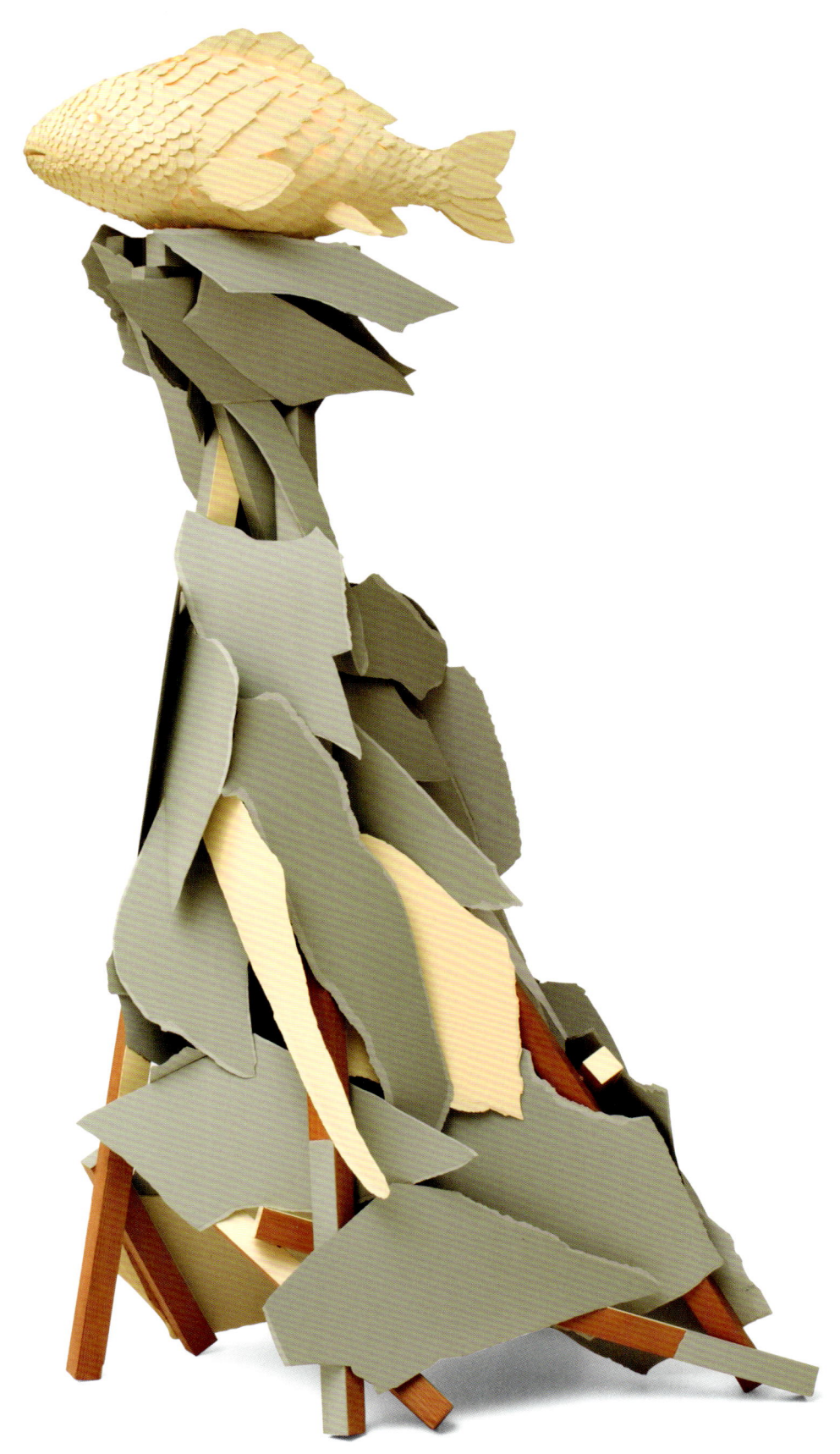

Frank O. Gehry : Design Process and the Lewis House : 2008–9
286. Frank O. Gehry : for New City Editions : *Fish* Lamp : c. 1983 : ColorCore, wood, silicone : H 5' 8 1/2" : 2008-263-1 (cat. 68)

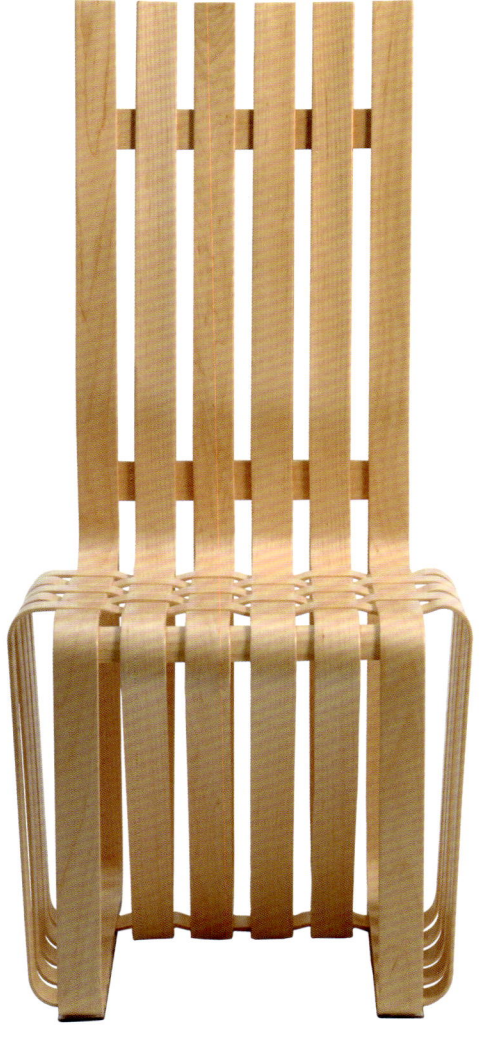
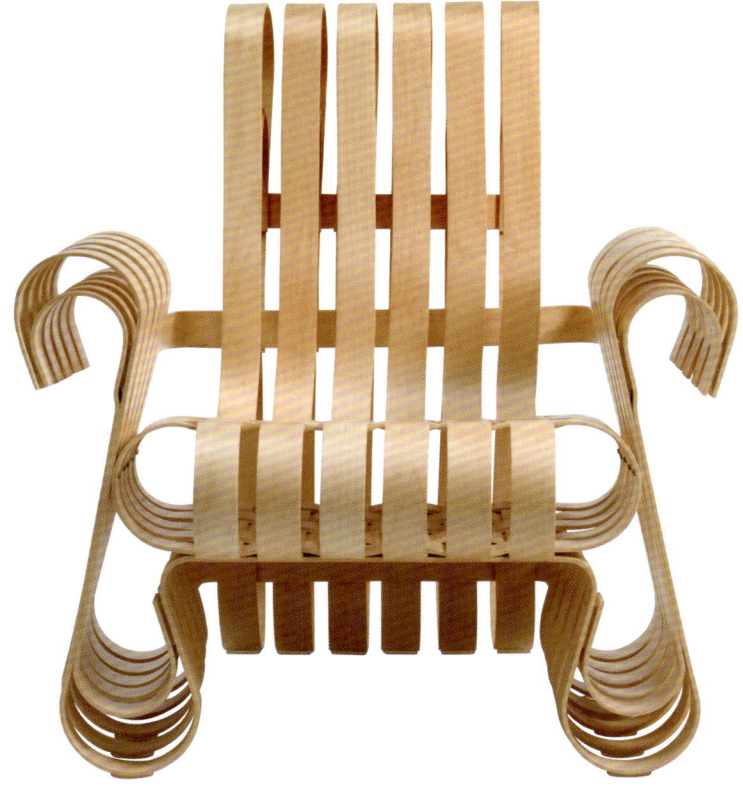

Tragically, Anne d'Harnoncourt, who dreamed the master plan this exhibition celebrated, never saw it. She had died unexpectedly in June 2008. In a message to the board of trustees, Gerry Lenfest and Gail Harrity (who became the Museum's interim chief executive officer following d'Harnoncourt's death) wrote: "As we mourn our great loss, it is also helpful to celebrate all that Anne gave us through almost four decades at the Philadelphia Museum of Art."[164] When earlier asked for an acquisitions "wish list" in connection with the master plan, d'Harnoncourt's "first response" was "contemporary art . . . because it's important to have contemporary expressions in all the fields in which we collect."[165]

In the months following d'Harnoncourt's sudden death in 2008, many works of art were given to the Museum in her memory, including a handsome stainless-steel vase of 2005 designed by Massimiliano Fuksas and Doriana Mandrelli for Alessi. The department redoubled its efforts to promote design at the Museum, dividing the Collab Gallery into two spaces after the Gehry exhibition closed in the spring of 2009 to make possible the presentation of two different exhibitions drawn from the collections. Donna Corbin organized *A Taste for the Modern: The Jeanne Rymer Gift of Twentieth-Century Chairs*,[166] celebrating the gift to the Museum through Collab of a collection assembled by Jeanne S. Rymer, retired professor and head of the interior

Frank O. Gehry : Design Process and the Lewis House : 2008–9

Above and opposite, left to right : **287. Frank O. Gehry** : for Knoll : *High Sticking* Chair : 1989–91 : laminated maple : H 43 3/8" : 2008-171-3 (cat. 71) **288. Frank O. Gehry** : for Knoll : *Power Play* Chair : 1989–91 : laminated maple : H 32 7/8" : 2008-171-1 (cat. 70) **289. Frank O. Gehry** : for Vitra : *Red Beaver* Armchair : 1986 : dyed corrugated cardboard : H 33 3/4" : 2009-58-3 (cat. 69)

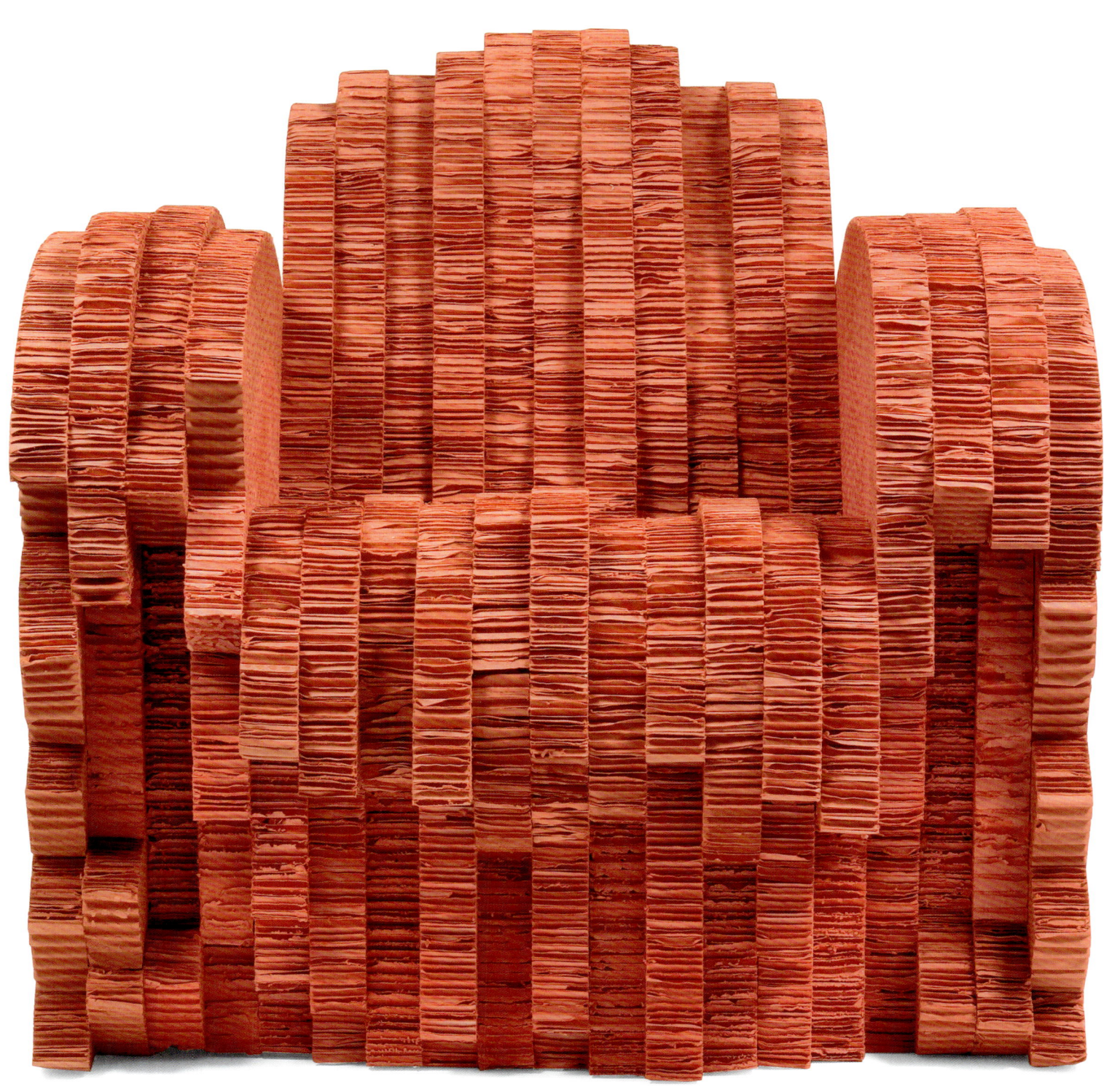

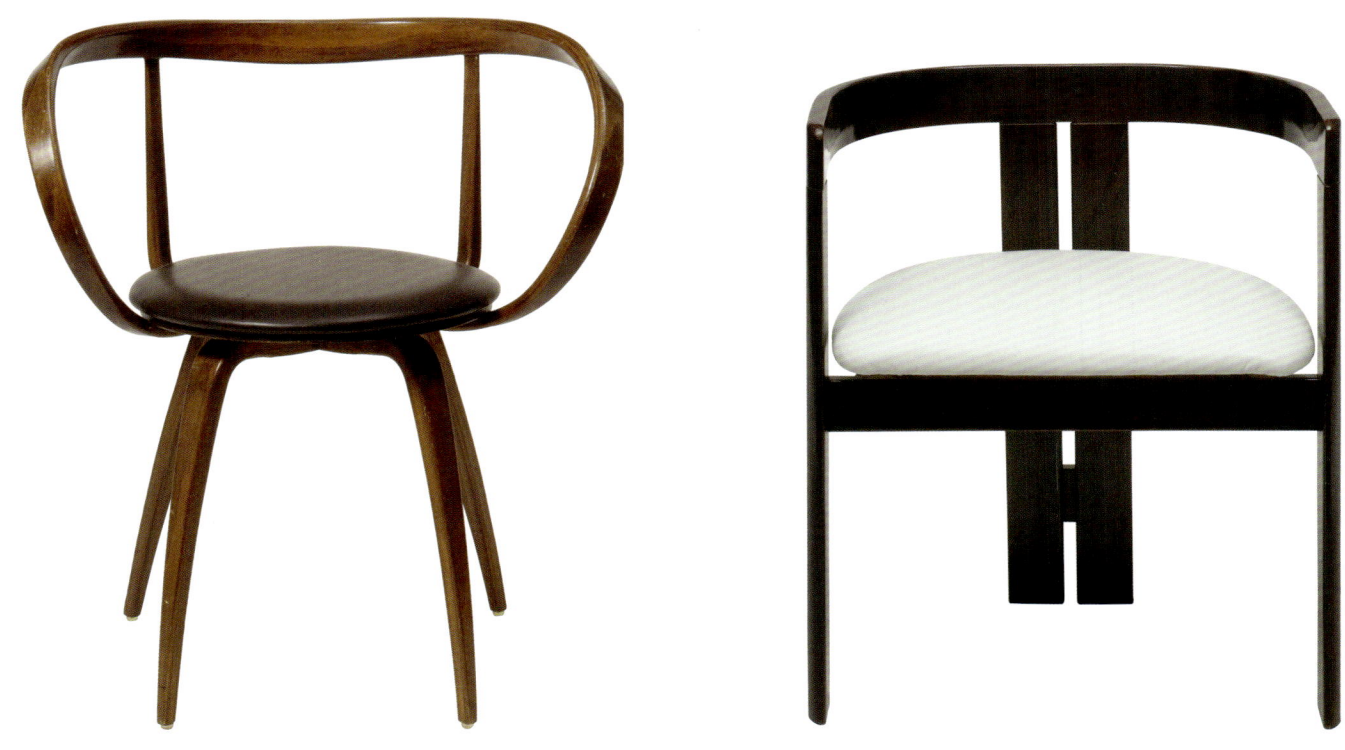

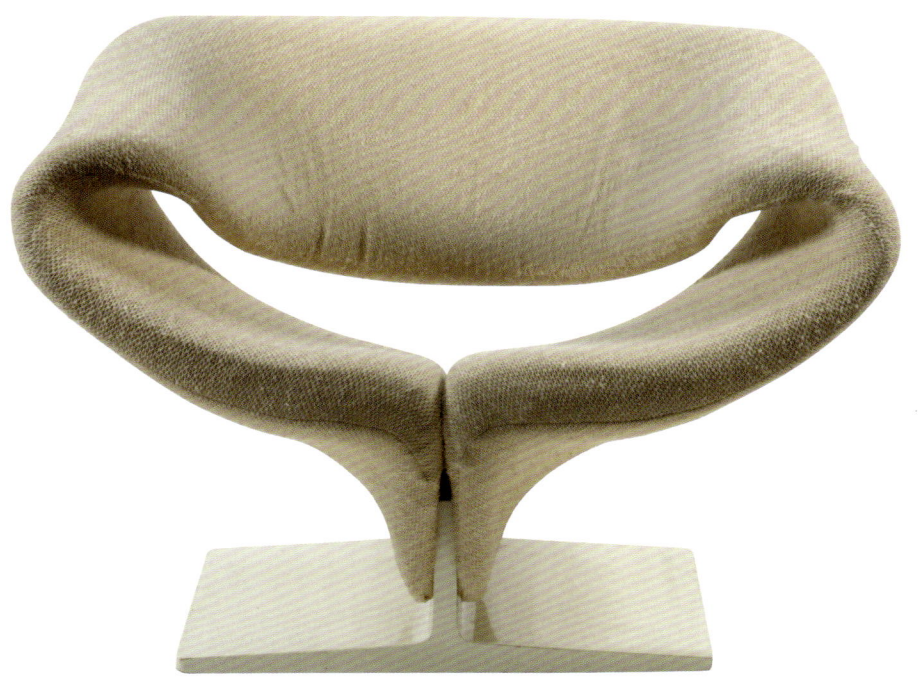

A Taste for the Modern : The Jeanne Rymer Gift of Twentieth-Century Chairs : 2009

Clockwise, from top left : **290. George Nelson with John F. Pile** : for Herman Miller : *Pretzel* Chair : 1957 : birch-faced laminated wood, leather : H 31" : 2007-186-28 (cat. 135)   **291. Tobia Scarpa** : for Gavina : *Pigreco* Armchair : c. 1956 : wood, cotton : H 27" : 2007-186-15 (cat. 171)   **292. Pierre Paulin** : for Artifort : *Ribbon* Chair #582 : 1965 : rubber, metal, acrylic, wood, fabric : H 27½" : 2007-186-18 (cat. 144)

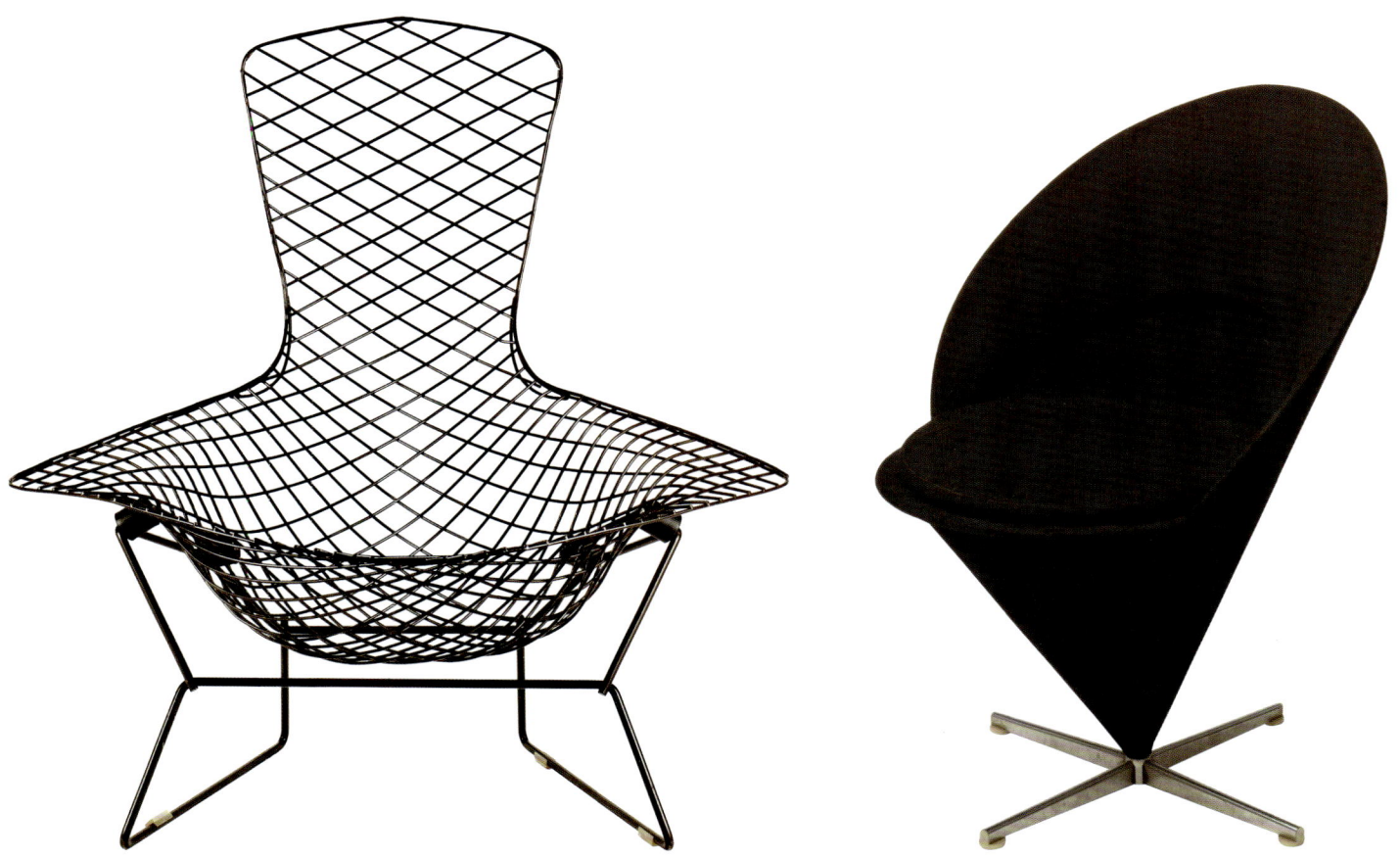

design program at the University of Delaware (figs. 290–94). In the other section of the Collab Gallery, *Visual Delight: Ornament and Pattern in Modern and Contemporary Design*[167] was organized by Diane Minnite around contemporary designers' fascination with embellishment; it included several new acquisitions, among them gifts from Collab and others as well as several manufacturers (figs. 295–301). At the same time, I organized the Museum's first outdoor exhibition on the Perelman Building's Café Terrace. *Richard Schultz: Five Decades of Design* featured a small selection of works created by the outdoor-furniture designer (fig. 302).[168] In conjunction with the exhibition, Schultz delivered Collab's 2009 spring lecture.

The *Philadelphia Inquirer* published a major review celebrating the designer and his classic furniture, a number of pieces of which entered the collection as gifts of Schultz (fig. 303).[169]

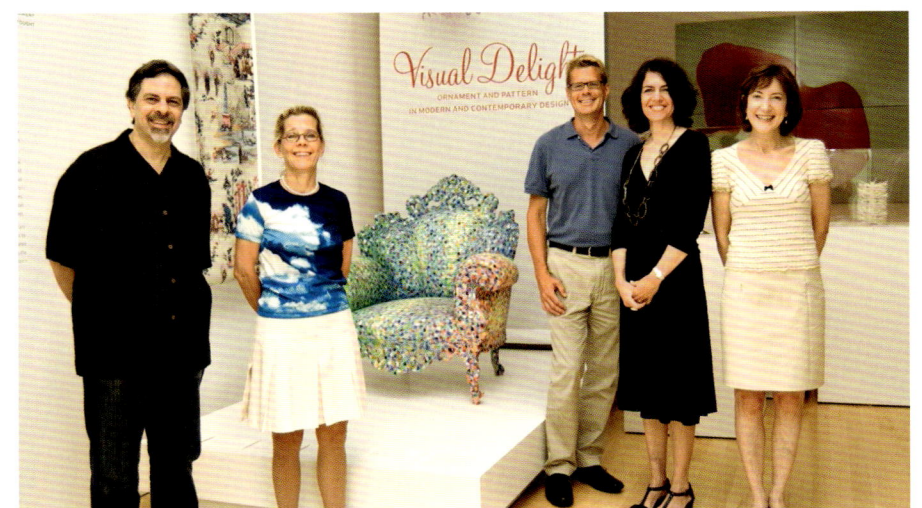

Top, left to right : **293. Harry Bertoia** : for Knoll : High-Backed Chair : 1950–52 : steel : H 38" : 2007-186-33 (cat. 19)   **294. Verner Panton** : for Plus-Linje : *Cone* Chair : 1958 : steel, wool upholstery : H 32" : 2007-186-13 (cat. 142)   **295.** Bottom, left to right : Collab member Robert Aibel, Associate Curator Donna Corbin, Collab Chair Neil Sandvold, Research Assistant Diane (Dee) L. Minnite, and Collab member Lisa S. Roberts

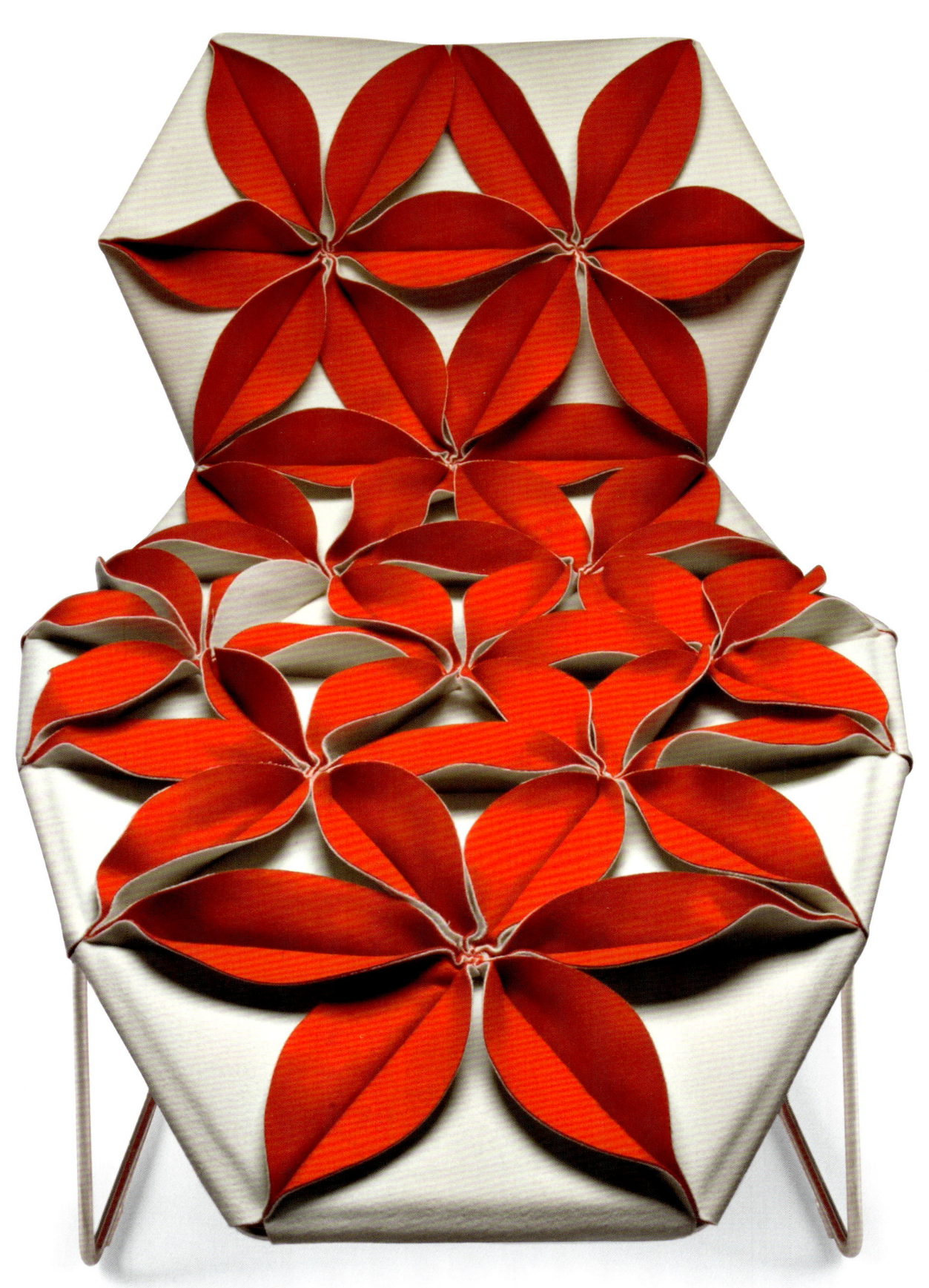

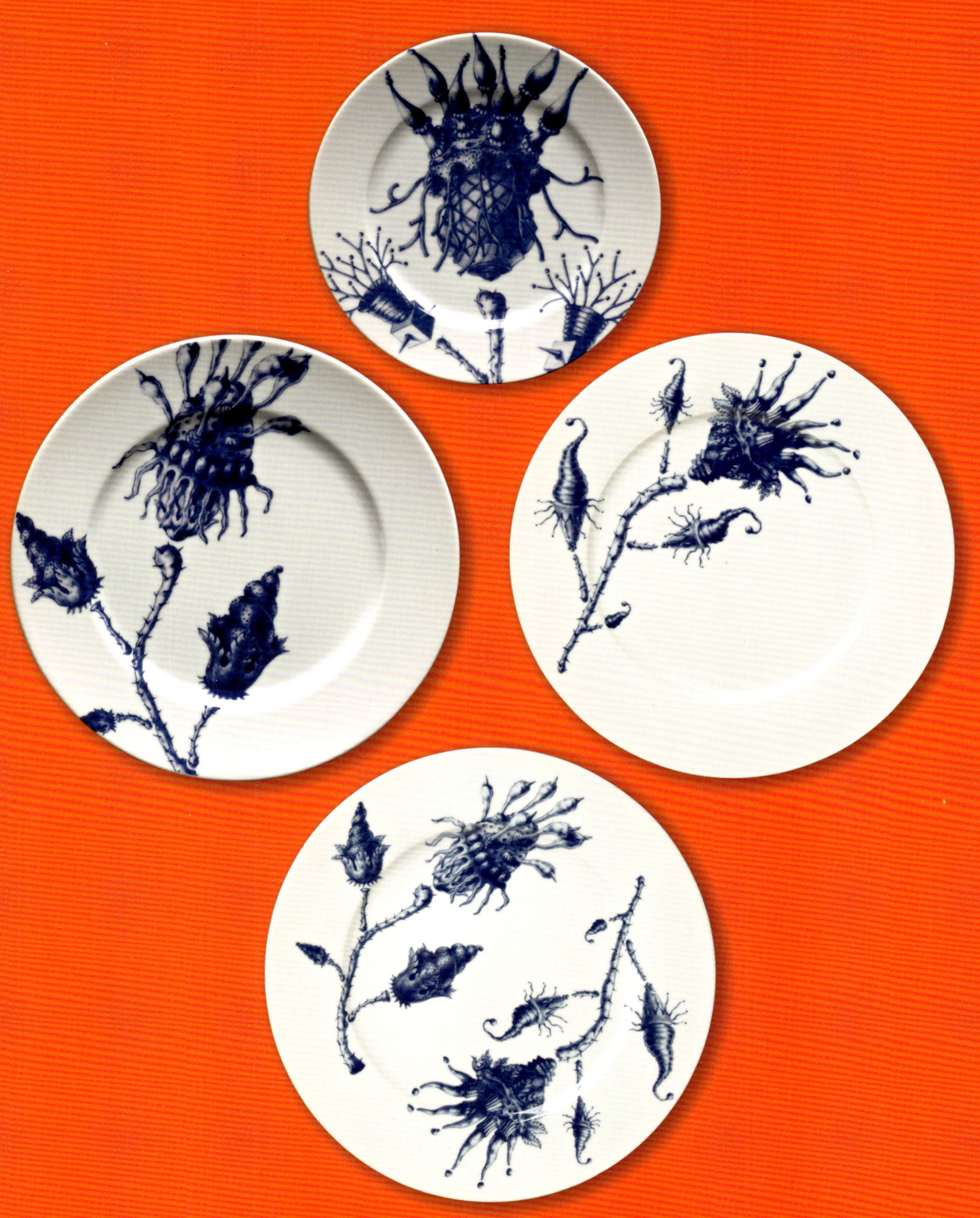

Visual Delight : Ornament and Pattern in Modern and Contemporary Design : 2009

Opposite : **296. Patricia Urquiola** : for Moroso : *Antibodi* Chaise : 2006 : stainless steel, PVC plastic, polyurethane, felt : L 5' 1 13/16" : 2008-57-1 (cat. 196)   Above : **297–300. Elizabeth Garouste and Mattia Bonetti** : for Porzellanmanufaktur Reichenbach and Anthologie Quartett : Plates from *Étrange Végetation* : 1992 : porcelain : D (large dinner plate, bottom) 11 13/16" : 2004-141-2,3,4,9 (cat. 64–67)

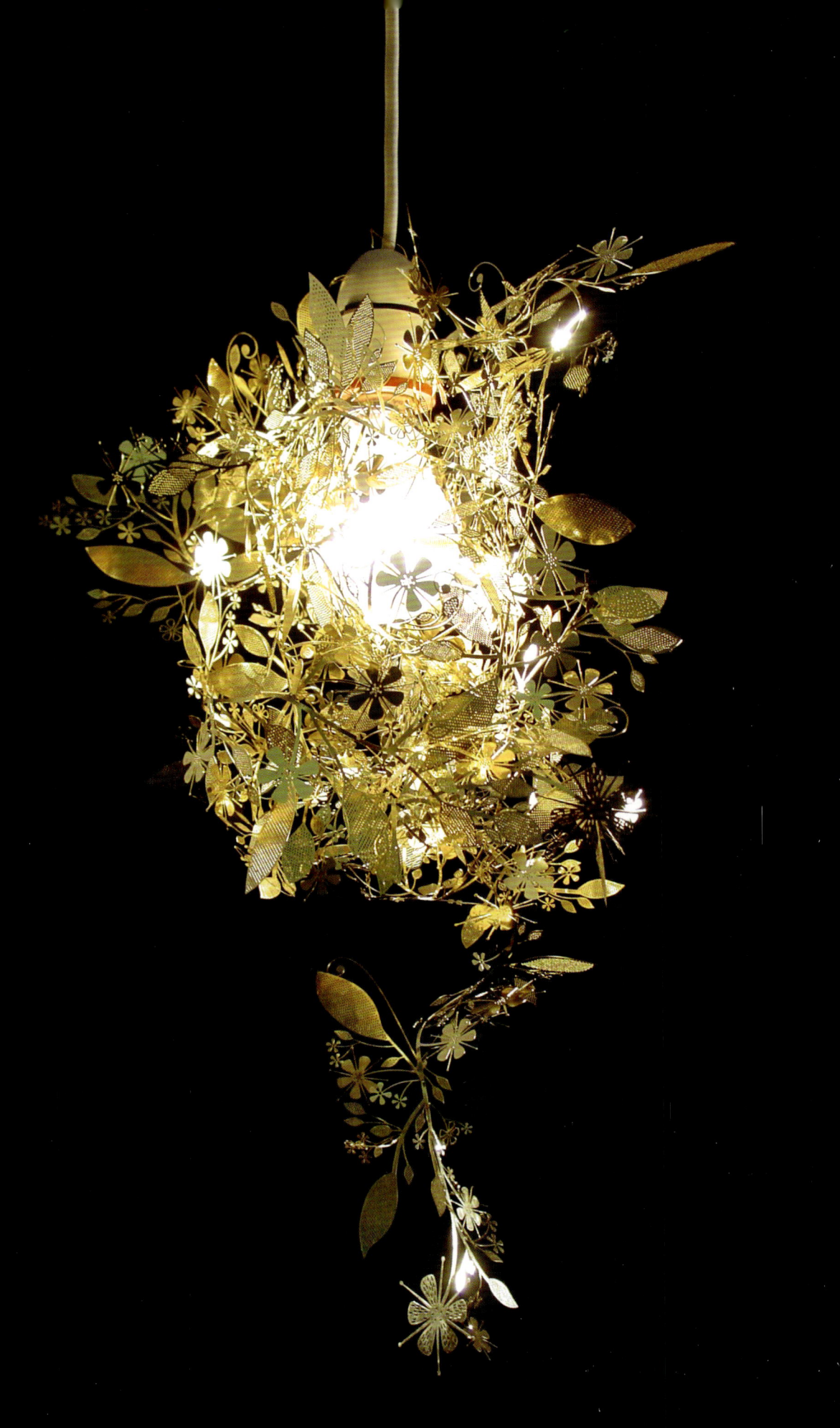

Visual Delight : Ornament and Pattern in Modern and Contemporary Design : 2009

301. Tord Boontje : for Artecnica : *Midsummer* Light : 2004 : Tyvek : H 30" : 2008-178-3 (cat. 22)

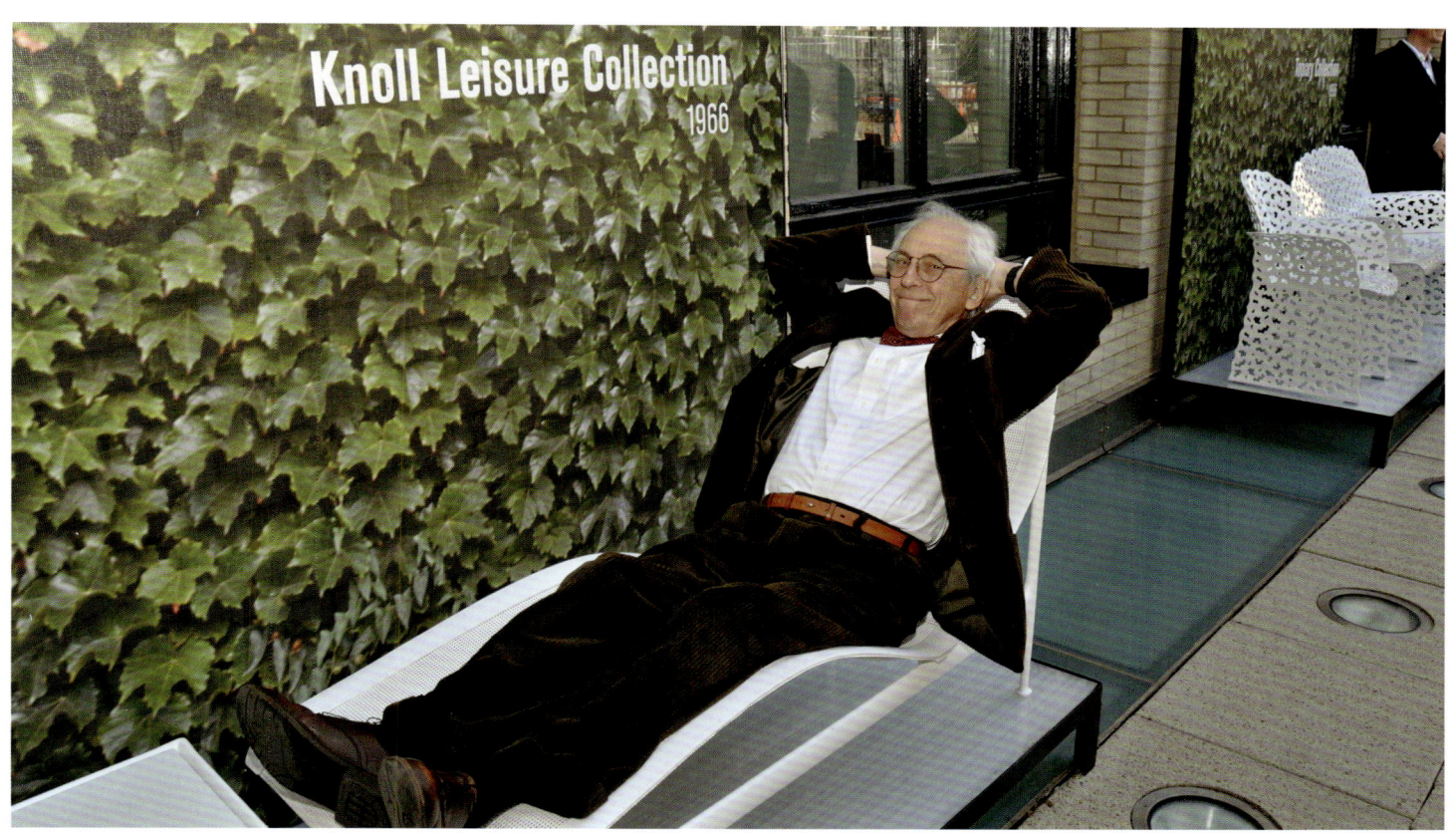

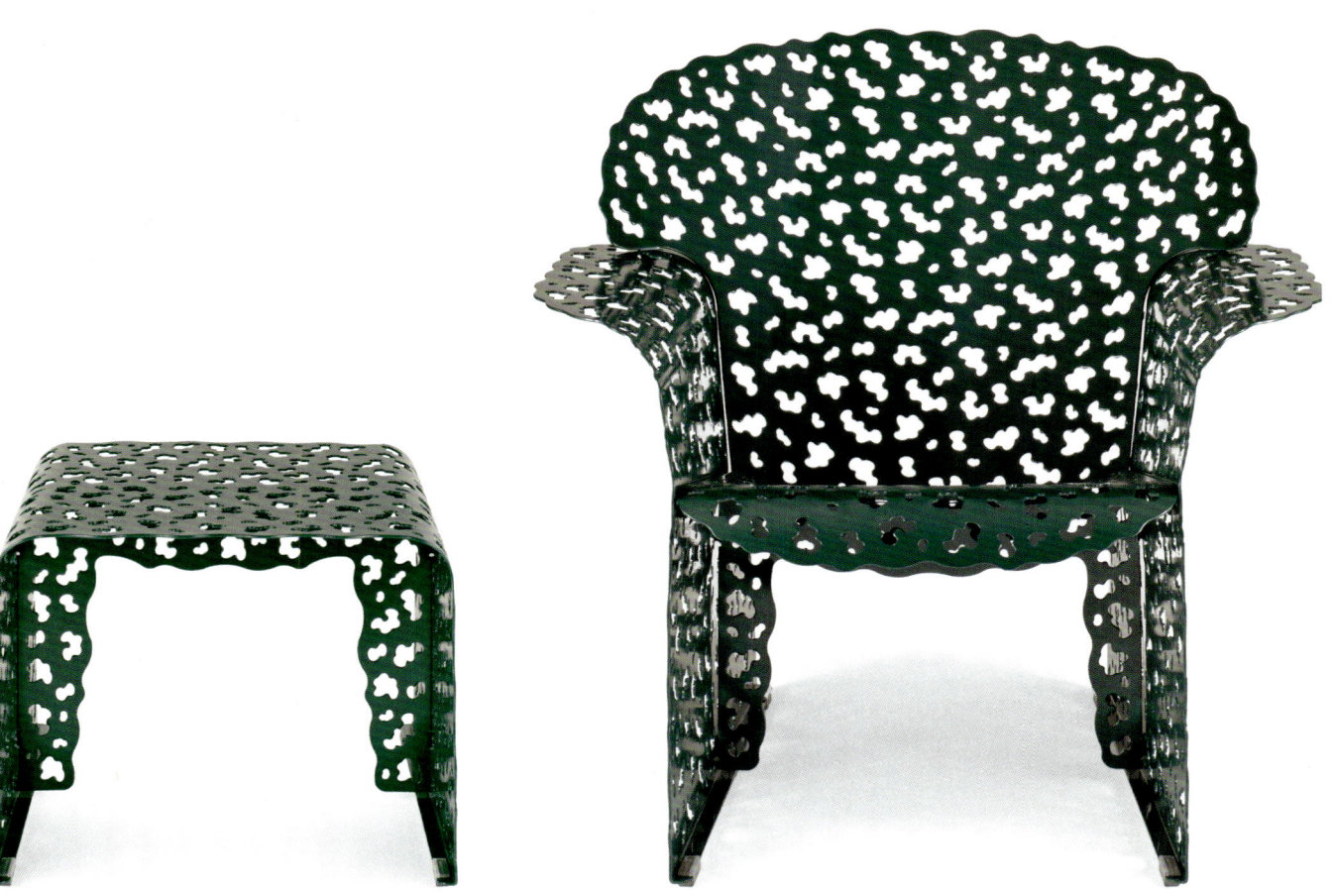

Richard Schultz : Five Decades of Design : 2009

Top : **302.** Richard Schultz at the exhibition   Bottom, left and right : **303. Richard Schultz** : for Richard Schultz Design : *Topiary* Lounge Chair and Ottoman : 1988 : aluminum with epoxy polyester powder coating : H (chair) 30 1/2" : H (ottoman) 15" : 2006-119-1,2 (cat. 175)

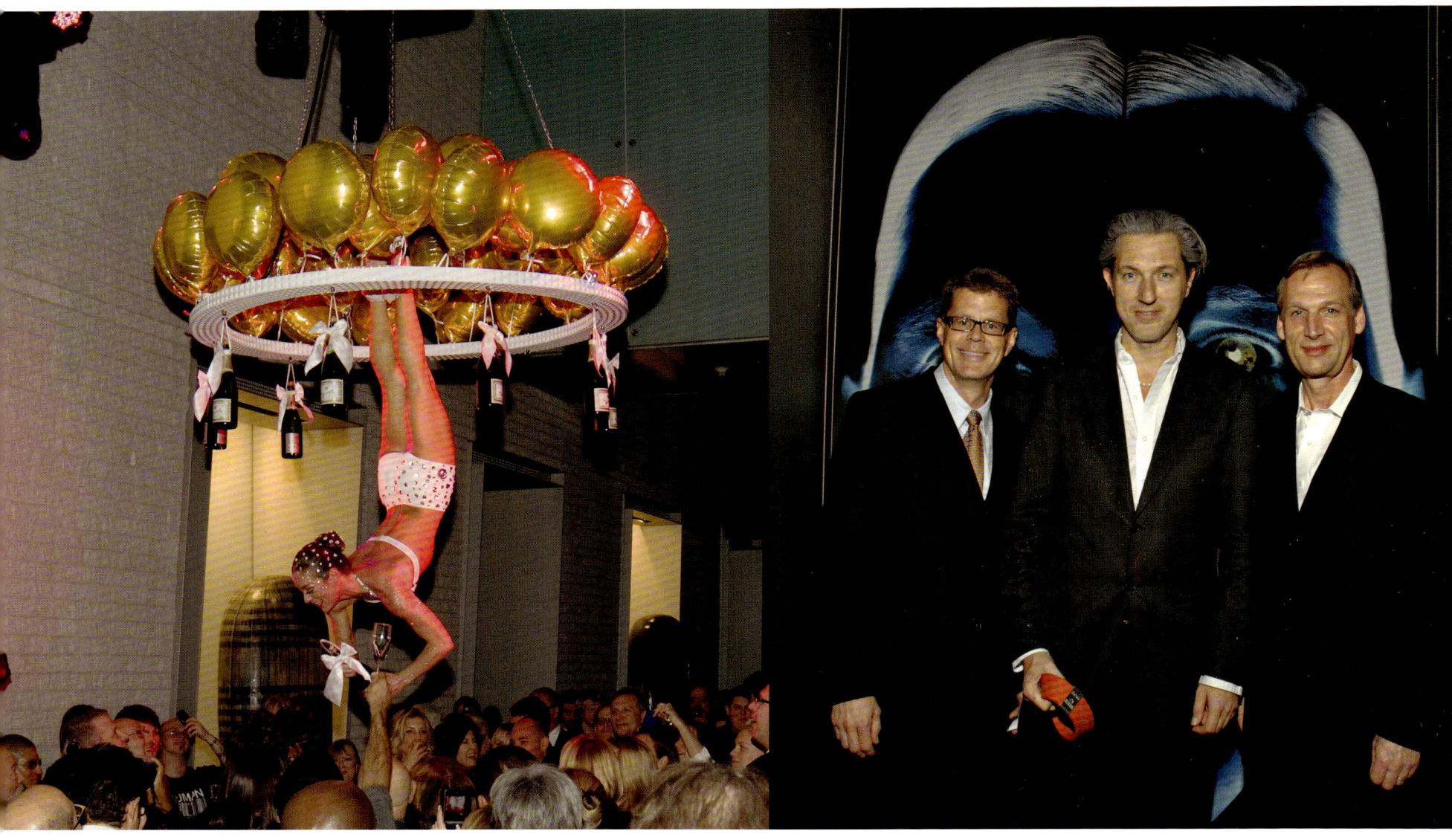

In June 2009, while modern and contemporary design was enjoying unprecedented visibility in these three simultaneous exhibitions, the Museum's board of trustees announced the election of Timothy Rub, at the time director of the Cleveland Museum of Art, as the institution's thirteenth director, succeeding the late Anne d'Harnoncourt.[170] Like Edwin Atlee Barber and Fiske Kimball generations earlier, Rub brought to the directorship a record of work, publications, and interest in the fields of decorative arts and architecture, with a particular taste for modernism. Trained at Middlebury College (B.A.) and New York University (M.A.), he served as curator at the Cooper-Hewitt Museum from 1983 to 1987, where he organized the exhibition *Vienna/New York: The Work of Joseph Urban*—described by the *New York Times* as "comprehensive . . . and unusually rich in the objects it contains."[171]

To the delight of Philadelphia's architecture and design community, the Museum's new director led a standing ovation for Dutch designer Marcel Wanders, the recipient of the Design Excellence Award at Collab 2009 (fig. 305), and at the reception afterward participated enthusiastically in the performance piece *Happy Hour Chandelier*, designed and conceived by Nanette Linning and Wanders (fig. 304).

Marcel Wanders : Daydreams : 2009–10

Above and opposite, left to right : **304.** *Happy Hour Chandelier* : 2009 : a performance piece conceived and designed by Nanette Linning and Marcel Wanders   **305.** Timothy Rub (right), named Museum director in 2009, with Neil Sandvold (left) and Marcel Wanders (center) at the exhibition opening   **306.** Gallery view

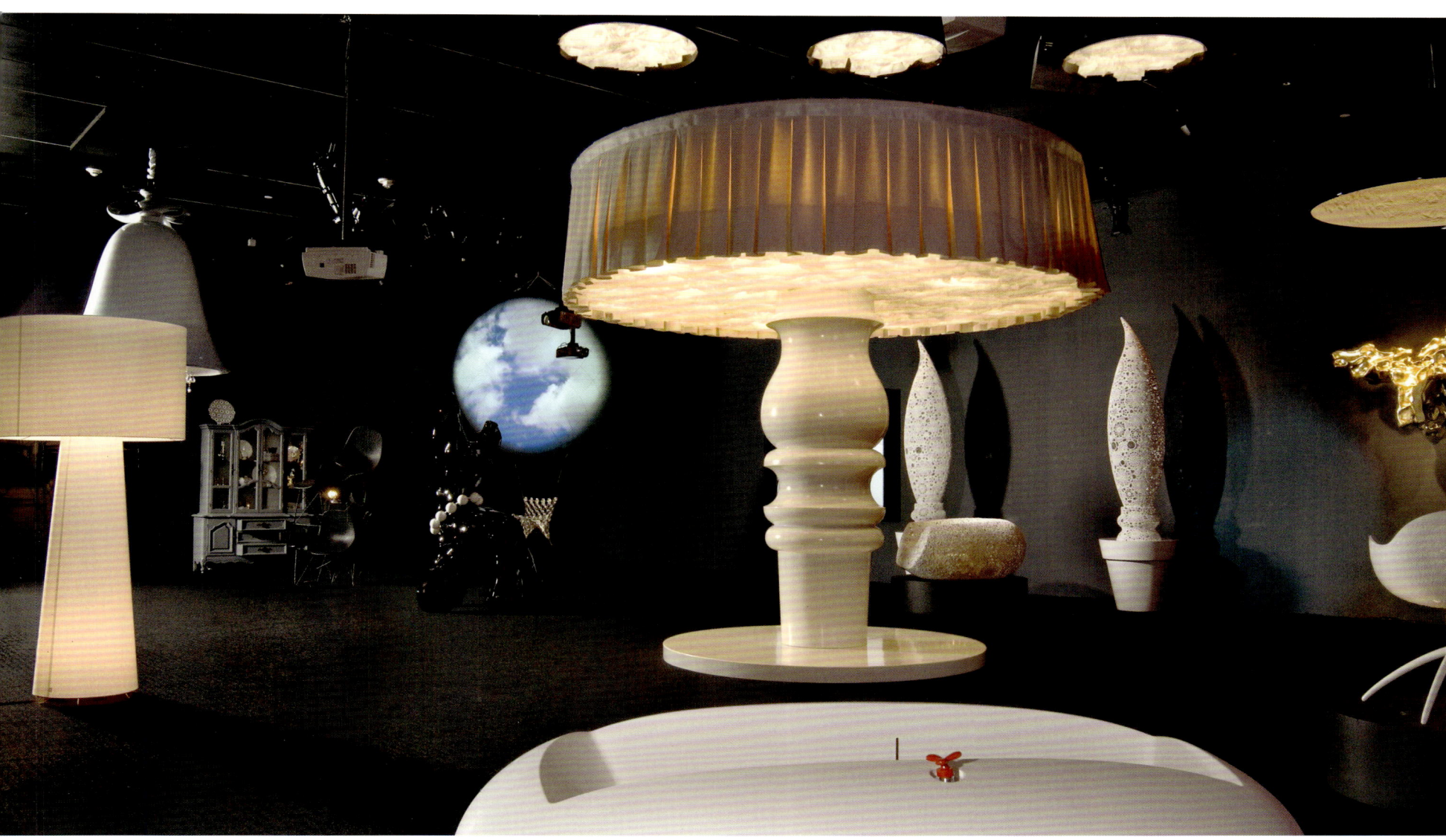

Marcel Wanders: Daydreams was the designer's first solo exhibition in the United States, for which he selected his favorite works of the last two decades and around them designed a unique multimedia installation in the Collab Gallery (fig. 306).[172] The shifting video images, light, and sound were choreographed with the Museum's first "show controller"—technology that can simultaneously operate multiple electronic devices—managed by the Museum's team of Stephen A. Keever, Jennifer Schlegel, and James J. Fraatz and resulting in the most complex audiovisual project in the institution's history. The exhibition's dazzling results were acclaimed to be "as surreal, exaggerated, and playful as its name suggests," according to the *Philadelphia Inquirer*.[173] Gifts to the design collections from the show came from several manufacturers, including Bisazza, Cappellini, Flos, and Wanders himself. At the final board of trustees meeting of 2009, Rub noted that he hoped the Museum would acquire Wanders's *Wallflower* light sculpture (as it did in 2010; fig. 307), a group of fifty-two color-changing LEDs dispersed through glass flowers—a wall-mounted circular bouquet that is intended to be programmed as a calendar, its color changes paced to celebrate different occasions.[174]

And so this history ends as it began, with the quest for acquisitions of contemporary decorative arts for the Museum. Collab marked its fortieth anniversary in 2010. It is safe to say that, powered by the group's advocacy and support of the last four decades, the Philadelphia Museum of Art can now lay claim to one of the most important modern and contemporary design collections to be found in any comprehensive museum. Supported by the Museum's directors and executive officers over many years, the program of design exhibitions large and small has driven the rapid growth of the collections, thanks to the generosity of manufacturers, designers, and many private individuals. This is a story with a happy ending in the present and the promise of a very bright future

Marcel Wanders : Daydreams : 2009–10

307. Marcel Wanders : for Flos : *Wallflower* Light Sculpture : 2009 : glass, aluminum, electronic components : D (overall) 55 1/8" : 2010-101-1 (cat. 205)

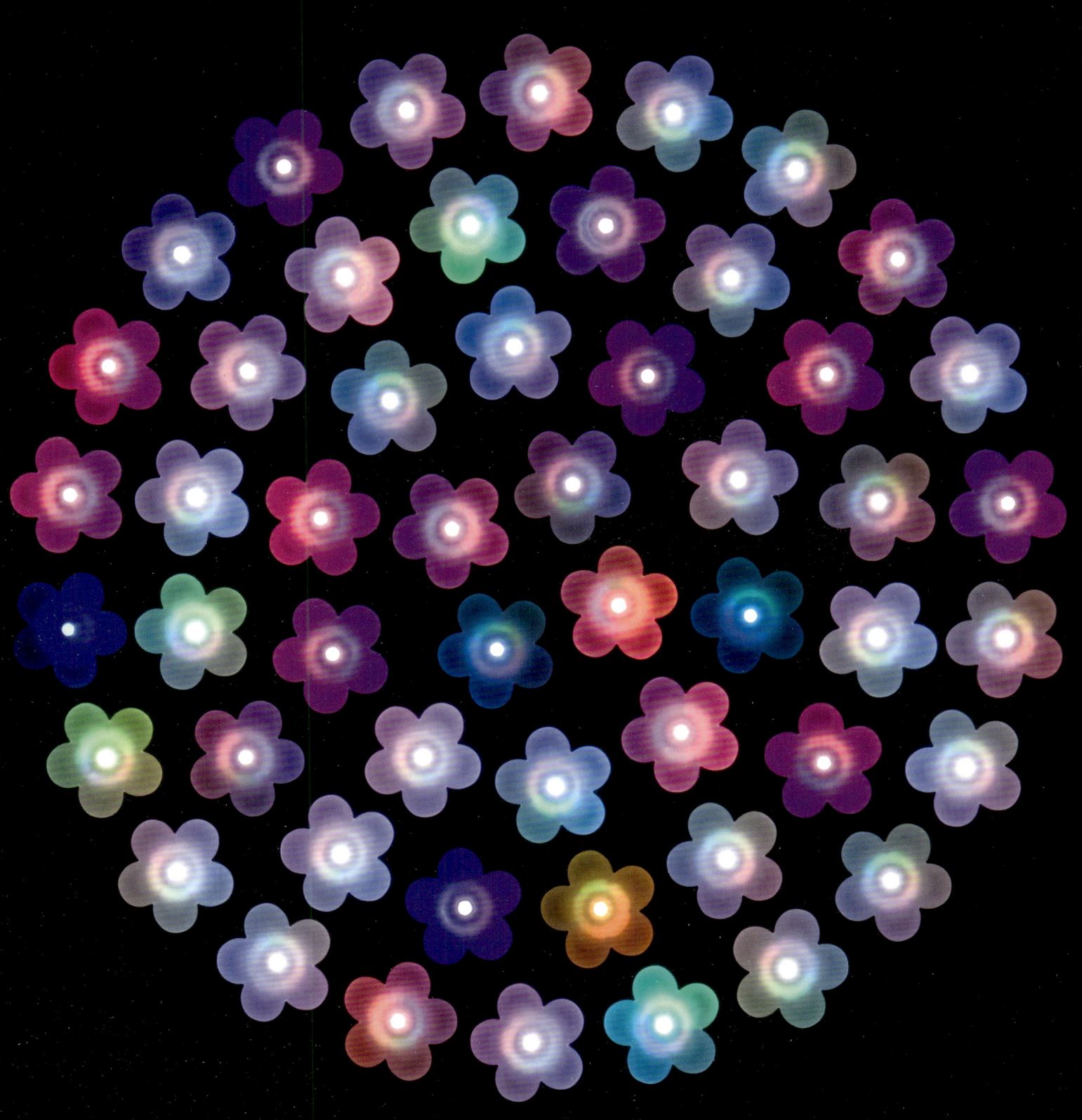

1. Board of Trustees Records, Minutes, April 3, 1963.

2. In 1967 the board approved Turner's plan to divide the department; see note 35 below. The title disappeared with Hathaway's retirement in 1972.

3. In 1963, Cooper Union for the Advancement of Science and Art, on Cooper Square in New York, decided to dispose of the collections of the Cooper Union Museum but was met with considerable resistance from various individuals and arts groups; in 1967 the Cooper Union Museum was formally transferred to the Smithsonian Institution; and in 1976 the Smithsonian's Cooper-Hewitt Museum of Design opened in the Carnegie Mansion on Fifth Avenue.

4. Calvin S. Hathaway to R. Sturgis Ingersoll, August 7, 1963, R. Sturgis Ingersoll Records, Correspondence.

5. John Coolidge to Ingersoll, August 13, 1963, Ingersoll Records, Correspondence.

6. McIlhenny to Ingersoll, July 16, 1963, Ingersoll Records, Correspondence. Announcing Turner's selection to the press, Ingersoll commented, "We wanted a young person, but we never thought we'd find one with so much knowledge and experience"; R. Sturgis Ingersoll quoted in Grace Glueck, "Art Notes: Out Ridgefield Way," *New York Times*, March 1, 1964, p. X24.

7. Cunningham also urged the creation of a long-range development plan to fund a program of distinguished exhibitions originating at the Museum, a broad educational program, and significant and important purchases. With regard to a new director, Cunningham's hope was that the Museum would find "an outstanding young man in his thirties or at best early forties, who could undertake this program, and in fifteen or more years feel that he has achieved his goal"; Charles Cunningham to Ingersoll, October 25, 1963, Ingersoll Records, Correspondence.

8. Board of Trustees Records, Executive Committee, Minutes, November 11, 1964; March 1, 1965; and May 12, 1965.

9. Claire McLean, typescript [July 24, 1964], Ingersoll Records, Correspondence.

10. Evan H. Turner, "A Message from the Director," *Philadelphia Museum of Art Bulletin*, vol. 60, nos. 283/284 (Fall 1964/Winter 1965): p. 5.

11. "Report of the Director," in "Annual Report, June 1, 1964–May 31, 1965," *Philadelphia Museum of Art Bulletin*, vol. 61, no. 286 (Summer 1965): p. 88.

12. Board of Trustees Records, Minutes, May 2, 1962.

13. "Department of Decorative Arts: The Year Past," in "Annual Report, 1964–65," p. 112.

14. Ibid., p. 113.

15. Ibid., p. 112.

16. Hathaway to Mlle Florence Marinot, September 21, 1966, European Decorative Arts after 1700 Files, Philadelphia Museum of Art.

17. Undated typescript, European Decorative Arts after 1700 Files.

18. "Report of the Director," in "Annual Report, June 1, 1968–June 30, 1969," *Philadelphia Museum of Art Bulletin*, vol. 64, no. 301 (October–December 1969): p. 80.

19. The design societies included the American Institute of Architects, American Institute of Interior Design, Interior Design Council of Philadelphia, National Home Fashions League, National Society of Interior Design, and Philadelphia Council of Professional Craftsmen.

20. "Decorative Arts after 1700," in "Annual Report, July 1, 1969–June 30, 1970," *Philadelphia Museum of Art Bulletin*, vol. 65, no. 304 (July–September 1970): p. 56.

21. Hathaway to Francis L. Rodebaugh, March 26, 1970, Decorative Arts Department Records, Calvin Hathaway Papers.

22. "Report of the Director," in "Annual Report, July 1, 1970–June 30, 1971," *Philadelphia Museum of Art Bulletin*, vol. 66, no. 306 (October–December 1971): p. 17.

23. Collab Records, Inter-Society Committee for Twentieth-Century Decorative Arts and Design, Minutes, October 7, 1970.

24. *Vincent van Gogh: Paintings*, February 28–April 5, 1970.

25. *Peace*, May 19–June 21, 1970.

26. *City/2*, June 10, 1971–January 2, 1972.

27. Turner to Bartine Stoner, Jr., October 20, 1970, "*Product Environment: New Furniture*," September 30–November 10, 1970, Exhibition Records. The exhibition venues included the City Art Museum of Saint Louis, April 24–June 7, 1970; Dallas Museum of Fine Arts, July 15–August 30, 1970; Philadelphia Museum of Art, September 30–November 10, 1970; and Albright-Knox Art Gallery, Buffalo, January 6–February 14, 1971.

28. Board of Trustees Records, Minutes, February 18, 1971.

29. Board of Trustee Records, Executive Committee, Minutes, March 12, 1969, and Minutes, June 11, 1969.

30. Sewell had previously headed the education department at the Smithsonian Institution's National Collection of Fine Arts (now known as the Smithsonian American Art Museum) in Washington, D.C.

31. Anne d'Harnoncourt began her career at the Museum in 1967 as curatorial assistant in the department of painting and sculpture; her first acquisitions included a Mexican painted-wood figure and stone angel, both from the eighteenth century (Board of Trustees Records, Minutes, April 9, 1969). She left Philadelphia in 1969 for a post at the Art Institute of Chicago, where she specialized in modern and contemporary art.

32. Board of Trustees Records, Executive Committee, Minutes, January 15, 1969.

33. Board of Trustees Records, Executive Committee, Minutes, March 12, 1969.

34. Board of Trustees Records, Minutes, June 19, 1971.

35. David DuBon was promoted to associate curator of decorative arts in 1964 to recognize his research and installation of the Constantine tapestries; Board of Trustees Records, Executive Committee, Minutes, December 2, 1964. In 1966 Turner suggested the advisability of dividing the department of decorative arts into two sections (May 11, 1966), and in 1967 the department was duly split between medieval and Renaissance decorative arts, headed by DuBon, and decorative arts after 1700, headed by Hathaway ("Report of the Director," in "Annual Report, June 1, 1967–May 31, 1968," *Philadelphia Museum of Art Bulletin*, vol. 63, no. 298 [July–September, 1968]: p. 177).

36. *Recent Acquisitions: Twentieth-Century Decorative Arts*, April 6–December 26, 1971.

37. In discussing the success of their programs months later, the format of Collab '71 was held up as an example; Collab Records, Inter-Society Committee, Minutes, May 14, 1973.

38. Hathaway to Charles Eames, April 21, 1972, Collab Records, Inter-Society Committee.

39. Collab Records, Inter-Society Committee, Minutes, "Rules of Organization," November 1, 1972.

40. Collab Records, Inter-Society Committee, Minutes, May 14, 1973.

41. Collab Records, Inter-Society Committee, Minutes, November 1, 1972.

42. *Industrial Design*, vol. 1, no. 6 (December 1954): p. 106.

43. The committee also proposed that the Museum develop a library of trade catalogues for reference, a policy continued to the present; Collab Records, Inter-Society Committee, Minutes, May 14, 1973.

44. *British Contemporary Design*, November 20–December 31, 1974.

45. Collab Records, Inter-Society Committee, Minutes, June 18, 1974.

46. "Annual Report, 1974–75, Department of European Decorative Arts after 1700," p. 2, European Decorative Arts after 1700 Files.

47. *A Touch of Gold*, November 23–December 15, 1974.

48. Board of Trustees Records, Minutes, February 15, 1978. These projects, largely completed by 1976 with support from the city's capital budget, also included new conservation laboratories; a new restaurant and cafeteria; a new shipping and receiving facility; the Wintersteen Student Center; completion of the study/storage and support service areas; design of new galleries and storage areas for the department of costume and textiles; installation of bronze railings in the Great Stair Hall; new crafts shops; and new employee facilities.

49. Board of Trustees Records, Minutes, June 10, 1968; April 19, 1978; June 21, 1978; and December 20, 1978. In December 1978 the city of Philadelphia purchased the building for use by the Museum. However, the board decided that the Museum should not assume title until sufficient funds were raised to cover all costs; Board of Trustees Records, Executive Committee, Minutes, October 9, 1979, attached memorandum from Carl Colozzi to the Executive Committee dated October 5, 1979.

50. *Philadelphia: Three Centuries of American Art*, April 11–October 10, 1976.

51. *The Second Empire: Art in France under Napoleon III*, Philadelphia Museum of Art, October 1–November 26, 1978; Detroit Institute of Arts, January 15–March 18, 1979; Grand Palais, Paris, April 24–July 2, 1979.

52. Hilton Kramer, "Art View: Blockbusters Weren't the Whole Show," *New York Times*, December 31, 1978, p. D1.

53. Ibid., p. D21.

54. Paul Richard, "Splendid Subversion, French Frivolity," *Washington Post*, October 8, 1978, p. H1.

55. Andrew Lins, who holds the Neubauer Family Chair of Conservation, remains the Museum's senior conservator of decorative arts and sculpture and head of the department of conservation.

56. *Gifts to Mark a Century: An Exhibition Celebrating the Centennial of the Philadelphia Museum of Art*, February 18–March 20, 1977.

57. John Canaday, "Philadelphia Refurbishes for the Bicentennial," *New York Times*, March 21, 1976, p. 83.

58. "Report of the President," in "Annual Report, July 1, 1975–June 30, 1976," *Philadelphia Museum of Art Bulletin*, vol. 73, no. 315 (January 1977): p. 3.

59. Evan H. Turner to William P. Wood [March 31, 1977], Evan H. Turner Biographical File. Turner would go on to become director of the Ackland Memorial Art Center at the University of North Carolina at Chapel Hill in 1978, and director of the Cleveland Museum of Art in 1983. In his reply Wood cited the "high standards" Turner had set and concluded that under his leadership, the Museum could "face its Second Century with confidence. Its magnificent collections are newly installed in a virtually completed building and its place is assured among the major art institutions of the world"; Wood to Turner, April 1, 1977, Turner Biographical File, Museum Archives, Philadelphia Museum of Art.

60. Board of Trustees Records, Minutes, April 20, 1977.

61. Diana Loercher, "Parting View from a Star Museum Director," *Christian Science Monitor*, April 11, 1977, p. 19; "Report of the Director," in "Annual Report, July 1, 1976–June 30, 1977," *Philadelphia Museum of Art Bulletin*, vol. 73, no. 319 (December 1977): pp. 8–10.

62. Collab Records, Minutes, April 4, 1977.

63. Philadelphia Museum of Art, "Museum Board Names Search Committee," news release, April 20, 1977.

64. A specialist in modern painting and a distinguished scholar awarded numerous honorary degrees, she had divided her career alternately between teaching (Mount Holyoke College; University of California, Riverside; Washington University, St. Louis; and Harvard University) and museum work (Art Gallery of Toronto and National Gallery of Canada).

65. Jean Sutherland Boggs, "Paintings and Sculpture at MOMA" [1979], typed manuscript solicited by *Art News*, Jean Sutherland Boggs Records, Correspondence.

66. Collab Records, Minutes, May 10, 1979. *Noguchi's Imaginary Landscapes*, which originated at the Walker Art Center, Minneapolis, was on view at the Philadelphia Museum of Art October 20, 1979–January 6, 1980.

67. "Report of the Director," in *104th Annual Report, July 1, 1979–June 30, 1980* (Philadelphia, Philadelphia Museum of Art, 1980), p. 9.

68. Boggs to the author, memorandum, October 19, 1981, Collab Records.

69. Additional funding for the cup was provided by Mr. and Mrs. Adolph Rosengarten, Jr., and the Fiske Kimball Fund.

70. Boggs to Pedro Rodriguez, December 22, 1981, Collab Records.

71. *Design Since 1945*, October 16, 1983–January 8, 1984.

72. George Nelson to Melanie Ingalls, May 9, 1983, Collab Records; first ellipses in original.

73. Kathryn B Hiesinger and George H. Marcus, eds., *Design Since 1945* (Philadelphia: Philadelphia Museum of Art, 1983).

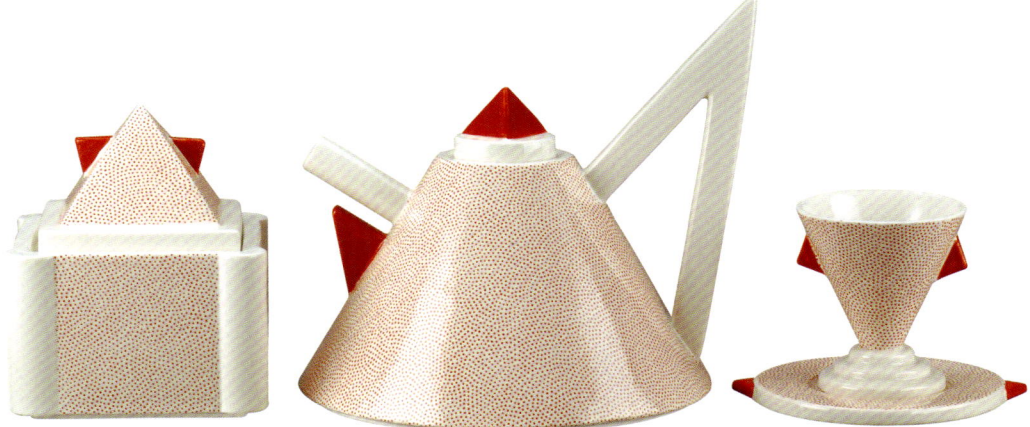

74. Suzanne Slesin, "A Close Look at Postwar Design," *New York Times*, October 13, 1983, pp. C1, C6.

75. Patsy Rogers, "Classics in Their Own Time," *Washington Post*, October 6, 1983, pp. 26, 29–30; Diana Loercher, "Design Since 1945: A Look at Functionalism in the Home," *Christian Science Monitor*, November 3, 1983, p. 29; Denise Cowle, "Fun Follows Function," *Boston Globe*, November 25, 1983, pp. 75, 80; Wolf Von Eckardt, "Design: Forms that Follow Function," *Time*, October 24, 1983, pp. 81–82; William H. Jordy, "The 'Big Picture' in Philadelphia," *New Criterion*, vol. 2 (January 1984): pp. 47–56; Anders Mortner, "Design eller Bara Dekoration?" *Svenska Dagbladet* (Stockholm), December 29, 1983, unpaginated; Aidan Dunne, "Shaping Up," *Sunday Press* (London), undated and unpaginated.

76. The two new institutions were the National Gallery of Canada in Ottawa and the National Museum of Man (now known as the Canadian Museum of Civilization) in Gatineau, Quebec.

77. See Collab Records, Minutes, November 16, 1979, and Board of Trustees Records, Minutes, February 18, 1981.

78. Member of a socially prominent, wealthy Philadelphia family, Scott had served as a trustee and unpaid president of the Museum, having succeeded William P. Wood.

79. By amendment to the Museum corporation's bylaws, the two were to report to each other as well as directly to the board and the executive committee. The new dual executive structure, with a salaried president as chief executive officer and a director as chief professional officer, continued until Scott's retirement in 1996.

80. Board of Trustees Records, Minutes, April 16, 1986.

81. Board of Trustees Records, Minutes, May 13, 1986.

82. Board of Trustees Records, Minutes, October 21, 1987. Madeira's death in 1993 was reported to the Board; Board of Trustees Records, Minutes, December 15, 1993. Earlier, trustee John T. Dorrance, Campbell Soup company executive and heir, who had been named chairman of the Museum's board at McIlhenny's death, died unexpectedly in 1989 and was succeeded by board vice chairman Philip I. Berman. Trustee and collector Mrs. Rodolphe Meyer de Schauensee died in 1990.

83. Louis C. Madeira to Robert Montgomery Scott, August 8, 1987, European Decorative Arts after 1700 Files.

84. In the same year David DuBon, who had been the Museum's curator of decorative arts since 1958, died, having retired in ill-health in 1984.

85. Alexa Aldridge quoted in Board of Trustees Records, Executive Committee, Minutes, June 9, 1993.

86. Board of Trustees Records, Executive Committee, Minutes, September 11, 1991. Like their predecessors, neither Evan Turner nor Jean Boggs had been expected to raise funds for the Museum; Turner confirmed that understanding in his letter to Sturgis Ingersoll accepting the position as director: "Whereas the Director is responsible for . . . creating the most favorable public image possible he does not carry a responsibility for fundraising although he will, naturally, do all he can to further it" (Turner to Ingersoll, February 14, 1964, Evan Hopkins Turner Records, Museum Correspondence).

87. *Masterpieces of Impressionism and Post-Impressionism: The Annenberg Collection*, May 21–September 17, 1989.

88. Preface to Collab '82 auction catalogue, Collab Records.

89. "Report of the Director," in *Biennial Report for the Years 1982–83 and 1983–84* (Philadelphia, Philadelphia Museum of Art, 1984), p. 10.

90. Alexander von Vegesack, in *Portrait d'une collection. Alexander von Vegesack*, by Marie-Laure Jousset, Vegesack, and Katarina V. Posch, exh. cat. (Paris: Centre Georges Pompidou, 1993), p. 14: "À la fin des années 70, je tombe en arrêt, au marché Paul Bert à Clignancourt, sur le High back chair d'Alvar Aalto—une pièce magnifique, noire, avec des bras en bois naturel. . . . Malheureusement, j'avais été contraint, entre-temps, faute d'argent, de m'en défaire au profit de Kathryn B. Hiesinger du musée de Philadelphie."

91. James L. Crowell and Grant Greapentrog, introduction to Collab '86 auction catalogue, Collab Records. As discussed in chapter 2, the Museum school had years earlier instituted an annual design award.

92. Philadelphia Museum of Art, "Collab Presents Award of Excellence to Vignelli Associates," news release [1988].

93. Massimo Vignelli to James L. Crowell, April 15, 1988, Collab Records.

94. Ralph Melick to Tom Hauserman, Jr., August 31, 1989, Collab Records.

95. *Building the City Beautiful: The Benjamin Franklin Parkway and the Philadelphia Museum of Art*, August 19–October 29, 1989.

96. In addition to the two books that I wrote, the series included *Glass* by Betty Elzea and *France, 1700–1800* by William Rieder.

308. Matteo Thun : for Ceramiche Flavia and Memphis : *Nefertiti* Tea Service : 1981 : enameled earthenware : H (teapot) 7⅞" : 1986-82-1a,b–3a,b (cat. 188)

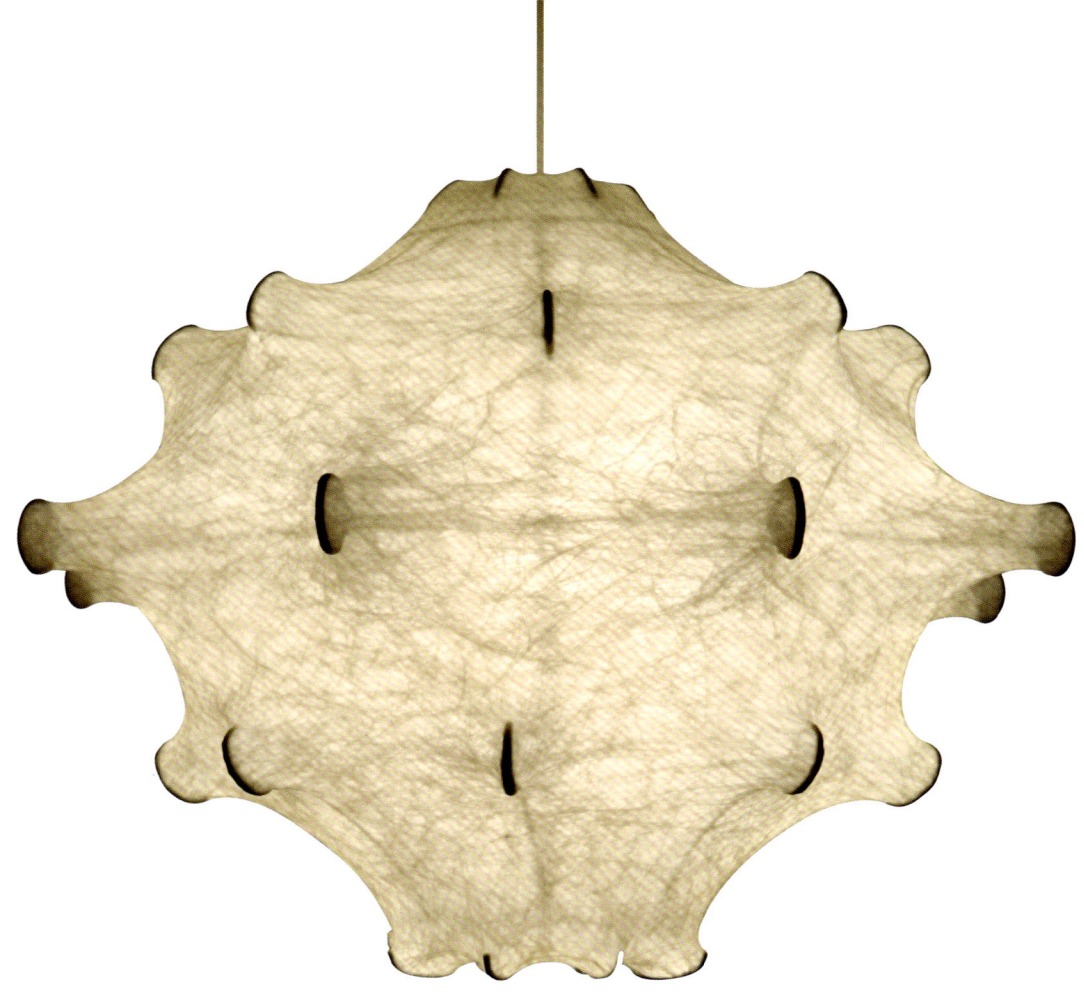

97. *Design, 1900–1940: From the Collections,* January 31–December 9, 1987.

98. *Art Nouveau in Munich,* Philadelphia Museum of Art, September 25–November 27, 1988; Los Angeles County Museum of Art, December 22, 1988–February 19, 1989; Saint Louis Art Museum, March 30–May 28, 1989; Münchner Stadtmuseum, June–July 1989.

99. Rita Reif, "Innovations from Munich's Masters of Art Nouveau," *New York Times,* October 23, 1988, p. H33.

100. Edward J. Sozanski, "Art Nouveau from Munich," *Philadelphia Inquirer,* September 25, 1988, pp. 1F, 6F.

101. W. W., "Neu präsentiert, neu gedeutet. Die Meister des Münchner Jugendstils," *Frankfurter Allgemeine Zeitung,* August 2, 1989, p. 19; my translation. See Kathryn B. Hiesinger, *Art Nouveau in Munich: Masters of Jugendstil from the Stadtmuseum, Munich, and Other Public and Private Collections* (Philadelphia: Philadelphia Museum of Art in association with Prestel, 1988); trans. as *Die Meister des Münchner Jugendstils* (Munich: Prestel, 1988).

102. *From the Collection: Objects Designed in the 1950s,* April 1–October 14, 1990; *Twentieth-Century Lighting,* opened May 7, 1991; *Timeline of Twentieth-Century Chairs,* opened February 21, 1995; *Scandinavian Design, 1930–1980,* March 17–October 1, 1997.

103. *Louis I. Kahn: In the Realm of Architecture,* Philadelphia Museum of Art, October 20, 1991–January 5, 1992; Centre Georges Pompidou, Paris, March 5–May 4, 1992; Museum of Modern Art, New York, June 14–August 18, 1992; Museum of Modern Art, Gunma, Japan, September 26–November 3, 1992; Museum of Contemporary Art, Los Angeles, March 7–May 30, 1993; Kimbell Art Museum, Fort Worth, TX, July 3–October 10, 1993; Wexner Center for the Arts, Ohio State University, Columbus, November 17, 1993–February 1, 1994.

104. *Japanese Design: A Survey Since 1950,* September 25–November 27, 1994; the exhibition also traveled as *Design giapponese. Una storia dal 1950,* Triennale di Milano, Palazzo dell' Arte, March 17–May 14, 1995; *Japanisches Design seit 1950,* Kunsthalle Düsseldorf, July 9–September 10, 1995; *Design japonais, 1950–1995,* Centre Georges Pompidou, Paris, February 14–April 29, 1996; and *Made in Japan, 1950–1994,* Suntory Museum, Osaka, May 24–July 24, 1996.

105. Emily Mitchell, "Setting the World Style," *Time,* vol. 144, no. 16 (October 17, 1994): p. 50.

106. Thomas Hine, "Made in Japan," *Philadelphia Inquirer,* September 25, 1994, p. N1.

107. Kathryn B. Hiesinger and Felice Fischer, *Japanese Design: A Survey Since 1950* (Philadelphia: Philadelphia Museum of Art, 1994).

108. Despite strong opposition from municipal labor unions, Rendell sought to privatize certain municipal functions, among them provisions for security, maintenance, and custodial staff at the Museum that had been established since 1929 by a contractual agreement between the city of Philadelphia and the Museum corporation. Under the contract the city was obligated to provide for these services with funds appropriated by the city council. However, over a period of many years predating and including the Rendell administration, in times of need the city had regularly cut its appropriation to the Museum, forcing the institution most visibly to close some or all of its galleries for lack of guards. In 1993 the *Philadelphia Inquirer* reported that the Museum required a complement of about 155 guards to remain fully open six days a week, and that currently the force was down to 80; Stephen Salisbury and Vernon Loeb, "Firms Get Jobs Held by City Workers," *Philadelphia Inquirer,* February 3, 1993, p. B5.

109. A *Philadelphia Inquirer* editorial further pointed out that the Museum's position was untenable under the city's labor agreements—rendering it powerless to "hire part-time staff, deploy its people more efficiently or put the work out to private bid"; "Rendell vs. Scott," editorial, *Philadelphia Inquirer,* March 27, 1992, p. A18.

110. Board of Trustees Records, Minutes, April 21, 1993.

111. Board of Trustees Records, Minutes, September 15, 1993.

112. Board of Trustees Records, Minutes, November 12, 1996. The mayor's initiatives included the City of Philadelphia Productivity Bank and the Greater Philadelphia Tourism and Marketing Corporation (GPTMC). The Museum received grants from the GPTMC and other civic agencies to promote its special exhibitions and other programs. Similar efforts to boost tourism occurred at the state level, also benefitting the Museum including in 1997 Pennsylvania Governor Thomas Ridge's Governor's Travel and Tourism Council.

113. *Design for the Table Top,* October 13, 1993–January 1994.

114. Venturi, Scott Brown and Associates, *Architecture and Decorative Arts: Two Naifs in Japan* (Tokyo: Kajima Institute, 1991). The exhibition *Two Naifs in Japan: Robert Venturi and Denise Scott Brown* was on view October 26, 1994–January 30, 1995.

115. *Michael Graves: The Architect and the Tea Kettle,* October 25, 1995–February 25, 1996.

116. *Richard Meier: Object and Furniture Design,* October 30, 1996–February 29, 1997.

117. Later Schrager said that Collab had given him "an enlightening and thrilling experience . . . the perfect way to start the exhibition"; Ian Schrager to the author, December 8, 1997, Collab Records.

118. *Philippe Starck Designs,* November 12, 1997–March 1, 1998.

119. *Cool Britannia: Recent British Design Selected by Sir Terence Conran,* November 11, 1998–March 7, 1999.

120. *Designing the Future: Three Directions for the New Millennium,* November 17, 1999–March 26, 2000.

121. *Milton Glaser: Design, Influence and Process,* November 15, 2000–January 21, 2001.

122. *Collab Collects: Notable Acquisitions in Design, 1970–2000,* November 14, 2001–April 21, 2002.

123. The latter was also published in French, as *Petit lexique des arts décoratifs de la Renaissance à l'art déco* (1997).

124. *Out of the Ordinary: The Architecture and Design of Robert Venturi, Denise Scott Brown and Associates,* June 10–August 5, 2001. The exhibition was supported by grants from the Philadelphia Exhibitions Initiative, the Annenberg Foundation, the Robert Montgomery Scott Endowment for Exhibitions, the Women's Committee of the Philadelphia Museum of Art; Alcoa Foundation; Elise Jaffe and Jeffrey Brown; Frances Lewis; Mr. and Mrs. J. Roffe Wike II; and Marion Stroud Swingle.

125. Paul Goldberger, "House Proud: Mies van der Rohe and Robert Venturi at Three Museums," *New Yorker,*

309. **Achille Castiglioni and Pier Giacomo Castiglioni** : for Flos : *Taraxacum 2* Lamp : 1960 : plastic resin, steel : H 25" : 2010-76-2 (cat. 28)

July 2, 2001, p. 79. Goldberger refers here to the exhibitions *Mies in Berlin*, Museum of Modern Art, New York, 2001; *Mies in America*, Canadian Centre for Architecture, Montreal, 2001–2; and *Frank Gehry: Architect*, Solomon R. Guggenheim Museum, New York, 2001.

126. Martin Filler, "The Spirit of '76," *New Republic*, July 9 and 16, 2001, p. 38.

127. Stanley Abercrombie, "Out of the Ordinary," review, *Interior Design*, September 2001, p. 184.

128. *Gifts in Honor of the Museum's 125th Anniversary*, September 29–December 8, 2002.

129. Cynthia Nalevanko, collections manager, Lannan Foundation, telephone conversation with the author, February 4, 1997.

130. Anne d'Harnoncourt to the author, memorandum, March 3, 1999, European Decorative Arts after 1700 Files.

131. Charles G. and Victoria Solin; their friend Benjamin Thompson, a member of the Architect's Collaborative with Walter Gropius, founded Design Research in 1953, a retail store in Cambridge, Massachusetts, that introduced many advanced European designs to the United States.

132. Philadelphia Museum of Art, "Museum Finds Room to Grow Through Purchase of a Nearby Art-Deco Landmark," news release, October 21, 1999.

133. Lisa S. Roberts and David Seltzer to Gail Harrity, March 2, 2000, Collab Records.

134. Board of Trustees Records, Minutes, December 20, 2001.

135. Lisa S. Roberts, *Antiques of the Future* (New York: Stewart, Tabori and Chang, 2006), p. 8.

136. The organizational assessment of Collab was undertaken by Jason D. Alexander from the firm Capacity for Change, West Chester, Pennsylvania.

137. *The Light Magic of Ingo Maurer*, November 20, 2002–March 30, 2003.

138. Within the installation for *Porca Miseria!* Ingo Maurer explained his goals and the source of the title in an object label: "My aim in this installation was to create a modern atmosphere within an eighteenth-century setting. I considered this to be a great challenge—respecting, rather than provoking, old traditions, and combining them, in harmony, with contemporary feelings. To protect the intimacy of this decorative and formal eighteenth-century salon, I created a room within a room. A mysterious, veil-like transparent wire mesh embracing the modern part allows the visitor a fluent transition between the different epochs. The centerpiece of the room within a room is the *Porca Miseria!*, a light sculpture made of broken porcelain dishes. Subversive feelings of anti-domesticity were the source of my creating the *Porca Miseria!*, which is lit invisibly from within. Originally I intended to name it *Zabriskie Point* after the famous movie; I was strongly impressed and inspired by the enormous explosions shown in slow motion in the film. When I presented the sculpture at the Euroluce lighting exhibition in Milan, however, many Italian viewers exclaimed 'porca miseria' (pig in misery), an Italian expression similar to 'oh, damn it.' I decided at that moment that *Porca Miseria!* was the perfect name for it." Ingo Maurer, artist's statement and gallery label, November 2002, Collab Records.

139. He explained that the genesis of the project lay in his invention, in the 1980s, of the first low-voltage lighting cable system, a breakthrough in lighting techniques: "Called 'YaYaHo,' the system invites the users to play with light and shadow, according to their own needs and interpretations. . . . Using elements of 'YaYaHo,' I created 'aha SoSo,' a sculpture that can be installed in many different ways. The name 'aha SoSo' (German for 'I see, I understand') is derived from the comments and expressions of astonishment uttered by spectators when they were first told about the system and understood its uniqueness. Different lighting components, such as mirrors and metal segments, along with personal elements, can be added." Ibid.

140. Kathleen Nicholson Webber, "Let There Be Light," *Philadelphia Inquirer*, November 22, 2002, pp. E1, E4; and Pilar Viladas, "The Illuminator," *New York Times Magazine*, January 5, 2003, pp. 38–43.

141. *Work in Progress: Gluckman Mayner Designs the Perelman Building*, November 19, 2003–April 4, 2004.

142. Inga Saffron, "Architecture's Good Showing," *Philadelphia Inquirer*, November 28, 2003, p. D6.

143. *On the Wall: Wallpaper and Tableau*, May 9–September 13, 2003.

144. *Have a Bite: 20th-Century Flatware from the Collection*, April 12–October 26, 2003.

145. *Florence Knoll Bassett: Defining Modern*, November 17, 2004–April 10, 2005.

146. *Gaetano Pesce: Pushing the Limits*, November 18, 2005–April 9, 2006.

147. Eils Lotozo, "If Looks Could Liberate," *Philadelphia Inquirer*, November 18, 2005, pp. E1.

148. *Georg Jensen Silversmiths*, November 17, 2006–April 1, 2007.

149. Museum trustee Barbara Rubenstein, energetic and committed, had chaired the committee after Louis Madeira's death in 1993 until her own untimely death in 2001.

150. Kise has noted this fact on several occasions, most recently at a departmental committee meeting, November 5, 2009.

151. Robert Montgomery Scott to James Nelson Kise, September 26, 1994, European Decorative Arts after 1700 Files.

152. Board of Trustees Records, Minutes, October 21, 1999. The transaction was heralded by the *Philadelphia Inquirer* in a front-page article; Edward J. Sozanski, "Art Museum's Latest Acquisition: More Space," *Philadelphia Inquirer*, October 22, 1999, p. A1.

153. Betty Marmon, Director of Development, Philadelphia Museum of Art, quoted in Board of Trustees Records, Minutes, October 20, 2005.

154. *Designing Modern*, September 15, 2007–September 14, 2008.

155. Edward J. Sozanski, "Five Opening Shows of Riches," *Philadelphia Inquirer*, September 9, 2007, p. 11.

156. Lee Rosenbaum, "An Expansion a Quaker Could Love," *Wall Street Journal*, December 19, 2007, p. D10.

157. Lisa S. Roberts to Kathryn B. Hiesinger, e-mail, September 1, 2007, Collab Records.

158. Board of Trustees Records, Minutes, October 20, 2005.

159. Board of Trustees Records, Minutes, September 21, 2006.

160. Philadelphia Museum of Art, "Philadelphia Museum Announces Selection of Frank O. Gehry for a Major Expansion of Galleries and Public Spaces over the Next Decade," news release, October 19, 2006. Gerry Lenfest stated, "We look forward to working with Frank and his talented staff to realize a project that began as a dream, and that today, in partnership with the city and the state, can begin to move full steam ahead"; ibid.

161. *Frank O. Gehry: Design Process and the Lewis House*, November 8, 2008–April 5, 2009.

162. "Frank O. Gehry: Design Process and the Lewis House," *Architect's Newspaper*, December 10, 2008, p. 28.

163. Frances McQueeny-Jones Macolo, "Frank O. Gehry: Design Process and the Lewis House," *Antiques and the Arts Weekly*, November 28, 2008, p. 41.

164. Board of Trustees Records, Minutes, June 19, 2008, Gerry Lenfest and Gail Harrity to the board, attached memorandum dated June 12, 2008.

165. Anne d'Harnoncourt quoted in Peter Dobrin, "Netting the Must Have Art," *Philadelphia Inquirer*, April 16, 2006, p. H6.

166. *A Taste for the Modern: The Jeanne Rymer Gift of Twentieth-Century Chairs*, May 16–September 20, 2009.

167. *Visual Delight: Ornament and Pattern in Modern and Contemporary Design*, May 16–September 20, 2009.

168. *Richard Schultz: Five Decades of Design*, April 5–August 23, 2009.

169. Eils Lotozo, "A Backseat to None," *Philadelphia Inquirer*, May 1, 2009, pp. E1, E8.

170. Board of Trustees Records, Minutes, June 18, 2009.

171. Paul Goldberger, "At the Cooper-Hewitt, Designs of Joseph Urban," *New York Times*, December 20, 1987, p. 175.

172. *Marcel Wanders: Daydreams*, November 22, 2009–June 13, 2010.

173. Christina Pellegrini, "A Marcel Wanders Exhibit," *Philadelphia Inquirer*, November 27, 2009, p. E11.

174. Board of Trustees Records, Minutes, December 17, 2009.

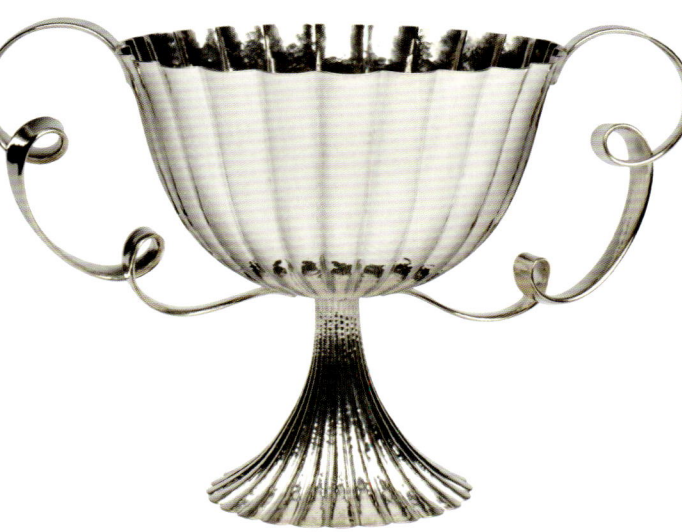

310. Josef Hoffmann : for Wiener Werkstätte : Footed Cup : c. 1926 : silver : H 7 1/4" : 1981-89-1 (cat. 83)

WORKS ILLUSTRATED

1. Alvar Aalto
Finnish, 1898–1976
Armchair, c. 1931–32
Made by Oy Huonekalu-ja Rakennustyötehdas AB, Turku, Finland
Birch-faced plywood, laminated birch frame, leather straps, H 37 1/2" (95.3 cm)
Purchased with funds contributed by Collab: The Group for Modern and Contemporary Design at the Philadelphia Museum of Art, in honor of Cynthia W. Drayton, and with the Fiske Kimball Fund, 1985-67-1
(fig. 200)

2. Tea Cart, designed 1936
Made by Oy Huonekalu-ja Rakennustyötehdas AB and Artek Oy Ab, Turku, Finland
Cork, laminated birch frame, H 23 1/2" (59.7 cm)
Purchased with funds contributed by Collab: The Group for Modern and Contemporary Design at the Philadelphia Museum of Art, in honor of Cynthia W. Drayton, and with the Fiske Kimball Fund, 1985-67-3
(fig. 199)

3. Attributed to Julian Abele
American, 1881–1950
Philadelphia Museum of Art: Perspective of the Stair Hall, c. 1927
Crayon on tracing paper, mounted on card, H 16" (40.6 cm)
PDP-1085
(fig. 65)

4. Gerald Abramovitz
English, born South Africa, 1928
Cantilever Desk Lamp, designed 1961
Made by Best & Lloyd Ltd., Birmingham, England
Aluminum, steel, H 20" (50.8 cm)
Gift of Duncan and Higgins, Ltd., 1974-58-1
(fig. 149)

5. Evelyn Hill Anselevicius
American, 1925–2003
Woven Fabric, 1951
Made by Knoll Textiles, New York
Wool, viscose, rayon, synthetic raffia, W 35" (88.9 cm)
Gift of Mr. and Mrs. George Anselevicius, 1983-42-2
(fig. 188)

6. Junichi Arai
Japanese, born 1932
Big Wave Fabric, 1988
Made by Nuno Corporation, Tokyo
Tie-resist dyed aluminum and polyester, W 50" (127 cm)
Gift of Nuno Corporation, 1991-125-1
(fig. 215)

7. *Ojo de Dios* Fabric, c. 1990
Made by K. K. Arai Creation System, Tokyo
Dyed and pleated polyester, W 38" (96.5 cm)
Gift of Junichi Arai, 1996-102-5
(fig. 213)

8. Artist/maker unknown
Caucasus
Pieced Cover, c. 1876
Wool, silk, H 19 3/4" (50.2 cm)
Purchased with Museum funds, 1876-507
(fig. 13)

9. Artist/maker unknown
England
Drawing Room from a Town House, Tower Hill section of London, c. 1763–66
Owned and remodeled by William Stead (English, 18th century)
Wood, H 22' 3 5/16" (6.8 m)
Purchased with funds contributed by Mr. and Mrs. John D. McIlhenny, 1922-8-1
(fig. 62)

10. Artist/maker unknown
France
Choir Screen from the Chapel of the Château of Pagny, 1536–38
Marble, alabaster, H 18' 9" (5.7 m)
Purchased from the Edmond Foulc Collection with funds contributed by Eli Kirk Price, 1930-1-84a–d
(fig. 75)

11. Artist/maker unknown
Italy
Brooch, c. 1850
Gold, mosaic, D 1 1/2" (3.8 cm)
The Bloomfield Moore Collection, 1899-923
(fig. 26)

12. Artist/maker unknown
Japan
Cabinet, c. 1876
Lacquered wood with horn, mother-of-pearl, jade, bronze, malachite inlay, H 5' 4 1/2" (1.6 m)
Purchased with Museum funds, 1876-1681
(fig. 24)

13. Artist/maker unknown
Turkey
Embroidered Quilt Facing (*Yorgan Yüzü*), c. 1300–1919
Linen plain weave with silk embroidery in surface darning stitch, W 50" (127 cm)
Purchased with Museum funds, 1877-18
(fig. 20)

14. Artist/maker unknown
United States
Centennial Handkerchief, 1876
Printed cotton, W 24 1/4" (61.6 cm)
Gift of Mrs. William D. Frishmuth, 1913-223
(fig. 3)

15. Hiroshi Awatsuji
Japanese, 1929–1995
Jitensha Art Screen, designed 1982
Made by Fujie Textile Co., Ltd., Tokyo
Screen-printed cotton, W 5' 10 7/8" (1.8 m)
Gift of Fujie Textile Co., Ltd., 1983-118-1
(fig. 212)

16. Peter Behrens
German, 1868–1940
The Kiss, 1899
Color woodcut: H (image) 10 3/4" (27.3 cm), H (sheet) 14 1/4" (36.2 cm)
Gift of Dr. and Mrs. Robert M. Walker, 1976-78-1
(fig. 51)

17. Electric Kettle, designed 1909
Made by Allgemeine Elektricitäts Gesellschaft (AEG), Berlin
Brass, cane, H (with handle) 8 5/16" (21.1 cm)
Purchased with funds contributed by Gregory and Emily Harvey, 1987-12-1a,b
(fig. 205)

18. Edwin Bennett Pottery Company, Baltimore
Pitcher, 1893
Glazed and gilt earthenware, H 12 1/2" (31.8 cm)
Gift of the Edwin Bennett Pottery Company, 1893-368
(fig. 32)

19. Harry Bertoia
American, born Italy, 1915–1978
High-Backed Chair, designed 1950–52
Made by Knoll, Inc., New York
Steel, H 38' (96.5 cm)
Gift of Jeanne S. Rymer, 2007-186-33
(fig. 293)

20. Acton Bjørn
Danish, 1910–1992
and Sigvard Bernadotte
Swedish, 1907–2002
Margrethe Bowls (5), designed 1950
Made by Rosti A/S, Ballerup, Denmark
Melamine, D (largest bowl) 9 7/16" (24 cm)
Gift of Rosti (U.S.A.), Inc., 1983-56-1–5
(fig. 187)

21. Tord Boontje
Dutch, born 1968
Garland Light, designed 2002
Made by Artecnica, Inc., Los Angeles
Etched brass, H 10" (25.4 cm)
Gift of Artecnica, Inc., 2008-178-5
(page 297)

22. *Midsummer* Light, designed 2004
Made by Artecnica, Inc., Los Angeles
Die-cut Tyvek, H 30" (76.2 cm)
Gift of Artecnica, Inc., 2008-178-3
(fig. 301)

23. Thomas John Bott, Jr.
English, 1854–1932
Ewer, Scene from the *Triumph of Scipio*, 1875
Made by Worcester Royal Porcelain Company, Worcester, England
Porcelain with enamel and gilt decoration, H 11 1/4" (28.6 cm)
Purchased with Museum funds, 1876-1623
(fig. 4)

24. Marcel Breuer
American, born Hungary, 1902–1981
Desk and Chair for James E. Rhoads Residence Hall, Bryn Mawr College, 1938
Maple plywood, L (desk) 50" (127 cm), H (chair) 33 1/2" (85.1 cm)
Gift of Bryn Mawr College, 1999-11-1–3
(fig. 123)

25. Mary Butterton
English, active c. 1874–94
Dish, c. 1876
Made by Doulton & Company, Lambeth, England
Lead-glazed earthenware with underglaze decoration, W 7 7/16" (18.9 cm)
Purchased with Museum funds, 1876-64
(fig. 11)

26. Fernando Campana
Brazilian, born 1961
and Humberto Campana
Brazilian, born 1953
Peneira Baskets (3), 2010
Made by Alessi S.p.A., Crusinallo, Italy
Stainless-steel mesh, natural fiber, D (largest) 15 3/4" (40 cm)
Gift of Museo Alessi, 2010-204-1a–c
(page 9)

27. Jean Carlu
French, 1900–1997
America's Answer! Production Poster, designed 1942
Printed by U.S. Government Printing Office, Office for Emergency Management, Washington, D.C.
Offset lithograph, H 29 7/8" (75.9 cm)
Purchased with funds contributed by Gregory M. Harvey in memory of Merrill P. Harvey, 2003-70-1
(fig. 103)

28. Achille Castiglioni
Italian, 1918–2002
and Pier Giacomo Castiglioni
Italian, 1913–1968
Taraxacum 2 Lamp, designed 1960
Made by Flos S.p.A., Brescia, Italy
Plastic resin, steel, H 25" (63.5 cm)
Gift of Collab: The Group for Modern and Contemporary Design at the Philadelphia Museum of Art, 2010-76-2
(fig. 309)

29. *Taccia* Table Lamp, designed 1962
Made by Flos S.p.A., Brescia, Italy
Aluminum, glass, H 21" (53.3 cm)
Gift of Atelier International, Ltd., 1977-199-1
(fig. 159)

30. Wendell Castle
American, born 1932
Molar Chair, 1973
Fiberglass-reinforced polyester, H 26" (66 cm)
Gift of the artist, 1973-99-1
(fig. 146)

31. Joe Colombo
Italian, 1930–1971
Mini-Kitchen, designed 1963
Made by Boffi S.p.A., Milan
Plastic-coated wood, plastic, stainless steel, H 37 3/4" (95.9 cm)
Gift of Mr. and Mrs. Benjamin Thompson, 2000-89-1
(fig. 249)

32. Armchair, designed 1964
Made by Kartell S.p.A., Milan, after 1964
Molded and painted plywood, H 22 3/4" (57.8 cm)
Gift of Collab: The Group for Modern and Contemporary Design at the Philadelphia Museum of Art, 2001-42-2
(fig. 247)

33. *Vademecum* Folding Lamp, 1968
Made by Kartell S.p.A., Milan, from 1969
ABS plastic, stainless steel, H 9 7/8" (25.1 cm)
Gift of Collab: The Group for Modern and Contemporary Design at the Philadelphia Museum of Art, 2001-42-4
(fig. 248)

34. *Boby* Trolley, designed 1970
Made by Bieffeplast S.p.A., Padua, Italy, from 1970
ABS plastic, H 28 3/4" (73 cm)
Gift of Collab: The Group for Modern and Contemporary Design at the Philadelphia Museum of Art, 2001-42-7
(fig. 251)

35. *Linea 72* In-Flight Service for Alitalia First Class, designed 1970
Made by Richard Ginori S.p.A., Sesto Fiorentino, Italy, from 1972
Porcelain, stainless steel, plastic, linen, L 7 1/16" (17.9 cm)
Gift of Collab: The Group for Modern and Contemporary Design at the Philadelphia Museum of Art, 2001-42-24a–r
(fig. 250)

36. Joe Colombo
Italian, 1930–1971
with Gianni Colombo
Italian, 1937–1993
Acrilica Table Lamp, designed 1962
Made by O-Luce Italia S.p.A., Milan, from 1963
Brass, Perspex, H 9 7/16" (24 cm)
Gift of O-Luce Italia S.p.A., 1983-134-1
(fig. 196)

37. W. T. Copeland & Sons, Ltd., Stoke-on-Trent, Staffordshire, England
Pitcher, c. 1876
Tin-glazed earthenware with polychrome decoration, H 10 1/2" (26.7 cm)
The General Hector Tyndale Memorial Collection, 1897-522
(fig. 23)

38. Hans Coper
English, born Germany, 1920–1981
Vase, 1974
Stoneware, H 7 3/4" (19.7 cm)
Gift of the American Institute of Interior Designers, 1975-46-2
(fig. 155)

39. Vase, 1974
Stoneware, H 9 1/8" (23.2 cm)
Gift of the American Institute of Interior Designers, 1975-46-3
(fig. 154)

40. Shirley Craven
English, born 1934
Five Fabric, 1967
Made by Hull Traders Ltd., Lancashire, England
Screen-printed linen and cotton, W 50" (127 cm)
Gift of Hull Traders Ltd., 1975-8-1a–c
(fig. 150)

41. Virginia Wireman Cute
American, 1908–1985
Cigarette Box, 1949
Silver, W 3 5/16" (8.4 cm)
Gift of the artist, 1970-202-1
(fig. 125)

42. Gene Davis
American, 1920–1985
Franklin's Footpath, 1971
414' 6" (126.4 m) long and 8 traffic lanes wide, Benjamin Franklin Parkway, Philadelphia
Painted March 1972 under the direction of the Philadelphia Museum of Art, Department of Urban Outreach
(fig. 142)

43. Robin Day
English, 1915–2010
Polyprop Stacking Chair, designed 1963
Made by Hille International Ltd., London, from 1964
Steel, polypropylene, H 29 3/4" (75.6 cm)
Gift of John Stuart International, Inc., 1974-150-1
(fig. 151)

44. Joseph-Théodore Deck
French, 1823–1891
Dish, 1863
Earthenware with underglaze and enamel decoration, D 18 13/16" (47.8 cm)
Purchased with funds contributed by Mr. and Mrs. Adolph G. Rosengarten, Jr., 1978-117-1
(fig. 22)

45. William J. Dodd
American, 1862–1930
Vase, c. 1902
Made by Teco Art Pottery Division, Gates Potteries, Terra Cotta, Illinois
Glazed earthenware, H 13 3/8" (34 cm)
Gift of John T. Morris, 1902-922
(fig. 49)

46. Dorflinger Glass Company, White Mills, Pennsylvania
Decanter and Wineglasses, 1876
Lead glass, H (decanter) 16 1/4" (41.3 cm), H (glass) 5" (12.7 cm)
Gift of the Dorflinger Glass Company, 1876-1693–1693ll
(fig. 7)

47. Marion Dorn
American, 1899–1964
Scarf, c. 1941–44
Screen-printed silk, W 36" (91.4 cm)
Gift of John F. Platt, 1971-42-1
(fig. 106)

48. James Dyson
English, born 1947
Dual Cyclone Vacuum Cleaner, designed 1995
Made by Dyson Appliances, Ltd., London
ABS plastic, polycarbonate, L (extended) 7' 10" (2.4 m)
Gift of Dyson Appliances, Ltd., 1998-113-1
(fig. 233)

49. Charles Eames
American, 1907–1978
and Ray Eames
American, 1912–1988
CTW Coffee Table, designed 1945
Made by Evans Products Company, Venice, California, and Grand Haven, Michigan, 1947–48, and by Herman Miller Furniture Company, Zeeland, Michigan, from 1949
Molded plywood, D 34 1/2" (87.6 cm)
Gift of Professor and Mrs. Eugene Schneider, 1999-106-1
(fig. 98)

50. *DCW* Chair, designed 1945
Made by Evans Products Company, Venice, California, and Grand Haven, Michigan, 1947–48, and by Herman Miller Furniture Company, Zeeland, Michigan, from 1949
Molded and bent plywood, rubber, metal, H 28 1/4" (71.8 cm)
Gift of Professor and Mrs. Eugene Schneider, 1999-106-3
(fig. 97)

51. *DCM* Chair, designed 1946
Made by Evans Products Company, Venice, California, and Grand Haven, Michigan, 1946–48, and by Herman Miller Furniture Company, Zeeland, Michigan, from 1949
Molded ash-faced plywood, steel, rubber, H 29" (73.7 cm)
Gift of Mrs. L. Talbot Adamson, 1972-37-2
(fig. 99)

52. Chair, designed 1948–50
Shell made by Zenith Plastics Company, Gardena, California, and others for Herman Miller Furniture Company, Zeeland, Michigan, from 1950
Molded fiberglass-reinforced plastic, steel, H 26" (66 cm)
Gift of Mrs. L. Talbot Adamson, 1972-37-1
(fig. 100)

53. *ESU D-10-C* Desk, 1950
Made by Herman Miller Furniture Company, Zeeland, Michigan
Masonite, birch plywood, steel, H 29 1/2" (74.9 cm)
Purchased with funds from the proceeds of the sale of deaccessioned works of art, 2009-107-1
(pages 4–5)

54. Lounge Chair, 1965
Made by Herman Miller Furniture Company, Zeeland, Michigan
Aluminum, steel, leather, latex foam, Dacron, plywood, H 35" (88.9 cm)
Gift of the Philadelphia Chapter, American Institute of Architects, 1970-113-1
(fig. 135)

55. Laurits C. Eichner
American, born Denmark, 1894–1967
Pair of Vases, 1937
Pewter, H 24" (61 cm)
Gift of Mrs. Rodolphe M. de Schauensee, 1944-92-1a,b
(fig. 108)

56. Max Ernst
American, born Germany, 1891–1976
Chess Set, designed 1944
Boxwood, H (queen) 4 15/16" (12.6 cm)
Gift of John F. Harbeson, 1964-91-35(1–32)
(fig. 131)

57. Bed-Cage, Screen, and Bedspread, 1974
Made for Modern Art Associates, Geneva
Walnut, alder, brass, mirror, offset lithograph collage, mink, H (bed) 7' 4" (2.2 m)
Gift of Lannan Foundation, Santa Fe, N.M., 1999-14-1a–c
(fig. 252)

58. Wharton H. Esherick
American, 1887–1970
Fireplace and Doorway from the Library of the Curtis and Nellie Lee Bok House (Gulph Mills, Pennsylvania), 1936
Carved oak, stone, copper, L 16' (4.9 m)
Acquired through the generosity of W. B. Dixon Stroud, with additional funds for preservation and installation provided by Dr. and Mrs. Allen Goldman, Marion Boulton Stroud, and the Women's Committee of the Philadelphia Museum of Art, 1989-1,2
(fig. 70)

59. Susan Frackelton
American, 1851–1932
Jar on Stand, 1893
Salt-glazed stoneware, H 25" (63.5 cm)
Gift of John T. Morris, 1893-309,a,b
(fig. 34)

60. Kaj Franck
Finnish, 1911–1989
Kremlin Bells Double Decanter, designed 1957
Made by Nuutajärvi Notsjö Glasbruk for Oy Wärtsilä Ab, Nuutajärvi, Finland
Blown glass, H 13 3/4" (34.9 cm)
Gift of Collab: The Group for Modern and Contemporary Design at the Philadelphia Museum of Art, 1982-33-1a–c
(fig. 178)

61. Émile Gallé
French, 1846–1904
Vase, c. 1900
Mold-blown glass with marquetry and carved decoration, H 8 1/8" (20.6 cm)
Gift of John T. Morris, 1900-219
(fig. 41)

62. Vase, 1900
Blown glass, cased with cameo-cut marquetry decoration, H 6 3/16" (15.7 cm)
John T. Morris Collection, 1921-46-71
(fig. 42)

63. Vase, c. 1903–4
Blown glass, cased, patinated, cut, and engraved with applied decoration and metal foil, H 11 1/2" (29.2 cm)
Purchased with the Joseph E. Temple Fund, 1905-46
(fig. 39)

64–67. Elizabeth Garouste
French, 1949
and Mattia Bonetti
French, born Switzerland, 1953
Étrange Végetation Service, designed 1992
Made by Porzellanmanufaktur Reichenbach GmbH, Reichenbach, Germany, for Anthologie Quartett, Bad Essen, Germany
Porcelain with underglaze decoration, D (dessert plate) 8 1/4" (21 cm), D (soup plate) 9 1/16" (23 cm), D (dinner plate) 9 13/16" (24.9 cm), D (large dinner plate) 11 13/16" (30 cm)
Gift of Anthologie Quartett, Bad Essen, Germany, 2004-141-2,3,4,9
(figs. 297–300)

68. Frank O. Gehry
American, born Canada, 1929
Fish Lamp, c. 1983
Made by New City Editions, Venice, California
ColorCore, wood, silicone, H 5' 8 1/2" (1.7 m)
Gift of Marion Stroud Swingle, 2008-263-1
(fig. 286)

69. *Red Beaver* Armchair, designed 1986
Made by Vitra GmbH, Basel, Switzerland, 2008
Dyed corrugated cardboard, H 33 3/4" (85.7 cm)
Gift of Vitra GmbH, Basel, Switzerland, 2009-58-3
(fig. 289)

70. *Power Play* Chair, designed 1989–91
Made by Knoll, Inc., New York, from 1992
Laminated maple, H 32 7/8" (83.5 cm)
Gift of Knoll, Inc., in honor of Kathryn B. Hiesinger, Curator of European Decorative Arts after 1700, 2008-171-1
(fig. 288)

71. *High Sticking* Chair, designed 1989–91
Made by Knoll, Inc., New York, from 1992
Laminated maple, H 43 3/8" (110.2 cm)
Gift of Knoll, Inc., in honor of Kathryn B. Hiesinger, Curator of European Decorative Arts after 1700, 2008-171-3
(fig. 287)

72. Milton Glaser
American, born 1929
Bob Dylan Poster, designed 1966
Made by Columbia Records, New York
Offset lithograph from an ink drawing with Cello-Tak overlay, H 32 5/8" (82.9 cm)
Gift of Collab: The Group for Modern and Contemporary Design at the Philadelphia Museum of Art, 2002-146-1
(fig. 236)

73. Carl Goetz
American, born Germany, active late 19th century
Centerpiece, 1892
Made by Ohio Valley China Company, Wheeling, West Virginia
Glazed and unglazed porcelain, H 25 1/2" (64.8 cm)
Gift of the Ohio Valley China Company, 1893-376a
(fig. 35)

74. Jules Goury
French, 1803–1834
and Owen Jones
British, 1803–1874
Plans, Elevations, Sections, and Details of the Alhambra
London: Owen Jones, 1842–45
2 vols., H 27 3/16" (69 cm) each
Collection of the Philadelphia Museum of Art Library, gift of Mrs. E. T. Stotesbury, 1939
(fig. 25)

75. Michael Graves
American, born 1934
Whistling Bird Teakettle, designed 1985
Made by Alessi S.p.A., Crusinallo, Italy
Stainless steel, polyamide, H 8 7/8" (22.5 cm)
Gift of the designer, 1996-27-1a,b
(fig. 228)

76. *Tea for Three*, 1995
Four-color screenprint, H 15" (38.1 cm)
Gift of Collab: The Group for Modern and Contemporary Design at the Philadelphia Museum of Art, 1995-154-1
(fig. 227)

77. Jacques Gréber
French, 1882–1962
Philadelphia Museum of Art: Perspective from East, Perspective of the Main Entrance, Steps of the Museum, 1917–18
Made for Borie, Trumbauer, and Zantzinger, Philadelphia
Crayon on tracing paper, mounted on card, W 34" (86.4 cm)
PDP-1086
(fig. 59)

78. June Groff
American, 1903–1974
Fabric, 1947
Hand screen-printed linen, W 54" (137.2 cm)
Gift of the artist, 1948-13-1
(fig. 115)

79. Fabric, 1947
Hand screen-printed cotton, W 41 1/4" (104.8 cm)
Gift of the artist, 1948-13-4
(fig. 117)

80. Hector Guimard
French, 1867–1942
Tray, 1909
Gilt copper, D 18 1/2" (47 cm)
Gift of Mme Hector Guimard, 1949-43-1
(fig. 124)

81. Chair, c. 1912
Cherry wood, leather, H 44" (111.8 cm)
Gift of Mme Hector Guimard, 1948-64-1
(fig. 114)

82. Wayne Higby
American, born 1943
Many Rocks Pass, 1976
Glazed and unglazed earthenware, H 12" (30.5 cm)
Gift of Collab: The Group for Modern and Contemporary Design at the Philadelphia Museum of Art, 1976-106-1
(fig. 156)

83. Josef Hoffmann
Footed Cup, c. 1926
Made by Wiener Werkstätte, Vienna
Silver, H 7 1/4" (18.4 cm)
Purchased with funds contributed by Collab: The Group for Modern and Contemporary Design at the Philadelphia Museum of Art, Mr. and Mrs. Adolph G. Rosengarten, Jr., and the Fiske Kimball Fund, 1981-89-1
(fig. 310)

84. Earl Horter
American, 1880–1940
The PSFS Building, c. 1932
Etching, aquatint, drypoint, H (image) 14 7/8" (37.8 cm), H (sheet) 16 11/16" (42.4 cm)
Gift of Samuel B. Sturgis, 1962-82-63
(fig. 83)

85. George Howe
American, 1886–1955
and William E. Lescaze
American, born Switzerland, 1896–1969
Lounge Chair and Ottoman, designed 1932
Made by Lloyd Manufacturing Company, Menominee, Michigan
Chromed steel, imitation leather, H (chair) 34 1/2" (87.6 cm), H (ottoman) 14 1/2" (36.8 cm)
Purchased for the Philadelphia Museum of Art with a grant from Preservation Pennsylvania, 2004-13-1,3
(fig. 84)

86. Maija Isola
Finnish, 1927–2001
Kivet Fabric, designed 1956
Made by Marimekko Oy, Helsinki
Screen-printed cotton, W 54" (137.2 cm)
Gift of Marimekko Oy, 1983-131-3
(fig. 194)

87. George Washington Jack
American, active England, 1855–1932
Secretaire Cabinet, c. 1889
Made by Morris and Company, London
Mahogany with hardwood inlay, H 51 1/2" (130.8 cm)
Purchased with funds contributed by the Friends of the Philadelphia Museum of Art and with the gift (by exchange) of Julia G. Fahnestock in memory of her husband, William Fahnestock, 1986-128-1a,b
(fig. 12)

88. Arne Jacobsen
Danish, 1902–1971
Egg Armchair and Ottoman, designed 1957
Made by Fritz Hansen Eft A/S, Allerød, Denmark
Molded plastic, leather, chromed steel, H (armchair) 42 1/2" (108 cm), H (ottoman) 17 1/2" (44.5 cm)
Gift of the National Society of Interior Design, Pennsylvania Chapter in memory of Jim Prosper, 1971-30-1,2
(fig. 136)

89–92. *Cylinda-line* Service, designed 1967
Made by Stelton A/S, Copenhagen
Stainless steel, nylon (coffeepot, teapot), H (coffeepot) 7 1/2" (19.1 cm), H (teapot) 4 5/16" (11 cm), H (creamer) 3 3/4" (9.5 cm), D (sugar bowl) 3" (7.6 cm)
Gift of Stelton A/S, 1982-53-5a,b–8a,b
(figs. 168–71)

93. Georg Jensen
Danish, 1866–1935
Dish, 1919
Made by Georg Jensen Sølvsmedie A/S, Copenhagen
Silver, D 14 7/16" (36.7 cm)
Gift of Louis V. Placé, Jr., 1936-33-1
(fig. 94)

94. Søren Georg Jensen
Danish, 1917–1982
Condiment Set for Salt, Pepper, and Mustard, *no. 965*, 1951
Made by Georg Jensen Sølvsmedie A/S, Copenhagen
Silver, H (pepper shaker) 3 1/8" (7.9 cm)
Gift of Mr. and Mrs. Louis Sherman, 1982-58-4a–c
(fig. 269)

95. Hella Jongerius
Dutch, born 1963
Repeat Dot Unique Fabric, 2002
Made by Maharam, New York
Cotton, polyester, rayon, W 55" (139.7 cm)
Purchased with funds from the proceeds of the sale of deaccessioned works of art, 2009-93-1
(back endpapers)

96. *Summer* Teapot from *Four Seasons*, 2007
Made by Porzellan Manufaktur Nymphenburg, Nymphenburg, Germany
Glazed hard-paste porcelain, silk, H 10 1/2" (26.7 cm)
Purchased with the John D. McIlhenny Fund, 2010-60-1a–d
(page 10)

97. Edward McKnight Kauffer
American, 1890–1954
Watch Out for Fire Poster, 1943
Printed by U.S. Government Printing Office for C.A.A. War Training Service, Department of Commerce
Lithograph, H 44 1/4" (112.4 cm)
Gift of Mrs. Marion V. Dorn, 1963-84-56
(fig. 107)

98. Isamu Kenmochi
Japanese, 1912–1971
Kashiwado Chair, designed 1961
Made by Tendo Mokko, Tendo, Japan
Lacquered Japanese cedar, H 24 3/4" (62.9 cm)
Gift of Tendo Company, Ltd., 1996-90-1
(fig. 216)

99. Toshiyuki Kita
Japanese, born 1942
Wink Chair, designed 1980
Made by Cassina S.p.A., Meda, Italy
Steel, Dacron-covered polyurethane-foam upholstery, L (extended) 6' 6 3/4" (2 m)
Gift of Collab: The Group for Modern and Contemporary Design at the Philadelphia Museum of Art, 1994-132-1
(fig. 208)

100. Florence Knoll
American, born 1917
Credenza, designed 1955
Made by Knoll, Inc., New York, 2004
Chromed steel, mahogany, marble, L 37" (94 cm)
Gift of Collab: The Group for Modern and Contemporary Design at the Philadelphia Museum of Art, in honor of Robert Aibel, 2005-20-1
(fig. 262)

101. J. Juriaan Kok
Dutch, 1861–1919
and Wilhelmus Petrus Hartgring
Dutch, 1874–1940
Tea Service, 1900
Made by Haagsche Plateelbakkerij Rozenburg, The Hague
Soft-paste porcelain with enamel decoration, W (tray) 12" (30.5 cm), H (cup) 2 13/16" (7.1 cm), D (saucer) 4 3/8" (11.1 cm), H (sugar bowl) 6 1/2" (16.5 cm), H (teapot) 7 1/2" (19.1 cm), H (creamer) 3" (7.6 cm)
Purchased with the Fiske Kimball Fund and the Marie Kimball Fund, 1975-18-1–6
(fig. 45)

102. Shiro Kuramata
Japanese, 1934–1991
Furniture in Irregular Forms: Side 2 Chest of Drawers, designed 1970
Made by Cappellini S.p.A., Arosio, Italy
Lacquered wood, H 5' 6 15/16" (1.7 m)
Gift of Cappellini S.p.A., Arosio, Italy, 1994-130-1
(fig. 221)

103. *How High the Moon* Armchair, designed 1986
Made by Vitra GmbH, Basel, Switzerland
Nickel-plated steel, H 28 1/4" (71.8 cm)
Gift of Collab: The Group for Modern and Contemporary Design at the Philadelphia Museum of Art, in honor of Gerard J. Jarosinski, Jr., 1993-1-1
(fig. 214)

104. René Lalique
French, 1860–1945
Tourbillons (Whirlwinds) Vase, designed 1926
Made by Lalique, Paris
Mold-pressed glass with enamel decoration, H 8" (20.3 cm)
The Henry P. McIlhenny Collection in memory of Frances P. McIlhenny, 1986-26-146
(fig. 95)

105. *Margaret* Vase, designed 1929
Made by Lalique, Paris
Mold-pressed and patinated glass, H 9 1/8" (23.2 cm)
Gift of Mr. and Mrs. Rodolphe M. de Schauensee, 1960-70-1
(fig. 91)

106. Jack Lenor Larsen
American, born 1927
Rémoulade Fabric, 1956
Woven by Richard Bolan, Patterson, New Jersey
Linen, jute, cotton, rayon, wool, silk, metallic yarns, other fibers, W 68" (172.7 cm)
Gift of Thomas Ashjean, 1984-26-1
(front endpapers)

107. *Magnum* Fabric, designed 1970
Woven by Jack Lenor Larsen, Inc., New York
Cotton, vinyl, nylon, polyamide, polyester, W 48" (121.9 cm)
Gift of Collab: The Group for Modern and Contemporary Design at the Philadelphia Museum of Art, 1983-186-2
(fig. 193)

108. Matthew Leibowitz
American, 1918–1974
H. L. Mencken: Speaking Album Cover, 1958
Made by Caedmon Records, New York
Letterpress on Lustro Gloss paper, H 12 1/2" (31.8 cm)
Gift of Lynn Leibowitz and Jan Bresnick, 2007-103-4
(fig. 104)

109. Charles Rennie Mackintosh
Scottish, 1868–1928
High-Back Side Chair, c. 1897
Probably made by Herbert Smith and Son, Glasgow
Stained oak, rush with horsehair, H 53 7/8" (136.8 cm)
Purchased with the Fiske Kimball Fund and the Thomas Skelton Harrison Fund, 1987-71-1
(fig. 56)

110. Enzo Mari
Italian, born 1932
Pago-Pago Vase, designed 1969
Made by Danese Milano, Bruno Danese S.r.l., Milan
ABS plastic, H 11 13/16" (30 cm)
Gift of Jacqueline and Bruno Danese, 1983-115-1
(fig. 189)

111. Maurice Marinot
French, 1882–1960
Bottle, 1923
Glass with encased enamel, H (bottle) 7 3/16" (18.3 cm)
Gift of Mlle Florence Marinot, 1967-98-10a,b
(fig. 90)

112. Vase, 1923
Acid-etched glass, H 7" (17.8 cm)
Gift of Mlle Florence Marinot, 1967-98-13
(fig. 88)

113. Bottle, 1924
Acid-etched glass with fused layers, H (bottle) 10" (25.4 cm)
Gift of Mlle Florence Marinot, 1967-98-16a,b
(fig. 89)

114. Bottle, 1932
Glass with encased enamel and bubbles, H (bottle) 4 7/16" (11.3 cm)
Gift of Mlle Florence Marinot, 1967-98-28a,b
(fig. 129)

115. Javier Errando Mariscal
Spanish, born 1950
Ensaladilla Fabric, 1978
Made by Marieta Textil, SA, Barcelona
Screen-printed cotton, W 63" (160 cm)
Gift of Marieta Textil, SA, 1983-8-1
(fig. 185)

116. *Hilton* Trolley, designed 1980
Made by Memphis Milano S.r.l., from 1981
Enameled metal, glass, H 31 3/4" (80.6 cm)
Gift of Abet Laminati S.p.A., 1983-104-1
(fig. 177)

117. *Floresta* Fabric, 1981
Made by Marieta Textil, SA, Barcelona
Screen-printed cotton, W 63" (160 cm)
Gift of Marieta Textil, SA, 1983-8-2
(fig. 176)

118. *Duplex* Stool, designed 1981
Made by B. D. Ediciones de Diseño, S.A., Barcelona
Metal, leather, H 32 1/2" (82.6 cm)
Gift of B. D. Ediciones de Diseño, S.A., 1983-44-1
(fig. 183)

119. Bruno Mathsson
Swedish, 1907–1988
Pernilla Chair and *Mifot* Footstool, designed 1941–43
Made by Karl Mathsson, Värnamo, Sweden, 1967
Laminated beech, bast fiber, H (chair) 39" (99.1 cm), H (footstool) 17" (43.2 cm)
Gift of Collab: The Group for Modern and Contemporary Design at the Philadelphia Museum of Art, 2003-33-1,2
(fig. 279)

120. Herbert Matter
Swiss, 1907–1984
En route pour la Suisse (En Route to Switzerland) Poster, designed 1935
Printed by Fretz Frères, S.A., Zurich
Rotogravure, H 39 1/2" (100.3 cm)
Purchased with the Bradburd Memorial Fund, 2003-71-1
(fig. 282)

121. Ingo Maurer
German, born 1932
Mozzkito Lamp, designed 1996
Made by Ingo Maurer GmbH, Munich
Metal, plastic, rubber, L 31 1/2" (80 cm)
Gift of Ingo Maurer GmbH, 1999-12-1
(fig. 258)

122. Ingo Maurer
and Dagmar Mombach
German, born 1958
Kokoro Lamp from *Les MaMo Nouchies* series, designed 1998
Made by Ingo Maurer GmbH, Munich
Pleated paper, metal, H 30" (76.2 cm)
Gift of Ingo Maurer, 2002-218-1
(fig. 259)

123. Paul Mayen
American, 1918–2000
Sand Urn and Waste Receptacle, designed c. 1965
Made by Habitat, Inc., New York
Trexiloy, H 25 3/16" (64 cm)
Gift of Habitat, Inc., 1970-206-3
(fig. 141)

124. Paul McCobb
American, 1917–1969
Planner Group Bench and Chest of Drawers, designed 1949
Made by Winchendon Furniture Company, Winchendon, Massachusetts, 1949–52
Maple, L (bench) 48" (121.9 cm), H (chest) 24" (61 cm)
Gift of Collab: The Group for Modern and Contemporary Design at the Philadelphia Museum of Art, 1983-5-2,3
(fig. 120)

125. *Planner Group* Buffet, designed 1949
Made by Winchendon Furniture Company, Winchendon, Massachusetts, 1949–52
Birch, *Madagaska* plastic-coated cloth, L 60" (152.4 cm)
Gift of Professor and Mrs. Eugene Schneider, 1999-106-4
(fig. 119)

126. Peter McCulloch
English, born 1933
Cruachan Fabric, 1963
Made by Hull Traders Ltd., Lancashire, England
Screen-printed cotton, W 48" (121.9 cm)
Gift of Hull Traders Ltd., 1975-8-2a,b
(fig. 152)

127. Giacinto Melillo
Italian, 1846–1915
Pair of Earrings, c. 1870
Gold, enamel, seed pearl, L 4 3/8" (11.1 cm)
Gift of Lydia Thompson Morris, 1925-27-337a,b
(fig. 21)

128. Alessandro Mendini
Italian, born 1931
Proust Armchair, designed 1978
Made by Atelier Mendini, Milan, 1998–99
Painted wood, painted fabric upholstery, H 42 1/2" (108 cm)
Gift (by exchange) of Mrs. Adolph G. Rosengarten, 2000-118-1
(fig. 198)

129. Ludwig Mies van der Rohe
American, born Germany, 1886–1969
MR20 Armchair and Stool, designed 1927
Made by Berliner Metallgewerbe Joseph Müller, Berlin, 1927–30; by Bamberg Metallwerkstätten, Berlin-Neukölln, 1931–32; and by Gebrüder Thonet, Vienna, after 1932
Chrome-plated steel, lacquered caning, H (armchair) 32 1/2" (82.6 cm), H (stool) 18 1/2" (47 cm)
Gift of Collab: The Group for Modern and Contemporary Design at the Philadelphia Museum of Art, in memory of Roland Gallimore, 1978-116-1,2
(fig. 85)

130. Joan Miró
Spanish, 1893–1983
Rug, c. 1934
Woven by unknown atelier, Aubusson, France
Wool and cotton knotted weave, L 6' 9 7/8" (2.1 m)
Gift of Mrs. John Wintersteen, 1940-2-1
(fig. 96)

131. Issey Miyake
Japanese, born 1938
Bustier, designed 1980
Made by Issey Miyake, Inc., Tokyo
Plastic, H 15" (38.1 cm)
Purchased with the Costume and Textiles Revolving Fund, 1992-136-1
(fig. 220)

132. Riokei Nakashima
Japanese, 1868–1912
Tray, c. 1875
Enameled and gilt earthenware, W 7 5/16" (18.5 cm)
Purchased with Museum funds, 1876-1665
(fig. 57)

133. Gertrud Natzler
American, born Austria, 1908–1971
and Otto Natzler
American, born Austria, 1908–2007
Bowl, 1945
Glazed earthenware, H 5 7/8" (14.9 cm)
Gift of Mrs. Herbert Cameron Morris, 1945-68-1
(fig. 127)

134. Camille Naudot, Fils et Cie., Paris
Bowl, c. 1900
Soft-paste porcelain with translucent enamel decoration, D 4 15/16" (12.6 cm)
Purchased with the Joseph E. Temple Fund, 1901-45
(fig. 40)

135. George Nelson
American, 1908–1986
with John F. Pile
American, active New York, 1952–2001
Pretzel Chair, designed 1957
Made by Herman Miller Furniture Company, Zeeland, Michigan
Birch-faced laminated wood, leather, H 31" (78.7 cm)
Gift of Jeanne S. Rymer, 2007-186-28
(fig. 290)

136. New York Architectural Terra-Cotta Company, New York
Panel, 1886–89
Terracotta, W 23 1/16" (58.6 cm)
Gift of the New York Architectural Terra-Cotta Company, 1889-169
(fig. 28)

137. Marcello Nizzoli
Italian, 1887–1969
Lettera 22 Typewriter, designed 1950
Made by Ing. C. Olivetti & C., S.p.A, Ivrea, Italy
Enameled metal, W 11 3/8" (28.9 cm)
Gift of James Nelson Kise, 1984-30-1
(fig. 270)

138. Isamu Noguchi
American, 1904–1988
Table Lamp, designed 1948
Made by Knoll Associates, Inc., New York
Plastic, wood, H 15 3/4" (40 cm)
Gift of Mr. and Mrs. James Dermody, 1977-85-1
(fig. 162)

139. *Akari* Floor Lamp, designed 1975
Made by George Kovacs Lighting, Inc., New York
Mulberry-bark paper, bamboo, metal, H 45" (114.3 cm)
Gift of the artist, 1979-87-1a–d
(fig. 161)

140. Edvin Öhrström
Swedish, 1906–1994
Vase, 1948
Made by Orrefors Glasbruk, Orrefors, Sweden
Glass with trapped-air decoration, H 4 7/16" (11.2 cm)
Gift of Mrs. Henry W. Breyer, Sr., 1967-17-8
(fig. 128)

141. Sinya Okayama
Japanese, born 1941
Kotobuki Shelves, designed 1989
Made by Daichi Company, Ltd., Tokyo
Lacquered wood, H 5' 4 1/8" (1.6 m)
Gift of Daichi Company, Ltd., 1990-25-1
(fig. 218)

142. Verner Panton
Danish, 1926–1998
Cone Chair, designed 1958
Made by Plus-Linje, Copenhagen
Steel, wool upholstery, H 32" (81.3 cm)
Gift of Jeanne S. Rymer, 2007-186-13
(fig. 294)

143. Nathalie du Pasquier
French, born 1957
Gabon Fabric, designed 1982
Made by Rainbow, Milan
Screen-printed cotton, W 60" (152.4 cm)
Gift of Furniture of the Twentieth Century, Inc., 1983-119-1
(fig. 174)

144. Pierre Paulin
French, 1927–2009
Ribbon Chair #582, designed 1965
Made by Artifort, Maastricht, The Netherlands
Upholstered rubber, metal, acrylic, wood, H 27 1/2" (69.9 cm)
Gift of Jeanne S. Rymer, 2007-186-18
(fig. 292)

145. Gaetano Pesce
Italian, born 1939
Up 5 Chair and *Up 6* Ottoman, designed 1969, reissued 1994
Made by C & B Italia S.p.A., Novedrate, Italy, 1970–72, and by B & B Italia S.p.A., Milan, 1973–81, 1984, and from 1994
Expandable polyurethane foam, stretch jersey fabric, H (chair) 40 1/2" (102.9 cm), D (ottoman) 22 1/2" (57.2 cm)
Gift of Collab: The Group for Modern and Contemporary Design at the Philadelphia Museum of Art, 2000-151-1,2
(fig. 278)

146. *I Feltri* Armchair (Lowback), designed 1986
Made by Cassina S.p.A., Meda, Italy, from 1987
Wool felt impregnated with thermosetting polyester resin, felt, cotton, and hemp string, quilted fabric upholstery, H 38 5/8" (98.1 cm)
Gift of Cassina S.p.A., Meda, Italy, 2006-32-1
(fig. 267)

147. *Nobody's Perfect* Chair, designed 2002
Made by Zerodisegno, a division of Quattrocchio S.r.l., Alessandria, Italy, 2002
Polyurethane-based resin, nylon pins, H (seat) 17 11/16" (44.9 cm)
Gift of Collab: The Group for Modern and Contemporary Design at the Philadelphia Museum of Art, 2003-136-1
(fig. 266)

148. *Spaghetti* Bracelet, 2005
Made by Fish Design, New York and Milan
Plastic resin, D 4 1/2" (11.4 cm)
Gift of Lisa S. Roberts, 2005-183-1
(fig. 264)

149. *Ribbon* Bracelet, 2005
Made by Fish Design, New York and Milan
Plastic resin, D 4" (10.2 cm)
Gift of Collab: The Group for Modern and Contemporary Design at the Philadelphia Museum of Art, 2005-102-2
(fig. 265)

150. Pablo Ruiz y Picasso
Spanish, 1881–1973
Woman with Loaves, 1906
Oil on canvas, H 39 13/16" (101.2 cm)
Gift of Charles E. Ingersoll, 1931-7-1
(fig. 76)

151. Gio Ponti
Italian, 1891–1979
Inverno (Winter) Plate from the *Four Seasons* Service, c. 1923–30
Made by Richard Ginori S.p.A., Sesto Fiorentino, Italy
Porcelain with enamel decoration, D 9" (22.9 cm)
Gift of Maude de Schauensee in memory of her parents, Mr. and Mrs. Rodolphe Meyer de Schauensee, 1990-102-1
(fig. 93)

152. Toilet, designed 1953
Made by Ideal Standard, Milan, 1954–71
Porcelain, H 15 1/8" (38.4 cm)
Gift of Ideal Standard, 1983-52-2
(fig. 147)

153. Jean Puiforcat
French, 1897–1945
Tureen, 1937
Made by Puiforcat, Paris
Silver, hematite, D 11 3/4" (29.8 cm)
Purchased with Museum funds, 1948-70-1a,b
(fig. 113)

154. Paul Rand
American, 1914–1996
IBM Rebus Poster, designed 1981
Made by IBM Corporation, Armonk, New York, 1982
Screenprint, H 36" (91.4 cm)
Gift of Collab: The Group for Modern and Contemporary Design at the Philadelphia Museum of Art, in honor of Lisa Benn Costigan, and with funds contributed by James Lapides, 2005-102-1
(fig. 283)

155. Karim Rashid
Canadian, born Egypt, 1960
Garbino Can, designed 1996
Made by Umbra, Ltd., Toronto
Molded polypropylene, H 13" (33 cm)
Gift of Umbra, Ltd., 1999-107-4
(fig. 235)

156. *Oh* Chair Prototype, designed 1998
Made by Umbra, Ltd., Toronto
Polypropylene, powder-coated steel, H 34" (86.4 cm)
Gift of Totem Design Group, 2000-155-1
(fig. 234)

157. Carlos Riart
Spanish, 1944
Desnuda Chair, designed 1973
Made by Temco, Barcelona, from 1979
Enameled iron, brass, fabric upholstery, H 39 3/8" (100 cm)
Gift of Carlos Riart, 1983-136-1
(fig. 184)

158. Lucie Rie
English, born Austria, 1902–1995
Bottle, 1974
Glazed porcelain, H 11" (27.9 cm)
Gift of the American Institute of Interior Designers, 1975-46-6
(fig. 153)

159. Richard Riemerschmid
German, 1868–1957
Chair, 1907
Made by Vereinigte Werkstätten für Kunst im Handwerk, Munich
Oak, leather, H 30 5/8" (77.8 cm)
Purchased with the Fiske Kimball Fund, 1991-17-1
(fig. 50)

160. Gerrit Thomas Rietveld
Dutch, 1888–1964
Zigzag Chair, designed 1932–33
Made by Gerard van de Groenekan, Utrecht, The Netherlands, c. 1935
Painted plywood, H 31 9/16" (80.1 cm)
Purchased with the Fiske Kimball Fund and with funds contributed by Collab: The Group for Modern and Contemporary Design at the Philadelphia Museum of Art, in honor of Eric B. Rymshaw, 1995-65-1
(fig. 229)

161. Rookwood Pottery Company, Cincinnati, Ohio
Plate, 1880
Glazed stoneware, D 8 3/4" (22.2 cm)
Gift of Mrs. James Cameron Bleloch, 1976-104-1 (formerly 1892-162, deaccessioned, and reacquired)
(fig. 33)

162. Rörstrand Fabriks, Stockholm
Plate, 1876
Lead-glazed earthenware, D 20" (50.8 cm)
The General Hector Tyndale Memorial Collection, 1897-617
(fig. 8)

163. Aldo Rossi
Italian, 1931–1997
Cabina dell'Elba Wardrobe, designed 1980
Made by Molteni & C. S.p.A., Milan
Particle board, plastic laminate, sheet brass, H 7' 6 1/4" (2.3 m)
Gift of Cecilia Metheny, 2000-70-2
(fig. 175)

164. Jacques-Émile Ruhlmann
French, 1879–1933
Chair, designed 1924
Rosewood, fabric upholstery, H 31 7/8" (81 cm)
Purchased with funds from Collab: The Group for Modern and Contemporary Design at the Philadelphia Museum of Art, and with the gifts (by exchange) of Mrs. Newell J. Ward and Dorothy Reed, 2006-77-1
(fig. 280)

165. Writing Desk, designed c. 1925
Macassar ebony with ivory inlay, suede lining, H 44 1/2" (113 cm)
Gift of Collab: The Group for Modern and Contemporary Design at the Philadelphia Museum of Art, 1976-227-1
(fig. 280)

166. Eero Saarinen
American, born Finland, 1910–1961
Grasshopper Chair, designed 1946
Made by Knoll Associates, Inc., and Knoll International, New York, 1948–65
Laminated birch, fabric upholstery, H 34" (86.4 cm)
Gift of Mr. and Mrs. Morton Weiss, 1984-34-1
(fig. 101)

167. *Pedestal* Chair, designed 1955–57
Made by Knoll, Inc., New York, from 1956
Fiberglass-reinforced plastic, lacquered cast aluminum, wool upholstery, H 31" (78.7 cm)
Purchased with funds contributed by Mr. and Mrs. Gregory M. Harvey, 1973-96-1
(fig. 102)

168. Roberto Sambonet
Italian, 1924–1995
Center Line Cooking Set (8), designed 1964
Made by Sambonet, Vercelli, Italy
Stainless steel, D (largest pot) 9 1/2" (24.1 cm)
Gift of Sambonet—Cutlery, Tableware & Holloware Manufacturers, 1983-141-1–8
(fig. 186)

169. Richard Sapper
Italian, born Germany, 1932
Tizio Table Lamp, designed 1972
Made by Artemide S.p.A., Milan, from 1972
ABS plastic, aluminum metal alloy, H (extended) 46 1/2" (118.1 cm)
Gift of Artemide, Inc., 1983-105-2
(fig. 192)

170. *9090* Espresso Coffeemaker, designed 1978
Made by Alessi S.p.A., Crusinallo, Italy
Stainless steel, cast iron, H 8 1/16" (20.4 cm)
Gift of Alessi S.p.A., 1983-41-1
(fig. 167)

171. Tobia Scarpa
Italian, born 1935
Pigreco Armchair, designed c. 1956
Made by Gavina S.p.A., Milan, from c. 1960
Wood, cotton upholstery, H 27" (68.6 cm)
Gift of Jeanne S. Rymer, 2007-186-15
(fig. 291)

172. Tobia Scarpa and Afra Scarpa
Italian, born 1937
Soriana Lounge Chair and Ottoman, designed 1970
Made by Atelier International, Ltd., New York, under license from Cassina S.p.A., Meda, Italy
Chromed metal, polyurethane, Dacron, leather, H (chair) 27" (68.6 cm), H (ottoman) 15 3/4" (40 cm)
Gift of Atelier International, Ltd., 1978-21-1a,b
(fig. 158)

173. Peter Schlumbohm
American, born Germany, 1896–1962
Water Kettle, designed 1949
Made by Chemex Corporation, Pittsfield, Massachusetts
Pyrex glass, cork, H (with stopper) 12 5/16" (31.3 cm)
Gift of Chemex Corporation, 1983-4-2a,b
(fig. 181)

174. Eugene Schoen
American, 1880–1957
Buffet, 1927
Made by Schmieg, Hungate & Kotzian, New York
Macassar ebony veneer, rosewood veneer, rosewood, walnut veneer, walnut, oak and oak plywood, cherry wood, light and dark wood inlay, brass, W 6' (1.8 m)
Gift of the Modern Club of Philadelphia, 1929-45-1a,b
(fig. 68)

175. Richard Schultz
American, born 1926
Topiary Lounge Chair and Ottoman, designed 1988
Made by Richard Schultz Design, Inc., Palm, Pennsylvania
Bent, stamped, and folded aluminum sheet, finished with epoxy polyester powder coating, H (chair) 30 1/2" (77.5 cm), H (ottoman) 15" (38.1 cm)
Gift of the designer, 2006-119-1,2
(fig. 303)

176. Kitaro Shirayamadani
Japanese, 1865–1948, active United States, 1887–1948
Vase, 1899
Made by Rookwood Pottery Company, Cincinnati, Ohio
Glazed stoneware, H 17 3/8" (44.1 cm)
Gift of John T. Morris, 1901-15
(fig. 44)

177. Olaf Skoogfors
American, born Sweden, 1930–1975
Decanter, 1966
Silver, rosewood, H (with stopper) 13 3/16" (33.5 cm)
Gift of the Friends of the Philadelphia Museum of Art, 1968-2-1a,b
(fig. 132)

178. Marc-Louis-Emmanuel Solon
French, 1835–1913
La Grace Vase, 1875
Made by Minton, Ltd., Stoke-on-Trent, England
Parian porcelain with pâte-sur-pâte and gilt decoration, H 15 3/16" (38.5 cm)
Purchased with Museum funds, 1876-1620,a
(fig. 5)

179. Marc-Louis-Emmanuel Solon and Alboine Birks
English, 1861–1941
Folie or *Jester* Vase, 1894
Made by Minton, Ltd., Stoke-on-Trent, England
Parian porcelain with pâte-sur-pâte and gilt decoration,
H 23 7/8" (60.6 cm)
Purchased with the Joseph E. Temple Fund, 1898-95
(fig. 58)

180. Ettore Sottsass
Italian, born Austria, 1917–2007
Nefertiti Desk, 1969
Made by Abet Laminati S.p.A., Bra, Italy
Plastic laminate–veneered chipboard, H 43 1/2" (110.5 cm)
Gift of Abet Laminati S.p.A., 1983-40-1
(fig. 197)

181. *Casablanca* Sideboard, designed 1981
Made by Abet Laminati S.p.A., Bra, Italy, for Memphis Milano S.r.l.
Plastic laminate–veneered wood and chipboard, H 7' 6 1/2" (2.3 m)
Gift of Collab: The Group of Modern and Contemporary Design at the Philadelphia Museum of Art and Abet Laminati S.p.A., 1983-113-1
(fig. 173)

182. Philippe Starck
French, born 1949
J. (Série Lang) Armchair, designed 1987
Made by Driade S.p.A., Fossadello di Caorso, Italy
Steel, aluminum, leather, H 33 3/4" (85.7 cm)
Gift of Collab: The Group for Modern and Contemporary Design at the Philadelphia Museum of Art, in honor of Lisa Roberts, 1997-183-5
(fig. 231)

183. *W.W.* Stool, designed 1990
Made by Vitra GmbH, Basel, Switzerland
Lacquered aluminum, H 38 3/16" (97 cm)
Gift of Vitra International AG, 1997-24-1
(fig. 232)

184. Robert Stocksdale
American, 1913–2003
Bowl, 1975
Indonesian boxwood, D 8 1/4" (21 cm)
Gift of Ellen Plotkin and Collab: The Group for Modern and Contemporary Design at the Philadelphia Museum of Art, 1976-107-1
(fig. 157)

185. Stumpf, Touvier, Viollet & Cie., Paris
Vase, c. 1900
Layered glass with wheel-cut decoration, H 8" (20.3 cm)
Gift of John T. Morris, 1900-145
(fig. 43)

186. Gebrüder Thonet, Vienna
Desk Chair, *Model No. 9*, designed c. 1870, made c. 1900–1903
Bent beechwood, caning, H 29 3/8" (74.6 cm)
Purchased with the Joseph E. Temple Fund, 1969-136-9
(fig. 9)

187. Chair, *Model No. 51*, c. 1890–1900
Bent beechwood, caning, H 36 5/8" (93 cm)
Purchased with the Marie Josephine Rozet Fund, 1969-136-8
(fig. 10)

188. Matteo Thun
Italian, born 1952
Nefertiti Tea Service, 1981
Made by Ceramiche Flavia, Montelupo Fiorentino, Italy, for Memphis Milano S.r.l.
Earthenware with enamel decoration, H (teapot) 7 7/8" (20 cm), H (sugar bowl) 5 1/8" (13 cm), H (cup) 3 9/16" (9 cm)
Gift of Mr. and Mrs. Frederick B. Henry, 1986-82-1a,b–3a,b
(fig. 308)

189. Louis Comfort Tiffany
American, 1848–1933
Vase, 1899
Made by Tiffany Glass and Decorating Company, New York
Favrile glass, H 10 3/4" (27.3 cm)
Purchased with the Joseph E. Temple Fund, 1901-59
(fig. 36)

190. Vase, c. 1900
Made by Tiffany Glass and Decorating Company, New York
Favrile glass, H 5 13/16" (14.8 cm)
Purchased with the Joseph E. Temple Fund, 1901-58
(fig. 37)

191. Vase, c. 1900
Made by Tiffany Glass and Decorating Company, New York
Cypriote Glass, H 9 3/8" (23.8 cm)
Purchased with the Joseph E. Temple Fund, 1901-63
(fig. 38)

192. Vase, c. 1905
Made by Tiffany Furnaces, New York
Favrile glass, H 13 1/8" (33.3 cm)
Purchased with the Joseph E. Temple Fund, 1905-167
(fig. 47)

193. Vase, 1911
Made by Tiffany Furnaces, New York
Favrile glass, H 5 1/2" (14 cm)
Purchased with the Joseph E. Temple Fund, 1912-1
(fig. 55)

194. David Tisdale
American, born 1956
Picnic Flatware, designed 1985
Made by David Tisdale Design, Inc., New York
Anodized aluminum, L (knife) 8" (20.3 cm), L (fork) 7" (17.8 cm), L (spoon) 6 1/2" (16.5 cm)
Gift of David Tisdale, 2003-14-1–3
(fig. 260)

195. Masanori Umeda
Japanese, born 1941
Ginza Robot Cabinet, designed 1982
Made by Memphis Milano S.r.l.
Plastic-laminated wood and chipboard, H 5' 8 7/8" (1.7 m)
Gift of Collab: The Group for Modern and Contemporary Design at the Philadelphia Museum of Art, in memory of Hava J. Krasniansky Gelblum, 1994-131-1
(fig. 219)

196. Patricia Urquiola
Spanish, born 1961
Antibodi Chaise, designed 2006
Made by Moroso S.p.A., Cavallicco, Italy
Stainless steel, PVC plastic, polyurethane, felt, L 5' 1 13/16" (1.6 m)
Gift of Fury Design, Inc., Philadelphia, 2008-57-1
(fig. 296)

197. Albert Robert Valentien
American, 1862–1925
Vase, 1886
Made by Rookwood Pottery Company, Cincinnati
Glazed stoneware, H 11 1/2" (29.2 cm)
Purchased with the Baugh-Barber Fund, 1976-45-1 (formerly 1893-269, deaccessioned, and reacquired)
(fig. 31)

295

198. Paolo Venini
Italian, 1895–1959
Glasses (4), c. 1921–25
Made by Venini S.p.A., Murano, Italy
Blown glass with enamel decoration, H 6 3/16"
(15.7 cm)
Gift of Maude de Schauensee and Maxine Lewis in memory of their parents, Mr. and Mrs. Rodolphe Meyer de Schauensee, 1990-22-2–5
(fig. 126)

199. Robert Venturi
American, born 1925
Gothic Revival Chair, designed 1979–84
Made by Knoll, Inc., New York, 1984
Bent laminated wood, painted plastic laminate, H 40 3/4" (103.5 cm)
Gift of Marion Boulton Stroud, 1999-158-1
(fig. 244)

200. Tea and Coffee Service, designed 1980–83
Made by Alessi S.p.A., Crusinallo, Italy, 1985
Silver with gilt decoration, H (teapot) 10 1/4" (26 cm), H (coffeepot) 8 7/8" (22.5 cm), H (cream pot) 4 3/4" (12.1 cm), H (sugar box) 3 9/16" (9 cm), W (tray) 14" (35.6 cm)
Purchased with the Richardson Fund, 1986-15-1a,b–5
(fig. 246)

201. *Notebook* Fabric, designed 1982–83
Made by The Fabric Workshop and Museum, Philadelphia
Screen-printed cotton, W 57" (144.8 cm)
Gift of Collab: The Group for Modern and Contemporary Design at the Philadelphia Museum of Art, 1987-99-1
(fig. 243)

202. *Grandmother* Fabric, designed 1982–83
Made by The Fabric Workshop and Museum, Philadelphia
Screen-printed cotton, W 57" (144.8 cm)
Gift of Collab: The Group for Modern and Contemporary Design at the Philadelphia Museum of Art, 1987-99-2
(fig. 245)

203. Dinner Plate from the *Flowers* Service, designed c. 1993
Made by Swid Powell, New York
Porcelain with overglaze transfer-printed decoration, D 12 1/4" (31.1 cm)
Gift of Swid Powell, 1993-140-2
(fig. 222)

204. Marcel Wanders
Dutch, born 1963
Skygarden Lamp, designed 2007
Made by Flos S.p.A., Brescia, Italy
Aluminum, polycarbonate, D 35 7/16" (90 cm)
Gift of Flos S.p.A., Brescia, Italy, 2010-156-2
(pp. 2–3)

205. *Wallflower* Light Sculpture, designed 2009
Made by Flos S.p.A., Brescia, Italy, 2009
Glass, aluminum, electronic components, D (overall) 55 1/8" (140 cm)
Purchased with the Walter E. Stait Fund, 2010-101-1
(fig. 307)

206. Riki Watanabe
Japanese, born 1911
Bench, 1960
Made by Tendo Mokko, Tendo, Japan
Douglas fir, L 5' 9 3/4" (1.8 m)
Gift of Tendo Company, Ltd., 1996-90-2
(fig. 217)

207. Franklin Chenault Watkins
American, 1894–1972
Portrait of Henry P. McIlhenny, 1941
Oil on canvas, H 47" (119.4 cm)
The Henry P. McIlhenny Collection in memory of Frances P. McIlhenny, 1986-26-38
(fig. 92)

208. Hans Wegner
Danish, 1914–2007
Round Armchair, *Model No. JH 501*, designed 1949
Made by Johannes Hansen Møbelsnedkeri A/S, Søborg, Denmark, 1949–69
Made by Knoll, Inc., New York, from 1969
Oak, caning, H 30" (76.2 cm)
Gift of Carl L. Steele, 1972-5-2
(fig. 145)

209. Daniel Weil
Argentine, active England, born 1953
Bag Radio, designed 1981
Made by Parenthesis, Ltd., London
Flexible PVC plastic, H 11 11/16" (29.7 cm)
Gift of Daniel Weil, 1983-58-1
(fig. 195)

210. Lori Weitzner
American, born c. 1960
Newsworthy Wallpaper, 2009
Made by Weitzner Ltd., New York
Newspaper strips, nylon, W 47" (119.4 cm)
Gift of Lori Weitzner and Vita DiBellis, 2010-170-1
(page 6)

211. Gunnar Gunnarson Wennerburg
Swedish, 1863–1911
Vase, 1903
Made by Gustavsberg Porslinsfabrik, Gustavsberg, Sweden
Tin-enameled earthenware, H 5 1/2" (14 cm)
Gift of John T. Morris, 1903-1693
(fig. 48)

212. Thompson Westcott
Centennial Portfolio: A Souvenir of the International Exhibition at Philadelphia
Philadelphia: T. Hunter, 1876
1 vol., H 7 7/8" (20 cm), W 11 7/16" (29 cm)
Collection of the Philadelphia Museum of Art Library, gift of Mrs. Samuel Hinds Thomas, 1935
(fig.1)

213. Tapio Wirkkala
Finnish, 1915–1985
Coreano Dish, designed 1970
Made by Venini S.p.A., Murano, Italy, 1983
Blown glass, D 15 3/4" (40 cm)
Gift of Venini S.p.A., 1983-151-3
(fig. 182)

214. *Bolla* Vase, designed 1970
Made by Venini S.p.A., Murano, Italy, 1983
Blown glass, H 13 3/8" (34 cm)
Gift of Venini S.p.A., 1983-151-4
(fig. 179)

215–18. Russel Wright
American, 1904–1976
American Modern Dinnerware, designed c. 1937–39
Made by Steubenville Pottery Company, Steubenville, Ohio, 1939–59
Glazed earthenware, W (chop plate) 12 5/8" (32.1 cm), W (platter) 13 5/8" (34.6 cm), W (gravy boat) 6 7/8" (17.5 cm), W (celery dish) 13 1/4" (33.7 cm)
Gift of Miss Joan Prentice, 1945-66-1,3,4,8
(figs. 109–12)

219. Covered Casserole from *Iroquois Casual China* Service, 1946
Made by Iroquois China, Syracuse, New York
Glazed porcelain, H 5 1/4" (13.3 cm)
Gift of Mr. and Mrs. Benjamin Bloom, 1983-45-1
(page 304)

220. Sori Yanagi
Japanese, born 1915
Butterfly Stool, designed 1954
Made by Tendo Mokko, Tendo, Japan
Plywood, metal, H 15 3/8" (39.1 cm)
Gift of Tendo Company, Ltd., 1983-11-1
(fig. 207)

221. Samuel Yellin
American, born Poland, 1885–1940
Lock, Key, and Handle, 1911
Wrought iron, mica (originally, now missing), W 19 3/4" (50.2 cm)
Purchased with the Joseph E. Temple Fund, 1911-237a–e
(fig. 52)

222. Marco Zanini
Italian, born 1954
Alpha Centauri Vase, designed 1982
Made by Toso Vetri d'Arte, Murano, Italy, for Memphis Milano S.r.l.
Molded and blown glass, H 15 5/8" (39.7 cm)
Gift of Collab: The Group for Modern and Contemporary Design at the Philadelphia Museum of Art, 1983-112-5
(fig. 180)

223. Marco Zanuso
Italian, 1916–2001
Ariante Fan, designed 1973
Made by Vortice Elettrosociali S.p.A., Milan, from 1974
Injection-molded ABS plastic, H 7 3/16" (18.3 cm)
Gift of Vortice Elettrosociali S.p.A., 1983-13-1
(fig. 191)

224. Marco Zanuso and Richard Sapper
Italian, born Germany, 1932
Grillo Telephone, 1965
Made by Italtel, Società Italiana Telecomunicazioni S.p.A., Milan
ABS plastic, L 6 5/16" (16 cm)
Gift of Italtel S.p.A., 1982-54-1
(fig. 190)

Tord Boontje : for Artecnica : *Garland* Light : 2002 : etched brass : H 10" : 2008-178-5 (cat. 21)

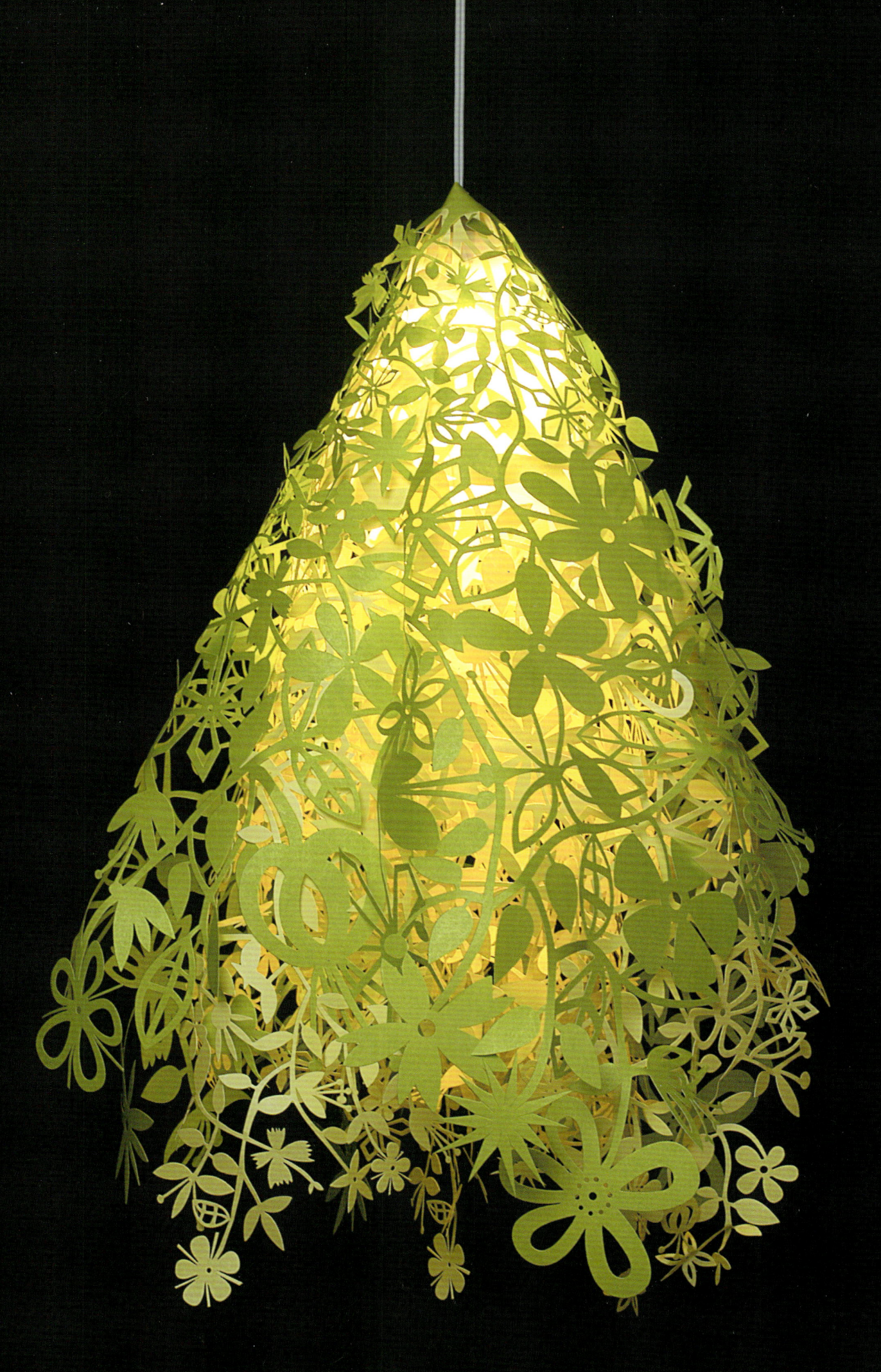

INDEX

A

Aalto, Alvar, 178, *200–201*, 285n90
Abele, Julian, *82*
Abet Laminati (Italy), *179*, 182, *198*
Abramovitz, Gerald, *159*, 160
Academy of Natural Sciences (Philadelphia), 25, 70n60
AEG (Allgemeine Elektricitäts Gesellschaft, Germany), 204
Agnew, Charles, 155
Aibel, Robert, 249, 255, *275*
Aldridge, Alexa, 285n85
Alessi S.p.A. (Italy), *9*, *176*, 225, *225*, 227, 238, *241*, 270, 272
Alexander, Jason D. (Capacity for Change), 287n136
American Academy (Rome), 123
American Association of Museums, 65, 83, *83*, 137n122; *A Selected Collection of Objects from the International Exposition of Modern Decorative and Industrial Art* (1925), *83*
American Federation of Arts (AFA), 77, 78, 84, 94, 99, 134–35nn23–26, 136n94; *International Exhibition of Ceramic Art* (Nov. 14–Dec. 12, 1929), 84, 135n55
American Institute of Architects, 145, 284n19
American Institute of Interior Design, 145, 160, 284n19
American Institute of Mining Engineers, 27
American Union of Decorative Artists and Craftsmen, 94–95
Anselevicius, Evelyn Hill, *190*
Anthologie Quartett (Germany), *277*
Arai, Junichi, 212, *212*, 214
Arai Creation System, K. K. (Japan), *212*
Arensberg, Walter and Louise (& collection), 125, 129, *131*, 132, 139n168, 146
Argyle Street Tea Rooms, 17
Armstrong Cork Company (United States), 143
Art Directors Club of Philadelphia, 116, 138nn148–49
Art Institute of Chicago, 135n29, 152, 284n31
Art Jury (Philadelphia), 134n2
Artecnica (United States), *278*, 297
Artek Oy Ab (Finland), *200*
Artemide S.p.A. (Italy), *193*
Artifort (Netherlands), *274*
Associate Committee of Women (Philadelphia Museum of Art), 39, 40
Atelier International (United States), *166–67*, 167
Atwater Kent Museum (Philadelphia), 111
Awatsuji, Hiroshi, *211*, 212
Ayer and Son, N. W. (Philadelphia), 150

B

B & B Italia S.p.A., *264–65*
B. D. Ediciones de Diseño (Spain), 182, *186*
Babral, Ludwig, *102*
Bach, Richard F., 78, 80, 88, 99
Bagian, James, 173
Bailey, Banks and Biddle (Philadelphia), 44
Baird, John, 16
Baker, Constance Amelia, 47
Balenciaga, Cristóbal, 138n128
Barber, Edwin Atlee, 41, *41*, 43, 47–48, 51–52, 55, 57, 58, 62, 65–66, 67, 68, 70n59, 69–70n60, 70n61, 70n83, 70–71n99, 71n102, 71n130, 73, 74–75, 79, 81, 86, 102, 111, 132, 134n23, 135n35, 142, 156, 280
Barnard, George Grey (& collection), 118, 129, 138n165
Barnes, Albert C., Dr., 74
Barr, Alfred H., Jr., 89
Bassett, Florence Knoll, 253, *253*, *254*, 255, 287n145
Bavarian National Museum (Munich), 66
Bayeux Tapestry, 39–40
BayGen (England), 231
Baylis, Trevor, 231
Behrens, Peter, 58, *63*, 78, 169, *204*
Bell, E. Hamilton, 74, 75, 91, 134n10
Benn, Lisa, 249, 266, *267*
Bennett Pottery, Edwin (United States), *43*
Berman, Philip I., 285n82
Bernadotte, Sigvard, *189*, 258
Bertoia, Harry, *275*
Best & Lloyd Ltd. (England), *159*
Best Products Company (United States), 238
Bieffeplast S.p.A. (Italy), *245*
Bignou Gallery (New York), 118
Birks, Alboine, *71*
Bisazza S.p.A. (Italy), 281
Bisque Radiators (England), 231
Bjørn, Acton, *189*
Blankenburg, Mrs. [Rudolph], 82
Bliss, Lillie P., 89
Boffi S.p.A. (Italy), *244*
Boggs, Jean Sutherland, 169, *169*, 173, 176, 285n86
Bok, Curtis, and Bok, Nellie Lee (house of), 86, *87*, 176
Bolan, Richard, *front endpapers*
Boontje, Tord, *278*, 297
Borie, Adolphe, 90, 94
Bott, Thomas John, Jr., 16, *16*
Brancusi, Constantin, 125, 137–38n128
Brandt, Edgar, *83*
Braque, Georges, 88, 116, 125
Breck, Joseph, 78
Breuer, Marcel, 128, *133*
Breyer, Mrs. Henry, 143
Bright, David, 255
Brinckmann, Justus, 66
Brinton, Mrs. McFadden, 82
Brocard, Philippe-Joseph, *29*, 31
Brodovitch, Alexey, 74, 90–91, 94, 95, *95*, 116, 136nn81–82
Brown, Denise Scott, 220, *222*, *223*, 225, 235
Brown, Jeffrey, 255, 286n124
Brownlee, David B., 205, 234, *234*
Bryn Mawr College (Bryn Mawr, Pa.), 128, *132*
Bulletin of the Pennsylvania Museum, 56, 57, 58, 65, 68, 73, 77, 83, 84, 93, 102, 106, 129, 135n35
Butterton, Mary, 17, *22*
Bye, Arthur Edwin, 79, 135n43, 136n83

C

Caedmon Records (United States), *117*
Calder, Alexander, 142
Caldwell Company, J. E. (Philadelphia), 202
Campana, Fernando, *9*
Campana, Humberto, *9*
Cappellini S.p.A. (Italy), 212, *219*, 281
Carles, Arthur B., 88
Carlu, Jean, 116, *116*
Carnegie Corporation, 78, 93–94, 99, 102, 103
Carnegie Institute, 135n29
Carnegie Museum of Art (Pittsburgh), 234
Carrière, Eugène, 58
Cassina S.p.A. (Italy), *166–67*, *207*, *257*
Castellani (Italy), 37, 111
Castiglioni, Achille, 167, *168*, 205, *286*
Castiglioni, Pier Giacomo, 167, *168*, 205, *286*
Castle, Wendell, 155, *156*
Centennial Exhibition of 1876 (Philadelphia), 13, *14*, 15, 16, 17, *18*, 25, 26, 27, 31, 37, 38, 47, 48, 69n45, 81, 111, 146, 202
Centre Georges Pompidou (Paris), 207, 285–86nn103–4
Cézanne, Paul, 112, 138n143
Chagall, Marc, 94
Chardin, Jean-Baptiste-Siméon, 103
Chemex (United States), *185*, 266
Cheston, George M., 146, 165, 166
Christo (Christo Vladimirov Javacheff), 146, *148*, *149*
City Art Museum of Saint Louis (Saint Louis Art Museum), 150, 284n27
City Parks Association (Philadelphia), 134n2
Civil Works Administration, 103
Clark, Charles D., 41
Clark, Clarence H., 16
Cleveland Museum of Art, 74, 280
Clifford, Henry, 91, 99, 104, 139n186
Cohn, Suzanne, 220
Collab, The Group for Modern and Contemporary Design at the Philadelphia Museum of Art, 145, 155–56, 159, 164, 165, 166–67, 169, 172, 173, 178, 182, 202–41, 243, 248, 249, 251, 253, 255, 256, 258, 260, 266–67, *267*, 270, 272–73, 275, *275*, 280, 281, 282, 284n37, 285n88, 285n91, 286n117, 287n136; Design Excellence Award, 202, 220, 225, 227, 231, 232, 249, 251, 255, 258, 266, 280; Student Design Competition, 220, 225, 227, 231, 232, 249, 251, 253, 255, 256, 258, 267
Collingwood, Peter, 160
Colombo, Gianni, *197*
Colombo, Joe, *197*, *242*, 243, *243*, 244, 245
Columbia Records (United States), *233*
Commercial Museum (Philadelphia), 111
Compagnia di Venezia e Murano (Italy), 40
Connelly, Henry, 133
Conran, Terence, Sir, 231, *231*, 286n119; Conran Stores, 231
Coolidge, John, 141
Cooper-Hewitt Museum (New York), 137n110, 141, 280; Cooper-Hewitt, National Design Museum (New York), 137n110
Cooper Union for the Advancement of Science and Art (New York), 83, 284n3; Cooper Union Museum (New York), 83, 99, 141, 284n3
Copeland & Sons, W. T. (England), *33*, 48
Coper, Hans, 160, *163*
Corbin, Donna, 204, 205, 232, 253, 272, *275*
Craven, Shirley, *160*, 161
Cros, Henri, 111
Crowell, James L., 202
Crown Corporation (Canada), 173
Cunliffe-Owen, Philip, Sir, 27
Cunningham, Charles, 141, 284n7
Cute (later Curtin), Virginia Wireman, 119, *135*
Cuttoli, Marie, 118, 138n151

D

Daichi Co., Ltd. (Japan), 212, *216*
Daley, William, 154
Dalí, Salvador, 128
Dana, Charles E., 38
Dana, John Cotton, 78, 135n28, 156
Danese Milano S.r.l. (Bruno Danese S.r.l., Italy), *191*
Daniell and Son, A. B. (England), 17, *18*, 27
Daroff, Karen (Daroff Design, Philadelphia), 232
D'Ascenzo, Nicola, 134–35n26
Davis, Gene, 152, *152–53*
Day, Robin, 160, *161*
Deck, Joseph-Théodore, 31, *32*
Delaherche, Auguste, 58, 86
De Long, David G., 205, 234, *234*

298

Derby House (Philadelphia Museum of Art), 84
Design Council of Great Britain, 159
Design Museum (London), 231
Deskey, Donald, 88, 95
Deutscher Werkbund, 135n29
Deutsches Museum (Hagen, Germany), 135n29
Dietrich, H. Richard, Jr., 133
Diffrient, Niels, 172, 202
Diller, Elizabeth, 243, 248, *248–49*
Dixon, Fitz Eugene, Jr., 133
Doat, Taxile, 58
Dodd, William J., *61*
Dolan, Thomas, 13, 16
Dorflinger Glass Company (White Mills, Pa.), 17, *19*
Dorn, Marion, *119*
Dorr, Benjamin, 37
Dorr, Dalton, 37, *37*, 40, 41, 43, 47, 48, 52, 57, 70n58, 70n63
Dorrance, John T., 285n82
Doulton & Company (England), 17, *22*
Downs, Joseph, 80–81, 83, 84, 88, 91, *91*, 94–95, 99, 137n109
Doyle, Joan, 220
Draveil, Château of (France), *250*
Drayton, Cynthia, 145, *145*, 178, 266
Drexel University (Philadelphia), 173
Driade S.p.A. (Italy), *228*
Drutt, Helen, 145, 159, 165
DuBon, David, 284n35, 285n84
Duchamp, Marcel, 125, 177
Dufy, Raoul, 116
Duke of Edinburgh, 159
Dunand, Jean, 89
duPont, Henry Francis, 137n109
Duveen, Joseph, 1st Baron, 103
Dyson, James (Dyson Appliances, England), *230*, 231

E

Eakins, Thomas, 26, 178
Eames, Charles, *4–5*, *112–13*, 113, 127, 128, 145, *146*, *154*, 154–55, 165, 172, 173, 266
Eames, Ray, *4–5*, *112–13*, 205
Eichner, Laurits Christian, 119, *120*
Eisen, Edward O., 202
Elkington and Company (England), 25, 111
Elkins, George W. (collection), 135n57
Elkins, Mrs. William L., 39, 122
Elkins, William L. (collection), 135n57
Elliott, C. Danial, 137n55
Elliott, Huger, 77, 80
Ernst, Max, *142–43*, 143, 243, *246–47*
Esherick, Wharton H., 86, *87*, 143, 176

F

Fabric Workshop and Museum (Philadelphia), 238, *238*, *241*, 253
Fairmount Park (Philadelphia), 65, 73, *73*, 79, 81, 134n2, 134n3, 139n176, 167; Fairmount Park Art Association, 134n2; Fairmount Park Commission, 73, 129, 134n2, 134n3, 139n176
Fashion Group (Philadelphia Museum of Art), 125, 145
Filipowski, Richard, 143
Fischer, Felice, 205–6, *207*, *210*
Fish Design (Italy & United States), *256*
Fisher, Bruce and Company (Philadelphia), 146
Flavia, Ceramiche (Italy), *285*
Fleisher, Samuel S. (& Art Memorial, Philadelphia), 111
Flos S.p.A. (Italy), *2–3*, *168*, 281, *283*, *286*
Fogg Art Museum (Cambridge, Mass.), 89, 141
Ford Motor Company (United States), 128
Foulc, Edmond (& collection), 93, 102–3, 129, 136n84, 138n165
Fouquet, Georges (Boutique Fouquet), *89*, 90
Fraatz, James J., 281
Frackelton, Susan, 44, *45*
Franck, Kaj, *184*
Franklin Institute (Philadelphia), 16, 111
Fraser, Elisabeth, *145*, 165, *166–67*, 169
Freeman, George, 165
Freeman and Company, Samuel T. (Philadelphia), 165
Fretz Frères (Switzerland), *268*
Friedeberg, Pedro, 243
Friends of the Philadelphia Museum of Art, 145, 173
Frishmuth, Mrs. William D., 17, 69n11
Fujie Textile Co., Ltd. (Japan), *211*
Fuksas, Massimiliano, 272
Fulton, James, 249, 251
Furniture of the 20th-Century (United States), 182

G

Gallatin, A. E. (& collection), 125, 129, *130*, 132
Gallé, Émile, 31, *50*, 51, *52*, 58, 86, 202
Gallimore, Roland, 159, 167
Gans, Herbert, 173
Garouste, Elizabeth, *277*
Garvan, Beatrice B., 154, 238
Gate, Simon, 78, 119
Gavina S.p.A. (Italy), *274*
Gehry, Frank O., 235, 270, *271*, 272, *272*, *273*, 287n160
Gelblum, Hava, *145*, 172, 212
Giacometti, Diego, 243
Gibson, Henry C., 13, 16
Gillespie, Elizabeth Duane, 39
Gimbel Brothers (Philadelphia), 113
Ginori, Richard, S.p.A. (Italy), 105, *107*, 244
Glaser, Milton, 232, *233*
Gluckman, Richard, 253
Gluckman Mayner Architects (United States), 253, 260, *260–61*, 266–67
Gobelins Manufactory (France), 81
Goetz, Carl, *46*
Goldberger, Paul, 235, 286–85n125
Goury, Jules, *35*
Graves, Michael, 169, *224–25*, 225
Greapentrog, Grant, 202
Gréber, Jacques, *73*
Groff, June, *124*, *126*
Gropius, Walter, 95, 287n131
Grueby Faience Company (United States), 55
Guimard, Adeline, 122
Guimard, Hector, 122, *123*, 134
Gustavsberg Porslinsfabrik (Sweden), 51, *60*
Gwathmey, Charles, 173

H

Habara, Shukuro, 206
Habitat, Inc. (United States), 150, *151*
Hacker, Marc, 220
Haines, Ephraim, 132
Hansen, Fritz, Eft AlS (Denmark), *147*
Hansen Møbelsnedkeri, Johannes, A/S (Denmark), *155*
Harbeson, John F., 142
d'Harnoncourt, Anne, 152, 176, 177, *177*, 178, 243, 258, *267*, 270, 272, 280, 284n31
d'Harnoncourt, René, 177
Harrison, Mrs. John, 41
Harrity, Gail M., 176, 243, 260, 272
Hartgring, Wilhelmus Petrus, 52, *55*
Hartranft, John F., 25
Harvard Society for Contemporary Art, 88, 89, 136n70; *The School of Paris* (1929), 88–89
Hathaway, Calvin S., 93, 99, 141, 142–43, 145, *145*, 150, 154, 155, 156, 165, 169, 284n2, 284n35
Hein, Piet, 258
Heine, Thomas Theodor, 78
Helme and McIlhenny (Philadelphia), 65
Heritage, Robert, 160
Heywood-Wakefield (United States), 95
Hiesinger, Kathryn Bloom, *172*, *173*, *210*, 285n90; *Antique Speak: A Guide to the Styles, Techniques, and Materials of the Decorative Arts, from the Renaissance to Art Deco* (1997; with George H. Marcus), 234, *234*; *Art Nouveau in Munich* (1988; ed.), 204–5; *Design, 1900–1940* (1986), 203, 204; *Landmarks of Twentieth-Century Design* (1993; with George H. Marcus), 234, *237*; *Out of the Ordinary: Robert Venturi, Denise Scott Brown and Associates* (2001; with David B. Brownlee and David G. De Long), 234, *234*; *Porcelain* (1984), 202; *Styles, 1850–1900* (1984), 202; *The Second Empire: Art in France under Napoleon III* (1978)
Higby, Wayne, 165, *164*
Higgins, Kathryn E., 270
Hille International (England), *161*
Hoentschel, Georges (collection), 66
Hoffmann, Josef, 169, 178, 287
Højsgaard, Hans-Kristian, 258
Horter, Earl, 74, 88, *98*, 137n128
Howe, George, 74, 83, 88, 90, 94, 95, *96*, 99, *100*, 103, 118
Hull Traders Ltd. (England), *160*, *162*
Huonekalu-ja Rakennustyötehdas (Finland), *200–201*

I

IBM (United States), *269*
Ideal Standard (Italy), *157*
Imperial Japanese Commission, 31
Ingersoll, Anna Warren, 74, 88, *90*
Ingersoll, Charles E., 93
Ingersoll, Jared, 88
Ingersoll, Marion, *90*
Ingersoll, R. Sturgis, 74, 88, 89, 90, *90*, 93, 94, 125, *125*, 128, 129, 132, 134n5, 139n191, 139n193, 141, 178, 284n6, 285n86
Institute for the Deaf and Dumb (Philadelphia), 40
Interior Design Council of Philadelphia, 284n19
Inter-Society Committee for Twentieth-Century Decorative Arts and Design (now Collab), 145, *145*, 146, 150, 154, 155, 156, 159. *See also* Collab
Iroquois China (United States), *304*
Isola, Maija, *195*
Isozaki, Arata, 205
Italtel S.p.A. (Italy), *192*
Ive, Jonathan, 232
Izenour, Steven, 220

J

Jack, George Washington, 17, *23*
Jackson and Graham (England), 31
Jackson and Ryan Architects (United States), 260
Jacobsen, Arne, 145, *147*, 172, *176–77*
Jaffe, Elise, 255, 286
Jahn, Roland, 145
Japan Industrial Designers Association, 206
Japanese Postal Savings Promotion Society, 238
Jarosinski, Gerard J., Jr., 212, 220
Jaulmes, Gustave, 81
Jayne, Horace H. F., 79, 89, *91*, 111, 132, 138n141, 139n181–82, 177
Jeffords, Walter, 132
Jenks, Ann, 90, 136n82
Jenks, John Story, 58
Jenks, John Story (nephew of John Story Jenks), 80, 80, 82, 90, 125, 136n81–82

Jensen, Georg (Georg Jensen Sølvsmedie A/S, Denmark), 78, 106, *108*, 138n129, 258, *258*
Jensen, Søren Georg, 258, *258*
Jessup and Moore, 37
Johns, Jasper, 146
Johnson, John G. (& collection), 74, 91, 103, 132, 134n3, 136n83, 173
Jolles, Arnold, 167
Jones, Owen, 31, *35*
Jongerius, Hella, *back endpapers*, 10

K

Kahn, Louis I., 205
Kaiser Friedrich Museum (Berlin), 139n175
Kartell S.p.A. (Italy), *242*, *243*
Katsui, Mitsuo, 207
Katzive, David, 146
Kauffer, Edward McKnight, 119, *119*
Kawasaki, Kazuo, 212
Keever, Stephen A., 281
Kelly, Ellsworth, 146
Kelly, John B., 139n176
Kenmochi, Isamu, 212, *215*
Keppel, Frederick P., 94, 102
Kiefer, Anselm, 178
Kienbusch, Otto von (collection), 132
Kimball, Fiske, 13, *81*, 81–82, 83–84, 86, *86*, 88–91, *91*, 93–94, 95, 99, 102, 103, 104, 105, 106, 111, 112–13, 116, 118–19, 122, 123, 125, 128, 129, 132, 135n60, 137n111, 137n122, 138n141, 139n175, 139n181, 139n182, 139n188, 141, 145, 152, 177, 178, 258, 280
Kimball, Marie, 129
Kinsman, Rodney, 231
Kirstein, Lincoln, 88
Kise, James Nelson, 173, 258, 270, 287n149
Kita, Toshiyuki, 206, *207*
Knoll, Inc. (United States), 113, *114*, *115*, *155*, *171*, *190*, 202, 227, 232, 238, *239*, 253, *254*, 255, 270, *272*, *274*, *275*
Kok, J. Juriaan, 52, *55*
Koppel, Henning, 258
Kovacs Lighting Inc., George (United States), *170*
Kunsthalle Düsseldorf, 207
Kurakawa, Kisho, 206
Kuramata, Shiro, 212, *213*, *219*
Kuriyama, Masako, 207

L

Lalique, René (Lalique, France), 86, 89, 105, *105*, *109*
Langenheim, F. D., 41
Lannan, J. Patrick (Lannan Foundation, Santa Fe, N.M.), 243
Lanvin, Jeanne, 137–38n128
Larsen, Jack Lenor (Jack Lenor Larsen, Inc., United States), *front endpapers*, 155, *194*
Lea, Arthur H., 106
Le Corbusier (Charles-Edouard Jeanneret), 83, 95, 143
Lee, Gabriele Windeck, 220
Lee, Jean Gordon, 177
Lee, Sarah Tomerlin, 154
Léger, Fernand, 116, 125
Leibowitz, Matthew, 116, *117*
Lenfest, H. F. (Gerry) and Marguerite (Lenfest Foundation), 260, 270, 272, 287n160
Léonard, Agathon, 52
Lescaze, William E., 94, 95, *96*, 99, *100*, 103, 136–37n105
Lewis, Francis W., 16
Lieberman, Alexander, 88
Lin, Maya, 232
Lindstrand, Vicke, 143
Linning, Nanette, *280*, 281
Lins, P. Andrew, 165, 284n55
Lloyd Manufacturing Company (United States), *100*
Lobmeyer, J. & L. (Austria), 40
Londos & Co. (England), 27
Longworth, Maria, 43
Lonhuda Pottery Company (United States), 43
Los Angeles County Museum of Art, 204
Louisiana Purchase Exposition of 1904 (Saint Louis World's Fair), 58
Lurçat, Jean, 116

M

Mackintosh, Charles Rennie, 17, 69
Madeira, Louis C., 123, 133, 138n164, 176–77, 285n82, 287n150
Magistretti, Vico, 167
Magnusson, Carl, 255
Maharam (United States), *4–5*
Maison Blanche (France), 90
Mandrelli, Doriana, 272
Man Ray (Emmanuel Radnitzky), 143
Marceau, Henri Gabriel, 91, 103, *103*, 104, 123, 129, 132, 132, 136n83, 139n181, 139n182, 139n188
Marcus, George H., *172*, *203*, 204, 234, *234*
Mare, André, 78
Mari, Enzo, *191*
Marieta Textil, SA (Spain), 182, *182*, 187
Marimekko Oy (Finland), *195*
Marinot, Florence, 143
Marinot, Maurice, 89, *104*, 105–6, *139*, 165
Mariscal, Javier Errando, 182, *182–83*, 186–87
Massier, Clement, 111
Mathsson, Bruno, 266, *266*
Mathsson, Karl, *266*
Matisse, Henri, 88, 94, 116
Matter, Herbert, 266, *268*
Maurer, Ingo (Ingo Maurer GmbH, Germany), *202*, 205, 250, 251, *251*, 287n138
Mayen, Paul, 150, *150–51*
Mayner, David (Gluckman Mayner Architects, United States), 253, 260, *260–61*, 267
McCahan Sugar Refining and Molasses Company, W. V. (United States), 106
McCarter, Henry, 88, 136n81
McClatchy, John H., 99, 136n92
McCobb, Paul, 127–28, *128–29*
McCulloch, Peter, 160, *162*
McFadden, John H., 65, 70n60
McIlhenny, Bernice "Bonnie." *See* Wintersteen, Bernice (Mrs. John)
McIlhenny, Frances (Mrs. John D.; mother of Henry P.), 125, 137n122
McIlhenny, Henry P. (son of John D.), 89, 103–5, *106*, 111, 113, 118, 122–23, 132, 133, 137n122, 141, 152, 154, 176, 285n82
McIlhenny, John (father of John D.), 71n127
McIlhenny, John D., 65, *65*, 74, 75, 77, 78, 80, 81, 82, 89, 103, 135nn35–36, 135n49
McLean, Claire, 141
McNeil, Robert L., Jr., 133, 152
Meier, Richard, 227, *227*
Melick, Ralph, 202
Melillo, Giacinto, *31*
Memphis Milano S.r.l., 179, 182, *183*, *184*, *217*, *285*
Mendini, Alessandro (Atelier Mendini, Italy), 182, *199*
Metropolitan Museum of Art (New York), 78, 80, 93, 99, 112, 137n109
Meyerson, Martin, 176
Mies van der Rohe, Ludwig, 95, *101*, 167
Mikolas, Karel, 155
Milan Exhibition of 1881, 38
Milan Triennale of 1995, 207
Miller, Leslie W., 40, 43, 57, 73, 77, 134n2
Miller Furniture Company, Herman (United States), *2–3*, *112–13*, 113, 127, 146, 274
Minnite, Diane "Dee" L., 232, 234, 253, 275, *275*
Minton (England), 17, *17*, *29*, 44, *71*
Miró, Joan, *111*, 116, 118
Miyake, Issey (Issey Miyake Inc., Japan), 212, *218*
Modern Age (United States), 227
Modern Club (Philadelphia), 84
Molteni & C. S.p.A. (Italy), *181*
Mombach, Dagmar, *251*
Montreal Museum of Fine Arts, 141
Moore, Bloomfield Haines, 37
Moore College of Art (Moore College of Art and Design; Philadelphia), 173
Moore, Clarence Bloomfield (son of Bloomfield Haines Moore), 41
Moore, Edward C., Jr., 78
Moore, Mrs. Bloomfield Haines, 37–38
Mora brothers (Italy), 40
Moroso S.p.A. (Italy), *276*
Morris and Company (England), 17, *23*
Morris and Company, I. P., (Philadelphia), 38
Morris, John T., 38, 40, 41, *41*, 43, 44, 47, 51, 52, 55, 57, 58, 62, 65–67, 68, 70n77, 71n123, 71n130, 74, 83, 102, 111, 142, 202, 249
Morris, Lydia T. (sister of John T. Morris), 44
Morris, Mrs. Herbert Cameron, 119
Mucha, Alphonse, *89*, 89–90
Mukai, Shutaro, 206
Münchner Stadtmuseum, 204
Murphy, Levy, Wurman (Philadelphia), 146
Musashino Art University (Tokyo), 206
Musée Carnavalet (Paris), *89*, 90
Museum für Kunst und Gewerbe (Hamburg), 66
Museum of Contemporary Art (Chicago), 146
Museum of Contemporary Art San Diego, 234
Museum of Contemporary Art, Los Angeles, 205
Museum of Fine Arts, Boston, 66, 81
Museum of Modern Art (New York), 89, 95, *95*, 113, 137n108, 169, 177; *Modern Architecture: International Exhibition*, 95, 137n103; *Organic Design in Home Furnishings* (Jan. 10–Feb. 16, 1942), 113, 138n145

N

Nader, Ralph, 173
Nakashima, George, 202
Nakashima, Riokei, 17, *70*
National Arts Club (New York), 76, 135n29; *German Applied Arts*, 76, 78, 135n29
National Association of Manufacturers, 40
National Gallery of Canada (Ottawa), 285n64, 285n76
National Home Fashions League, 145, 284n19
National Museum of Man (Canadian Museum of Civilization; Quebec), 285n76
National Society of Interior Design, 145, 284n19
Natzler, Otto and Gertrud, 119, 122, *137*
Naudot, Camille, Fils et Cie. (France), 51, *51*
Negroponte, Nicholas, 173
Nelson, George, 128, 154, 172–73, *173*, 274
Neuhart, John and Marilyn, 205
Newark Museum Association (Newark Museum), 78, 79, 156
New City Editions (United States), *271*
New York Architectural Terra-Cotta Company, *39*, 40
New York Museum of Science and Industry, 90
New York World's Fair of 1939, 122
Newhall, Beaumont, 93, 137n108
Nielsen, Harald, 258
Nizzoli, Marcello, *259*

Noguchi, Isamu, 169, *170–71*, 285n66
Norris, Isaac, 38
Noyes, Eliot, 113, 128
Nuno Corporation (Japan), *214*
Nuutäjarvi Notsjö Glasbruk (Finland), *184*
Nymphenburg, Porzellan Manufaktur (Germany), *10*

O

Oak Lane Country Day School (Blue Bell, Pa.), 99
Ohio Valley China Company (United States), 43, *46*
Öhrström, Edvin, *138*, 143
Okayama, Sinya, 212, *216*
Olin, Laurie (Olin Partnership; Philadelphia), 232
Olivetti, Ing. C., & C., S.p.A. (Italy), 258, *259*
O-Luce Italia S.p.A., *197*
OMK Design Ltd. (England), 231
Orrefors Glasbruk (Sweden), 119, *138*, 143, 146
Osthaus, Karl Ernst, 135n29
Ottomeyer, Hans, 204
Oud, J. J. P., 95
Ozenfant, Amédée, 165

P

Page, Louis Rodman (& Gallery of Miniatures), 89, 136n76
Pagny, Chateau of (France), choir screen, *92*
Pantin, Cristallerie de (France), 51
Panton, Verner, *275*
Parenthesis Ltd. (England), *196*
Paris Universal Exposition: of 1878, 31; of 1889, 44; of 1900, 39, 51, 52, 202; of 1925 (International Exposition of Decorative and Industrial Arts), 82, *82*, 83, 135n51; of 1945, 111; of 1949, 111
Pasquier, Nathalie du, *180*, 182
Paulin, Pierre, *274*
Peale, Charles Willson, 16
Pedersen, Erling, *91*, 99, 136–37n105
Pell, Alfred Duane, Rev., 48, 70n83
Penn, Irving, 91
Pennsylvania Academy of the Fine Arts (Philadelphia), 26, 39; *Art Applied to Industries* (Jan.–March 1877), 26–27
Pennsylvania Museum and School of Industrial Art (1876–1938; now Philadelphia Museum of Art), 13, *14*, 25, *27*, 27, *28–29*, 67, 75, 79, 113, 139n171; *Art Applied to Industries* (May 1877), 26–27; *Catalogue of the Exhibition of American Pottery and Porcelain, including a Competition of American Workmen* (1888), 40, 69n51; *Design for the Machine: Contemporary Industrial Art* (Feb. 20–March 20, 1932), 94–95, 96–97, 136n96, 142, 172, 173; *Etchings and Engravings by Contemporary Artists of Holland* (1925), 81, 135n43; *Exhibition of American Handicrafts Assembled and Circulated by the American Federation of Arts* (Dec. 5–25, 1922), 77, 134n25; *Living Artists* (Nov. 20, 1931–Jan. 1, 1932), 94, 136n95; *Loan Exhibition of Contemporary Painting and Sculpture from the Collections of Miss Anna Warren Ingersoll and Mr. & Mrs. R. Sturgis Ingersoll* (Nov. 4–Dec. 6, 1933), 90, *90*; *Pottery and Porcelain Exhibition, including a Competition for American Workmen* (1888), 40, 70n51
Penrose, Boies, 99, 135n43, 139n167
Pepper, George Wharton, 137n113
Pepper, William, Dr., 13, 38
Pepper, William Platt, 13, 16, 37, 38, 40, 41, 43, 44, 51, 52, 65, 69n6, 70n58, 70n63, 70n77, 70n99
Perelman, Raymond G. and Ruth, 164, 253, *260*, 260–80
Perry, Commodore Matthew, 17
Pesce, Gaetano, 256, *256*, *257*, 264–65

Philadelphia Art Teachers Association, 88
Philadelphia College of Art, 25, *72*, 73, 79, *86*, 88–91, 99, *102*, 103, 127, 129, 137n113, 138–39n171, 146, 164, 167, 173, 202, *270*
Philadelphia Council of Professional Craftsmen, 284n19
Philadelphia Craft Show, 155, 164
Philadelphia Museum College of Art (1959–64), 127
Philadelphia Museum of Art, exhibitions at: *Art in Advertising in Collaboration with the Art Director's Club of Philadelphia* (Feb. 26–Mar. 29, 1942), 116, 138n146; *Art Nouveau in Munich* (Sept. 25–Nov. 27, 1988), 204, *204*, 205, 286n98; *British Contemporary Design* (Nov. 20–Dec. 31, 1974), 156, *158*, 159, 160, *160*, *161*, *162*, *163*, 164, 284n44; *Building the City Beautiful: The Benjamin Franklin Parkway and the Philadelphia Museum of Art* (Aug. 19–Oct. 29, 1989), 202, 285n95; *City/2* (June 10, 1971–Jan. 2, 1972), 146, 152, 284n26; *Collab Collects: Notable Acquisitions in Design, 1970–2000* (Nov. 14, 2001–Apr. 21, 2002), 232, 286n122; *Connelly & Haines, Cabinetmakers: Philadelphia Sheraton Furniture* (Mar. 20–Apr. 19, 1953), 132, 139n184; *Contemporary Sculpture*, 103; *Cool Britannia: Recent British Design Selected by Sir Terence Conran* (Nov. 11, 1998–Mar. 7, 1999), *230*, 231, 286n119; *Dalí Jewels* (Jan. 15–Feb. 13, 1955), 128, 139n175; *Design, 1900–1940: From the Collections* (Jan. 31–Dec. 9, 1987), *203*, 286n97; *Design for the Table Top* (Oct. 13, 1993–Jan. 1994), 220, *221*, 286n113; *Designing Modern* (Sept. 15, 2007–Sept. 14, 2008), 260, *260–69*, 266, 267, 287n154; *Designing the Future: Three Directions for the New Millennium* (Nov. 17, 1999–Mar. 26, 2000), 231, 232, *232*, 286n120; *Design Since 1945* (Oct. 16, 1983–Jan. 8, 1984), 172–97, 202, 204, 205–6; *Designs of the 1950s* (1990), 205; *Design This Day: Industrial Design* (Dec. 26, 1942–Apr. 18, 1943), 118, 119, 122, 138n152, 138n160; Diamond Jubilee exhibition (1951), 139n175; *Florence Knoll Bassett: Defining Modern* (Nov. 17, 2004–Apr. 10, 2005), 253, *253*, *254*, 255, *255*, 287n145; *Frank O. Gehry: Design Process and the Lewis House* (Nov. 8, 2008–Apr. 5, 2009), 270, *271–73*, 272, 287n161; *From the Collection: Objects Designed in the 1950s* (Apr. 1–Oct. 14, 1990), 286n102; *Gaetano Pesce: Pushing the Limits* (Nov. 18, 2005–Apr. 9, 2006), 256, *256*, *257*, 287n146; *Georg Jensen Silversmiths* (Nov. 17, 2006–Apr. 1, 2007), 258, *258*, 287n148; *Gifts in Honor of the Museum's 125th Anniversary* (Sept. 29–Dec. 8, 2002), 242–47, 287n128; *Gifts to Mark a Century: An Exhibition Celebrating the Centennial of the Philadelphia Museum of Art* (Feb. 18–Mar. 20, 1977), 165, 285n56; *Have a Bite: 20th-Century Flatware from the Collection* (Apr. 12–Oct. 26, 2003), 253, 287n144; *Japanese Design: A Survey Since 1950* (Sept. 25–Nov. 27, 1994), 205–19, 220, 225, 232, 286n104; *The Light Magic of Ingo Maurer* (Nov. 20, 2002–Mar. 30, 2003), *250–51*, 251, 287n137; *Louis I. Kahn: In the Realm of Architecture* (Oct. 20, 1991–Jan. 5, 1992), 205, 286n103; *Marcel Wanders: Daydreams* (Nov. 22, 2009–June 13, 2010), 249, 280, *280*, 281, *281*, *283*, 287n172; *Masterpieces of Impressionism and Post-Impressionism: The Annenberg Collection* (May 21–Sept. 17, 1989), 178, 285n87; *Michael Graves: The Architect and the Tea Kettle* (Oct. 25, 1995–Feb. 25, 1996), *224*, 225, 286n115; *Milton Glaser Graphic Design: Design, Influence, and Process* (Nov. 15, 2000–Jan. 21, 2001), 232, *233*, 286n121; *Modern Architecture: International Exhibition* (March 20–April 30, 1932), 95, 99, 136n103; *Noguchi's Imaginary Landscapes* (Oct. 20, 1979–Jan. 6, 1980), 169, 285n66; *On the Wall: Wallpaper and Tableau* (May 9–Sept. 13, 2003), 253, 287n143; *Organic Design in Home Furnishings* (Jan. 10–Feb. 16, 1942), 113, 116, 138n145; *Out of the Ordinary: The Architecture and Design of Robert Venturi Denise Scott Brown and Associates* (2001), 234–41; *Paintings and Drawings by Vincent van Gogh* (Jan. 13–Feb. 28, 1954), 128, 139n175; *Peace* (May 19–June 21, 1970), 146, *148–49*, 284n25; *Philadelphia International Salon of Photography* (69th Street Branch, 1932), 137n103; *Philadelphia Silver* (Apr. 14–Sept. 9, 1956), 132, 139n184; *Philadelphia: Three Centuries of American Art* (Apr. 11–Oct. 10, 1976), 164, 284n50; *Philippe Starck Designs* (Nov. 12, 1997–Mar. 1, 1998), 227, *228*, *229*, 286n118; *Product Environment: New Furniture* (Sept. 30–Nov. 10, 1970), 150, *150–151*, 284n27; *Recent Acquisitions: Twentieth-Century Decorative Arts* (Apr. 6–Dec. 26, 1971), 154, *154*, 284n36; *Richard Meier: Object and Furniture Design* (Oct. 30, 1996–Feb. 29, 1997), 227, *227*, 286n116; *Richard Schultz: Five Decades of Design* (Apr. 5–Aug. 23, 2009), 275, *279*, 287n168; *Scandinavian Design, 1930–1980* (Mar. 17–Oct. 1, 1997), *204*, 205, 286n102; *The Second Empire: Art in France under Napoleon III* (Oct. 1–Nov. 26, 1978), 164–65, 167, 284n51; *The Shakers: Their Arts and Crafts* (April–May 20, 1962), 132, 139n184; *Styles in Silver: Period Silver in Period Settings* (Apr. 13–May 19, 1946), 122, 138n160; *Tapestries by Contemporary French Painters lent by Madame Marie Cuttoli* (Apr. 18–June 14, 1942), 118, 138n151; *A Taste for the Modern: The Jeanne Rymer Gift of Twentieth-Century Chairs* (May 16–Sept. 20, 2009), 272, *274*, 287n166; *Timeline of Twentieth-Century Chairs* (1995), 205, 286n102; *A Touch of Gold* (Nov. 23–Dec. 15, 1974), 164, 284n47; *Tucker China* (May 3–Sept. 9, 1952), 132, 139n184; *Twentieth-Century Lighting* (opened May 7, 1991), 205, 205, 286n102; *Two Naifs in Japan: Robert Venturi and Denise Scott Brown* (Oct. 26, 1994–Jan. 30, 1995), 220, *222*, *223*, 286n114; *Vienna Art Treasures* (1952), 128, 139n175; *Vincent van Gogh: Paintings* (Feb. 28–Apr. 5, 1970), 146, 284n24; *Visual Delight: Ornament and Pattern in Modern and Contemporary Design* (May 16–Sept. 20, 2009), 275, *276–78*, 287n167; *Work in Progress: Gluckman Mayner Designs the Perelman Building* (Nov. 19, 2003–Apr. 4, 2004), 253, 287n141
Philadelphia Museum School of Art (1949–1959), 127
Philadelphia Photographic Society, 137n103
Philadelphia Saving Fund Society Building, 95
Philadelphia Textile Institute (Philadelphia College of Textiles and Science; Philadelphia University), 69n15, 127
Philadelphia Textile Manufacturers Association, 40
Philadelphia Water Color Club, 38
Philco (Philadelphia Storage Battery Company), 127, 172
Picabia, Francis, 125
Picasso, Pablo (Pablo Ruiz y Picasso), 88, 93, *93*, 125, 139n182
Pile, John F., *274*
Placé, Louis V., Jr., 106
Plus-Linje (Denmark), *275*
Poli brothers (Italy), 38
Ponti, Gio, 105, *107*, 156, *157*
Powel House (Philadelphia), 84
Powell, David, 160

301

Prentice, Joan, 118, 119, 122, 123
Price, Eli Kirk, 73, 82, 84, 93, 94, 102, 134n2, 137n113
Priestman, Paul, 231
Puiforcat, Jean, 78, 122, *122*, 165

Q

Quattrocchio S.r.l. (Italy), *256*

R

Radio Corporation of America (United States), 127
Rainbow (Italy), *180*
Rams, Dieter, 172
Rand, Paul, 266, *269*
Randolph, Rachel, 118
Randolph and Jenks (Philadelphia), 58
Rashid, Karim, *231*, 232, *232*
Rea, Paul H., *91*
Reichenbach, Porzellanmanufaktur (Germany), *277*
Rendell, Edward G., 207, 220, 286nn108–9
Renoir, Pierre-Auguste, 93
Riaño, Juan, 27, 69n26
Riart, Carlos, 182, *186*
Richards, Charles, 83, 90, 94
Richardson, Joseph, 119
Ridge, Thomas, 286
Rie, Lucie, 160, *163*
Riemerschmid, Richard, 58, *62*, 78, 205
Rietveld, Gerrit Thomas, 225, *226*
Rishel, Joseph J., 164
Roberts, Lisa S., 220, 227, 231, 248–49, 266, 267, *267*, 275; *Antiques of the Future* (2006), 249
Rockefeller, Abby Aldrich, 89
Rodebaugh, Francis L., 145
Rodin Museum (Philadelphia), 99, 103, 167
Rogers, Fairman, 13, 16
Rohde, Gilbert, 95, *97*
Rohde, Johan, 258
Rookwood Pottery Company (United States), 39, *42*, 43, *44*, 47, 52, *54*, 70n70, 70n77, 111
Root, Elihu, 134n24
Rörstrand Fabriks (Sweden), *20*, 51, 58
Rose, Ben, 91
Rosengarten, Mr. and Mrs. Adolph G., Jr., 165, 285n69
Rosenquist, James, 146
Rossi, Aldo, *181*, 182
Rosti A/S (Denmark), *189*
Rouault, Georges, 116
Royal Copenhagen Porcelain Manufactory, 51
Royal Porcelain Manufactory (Germany), 51, 74
Rozenburg, Haagsche Plateelbakkerij (The Netherlands), *55*
Rub, Timothy, 280, *280*, 281
Rubens, Peter Paul, 139n175
Rubenstein, Barbara, 287n150
Rubenstein, Mark, 270
Ruhlmann, Jacques-Émile, 78, 165, 266, *267*
Ruskin Pottery (England), 58
Russell, Lewine, 164
Rymer, Jeanne S., 272, 274, 275
Rymshaw, Eric, 220, 225

S

Saarinen, Eero, 113, *114*, *115*
Sachs, Keith, 270
Sachs, Paul J., 89, 93, 99, 103, 122, 137n108
Sailer, John (collection), 143
Saint Louis Art Museum, 135n29, 204, 286n98
Saito, Makoto, 212
Salviati (Italy), 38
Sambonet, Roberto (Sambonet–Cutlery, Tableware & Holloware Manufacturers; Italy), *188*
Sandvold, Neil, 238, 249, *275*, *280*
Sapper, Richard, *176*, *192*, *193*
Sartain, John, 26
Scarpa, Afra, *166–67*, 167
Scarpa, Tobia, *166–67*, 167, *274*
Scharff, Allan, 258
de Schauensee, Rodolphe Meyer, 105, 137n128
de Schauensee, Williamina, 105, 119, 133, 137n128, 285n82
Schiaparelli, Elsa, 137–38n128
Schlechter, Jack, 255, 258, 270
Schlegel, Jennifer, 281
Schlumbohm, Peter, *185*
Schmieg, Hungate & Kotzian (United States), *85*
Schneider, Michael, 253
Schoen, Eugene, 84, *85*
Schrager, Ian, 227, 286n117
Schultz, Richard (Richard Schultz Design, Palm, P.A.), 155, 275, *279*
Scofidio, Ricardo, 243, 248, *248*–49
Scott, Robert Montgomery, 176, 177, 178, 220, 285n78, 285n79, 286n109, 286n124
Search, Theodore C., 40, 70n58, 75, 134n1
Sellers, Coleman, 16
Seltzer, David, 248, 249, 266, *267*
Sèvres, Manufacture Nationale de (France), 52
Sewell, Darrel, 152, 154, 284n30
Shepheard, Peter, Sir, 159
Shepheard, Raymond, 154
Shirayamadani, Kataro, *54*, 55
Simeti, Francesco, 253
Sixty-ninth Street Arts and Crafts Community Center (Upper Darby, Pa.), 94
Skoogfors, Olaf, *144*, 145
Smith, Herbert, and Son (Scotland), *69*
Smithsonian Institution, 74, 137n110, 141, 284n3, 284n30
Solon, Marc-Louis-Emmanuel, 17, *17*, 44, 52, *71*
Sony Corporation (Japan), 172, 225
Sottsass, Ettore, 172, *179*, 182, *198*
South Kensington Museum (London; now Victoria and Albert Museum), 25, 27, 69n26
Staffel, Rudolf, 145
Starck, Philippe, 227, *228*, *229*
Starr, Stephen, 232
Steel, Sophy T., 66
Steele, Carl, 155
Steichen, Edward, 130
Stein, Gertrude, 251
Stelton A/S (Denmark), *176*–77
Stephensen, Magnus, 258
Stern, Robert, 173
Stetson Company, John B. (Philadelphia), 40
Steubenville Pottery (United States), *121*
Stieglitz, Alfred, 125, 139n167
Stocksdale, Robert, 165, *165*
Stokes, J. Stogdell (Stokes & Smith; Philadelphia), *91*, 102, 103, 106, 116, 118, 125, 136n85, 138n141, 138n165
Stoner, Bartine, 150
Stotesbury, Edward T., 65, 73, 134n2
Stroud, Marion Boulton (Swingle), 238, 253, 270, 286n124
Stumpf, Touvier, Violett, & Cie. (France), 52, *53*
Süe, Louis, 78
Sullivan, Mary Quinn, 89
Sunar Hauserman Inc. (United States), 202
Suntory Museum (Osaka), 207, 286n104
Swid Powell (United States), 220, *221*

T

Talbert, Bruce, 31
Tanabe, Reiko, 212
Taylor, Francis Henry, 91, *91*, 93
Taylor, William Watts, 43, 47
Teague, Walter Dorwin, *96*, 118
Teco Art Pottery (United States), 58, *61*
Temco (Spain), *186*
Temple, Joseph E. (Fund), 39, 40, 44, 52, 57, 58, 65, 71n130
Tendo Mokko (Japan), *206*, 212, *215*
Thesmar, André Fernand, 58
Thomas Jefferson University (Philadelphia), 178
Thomas, W. H., 58, *62*
Thompson, Benjamin, 243, 287
Thompson, Mrs. Benjamin, 243
Thonet, Gebrüder (Austria; & Michael Thonet), 17, *21*, 143; 169
Thun, Matteo, 182, *285*
Tiffany, Louis Comfort (Tiffany Glass and Decorating & Tiffany Furnaces; United States), *48*, *49*, 51, 52, 58 *59*, 62, 67, *68*, 111, 143, 270
Tisdale, David (David Tisdale Design; United States), *252*, 253
Toft, Charles, *29*
Toso Vetri d'Arte (Italy), *184*
Toulouse-Lautrec, Henri, 103–4
Treaty House (New Place) (now Philadelphia Museum of Art), 84
Tucker China (manufactory; Philadelphia), 70n77, 132
Turner, Evan H., *141*, 141–42, 143, 145, 146, 150, 152, 154, 155, 156, 159, 164–67, 284n2, 284n6, 284n35, 285n59, 285n86
Twombly, Cy, 178
Tyndale, Hector, General, 48
Tyndale, Julia N., 48
Tyson, Carroll S., Jr., 88, 89, 90, 94, 123

U

Uffizi Gallery (Florence), 132
Umbra, Ltd. (Canada), *231*, *232*
Umeda, Masanori, 212, *217*
University Museum (University of Pennsylvania Museum of Archaeology and Anthropology; Philadelphia), 111, 112, 125
Urquiola, Patricia, *276*
U. S. Government Printing Office, *America's Answer! Production Poster* (for Office for Emergency Management), *116*; *Watch Out for Fire!* poster (for C.A.A. War Training Service, Department of Commerce), 119, *119*

V

Valentien, Albert Robert, *42*
Valentiner, W. R., 66
van de Groenekan, Gerard (The Netherlands), *226*
van der Rohe, Georgia (daughter of Mies van der Rohe), 169
Van Doren, Harold, 127
van Gogh, Vincent, 128, 139n175, 146
Vechte, Antoine, *29*
Vegesack, Alexander von, 178, 285n90
Venini, Paolo (Venini S.p.A.; Italy), 105, *136*, *184*–85
Venturi, Robert, 143, 154, 220, *221*, *222*, *223*, 225, 234, 235, *238–41*, 260
Venturi, Scott Brown and Associates (Philadelphia), 220, 234, *234–39*, *241*, 286n114, 286n124; Venturi, Rauch and Scott Brown, 173
Véra, Paul, 78
Vereinigte Werkstätten für Kunst im Handwerk (Germany), 58, *63*

Vignelli, Massimo and Lella, 202
Vitetta Group (Philadelphia), 260
Vitra Design Museum (Weil am Rhein, Germany), 178
Vitra International (Switzerland), *213, 227, 229*, 270, *273*
Vortice Elettrosociali S.p.A. (Italy), *192*

W

Wadsworth Atheneum (Hartford), 141
Wagenfeld, Wilhelm, 95, 205
Wagner, H. Dumont, 31, 37
Wagner, Samuel, Jr., 13, 16
Walker, John, 88
Wanamaker, John, 71n112
Wanders, Marcel, *copyright page*, 249, 280, *280*, 281, *283*
Warburg, Edward, 88
Warhol, Andy, 253
Warner, Langdon, 74, 75, 77, 78, 79–80, 134n14, 134–35n26, 135n28, 135n33–36
Washburn, Gordon, 103
Watanabe, Riki, 212, *215*
Watkins, Franklin Chenault, 88, *106*
Weber, Kem, 95
Weber, Mary Ellen, 202, 205
Wegner, Hans, 155, *155*
Weightman, Mrs. William, 43
Weightman, William, 40
Weil, Daniel, *196*
Weitzner, Lori (Weitzner Ltd.; United States), 6
Wells, Suzanne F., 164, 167
Wennerburg, Gunnar Gunnarson, *60*
Westcott, Thompson, *14*, 17
Whitaker, William, 234
White, Samuel S., III, 88, 89
White, Vera, 88
Widener, George D., 133, 139n192
Wiener Werkstätte (Austria), *287*
Wike, Mr. and Mrs. J. Roffe, II, 286n124
Willett, Anna Lee, 134–35n26
Wilson, Edward L., *28–29*
Wilson, Robert, 243
Wilstach, William P. (& collection; fund), 38, 134n3, 136n90, 138n143, 139n175
Winchendon Furniture (United States), *128, 129*
Wind, Yoram "Jerry," 220
Winokur, Paula, 145
Wintersteen, Bernice "Bonnie" McIlhenny (Mrs. John), 118, 125, 132, 142, 146, 176
Winterthur Museum (Wilmington, Del.), 137n109
Wirkkala, Tapio, 172, *184*, *185*
Women's Committee of the Philadelphia Museum of Art (Associate Committee of Women; Women's Centennial Executive Committee), 69n45, 82, 155, 164, 202, 286n124
Wood, William P., 166, 285n59, 285n78
Woodhouse, Samuel W., Jr., 75, 79, 80, 81–82
Worcester Art Museum, 93
Worcester Royal Porcelain Company (England), 16, 17, 202
Work Projects Administration (WPA; Works Progress Administration), 103
World's Columbian Exposition of 1893 (Chicago), 40, 43, 47, 74
Wright, Frank Lloyd, 176
Wright, Russel, 95, 119, 155–56, *121*, *304*
Wurman, Richard Saul, 146, 159

Y

Yanagi, Sori, 206, *206*
Yellin, Samuel, *64*, 65, 74, 77, 134–35n26
Youtz, Philip N., 94, 99, 137n103

Z

Zanini, Marco, 182, *184*
Zanuso, Marco, 172, *192*
Zerodisegno (Italy), *257*
Zieget, Julius, 139n186
Zigrosser, Carl, 139n167
Zsolnay (Hungary), 51

PHOTOGRAPHY CREDITS

Objects in the collection of the Philadelphia Museum of Art were photographed by Graydon Wood, Lynn Rosenthal, Andrea Nuñez, and Jason Wierzbicki except as noted.

Alessi S.p.a., Crusinallo, Italy: p. 9

Annual Report, Pennsylvania Museum and School of Industrial Art (Philadelphia, 1878): fig. 15; (Philadelphia, 1903): fig. 27; (Philadelphia, 1911): fig. 54; (Philadelphia, 1916): fig. 60

Bulletin of the Pennsylvania Museum, vol. 3, no. 10 (April 1, 1905): fig. 29; vol. 15, no. 57 (January 1917): fig. 30; vol. 18, no. 76 (April 1923): fig. 62; vol. 21, no. 99 (January 1926): fig. 53; vol. 22, no. 107 (November 1926): fig. 67; vol. 23, no. 117 (December 1927–January 1928): fig. 69; vol. 26, no. 142 (May 1931): fig. 77; vol. 30, no. 165 (January 1935): fig. 87

Bulletin of the Philadelphia Museum of Art, vol. 49, no. 242 (Summer 1954): fig. 118; vol. 60, nos. 283/84 (October 1, 1964): fig. 130; vol. 61, nos. 287/88 (October 1, 1965): fig. 74; vol. 65, no. 304 (July–September 1970): fig. 138

John Condax: figs. 116, 160

Sigurd Fischer: fig. 71

Flos S.p.A., Brescia, Italy: pp. 2–3.

Free Library of Philadelphia, Print and Picture Collection: figs. 6, 14

Mark Garvin: fig. 271

John Getting, courtesy of Maharam: back endpapers

Andrew Harkins: fig. 65

Kelly & Massa: figs. 201, 281, 303

Andrea Nuñez: fig. 295

Philadelphia Museum of Art, Archives, Decorative Arts Department Records: figs. 253–56; Founding Documents Collection: figs. 16–19; Records of the Directors, Exhibition Records: fig. 137; Special Format, Architectural Drawings: fig. 86

Philadelphia Museum of Art, Library: figs. 1, 2

Matt Wargo, courtesy of John Izenour, Venturi, Scott Brown and Associates: figs. 223, 224

Stuart Watson Photography: p. 303

James Jason Wierzbicki: figs. 284, 302

ABOUT THE AUTHOR

Kathryn Bloom Hiesinger is curator of European Decorative Arts after 1700 at the Philadelphia Museum of Art, a position she has held since 1972, and has also taught and lectured widely. She was educated at Wellesley College and Harvard University, where she received her A.M. and Ph.D. in the history of art. Her interests and publications have ranged from sixteenth-century Italian tomb monuments to the decorative arts of the French eighteenth century and Second Empire to contemporary design. She is the recipient of numerous honors and awards including France's Chevalier of the Order of Arts and Letters.

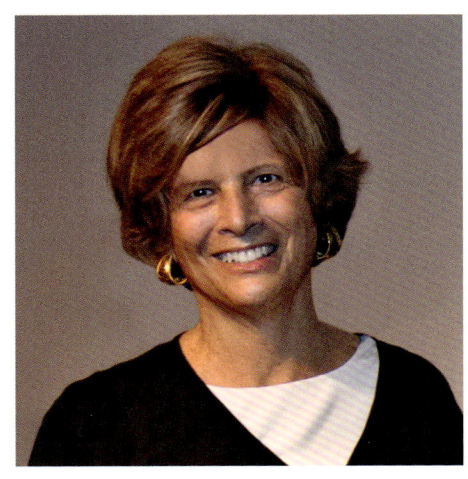

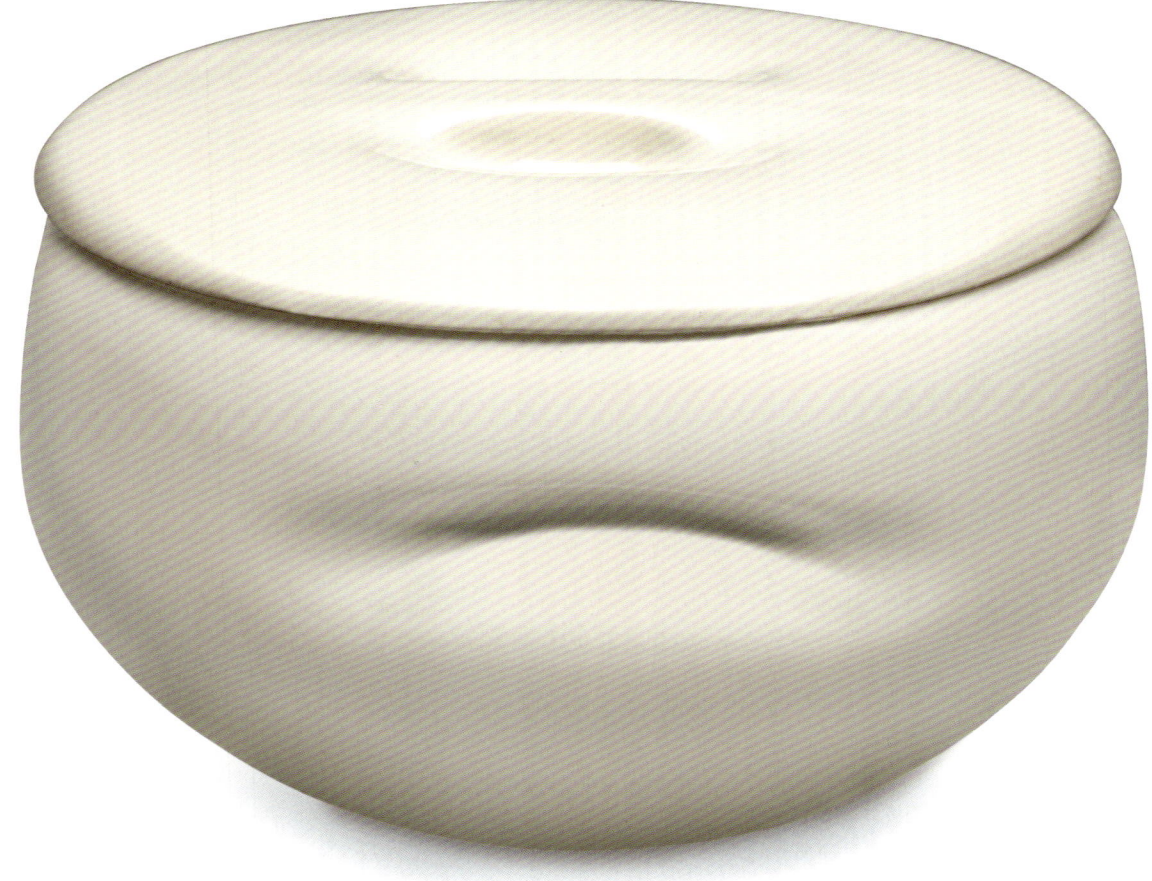

Russel Wright : for Iroquois China : Covered Casserole from *Iroquois Casual China* Service : 1946 : glazed porcelain : H 5 1/4" : 1983-45-1 (cat. 219) :
The author dined on Wright's *Iroquois Casual China* at her family's home; the casserole was a gift of her parents, Mr. and Mrs. Benjamin Bloom, in 1983.

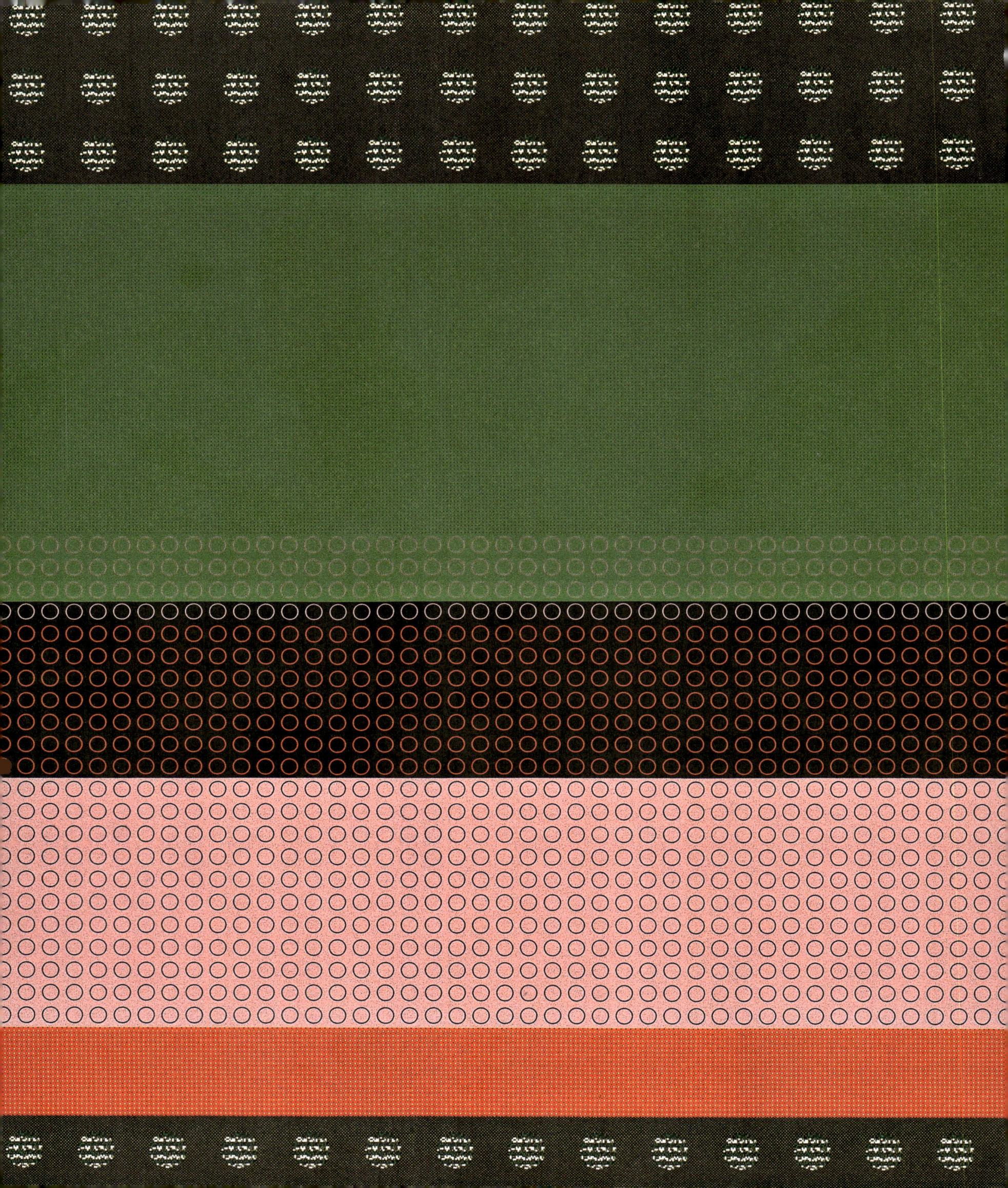